MORE PRECIOUS THAN PEACE

MORE PRECIOUS THAN PEACE

A New History of America in World War I

JUSTUS D. DOENECKE

University of Notre Dame Press
Notre Dame, Indiana

University of Notre Dame Press
Notre Dame, Indiana 46556
undpress.nd.edu

Copyright © 2022 by the University of Notre Dame

Published in the United States of America

Library of Congress Control Number: 2021948510

ISBN: 978-0-268-20185-2 (Hardback)
ISBN: 978-0-268-20184-5 (WebPDF)
ISBN: 978-0-268-20187-6 (Epub)

This book is dedicated to

———————————

June and Elliot Benowitz

Susan Matthews

Scott Perry

Marsha and Frank Samponaro

It is a fearful thing to lead this great peaceful people
into war, into the most terrible and disastrous of all wars,
civilization itself seeming to be in the balance.
But the right is more precious than peace,
and we shall fight for the things which
we have always carried nearest our hearts.

—President Woodrow Wilson,
War Message to Congress, April 2, 1917

CONTENTS

Acknowledgments   ix

Abbreviations in the Notes   xi

Maps   xiii

Introduction   1

ONE   Raising an Army   7

TWO   The Naval War   31

THREE   Mr. Creel Administers a Committee   45

FOUR   Legislating Unity   63

FIVE   The Ramparts We Watch   81

SIX   Foes of Our Own Household   95

SEVEN   The Anti-Radical Crusade   117

EIGHT   "Living on a Volcano": Russia Amid Revolution 147

NINE   "Walking on Eggs": The Decision to Intervene 177

TEN   Wrestling with War Aims, 1917   203

ELEVEN   Wilson's Peace Offensive, 1918   231

TWELVE   The Matter of Preparation   257

THIRTEEN   Checking Ludendorff   279

FOURTEEN   Towards Allied Victory   293

FIFTEEN   Final Negotiations with the Germans   305

SIXTEEN   The Colonel's Last Mission   329

SEVENTEEN   "Not Ordinary Times": The 1918 Elections   341

EIGHTEEN   Armistice   359

             Conclusion   367

             Notes   377

             Bibliographic Essay   445

             Index   471

ACKNOWLEDGMENTS

IN THIS CASE, AS WITH MY OTHER WORKS, THIS BOOK could never have been written without the aid of others. I first developed my interest in World War I through the stimulating seminars of Arthur S. Link and Arno J. Mayer; it was renewed years later by David F. Trask. My wife, Carol, read this entire manuscript in its most embryonic form. June Benowitz, Irwin Gellman, Scott Perry, and Frank Samponaro have gone over the entire text with care. John Belohlavek has offered more critical input than any author has a right to expect. John Milton Cooper Jr. made extremely valuable suggestions. Perceptive comments on the broad themes of the book have been made by Lloyd Ambrosius, George H. Nash, Charles E. Neu, and John A. Thompson. Mark Stoler, Landy Nelson, Michael Clay, and particularly Jack Tunsell have been invaluable concerning military matters. My gratitude, as so often in the past, extends to the dedicated staff of the Jane Cook Library, New College of Florida. Steve Wrinn, director of the University of Notre Dame Press; Rachel Kindler, assistant acquisitions editor; Matthew F. Dowd, managing editor; and copyeditor Scott Barker could not have been more supportive.

ABBREVIATIONS IN THE NOTES

ATR	*Appeal to Reason*
CO	*Current Opinion*
CR	*Congressional Record*
DD	*The Cabinet Diaries of Josephus Daniels, 1913–1921*, ed. E. David Cronon (Lincoln: University of Nebraska Press, 1963)
DRF	David Rowland Francis
EMH	Edward Mandell House
EMHP	Edward M. House Papers, Yale University Library, New Haven, Conn.
FR	*Foreign Relations of the United States, 1917–1918* (Washington, DC: Government Printing Office, 1931–1933)
FR-LP	*Foreign Relations of the United States: The Lansing Papers, 1914–1920*, 2 vols. (Washington, DC: Government Printing Office, 1939–1940)
HCL	Henry Cabot Lodge
HCLP	The Papers of Henry Cabot Lodge, Massachusetts Historical Society, Boston
I&E	*Issues and Events*
JJP	John J. Pershing
LD	*Literary Digest*
LP	*The Lansing Papers, 1914–1920*, 2 vols. (Washington, D.C.: Government Printing Office, 1939–40)
LTR	*The Letters of Theodore Roosevelt*, 8 vols., ed. Elting E. Morison (Cambridge, Mass.: Harvard University Press, 1951–54)
N	*Nation*

NAR	*North American Review*
NARWW	*North American Review War Weekly*
NDB	Newton Diehl Baker
NR	*New Republic*
NYA	*New York American*
NYT	*New York Times*
NYTr	*New York Tribune*
O	*Outlook*
PCM	Peyton C. March
PWW	*The Papers of Woodrow Wilson*, 69 vols., ed. Arthur S. Link (Princeton, N.J.: Princeton University Press, 1966–93)
RL	Robert Lansing
SFE	*San Francisco Examiner*
THB	Tasker H. Bliss
TR	Theodore Roosevelt
VTAW	*Viereck's: The American Weekly*
WHT	William Howard Taft
WHP	Walter Hines Page
WW	Woodrow Wilson

MAPS

English Channel

Dunkirk
Calais
Boulogne
Passchendaele
Ghent
Brussels
FLANDERS
Lys River
Armentières
Vimy Ridge
Arras
Cambrai
Abbeville
Somme River
Amiens
St. Quentin
Cantigny
Chemin des Dames
Compiègne
Soissons
Aisne River
Rheims
Seine River
Paris
Marne River

BELGIUM
Meuse River

Sedan
LUX.
Verdun
Thionville
LORRAINE
Metz
St. Mihiel
Seicheprey
Nancy
Sommerviller
ALSACE

GERMANY
Cologne
Coblenz
Mainz
Rhine River

FRANCE

Loire River

The Western Front, 1917-1918

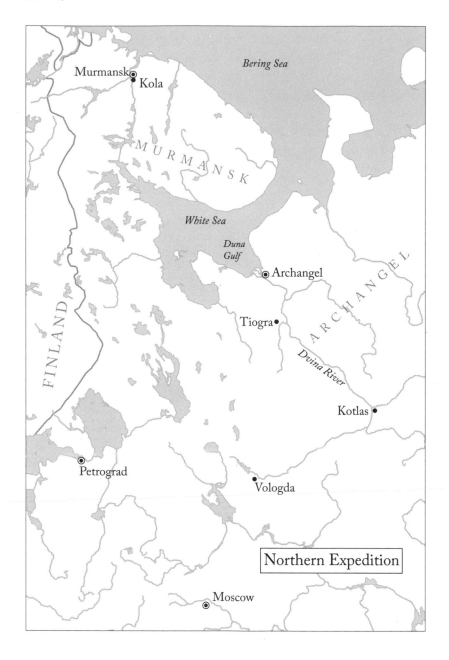

Bering Sea

Murmansk

Kola

M U R M A N S K

White Sea

Duna
Gulf

Archangel

A R C H A N G E L

Tiogra

Devina River

Kotlas

FINLAND

Petrograd

Vologda

Northern Expedition

Moscow

Siberian Involvements

Trans-Siberian Railroad
Chinese Eastern Railroad

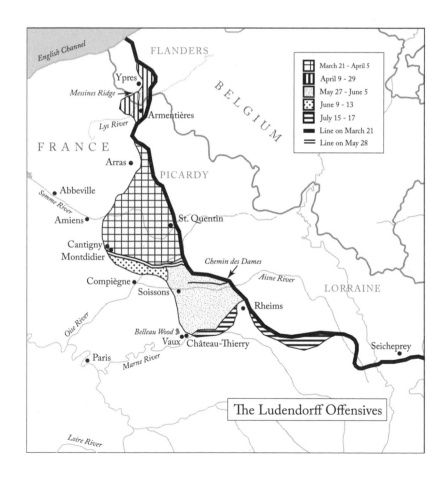

The Ludendorff Offensives

	March 21 - April 5
	April 9 - 29
	May 27 - June 5
	June 9 - 13
	July 15 - 17
	Line on March 21
	Line on May 28

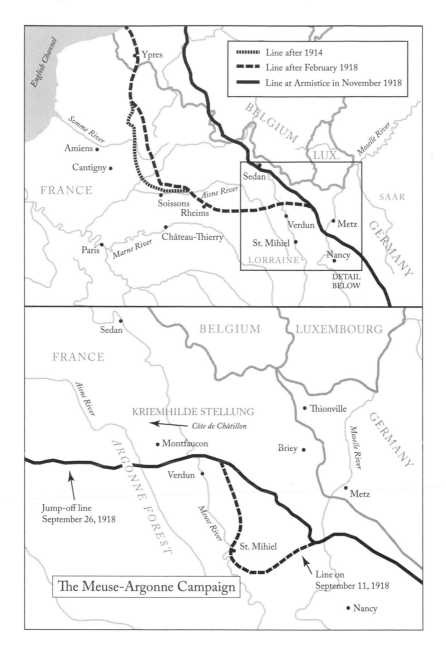

Line after 1914
Line after February 1918
Line at Armistice in November 1918

English Channel

Ypres

BELGIUM

LUX.

Moselle River

Somme River

Amiens

Cantigny

FRANCE

Sedan

SAAR

GERMANY

Aisne River

Soissons
Rheims

Verdun   Metz

Paris   Marne River   Château-Thierry

St. Mihiel

Nancy

LORRAINE

DETAIL
BELOW

Sedan

BELGIUM   LUXEMBOURG

FRANCE

Aisne River

KRIEMHILDE STELLUNG

Thionville

Côte de Châtillon

GERMANY

Montfaucon

Briey

Moselle River

ARGONNE FOREST

Verdun

Jump-off line
September 26, 1918

Meuse River

Metz

St. Mihiel

The Meuse-Argonne Campaign

Line on
September 11, 1918

Nancy

INTRODUCTION

WORLD WAR I MARKS ONE OF THE MOST REMARKABLE periods in our nation's history. The United States sent nearly 2 million troops overseas, created an unparalleled war machine, and established a propaganda apparatus the envy of any land. Such efforts are particularly extraordinary in a nation whose leadership was totally inexperienced in such matters. A decade before America entered the conflict, its president headed a major eastern university, its secretary of war served as a solicitor of a leading midwestern city, its secretary of the navy edited a metropolitan daily in the South, and the secretary of the treasury had just helped create a subway connecting Manhattan to Jersey City. Its postmaster general was attorney for a judicial district outside of Austin, Texas. Its leading general administered a fort outside of Manila. The man who headed the nation's war propaganda ran a newspaper in Kansas City. The president's alter ego, a confidant who would be entrusted with the most delicate of diplomatic missions, had recently been an intimate of several Texas governors and was just becoming immersed in national Democratic politics. Only the secretary of state had some experience befitting his station as a respected international lawyer whose specialty lay in arbitration. Of all the wartime ambassadors to Europe, just one had ever held a diplomatic post before.

Given such lack of experience, in some ways the U.S. war effort achieved remarkable success, especially since the United States participated as a belligerent for merely a year

1

and a half. While still a newcomer to the coalition fighting the Central Powers, President Woodrow Wilson articulated peace aims that forced all the warring leaders, friend or foe, to respond to his agenda. Presenting an alternative vision to V. I. Lenin's dictum of an immediate peace with no annexations or reparations, Wilson captured the popular imagination both at home and overseas with his stress on self-determination of peoples and an entirely new global order, thereby strengthening liberals everywhere. Even his military intervention in Russia drew little contemporary dissent, with quarrels over his motives remaining for historians to debate decades later.

Certain other cabinet members possessed genuine strengths. Secretary of State Robert Lansing framed an agreement with Japan, nebulous to be sure, that reduced tensions at a critical point in the conflict. Navy Secretary Josephus Daniels directed massive convoy operations and engineered a "Bridge of Ships" that sent hordes of doughboys overseas with few losses. William Gibbs McAdoo, secretary of the treasury, raised $17 billion in massive publicity drives while authorizing $7.3 billion in loans to the Allies, money crucial to their survival. He also coordinated a complex U.S. railroad system, one that had been so chaotic that briefly in the winter of 1917–18 much of the economy was barely functioning.

The Wilson administration suffered less corruption than had existed under Abraham Lincoln. It showed more imagination than did a host of subsequent wartime presidents, ranging from Franklin D. Roosevelt to George W. Bush, particularly in the ability to propagate the nation's war aims. Waging its first total overseas conflict in its entire life — manpower, factories, farms, indeed its thinking — the United States was welded into a militarized behemoth. As part of a production miracle, several million inductees were supplied with 30.7 million pairs of shoes, 21.7 million blankets, 13.9 million wool coats, and 131 million pairs of socks. George Creel, chairman of the Committee on Public Information (CPI), distributed about 75 million pieces of literature throughout the world. Most important of all, U.S. shipments to Europe, ranging from steel and copper to textiles and raw cotton, were crucial in making victory possible. Furthermore, in the fall of 1918, the American Expeditionary Force (AEF) played a major role in the Allied triumph.

As expected, the Wilson administration set a premium on national unity. Americans, the president pledged in his war message of April 2, 1917, would "dedicate our lives and fortunes, everything that we are and everything that we have" to the common effort. Two weeks later, in a proclamation urging sacrifice, he remarked, "We must all speak, act, and serve together!" In his Flag Day address delivered in June, he warned, "Woe be to the man or group of men that seek to stand in our way in this day of high resolution." Speaking to Congress close to a year later, in May 1918, Wilson went so far as to claim "politics is adjourned."[1]

The story of the war, however, is not one of consensus. Although the success of four Liberty Loan campaigns indicates massive popular support for the military effort, few realize the degree of dissidence manifested in the nation. Not only was politics never "adjourned," but from the time the country entered the war, attacks on the Wilson administration remained strong and bitter. Early in April 1917, six senators and fifty members of the U.S. House of Representatives voted against entering the conflict. At the time, at least four other antiwar senators and up to fifty representatives still opposed full-scale U.S. participation in the war. However, they did feel pressured by the need to express national unity and, if they were southerners, by Democratic Party loyalty. Final congressional tallies supporting conscription belie strong initial dissent over the matter, expressed over several weeks and lodged within the highest ranks of the president's own party. The CPI and particularly Director Creel drew impassioned congressional attack, as did the original espionage bill of June 1917 and the Sedition Act of May 1918. The nation experienced persecutions of German Americans, an ethnic group totaling at least 8 million. It saw wide-sweeping repression of political radicals, who nonetheless offered surprising resistance that continued well into the war.

Moreover, in other ways the war was no success story, the administration showing itself woefully inept and occasionally downright destructive. Postmaster General Albert Sidney Burleson refused mailing privileges to scores of dissident journals, especially if they were on the political left. Before the United States entered the conflict, Colonel Edward Mandell House, Wilson's primary adviser, had already proven himself out of his depth in negotiating with the British. Critically, as the war drew to an end, U.S. and Allied obstinacy concerning any sort of negotiated peace cost countless lives on all sides.

The sheer waging of war had its own problems. Secretary of War Newton Baker was hesitant in grasping the full implications of the struggle, long permitting War Department bureau chiefs to exercise an autonomy that resulted in painful slowdowns. For close to a year, army chiefs of staffs remained equally inept, overwhelmed by the complexities of modern warfare. U.S. Army commander John J. Pershing's stress on a frontal assault, unaccompanied by supporting artillery, led to many needless casualties.

Particularly within the past decade, amid the centennial of World War I, many fresh accounts have been written concerning the U.S. role in the struggle. Some narratives paint with a broad brush, covering such matters as the nature of Wilsonianism and the United States' rise to global financial dominance. Not surprisingly, the story of U.S. ground forces has received fresh treatment, with attention now given to the role played by war correspondents. New biographies have been written on such diverse figures as President Wilson, Colonel House, Theodore Roosevelt, Robert Lansing, William Gibbs McAdoo, Newton D. Baker, Josephus Daniels, and journalist Roy W. Howard.

My account in this book often deals with the domestic controversies regarding the nature of U.S. participation. As one who has spent much of his career examining Americans who took a dim view of U.S. foreign policy from 1931 to the early Cold War, I am now continuing to examine foes of U.S. intervention, this time scrutinizing their opposition to the way the nation waged World War I. Hence, I offer extensive coverage of critics of Wilson's policies, both those who found him insufficiently belligerent and those who sought immediate negotiation with the Central Powers. I explore diplomatic ineptitude, as reflected in a Russian policy singularly incompetent in execution; production snags, leading to AEF reliance on Allied weapons during the entire involvement; and military incompetence, as revealed in crucial battles and campaigns. When historians have differed over various topics, their diverse views are included.

My narrative is the second in a series dealing with the administration of Woodrow Wilson in regard to World War I and its aftermath. My first volume, *Nothing Less Than War: A New History of America's Entry into World War I* (2011), covers the period beginning in August

1914, when the European powers found themselves embraced in deadly struggle, and it ends in April 1917, when the United States entered what was once known as the Great War.[2] As with the previous volume, I hope to share with both the general reader and the specialist my research in both primary sources and secondary literature.

This book begins with the first great controversy of the war, the conscription issue, and in the process reveals lively debates as to what America's general role should be in the conflict. It moves to the nation's first military participation in the war, that involving the navy, which played a crucial part as the United States initially entered the conflict. Because, from the outset, the Wilson administration deemed national unity essential to achieving victory, the book takes up in turn the Creel Committee, legislation designed to suppress dissident opinion, the activities of those responsible for enforcing "100% Americanism," ethnic targets of the "patriotic" crusades, attacks on publisher William Randolph Hearst and Senator Robert M. La Follette, and assaults on the political left. The narrative continues with U.S. reaction to the Russian revolutions of March and November 1917, events that challenged war aims throughout the entire West, increased radical sentiments everywhere, and soon led to Allied military intervention. These topics are succeeded by Wilson's vision of a just peace, scandals in military training and production, and U.S. combat in Western Europe. After describing the nation's final negotiations with both the Germans and Allies and the politics leading up to the 1918 congressional elections, the book concludes with the armistice of November 11.

The published Wilson Papers, the *New York Times*, and the *Congressional Record* remain indispensable. Certain vehicles of opinion have proven particularly helpful. Both the *Literary Digest* and *Current Opinion* combine news accounts with press summaries. The *Nation* strongly reflected the views of pacifist leaning Oswald Garrison Villard, who in January 1918 became editor in chief. The *New Republic*, another liberal weekly, harbored editors who were personally close to Colonel House. Lyman Abbott's *Outlook* shared the views of Theodore Roosevelt, who had resigned as contributing editor just before war broke out in Europe. The conservative *North American Review* published its own *War Weekly* (hereafter referred to as George Harvey's *War Weekly*), which became an increasingly venomous critic of the Wilson administration. There existed the pro-German weeklies, such as *Viereck's: The American Weekly* and *Issues and Events*, both of which miraculously escaped the sting of Post Office Department censors. An analysis of the newspaper chain of William Randolph Hearst puts to rest many stereotypes, for the press mogul strongly backed the Wilson administration while casting aspersions on almost every U.S. ally.

Seeking to keep references under control, I have often limited notes to direct quotations, diplomatic documents, and the contemporary press. When several newspapers treat an event, I have sought to cite the one with the largest circulation. For readers who seek to ascertain my sources for sheer narrative, be the topic violations of civil liberties, the turmoil in Russia, or battles fought by U.S. troops, I have provided an extensive bibliographic essay.

ONE
RAISING AN ARMY

ON JULY 20, 1917, AT 2:40 P.M., IN THE JUDICIARY CHAMBER
of the Senate Office Building, a slightly built, youthful-
looking, bespectacled man told several hundred people, "This
is an occasion of great dignity and some solemnity. The young
men selected today are honored by the privilege of serving
their country." Then, wearing a blindfold, Secretary of War
Newton Diehl Baker reached into a large glass container fifteen inches high and thirty in circumference. He drew a cap-
sule from the 10,500 in the bowl and remarked, "I have drawn
the first number," giving the object to Provost Marshal Enoch
Crowder, who intoned "Number 258." Except for the whirl
of a movie camera, the room was silent, for those present were
breathless. All realized that the 258th man in each of 4,557
local boards would be immediately called up for the draft.
Once called up for a physical examination, Number 258 faced
the strong possibility that he would soon be part of the U.S.
Army. Subsequent drawings were made in turn by the chairmen of the Senate and House Military Affairs committees and
by the ranking minority members.[1] For the next sixteen hours
and forty-six minutes, other officials dipped into the bowl
until 2:16 the following morning. It had taken the wartime
United States several months and much congressional debate

to reach this step—the United States had only become a belligerent power on April 6.

On the eve of entering the conflict, the United States remained woefully unprepared. Its army was antiquated, ranking seventeenth among the nations of the world. Historian Robert H. Ferrell labeled it "a home for old soldiers, a quiet, sleepy place where they killed time until they began drawing their pensions." Because the bulk of its soldiering had been on the Great Plains, military scholar David R. Woodward finds it essentially a constabulary force usually fighting Native Americans.[2] The regular army numbered 121,000 men; about 180,000 were enrolled in the National Guard, long an entity of dubious quality.

As for weaponry, the army fell short in just about every essential—tanks, mortars, grenades, gas masks, flamethrowers, heavy howitzers—and had fewer than two thousand machine guns. Field artillery did not have enough rounds to sustain a bombardment for more than a few minutes. If the Springfield rifle was possibly the world's best, there were far too few of them to outfit a massive expeditionary force. The fifty-five aircraft were obsolete, and in any case only thirty-five officers knew how to fly. Lacking motorized transport, troops depended on horse and mule. Ammunition sufficed for just one and a half days of combat. Organized field armies, army corps, and combat divisions did not exist; the very few surviving regiments were undermanned. The small National Guard was most inadequate, despite its recent service on the Mexican border. Since the Spanish–American War, only Major General John J. Pershing had commanded a large body of combat troops. War Secretary Baker possessed practically no military experience, having been mayor of Cleveland before occupying his post. Relatively speaking, the United States had been better prepared in the American Revolution and the War of 1812.

Existing war plans bore little semblance to reality: they ignored the creation of an industrial base needed for mobilizing massive forces, much less the needed reorganization of all of American society. Until Germany announced unrestricted submarine warfare, the U.S. General Staff had focused solely on the defense of the North American continent—with one exception, a harebrained scheme hatched late in 1916 to send half a million men to the Balkans.[3]

Once Uncle Sam had committed himself, the U.S. Army War College took a quite different direction. It sought the conscription of

1.5 million men, a force not immediately scheduled for overseas duty; instead, U.S. troops would receive extensive training at home until they became battle-ready. As Major General Tasker H. Bliss, assistant chief of staff under Major General Hugh L. Scott, summarized War College studies on March 31, 1917, U.S. cooperation must initially be limited to naval and economic support. Only after two years, Bliss maintained, would the United States possess the ground troops needed to fight on the western front against Germany.[4]

Others concurred. In mid-March, Colonel Edward Mandell House, by far Woodrow Wilson's closest adviser, had written the president concerning Allied needs. He claimed that the British and French governments, with whom he was in contact, stressed the delivery of matériel, France in particular focusing on steel, coal, and other raw materials: "No one looks with favor upon our raising a large army at the moment, believing that it would be better if we would permit volunteers to enlist in the Allied armies." Treasury Secretary William Gibbs McAdoo doubted America's ability to furnish troops in Europe, stressing loans as the chief form of aid.[5]

During the debate of early April 1917 over U.S. entry into the war, several members of Congress surmised that the nation's role would be limited to shipping supplies and conducting naval operations. Seldom was full-fledged combat on the European continent mentioned. Fiorello La Guardia (R-N.Y.), at the time a newly elected member of the U.S. House, later maintained that at least 60 percent of those House members who voted for war did not think the United States would send a single soldier overseas.[6]

Through April most of the administration agreed, assuming that the navy would do most of the fighting. Any expeditionary force would be a token one, composed of army regulars and volunteers. In early May, British prime minister David Lloyd George told Allied leaders that the United States lacked the shipping needed to send a large force to Europe. "America is still an unknown," he said. "We must not count upon her aid in a military way for a long time to come."[7]

Yet raising large masses of ground troops for combat soon became a crucial matter. On March 5, 1917, a month before the United States entered the conflict, the War Department submitted a plan providing for the mobilization of half a million men within six months. Wilson and Secretary Baker had been cool to a draft, believing that voluntary enlistment was sufficient and also in best accord with the American tradition. Only late that month did both men deem conscription necessary.

In his April 2 war message, Wilson called for half a million men, preferably through "universal military liability to service," a request that drew particularly strong applause. On the 5th, Baker submitted his draft proposal to Congress. The war secretary sought a regular army that would reach almost 300,000 men; a "federalized" National Guard that would tally 440,000; and a conscripted force of half a million between the ages of nineteen and thirty-five. If necessary, another 500,000 could be drafted. In this way, at least 1.2 million troops could be raised.[8] Not surprisingly, except for the declaration of war, the draft produced more letters to Congress than did any other issue of the year. The subsequent debates forced the legislators to deal with the most fundamental of questions: What would be the nature and scope of the nation's commitment and how could the United States best fulfill any major military enterprise?

Groups reacted differently. Samuel Gompers, president of the American Federation of Labor (AFL), claimed that organized labor had always opposed conscription, for "institutions and relations of a free people can and should be based upon the voluntary principle." The Black community was divided, but most of its leaders, including *Crisis* editor W. E. B. Du Bois, saw a chance to gain equality. Urban support for the draft was revealed when 383 mayors of cities of more than 5,000 people backed universal military training, including James M. Curley of Boston and John Purroy Mitchel of New York City. Various preparedness societies supported the bill, including the National Security League (NSL), the American Defense Society (ADS), and the American Rights League. In noting a NSL survey of 470 newspapers taken in mid-April, the *Literary Digest* reported that 270 favored universal training, 49 opposed it, and 157 were uncommitted.[9]

At first the issue seemed in doubt. On April 10, a dispatch from the *New York Tribune*'s Washington Bureau reported that if all members of the House voted the way they talked, "the majority against the President's conscription plan would be tremendous." A day later, Congressman Edward William Pou (D-N.C.), chairman of the House Rules Committee, wrote Wilson aide Joseph Tumulty, saying that

House sentiment overwhelmingly favored the voluntary system. He predicted a bitter and uncertain floor fight were the matter challenged. On April 21, a poll of the House showed only 43 percent of the membership favored an immediate draft.[10] Much of the congressional establishment opposed conscription, including such political powerhouses as Speaker of the House Champ Clark (D-Mo.), House majority leader Claude Kitchin (D-N.C.), House minority leader James Mann (R-Ill.), and former Speaker Joseph G. Cannon (R-Ill.).

The House and Senate military committees split over the matter. The House Committee on Military Affairs chair, Hubert S. Dent Jr., a conservative Democrat and lawyer from Montgomery, Alabama, introduced legislation that undercut administration plans. His bill did establish a selective service system with accompanying registration, but only if and when the president had determined that voluntarism had failed. By creating both volunteer and conscripted forces, it raised the possibility that only volunteers would serve overseas.

Passing the committee 13 to 8 on April 18, the bill was backed by southern and western congressmen but opposed by easterners and such westerners as Julius Kahn (R-Calif.), who led the House's pro-conscription forces. Born in the Grand Duchy of Baden and moved to California at age five, the colorful Kahn—the son of a cattle rancher—had performed on the stage with Edwin Booth before becoming a trial lawyer and representing San Francisco in Congress. Ironically, it was therefore a German-born Republican who spearheaded administration policy on the House floor.

Conscription had an easier time in the Senate Military Affairs Committee, which reported the bill in the form desired by Wilson, Baker, and the General Staff. The committee chair, George E. Chamberlain (D-Ore.), had introduced a bill for universal military service two years earlier. After narrowly voting down a two-track measure similar to the Dent bill and sponsored by Kenneth McKellar (D-Tenn.), on April 18 the Senate committee voted 10 to 7 to back the administration. The lineup was usually regional, with the South and West often opposing the president and metropolitan districts in the Northeast or on the West Coast supporting him.

By now debate was bitter, for it quickly involved the entire role the United States should play in the conflict. Seldom, if ever, during the war would the United States experience such impassioned arguments. Congressman Robert Crosser (D-Ohio) called the matter "the gravest question which has confronted this country in a half century, if not in its whole history."[11] If Crosser was exaggerating, an examination of the congressional debates shows that the stakes were enormous.

Nevertheless, contrary to stereotype, the issue, at least in the House, was not voluntarism versus draft but giving voluntarism a trial run before conscription was instituted. As conscription historian John Whiteclay Chambers II notes, despite public protestations, many rural southern Democrats and midwestern Republicans believed in a wartime draft but sought a measure acceptable to their constituents. Hence, they desired to first try the volunteer system or at least permit the raising of volunteers while the draft was put into effect.[12]

For some supporters of conscription, imperial Germany put the entire world in peril. To Senator Frank B. Kellogg (R-Minn.), the Reich was "the greatest military power in the world history." Senator Henry Myers (D-Mont.) saw the kaiser ranking with Julius Caesar, Alexander the Great, and Napoleon. Senator Thomas ("Tom-Tom") Heflin (D-Ala.) warned, "A mad monarch, dreaming of world power, now threatens every free government in the world."[13]

Certainly, so pro-draft legislators argued, the United States was directly threatened. Were Britain and France defeated, so warned Congressman Clifton McArthur (R-Ore.), "the common enemy will be on our shores, with a combined fleet outnumbering ours two to one with a seasoned army of millions of veteran soldiers." Senator Albert B. Fall (R-N.Mex.) feared that if the Germans reached Paris, they—accompanied by 15 million Mexicans—would "next reach Chicago and cut your great United States in two."[14]

Little wonder many such legislators agreed with Congressman Irvine L. Lenroot (R-Wis.): "We must fight autocracy in Germany in order to preserve democracy in America." Given the danger of Russia's collapse, so both Representatives Asbury Lever (D-S.C.) and Royal C. Johnson (R-S.Dak.) admonished, the United States might have to bear the brunt of the war. At any rate, this conflict, warned Congressman Thomas D. McKeown (D-Okla.), was no mere "gala occasion for the American Navy to engage in a little target practice and our torpedo destroyers to have a little game of hide and seek upon the high seas with a few German submarines."[15]

To its defenders, it was the draft that was more democratic. Conscription, several congressmen argued, was no more coercive than taxation, jury duty, or compulsory education. Indeed, the draft could be downright wholesome. John Miller (R-Wash.) said, "Bring the young fellow out of the poolroom, away from the bright street lights of the night, jerk him away from his cigarettes and let us make a man of him of some use to his country—let us compel him to be a man." Outside of Congress, administration publicist George Creel found conscription regenerating "the heart, liver, and kidneys of America," all in "sad need of overhauling."[16]

Some senators conceded a loss of freedom but found it necessary. To Wesley Jones (R-Wash.), the United States could not win victories without militarism. Hiram Johnson (R-Calif.) conceded that the war would temporarily destroy "the last proud tradition that made us a Nation of sovereign free men," but spoke of the need to foster democracy in a wider world.[17]

To conscription advocates, the volunteer system would always be found wanting. Chamberlain called the arrangement "undemocratic, unreliable, extravagant, inefficient, and, above all, unsafe." Only Nevada, noted Congressman John M. C. Smith (R-Mich.) in late April, supplied its quota of volunteers. Speaking more cautiously, Congressman Kahn asserted, "Some days volunteering is good; some days it is bad." At the current rate of a thousand volunteers a day, commented Senator John Sharp Williams (D-Miss.), it would take three years to create an army.[18]

To some draft backers, their opponents might be suspect in their loyalties, indeed downright subversive. Heflin claimed that "every German agent and sympathizer in the United States is to-day advocating the voluntary system." John Sharp Williams saw conscription separating "the loyal from the disloyal."[19]

Draft opponents sought to meet all such arguments. None was more pronounced in denying any threat to the United States than the Senate's most outspoken dissenter, Robert Marion La Follette. In a speech lasting close to two and a half hours and delivered on April 27, the Wisconsin Republican maintained that no German soldier or battleship could endanger America's coasts. If the Germans could not crack the submarine blockade so as to feed their hungry people, then surely they could not spare ships to transport troops across the Atlantic. Conversely, hundreds of thousands of U.S. soldiers might be caught in a situation similar to Britain's "desperate and foolish under-taking at the Dardanelles or face "the double risk of being blown up at sea and being killed in the trenches."[20]

Indeed, conscription foes argued that the Allies were not en-dangered. Congressman James L. Slayden (D-Tex.) commented that Britain itself had not yet been invaded. House colleague Harvey Helm (D-Ky.) claimed that the Entente was smashing the Hindenburg Line on the western front and driving the Turks back to their own borders. With Berlin's manpower being exhausted at a tremendous rate, Ger-many resembled the U.S. South in the closing year of the Civil War.[21]

Moreover, one lawmaker argued, a United States with limited war aims would have no need for conscription. To Representative Denver Church (D-Calif.), "We are simply fighting to establish the right to run the German submarine blockade, and we would be able to do that at the end of the war just the same whether we enter it or not."[22]

Above all, according to anticonscription legislators, the United States had no business fighting for the material goals of the Allies. Once it deposed the kaiser, Congressman Isaac R. Sherwood (D-Ohio) asked, was the United States going to overthrow the monarchs of Spain, Rumania, Serbia, Denmark, Sweden, and Norway, or the Sultan of Turkey and the Mikado of Japan? Senator Thomas W. Hardwick (D-Ga.) opposed sending young Georgians into the trenches "to de-cide who shall have Alsace or Lorraine or Bosnia or Herzegovina, or some other outlandish country over there." The lone Socialist con-gressman, Meyer London (N.Y.), was not surprised that only one out of every 20,000 eligible men had volunteered: "They do not under-stand what it means to be asked to fight for democracy in Germany or Austria-Hungary and Turkey and Bulgaria so as to fix the boundary lines between contending European nations.... Most of the people do not know whether Hamburg is in Switzerland or in Palestine."[23]

Certain House members who favored retaining the volunteer system stressed matters of ability, willpower, and morale. To Henry I. Emerson (R-Ohio), one volunteer equaled two conscripts. James W. Wise (D-Ga.) proclaimed, "I want an army of free men; not slaves."[24]

Conversely, House conscription foes scorned draftees. Asked James F. Byrnes (D-S.C.), "Are you going to defeat Germany with an army of pool-room sharks?" Addressing his colleagues for more than an hour, Speaker Clark drew much attention for saying, "I protest with all my heart and mind and soul against the slur of being a conscript placed upon the men of Missouri! In the estimations of Missourians, there is precious little difference between a conscript and a convict." John M. C. Smith took particular exception to Champ Clark's convict analogy: "There is no more connection between conscript and convict than there is between preacher and prisoner."[25]

To conscription foes, however, draftees were far too young to serve overseas. One should not, argued Congressman John Morin (R-Pa.), send America's youth to Europe, where women were treated disdainfully and the Christian Sabbath not observed. Senator William F. Kirby (D-Ark.) saw in the draft corroboration of the old statement of "a rich man's war and a poor man's fight." Congressman Mark Bacon (R-Mich.) spoke of "sons between the age of 18 and 21 . . . shot down or [who] return sightless, armless, legless, dying of disease, or their health wrecked for life."[26]

Some conscription opponents saw sinister interests behind the draft. Senator Lawrence Sherman (R-Ill.) condemned the belligerency of "the metropolitan newspapers." Representative Daniel R. Anthony (R-Kans.) attacked the pressure exercised by such "bogus" organizations as the American Defense Society, accusing many of their members of holding munitions stocks. (Congressman Jouett Shouse (D-Kans.) sought to meet Anthony's accusation by asking how a stockholder in a munitions factory would profit more through selling munitions under the conscription system than under the volunteer one.) Alabama representative George Huddleston (D), noting that New York's prestigious Union League Club had endorsed the draft, found such backers needing "big armies and navies to protect their investments in foreign lands, to secure for them the safe return of dividends from concessions of mines, railroads, and so forth, and the exploitation of weak and undeveloped peoples." U.S. entry into the war, he continued, was merely the last in a series of capitalist involvements, ranging from "seizure" of the Philippines to the sending of troops to Haiti, Santo Domingo, and Costa Rica.[27]

The nation, draft critics warned, was losing its democratic character. Congressman Thomas Sisson (D-Miss.) saw the arrival of "Prussianism." Representative Harold K. Claypool (D-Ohio) commented that Russia's czar would have blushed at such a system. Senator Hard-wick said conscription conferred more power "than was ever con-ferred upon any German Hohenzollern, Russian Romanoff, or any Roman Caesar, or any despot in the history of the world." To Con-gressman Robert Y. Thomas Jr. (D-Ky.), conscription was simply an-other name for slavery.[28]

Conscription foes saw the present system working. If the presi-dent called for a million volunteers, Daniel E. Garrett (D-Tex.) prom-ised, "men would be standing at the doors waiting." At the current enlistment rate of two thousand a day, remarked Senator James A. Reed (D-Mo.), the nation could raise from three to five first-class regi-ments within twenty days; the regular army would be at full war strength within seventy-five.[29]

Draft foes cited the role of the British Empire in the ongoing con-flict. Congressman Edward E. Browne (R-Wis.) pointed to the ex-amples of Britain, Canada, New Zealand, and Australia, all of which currently or just recently had depended on a volunteer army. Repre-sentative Wise reported that Britain was able to raise half a million troops under the volunteer system, Canada between 400,000 and 500,000, and Australia between 300,000 and 400,000, with New Zea-land and Ireland doing equally well. Senator Reed even went so far as to claim that the English and Canadian volunteer, once trained and equipped, was a better fighting man than the German.[30]

Race played a role in the debate. Even before the congressional debates began, arch-racist James K. Vardaman (D-Miss.) warned that drafting African Americans would lead to "arrogant strutting rep-resentatives of the black soldiery in every community." Conversely, Alabama's Heflin claimed that southern white men were willing to volunteer but did not want to "leave the negro boys at home to be-come the tools of German spies and agents in stirring up trouble for our people."[31]

At times, the debate became frivolous. Representative Alben Bark-ley (D-Ky.) quipped that "Moses himself was a drafted man." Con-gressman William Adamson (D-Ga.) added that "Jesus selected or drafted all of his Disciples, and when Judas went out his successor was selected."[32]

By April 28, the anticonscription forces were worn down. Within three weeks, the House had completely reversed itself, pivoting—in historian Chambers's words—"like a weathervane in a wind." First, Dent's volunteer plan was voted down 313–109 in favor of the Kahn amendment embodying the draft. Then the House approved conscription 397–24, with 10 not voting. At this point even Chairman Dent and Speaker Clark supported it. The majority staged a great demonstration as the administration victory was announced, with several members engaging in a snake dance down the aisle.[33]

On the same day a few minutes before midnight, the Senate passed conscription 81–8. The success did not alleviate some bitterness. Senator Henry Cabot Lodge (R-Mass.) wrote a close friend concerning President Wilson: "He has not even the decency to say 'thank you' to the Republicans of the military committee who are standing by him. He did right in going to war but he is not the kind of animal who changes his spots."[34]

Two other matters came before the Senate that day, showing that certain issues still needed resolution. First, the House had fixed the age range between twenty-one and forty, the Senate twenty-one to twenty-seven. The General Staff had sought all men between nineteen and twenty-five. Second, the Senate, by a vote of 56–31, adopted the amendment of Warren Gamaliel Harding (R-Ohio) that in essence gave permission for Theodore Roosevelt to lead four volunteer infantry divisions. Twenty Democrats favored the TR proposal, including such long-standing Wilson critics as Reed, Vardaman, Hardwick, and Thomas P. Gore (D-Okla.). On the previous day, April 27, the House had rejected the Roosevelt proposal by 170 to 106.[35]

Once it had become clear that the United States had broken off diplomatic relations with Germany, Roosevelt (often called "colonel") had sought to head a division, possibly totaling 54,000 men. An ardent militarist, TR once claimed that "no triumph of peace is quite so great as the supreme triumph of war." In the spring of 1917, he offered to raise a force that would complement, not replace, universal service, which he had always endorsed. As early as February 16, he promised French ambassador Jules Jusserand and British ambassador Sir Cecil Arthur Spring Rice he could supply the trenches with 20,000 men within six months: "I should be profoundly unhappy unless I got into the fighting line." Such a gesture, he believed, would raise Allied morale while terrifying the German high command. As he wrote a friend on March 7, a month before the United States became a belligerent, "I shall endeavor to free this country from the disgrace of seeing it embark in a war without fighting, for such a war can only be ended by a peace without victory."[36]

Weeks before the United States entered the war, Roosevelt wrote Newton Baker three times, asking permission to raise his division. In the last letter he referred to having been a past commander in chief of the army, a title that came with the presidency, and to his leading the Rough Riders in the war with Spain. On March 30, TR spoke at New York's Union League Club, declaring he expected to die in France and to be buried on French soil. Former secretary of state Elihu Root responded, "Theodore, if you can convince Wilson of that I am sure he will give you a commission."[37]

The administration was always discouraging. Baker's responses were perfunctory, replying that the War Department would call upon Roosevelt if needed. Four days after the United States entered the war, TR visited the White House, conversing with the president for twenty-five minutes. "He is a great big boy," Wilson later told his secretary, Joseph Tumulty. "I was, as formerly, charmed by his personality. There is a sweetness about him that is very compelling. You can't resist the man." Three days after the meeting, Roosevelt admitted to journalist John Callan ("Cal") O'Laughlin that all his former attacks on his successor were "true and justified and necessary to say." (As late as November 1916, TR had accused Wilson of downright cowardliness, attacking the president's efforts to maintain neutrality.) He went on to remark, however, that he would "let it all drift into oblivion" if the president "will now go into the war with all his heart, and with single-minded patriotism serve this country."[38]

Any surface cordiality went for naught when, on April 13, Baker wrote Roosevelt that the Army War College had unanimously recommended against his proposal. The decision, wrote the secretary of war, was "purely military," based on the tenet that any expeditionary force should be commanded by experienced professional officers. Baker wrote economist Alvin Johnson, "We could not risk a repetition of the San Juan Hill affair, with the commander rushing his men into a situation from which only luck extricated them."[39]

There were several reasons for administration reluctance. Wilson biographer John Milton Cooper Jr. notes that the president "would not have been human if thoughts of foiling a bitter rival had not crossed his mind. Moreover, Roosevelt could not hide his desire to horn in on running the war." Certainly, Wilson recalled TR's desire for "an all-out, shoulder-to-shoulder crusade" against all the Central Powers at the very time Wilson sought to avoid military involvement. More important, the old colonel would seek a total triumph, not a "peace without victory." Obviously Wilson recalled his predecessor's remarks during the 1916 presidential campaign, when TR found Wilson's neutrality policy revealing him as worse than Pontius Pilate.

Yet Cooper downplays motives of personal revenge and political considerations, claiming that Wilson realized that the Rough Rider, cavalry-charge style of war was tragically outmoded in twentieth-century technological warfare. Roosevelt was now fifty-eight years old, blind in one eye, and at times victim to poisoning created by equatorial fever, a consequence of his 1913 journey down the Amazon River. He had not seen combat for nearly two decades. Most important of all, TR's crusading stance, desire for "total victory," and closeness to the Entente contrasted strongly with Wilson's more distant and dispassionate approach. Historian Chambers goes so far as to find Wilson's endorsement of the draft the direct result of TR's challenge.[40]

Besides, the War Department convincingly argued that TR's zeal would hamper efficiency, for he planned to recruit the most experienced officers for his volunteer force. The War Department's Tasker Bliss remarked that Roosevelt's plan would result in poorly trained troops experiencing excessive losses. Lieutenant General George Bridges, chief military adviser to British foreign secretary Arthur Balfour, convinced his superiors that conditions were too serious for any such amateurs.[41]

Two days after Baker turned TR down, Roosevelt publicly asked Congress to take up the matter. In a letter to Senator Chamberlain and Representative Dent, he spoke in terms of a division of three regimental infantry brigades, one divisional brigade of cavalry, an artillery brigade, a regiment of engineers, a motorcycle machine-gun regiment, an air squadron, a signal corps, and a supply service. He referred to "intensive training in gas-work, bomb-throwing, bayonet-fighting, and trench work." Senator Lodge soon recruited Senator

Harding to introduce a resolution authorizing Roosevelt to raise and command three divisions. The bid to Harding would foster intraparty unity, for as chairman of the 1916 Republican Convention, the Ohio senator had maneuvered to block TR's presidential nomination. Within days Harding expanded the amendment, empowering the president to appoint up to four volunteer divisions. Though Roosevelt was not specifically named, the intent of the proposal was obvious. Harding claimed that TR bore the standard "New World liberty, New World Civilization, and New World humanity," leading a force that would "put new life in every allied trench and a new glow in every allied campfire."[42]

Serving with Roosevelt would be Major General Leonard Wood, former army chief of staff and an outspoken TR protégé. Captain Frank McCoy would be divisional chief. McCoy had been wounded in the Spanish–American War, helped suppress the Philippine rebellion, served in the occupation of Cuba, and spent two years as military aide to President Roosevelt. Henry L. Stimson, William Howard Taft's secretary of war, would be commissary general. TR even offered Wilson aide Joe Tumulty a commission.[43]

TR was quick to find volunteers. Among the thousands who offered to serve under him were Senator William E. Borah (R-Idaho), who had voted against conscription, and War Secretary Baker's own brother Julian. So did a budding army captain in San Antonio named Dwight David Eisenhower. Evangelist Billy Sunday told an audience of 2,000 gathered at New York's Tabernacle that he would join the colonel's expedition, "if it was just to black his boots."[44]

For Roosevelt advocates, his celebrity status was a crucial factor. William Randolph Hearst's *New York American*, conceding it had "never worshipped at Mr. Roosevelt's shrine," remarked that "there is no other American who looms up so large in the eyes of Europe." To Congressman Augustus P. ("Gussie") Gardner (R-Mass.), Roosevelt was "one of the greatest moral forces that the modern world has ever known," a man who had commanded in "the biggest land battle the U.S. had fought since the Civil War."[45]

Roosevelt's backers made other points. Chicago congressman William E. Mason (R) accused the hostile General Staff of jealousy. Representative Walter M. Chandler (Prog.-N.Y.) compared TR favorably to John J. Pershing, whom Wilson had designated to lead the American Expeditionary Force (AEF) in Europe, calling "Black Jack" "the man who could not capture [Pancho] Villa after several months of trial." Congressman William S. Vare (R-Pa.) denied that Roosevelt's efforts would interfere with the conscription system, for men called by selective service had already volunteered for his division. "Uncle Joe" Cannon denied he was ever a Roosevelt backer but wryly found it "more dangerous to leave him at home."[46]

Roosevelt drew Republican opposition too. Many among the Old Guard had never forgiven Roosevelt for his "Bull Moose" bolt in 1912, as the resulting schism had cost the Grand Old Party the election. The party's pro-war faction had never been large. Antiwar representatives, centering around James Mann and other midwesterners, could not forget that Roosevelt had called them traitors when they backed Wilson's "peace without victory" position.

Such critics found TR's reputation much overrated. On April 9, ex-president William Howard Taft wrote James Bryce, former British ambassador to the United States: "It would involve great risk to entrust 25,000 men to a commander so lacking in real military experience and so utterly insubordinate in his nature." Congressman Tom Connally (D-Tex.) exclaimed that "the charge of the Light Brigade was a magnificent thing, but it slaughtered great numbers of soldiers uselessly." Senator William J. Stone (D-Mo.) even attacked Roosevelt's Cuban record, claiming his regiment in Cuba would have been cut to pieces had it not been rescued by Black troops of the regular army. The ultraconservative *North American Review*, edited by Wilson critic George Harvey, suggested that TR's "Western cowboys and Eastern sports" patrol the Mexican border![47]

More important, Wilson backers realized that some pro-volunteer forces were obviously using TR's cause as a means of avoiding conscription altogether. The *New York Times*, though finding Roosevelt's bid "a manly act," claimed it would "derange" the plans of the War Department. New York's *World* commented: "The volunteer system is vicious and indefensible except when he personally wishes to raise a division of volunteers." In a public letter, Joseph Leiter, president of the Army League and Chicago grain merchant, went so far as to accuse Roosevelt of "giving aid and comfort to the enemy in Congress."[48]

For a brief time, it looked as if the "Roosevelt Volunteers" amendment had a chance. On May 10, after setting the draft age between twenty-one and thirty, the three Republican delegates to the conference committee agreed to eliminate all proposals for raising volunteer units. However, it gave the president the option of bestowing a general's commission on the old colonel in the newly created forces. A day later, TR cabled Senator Harding and Congressman Gardner, saying he did not want his proposal to hold up conscription legislation. Nonetheless, he claimed, his own expeditionary force could have "sailed for France tomorrow."[49]

A surprise House motion presented by Daniel R. Anthony on May 12 would recommit the conference report with instructions to support the provision giving TR an independent command. Percy E. Quin (D-Miss.) accused the Roosevelt forces of "waving a red flag in the face of the War Department," thereby delaying the passage of the draft bill. Charles P. Caldwell (D-N.Y.) alleged that the whole purpose of the amendment was to turn Roosevelt into a martyr, hence advancing his presidential hopes in 1920. Gardner countered that there was no more politics in the Anthony proposal than there had been when President William McKinley gave Confederate general "Fighting Joe" Wheeler a command in the Spanish–American War.[50]

After such spirited debate, the House voted that day 215–178 to accept Roosevelt's offer. Forty-five Democrats voted with the majority of the Republicans. Historian Chambers notes that the antiadministration Republicans and antidraft Democrats from the South and Midwest reflected considerable national sentiment.[51]

Four days later, May 16, the conferees had reached a final compromise. The president was *permitted* but not required to accept up to half a million men in four volunteer divisions, something that—in the words of historian Thomas Fleming—"every man, woman and child over the age of six knew was never going to happen." On the same day, the House adopted the conference report without a roll call. A day later, the Senate, voting 65 to 8, adopted the conference report. Never gracious in defeat, Roosevelt immediately wrote his sister Anna, "It is exactly as if we were fighting the Civil War under Buchanan—and Wilson is morally a much worse man, and much less patriotic, than Buchanan."[52]

The president merely added to Roosevelt's humiliation by publicly saying such a move "would contribute practically nothing to the effective strength of the armies now engaged against Germany." "The business now in hand is undramatic, practical, and of scientific definiteness and precision." Responding directly to TR's cable seeking permission to raise two divisions, Wilson replied, "I need not assure you that my conclusions were based entirely upon imperative considerations of public policy and not upon personal or private choice." Pershing privately backed the president. Opposing the calling of any volunteers, he believed that the day of waving your hat, yelling "Come on, boys!" and charging up a hill was past. As the general's biographer Donald Smythe notes, "The Germans were not the Spanish."[53]

Roosevelt would not let the matter go. Writing Baker directly, he accused the secretary of listening to the "doubtless well-meaning military men, of the red-tape and pipe-clay school, who are hidebound in the pedantry of . . . wooden militarism." In a public statement disbanding his skeleton force released on May 20, TR noted "certain errors" in Wilson's announcement. He did not want an "independent" command in Europe but only to serve under such generals as Pershing and Wood. His initial division would only have about fifty regular officers, one-tenth of the number going to Europe with Pershing. Wilson's plan, he claimed, would take ten times as many men as his. He also envisioned German American and African American regiments, the latter officered by white men.[54]

The Roosevelt controversy would not die. Meeting with TR in May at a private dinner in New York's Frick Mansion, French general Joseph Joffre — serving as part of an Allied mission in the United States — told him that a march by his troops down the Champs-Élysées would electrify French morale. Later that month, Georges Clemenceau, head of the French senate's commission on the army, appealed publicly to Wilson. Writing in his own paper, *L'Homme Enchaîné*, the future premier said that to French troops Roosevelt's mere name was magic. In his reply, TR maintained that the first division of 25,000 men could head for France immediately, other divisions departing at intervals of fifteen to thirty days. Wilson, TR remarked, "is merely a rhetorician, vindictive and yet not physically brave," a man who "cannot really face facts."[55]

Historians differ concerning the wisdom of Roosevelt's proposal. Richard Striner finds Wilson missing "a priceless opportunity to turn an enemy into a friend — and an asset." Furthermore, there was no reason why the training of Roosevelt's men would have impaired the training of other units. Conversely, to David R. Woodward, the scheme threatened to politicize U.S. land forces and, because of TR's pro-British leanings, hinder Wilson's efforts to effect a balanced peace. David M. Kennedy suspects that "the aging Colonel and his ill-trained hodgepodge of glory-seekers would have blustered about in France, and, if the fates were not too cruel, retired with minimum harm done to the Allied cause and only a few lives squandered."[56]

One could well argue that temperament alone would disqualify Roosevelt from any commanding role, for the ex-president was constitutionally unable to accept any subordinate position. Even a general of Pershing's far more lengthy experience found it difficult to adjust to the type of mechanized warfare being waged in Europe. For TR, the challenge would have been much more daunting.

As the final touches were being put on conscription legislation, Allied pressure for an overt troop commitment in Europe became increasingly intense. A mission led by British foreign secretary Arthur Balfour and René Viviani, recently France's prime minister, pressed the matter. French general Joseph Joffre, who had received wide acclaim for repulsing Germany's initial offensive on the Marne in September 1914, spoke with urgency. Conversing with Wilson in early May, Joffre stressed the need for a division, asserting it would boost morale. He had fifteen to twenty more in mind by the next calendar year, that is, 300,000 to 400,000 men. The president responded that such a force would be sent as soon as possible.[57] Because the United States possessed only a small number of trained troops, the General Staff opposed the move, but Wilson saw the need to "show the flag." Neither the president nor his military realized just how weak the Allies were; most Americans still thought that shipping, loans, materials, and naval support would suffice.

On May 18, 1917, Wilson signed the conscription bill, which required 10 million men between ages twenty-one and thirty-one to register. Wilson's proclamation stressed that the draft was "in no sense a conscription of the unwilling" but rather "selection from a nation which has volunteered in mass." Certainly, as future chief of staff General Peyton C. March later noted, the law embodied the single most important piece of legislation Congress passed during the entire war. Historian Edmund Morris writes, "This stroke of the pen made him [Wilson] the most powerful commander in chief in American history."[58]

Recalling the New York draft riots of 1863, when it took four days before federal troops could restore order, Provost Marshal Crowder turned responsibility for meeting quotas over to more than 4,500 local boards. Civilian officials—mayors and governors—offered supervision. All potential draftees registered at their local polling precinct, giving the illusion of making the process as easy as casting a ballot. Forty-three percent of all registrants were married men with dependents and thus deferred. So, too, were many farmers and workers employed in defense industries. Exemption decisions were made by one's own neighbors.

Yet the War Department was taking no chances. Even before the draft act had become law and the needed funds appropriated, Secretary Baker had the Government Printing Office secretly print more than 10 million blank forms. The cellar of the Washington Post Office was stacked to the ceiling with them, but both public and Congress remained ignorant. Local sheriffs maintained confidentiality.

The officer in charge, Major Hugh Johnson, later a top New Deal administrator, acted without legal authority. His assistant, Major Cassius M. Dowell, later told Crowder that "success would mean a medal of honor, failure would spell court-martial. . . . Delayed and inefficient action will merely confirm Germany in her notion that we are militarily impotent."[59]

Even before registration, anticonscription activity was taking place. Anarchist Emma Goldman predicted to novelist Upton Sinclair that antidraft rioting would resemble civil war. Speaking at New York's Harlem River Casino on May 18, two days after the Senate vote ensured the bill's passage, Goldman told 5,000 people that the city alone contained 50,000 people who would refuse to fight. The nation's leading Socialist weekly, the *Appeal to Reason*, found conscription unconstitutional; it specifically denied that the conflict was either "a war for defense or a war for liberty." In Snyder, Texas, seven men were charged with seditious conspiracy for "planning to resist conscription by force." By June 1, similar arrests had taken place in such cities as Minneapolis, Detroit, Milwaukee, Cleveland, Cincinnati, and Chicago.

In at least six hundred towns, more than 80,000 members of the American Protective League (APL), a vigilante group, patrolled the streets, ordering police to arrest summarily any antidraft agitators. Since most of those seized were radicals—socialists, anarchists, members of the Industrial Workers of the World (IWW)—historians H. C. Peterson and Gilbert C. Fite suspect such action was aimed at the wider purpose of suppressing dissident groups altogether.[60]

June 5 marked Registration Day. The law could have been administered within a week of the bill's signing, but officials decided to allow more time for publicity. Throughout the nation, between 7 a.m. and 7 p.m., more than 9.5 million men registered at 12,000 local registration boards staffed by 125,000 personnel. In a speech that day given in Washington to the United Confederate Veterans, the president used typically Wilsonian rhetoric: "Now we are to be an instrument in the hand of God to see that liberty is made secure for mankind." Most of the press found the event most significant, the *New York Telegram* calling it "the most eventful day, perhaps, in the history of the world's greatest democracy."[61]

The tone was often one of celebration, in the words of historian Fred Davis Baldwin, "half carnival, half Lent." A month before, Baker had written the president, saying that he hoped to make Registration Day "a festival and patriotic occasion." Now everywhere mayors, clergy, and Chamber of Commerce leaders addressed the young men in rousing terms, all conveying the sentiment that the war would be a great adventure. In Hollidaysburg, Pennsylvania, citizens sent draftees off with a bonfire of German textbooks, the band playing "Keep the Home Fires Burning." In a Philadelphia suburb, a goat carried the sign "Frog Hollow will get the Kaiser's goat." At Versailles, Indiana, as a train of volunteers rolled away, a citizen yelled, "Get the sons of bitches, men! Get the sons of bitches!"[62]

By Armistice Day, November 11, 1918, slightly less than a year and a half away, 44 percent of American males, about 24 million men, had registered. 2.8 million draftees received the telegram that began, "Greetings from the President of the United States. You have been selected by a committee of your neighbors for service in your country's armed forces." Of the over 4.5 million mobilized soldiers, more than 67 percent were draftees. The rest included 1.5 million enlisted in the army, 520,000 in the navy and marines. Within a year the U.S. Army had increased twentyfold, now with 4.75 million men and women. Eventually, more than 2 million U.S. troops were in Europe, together with 45,000 horses, nearly 40,000 cars and trucks, and 2,000 airplanes.

Nationwide reports, however, revealed that the majority of registrants claimed exemptions, with the national average being 60 percent. Of the 315,000 who registered in Chicago, 151,000 sought immunity. Outside of Chicago's Cook County, 60 percent of Illinois's registrants made similar appeals. Figures for Ohio ran up to 60 to 70 percent.

Not all males obeyed the summons. Provost Marshal Crowder himself estimated that as many as 3.6 million never registered. Of those who did register and were deemed fit, 12 percent—around 2.8 million—were draft dodgers, some fleeing the training camps for Canada or Mexico, although nearly half the offenders were eventually apprehended. Crowder noted an unusual number of self-mutilations, including blinding an eye or removing a finger or toe.[63]

Usually it was not, however, cosmopolitan, young, middle- or upper-class radicals who failed to register. Rather, most were poorer men, such as agricultural laborers hailing from the Appalachian Mountains. They would come from backcountry areas of Louisiana, Missouri, Oklahoma, Texas, and southern Illinois, and the lumber, farming, and mining regions of Minnesota and Colorado. Many arrests took place among unskilled ethnic immigrants populating such cities as Boston, New York, Jersey City, Paterson, Cleveland, and Detroit.

Registration Day itself did not go unopposed. On its eve, soldiers charged 10,000 protesters in the Bronx. Along the California coast, IWW members distributed antidraft material. In Rockford, Illinois, two hundred resisters marched to the courthouse, where they were immediately arrested. In a few places, locals took up arms, fighting a few pitched battles that resulted in from fifteen to twenty deaths. On July 30, Wilson wrote Tumulty: "Anybody is entitled to make a campaign against the draft law provided they don't stand in the way of the administration of it by any overt acts or improper influences."[64]

One of the most visible protests took place in southeast Oklahoma. On August 3, tenant farmers cut telephone and telegraph wires and blew oil pipelines leading out of the town of Healdton. These radicals hung posters such as this:

Now is the time to rebel against this war with Germany boys. Get together boys and don't go. Rich mans war. Poor mans fight. If you don't go J. P. Morgan Co. is lost. Speculation is the only cause of the war. Rebel now.

Joined by several Blacks and Native Americans and calling themselves the Working Class Union, they gathered along the banks of the South Canadian River to begin a march on Washington, D.C., living on beef and corn as they traveled. Like Coxey's Army, a massive nationwide march of the unemployed that took place in 1894, they expected to recruit huge numbers of protesters along the way. They had not gone several miles when a posse routed them. After some bloody skirmishes with backwoods renegades, about seventy-five were imprisoned.[65] What became known as the Green Corn Rebellion ended quickly.

Legislative dissenters were not entirely through with the matter. In a poll of his constituents, Representative Ernest Lundeen (R) found three-to-one opposition in his Minnesota district. In a similar survey, Chicago's William Mason declared that 90 percent of his respondents opposed conscription. On June 19, he cited a pamphlet by Hannis Taylor, constitutional expert and former U.S. minister to Spain, claiming that Congress had no authority to send conscripted men overseas. The leaflet had already upset the president's cabinet, with Wilson saying, as reported by Navy Secretary Josephus Daniels, "some examples must be made of men who circulated statements calculated to aid the enemy." When Mason proposed an amendment to a pending food bill specifying that only volunteers should be sent to the European front, Congressman William W. Hastings (D-Okla.) accused the Illinois congressman of treason. He withdrew his words after House members sought to halt a personal altercation.[66]

In mid-August, Senator Thomas P. Gore offered an abortive amendment to the War Revenue Bill forbidding the sending of drafted men overseas if they had not so volunteered. Citing the protests in his home state of Oklahoma, he claimed the new law infringed on "the Constitutional right to the pursuit of peace and happiness." Furthermore, so he argued, the Allies needed not men but munitions, which the United States could supply better than any one else. Indeed, the

United States could possibly maintain a Chinese army of 5 million at less cost than maintaining an American one of 2 million.[67]

In early September, Senator Hardwick introduced a provision to an income tax bill that would require a $50-a-month bonus to any enlistee or draftee serving abroad. When the United States had entered the war, he claimed, Americans assumed that the conflict would largely be a naval one, conducted on the high seas, where the nation's rights had been denied. John Sharp Williams accused his Georgia colleague of endorsing illegal resistance to the draft, by which "some poor, ignorant devil will be thrown in jail." Knute Nelson (R-Minn.) found such a "bribe" insulting, recalling that as a Civil War corporal he received only $11 a month, payment eventually being raised to $16. The amendment mustered only five votes, drawing Reed, Vardaman, Hardwick, La Follette, and Asle Gronna (R-N.Dak.) to its support.[68]

The general debate over conscription revealed one thing above all: despite the nation's declaration of war, there remained strong skepticism concerning any full-scale undertaking. Even echoes of Senator George Norris's (R-Neb.) accusation of putting the dollar sign on the American flag remained among several dissenters.[69] Wilson skillfully bided his time until the opposition exhausted itself. In the end, however, it was Republican Party support that gave the president the backing he needed. It remains uncertain, however, whether he fully realized this fact. He certainly did not publicly acknowledge it. Historian Chambers cites army authorities to support the claim that extensive enlistment by volunteers could have easily produced a million men in 1917.[70] One wonders, though, if after the great German spring offensive of 1918, it would have been hard getting U.S. recruits, particularly in the face of increasingly severe casualties suffered by the AEF.

If conscription was still meeting with occasional protest, far more significant events were taking place abroad. On the western front, Allied offensives were failing and the U.S. Navy was becoming the first branch of the armed forces to see action.

TWO
THE NAVAL WAR

THE U.S. CONSCRIPTS WOULD SOON ARRIVE AT A WESTERN front that was in stalemate. All through the spring and summer of 1917, Allied attacks had failed. On April 9, British general Edmund Allenby's Third Army launched a major offensive from Arras, France. Nearly 6,000 German prisoners were taken, and Canadian troops captured Vimy Ridge. Yet the assault could not be maintained. When, on May 4, Britain called it off, it only had advanced four miles while producing more than 4,000 casualties per day. In July, the British Fifth Army under General Sir Hubert Gough began a fresh drive at Passchendaele, Belgium, that ended only in November. Here the British lost 310,000 men, the French 8,500; the entire advance gained only five miles.

On April 16, a French assault under General Robert Nivelle proved equally disastrous, for only the strategic ridge of Chemin des Dames was captured. The Germans had foreknowledge of the strike and were able to repulse the attack within three days. In mid-May, General Henri Philippe Pétain assumed his nation's command amid a massive army mutiny involving whole companies that refused to "go over the top." One rebellious division even tried to march on Paris. In the words of military historian John Keegan,

"Defend the homeland the soldiers of France would; attack they would not." Experiencing the greatest crisis faced by the Allies, Pétain said, "We shall wait for the Americans and the tanks."[1]

Americans were far from optimistic. Not surprisingly, George Sylvester Viereck's *American Weekly* pointed to Entente setbacks as reason for U.S. restraint. Since 1914, the journal had been the leading voice of German American sentiment. Its "military expert," noting propagandistic press reports of Entente success, caustically asked, "Why should we raise a large army if the Allies are so successful?" The journal even opposed shipping food overseas unless the United States could be assured it could feed its own people first.[2]

Some in Congress felt similarly. Early in May, Chicago congressman Fred ("Pop-Gun") Britten (R) introduced a resolution accusing the British of imposing trade restrictions in Latin America, censoring U.S. mail, and blockading the Netherlands and the Scandinavian countries. In late June, Senator Asle Gronna told his North Dakota constituents that Britain was selfishly withholding 2.5 million troops while such allies as France were exhausting their manpower.[3]

More traditionally interventionist voices were at best cautious as to the war's eventual outcome. In April 1917, Henry Cabot Lodge envisioned Allied victory, but not before "terrific fighting and universal suffering." In May, the *North American Review* foresaw deadlock, the conflict ending within a year: Germany's armies were experiencing stalemate, its people were starving, and its allies weakened to the point of exhaustion. To the prominent *New York Tribune* correspondent Frank Simonds, the struggle would last as long as the American Civil War; certainly Germany could not be conquered within the year. Former assistant attorney general James M. Beck, who had written several books stressing German atrocities, mourned, "this is the darkest hour of the greatest conflict in history."[4]

The Wilson administration manifested alarm. In early June, Assistant Secretary of the Navy Franklin Delano Roosevelt warned, "Unless haste is made we stand a chance of losing the war." Walter Hines Page, U.S. ambassador to Britain, envisioned a Europe-wide famine. Late in May, War Secretary Newton Baker had told newspaper editors that the Allies were so exhausted that only U.S. power could establish permanent peace. In his diary, Wilson's confidant Colonel House questioned whether France could sustain itself for the rest of the year. When in mid-June, Pershing's principal adviser, Colonel James G. Harbord, arrived in France, he confided to his diary that a coup there would not be surprising. Slightly more optimistic, Pershing wrote Baker in July, predicting that France could hold on until the next spring, but that it was "very tired of this war."[5]

Financially, Britain had been threatened with bankruptcy for several months. Since October 1916, Britain and France had needed massive funds to continue the war. Britain was in so much peril that Wilson could have pressed it to abolish the blacklist and loosen its continental blockade. Early in the war, the British had begun to seize ships of neutral nations suspected of transporting goods bound for the Central Powers. In July 1916, Britain banned its subjects from trading with firms suspected of dealing with Germany and its allies. On June 29, 1917, British foreign secretary Balfour warned Colonel House of a financial disaster "worse than defeat in the field." Realizing Britain's total dependence on U.S. credit, the British press mogul Alfred Harmsworth, commonly known as Lord Northcliffe, cautioned, "If loan stops, war stops." Ambassador Page spoke in terms of "general collapse," the "brink of a precipice."[6] July 1 marked the due date for a $400 million overdraft with J. P. Morgan and Company. In the last days of June, Britain came within hours of insolvency. Fortunately for Britain, Treasury Secretary William Gibbs McAdoo responded by lending it well over a billion dollars over a three-and-a-half month period.

The two major Allies faced other problems. On May 1, more than 250,000 British engineering workers went on strike, protesting long hours, low wages, and food and fuel shortages. Cabling Baker concerning France in early July, Pershing pointed to heavy taxes and astronomical food prices. Even Germany was experiencing severe difficulties: there were reports to the State Department in April of 125,000 demonstrators in Berlin protesting a cut in bread rations.[7] Moreover, 300,000 workers there went on strike.

And if all this were not enough, there was a far more immediate crisis at hand: German submarines imperiled the British Isles. Henning von Holtzendorff, chief of the German admiralty, calculated that the sheer existence of Britain depended on 11 million tons of shipping. Were Germany to destroy an average of 600,000 tons per month for six months and were 1.2 million tons of shipping from neutral powers warded off the high seas, Britain would lose 39 percent of its tonnage, a "final and irreplaceable loss." Erich Ludendorff, first quartermaster general of the German army, boasted that "at sea, the U-boats were operating more successfully than the Admiralty predicted."[8] If, in addition, Germany could take sufficient advantage of turmoil within Russia to shift massive numbers of troops to the western front, its prospects would be suddenly and radically improved.

During the month of April 1917, 120 of Britain's oceangoing vessels were fatally struck. Between April 24 and 29 alone, it lost seven to nine merchant ships a day. In one two-week period in April, one of every four ships leaving the United States was sunk. Fuel could only last six more weeks, grain only eight, food between three and ten. In short, Britain was facing starvation. Not unexpectedly, food prices rose sharply. Furthermore, France and Italy were experiencing coal shortages. In total, from February 1 to August 1, 1917, U-boats sunk on the average 640,000 tons a month. Moreover, British vessels were being lost at more than twice the rate of any possible replacement.

Britain now faced slow and inexorable strangulation, the island nation living on borrowed time. The very outcome of the war lay in the balance. As First Sea Lord John Jellicoe remarked, "They will win, unless we can stop these losses—and stop them soon."[9] Had Britain been forced to surrender, France, Italy, and Russia would probably have faced capitulation. Certainly, the United States would have been totally unable to intervene.

At first, the U.S. Navy appeared in little condition to offer help, for it was in poor shape. When war broke out, as Assistant Navy Secretary Roosevelt noted, it was the world's third largest, possessing more than 360 ships.[10] In 1916, Congress had launched a program consisting of four battleships and four battle cruisers, in total eight capital ships, marking the largest expansion yet in U.S. history. Yet the fleet remained outdated and undermanned, possessing few cruisers and destroyers. The nation lacked troop transports capable of making a round trip to Europe.

In affirming the vision of theorist Alfred Thayer Mahan, who foresaw massive engagements of capital ships, the U.S. naval agenda proved itself totally irrelevant to the current European war. Planners envisioned a contest in the distant future in which the United States might face a coalition fighting in both oceans—Great Britain, which possessed the world's largest navy, and Germany and Japan, which also possessed major fleets. Even in January 1917, the navy's General Board visualized U.S. domination of the western Pacific, obviously at Japan's expense. Contingency plans for a war with Germany focused on only a major engagement in the western Atlantic, with the Caribbean being the likely place of action.[11] The day before Congress voted for war, the board recommended that Navy Secretary Josephus Daniels increase "the fighting line of battleships," for which in reality there was no pressing need.

Daniels had begun his tenure as very much the landlubber, having simply been editor and publisher of the prominent *News and Observer* of Raleigh, North Carolina. Like William Jennings Bryan, whom he idolized, he had been strongly antimilitarist. He was, however, an ardent reformer, stressing naval education, requiring sea duty for promotion, successfully fending off the armor-plate lobby, and, most important of all, pushing expansion of the fleet. He protected government oil reserves, generally sided with labor, and was quite public relations conscious. To meet a shortage in clerical help, he welcomed 11,000 female yeomen and 269 female marines, who were called "yeomanettes" and "marinettes."

Admittedly, Daniels was often ridiculed for his rustic demeanor, his urbane assistant secretary, Roosevelt, at best patronizing him. Roosevelt also found Daniels painfully indecisive, observing that the navy's business methods had "not changed since Christopher Columbus." More important, Daniels appeared reluctant to delegate authority, even to his most able admirals. As historian Edward M. Coffman notes, "A more understanding or diplomatic man should have been able to retain civilian control without the bitterness and without sacrificing maximum efficiency."[12]

Roosevelt's own record was mixed. He wisely pushed construction of submarine chasers and fostered the mining of British waters, but he foolishly harassed the entire department to promote almost worthless patrol boats.

Initially, the U.S. Navy focused on defending the East Coast, acting in the fear that German U-boats would cross the Atlantic. Were the Allies defeated on both sea and land, officers feared that the United

States itself lay exposed. Rear Admiral William S. Benson, chief of naval operations, later wrote, "My first thought in the beginning, during, and always was to see first that our coasts and our own vessels and our own interests were safeguarded. Then . . . to give everything we had . . . for the common cause." Ever fearful of Perfidious Albion, however, he warned, "Don't let the British pull the wool over your eyes," adding that it was none of America's business "pulling their chestnuts out of the fire. We would as soon fight the British as the Germans."[13] On April 10–11, Daniels and his staff reached an agreement with British and French admirals whereby the U.S. Navy would patrol the Western Hemisphere while Britain's fleet would concentrate on defending home waters.

American anxieties were ill founded, for at first Germany avoided extensive submarine activity in U.S. waters. Kaiser Wilhelm II and Foreign Secretary Arthur Zimmermann successfully bucked their own admiralty, hoping to divide American opinion by placating the more isolationist West and Midwest. Besides, thanks to the Battle of Jutland, fought in the spring of 1916, the German fleet remained bottled up in the North Sea.

In late March 1917, Daniels had secretly sent Rear Admiral William Sowden Sims, who had just been made president of the U.S. Naval War College, to Britain. Sims's mission: to discuss naval coordination with First Sea Lord Jellicoe. Incredibly handsome, possessing an athletic frame and sporting a white spade beard, the able Sims could appear arrogant and disingenuous. In 1910, while speaking informally at London's Guildhall, the Canadian-born officer had pledged that Britain, if ever endangered, would receive support in the form of "every man, every dollar, every drop of blood" from "your kindred across the sea."[14] President Taft felt forced to respond with an immediate reprimand. In early 1918, King George V found Sims sufficiently pro-British that the monarch wanted to make him an honorary member of the British Admiralty, a proposal that Wilson and Daniels vetoed. Admiral Sims's sentiments were so pronounced that American journalist Ray Stannard Baker reported:

> He would decapitate all the Irish, thought that Irish conscription could be enforced with "trifling losses." He would hang certain

members of Parliament, and as for the pacifists and labor leaders, why, they should simply be shot. As for the war in France, let the British and American armies withdraw and fight the Germans on the sea for twenty years if necessary. The navy would do it! . . . He was an efficient man, I should say, but think of a world ruled by men of that type![15]

By late April, Daniels made Sims commander of the U.S. Naval Forces Operating in European Waters. The post had first been offered to Captain Henry B. Wilson, who led the patrol force of the Atlantic Fleet, but the captain preferred sea command. Formal supervision remained with Admiral Henry T. Mayo, commander of the Atlantic Fleet, whose actions in Mexico had led in 1914 to the U.S. occupation of Vera Cruz.

Sims wasted no time in reporting Britain's dire condition, finding that any possible damage inflicted upon the United States was negligible compared with that being done off the Irish coast. His first cable from London, dated April 14, was stark: "The submarine issue is very much more serious than the people realize in America. The recent success of operations and the rapidity of construction constitute the real crisis of the war." Just a week later, Sims again pleaded with Daniels: "Situation here is critical, serious, and daily growing worse. During last 24 hours, 13 ships, 44,000 tons lost, not counting 4 mine sweepers, mostly southwest of Ireland." Though Washington immediately replied that thirty-six destroyers would be sent, Sims again telegraphed Daniels on July 7, "Briefly stated, I consider that at the present moment we are losing the war." The admiral was particularly furious that the Navy Department persisted in maintaining patrols along the East Coast, in Sims's words, "three thousand miles from where the vital battle of the war is going on."[16]

The admiral was not alone. On April 28, Ambassador Page cabled Secretary of State Robert Lansing: "If the present rate of destruction can be kept up, we shall have to contemplate the defeat of Great Britain." In mid-June, he again reported to the secretary: "It is the most serious situation that has confronted the Allies since the battle of the Marne." Later that month, U.S. Navy headquarters in London informed Page that "the enemy is winning the war."[17]

Submarines, however, had their limitations. They were extremely vulnerable, being light, flimsy, and slow. Forty crew members worked in intense heat. Oil and carbonic gas created a continual stench. The periscope's vision could be obscured by waves, fog, darkness, a hazy horizon, and poor light at dawn or dusk. Stormy weather forced U-boats to submerge, making it most difficult to launch a torpedo through the mountainous waves. Shooting too close to the target could damage, even sink, the sub itself. But if one fired from too great a distance, the torpedo might fizzle out. Besides, torpedoes traveled at a speed much slower than that of a projectile fired by a gun. The farther it traveled, the less likely to hit its target. In its wake, it left a telltale trail of exhaust bubbles that, if spotted, could permit the enemy to escape destruction. The British Admiralty possessed a most efficient intelligence service, capable of tracking the course of U-boat routes and giving some warning.

The U.S. military became particularly frustrated by Britain's failure to convoy their own merchant vessels, that is, send them out in groups under military escort. Admittedly, the Admiralty had legitimate reasons for skepticism. Convoys might be too large a target, thereby inviting attack. They guaranteed sluggishness, because they could not go faster than their slowest ship. Their arrival at port temporarily created bottlenecks, for suddenly all craft would arrive at once. Fog could create much confusion. Captains were by nature undisciplined, used to keeping their own schedules; they would not adjust easily to such practices as zigzagging, keeping regular distance, and sailing without night lights. Moreover, Britain, lacking sufficient escort ships for total protection, sought to concentrate on protecting its Grand Fleet and Channel crossing.

Only on April 26 did British rear admiral Alexander L. Duff, who supervised antisubmarine activity, call for the convoy system, a recommendation that Admiral Jellicoe immediately accepted. On May 10, the Admiralty introduced transatlantic escorts. An experimental convoy of seventeen ships, accompanied by two escorts, left Gibraltar, arriving safely twelve days later in Britain.

That spring, Wilson instituted convoys for U.S. ships. On the high seas, cruisers and armed merchantmen escorted commercial shipping; in danger zones, close to European ports, destroyers took over. U-boats were forced closer inshore, where they were more vulnerable to mines and submarine chasers. The United States could now send men overseas. Thanks to such convoys, in July British losses had dropped to 500,500 tons, in November to 200,000. By the end of August, Germany had sunk less than 1 percent of the thousands of ships moving in convoy.

For both the United States and Britain, the convoy system proved invaluable. Convoys were difficult to locate and, because of the protection shield they provided, hard to attack. Now it was German submarines that were in peril. An average of seven men with supplies were put ashore every minute day and night. Eventually U.S. naval units made almost two thousand sorties against enemy submarines, sinking between four and six U-boats and damaging seventeen others. In addition, meager success caused many U-boats to abandon U.S. waters, restricting their hunting to such areas as the English Channel.

Yet even in early July, Wilson felt stymied by British inertia, writing Sims, "In the presence of the present submarine emergency they [the British] are helpless to the point of panic. Every plan we suggest they reject for some reason of prudence." In mid-August, speaking confidentially near Norfolk to officers of the Atlantic Fleet, Wilson complained about the hidebound attitudes of the British Admiralty: "We have got to throw tradition to the wind." He compared the professionalism of Germany, which approaches matters "out of the book," to the amateur status of the United States, which knew so little about a task that it is "fool enough to try the right thing." Referring to the U-boat threat, Wilson asserted he would sacrifice half the U.S. and British navies in order to "crush that nest, because if we crush it, the war is won."[18]

The president was similarly distressed that the Admiralty would not launch a close-in offensive against German naval bases. Such a measure, however, was quite risky. British craft would be highly vulnerable. Belgium feared further damage on its own soil. The Dutch might find themselves forced into German hands. France could fear an increased British presence across the Channel.

By the second half of 1917, because of stalemate on the western front, Berlin no longer felt so confident. Walther Rathenau, who directed Germany's War Materials Department, reproved the U-boat command, telling Erich Ludendorff, formally first quartermaster general and in reality Germany's most powerful leader, that the U-boat war was failing: the United States and Britain were fully replacing the craft Germany was sinking. Similarly, Chancellor Theobold von Bethmann Hollweg saw no cause for optimism: Austria-Hungary probably would not survive the year; Britain would not be vanquished by autumn; no victory in Russia could compensate for failure in the West; France would not collapse.[19] In a further attempt to alleviate the submarine menace, Wilson suspended massive construction of battleships. On the very day Congress had approved the war resolution, London had notified Washington that antisubmarine craft, not battleships, were essential. Hence the president focused on building destroyers, torpedo boats, and small antisubmarine craft. On April 13, 1917, he sent six destroyers across the Atlantic, soon to be followed by twenty-six more.

The president was wise. The immediate necessity lay not in creating an independent battle fleet to serve as the basis of a "balanced" navy. Rather it lay in sinking German U-boats, thereby sustaining the Allied civilian population of the cities and the armies in the field, not to mention transporting a huge AEF to Europe. Wilson was taking a political risk, but he realized the desperateness of the situation and the need for immediate action. "Rarely in the national experience of war," writes historian David F. Trask, "has the exercise of force and diplomacy been so consistently coordinated and so broadly accepted within the armed services."[20]

The United States itself faced one brief submarine scare, which took place more than a year after it had entered the war. Beginning on June 5, 1918, press reports appeared daily of submarine attacks on U.S. ships off the Atlantic coast. New York and Boston dimmed lights and manned antiaircraft guns. Franklin Roosevelt warned his wife, Eleanor, who was summering at Campobello Island with their children, to hide in the woods if the Germans attacked. Uncle Theodore hoped the fear of imminent attack might bring the war "home to our people" as never before. On July 22, the press reported that U-boats sank four barges off Cape Cod. Yet, when Republican senators Boies Penrose (Pa.) and Frank Brandegee (Conn.) accused Daniels of faulty priorities, Henry Cabot Lodge defended him. Better to use destroyers to convoy troops than to chase submarines far afield, which was "something like searching for a needle in a haystack."[21] But during the entire war, only four U.S. Navy warships were lost to the enemy. In October 1918, the Germans sank only 112,000 tons.

German sea warfare was seriously flawed. Berlin's command structure lacked unity. The secretary of the naval office, the chief of the naval cabinet, the chief of the naval staff, the commander of the High Seas Fleet, the commander of the Baltic Fleet, and the kaiser were all separate players, at times acting independently of each other. Such disorganization delayed the use of U-cruisers, a larger submarine class with the capacity to remain at sea for longer periods. It also hindered plans to expand repair facilities in the Adriatic while playing havoc with the ever-growing convoy system. Tensions between military and civilian leadership proved a fatal weakness, as military leaders constantly overruled the initiatives of diplomats.

When Ludendorff finally prioritized submarine construction, it was too late. During the entire year of 1918, Germany built only seventy-four U-boats. By spring, the general conceded that submarines could not prevent U.S. doughboys from reaching the western front. U.S. troop transports sailed at a good pace, altered course regularly, and used unexpected routes, hence usually avoiding attack. As U-boats stationed close to the British Isles were increasingly challenged, they were forced either to operate in increasingly distant seas or remain extremely close to shore. Either way, their effectiveness was severely reduced—in short, they were increasingly bottled up.

By early summer of 1918, Kaiser Wilhelm defied his generals by canceling the U-boat offensive in U.S. waters, arguing that his nation lacked the resources to continue. Only a month before the armistice in November 1918 did Ludendorff develop a comprehensive U-boat program. Indeed, Germany never mounted a serious campaign; its large submarine cruisers proved unfit for combat. Even improved models were ineffective.

Only in the Mediterranean alone did U-boats of the Central Powers operate effectively against Allied shipping. During the first half of 1918, Admiral Sims proposed that the U.S. Navy take offensive action there. In January, his command recommended attacking Austria, as the dual monarchy of Austria-Hungary was increasingly called. American ships would enter the Adriatic Sea, spearheaded by a raid on the Austrian base at Cattaro (now Kotor) on the Dalmatian coast. Britain backed the scheme, but France and Italy successfully objected.

As far as transporting U.S. troops was concerned, over 2 million arrived safely in France after 1,142 sailings. Moreover, the ships carried an average of four tons of supplies for each soldier. Such a movement of manpower across 3,000 miles of ocean had never been organized in history. Forty-nine percent of the American Expeditionary Force traveled to France on British transports, 45 percent in U.S. ships, and the rest in ships belonging to other Allies. British vessels carried slightly more than a million men to France and U.S. ships more than 900,000, some on old tubs, others on large, fast transports. The troop carriers outpaced submarines and were well guarded by destroyers. They were hard to locate because they moved through danger areas at night.

There was some toll. In October 1917, German U-boats sank the first of several U.S. troopships, the *Antilles*, killing sixty-seven men in less than five minutes. In 1918, two other troopship sinkings took place during the return voyage from France to the United States, thereby minimizing casualties. During the spring of 1918, German subs destroyed other U.S. craft, the *U-151* alone managing to sink twenty-three merchant ships off the Atlantic coast. When one troopship, the Cunard liner *Tuscan* was sunk off the Irish coast on February 5, 1918, more than two hundred U.S. troops and British crew were lost.

For both crew and passengers, the voyage was most unpleasant. Incredible crowding, bunks jammed to the ceiling, the continued swaying of the ship, and the frequency of seasickness all made ten days on the transport a miserable experience.

Convoys were not the only U.S. naval contribution. In mid-June 1917, fearing that Germany would undertake U-boat operations in the mid-Atlantic or even in waters adjacent to the U.S. coast, the U.S. Navy began laying mines across the North Sea to Norway. Both Admiral Sims and the British Admiralty disapproved of the practice, and with good reason. For months the needed mines were scarce. Moreover, they were difficult to maintain in bad weather. If they broke loose, they endangered friendly vessels. It remained difficult to specify just where Allied ships could themselves avoid being struck.

Nevertheless, despite enemy activity, bad weather, and the enormous range involved, by war's end the U.S. Navy had placed a total of 56,570 sea mines, creating a 300-mile barrier against Germany that stretched from Scotland to Norway. The armistice of November 1918 took place before the mining mission had been completed. Its effect was relatively small, but mining did seriously damage at least six U-boats and weakened the morale of many a submarine crew.

One should not exaggerate the U.S. role in the wider naval war. Many U.S. battleships remained in Atlantic coast ports during the entire conflict. Britain's Royal Navy contributed the overwhelming proportion of ships engaged in fighting U-boats. Indeed, the United States contributed less than 10 percent of Allied units fighting the submarine.

If, however, the Americans played a supporting role at sea warfare, primarily serving as a backup for the British navy, it was nonetheless an important one. In addition to transporting massive numbers of doughboys to Europe, U.S. ships supplied more than a quarter of the convoy escort, more than 10 percent of the battleships used by the British Grand Fleet, and maintained twenty-three naval stations along Allied coasts. The United States' 368 craft in European waters included 128 submarine chasers and 85 auxiliary vessels; 75,000 ordinary seamen served, as did 5,000 officers.[22]

In conducting the naval war, Wilson experienced a major administrative headache that involved a dispute over construction of merchant vessels. George W. Goethals, famed for directing the construction of the Panama Canal and general manager of the U.S. Shipping Board's Emergency Fleet Corporation, wanted ships made of steel. William Denman, chairman of the Shipping Board and a heavy Democratic Party contributor, favored the more antiquated wooden craft. Eventually Denman realized the importance of producing steel tonnage, and Goethals did place orders for many wooden ships, but the two men remained unable to work together. By late July 1917, Wilson was exasperated by the bitter infighting, squandering of public funds, destructive publicity prompted by Goethals's leaks to the press, and—most important of all—an actual standstill in shipbuilding operations. Hence, he fired both men, replacing them with financier Edward N. Hurley, who successfully reorganized the entire shipbuilding program. Shipping still remained the most important failure of the nation's war effort, with Hurley's Emergency Fleet Corporation delivering well under 500,000 tons of the 15 million promised by September 1918.

Occasionally, long-standing commercial rivalries with Britain surfaced. In late June 1917, Treasury Secretary McAdoo wrote Andrew Bonar Law, chancellor of the exchequer, accusing Britain's naval construction program of focusing as much on postwar supremacy as on present needs. Consequently, it should be reduced. Towards the end of October, British ambassador Sir Cecil Arthur Spring Rice reported to Balfour from Washington on "an undercurrent of feeling that, by the end of the war, America will have all the ships and all the gold of the world, and that the hegemony probably of the world, and certainly of the Anglo-Saxon race, will pass across the Atlantic."[23]

Just a year later, in October 1918, Sir Eric Geddes, first lord of the admiralty, feared that whereas his own nation had been forced to concentrate on building warships, the United States was building a merchant marine threatening to surpass Britain's. In a futile mission that only resulted in antagonizing Wilson, he traveled to Washington, seeking compensation in the form of destroyers for lost British tonnage. Moreover, he desired retention of prewar ratios of merchant ship to warship construction. He reported home that the United States sought a naval force "equivalent of, or greater than, the sea power of the British Empire." Colonel House's assurance that the new League of Nations would control excessive rivalries did not assuage him.[24]

Geddes was quite correct in his suspicions. Two months before his visit, the U.S. Navy's General Board recommended a building program wide enough in scope as to create a U.S. sea force that, in its own words, would by 1925 be "equal to the most powerful maintained by any other nation in the world." On October 16, 1918, Wilson approved a three-year construction program involving 10 battleships, 6 battle cruisers, and 140 smaller vessels.[25] If the war's end saw the destruction of German naval power, a dangerous Anglo–American rivalry lay in the offing.

In the meantime, the Wilson administration realized that mobilization required more than conscripts and convoys. American minds needed to be mobilized too.

THREE
MR. CREEL ADMINISTERS A COMMITTEE

THE ALLIED DEMAND FOR TROOPS AND THE PERIL TO BRITAIN clearly indicated the need for a united home front in the United States, one squarely behind the administration's mobilization efforts. "Consensus" immediately became the watchword. President Wilson set the tone: "The supreme test of the Nation has come. We must all speak, act, and serve together!" AFL president Samuel Gompers pledged his organization's backing. Former secretary of state William Jennings Bryan cabled Wilson: "Please enroll me as a private whenever I am needed, and assign me to any work that I can do." Bryan wrote Baker that he would even volunteer to serve as a regimental "assistant chaplain." At the behest of Elihu Root, the Republican Club of New York unanimously adopted a resolution approving of Wilson's war message. He personally commented, "We must have no criticism now. The fate of our country is involved." Senator William Calder (R-N.Y.) hoped the president "will avail himself of the services of the intrepid Roosevelt, the wise Taft, and sagacious Root." In August 1917, Senator Warren Harding went so far as to favor absolute power for the president, even if the White House was occupied by a

Democrat: "Not only does this country need a dictator, but in my opinion is sure to have one before the war goes much further."[1]

Various ethnic and racial groups pledged support. New York corporation lawyer Samuel Untermyer organized the Jewish League of American Patriots. Tammany judge Daniel F. Cohalan, leader of the fiercely anti-British Clan na Gael ("party of the Irish"), asked all Americans to stand "unwaveringly, unfalteringly and uncompromisingly" behind the U.S. government. Similarly, George Sylvester Viereck's pro-German *American Weekly* claimed that Washington needed "the undivided support of all its sons." At its May convention, the National Association for the Advancement of Colored People (NAACP) endorsed the conflict. However, it reminded the nation that "absolute loyalty in arms and civil duties need not for a moment lead us to abate our just complaints and just demands."[2]

The churches joined the effort. The Federal Council of Churches resolved: "We are as one in loyalty to our country and in steadfast and wholehearted devotion to her service." America's leading Roman Catholic cleric, Baltimore cardinal James Gibbons, pronounced, "The hands of the chief executive must be upheld." The famed Manhattan politico Bourke Cochrane told a Knights of Columbus rally that the United States was fighting "the most distinctively Catholic war ever waged since the Crusade." By early 1918, evangelist Billy Sunday preached in Carnegie Hall: "I tell you it is [Kaiser] Bill against Woodrow, Germany against America, hell against heaven."[3]

Such hearkening was accompanied by calls for repression of "subversive" elements. In August 1917, Elihu Root told New York's Union League Club: "There are men walking about the streets of this city tonight who ought to be taken out at sunrise tomorrow and shot for treason." He sought similar treatment for "some newspapers in this city," an undoubted reference to the Hearst chain. (One Harvard psychiatry professor, who witnessed the speech, claimed that Root suffered from emotional dementia.) A month later, in speaking to the Banker's Association of West Virginia, Treasury Secretary McAdoo labeled every pacifist speech "treasonous," to be met with government suppression. That November, Attorney General Thomas Gregory said of the "disloyal": "May God have mercy on them, for they need expect none from an outraged people and an avenging government."[4]

Even more sober individuals were far from sanguine about such matters. Philip Marshall Brown, professor of international law at Princeton, found it "tantamount to treason" to question U.S. participation in the conflict. Harvard philosopher Ralph Barton Perry warned in the *Yale Review* that people who "willingly give their lives or the lives of their sons" could not "view with cool magnanimity the indifference or obstructiveness of their neighbors."[5]

Amid such a climate, the Bill of Rights lost its traditional meaning. In his monthly *Commoner* column of August 1917, Bryan warned against aiding the enemy under the cloak of free speech: "There are only two sides to a war—every American must be on the side of the United States." The *Outlook*, a progressive weekly that combined Protestant moralism with Rooseveltian stridency, felt similarly: "Freedom of the press and of speech does not mean freedom to foment sedition, freedom to slander our allies, or freedom to give aid and comfort to our enemies." Examples of unpatriotic actions included discouragement of recruiting or advocating tax policies that hamstrung the general struggle.[6]

Some legislators were quite vocal on the matter. Early in September 1917, John Sharp Williams told his Senate colleagues, "We have not and will not 'tolerate' disloyal speech . . . because that is 'aiding and abetting the enemy.'" Late that month, Senator J. Hamilton Lewis (D-Ill.) remarked, "The country guarantees free speech to every American but that man who uses free speech against America is not the American to whom free speech is guaranteed." In March 1918, Senator Harding, addressing the Maryland Council of Defense in Baltimore, called for shooting "the man with the bomb and the torch . . . against the wall." Later that month, Representative Julius Kahn, in opposing the "seditious or traitorous voice," told his coreligionists at a New York synagogue, "I hope that we shall have a few prompt hangings, and the sooner the better."[7]

Admittedly, not all opinion leaders shared such views. Frank Cobb, chief editorial writer of the New York *World*, approvingly quoted prominent Gilded Age jurist Thomas Cooley: "Repression of full and free discussion is dangerous to any government resting upon the will of the people." Several weeks after the United States went to war, a host of progressives—settlement workers Jane Addams and

Lillian Wald and *New Republic* editor Herbert Croly among them—
petitioned the president, noting that already protest meetings had been
broken up, speakers arrested, and censorship exercised, all to prevent
the free discussion of public issues. After two weeks, Wilson replied
to the reformers, maintaining that their letter "chimed in" with his own
"feelings and sentiments" and promising to act "at the right time."[8]

In August 1917, the American Union Against Militarism (AUAM),
led by such reformers as Wald and pacifist leader Crystal Eastman,
wrote the president attacking "these invasions of established rights
at the hands of over-zealous officials." Supporting evidence included
arrests without warrant, unlawful seizure of private papers, the closing of New York's Carnegie Hall and Cooper Union to peace meetings, and the arrest of a Manhattan man for distributing leaflets that
simply contained excerpts from the U.S. Constitution and Declaration
of Independence.[9]

Despite such expressions of unity and early signs of outright intimidation, pockets of opposition to the draft had revealed that seg-
ments of the nation did not fully back mobilization. In fact, few
Americans knew clearly why their nation was fighting. Because there
had been no frontal attack on U.S. territory, initial support for the war
effort was relatively weak. In mid-June, James G. Harbord, just appointed chief of staff of the AEF, confided to his diary: "Our American
people are not, in my judgment, very keen for the war. They do not
realize its perils." On May 23, the *American Press Résumé* had noted
that many regions betrayed a sense of inevitability more than one of
enthusiasm. In mid-August, Senator William S. Kenyon (R-Iowa)
supposedly claimed that two-thirds of Americans opposed the war.
If, indeed, the Germans captured New York, his fellow Iowans would
rejoice. In November, William Howard Taft noted "a lack of affir-
mative and aggressive support for the war in many small centers."
A month later, journalist Lincoln Steffens found apathy, with only
business and the "upper class" favoring the conflict. In his memoirs,
George Creel observed that western sentiment in particular remained
isolationist; the Northwest perceived a "rich man's war," waged to rescue Wall Street loans; those of Irish stock were "neutral," not caring
who "whipped England"; and that in every state "demagogues" raved
against "warmongers."[10]

The administration's major effort to foster national unity centered on the CPI (Committee on Public Information) headed by journalist Creel. Even before April 1917, two progressive journalists, Walter Lippmann and David Lawrence, pressed Wilson to establish a government publicity bureau. So did the muckraking reporter and novelist Arthur Bullard, once editor of a Socialist daily, the *New York Call*. In fact, Bullard's memos to Colonel House did much to outline the structure of the committee. Americans, Bullard said, must be made to desire mobilization.

George Creel had been an editor in Denver and Kansas City, worked for William Randolph Hearst in New York, been police commissioner of Denver, and served in 1916 as publicity director for the Democratic Party. His campaign tract, *Wilson and the Issues*, ardently defended Wilson's neutrality policies. A quintessential muckraker, Creel pushed for child labor laws, anticorruption practices, woman suffrage, the single tax, and public ownership of utilities. He was an outspoken opponent of Tom Pendergast's Kansas City machine.

A man of boundless energy, Creel proved himself an efficient and enthusiastic administrator. His self-confidence was legendary. A journalist friend said, "To Creel there are only two classes of men. There are skunks and the greatest man who ever lived. The greatest man is plural and includes everyone who is on Creel's side in whatever public issue he happens to be concerned with."[11]

As one reporter described him, Creel was a "fascinating talker who looked like a gargoyle." He possessed a brash personality, an acid tongue, and an absolute gift for creating opponents. Historian Walton E. Bean contends, "He seemed to have the capacity to make an enemy for life in a sentence or two." Creel would compare the mind of Henry Cabot Lodge to the soil of New England: "highly cultivated, but naturally sterile." He found Senator Hiram Johnson appearing always in "a state of chronic inflammation." He dismissed archconservative publisher George Harvey as simply "vermin." Some reformers—Albert Jay Nock, Amos Pinchot—praised him highly, but journalist Mark Sullivan wrote, "President Wilson might just as appropriately have appointed Billy Sunday."[12]

Wilson launched the CPI on April 14, 1917, by executive order. He had first wanted Frank Cobb to head the agency, choosing Creel only when Cobb declined. Formally, the CPI consisted of Secretary of State Lansing, Navy Secretary Daniels, and War Secretary Baker, with Creel as chairman. Creel met only once with the three men, never conferring with them again. In fact, Lansing's State Department refused to co-operate, finding foreign policy too delicate to be turned over to amateurs.

The CPI was originally conceived to act as a censor, something Creel later called "criminally stupid and bound to work untold harm." No one dreamed that he would immediately turn his agency into a massive operation dedicated to presenting positive information con-cerning the war effort, or to issuing "propaganda," to use a word that had not yet received opprobrium. Americans must be unified "into a white-hot mass instinct of fraternity, devotion, courage, and deathless determination." The government, Creel said, must issue "big, ringing statements"; policy "must be dramatized and staged, and every energy exerted to arouse ardor and enthusiasm." He saw himself engaged in "a plain publicity proposition, a vast enterprise in salesmanship, the world's greatest adventure in advertising," or, to use Newton Baker's phrase, "mobilizing the mind of the world."[13]

As the most gigantic propaganda campaign ever in U.S. history, the CPI was a huge success. Historian Carol A. Gruber observes that "an American couldn't step on a street car, go to the store, open a magazine or a newspaper, go to church, or attend a movie without being exposed to the CPI's message." The CPI publicized the govern-ment's war aims skillfully and with imagination, popularizing the no-tion that America was involved in a great struggle to serve democracy. It acted as a nationalizing agent, fostering such collective allegiance that—in the words of committee historian Stephen L. Vaughn—at times the CPI preached a secular religion. By the end of the war, it had achieved its essential aim: most Americans accepted its case against German militarism.[14]

Statistics supported these claims. All told, the CPI distributed 75 million copies of more than thirty pamphlets. It issued 6,000 press releases. Six hundred thousand schools received the committee's *National School Service*, a sixteen-page bimonthly designed, in the CPI's own words, to inculcate "unswerving loyalty" by using the teacher as "an officer of the state." The CPI printed the first government daily, the *Official Bulletin*. In reality a glorified release sheet, it was posted in nearly every military camp and 54,000 post offices.

Four Minute speakers were a particularly unique way of conveying the war message. Just as the United States entered the conflict, a prominent Chicago citizen, Donald Ryerson, gave a short patriotic speech during intermission at the city's Strand Theater. With this impromptu event, a new means of war propaganda was created. Envisioning themselves as something of a reincarnation of the Revolutionary War volunteers, about 74,500 Four Minute Men delivered 7.5 million speeches to 134 million people. Movie theaters remained a prominent venue, but speakers also addressed fraternal organizations, labor unions, lumber camps, houses of worship, and even Indian reservations. Women, college, and youth divisions were established.

Speaking was not limited to Four Minute Men. The CPI sponsored lecture tours by members of the Wilson cabinet and other administration officials. Some leading women were included, such as suffragist Anna Howard Shaw and muckraker Ida Tarbell. Even Jane Addams, the nation's most prominent pacifist, spoke under CPI auspices, stressing the need for conservation so as to feed the world's hungry.

As far as the brigades of CPI journalists were concerned, the war waged by the Creel Committee was the liberal's war. The CPI attracted reformers of all shades, its roster reading like a who's who of the progressive movement. Among those working for the Creel Committee were political scientist George H. Sabine; historians Sidney Bradshaw Fay and Carl Becker; muckrakers S. S. McClure and Samuel Hopkins Adams; and novelists Booth Tarkington and Upton Sinclair. Several leading Socialists, including Charles Edward Russell, William English Walling, Algie M. Simons, and John Spargo, labored enthusiastically for the CPI. So did business analyst Roger W. Babson, advertising executive Edward L. Bernays, film director D. W. Griffith, illustrator James Montgomery Flagg, and journalist Heywood Broun. One of the nation's most prominent political scientists, the University of Chicago's Charles E. Merriam, headed CPI offices in Italy.

To many CPI personnel, the war would not only preserve democracy. It would reform international relations, globalizing what they saw as the crusade against exploitation and oppression. Committee members often perceived life in general, and politics in particular, as a holy war of good against evil, or, to use the metaphor of Interior Secretary Franklin Knight Lane, "the world of Christ . . . come again face to face with the world of Mahomet, who willed to win by force." To them, the kaiser was committing—on a much greater scale—the sins of Tammany Hall and Standard Oil. In the words of historian Stephen L. Vaughn, "Not only would the war be won but reform would be made international, the world Americanized and made safe for democracy." The CPI's ideological campaign would provide social stability, something that the progressives found sorely lacking amid the turmoil created by industrialization, immigration, and the war itself. The committee would "hold fast the inner lines," reinforcing a traditional America, where, as one historian notes, "old landmarks were losing their familiar contours."[15]

With such a perspective, it was hardly surprising to find CPI writers advocating various forms of government intervention. Not only did the CPI defend the excess profits tax, but one of its bulletins found the income tax rooted in the "copartnership of mankind, a certain vague sense of the brotherhood of man." An editor of the CPI's *War Cyclopedia*, U.S. Constitution expert Edward S. Corwin, claimed that the state needed broad powers to promote the general welfare; the Princeton scholar saw Lincoln's temporary suspension of civil liberties during the Civil War as a model for Wilson to follow. Economist John R. Commons predicted a universal eight-hour day: "American labor will come out of this war . . . with as much power to fix its own wages by its own representatives as employers have." Creel himself asserted that military training was bound to increase public health and civic virtue. Indeed, the CPI's reformist thrust was so strong that historian Guy Stanton Ford later regretted that "the Germans spoiled some perfectly good enterprises by ending the war as they did."[16]

CPI writers promoted a militant form of nationalism. Interior Secretary Lane told his countrymen to love the United States because it was "holy ground." Katherine Lee Bates, author of "America the Beautiful," offered "The New Crusade," a poem that began "Life is a trifle / Honor is all / Shoulder the rifle / Answer the call." Stuart P. Sherman, later an editor of the *Cambridge History of American Literature*, believed—in the words of historian Vaughn—that any person not indoctrinated with American ideals was a menace to the republic. Historian Carl Becker, deploring the disappearance of the frontier, found the conflict a war "to save our own soul," by which he meant to prevent Americans from backsliding into a class struggle. "Free education," added Becker, aims at creating "good citizens rather than good scholars."[17]

In its effort to impose unity, the CPI fostered a powerful presidency. Wilson asked his countrymen to think of him as a symbol of "the power and dignity and hope of the United States." Creel concurred, once claiming that "a President of the United States, in time of war, is either a *dictator* or a *traitor*, for dictatorship in war is the Constitution's direct intent."[18]

The CPI encouraged domestic spying, urging citizens to report "defeatist" rumors to the Department of Justice. Said one CPI advertisement, "Do not wait until you catch someone putting a bomb under a factory. Report the man who spreads pessimistic stories, divulges— or seeks—confidential information, cries for peace, or belittles our efforts to win the war." Soon the Justice Department was receiving a thousand letters a day. Creel confessed that his agency exhibited "suppressive features," but he hoped that they would be overshadowed by positive ones. The CPI chief sought to ban publications portraying the United States unfavorably or containing material deemed too dangerous for the public. Among such "dangerous" material were books "laudatory of Germany." Although the committee itself lacked the power of censorship, it publicized statements—some made by reformers— advocating the suspension of free discussion. (Quotations by Bryan, Corwin, and attorney Clarence Darrow did quite nicely.)[19]

Scholars were quick to apply their skills to the effort. In the CPI's *War Cyclopedia: A Handbook for Ready Reference*, a 332-page work put together by twenty historians, Columbia's Charles A. Beard contributed entries on "atrocities," "Rheims," and "frightfulness" (*Schrecklichkeit*); Smith College's Sidney Bradshaw Fay wrote on "Berlin to Bagdad," "Place in the Sun," and "Bernhardi," the last item referring to a German military theorist who had written a belligerent book in 1911.[20]

Attacks on Germany approached the hysterical, with scholars willingly adding their imprimatur to the cause. Historian Wallace

Notestein used highly selective quotations to bolster his claim that the Second Reich sought world domination. The Cornell scholar also accused the Teutons of viewing the state as "something almost divine," the very same claims about the United States that Franklin K. Lane and Stuart Sherman were making.[21]

The CPI played upon fears of invasion. In a pamphlet with a circulation of 750,000, a Stanford professor of English described a possible German capture of New York City and the German pillaging of Lakewood, New Jersey. The CPI distributed a map of a German-occupied United States. (Milwaukee was renamed "Prosit"; Savannah, "New Vienna.") One script for Four Minute Men warned that under German occupation "wives, mothers, sisters and daughters will be dragged from their families, mistreated and forced to become mothers by German fathers." Purdue historian Thomas Moran pictured the enemy "coming across the Rio Grande and sweeping up through the Middle West." He asked, "Which would you rather do—fight the Germans in Indiana and Illinois or fight them on the western front?"[22]

Sometimes the committee fabricated atrocity stories, with Four Minute Men being bluntly told to arouse fear. Illustrator Charles Dana Gibson sought posters that were deliberately inflammatory. One drawing showed German officers chopping off the hands of a boy; another portrayed a soldier ready to commit rape.[23]

In an effort to win African American support, the committee claimed that Germany was no place for Blacks—Kaiser Wilhelm II himself favored slavery. Such arguments did not prevent committee films from stereotyping African Americans. One CPI film showed Black troops tap-dancing, with the caption indicating that they were exhibiting as much "rhythm" in France as they did in the U.S. South.[24]

U.S. history was reinterpreted. Evarts B. Greene of Columbia, a specialist in the American Revolution, found global-mindedness in such figures as George Washington, James Madison, and even John C. Calhoun! Harvard's Frederick Jackson Turner called upon historians to stress close ties to Britain and France. The University of Rochester's Dexter Perkins pointed to what he called "the impossibility of our maintaining our older isolation." Carl Becker argued that 2 million doughboys in France was the logical implication of the Monroe Doctrine.[25]

The committee performed extensive work among trade unions. Born in London, the AFL's Samuel Gompers was strongly pro-Ally. More important, he realized that in wartime every nation sought to suppress strikes and freeze wages. Therefore, he sought administration protection for union growth, high pay, and decent working conditions. In turn, the government needed to recruit labor behind the president's war aims and to check antiwar sentiment within its ranks. Particularly threatening was the People's Council of America (PCA), which had a strong socialist-labor base. The PCA continually denounced the war as an imperialistic conflict and sought a negotiated peace.

Hence, in late July 1917, the CPI financed the American Alliance for Labor and Democracy (AALD), created—in Gompers's words— to combat those "suspicious bodies in our midst" aiding "the forces of reaction and autocracy." Creel had advised Gompers, "I am ready to get behind you and the Central Federated Union in your attempt to Americanize the labor movement."[26] Though several pro-war socialists were on the advisory council, it was weighted heavily with AFL leaders. The AALD was directed by Robert Maisel, who headed the National Labor Publicity Organization, a body organized to promote the labor press.

At its convention in Minneapolis, September 7–9, 1917, the AALD passed resolutions backing Wilson's war aims, denouncing the People's Council, opposing a negotiated peace, and seeking to stamp out "pro-German" societies. Mindful of its constituency, it issued a "Declaration of Principles," which endorsed taxing incomes, excess profits, and real estate, plus government control of strike-torn industries.[27] Within six months after its founding, the AALD had established 150 branches in forty states, conducted 200 mass meetings, distributed nearly 2 million pamphlets, and produced 10,000 newspaper columns.

In July 1918, the Creel Committee sponsored the American Socialist and Labor Mission, composed of a small group of pro-war Socialists. After the Socialist Party refused to back the struggle, a minority faction had formed the Social Democratic League (SDL). Setting sail for Europe on July 1, the SDL delegates spent three weeks meeting with Allied labor and radical leaders, seeking to promote Wilsonian war aims and disparage peace talk. Results were mixed: the group met with pessimism in Britain, moderate warmth in France, and indifference in Italy. One delegate, Marxist editor Algie Simons, wrote home, "The world is completely torn to pieces. . . . It is like sitting at the side of the French Revolution."[28]

Both the AFL and the Creel Committee benefited from the relationship. The AFL experienced prodigious growth, received administration recognition, and won wage increases and better working conditions. The CPI gained an effective voice in its battle to win over the public to Wilsonian war aims. There was, however, a price to be paid. As historian Ronald Radosh notes, a vital part of the progressive movement took an active role in suppressing dissenting views when they were more needed than ever. Because the CPI funding and direction was secret, a dangerous precedent was set for further surreptitious subsidies of ostensibly private groups.[29]

The CPI did much work overseas. It fostered separatist movements in Germany and Austria-Hungary. It encouraged neutral nations either to join the Allies or at least not back the Central Powers. Within the Allied nations, it promoted Wilson's war aims, even at times over heads of government. Two CPI staffers played particularly prominent roles in Russia. In June 1917, Socialist journalist Arthur Bullard, an associate CPI chairman, directed committee activities there. Another associate chairman, Edgar Sisson, once editor of Hearst's *Cosmopolitan* magazine, distributed Wilson's speeches and released documents, later found bogus, claiming that Bolshevik leader Lenin was in the pay of the Germans.

Several incidents exposed Creel to particularly strong attack. One involved Edward S. Rochester, editor of the *Official Bulletin* and a former editor of the *Washington Post*. Assigned to obtain overseas endorsement of U.S. war aims, Rochester addressed European monarchs as "Dear King" and asked for a five- or six-hundred-word pronouncement from them. When criticized for his casualness, Rochester snapped: "Insult, hell! All of 'em shot back three times as much as I asked for, and I'm still blue-penciling. And that little Italian bird Victor Emmanuel wants to become a regular customer." Lansing wanted Rochester fired, but Wilson suggested that he be sent abroad as roving ambassador: "His direct methods might get us somewhere."[30]

Given Creel's impudence, flamboyance, and militant progressivism, trouble began for the CPI almost instantly. On July 2, 1917, the

CPI announced that the first major U.S. transport convoy had sunk at least one U-boat in a spectacular engagement. "The attack was made in force," said Navy Secretary Daniels in a CPI memorandum, "although the night made impossible any exact count of the U-boats gathered for what they deemed a slaughter." When a U.S. general and various other officers interviewed at the port of St. Nazaire denied anything had happened, Senator Boies Penrose demanded a Senate inquiry, soon referring to a sensational account of a battle that had never occurred reported by a "committee on misinformation." Representative Joseph Walsh (R-Mass.) called the Daniels-to-Creel cable "a fable," "worthy of a chronicle of Capt. Kidd."[31]

Democrats were quick to respond: Senator Ollie James (D-Ky.) accused CPI critics of "copperheadism." The partisan controversy was only put to rest when, early in August, Rear Admiral Albert Gleaves, who commanded the convoy, filed his report, saying at least two U-boats sought to sink his flagship and that his forces sank one submarine.[32]

Another such controversy took place in February 1918. The CPI reported that "the first American-built battle-planes are to-day en route to the front in France." Investigation revealed that only one was involved and this lone aircraft was simply passing from the factory to an American aviation field for a radiator test. In the same optimistic spirit, the CPI gave out four photos of airplanes that were, as Creel himself later confessed, "flamboyant and over-colored."[33]

Ironically, the CPI was more often attacked for its moderation than for any extremism. Despite the committee's decidedly negative depiction of Germany, several attacks on Creel involved his supposed softness towards the Germans. In instructions to its speakers, the CPI warned that "there must be no preaching of hate." Colonel George Harvey's *War Weekly*, a supplement to his *North American Review*, accused the CPI of saying that "the Huns must be treated gently as neighbors and loved as ourselves. . . . That is to say, we may hang our clothes on a hickory limb but not approach the water and must fight the barbarians, if at all, with gloves on." Even the claim that "Germany may even yet become one of the leading nations for the preservation of the peace of the world" brought attack from the archnationalist American Defense Society. In April 1918, Creel responded, "It is not our duty to deal in emotional appeals, but to give the people the facts from which conclusions may be drawn."[34]

The man himself was berated. Creel's earlier newspaper columns became another target. In 1910, while writing for the *Rocky Mountain News*, he compared America's brand of democracy to tsarist Russia: "We have no more real control over an elected official than if he were Nicholas and we poor pouliks in the fields." A year later, citing political scientist J. Allen Smith, he asserted, "the Constitution was framed by rich men for the protection of their property; by aristocrats for the preservation of aristocratic privileges." One year after that, Creel propounded, "The law winks complacently or else groans impotently at the crimes of those in high places." Such "seditious utterances," proclaimed Senator James E. Watson (R-Ind.) in April 1918, demanded Creel's removal from office. Borah recommended the penitentiary.[35]

Creel's problems continued. On April 8, 1918, speaking to the National Conference of American Lecturers, an umbrella group of educational and patriotic societies, he boasted that the nation experienced "no rush of preparation" before Wilson gave his war message. Otherwise, he argued, the United States would have been hypocritical in claiming that it would not fight until it had "exhausted every resource at our command."[36]

Again, calls were loud for Creel's dismissal. To Congressman Nicholas Longworth (R-Ohio), who was Theodore Roosevelt's son-in-law, "no more unpatriotic, un-American sentiment" had ever been uttered by any American since the war began. Representative Martin B. Madden (R-Ill.) maintained that a private citizen would have been arrested for such comments. Senator Sherman remarked, "He has all the elements of a Red, of a destroyer of civil society, one that dissolves all the restraints of communities and the protection of persons and property." The *New York Times*, claiming that the usefulness of the CPI had never been satisfactorily demonstrated, argued that at the very least Creel's committee needed a new head. (Hearst's *New York American* dissented, claiming Creel's critics were themselves indifferent to preparedness before the United States entered the war.)[37]

Creel's problems soon peaked. On May 12, in an address at New York's Church of the Ascension, a participant asked him, "Do you think every Republican and every Democrat in the Senate and House has a loyal heart?" He replied, "I don't like slumming, so I won't explore the heart of Congress for you."[38] The reaction was instantaneous. A member of the Trenton city commission wrote Wilson, "Is George Creel a damn fool or just a plain nut?" Representative Edward Pou claimed never to have seen Congress so angry. Congressman Claude Kitchin saw the comment as unworthy of the respect of any decent citizen. "Mr. Creel," commented Representative Daniel Garrett, "does not dislike Congress any more than Congress dislikes him." Colonel Harvey's *War Weekly* accused Creel of "criminal neglect" and acting as "a damned fool."[39]

Wilson, Daniels, and Pou all stressed the need to respond quickly. Five days after he spoke, Creel wrote Pou: "I made a quick and thoughtless answer that left itself open to exaggeration and distortion." His apology halted an inquiry into the matter fostered by Representative Allen Treadway (R-Mass.). Creel later wrote that his remark was aimed at such bitter antiadministration foes as James A. Reed, Boies Penrose, and James E. Watson.[40]

Fortunately for Creel, he always had the president in his corner. After Creel's preparedness remarks of April 1918, Wilson told his cabinet that he was willing to act as Creel's attorney and say, "It's me you are after. Here I am. Be brave enough to go after me." According to a magazine article Creel wrote years later, Wilson responded to the "slumming" comment by telling a Senate delegation demanding Creel's discharge, "Gentlemen, when I think of the manner in which Mr. Creel has been maligned and persecuted, I think it is a very human thing for him to have said." Wilson's case was strengthened by the fact that almost every congressional critic was either a Republican or Creel's personal enemy.[41]

Early in June, Creel faced a grilling from the House Appropriations Committee that lasted eight hours a day for three days. All committee members were hostile. "Uncle Joe" Cannon remarked that Creel "ought to be taken by the nape of the neck and the slack of the pants and thrown into space." Senator Porter McCumber (R-N.Dak.) had just made the claim that the CPI had spent $10 million distributing "socialistic literature." Yet not only did Creel receive unanimous committee support, but the entire House voted $1.25 million for the CPI without calling the roll. Congressman James F. Byrnes noted that only four CPI statements had ever been questioned, a record surpassing that of any private press association.[42]

Creel's problems were still not over. He had written an introduction to a reference book, *Two Thousand Questions and Answers about the War*. The book's publisher, the Review of Reviews Company, released the book on June 20, printing between four and five thousand copies. Some material was based upon "A Catechism of the War," a semimonthly feature of questions and answers appearing in an Australian journal, *Stead's Review*. Within a week, Creel wrote the publisher, Albert Shaw, saying that the volume had "certain disturbing points."[43] The publisher immediately withdrew all unsold copies, revoked orders for a second printing, and made plans for drastic revision.

Yet in early July 1918, Guy Stanton Ford, CPI director of civil and educational publications and University of Minnesota historian, attacked the work, claiming that it had stressed British navalism and aggression towards the Boers, praised German education and suffrage policies, and skirted U-boat and Zeppelin warfare. Claude H. Van Tyne, educational director of the National Security League's Bureau of Education and historian at the University of Michigan, argued that the work found the Germans ethnically predominant in Alsace-Lorraine, maintained that the Reich had issued warnings before sinking the *Lusitania*, and asserted that Britain controlled "nearly the whole colonial area" of the Earth's surface. In the Senate, Lodge called the book German propaganda of "the worst and most insidious kind." Reed asked why its author was not turned over to the Justice Department.[44] Due, however, to the burst of Allied victories in October and the subsequent armistice, the controversy quickly became moot.

Historians place different emphases on the CPI's work. Stephen L. Vaughn finds much of the committee's work "well intentioned," indeed "worthwhile," for the committee often stressed "antimilitarism, antiauthoritarianism, and the defense of democratic government." Far from harassing any immigrant group, it went out of its way to stress that German Americans in particular were loyal. He sees historian Guy Stanton Ford, who directed a CPI division employing several hundred scholars, attempting to uphold high standards of documentation and even forbidding the use of the word "Hun." Vaughn stresses that the most severe repression of civil liberties did not come from the

Creel Committee; rather, it emerged from the state Councils of Defense and from such private organizations as the National Security League and the American Defense Society. Nevertheless, he finds its record a flawed one, particularly as it led to confusing Americanism with subordination of the individual to the will of the state.[45]

Several historians challenge the postwar view that the CPI bamboozled an unsuspecting public. During the war, notes Walton E. Bean, no such criticism existed. Indeed, the majority of the public was *"plus royaliste que le roi."* In their study, James Robert Mock and Cedric Larson offer a similar view, claiming that the CPI articulated views already widely shared, taking advantage of "a burning eagerness to believe, to conform, to feel the exaltation of joining in a great and selfless enterprise." At the same time, it contributed to a climate wherein symbols were substituted for thought, stereotypes for analysis. Indeed, its methods and rhetoric created an atmosphere of such hate and fear that it actually endangered national safety, in the process undercutting Wilson's "concentrated mission."[46]

John Milton Cooper Jr. concurs. If, he writes, the Creel Committee was essential to prosecuting the war, it ultimately undermined Wilson's political values. Its crude salesmanship and Manichean view of the war fell far short of the president's own far more complex justification of intervention. The CPI's very existence reveals that the president was failing at a primary task: educating the public to the complexity of the struggle and the sacrifice it would involve. Instead, rather than articulating his sophisticated views concerning the conflict, he wholeheartedly backed the CPI's simplistic portrayal of the forces at work.[47]

No aspect of the American crusade so reflected the dual nature of the Progressive movement, for the Creel Committee showed that reform and repression could exist in tandem. The very agency that portrayed the global struggle as a crusade for righteousness endorsed informing on fellow citizens and demonized the Hohenzollern dynasty and the German nation. Although the matter transcends Creel's prickly personality, it remains regrettable that the wiser and more balanced Frank Cobb turned down Wilson's invitation to head the agency.

The problem is particularly heightened when scholars are recruited for promoting the war effort. The professors working for the

CPI undoubtedly had the purest of motives. Often too old for military service, they hoped to apply their learning to advance their nation's cause. It would, however, take almost superhuman qualities to refrain from "making the case" for the Allied cause and presenting, even if inadvertently, a more jaundiced analysis. Far too often, one's professional responsibility was abdicated.

At any rate, the administration was not about to leave national mobilization to sheer persuasion. It soon resorted to legal measures seldom, if ever, undertaken by the United States before.

FOUR
LEGISLATING UNITY

TO THE WILSON ADMINISTRATION, MOBILIZING OPINION WAS not enough. Espionage and sabotage could be serious dangers, particularly given such incidents as the Black Tom explosion of July 1916, which blew up a huge munitions dump in New York harbor. The impact was great enough to be felt in Philadelphia and Maryland. Furthermore, just four days after the United States entered the war, 125 people were killed when the Eddystone Ammunition Plant exploded in Chester, Pennsylvania. Even if the cause was never determined, the event added to the nation's anxiety.[1] There emerged an absolute spy mania, reaching voices usually more judicious. Wild rumors were afloat, ranging from fears of a Black uprising in the South to mines due to explode when conscription went into effect. It was hard to find a newspaper that did not refer to the permeating influence of "the enemy within."

Soon greater dangers were perceived, wider nets cast. Constitutional guarantees concerning a free press immediately became a focal point. Why, it was asked, should the federal government force men to give their lives for their nation while publications attempting to obstruct the war effort remained free?

On April 6, 1917, the day the nation entered the conflict, Wilson's cabinet had been divided concerning government censorship. War Secretary Baker and Navy Secretary Daniels would only restrict sensitive military news. Lansing wanted to ban the entire German-language press. Postmaster General Albert Burleson sought to suppress any newspaper that criticized U.S. policy.[2]

On April 13, the Department of Justice prepared an espionage bill that was approved by the Senate Judiciary Committee on the following day. Charles Warren, an assistant attorney general in the Justice Department, had drafted the original legislation in September 1915. At first its focus was in preventing sabotage. Yet the omnibus bill would not only repress spies and saboteurs but censor all publications and exclude "treasonous" materials from the mails. Wilson, who never liked the press, strongly favored the legislation, as did his secretary of state, attorney general, and postmaster general.

Once Congress saw the proposed legislation, protests immediately surfaced, particularly among Republican senators. Borah found the bill flying "into the very teeth of the language of the Constitution." Lodge saw a broad distinction between publishing information aiding the enemy and legitimate criticism. Frank A. Brandegee spoke of "an unknown guillotine" over Americans' heads. "We may well pause," warned Hiram Johnson, "lest in our tenderness for democracy abroad we forget democracy at home."[3]

The Republicans were not alone. Senator Hoke Smith (D-Ga.) claimed the bill could outlaw causal conversations if a vigilante deemed them of value to the enemy. House Speaker Champ Clark feared that the bill would censor reports of military incompetence, such as the "rotten beef" scandal of the Spanish–American War. Socialist Meyer London, who represented New York's Lower East Side, objected to the barring of "anarchistic" material: "Do not try to suppress ideas by law. You can not do it."[4]

Understandably many newspapers protested. The *Los Angeles Times* referred to "Prussian autocracy." Hearst's *New York American*, noting that the British government had concealed news concerning the Russian Revolution ("the greatest single event in human history"), cried, "Trim this espionage bill to the bone." The *New York Tribune*, accusing Wilson of adopting "the chief instrument of the Czar and the

Kaiser," claimed that no U.S. president had ever acted in such a manner. The *New York Times* carried many editorials attacking the legislation, one warning that "a newspaper correspondent might be imprisoned for merely entering a Government building in quest of news." It continued that public knowledge of the abortive Dardanelles expedition of 1915, where an Allied operation at Gallipoli failed miserably, might have helped avert the disaster.[5]

On April 20, Hearst editor Arthur Brisbane wrote Wilson, fearing that the bill embodied "the proposition to nullify, by war legislation, the Constitutional Amendment guaranteeing freedom of the press." "Some statesmen," he added, "appear eager that the nation should embark on the present serious enterprise with comment and criticism muzzled in advance." Five days later, the president, in a much publicized letter, sought to assuage him, saying he opposed any "censorship that would deny to the people of a free republic like our own their indisputable right to criticize their own public officials."[6]

Several senators backed administration censorship. Lee Overman (D-N.C.) replied, "If we cannot give our Executive power, then God help this country." Knute Nelson recalled that both Union and Confederate armies had been hampered by irresponsible press reporting. "All rules of law," remarked Albert Fall, "are set aside in the face of national necessity, of self-preservation." William J. Stone found that unrestricted freedom of speech might be dangerous, giving as an example Britain publicizing the location of antisubmarine mines in the North Sea. Similarly, Congressman Edwin Webb (D-N.C.) noted that Germany possibly relied upon press reports to mine a British harbor the day before a U.S. Navy destroyer fleet was scheduled to arrive.[7]

Even elements of the press sympathized with Wilson's goal. The *Outlook* warned that all information published by the nation's newspapers was automatically revealed to its enemies. The New York *World* endorsed "a sane censorship" limited to protecting vital military secrets.[8]

Passage of the espionage bill was complicated. After extensive parliamentary maneuvering, on May 4, by a 260–106 vote, the House adopted the general bill with strong Democratic support. Sixty-two members abstained. The legislation had been watered down but still contained Title Nine, which barred material of a "treasonable or anarchistic nature" from the mails. Postmaster General Albert S. Burleson engaged in strong lobbying. President Wilson issued a forceful message in which he claimed that the censorship provision remained "essential for the successful conduct of the war." Ten days later, the Senate, in a nonpartisan manner, voted 77–6 for a bill that eliminated censorship entirely.[9]

Wilson kept up the pressure. On May 22, he sent a public letter to Congressman Webb, chairman of the House Judiciary Committee, stressing that certain censorship powers were "absolutely necessary to the public safety." The great majority of newspapers would never print anything injurious, but there remained some "whose interests or desires will lead to actions on their part highly dangerous to the nation in the midst of war." A day later, the president wrote *World* editor Frank Cobb, saying that ninety-nine out of every hundred papers constituted no problem. Yet he found "some papers and some news agencies which we simply cannot trust," adding that "the safety of the country" was at stake.[10] Wilson was undoubtedly referring to the massive media empire of William Randolph Hearst, which kept up a running barrage of criticism against most U.S. allies.

After a further week of deadlock, conferees agreed on a modified form of censorship, but on May 31 the House voted this compromise down 184–144. Thirty-seven Democrats and four independents joined 143 Republicans in defying the president. Ninety-six members did not vote.[11] At this point Wilson gave up the fight, on June 15 signing an espionage bill lacking the provision giving the president broad power to define sensitive information. The event was practically unreported.

Historian David M. Kennedy notes that Congress was far more moved by partisan criticism of the Wilson administration than by any principled devotion to a free press. All the same, as the scholar Seward W. Livermore observes, Wilson's public prestige had been damaged. So, too, had his relations with the press. To deny the president censorship power in a time of war, writes civil liberties authority Ernest Freeberg, embodied "a remarkable victory for the First Amendment."[12]

Once major newspapers were reassured they would not be suppressed, they lost interest in the legislation. Few noted Title Twelve, which gave the postmaster general the right to determine just what mailed matter was "advocating treason, insurrection, or forcible resistance to any law of the United States." He could also decide just what determined "willful obstruction to the progress of the war." Indeed, he would be given the authority to make such decisions solely upon his personal opinion. Offenders would face up to twenty years imprisonment and/or a fine up to $10,000 for making false reports to help the enemy, inciting rebellion among the armed forces, or attempting to obstruct recruiting or the operation of the draft.

The bill had been initiated to prevent spying and disclosing information potentially valuable to the enemy. The Justice Department, however, did not convict a single German spy or saboteur under its terms. It soon became an instrument for a massive assault on the First Amendment. The day after Wilson signed the legislation, Burleson secretly wrote the nation's postmasters across the country, urging them to be alert to matter calculated "to *embarrass* or hamper the Government in conducting the war."[13]

Burleson had been a Texas congressman who received his appointment thanks to Colonel House. Until 1917, he had focused on patronage matters, which had always been the main concern of a postmaster general. A stereotypical southern legislator, complete with black coat, winged collar, and rolled umbrella, the pompous Burleson saw himself speaking for small business and agriculture. If, he mused, a day laborer could not rise as high as financier J. P. Morgan, it was because his brain was too small. As House himself privately noted in February 1918, Burleson was "the most belligerent member of the cabinet," speaking with equal vehemence against Germans, labor, and pacifists. A man of profound ignorance, he was—in the words of radical leader Norman Thomas—a person who "didn't know socialism from rheumatism." In September 1918, he told Thomas, after depriving Thomas's journal, the *World Tomorrow*, of second-class mailing privilege, "If I had my way, I'd not only kill the magazine but send you to prison for life." Only the intervention of John Nevin Sayre, the pacifist brother of Wilson's son-in-law, saved the journal. Burleson's aide, department solicitor William H. Lamar, was heard to remark, "I am after three things and only three things—pro-Germanism, pacifism, and 'high-browism.'"[14]

Ironically, most popular magazines and large city newspapers were bland, offering little discussion of the war and its meaning, much less addressing themselves to controversies over such matters as conscription or a negotiated peace. Hence, they did not need censoring. It was those of a reformist or radical bent that found themselves on borrowed time, particularly if they possessed outright socialist leanings. To be sure, Burleson did not prohibit actual publication, but he suspended second-class mailing rates, thereby preventing circulation beyond a local area. By the end of June, an issue of the *Appeal to Reason*, America's leading Socialist weekly, was thus outlawed. Within several months, sixty socialist newspapers received the same treatment as did Tom Watson's populist weekly *The Jeffersonian*, which opposed the draft.

At times, such censorship was defended. Historian James Harvey Robinson called it a transient measure that "need not be a serious cause of apprehension to any one." Nevertheless, there were occasional protests. The reformist *New Republic*, noting that officials often told journals that their "spirit" or "tone" was objectionable, claimed that "the effect is to terrorize all criticism." Hearst's *New York American* opposed any ban on Socialist journals, appreciating their call for municipal ownership of street railways, telephone companies, and gas and electric plants. It warned that a future administration could suppress journals of the major parties.[15]

In mid-July, Socialist representative Meyer London introduced a resolution calling upon the postmaster general to offer reasons for suspending mailing privileges. "The man has not yet been born," said the congressman, "upon whom the American people are ready to confer the power of determining what people shall think and what they shall say." Within three weeks, the House turned down London's resolution without debate. In a letter to Senator John Bankhead (D-Ala.), Burleson called London's move "incompatible with the public interest," adding that the department had done nothing to "suppress free criticism, right or wrong."[16]

Wilson himself was always equivocal. Upon learning in mid-July of protests made by radical editors (Max Eastman, Amos Pinchot, John Reed) and by New York publisher Oswald Garrison Villard, the president told his aide Tumulty that the offending journals "contained matter explicitly forbidden by law." In early August, Wilson appeared to backtrack slightly, writing reformist attorney Clarence Darrow that he hoped to work with Burleson towards a solution "in conformity with law and good sense." Just a month later, however, Wilson again doubled-back: "You know that I am willing to trust your judgment after I have called attention to a suggestion." "The line is manifestly exceedingly hard to draw," he informed Eastman, "and I cannot say that I have any confidence that I know how to draw it."[17]

Theodore Roosevelt accused the government of hypocrisy, writing privately in September, "The great Hearst papers and most of the German-American press have been far more vicious and dangerous [and] should, beyond all pressure, be forbidden the mails." Conversely, Tom Watson, TR maintained, was simply continuing to articulate positions Wilson himself had maintained before the United States entered the war.[18]

The Trading with the Enemy Act of October 1917 created more repression. It came in the form of an amendment introduced by Senator William H. King (D-Utah), who referred to treasonous "vipers." The bill required all foreign-language newspapers, in advance of publication, to submit to the Post Office Department English translations of any articles or editorials regarding "any nation engaged in the present war, its policies, international relations, the state or conduct of the war, or any matter relating thereto."[19]

Making no secret of his intent, in late summer Burleson had told the Washington correspondent of the *New York Evening Post* that he opposed "newspapers preaching disloyalty, newspapers that are really German at heart and in secret sympathy with the German Government with which we are fighting, newspapers which are trying to make the masses in this country believe that this is a capitalistic war." In a separate interview he maintained that no publication would be permitted to say that "this Government got into the war wrong, that it is in it for the wrong purposes, or anything that will impugn the motives of the Government for going into the war." Nor could they assert that "this Government is the tool of Wall Street."[20]

During the debate, there was dissent, in and out of Congress. Senator George Norris referred to "a desperate method of putting a newspaper out of business." Norris accused the postmaster general of seeking to make it unlawful for anyone to distribute a journal by automobile or sell it at a newsstand. Senator Albert B. Cummins

(R-Iowa) found no provision for a trial or an injunction, while James K. Vardaman accused the law of making the postmaster general "censor by statute." The National Civil Liberties Bureau (NCLB), which had just splintered off from the pacifist American Union Against Militarism, commented that the bill "makes possible the practical wiping out of a free press in the United States and completely sets adverse [subverts] constitutional rights." *Nation* publisher Oswald Garrison Villard wrote Tumulty, saying the proposed act surpassed anything enacted in either Germany or Russia. It would only create more sedition and anarchy, he added, driving "extreme radicals and agitators" underground. The pro-German *Issues and Events* noted that the Allied nations did not censor their war reports. It observed that all London and Paris papers were circulated without restraint. In fact, American correspondents returning from Germany found no restriction placed on its press.[21]

On October 6, Wilson signed the bill. The House did not even seek a roll call. The Senate passed it by voice vote. Meyer London immediately told the House, "We have made every assistant district attorney an expert on internationalism, politics, economics, and the guardian of the people's liberties."[22]

The law soon achieved the intended result. Meanwhile, the general censorship continued unabated — as did protests against it. In banning such Socialist papers as the *Milwaukee Leader* and the *New York Call,* Burleson drew criticism from more conventional sources — mainstream newspapers, pro-war Socialists, the *New Republic*, and Colonel House. In mid-October, journalist Walter Lippmann wrote House, asking why "the government is apparently more apprehensive about what an obscure and discredited little sheet says about Wall Street and munition makers than about Mr. Roosevelt's malicious depreciation of the American army," as evidenced by TR's antiadministration columns that were syndicated nationally. The *New Republic* editor added, "A great government ought to be contemptuously uninterested in such opinion and ought to suppress only military secrets and advice to break the law or evade it." House, in forwarding Lippmann's letter to Wilson, added that it was better to err on the side of leniency than repression.[23]

Again, Wilson first appeared to advocate tolerance. In early October, the president called upon the postmaster general to "act with the

utmost caution and liberality." Just a week later, he wrote a Boston reformer that Burleson was "as anxious as I am to see that freedom of
criticism is permitted," that is, unless a journal puts "insuperable obstacles in the way of the Government in the prosecution of the war."
At the same time, Wilson wrote Burleson in reference to the *Milwaukee Leader*: "There is a wide margin of judgment here and I think that
doubt ought always to be resolved in favor of the utmost freedom of
speech."[24]

Any such sentiment was short-lived. When *New Republic* editor
Herbert Croly warned Wilson that censorship was recruiting Socialist
voters, reinforcing the argument for the war being fought to enhance
capitalism, the president defended his postmaster general, replying
that Burleson was acting in "a very just and conciliatory manner." In
a letter to George Creel, Wilson referred to such "disloyal newspapers" as the *Vorwärts* (later the *Forward*), saying he thought the censorship matter was "being worked out with some degree of equity and
success." Early in November, the pro-war Socialist John Spargo protested against permitting censorship to reside in the hands of "men
who are entirely out of touch with the great liberal and radical movements of our time." The president replied that the ban was only being
applied to "very few papers indeed, only to those indeed whose offenses against the law are manifest and flagrant." In his annual message
delivered to Congress on December 4, 1917, the president appeared to
strike a more liberal stance, claiming that "noisily thoughtless and
troublesome" elements "may safely be left to strut their uneasy hour
and be forgotten," for they did not threaten "the calm, indomitable
power of the nation."[25]

Concern remained that the 1917 Espionage Act did not sufficiently restrict opinion hostile to the war. In particular, fear existed
concerning such radical labor organizations as the Industrial Workers
of the World, which promoted paralyzing strikes in the mining and
lumber industries, both critical to the war effort. In January 1918,
Congressman Edwin Webb introduced a sedition bill. Whereas the
Espionage Act of May 1917 had forced the government to prove that
injurious consequences would result directly from seditious remarks,
the 1918 sedition bill contained no such restraint. It forbade "disloyal,
profane, scurrilous, or abusive language" concerning the U.S. form of
government, flag, or uniform. Indeed, it banned any language intended

to incite resistance to the United States or to promote the cause of its enemies. The postmaster general could deny the use of the mails to any person who, in his own opinion, used the mail service to violate the act. The penalty was the same as the Espionage Act: a $10,000 fine and or up to twenty years in jail. The bill was modeled after a recent statute in Montana, where the IWW was active.

On March 4, 1918, after just minutes of debate, the House passed the legislation by voice vote. Even during this brief exchange, it was clear that members of the House wanted legislation that would not so much strike at spies as silence hostile opinion about the war and in particular curb the IWW. Representative William E. Cox (D-Ind.) feared those "talking about a revolution to come." Clarence B. Miller (R-Minn.) warned that the IWW was encouraging farmhands to strike, thereby crippling agricultural production.[26]

In early April, the Senate took up the legislation. In reporting the bill, Thomas Walsh (D-Mont.) found it necessary to punish those derogating the sale of Liberty Bonds and hampering the success of the armed forces. Not simply actual obstruction but the attempt to create obstacles must be made illegal. To Lee Overman, who again led the fight for the proposal, the country faced the choice of passing the administration bill or witnessing ad hoc action by vigilantes. He warned, "The people of this country are taking the law in their own hands on the ground that Congress is not doing its duty." Miles Poindexter (R-Wash.) asked why opponents "attach so much more importance to the right of free speech, while at the same time we take men's bodies, conscript them into the Army, and subject them to the dangers of the firing line?" Even to claim that Germany did not seek world conquest deserved punishment. Kenneth McKellar (D-Tenn.), noting that the Socialists drew close to 100,000 votes in a recent Wisconsin senatorial election, claimed to have "had no idea there were so many disloyal people in this country." James Watson went so far as to seek extending the law to peacetime statements, giving George Creel's prewar editorials as an example.[27]

Other senators, however, protested vehemently. Hiram Johnson feared the bill would bring autocracy to the United States: "We are at war against a ruthless enemy. But good God, Mr. President, when did it become a war upon the American people?" Making analogies ranging from the 1798 Alien and Sedition Acts to the Romanov dynasty, Thomas Hardwick accused the administration of creating "an engine of persecution where[by] perfectly loyal men who have honest differences of opinion can be punished." James Reed could not find a single instance that justified this legislation. Thomas P. Gore accused proponents of turning "an X ray into the hearts and minds of men" and of cutting "the tongues out of the throats" of honest dissenters. James K. Vardaman feared that the law would silence people who desired to finance the war by income and excess profits taxes rather than by the prevailing system of war bonds. Lawrence Sherman claimed to have heard more abusive language about the government from the National League for Popular Government than from "a meeting of red-handed anarchists on the lake front in Chicago."[28]

Lodge found it disingenuous to use the pretense of antiespionage legislation to curb "certain classes of agitators." "The spies or agents do not go around uttering, publishing, and writing. The dangerous men keep quiet." Better to turn saboteurs over to a military tribunal that would employ a firing squad. Former president Taft concurred.[29]

Even Theodore Roosevelt was vehement on the matter. "Our loyalty," he wrote in his syndicated column in April, "is due entirely to the United States. It is due to the President only and exactly to the degree in which he efficiently serves the United States." Indeed, the proposed law was "sheer treason," for under it Abraham Lincoln would have been imprisoned for his attacks on such antebellum presidents as James K. Polk, Franklin Pierce, and James Buchanan. (Senator William J. Stone denied that the bill ever embodied such a notion, accusing TR of merely wanting "to get out of the zone of danger himself and leave everything else and everybody else subject to criticism, to arrest, and to indictment.") In early May, TR admonished Congress to "guarantee the right of the press and people to speak the truth freely of all their public servants, including the president, and to criticize them in the severest terms of truth whenever they come short in their public duty." This limited defense of free speech, notes historian John Milton Cooper Jr., was the closest Roosevelt ever came to sympathizing with victims of official repression.[30]

On April 10, the Senate version of the sedition bill passed by voice vote. When the conference committee reported back twelve days later, it had eliminated an amendment by Senator Joseph France (R-Md.) proposing that nothing in the new law should impair "the right of any individual to publish or speak what is true, with good motives, and for justiciable ends." Assistant attorney general John Lord O'Brian argued that the France amendment would seriously interfere with the law's successful execution, adding that "motives promoting propaganda are irrelevant" and would only create "confusing legal technicalities." He gave the example of a father who steals bread for his starving children. Certain assertions could be most destructive, such as citing pacifist passages from the Bible, claiming that the war was fundamentally between capitalist and proletariat, and criticizing the status of "the negro" in the South. Obviously the Justice Department did not want the burden of proof lying on the matter of motive. Hiram Johnson called for restoring France's amendment, but Albert Fall asserted that "better that 10 innocent men should sacrifice their blood than that the country should not be saved. That is harsh doctrine, but war is harsh."[31]

On May 4, the Senate accepted the conference report, 48 to 26, with 16 not voting. Three days later the House approved the bill 293 to 1. The lone dissenter, Meyer London, found something wrong with a war that invalidated "the right of the people to hear the truth and speak the truth." Congressman Percy Quin retorted that London's sentiments meant "stabbing in the back the brave boys who have gone yonder in Flanders to go 'over the top' to save the American Republic."[32] On May 16, 1918, Wilson signed the Sedition Act, enacted as a series of amendments to the 1917 Espionage Act.

Again, technically the postmaster general was not involved in "suppressing" periodicals, but only in withdrawing second-class mailing privileges. Socialist urban dailies, such as the *New York Call*, could remain active, for they relied primarily on street sales and their own carriers for home delivery. Yet historians H. C. Peterson and Gilbert C. Fite write that "dissent of nearly every imaginable form was to be silenced or punished under this bill. Freedom of speech and of the press were subjected to the severest restrictions in American history."[33]

Although O'Brian, Attorney General Thomas W. Gregory, and President Wilson all had misgivings about the sweep of the measure, the Sedition Act was so popular that the fledgling National Civil Liberties Bureau did not struggle against it. The NCLB did note that by May the Post Office Department had interfered with more than seventy-five publications, more than half of them Socialist. The daily press paid little attention to the signing. The *Nation* saw the act as so extreme that it could be construed to forbid any African American advocacy of civil rights or opposition to lynching. The *New Republic* observed the censorship of opinion was "as drastic as any censorship can well be."[34]

Late in May, Attorney General Gregory wrote a Georgia superior court judge that all law-abiding persons, including aliens, should not be subject to unfounded suspicion. In August, in a communication to Wilson, he conceded that many targets of the Espionage Act lacked the slightest sympathy with Germany. They gave, however, "public voice to sentiments which are deemed by the Department of Justice and the trial court and jury to be obstructive of the prosecution of the war." Historian Richard Striner aptly calls Gregory's answer "a very strange mixture of insight, banality, and something that bordered on cowardice."[35]

By early September, Americans learned that Secretary Baker had banned more than twenty books from the libraries of army camps. Some works were pro-German (e.g., John W. Burgess, *European War of 1914*; F. F. Schrader, *German-American Handbook*); others pro-Irish (e.g., James G. McGuire, *What Germany Could Do for Ireland*); others pacifist (e.g., Emily Greene Balch, *Approaches to the Peace Settlement*; Rufus Jones, *A More Excellent Way*); still others left-wing (e.g., Frederick C. Howe, *Why War?*; Alexander Berkman, *Prison Memoirs of an Anarchist*). Senator Lodge backed Baker on the matter, finding the books "as thoroughly mischievous as anything that can be imagined." A subsequent list included pro-German writers (e.g., ex–New York Mayor George B. McClellan and journalist Edward Lyell Fox), pacifists (e.g., Madeline Doty and David Starr Jordan), and African Americans (e.g., Kelly Miller, dean of Howard University).[36]

The censorship of journals continued. In early September 1918, the Post Office Department held up the foreign edition of the *Outlook*, which spoke for Theodore Roosevelt's brand of progressivism, because it held Secretary Baker personally responsible for a major aircraft scandal. The editorial said, "To supply our fliers with machines

in which they have no faith because they have tried them and discovered their weakness is nothing less than a crime." Wilson backed
Burleson, saying circulation overseas might furnish useful material to
the enemy. The month also marked the detainment of the *Nation*
magazine, edited and published by reformer Oswald Garrison Villard.
An editorial in the September 14 issue criticized a mission of Samuel
Gompers overseas, referring to the labor leader as representing "sheer
bagmanism."[37]

Though Wilson soon rescinded the *Nation* ruling, by fall criticism
of the administration considerably increased. The New York *World*
accused the Wilson administration of undertaking "the Prussianiza-
tion of American public opinion." The *New Republic* called upon
other editors to oppose such repression. Colonel Harvey's *War Weekly*
found the action "not of mere injustice but of sheer idiocy." In any
other country, it continued, a cabinet officer thus criticized would resign instantly. Radical reformer Amos Pinchot quipped that Wilson
"puts his enemies in office and his friends in jail."[38]

Late in October, Wilson wrote Burleson, seeking to withdraw
mailing privileges from Harvey's *War Weekly*. It had published a cartoon depicting worried German warriors having a vision of Wilson at
his typewriter and carrying the caption "Their Only Hope." The president confessed to Burleson that he had "no interest in or sympathy
with the business of punishing people, little or big, for expressing
ideals, however abhorrent to me." He did, however, sympathize with
journalist John Palmer Gavit. The writer accused the administration
of being "ruthless toward the little fellows," such as the *Masses* or even
towards Oswald Garrison Villard, but revealed itself "palsied, its
bowels turned to water, in the presence of precisely the same conduct
on the part of the great ones." Burleson replied that such publishers
were "extreme advocates of extermination of the German people," but
he held that their views did not indicate disloyalty.[39]

Undoubtedly it was the suppression of the *Masses* that drew the
most extended attention, for it resulted in two highly visible court
cases. Founded in 1911, the radical monthly boasted such able contributors as poet Louis Untermeyer, novelist Upton Sinclair, critic
Randolph Bourne, journalist Charles Edward Russell, and artists Art
Young and John Sloan. All editorial policy rested in the hands of Max

Eastman, who later found socialism "never a philosophy of life, much less a religion, but an experiment that ought to be tried." Milder than many leftists, Eastman mocked any notion of inevitable revolution; socialism, he maintained, would not solve all social problems.[40]

In April 1917, Eastman claimed that Wilson should state U.S. war aims before he began conscripting civilians. A month later, he denied that the conflict represented a war for democracy. His June editorial endorsed the antiwar St. Louis platform of the Socialist Party, which called for opposing the conflict.[41]

It took little time for Burleson to withdraw mailing privileges. On July 5, 1917, the New York Post Office moved against the August issue of the *Masses*, citing several violations of the newly passed Espionage Act. One involved a drawing titled "Conscription," depicting two naked young men, "Labor" and "Youth," chained to a cannon and a naked woman. Another showed a figure of "Democracy" lashed to a wheel. Elihu Root, recently special emissary to Russia, was represented preparing a noose for the Petrograd Soviet. Art Young had drawn a cartoon representing a group of big businessmen studying "War Plans" with Congress hat in hand at the door. Eastman himself praised anarchists Emma Goldman and Alexander Berkman, both under indictment for opposing draft registration.[42]

In late July, Judge Learned Hand of the U.S. Court for the Southern District of New York sustained the editors, saying that the material fell within the scope of the "right to criticize." Even, however, as an appeal was pending, the August issue had not been mailed. Hence, as an "irregular" publication, its postal privileges remained revoked. By October, Burleson was telling a journalist that the *Masses* was spewing out "poison." In early November, the U.S. Second Circuit Court of Appeals reversed Hand's decision, Judge Henry Rogers ruling that "liberty of circulating may be essential to freedom of the press, but liberty of circulating through the mails is not."[43] The editors published through December but sales were limited to newsstands.

In July, while the case was under appeal, Max Eastman, John Reed, and Amos Pinchot had written a joint letter to Wilson, protesting against the suppression not only of the *Masses* but several other major Socialist journals. They quoted department solicitor Lamar, who had refused to specify any particular *Masses* article but had simply found that the "general tenor" of the magazine made it unmailable. When the joint letter was forwarded to Burleson, the postmaster general told Wilson the journal was seeking to "obstruct the Government in its conduct of the war." According to a later account, Wilson replied that the editors were "well-intentioned people," adding, "Let them blow off steam!" Yet, when Burleson responded in turn that "these men are discouraging enlistments," the president said, "Well, go ahead and do your duty." In September the president wrote Eastman concerning the legal and illegal dissent: "I can only say that a line must be drawn, and that we are trying, it may be clumsily but genuinely, to draw it without fear or favor or prejudice."[44]

Liberals protested strongly. To the *New Republic*, the tactics appeared those of "the landlady who ejected a boarder because he had scarlet fever and then billed him for leaving without notice." Upton Sinclair told Wilson that the treatment of the *Masses* was disgraceful. Better to require such journals to publish an official government response in their columns.[45]

In November 1917, the Second Court of Appeals overruled Learned Hand's decision. In April 1918, four editors, including Eastman, were again tried in New York's Court for the Southern District. This time Augustus N. Hand, the cousin of Learned Hand, served as judge. The defendants were accused of seeking to "unlawfully and willfully obstruct the recruiting and enlistment service of the United States." Socialist leader Morris Hillquit was general counsel, assisted by reformist attorney Dudley Field Malone. CPI director George Creel testified as a witness for the government, finding treasonous an advertisement in the June issue involving a pledge of "I will not kill nor help to kill my fellow man." By now, Eastman was endorsing the war effort, calling the conflict one "for liberty and freedom" and denied any middle ground between loyalty and disloyalty. After forty-two hours of deliberation, the jury could not reach a verdict, the deadlock being ten to two for conviction.[46]

In early October, a second trial took place, in which contributor John Reed claimed that war between capitalism and the working classes was the only justifiable conflict. Eastman, addressing the jury for an hour, denied that the *Masses* had ever sought to interfere with participation in the war. After an hour of deliberation, the jury voted eight to four for acquittal.[47] In February 1918, Max and his sister Crystal had begun a new monthly, the *Liberator*, named after William Lloyd Garrison's famous abolitionist weekly and devoted to war aims espoused by both Wilson and V. I. Lenin.

As during the previous year, occasionally the president did speak for civil liberties. In April 1918 he successfully opposed a bill sponsored by Senator Chamberlain that would have subjected outspoken dissenters to court-martial and the death penalty. Calling it unconstitutional, he claimed it "would put us nearly upon the level of the very people we are fighting and affecting to despise." Writing philanthropist Anita McCormick Blaine, he privately declared his "very great passion for the principle that we must respect opinion even when it is hostile."[48]

Yet these doubts did not prevent 2,168 persons from being prosecuted, 973 of whom were convicted. Only during the last weeks of the war did the Justice Department instruct federal district justices to avoid prosecuting offenders unless it gave explicit approval.

If Wilson held reservations concerning such blatant violations of the Bill of Rights, he never expressed them publicly. It was bad enough when isolated individuals, local officials, and state Councils of Defense demanded censorship. For the president of the United States to remain silent when the First Amendment was so flagrantly violated was far more irresponsible. Wilson's instincts were often on the side of leniency, but he never followed through on them. No president should entrust someone as ignorant as Burleson with suppressing material of an ideological nature. For one of the most educated individuals in the United States, particularly in regard to matters of governance, to give such a postmaster general carte blanche was more than irresponsible.

There remained, however, powerful Americans, operating in the private sector, who shared Burleson's views and who did not want repression limited to the press. They sought to impose a far more wide-sweeping unity on the nation.

FIVE
THE RAMPARTS WE WATCH

THE DRIVE FOR NATIONAL UNITY WENT FAR BEYOND GOVERNMENT propaganda and censorship. Among the semiofficial groups aiming at suppressing general opposition to the war were the Home Defense League, the Liberty League, the Knights of Liberty, the American Rights League, the Anti-Yellow Dog League, the American Anti-Anarchist Association, the Boy Spies of America, the Sedition Slammers, and the Terrible Threateners.[1] Moreover, each state had its own Council of Defense, with branches in every county and city, often focusing upon the German American "threat."

Certain voluntary organizations were particularly active. In November 1916, four professional writers founded the Vigilantes, a group organized to foster the preparedness movement. Defining itself as a "patriotic, anti-pacifist, nonpartisan organization of Authors, Artists and others," with offices on New York's Fifth Avenue, by mid-1918 it included many prominent figures. Among them were novelists Booth Tarkington and Gertrude Atherton; muckrakers Mark Sullivan, Samuel Hopkins Adams, and Ida Tarbell; publicist Bruce Barton; columnist Don Marquis; editors Lyman Abbott and William Allen White; historian Albert Bushnell Hart; philosopher Ralph Barton Perry; and former

Yale football coach Walter Camp. Several Wall Street financiers bank-rolled the effort, including Vincent Astor, First National Bank's George F. Baker, and Kuhn, Loeb's Jacob Schiff. Theodore Roosevelt contributed generously.

The Vigilantes promoted Liberty Loans, conservation of food and fuel, and the War Savings campaign while fighting the Socialist Party, the Hearst publications, pacifist groups, the German-language press, and the teaching of German in primary and secondary schools. Its vol-unteer authors contributed to 15,000 newspapers serving 53 million readers.

George Creel found the group suspect. When eighty Vigilante writers offered their service to the Committee on Public Information (CPI), he replied, "We don't want you. You're all Roosevelt men!"[2] Vigilante illustrators Charles Dana Gibson and James Montgomery Flagg did, however, work closely with the CPI.

The National Security League was far more visible—and contro-versial. It had been founded in 1914 by Solomon Stanwood Menken, a prominent Manhattan lawyer, to warn against a German military at-tack and to make U.S. forces combat-ready. When honorary president Joseph H. Choate, jurist and diplomat, died in May 1917, he was re-placed by Elihu Root. As early as that June, the NSL boasted 290 branches; it had established ninety Home Defense bodies, held several thousand meetings, and distributed 20 million pieces of literature. During the conflict, it sponsored five hundred speakers. Much financ-ing came from Henry Clay Frick, Cornelius Vanderbilt III, and the Carnegie Corporation. In the spring of 1918, Theodore Roosevelt toured the Middle West under NSL auspices. By the end of the war, it claimed 85,000 members and branches in twenty-two states.[3]

Once the United States became a full-scale belligerent, the NSL stressed internal security and the dangers of "hyphenated Ameri-canism." It took the lead in advocating military tribunals for spies, enemy aliens, and Americans opposed to the war. In time it called upon educational institutions to inquire carefully into the loyalty of their faculty. Its educational director, Princeton historian Robert McElroy, mourned that "the melting pot has not melted" as he toured nine states and addressed 45,000 people. After the war, Harvard his-torian Albert Bushnell Hart, who had preceded McElroy as NSL educational director, admitted to a Senate subcommittee that effective propaganda required simplistic arguments, uncluttered with academic complexities.[4]

On April 6, 1918, McElroy attracted much controversy when, in a speech in Madison, Wisconsin, he told several thousand people that "this state has been on trial as to whether it is American or German." Weary rain-soaked university cadets, listening to three hours of speeches in an unheated arena, showed their irritation by fidgeting, shuffling their feet, and clicking their rifle triggers. McElroy snapped, "By God, I believe you are traitors!" After the meeting, he claimed that at least 60 percent of the audience was disloyal. Even after NSL president Menken traveled to Madison and reported that McElroy should apologize, the executive committee endorsed the professor's remarks. Creel was furious. In a letter to William E. Dodd, historian at the University of Chicago, he wrote, "Few instances have struck me as more disgraceful than the McElroy affair. . . . The National Security League seems to put press notices above patriotism."[5]

In late June 1918, Menken, a Democrat with reformist leanings, praised the Hearst papers for their pro-military stance, encomiums that met with Theodore Roosevelt's scorn and Root's threatened resignation. He immediately found himself replaced by attorney Charles E. Lydecker, a conservative Republican who proved to be a weak leader. Members of the Hearst staff, including the publisher himself, had contributed to the NSL from its inception. Feeling strongly insulted, the publisher commented, "Poor little Menken, long-time cabin boy of the black craft Plunderbund, has at last been made to walk the plank by its brethren."[6]

If anything the American Defense Society, founded in 1915, was more militant. Like the NSL, it was established to agitate for a larger army and navy. Unlike the NSL, however, it directly attacked the Wilson administration. Formally chaired by Elon Hooker, who headed a New York electrochemical concern, it was dominated by Theodore Roosevelt, who in January 1918 became the honorary president. Early in 1917, the advisory board was headed by David Jayne Hill, who had been TR's ambassador to Germany. Other members included TR himself; Robert Bacon, President Taft's ambassador to France; banker Perry Belmont, vice president of the Navy League; Charles J. Bonaparte, in turn TR's secretary of the navy and attorney general; Princeton president John Grier Hibben; automobile manufacturer

Henry B. Joy; and military inventor Hudson Maxim. A year later, Charles Stebbins Fairchild, Grover Cleveland's secretary of the treasury, was added. Not surprisingly, most members backed the writers group, the Vigilantes. In January 1918, C. S. Thompson, ADS founder and chairman of its publicity committee, embarrassed the organization when he was investigated by the Justice Department for spreading false rumors concerning alleged U.S. arms shipments to Germany.[7]

Upon U.S. entry into the war, the ADS stressed "100% Americanism." It pushed loyalty oaths for teachers, opposed the teaching of German in city schools, wanted all German-owned insurance companies closed, and sought to expel Robert La Follette from the Senate for giving a supposedly seditious address. In late August 1917, the ADS created an American Vigilante Patrol that would charge "seditious" street orators with disorderly conduct. Early in 1918, it sought to organize small groups of citizens in each community who would divide all residents into the categories of "loyal," "disloyal," "doubtful," and "unknown." By August, the ADS reported that 200,000 had signed its pledge to boycott German goods for the rest of their lives. An ADS pamphlet by William T. Hornaday, director of the New York Zoological Park, advocated dropping German language instruction for all schools. He opposed the importing of German wares for the next hundred years. He continued, "After the war is over, the less we hear in America of the German language and of German literature, art, music, art and science, the better for all concerned."[8]

The Wilson administration found the ADS destructive. In September 1918, the president wrote former California congressman William Kent (Prog. Rep.): "It is astonishing to me that some of the responsible men whose names are given as Vice Presidents or Trustees should lend their authority to such damnable stuff—for it is nothing less." In his memoirs, Creel saw both the NSL and the ADS as singularly obnoxious: "At all times their patriotism was a thing of screams, violence, and extremes, and their savage intolerances had the burn of acid." Even TR, irritated by scandals and mismanagement, threatened to resign from the ADS.[9]

The largest of such organizations, "vigilante" in the true sense, was the American Protective League. Membership fluctuated widely over a year and a half, but it boasted almost half a million in its ranks by war's end. Just after Germany had declared unrestricted submarine warfare, Albert Briggs, president of a Chicago outdoor advertising firm and veteran of the Spanish–American War, sought to ferret out spies and German sympathizers, doing so by recruiting private citizens as a volunteer auxiliary to the government. Because of his extensive business contacts, he appeared ideal for this task. He approached Hinton Clabaugh, head of the Chicago branch of the Justice Department's Bureau of Investigation (BOI), who accepted their offer. Bruce Bielaski, national BOI chief with headquarters in Washington, realized that his agency was greatly understaffed and welcomed the volunteers.[10]

Briggs took the name American Protective League, first used by an old secret society in Maryland, for his new organization. Headquarters were initially established in Chicago's People's Gas Building, rooms having been donated by utilities mogul Samuel Insull. In November, the offices were moved to Washington, where they occupied an entire building.

At the time of Wilson's war message, about a hundred APL branches were being organized. The Eddystone explosion on April 10, 1917, caused factory owners to seek the protection that neither federal nor state governments appeared able to provide. On paper the organization appeared most effective, having a quasi-military structure of lieutenants, captains, and operatives. It drew from the more affluent and influential levels of society, recruiting a disproportionate number of bankers, hotel managers, retired police chiefs, insurance executives, railroad presidents, and company directors.

At first, however, APL administration was chaotic. Local units were practically autonomous. Briggs himself served as the only link between the branches and Washington. He lacked control over his membership, unable to impose discipline. Only when headquarters were moved to Washington did some semblance of order ensue.

Almost immediately, the APL was caught in turf wars between the Justice and Treasury Departments. In mid-May, Treasury Secretary William Gibbs McAdoo, who had hoped for a unified intelligence bureau under his control, warned Wilson. If, he said, the APL was allowed to continue, "suspicion will be engendered among our people, smoldering race antagonisms will burst into flame, and the melting pot of America will be a melting pot no longer, but a crucible out of which will flash the molten lead of suspicion and dissension." Writing Attorney General Thomas W. Gregory early in June, he accused the Justice Department of promoting a scheme whose very existence "is fraught with the gravest danger of misunderstanding, confusion and even fraud." In a letter to Wilson, the treasury secretary compared the danger to the injustices performed by the Sons of Liberty during the American Revolution. Within a week, Gregory replied to McAdoo, claiming that the APL volunteers had been most valuable.[11]

By this time, the president had entered the controversy. On June 4, Wilson wrote Gregory, finding such an association "very dangerous." "I wonder if there is any way we could stop it." The attorney general countered that the APL was a patriotic organization. Possessing up to 100,000 members, it had been a tremendous help to the Justice Department's BOI. The president, satisfied with Gregory's explanation, dropped the matter. Historian David M. Kennedy observes of its members: "They went their meddlesome and noxious way, unmolested and even supported by the administration."[12]

In late June, Bielaski permitted the APL to bear the title of "Organized with the Approval and Operating Under the Department of Justice of the United States." By August the first news story concerning the APL appeared. The *Chicago Tribune* reported that more than 200,000 members were on guard in "every city, town, and hamlet"; a million people served as intelligence field operatives. "Your own banker is just as likely to be a secret agent as your haberdasher or your chauffeur. . . . A street car conductor is welcomed just as graciously as a capitalist." In Cleveland, St. Louis, and San Francisco, women were members, but in July 1918 the directors banned females.[13]

It took little time for the APL to make its presence felt. From rounding up aliens to illegally arresting "slackers," it acted with abandon. Enrollees would tap phones, bug offices, and even would pose as plumbers and gas repairmen to enter homes illegally. Clergy would be asked about congregants, teachers about pupils. Nothing was sacred— bank accounts, medical records, real estate transactions, even the mails. In Minnesota, the police deputized APL members, which allowed them to arrest citizens. Recruits could pose as reporters, salesmen for autos or Liberty Bonds, or representatives of credit bureaus or insurance companies. Members loved to play detective, lurking at street corners and in hotel lobbies and sporting official-looking badges labeled "American Protective League—Secret Service" that one could purchase for seventy-five cents.

Some activities were authorized, such as making character investigations of civil service positions, enforcing laws against bootleggers, checking on jury qualifications, enforcing vice and liquor bans around military camps. In New York City, APL volunteers asked would-be army officers if they had approved of the German invasion of France and Belgium or the sinking of the *Lusitania*. Were they susceptible to bribery, blackmail, or "bad women"? The Brooklyn Navy Yard allowed the APL to investigate its 16,000 employees.[14]

McAdoo kept up his opposition. Writing Attorney General Gregory early in January 1918, he pointed to the APL's "many abuses," adding:

> I am frank to say that if I were a German spy I should want nothing better than the opportunity of joining this organization, getting one of its "Secret Service" badges, and carrying on my nefarious activities under the guise of this organization. . . . No volunteer organization should, in my opinion, be entrusted with power of this character, which can be irresponsibly exercised with resultant injustices of the gravest sort to the people.[15]

Thomas Gregory remained supportive, though he did call upon APL directors to oppose an increasing wave of hysteria. At times members heeded his request. One intervened when a New York factory woman was about to whip a fellow employee for pro-German remarks; others rescued a man about to be personally painted yellow for opposing a Liberty Bond drive; still others foiled an armed vigilante attack on a German American community.[16]

In 1918, APL activities were extended. In June, it authorized movie director Cecil B. De Mille, who owned one of the few planes in California, to organize an "Aerial Division" on the West Coast; its task involved engaging in air intelligence. That month, thanks to a distressed Polish woman living in Chicago concerned about her husband, APL members arrested an entire Jehovah's Witnesses congregation. Because of APL evidence, Joseph F. Rutherford, president of the International

Bible Students Association (the formal name of the Witnesses), and seven other members were sentenced to Atlanta Penitentiary for the rest of the war. The APL undertook investigations for the Food and Fuel Administration, reporting on enemy employees. Its Washington State unit merged with the State Minute Men, a private organization focusing on suppressing units of the Industrial Workers of the World. The newly formed cadre extended anti-IWW activity and purged German influences in the schools. In late July, the APL served as the field office for Alien Property Custodian A. Mitchell Palmer, searching out German-held assets.[17]

Almost from the outset, though, the APL faced obstacles. Relations with the Justice Department were always shaky. Intelligence work was taken over by the Secret Service, the War and Navy Departments, and the Industrial Plants Division of the Labor Department. State Councils of Defense and commissions of public safety rivaled APL work.

Several incidents made the APL look foolish. In New Orleans, the local leader sought to outlaw all horse racing. George Creel protested to Bielaski that APL staffers were investigating his friends. The State Department complained that members sought information directly from U.S. consuls overseas. One rural North Carolina member dressed up as a self-styled marshal, wearing an old Texas Ranger uniform, sporting a high-powered Winchester, and pocketing a $50 bounty for every deserter he rounded up.[18]

During the summer of 1918, as U.S. troops were engaging German forces in Europe, APL volunteers played a prominent role in rounding up men suspected of being draft dodgers. City after city experienced "slacker raids," including Milwaukee, Cleveland, Minneapolis, Detroit, Galveston, Trenton, and Sacramento. Theaters, vaudeville houses, cabarets, bars, poolrooms, restaurants, railway stations—no public place seemed immune. In mid-July, the Cubs' Weeghman Park in Chicago was raided. So, too, was the Barnum and Bailey Circus.[19]

On September 3, the APL took a leading role in the massive "slacker raids" of New York City. Acting alongside soldiers and sailors, members assumed posts at all subway exits, rounding up thousands, who stretched the city's armories beyond capacity. The raids continued two more days, corralling 60,187 men but yielding only

1,999 draft dodgers. Even Wall Street was not immune—vigilantes interrupted trading. A U.S. marshal congratulated APL director Briggs for "splendid work."[20]

Outrage was instantaneous, even reaching the Senate. Hiram Johnson likened the APL actions to the French Revolution's Reign of Terror. Only in Bolshevik Russia, remarked Albert Fall, could such actions take place. Reed Smoot (R-Utah) introduced a resolution calling for a national investigation. The New York *World*, referring to APL operatives, noted that arrests were made without warrants by "men destitute of official standing."[21]

A minority defended the roundup. Senator Andrieus Jones (D-N.M.) praised the "most patriotic" people involved, saying that "the results justify the means." Senator Miles Poindexter declared that the raids had imposed no "great hardship" or "serious mistreatment" upon anyone. To Hearst columnist Arthur Brisbane, those who objected were "like the young English lady who wanted the war to stop because she could no longer get the right kind of dog biscuit for her poodle."[22]

Attorney General Gregory had long protected the APL. Now he hedged on the matter, reporting to President Wilson that the organization betrayed an "excess of zeal for the public good." Conceding that "a considerable number of persons" were detained unjustly, he remarked in a letter made public, "Such mistakes always occur in exercising the power of arrest."[23] Neither Gregory nor Wilson ever disavowed these raids.

Yet, given the extensive negative publicity, the APL soon fell apart. The organization had caught no saboteurs and entrapped no spies. Stripping the APL of its quasi-official status, Bielaski told APL agents that they had never possessed the authority to make arrests. In October, the association's New York City chief ordered that all operators turn in their badges. The ending of draft calls, the influenza epidemic, and of course the armistice showed no further demand for such an organization. On February 1, 1919, it disbanded.[24]

APL chronicler Joan M. Jensen concludes that none of those arrested was accused of espionage: all had simply opposed the war or were against Wilson's means of waging it. Historian David M. Kennedy writes that the sheer existence of such organizations reveals "the unusual state of American society in World War I, when fear corrupted usually sober minds, and residual suspicions of strong government disposed public officials to a dangerous reliance on private means."[25] In retrospect, what is particularly disconcerting is the informal deputizing of a nondescript band of citizens to take on what are usually police functions, often violating constitutional rights in the process.

No prominent American embodied the drive for imposed unity as much as Theodore Roosevelt, and none stirred such controversy. His attacks against "hyphenated Americans" were long-standing, the nation's entry into the war simply intensifying them. Not only did he make many public addresses. He wrote a monthly column for the *Metropolitan* magazine and, more important, contributed a newspaper column several times a week for the *Kansas City Star*. Beginning with the issue of September 17, 1917, the column was syndicated in fifty leading dailies throughout the country. For Roosevelt the war served as a time of political recovery, allowing him to heal the 1912 breach with his party's Old Guard and receive consideration as the leading presidential prospect in 1920.

No friend of civil liberties, TR wanted the entire nation subject to martial law. In fact, he maintained that military courts should try all dissenters. Conscientious objectors should be made to perform army service, but without bearing arms. If they refused, they must be subjected to hard labor behind the French lines. All church services and Sunday School classes ought to be conducted in English, which should be the nation's only language. The German American writer George Sylvester Viereck, in 1912 a leading Roosevelt backer, deserved jail. Directly naming the *New Yorker Staats-Zeitung* and the Hearst chain, Roosevelt called them "enemies of America." In August 1917, TR appealed to the police to make "short shrift" of dissenting newspapers and "street-talking traitors." By April 1918, he sought the imprisonment of any American who "directly or indirectly, assails any of our allies, notably England, but also Japan." A month later, he called pacifists "the tools of alien militarism." If one wrote him criticizing the U.S. government or the Allies, TR would turn the letter over to the Justice Department for investigation and prosecution.[26]

TR's attacks on Wilson marked him off from many who sought an imposed patriotism. The administration's rejection of a Roosevelt army division simply added to his bitterness. In a work titled *The Foes of Our Own Household*, published late in 1917, TR wrote, "The leaders who have led us wrong are these foes." TR biographer John Milton Cooper Jr. notes that it is not difficult to guess just who these foes were. Just two weeks before the armistice, the former president approvingly quoted a supposed slur made informally in the U.S. House: "Here's our Czar, last in war, first toward peace, long may he waver."[27]

Some longtime Roosevelt foes believed that he nevertheless served a useful purpose. Mainline Republicans saw in TR's columns evidence that Wilson had not totally succeeded in muzzling the press. The far more radical *Nation* remarked, "It is largely to him that we owe our ability to discuss peace terms and to criticize at all."[28]

Given his views, TR found himself strongly attacked. German Americans were particularly incensed. In a 1917 Fourth of July speech, Roosevelt assailed those who, though favoring the United States against Germany, still sided with Germany against Britain. *Issues and Events* accused the former president of demanding that "every German must kiss the English colors and pray to hear of their sons and brothers slaughtered by English Zulus and Maoris, and Berlin sacked, as our English cousins sacked Washington in 1812."[29]

Others felt similarly. In October 1917, Hearst's *New York American* claimed that TR had "ceased to think sanely any more." In May 1918, it accused TR of suffering from "mental and moral deterioration" and "the childish mental processes" of old age. The newspaper carried a cartoon of this "moral traitor" showing the kaiser patting TR on the back, saying, "He's Good Enough for Me."[30]

The literary critic Stuart P. Sherman wrote, "Victory for Mr. Roosevelt means the permanent establishment of militarism in the United States," for the ex-president sought permanent universal military service and seemed grimly determined to keep the population mobilized for "the next war." In September 1917, the *Chicago Tribune*, an overtly nationalistic organ, urged him to moderate his criticism, rebuking him for "digging into the rubbish heap of past mistakes to assail the Administration." When Kermit Roosevelt accepted a commission in the British army, Viereck's *American Weekly* accused TR's son of placing the Union Jack above the Star-Spangled Banner in order to realize Cecil Rhodes's dream of an Anglo–American union.[31]

Wilson's cabinet was furious over TR's broadsides. In October 1917, Daniels argued that Roosevelt's writings were aiding Germany more than those of "the little fellows" being arrested for sedition. Burleson considered banning the *Kansas City Star* from the mails. A month later, McAdoo referred to the former president's "utter hypocrisy and lack of patriotism."[32]

Obviously aware of TR's popularity, the administration realized it could do nothing. A postal inspector did visit the offices of the *Kansas City Star* yet no action resulted. In an interview in the fall of 1917, Burleson commented, "What he says is not true, but I don't think it would affect the morale or fighting spirit of our soldiers." In December 1917, Wilson articulated his attitude: "I really think the best way to treat Mr. Roosevelt is to make no notice of him. That breaks his heart and is the best punishment that can be administered." Just after the armistice, journalist Ray Stannard Baker remarked, "Nothing could have been better calculated to infuriate a man of Roosevelt's temperament more than this. It drove him wild!"[33]

By the beginning of 1918, however, Wilson's backers were increasingly vocal in their response. On January 21, during a three-hour Senate debate that was the most tempestuous since the one over conscription, William J. Stone called Roosevelt "the most potent agent the Kaiser has in America." Lodge snapped back, "Is it treason to say that our lack of preparation has cost thousands and thousands of lives of our allies, hundreds of lives already of our own men, and uncounted millions of money?"[34]

Certain facts about Roosevelt are not commonly known. All during the conflict, his health was deteriorating. Prone to irrational rages, in October 1917 he became so fatigued that his wife, Edith, sent him to a health farm in Connecticut. In February 1918, suffering from fevers contracted four years earlier on the Amazon, TR underwent surgery on his inner ear. At one point, the surgeon called his situation "hopeless." Roosevelt had a sense of increasing irrelevance, writing his son Archie that month, "I am not in sympathy with the bulk of my fellow countrymen, and therefore am no longer fit to lead the public men or politicians."[35]

All four of Roosevelt's sons saw military service overseas. The loss of his son Quentin, an AEF pilot shot down behind German lines in

July 1918, was a blow from which he never recovered. On the very day of the armistice, TR was rushed to New York's Roosevelt Hospital, and on January 6, 1919, he died, having suffered six weeks of pain in his legs, arm, and hand.

There is a risk, however, in stereotyping Roosevelt as a crude advocate of repression. During the July 1917 riots in East St. Louis, in which nine whites and thirty-nine Blacks were killed, TR offered far more condemnation than any other leader, including President Wilson; he claimed there had been "no real provocation" for this mob violence. His address in New York's Carnegie Hall on the matter almost resulted in a fist fight with labor leader Samuel Gompers, with whom he shared a platform. Amid the anti-German hysteria, to which he strongly contributed, he claimed that discrimination against loyal Americans of German stock was "base infamy," doing so as he cited the heroism of AEF pilot Eddie Rickenbacker. (In reality, Rickenbacker was born in Columbus, Ohio, of Swiss ancestry.) Indeed, TR boasted of the "German blood" in his own veins. Unfortunately, writes biographer Kathleen Dalton, "that fine distinction was lost on audiences already inclined toward nativism."[36]

In regard to domestic policy, TR very much remained the Bull Moose reformer. In a 1917 Labor Day speech in Chatham, New York, Roosevelt called for an 80 percent excess-profit tax and continued long-standing pleas for health, old-age, and unemployment insurance; he favored heavily graduated income and inheritance taxes. "After declaring," he told his daughter Ethel in December, "that all men are equal we cannot expect that permanently the 3% will own the property and have the power: the 97% will become restless, are restless." In March 1918, he wrote a California progressive that the British Labor Party was "about 90% right." A month later, TR told reformist editor William Allen White, "If the Romanovs of our social and industrial world are kept at the head of our government the result will be Bolshevism, and Bolshevism means disaster to liberty writ large across the face of this continent."[37] His domestic policy certainly rivaled the progressivism of the Democrats.

Biographers offer varied appraisals of the old Rough Rider's role. Kathleen Dalton notes that TR eagerly sought to advance domestic reform even as the press continually focused on "bugle call" messages.

However, the great bulk of his writings and speeches were devoted to issues of mobilization and loyalty, not to the progressive cause. In addressing Roosevelt's wartime stridency, Cooper notes that TR's stress upon service and sacrifice in 1917–18 allowed him to integrate his views on domestic and foreign policy better than at any time since 1912. His continued attacks on "materialism" revealed that he had certainly not forsaken the cause of renewal at home. No shallow, juvenile romantic, the ex-president welcomed the grim and brutal aspects of war, for only by passing through suffering could men gain full humanity. As TR himself wrote in September 1917, "To my fellow Americans I preach the sword of the Lord and of Gideon."[38]

As for the ultrapatriotic leagues, any positive effect gained by their activities was far exceeded by their destructive force. In many ways, however, the "countersubversive" activities of the National Security League and the American Defense Society are the logical outcome of their prewar undertakings, with their continual focus on a German menace. The American Protective League was a somewhat different matter, for relatively obscure leaders were engaging in major vigilante action. As in the case of Burleson's censorship activities, Wilson was acquiescent. Roosevelt could have served as a positive force, rallying both reformers and many mainline Republicans in support of the general war effort. As we will see, Roosevelt had legitimate concerns over abysmal training conditions and snags in weapons production. He could not, however, separate valid criticism from vindictive assaults. Serving as a antithetical model to such GOP leaders as William Howard Taft and Charles Evans Hughes, in reality he became something of a pathetic individual.

To see the antisubversion crusade, one must take a close look at its targets.

SIX

FOES OF OUR
OWN HOUSEHOLD

THEODORE ROOSEVELT IMPLIED THAT THE "FOES OF OUR own household" lay primarily among his opponents in the Wilson administration. Many Americans, however, thought in terms of a far wider scope. Seldom if ever had the United States seen so much repression, legal or otherwise. Not since the presidency of John Adams had Congress passed a law to punish seditious speech and that legislation was short-lived. British publicist Norman Angell later recalled that "the mob mind in the United States often outdid that of Britain in violence and silliness." Only 10 out of 1,500 Americans arrested under the Espionage Act were actually accused of being German agents. Much suppression took place below the federal level, particularly in the West. State and municipal agencies, often working through Councils of Defense, were supplemented by private vigilante activity. In Minnesota, for example, the Commission on Public Safety was a de facto agent of the state government, with the state courts enforcing its edicts.[1]

Of all the ethnic groups in the United States, German-Americans were the most suspect. In 1917 they were a markedly distinct element in society, seeking to preserve their own identity and asserting themselves with vigor whenever their ancestral land came under attack. According to the 1910 census, of the nation's nearly 92 million people, more than 8 million were either born in Germany or had a German parent. At least 14 percent of Nebraska's population was of Teutonic stock, in Wisconsin nearly 29 percent.

Yet, to many Americans, the words "German" and "atrocity" were synonymous. Recalled were the German U-boat sinking of the *Lusitania* passenger ship in 1915 and the Black Tom incident of 1916. By January 1918, Harvey's *War Weekly* reported that Canadian prisoners were literally crucified, nailed to the cross and left to die in agony (no locale was given). Its publisher, Colonel George Harvey, blamed the nation's entire German population: "It is the German people who murder and crucify and mutilate." That same month, William Kenyon told his Senate colleagues that the Germans shelled Red Cross hospitals, killed the wounded after battle, and placed women and children in advance of soldiers attacking French troops. "Germany has lost its soul," he commented. In July, the Reverend Henry Van Dyke, recently U.S. minister to the Netherlands, reported German mutilation of children and the killing of old women. Novelist Gertrude Atherton was undoubtedly not alone in saying, "Better to extirpate the whole breed, root and branch." Nor was Princeton's Robert McElroy isolated in finding the German soul "as black as hell itself."[2]

Some sought to counteract such rumors. In July 1918, AEF commander John J. Pershing denied that the Germans gave poison candy to children and hand grenades to play with, infected U.S. troops with tubercular germs, and rejoiced at children's dying writhings. In October, War Secretary Newton Baker declared that the U.S. Army found only two certifiable stories of German barbarism.[3]

In offering an invocation before the House of Representatives, Billy Sunday prayed:

> Thou knowest that Germany has drawn from the eyes of mankind enough tears to make another sea; that she has drawn enough groans and shrieks from the hearts of men, women, and children to make another mountain. We pray Thee that Thou wilt make bare Thy mighty arm and beat back the great pack of hungry, wolfish Huns, whose fangs drip with blood and gore.

At one point, the evangelist remarked, "If hell were turned upside down you would find 'made in Germany' on the bottom of it."[4]

American Germanophobia manifested itself in numerous ways, ranging from the utterly ridiculous to the utterly savage. By the fall of 1917, the nation was experiencing a hatred for everything Teutonic. To members of the American Protective League (APL), a German surname made one subject to investigation. Words such as "Hun" (barbaric Germans), "Boche" (German soldiers), "Schrecklichkeit" (frightfulness), and "Kultur" (bestial ideals) were tossed about with abandon. Socialist journalist William English Walling thought the East St. Louis race riots of early July 1917, in reality rooted in southern white malice, were fostered by German spies.[5] Sauerkraut became "liberty cabbage," German measles "liberty measles." Cincinnati saloons no longer offered free pretzels.

Germany's much touted culture was assailed. To New York mortgage lawyer Richard M. Hurd, board chairman of the American Defense Society in 1918, "everything German has to go." Former state senator Lafayette Young (R), chairman of the Iowa Council of Defense, saw Germany's much touted civilization as the most overrated in the world. He claimed that Gutenberg was the last major German inventor and that no German author had ever equaled Shakespeare.[6]

Congress's passage of the Espionage Act in June 1917 by no means allayed public fears. In 1920, George Creel noted that every fire, explosion in a munitions plant, or accident on land or seas was credited to the German "spy system." A cut in a child's hand that didn't heal quickly was because of Teutonic germs in the court plaster. If an experiment in a submarine or aircraft factory failed, German "spies" had tampered with the mechanism. If a woman's headache was not cured, the "Germans" had "doped" the particular pill or powder.[7]

In a July editorial titled "Spies" that addressed subversive elements within the German embassy, the *New York Times* warned that the government "should not wait until it has the quality of legal evidence that would justify a Grand Jury indicting a man for murder in the first degree." During the same month, Senator Benjamin ("Pitchfork Ben") Tillman (D-S.C.) demanded that "the German devils" infesting the government be "ferreted out and hanged." In November, the AFL's Samuel Gompers claimed that "German spies and Teutonic agents" had honeycombed his organization's convention. At the end of the month, the *Literary Digest* warned of "furtive, ununiformed armies whose weapons are spying, sabotage, bomb-planting, incendiarism, murder, and a hundred forms of insidious and demoralizing propaganda." The article was titled "The Kaiser's Secret Army Here." From December 1917 through March 1918, muckraker Samuel Hopkins Adams wrote a series for *Everybody's Magazine*, "Invaded America," that even found disloyalty among Lutheran clergy. Nova Scotia-born Charles A. Eaton, minister of New York's Madison Avenue Baptist Church, called for the lynching of all spies and "propagandists," telling Newark ship workers, "You know where to get the rope, I'm sure."[8]

In his April 2, 1917, war message, Wilson had claimed that most German Americans were "true and loyal Americans," who "will be prompt to stand with us in rebuking and restraining the few who may be of a different mind and purpose." Yet the speech did contain a caveat: any disloyalty would be met with "a firm hand of stern repression."[9]

It did not take long for the president to change his tone. In his Flag Day address of June 14, 1917, Wilson warned that Germany "has many spokesmen here, in places high and low." They discretely keep within the law and do not engage in sedition, but they "proclaim the liberal purposes of their masters; declare this a foreign war which can touch America with no danger to either her lands or her institutions; set England at the centre of the stage and talk of her ambition to assert economic domination throughout the world; appeal to our ancient tradition of isolation in the politics of the nations; and seek to undermine the government with false professions of loyalty to its principles." Historian Michael Kazin finds that the president "all but equated opposition to the war with treason."[10]

One accusation of disloyalty led to a wrestling match on the House floor. In mid-September, Representative Tom Heflin implied that back in January at least thirteen members of Congress had received German bribes, the money being funneled through a Washington gambling house where "slackers and pacifists played cards." Moreover, funds from Berlin were financing an antidraft bill of Congressman William Mason as well as legislation advanced by Congressman Fred A. Britten exempting German Americans from overseas service. On September 28, Congressman Patrick Norton (R-N.Dak.), believing that Heflin had slandered him, almost pushed the Alabama legislator through an adjacent table. Each took one swing at the other, then clinched and rolled to the floor. At this point, Congressman John M. Baer (Non-Partisan League-N.Dak.) took Norton by the neck, lifting him out of the way. Within a week, Heflin admitted he had no substantiating evidence. In October a special House investigating committee found all the accused innocent.[11]

German law allowed emigrants to retain full citizenship rights, a circumstance that added to charges of dual loyalty. The day he signed the war declaration, Wilson immediately forbade German aliens from owning firearms or coming within a half mile of military facilities. The *Providence Journal*, edited by the former Australian John Revelstoke Rathom, saw all German and Austrian aliens as spies until proven innocent. *New York Tribune* columnist Frank Simonds cried, "Intern all enemy aliens."[12]

Between April and November 1917, more than 4,500 aliens were arrested, of whom 1,200 were interned. On November 20, all German aliens older than thirteen were forced to register with the government. They were barred from wharves, canals, and railroad depots; more than five thousand were expelled from the District of Columbia. They needed permission to travel within the country and change their residence while being denied access to all ships but public ferries.

Tremendous pressure was put on German-language newspapers, which in 1914 had totaled 557 journals possessing a circulation of nearly 800,000. In certain localities, they drew more readers than their English-language rivals.

In July 1917, the *Atlantic Monthly* printed an article, "The Disloyalty of the German-American Press," by Frank Perry Olds, foreign-language editor of the *Milwaukee Journal*. Olds stressed the press's opposition to loans, food, and troops to the Allies, stances that gave "comfort to the enemy." A similar attitude was expressed by Hermann Hagedorn, a German American writer and intimate of Theodore Roosevelt, who informed *Outlook* readers how many German papers sneered at America's motives, abused Britain and France, and praised Kaiser Wilhelm II and Field Marshal Paul von Hindenburg: "These newspapers are as wreckers on treacherous shores, flashing false signals to signs at sea." By August, the National Security League insisted that 450 German American newspapers make a public confession of faith that included affirmation of Allied war aims, condemnation of German ones, and "the permanent effacement of the present Germany dynasty."[13]

At first the censors felt frustrated. In July, Attorney General Gregory told Wilson that many German American papers still printed disloyal material, but "there seems to be no way in most cases in which this can be prevented lawfully." In October 1917, Postmaster General Burleson personally asked pro-German editors: "Have you printed that Germans dropped bombs on Red Cross hospitals? Have you printed any atrocities practiced by Germans?" The Trading with the Enemy Act of that month required English translations of all war coverage before the Post Office Department would bestow mailing privileges. Realizing that translation was costly and could create crippling delays, practically all German American papers either stopped publishing or fell in line, voicing an ostentatious patriotic position. By 1920, only fifty-six daily German language journals remained, with circulation falling below 250,000.[14]

In April 1918, during the debate over the Sedition Act, Senator Lodge briefly proposed that all German publications sent through the mails must include a parallel English translation. Some legislators balked, Senator Nelson calling the proposal "a direct insult to the large German population." Warren Harding replied that many German-language newspapers carried "the finest utterances of American devotion." "Let us," said Senator Borah, "not discriminate against men because they are Germans."[15]

Language was deemed a particular threat. More than 9 million Americans spoke German as their first language. Twenty-four percent of American high school students studied German. It was the primary teaching language in many midwestern parochial schools and in certain institutions in Cincinnati, Cleveland, and Milwaukee.[16]

By March 1918, 149 schools had discontinued German language study and numerous cities had outlawed the use of German in public places. In Montana, German was banned from pulpits and schools. Thanks to Iowa governor William Harding, conversations on streetcars and over telephones were monitored. Books were often burned.

In calling for the disappearance of the German tongue, the American Defense Society warned, "The time for sentiment about Goethe and Schiller has gone by." Said the *North American Review*, "The speech of the Hun must be abolished in America." The ADS sought to change the names of any city bearing the names of Bismarck, Bremen, Dresden, and Hanover.[17]

Wilson's response to the general repression was uneven. In late March 1917, when a White House housekeeper told the president that the building's heating fires were tended by a German, the president remarked, "I'd rather the blamed place should be blown up rather than persecute inoffensive people." In July, St. Louis congressman Leonidas C. Dyer (R) wrote Wilson concerning "a campaign of slanderous attacks" upon German Americans, to which the president affirmed his "confidence in the entire integrity and loyalty of the great body of our fellow-citizens of German blood." In October, Wilson expressed concern to the cabinet upon hearing that the owner of the town hall of Aspinwall, Iowa, had been arrested for not permitting a Liberty Loan meeting. In April 1918, Wilson wrote Tumulty, saying he found opposition to teaching German "ridiculous and childish" but added that he did not want to get "involved" in the matter.[18]

At times even German music was forbidden. The ADS's Hurd warned, "Music is one of the most dangerous forms of German propaganda, because it appeals to the emotions and has the power to sway an audience as nothing else can." The *Los Angeles Times* called German music "the music of conquest, the music of the storm, of disorder and devastation." The *Outlook* expressed no hostility to Bach, Brahms, and Beethoven, but opposed works by Richard Strauss and also Richard Wagner's *Tristan und Isolde* and *Siegfried*. Such music, it warned, "sets forth an ideal which German guns and German poisoned gasses and German atrocities are making repugnant to the world. " In Milwaukee, vigilantes set up a machine gun to prevent the performance of Schiller's *Wilhelm Tell*, ironically a play protesting against tyranny.[19]

Several journals opposed such suppression. The *Chicago Tribune* remarked, "We disapprove of the Kaiser and his projects. Therefore we punish him by snubbing Beethoven." Noting in July 1918 that German music had been banned from the Los Angeles public schools, the *Nation* observed that Sir Henry Wood still played Brahms and Beethoven at Queen's Hall, London.[20]

Even musicians and conductors were not immune to the growing hysteria. In November 1917, the directors of New York's Metropolitan Opera House unanimously adopted a resolution to ban German opera. "Loyal" singers of German birth could appear in French and English works. March 1918 saw Austrian violinist Fritz Kreisler canceling all U.S. engagements because he had served as a lieutenant in his nation's army earlier in the war. The Bavarian-born conductor Karl Muck had been sufficiently pro-German to have endorsed the sinking of the *Lusitania*. In November 1917, he at first refused to play the "Star-Spangled Banner" at concerts of the Boston Symphony, declaring that "patriotic airs" had no place in a symphony program. Within several months he felt himself forced to relent. Muck, too, felt forced to resign his position and was jailed in Fort Oglethorpe, Georgia, for a year as an alien who threatened national security.[21]

When the matter of German music came up, the president again was equivocal. In early April 1917, the Metropolitan Opera asked Wilson if performances in German, sung by German artists, should be permitted. Wilson simply told Tumulty that "it would not be wise to express an opinion in regard to this matter, and yet personally I should hate to see them stop German opera." In November 1917 in response to an inquiry from the Florida Federation of Women's Clubs, the chief executive replied that he did not find "any good music" unpatriotic. When, however, in August 1918, Leopold A. Stokowski, conductor of the Philadelphia Orchestra, asked the president whether such composers as Bach, Beethoven, Mozart, and Brahms should be performed during the war, Wilson responded, "It is not a question which can be decided on its merits, but only on the feelings and present thoughts of the audiences to whom the Philadelphia Orchestra and the other orchestras of the country play."[22]

Lynching remained the ultimate form of repression. On April 4, 1918, at 9 p.m. in the town of Collinsville, Illinois, a mining town near East St. Louis, a mob executed Robert Paul Prager, a baker born in Germany. He had attempted to enlist in the navy, but a glass eye caused him to be rejected. A group of town drunks accused him of being a spy, stripped him of his clothing, wrapped an American flag around him, and—an hour later—hanged him.[23]

The following afternoon, Wilson's cabinet condemned the action. Attorney General Thomas Gregory, however, told the press that only the state of Illinois could deal with the matter. Illinois's senator Sherman claimed that every man who participated in the lynching should be hanged. To the *Washington Post*, however, "enemy propaganda must be stopped, even if a few lynchings may occur."[24]

In mid-May, eleven of the lynchers began a three-week trial for murder. The jury took twenty-five minutes to return verdicts of not guilty, arguing that the evidence was contradictory and that, because the crime scene was dark, one could not say just who the guilty persons were. One juror shouted, "Well, I guess nobody can say we aren't loyal now." Governor Frank Lowden called the decision "a lamentable failure of justice." Colonel Harvey's *War Weekly* found that Prager lacked loyalty, but continued, "We cannot approve lynch law, not even for traitors." After making a thorough survey, historian Donald R. Hickey notes that most public statements were timid and qualified. The *New York Times*, for example, though condemning the "mob mind," praised the government's "almost saintlike patience" in dealing with "disloyal editors," "German propagandists," and "suspects generally."[25]

Prager was not the only victim of such murder. That April one S. J. Walker, though not a German American, was shot in Honolulu for calling the naval ensign "a dirty rag." A jury acquitted the assailant after deliberating six minutes. He received congratulations from the judge and was honored by a parade. In late July, Wilson issued a statement condemning the "many lynchings" and "the mob spirit" that had "shown its head among us," but he cited no examples.[26]

German American reaction to the war itself was mixed. According to historian Frederick C. Luebke, most were neither pro-kaiser nor superloyalist. Not surprisingly, particularly with immigration rates falling off, the younger generation focused more on the United States than on any ancestral homeland. Despite the vehement attacks, a healthy majority of German-language newspapers backed Wilson's policies, so much so that Luebke found them to be vehicles of patriotic propaganda. German Americans responded to the draft as willingly as any other group. In fact, 10 to 15 percent of the AEF was of German descent or birth; Pershing was himself of German stock, his family originally named Pfoershing. Nevertheless, as Luebke observes, German Americans found themselves in a bind. If they remained silent on the subject of the war or assented passively to it, as did most, they would likely face accusations of lukewarm patriotism. If, however, they voiced enthusiasm for the conflict, they could be accused of hypocritically hiding their disloyalty.[27]

Some German Americans ostentatiously tried to prove their Americanism. Kuno Francke, honorary curator of Harvard's Germanic Museum, publicly remarked: "Germany is for the time being my country's enemy." In August 1917, New York publisher Bernard Ridder wrote Wilson, praising the "splendid attitude which the Administration has taken in its treatment of German subjects." Just a year later, Ridder's prominent *New Yorker Staats-Zeitung* condemned the German war record, remarking that "for a long time German-Americans were unable to see the peril, and rude was their awakening."[28]

One particularly scandalous case involved the Hamburg-born German-Jewish banker Paul M. Warburg, who felt forced to resign as vice governor of Federal Reserve Board. One of his brothers was serving as financial adviser to the German government and another represented the family banking firm in Sweden. Warburg had not communicated with either individual since the United States entered the war. Moreover, his only son had joined the AEF aviation service. In August 1918, Wilson publicly called the resignation a serious loss.[29]

That year Hermann Hagedorn wrote *Where Do You Stand? An Appeal to Americans of German Origin*, in which he accused the German American of being "the-man-without-a-country." "America is his wife, but he keeps Germany as his soul-mate," he added. Accusing his kinsmen of being pro-German before April 1917, Hagedorn feared a U.S. war against "a stronger Germany, not on our shores, perhaps, but in South America in defence of the Monroe Doctrine." Now his kinsmen "stand at the cross-roads" having to make a clear-cut choice.[30]

The National German-American Alliance (NGAA) (Deutsch-amerikanischer Nationalbund) remained subject to tremendous attack. Founded in 1901 and originally focused on fighting prohibition, the NGAA was a federation of various local clubs and societies. Though boasting 3 million members, it largely remained a paper organization. Before the United States entered the war, the group took a strong pro-German position, but once war was declared, it became ardently patriotic, participating in several Liberty Bond drives.[31]

In December 1917, the NGAA agreed not to hold a general congress, but it still faced strong hostility. The *Louisville Courier-Journal* claimed most NGAA leaders were German spies. In February 1918, the Senate Judiciary Committee investigated its operations. Henry C. Campbell, assistant editor of the *Milwaukee Journal*, saw in it one single purpose: to "Germanize America." Toledo lawyer Gustavus Ohlinger, president of his city's chamber of commerce, called the NGAA the "core of the Kultur cyst in the American body politic." Early in April, its executive committee voted to disband the organization. On July 2, by voice vote, the Senate adopted a resolution by William King annulling its charter.[32]

Some German Americans sought to prove their patriotism by establishing a new organization. In the fall of 1917, New York attorney Franz Sigel, son of the noted Civil War general, established the Friends of German Democracy. Abraham Jacobi, a famous physician whom the German government had once imprisoned for "high treason," was chosen honorary president. Renowned German-Jewish bankers Jacob Schiff and Otto Kahn each contributed a thousand dollars. Its secretary, Frank Bohn, war correspondent for the *New York Evening Post*, engaged in contacts with the European left. The organization sought a popular revolution against Junker rule, claiming the United States would make peace with a popularly chosen government. Never a large group, practically speaking the Friends served as an appendage of the Creel Committee.[33]

Surprisingly enough, the German-American *Issues and Events* survived until the summer of 1918. Edited by Frederick Franklin Schrader, former drama critic for the *Washington Post*, the weekly opposed loans to the Allies: "Our money, like our armies and our fleets, should be concentrated at its home bases and not dispersed abroad." The journal warned that Cecil Rhodes and Andrew Carnegie had sought to reintegrate the United States into the British Empire, a stock argument of Anglophobes. By backing conscription and pushing Liberty Loans, however, the weekly was able to ward off many attacks.[34]

More important, George Sylvester Viereck's journal generally remained in circulation throughout the war. Only thirty-two years old when the United States entered the conflict, he had been best known as a poet of "decadence" until 1914, when he began publishing *The Fatherland*, a magazine that defended Berlin at every turn. Nothing if not shrewd, in March 1917 he changed the title of his periodical to *Viereck's: The American Weekly*, which in September 1918 became a monthly. The Post Office Department only withdrew one issue from circulation; it had criticized "entangling alliances" and found Wilson a hypocrite.[35] An anonymous column, "With the Military Experts," continually offered pessimistic reports of the western front. In issue after issue, Viereck gleefully reprinted attacks upon him verbatim, not even bothering to reply.

Within a week after Wilson delivered his war message, Viereck wrote that the conflict must be "for American principles only," not for "the Cecil Rhodes conspiracy for the reunion of the English-speaking world under the Union Jack." On May 9, 1917, he noted reports from American correspondents denying that Germany was sending U-boats into U.S. waters. He continually backed peace proposals, be they from the pope, the Reichstag, Russian revolutionists, remnants of the Second International seeking to meet at Stockholm, and Wilson himself, as manifested in the president's "peace without victory" speech of January 1917.[36]

In October 1917, Viereck summarized his platform, which included universal military service; a powerful army and navy; arbitration of international agreements; the initiative, referendum, and recall; U.S. acquisition of all foreign possessions in the Western Hemisphere; public ownership of national resources; protection of labor on the factory and farm; and a nonannexationist peace. The journal often endorsed Liberty Loans. By the beginning of 1918, one finds a push for such disparate causes as food conservation, woman suffrage, confiscation of wealth, termination of prohibition, and the continuation of German language teaching in American schools.[37]

In August 1918, Viereck proposed an entire slate of candidates: Robert La Follette for president, Stanford's former chancellor David Starr Jordan for vice president, and William Randolph Hearst for New York governor. Socialist leader Morris Hillquit would be New York City's mayor; *Masses* editor Max Eastman and Tammany judge Daniel F. Cohalan would represent New York State in the Senate.[38] Though the group was nothing if not varied in nature, all had strongly opposed U.S. participation in the conflict. Not surprisingly, Viereck often promoted anti-interventionist programs of the Socialist Party and the Nonpartisan League.

In May 1917, Viereck organized an Agricultural and Industrial Labor Relief Bureau. He boasted that this agency found employment for about two thousand people, mainly aliens, and was endorsed by many state governors. When in July 1918 New York deputy attorney general Albert L. Becker accused the Bureau of massive fraud, Viereck could not produce records in its defense. The organization soon disbanded.[39]

During the debate over conscription, Viereck sought a legislative amendment exempting German American draftees from overseas service. "Let us not compel them to fight against their own kin," he wrote. "We can ask from a son no more appalling sacrifice than that he slay his own mother." Such troops could patrol the Mexican border, guard the nation's coastal defenses, or work on farms. In a letter to David Starr Jordan, he noted the attempted suicide of one young German American and actual suicide by another.[40]

Congressman Fred Britten, who had voted against entering the war, introduced such a bill, his Chicago district being home to many German-Americans. Several legislators who had long opposed Wilson's foreign policy backed the plan, as did poet Edwin Markham. The Socialist *New York Call* went further, wanting all unwilling soldiers exempted, including Irish Americans.[41]

Not surprisingly, the proposal met with much opposition. Mississippi governor Theodore G. Bilbo remarked: "Strictly speaking, there are no German Americans, and if a man hesitates to fight for America in this crisis because of his relationships, he should either be interned or shot at sunrise." Ohio governor James M. Cox (D) commented: "All of us are Americans and this is America's war, in which there can be no thought of individual desires." President Wilson burned his copy of the resolution. Theodore Roosevelt called the proposal treason. Suppose, during the American Revolution, those of English descent decided not to join the patriot army.[42] By fall, the proposal was dead.

Viereck did face some harassment. Once the 1917 Espionage Act was passed, his offices were raided and his book-distributing agency confiscated. Senator Miles Poindexter claimed the journal should be called the *German Weekly*, not the *American Weekly*. In July 1918, the Poetry Society of America, of which he was a founder, asked him to resign. He refused to do so, being supported by such prominent figures as Edgar Lee Masters, Harriet Monroe, Conrad Aiken, and George Bernard Shaw. When that month the Authors' League of America expelled him, stressing that no member should ever mention his name or writings, Viereck mused, "This is charmingly medieval." At one point, after confronting hostile demonstrations, he abandoned his home in Mount Vernon, New York, to live in Manhattan.[43]

German Americans were not the only controversial ethnic group. Such groups as the United Irish-American Societies of New York pledged loyalty to the war effort but still advocated immediate establishment of an Irish republic. In April 1917, Wilson wrote Secretary of State Robert Lansing that the granting of "substantial self-government" would add much "satisfaction and enthusiasm" to American–British cooperation. When in January 1918, however, an Irish American delegation led by Senator James D. Phelan (D-Calif.) suggested that the president endorse nationhood for Ireland, Wilson replied that current British–Irish negotiations made it inappropriate for him to comment. Privately, Wilson was furious, finding such talk "almost treasonable." By April he was linking "Irish and Catholic intrigue" in the United States to "German intrigue."[44]

The Irish nationalist cause did receive some congressional support. Late in April 1917, 168 members of the House petitioned British prime minister David Lloyd George to settle the matter in accord with Wilsonian principles. The Hearst press preached "justice" for the Emerald Isle while expressing suspicions over British intentions there. Theodore Roosevelt privately hoped that Ireland, if not granted complete independence, would have representatives offering "a voice" within Parliament on major military and diplomatic matters. Yet sympathy only went so far. William Howard Taft conceded that Britain had misgoverned Ireland. However, Wilson's predecessor lacked sympathy for militant Irish American groups and found the nationalist cause "incidental" in relation to "the black threat of German domination."[45]

Militant Irish American journals and leaders kept up their attack. The *Gaelic American*, the organ of the Clan na Gael, responded to Wilson's war message by claiming that the president entered the conflict to save Britain. A victorious Britain would keep Ireland subject to "oppression and robbery." More important, the United States would be facing a superpower whose mastery of the seas could menace the entire human race. In November 1917, at a meeting held at Boston's Hibernian Hall, the journal's editor, John Devoy, defended Germany's execution of British nurse Edith Cavell in 1915 for helping Allied prisoners escape captivity. He also found German cruelty "nothing" compared to Britain's record in Ireland.[46]

In September 1917, government-released documents implied that New York Supreme Court justice Daniel Cohalan had conspired with the Germans. In 1916, Cohalan had been in secret contact with the German embassy, suggesting that the Reich attack Britain from the air while the Irish begin a rebellion. Soon such journals as *Bull*, the *Irish World*, the *Freeman's Journal*, and the *Gaelic American* were temporally barred from the mails.[47]

In early 1918, the Justice Department indicted Jeremiah O'Leary, a New York attorney who headed the American Truth Society, an anti-British organization. As editor of the *Bull*, O'Leary was charged with advocating insubordination in the U.S. armed forces, thereby violating the Espionage Act. O'Leary escaped to Washington State, where he lived under an assumed name and raised chickens. Once arrested, he experienced a mistrial and then a new trial for treason, from which he was acquitted.

Such repression did not cool down the rhetoric of the archnationalists. At a meeting in mid-May 1918 of the Friends of Irish Freedom, held in New York's Central Opera House, the audience of a thousand cheered one indictment of Britain after another: the British controlled the American press, were committing atrocities in Ireland, and were seeking the landing of U.S. Marines there. They were rushing U.S. troops to the front lines in France in order to release British soldiers to "massacre" the Irish people. Every member of Congress opposed to the nationalist Sinn Fein Party should be defeated in November.[48]

In the spring of 1918, the British government sought to conscript Irish males even if it would not enforce the policy until a new home rule bill was passed. The Irish and their American supporters were outraged, yet the American press generally supported the move. Colonel Harvey's ardently pro-Allies *War Weekly* commented, "Self-government is not to be secured by playing the part of catspaw to the Hun." By September, the *Outlook* went so far as to oppose Irish independence on the grounds that its harbors would nest German U-boats. When the war ended, it went on, Britain should establish a federal system in which local self-government could be combined with participation in the broader empire.[49]

Quite a different opposition to the war came from William Randolph Hearst, the most powerful—and hated—publisher in the United States. Beginning with his acquisition of the *San Francisco Examiner* in 1887, by mid-1918 he owned seven magazines and eleven newspapers: three in New York; two each in Chicago, Boston, and Atlanta; and one each in San Francisco and Los Angeles. His magazines drew an average circulation of more than 2 million readers, his newspapers more than 2.5 million. In April 1917, the *New York American* alone boasted 413,000 purchasers. Never in U.S. history had a single individual controlled so much of the nation's press.

Before April 1917 Hearst stood for a far more rigid neutrality than had President Wilson, but now he claimed wholehearted support for the war effort. Once the United States entered the conflict, he strongly favored conscription and backed the drive for Liberty Bonds. His *New York American* immediately established recruiting stations. The anti-German cartoons of Dutchman Louis Raemaeker often appeared on Hearst's front pages.

From the outset of U.S. entry into the war, the Hearst press pushed one great panacea for winning the war: air power. In June 1917, the *New York American* asserted that fifty thousand U.S. aircraft, each dropping a hundred "dynamite bombs" daily on German soil, would win the war. Most bombs would not take human life but would instead kill livestock, which would "make the German peasant determine that he MUST HAVE PEACE." By August it was demanding a hundred thousand planes.[50]

Yet if Hearst backed U.S. belligerency, it was decidedly on his own terms. In April 1917, his chain warned against "further drainage of our food supplies and our military supplies and our money supplies to Europe." His New York German-language paper, *Deutsches Journal*, denied Allied claims of fighting for humanity and the rights of small nations: "This war is nothing but a business proposition." A month later, his papers proclaimed that the United States should compel Germany to fight in U.S. waters ("see how she likes the taste of OUR GRANITE"). In June the Hearst press predicted that the war might last ten years, the United States eventually having to fight alone against a coalition of Germany, Russia, and Japan. The *New York American* approvingly quoted "a diplomat" who called the present conflict "a

European war for European ambition and aggression." By July the publisher sought a war referendum and also U.S. insistence that Germany, France, Russia, and Britain do likewise. Under such practice, he argued, Austria would never have made war in revenge for the assassination of "a worthless Grand Duke." In a signed editorial, Hearst wrote, "Better to make peace now than to look forward to year after year of such national and individual sorrow and sacrifice."[51]

Britain in particular met with Hearst's scorn. As the United States entered the war, his *New York American* accused it of simply reinforcing Britain's future aggrandizement. In June the *American* accused Britain of allowing France to maintain nine-tenths of the western front while it sat "comfortably at home, for the most part, surrounded by her steel wall of ships, accessible only occasionally to Zeppelin and aeroplane raids of no actual importance. . . . France has been allowed to sacrifice herself to protect England on land, and we will be allowed to sacrifice ourselves to protect England at sea."[52]

Needless to say, such views met with bitter opposition, particularly from the *New York Tribune*, a Republican paper that had long attacked Wilson's foreign policy for lacking the needed belligerency. In late September 1917, muckraker Samuel Hopkins Adams contributed an entire series on Hearst: "Behind the pretense of patriotism and the outward flag-flying of his newspapers lies a spirit that speaks subtly with a Prussian accent." Since the United States entered the war, so the *Tribune* claimed in September 1918, Hearst papers had defended Germany seventeen times, published sixty-three pieces of antiwar propaganda, and made seventy-four attacks upon the Allies. Even the far more liberal *Nation* remarked of Hearst himself in June 1918: "We doubt if any journalist in history has blacker acts to his discredit. . . . There is nothing sincere in any position that he takes."[53]

Other Hearst enemies were equally vocal. Former assistant attorney general James Beck publicly called the publisher the fountainhead of American pro-Germanism, his power for evil being "immeasurable." On October 2, 1917, New York mayor John Purroy Mitchel warned, "Mr. Hearst puts the Star-Spangled Banner on the front page and tries to stab his country in the back in his editorial columns." In a private letter, Theodore Roosevelt found him "the most sinister pro-German traitor in the country and much the ablest and most dangerous." Publicly, TR called Hearst a leader in "the cult of disloyalty."[54]

By the fall of 1917, Hearst's enemies accused him of having secretly met in 1916 with Paul Bolo Pasha, publisher of the *Paris Journal*, whom the French later executed for being in the pay of the Germans. New York State attorney general Merton E. Lewis claimed that Hearst had conspired with Bolo to raise $1.7 million to finance subversive activities in France. A year earlier, charged Lewis, the publisher had hosted German military attaché Franz von Papen and naval attaché Karl Boy-Ed in New York, both expelled from the United States for espionage activities. Hearst was easily able to refute such charges, noting that he only conversed with Bolo about how the Parisian could get the best and cheapest paper for his newspaper. In mid-1918, New York State deputy attorney General Albert L. Becker accused William Bayard Hale, Berlin correspondent for the *New York American*, of acting in Rumania in 1916 as an agent of the German Foreign Office, a charge soon proven unfounded.[55]

These assaults took their toll. In May 1918, the city council of Mount Vernon, New York, adopted a resolution—later overruled by the state supreme court—prohibiting the circulation of Hearst papers. At the same time, a group of National Guardsmen in Poughkeepsie burned copies of the *New York American*. In Cincinnati, librarians removed all Hearst dailies from their reading rooms. The Albuquerque Rotary boycotted Hearst's California papers. Chicago bartenders banned their city's counterparts. From Nutley, New Jersey, to Pasadena, California, citizens sought to prevent vending of Hearst papers.[56]

Hearst realized he was under fire. On Christmas Day 1917, he launched a massive fundraising drive to restore six French cities destroyed by the Germans. In this effort, he probably drew as much consensus as ever in his entire career. He won praise from people as varied as Colonel House, Harvard president A. Lawrence Lowell, architect Ralph Adams Cram, Boston cardinal William H. O'Connell, Supreme Court justice Louis D. Brandeis, and University of Chicago football coach Amos Alonzo Stagg. Only Theodore Roosevelt appeared to dissent, writing French premier Georges Clemenceau that Hearst was "as sinister and efficient a friend of Germany as is to be found in all the world."[57]

The Hearst press tried to meet such attacks by continually defending leading members of the Wilson administration. It called Daniels one of the most successful secretaries of the navy the nation had ever seen. In time, similar praise fell upon Treasury Secretary McAdoo and Edward N. Hurley, chairman of the U.S. Shipping Board.[58] The chain even sought to prove its Americanism in small ways. For a brief time, Hans and Fritz of the cartoon "The Katzenjammer Kids" became Mike and Aleck of the "The Shenanigan Kids."

In September 1917, the *New York American*'s editorial director wrote Wilson: "I most heartily believe in you and your course." By October, Hearst papers editorialized, "The American people stand behind the President in the determination to fight this war to a finish." At a Fourth of July luncheon in 1918 at New York's Holland House, Hearst toasted the president.[59]

Wilson himself was less than enthusiastic about such an endorsement, writing Burleson that he regretted Samuel Hopkins Adams had found that the publisher, though "outrageous," had done nothing illegal. In the summer of 1918, however, Wilson aide Tumulty congratulated Hearst editor Arthur Brisbane for adding the *Chicago Herald* to the chain. Newton Baker fired Dr. James A. B. Scherer, Lutheran missionary and Japan expert, as chief field agent of the Council of National Defense for calling the Hearst press disloyal.[60]

Hearst did have some supporters. Forty-nine members of Congress, including five senators, accepted the publisher's invitation to view his 1918 Fourth of July loyalty parade in New York. Champ Clark declared, "Hearst has done a heap more good than all of those fellows together who are bully-ragging him." (Clark had been Hearst's original choice for president in 1912.) James Reed remarked of Hearst's critics, "They have employed the methods of cheap demagogues, the same from the days of Alcibiades on the streets of Athens, to the modern type."[61]

Hearst's leading columnist, Arthur Brisbane, himself owner of the *Washington Times*, stressed his own patriotism in his daily column titled "Today." Amid blasts against Wall Street, big business, and war profiteers, he continually denounced Germany. In September 1918, he wrote of the kaiser: "He secretly planned wholesale murder for years, preparing army and navy, drilling millions of men, then struck the treacherous blow against Belgium, the weak, brave nation." He also commented, "Every bullet that goes from an American rifle through the head or the heart of a Prussian is a good bullet that does good work."[62]

Such disclaimers did not prevent the *New York Tribune* from lumping Brisbane together with Hearst. *Tribune* staffer Kenneth Macgowen accused Brisbane of bitterly attacking Britain. Brisbane, claimed Macgowen, accused Japan of threatening the United States, portrayed Mexico as a danger, constantly emphasized the horror of warfare itself ("international murder"), and opposed food shipments to the Allies on the plea that American children were starving.[63]

If the Hearst chain ended up backing the Wilson administration and the man personally had never collaborated with the Germans, historian Ian Mugridge finds the publisher guilty of tactical errors and too often taking the approach of "a plague on both your houses."[64] Certainly Hearst was his own worst enemy. One could well argue that his portrayal of certain U.S. allies lacked any balance. Therefore, they could not help but undercut any coalition against the Central Powers.

Only one other figure as prominent as Hearst received such vilification. Senator Robert Marion La Follette had spoken for four hours against Wilson's war message. After the United States entered the conflict, La Follette fought conscription and the Espionage Act. He sought a 50 percent increase on the taxes millionaires must pay. On August 11, 1917, he introduced a resolution asking the Allies to restate their peace terms, warning that the Entente was fighting for punitive damages and annexation of new territory. "The people," he demanded, "have a right to know with certainty for what end their blood is to be shed and their treasure expended."[65]

La Follette's resolution drew little support. Historian Claude H. Van Tyne compared "the little Badger Napoleon" to Aaron Burr. The *New Republic* saw all penalties and annexations dependent upon Germany's good behavior. The *Outlook* warned that Berlin would use the senator's resolution to discredit the Allied cause. To Commerce Secretary William C. Redfield, La Follette's resolution stabbed the United States in the back.[66]

Such opprobrium was nothing, however, compared to the reaction to LaFollette's address delivered on September 20 to a Nonpartisan League audience of possibly 15,000 in St. Paul, Minnesota. He attacked the "kept press" and claimed that Congress had shirked its responsibility. In discussing the sinking of the *Lusitania*, La Follette asserted that Secretary of State William Jennings Bryan had warned

Wilson beforehand that the ship was transporting 6 million pounds of munitions to Britain. Even more significant, the senator was quoted as saying that "I wasn't in favor of beginning the war. We had no grievance." Within four days, La Follette stressed that his remarks had been deliberately misconstrued, but his denial was ignored.[67]

Seldom in U.S. history had a speech met with such scorn. Bryan denied he had foreknowledge of the *Lusitania*'s cargo. It was, however, La Follette's supposed statement of "no grievance" that led to many calls for his expulsion from the Senate. Such demands came from public safety commissions, chambers of commerce, merchants' and manufacturers' associations, service clubs, Councils of Defense, the National Security League, and the American Defense Society. Included was the Chattanooga Bar Association, the Rotary Club of Ithaca, the Massachusetts Republican State Convention, the U.S. Grant Post of the Grand Army of the Republic in Brooklyn, and a flying squadron of a thousand Liberty Bond salesmen. In Sheboygan he was hanged in effigy, an event later repeated on the state university campus in Madison. Theodore Roosevelt called the Wisconsin senator American democracy's "most sinister foe." To pro-war Socialist Charles Edward Russell, "La Follette is simply a big yellow streak." Taft referred to traitorous activities and seditious speech. Columbia University president Nicholas Murray Butler found his remarks akin to poisoning every U.S. soldier who went to war. When Wilson learned that the Wisconsin state and county councils of defense demanded La Follette's resignation, he told Tumulty to communicate "my warm appreciation of the patriotic feeling and purpose involved."[68]

On October 6, La Follette sought to defend himself before his Senate colleagues. He ignored his St. Paul speech, the focus of calls for his expulsion. Rather, his three-hour address stressed the duty of dissenting in wartime and the need for a popular war referendum and a declaration of U.S. war aims. The United States should frankly say, "We are not seeking to dictate a form of government to Germany or to render more secure England's domination of the seas."[69]

Rebuttals from his Senate colleagues came immediately. Just after La Follette spoke, Frank B. Kellogg, who had introduced an expulsion resolution, denied that the country entered the conflict so its citizens could ride on ships loaded with munitions or to assure the profits of munitions makers. Joseph Robinson (D-Ark.), calling the conflict "a holy war," asserted that if the Wisconsin senator had his will, "liberty would become a memory." Albert Fall found that "no more dangerous doctrine has been preached." La Follette's only support came from James K. Vardaman, who pointedly shook his hand as debate ended. The Senate unanimously endorsed the creation of a subcommittee of the Committee on Privileges and Elections to examine the St. Paul speech.[70]

In February 1918, La Follette's own Wisconsin state senate passed a loyalty resolution 26 to 3 condemning the senator. One F. A. Huber dissented, seeing a conspiracy sparked by "all the war-profiteers that have so recently created a stench in the nation that smells to high heaven." After a stormy seventeen-hour session held that March, the state assembly concurred with the state senate, 53 to 32.[71]

Few opinion leaders came to La Follette's defense. Viereck's weekly reprinted major excerpts of the senator's October 1917 speech. Philosophy professor Horace Kallen of the University of Wisconsin bucked the overwhelming anti-La Follette sentiment of his faculty colleagues, finding the senator properly reflecting the progressivism of Wisconsin voters.[72]

Eventually the controversy died. Throughout 1918, La Follette was absent from the Congress, caring for an ill son. In late May, the Associated Press admitted it had misquoted the senator. Noting that the AP served a thousand newspapers, the *Nation* lamented, "No amount of apology can undo the serious wrong done by this error." After the 1918 congressional elections, the Republican Party, now holding only a 49–47 margin in the Senate, immediately realized it needed La Follette's vote. Hence, in January 1919, the Senate voted 50–21 to drop all charges. Practically every Republican backed La Follette, but such Democratic stalwarts as Thomas Walsh (D-Mont.), Key Pittman (D-Nev.), and Morris Sheppard (D-Tex.) still favored expulsion. To John Sharp Williams, the Wisconsin senator's remarks concerning the *Lusitania* were "an everlasting lie."[73]

To some promoters of national unity, the threat went well beyond unpopular ethnic groups, a flamboyant publisher, and a recalcitrant senator. The American left underwent blistering attack.

SEVEN
THE ANTI-RADICAL CRUSADE

the German American community, much less the Irish one. Nor was it followers of Hearst or La Follette. It lay in various left-wing movements, spearheaded by the Socialist Party.

The party itself had been in decline. Though its presidential candidate, Eugene Victor Debs, had won almost 900,000 votes in 1912, its 1916 standard-bearer, journalist Allan Benson, drew fewer than 600,000. Party membership dropped from its 200,000 high, reached just after the 1912 election, to 77,000 once the United States entered the war. In roughly the same time span, the circulation of the *Appeal to Reason* of Girard, Kansas, one of the widest circulated weeklies in the world, had dropped from 761,742 to 529,172. By 1916, only two Socialist dailies remained, the *New York Call* (circulation 15,000) and the *Milwaukee Leader* (circulation 37,000). Demographically, the base of the party was shifting from the agricultural and mining areas of the West and Southwest to midwestern and northeastern cities, where it found support among Germans, Poles, and Russian Jews.

In 1914, at the outbreak of the conflict triggered in Sarajevo, the party's executive committee claimed, "The Socialist Party is opposed to this and all other wars." The day

117

after Wilson's war message, the party's national executive committee held an emergency meeting in St. Louis's Planters' Hotel. Debs was unable to attend, being bedridden with back pain, digestive ailments, and a weak heart. New York labor lawyer Morris Hillquit, the group's keynoter, set its tone: "We have been violently, needlessly, criminally drawn into this conflict."[1]

The two hundred delegates from fourteen states selected created a Committee on War and Militarism, which took three days to draft the party's response to the war. The party saw no reason to change its long-held antiwar position. The majority report, signed by eleven of the fifteen drafters, became the official position, gaining the votes of 140 delegates. It was approved by both its press and 90 percent of its membership, as expressed in a national mail referendum with a vote of 21,639 to 2,752. Primarily written by Hillquit, this report remained the authorized Socialist stance until the November 1918 armistice. Offering standard socialist doctrine, it blamed U.S. entrance into the war upon predatory capitalists seeking war profits, noting that business moguls always sought foreign markets to dispose of surplus wealth. Attacking the "false doctrine of national patriotism," it pledged to uphold the "ideal of international working class solidarity." "In support of capitalism we will not willingly give a single life or a single dollar; in support of the struggle of the workers for freedom we pledge our all." It demanded "continuous, active, and public opposition to the war through demonstrations, mass petitions, and all other means within our power," adding a plea for "unyielding opposition to all proposed legislation for military or industrial conscription." As far as financing the war was concerned, "Let those who kindle the fire furnish the fuel."[2] The St. Louis resolution made the Socialists of America almost unique among belligerents, for the official Socialist and Labor Parties of Britain, Germany, France, and Austria had all rallied to the colors. It would be hard to find another major national organization so open in its condemnation of U.S. participation in the conflict.

At St. Louis, a rival report, drafted by legal expert Louis Boudin, spoke for one minority of the platform framers. It called the U.S. declaration of war "a crime against the people of the United States and against the nations of the world"; it did not advocate resistance, however, and the statement drew only thirty-one votes. The second mi-

nority report, written by English-born muckraker John Spargo, denied
that nationalism was incompatible with true internationalism. He attacked the Germans for brutal lawlessness, even against law-abiding
neutral nations. In Spargo's eyes, the greatest autocracies in the world
were fighting the world's most progressive and democratic nations.
Certainly the founders of socialism—Karl Marx, Friedrich Engels,
August Bebel—all believed in national self-defense. Only thirteen
delegates supported Spargo's measure.[3]

Even before April, several prominent Socialists had opposed the
party's uncompromising position, among them novelist Upton Sinclair; journalists Charles Edward Russell of New York and Algie M.
Simons of Chicago; and Spargo, a former member of the national executive committee. In March, James Graham Phelps Stokes, a pro-Ally
millionaire who helped bankroll the party, had written, "To refuse
to fight against international crime is to be unworthy of the name
socialist."[4]

Once the party took its militant stand, a virtual exodus of its leaders took place. Allan Louis Benson, presidential candidate in 1916, had
written *Inviting War to America* that year, in which he called intervention "monumental folly." Charles Edward Russell, a Hearst editor
from 1897 to 1902, was the party's gubernatorial candidate in New
York in 1910 and 1912, mayoral nominee for New York City in 1913,
and his party's senatorial aspirant in 1914. Stokes had been the Socialist
candidate for the New York Assembly in 1908 and for mayor of Stam-
ford, Connecticut, in 1916. In 1912, William G. Ghent had served as
secretary to the platform committee of the national convention. Said
Socialist publicist William English Walling, himself now cast out by
the antiwar majority, "We are facing a disruption which will shake the
party to its very foundation."[5]

A pro-war stance did not constitute conversion to domestic con-
servatism. Several defectors were nationally known reformers. Spargo's
most popular work had been *The Bitter Cry of the Children* (1906),
based upon personal investigations of New York City. Both Russell
and Walling had been instrumental in founding the NAACP. Walling
had been part of the party's left wing, which opposed all intermediate
reforms, and had attacked Germany's Social Democrats for voting war
credits in 1914. Jack London and Upton Sinclair, who particularly

feared a German invasion, were popular novelists whose work exalted proletarian rebellion. Ernest Poole's *The Harbor* (1915) glorified a strike on New York's waterfront. Social worker Robert Hunter wrote a searing indictment of American society titled *Poverty* (1904). William J. Ghent's *Our Benevolent Feudalism* (1902) warned of an incipient despotic society, which would later be termed "fascist." Algie Simons had edited the *International Socialist Review*, helped found the Industrial Workers of the World, and was a delegate to international socialist conventions in Copenhagen and Stuttgart. In fact, of the most prominent party figures, only Debs, Hillquit, and Victor Berger, a former congressman and editor of the *Milwaukee Leader*, remained in the party.

Such dissidents quickly denounced their antiwar rivals. Midwestern party members often came from German stock. Eastern members were often Jews who had emigrated from the German, Hapsburg, and Russian empires and who occupationally were based in New York City's garment trades. Not so much pro-German as anti-Russian, acting in reaction to tsarist anti-Semitism, they were nonetheless branded as instruments of the kaiser. Simons referred to a "mad devotion to German autocracy." Spargo called the April 1917 St. Louis proclamation "essentially unneutral, un-American, and pro-German." Benson claimed that the manifesto verged on treason. Ghent accused the party of sanctioning German spies and found it starting "a brush fire war in the rear." Walling called Hillquit ("the absolute boss of the Socialist Party here") "probably the most valuable individual to Germany in this country, now that [Ambassador] von Bernstorff has left." Privately, Russell referred to "the bitter, malignant, covert but insatiable hatred that many Jews in America feel for the United States." Wisconsin state senator W. R. Gaylord, who once spoke for his state's party, accused his former associates of advocating mob rule. Stokes made the peculiar observation that the party was both "anarchistic and Leninistic."[6]

In late April, several former Socialists met in Stokes's Manhattan home to form a rival group, the Social Democratic League (SDL). Spargo called upon the socialist movement to "abandon the antiquated notions that society consists of capitalists and proletarians." Rather it should recruit "former proletarians who have a little property or money in the bank" and "vast numbers of small investors who live by useful trades and occupations." By early July, Spargo was SDL chairman, Stokes its treasurer. Members included Allan Benson, Algie Simons, and journalist Frank Bohn.[7]

The SDL lay stillborn. Only middle- and upper-class Socialists were attracted. Its one major effort centered on a trip, made in the summer of 1918, to encourage western European labor to remain in the war. Among the six delegates were Spargo, Russell, and Louis Kopelin, an editor of the *New Appeal*, successor to the *Appeal to Reason*. Algie Simons chaired the group. Financed primarily by Baltimore industrialist William Cochran Jr., the group reported to Robert Lansing on their mission, informing the secretary of state that Allied Socialists needed assurance that the coming peace would be a Wilsonian one.[8]

In October 1917, pro-war Socialists embarked upon another effort to create an alternative organization. Such erstwhile party leaders as Spargo and Upton Sinclair joined with ex-Progressives, prohibitionists, single-taxers, and left-leaning Democrats and Republicans to form the National Party. The platform duplicated the 1916 Socialist plank, adding prohibition of alcoholic beverages and endorsement of both the war effort and Wilsonian peace aims. Spargo soon claimed 2,500 dues-paying members. From its outset, however, the organization lacked funding and grassroots support. It found the Wilson administration apathetic and faced the hostility of the influential William English Walling, who opposed Spargo's advocacy of free speech for the antiwar minority. Hence, the National Party, too, was an abortive effort.[9]

Other Socialists refused to recant. In late April, the most popular of the party weeklies, the *Appeal to Reason*, claimed that the war resulted from the "determination of American capitalists to carry on business as usual in spite of military operations abroad." In May, a group of Socialists, sporting their educational credentials, defended the party against accusations of being pro-German, among them critic Randolph Bourne (Columbia), editor Max Eastman (Williams), and writer Freda Kirchwey (Barnard).[10]

In mid-April, Socialists from European neutral countries—the Scandinavian nations plus the Netherlands—had invited all groups affiliated with the Second International to explore peace terms in Stockholm. Originally scheduled for May 15, 1917, the assembly would be led by Hjalmar Branting, a leading member of the Swedish delegation. From the outset, the majority of socialists in Britain and France were hostile. In Germany, both the official party and a separate group called the Independent Socialist Party agreed to participate. In Russia, the Menshevik Party accepted the bid, as did the entire Petrograd Soviet within two months.

The American Socialist leaders—Hillquit, Victor Berger, former New York mayoral candidate Algernon Lee—applied for passports. Hillquit declared, "The American delegation to the congress is not to be either pro-Ally or pro-German. The men who will go from this country will be pro-Socialism and pro-peace." He claimed that the conference's leading light would be Camille Huysman, a Belgian Socialist who was as "anti-German as any Belgian could possibly be."[11]

On May 23, Robert Lansing refused to grant the delegation permission to leave, warning that any American taking part in the negotiations would be liable to severe punishment. The secretary of state cited the Logan Act, which punished unauthorized persons who directly or indirectly dealt with foreign officials regarding U.S. controversies. In 1799, Congress had passed the act after Dr. George Logan, a Quaker and leader in Pennsylvania politics, toured France to relieve tensions with the United States. (Hillquit pointed out that the Logan Act only concerned governments, not such private entities as political parties.) Lansing feared that the conference might create international sentiment for a separate peace, which in turn would stifle efforts to keep Russia in the war and thereby keep Germany fighting on two fronts. In a personal letter to Senator Lodge, Lansing maintained that U.S. participation might be considered as "giving aid and comfort to the enemy," part of the Constitution's definition of treason. Three obscure radicals did journey to Stockholm claiming to represent American socialism, but Berger was quick to comment that none were members of the Socialist Party.[12]

Obviously, some on the left were less than convinced of Lansing's wisdom. The Socialist daily *New York Call* quipped that

Berger, Hillquit and Lee one night
Planned a cruise across the sea;
"Oh dear no," said Woodrow, "we're in this fight
To make the oceans free."[13]

To Simeon Strunsky, editorial writer for the *New York Evening Post*, "democratic America" was violating the very freedom of thought and action that the German government was allowing its own Socialists. The *New Republic* suggested that the United States could have been represented by pro-war Socialists. Even Walling, who labeled the Stockholm conference "the most dangerous of all the Kaiser's plots for cashing in his military victories," argued that the ban would turn the would-be delegates into martyrs. Hearst's *New York American* accused the Western powers of making a huge mistake; they were allowing Germany to take the initiative among revolutionaries who may everywhere decide the fate of Europe. *Viereck's: The American Weekly* went much further, calling the conference the most important event since the Philadelphia meeting of the Second Continental Congress that produced the Declaration of Independence.[14]

Historian Ronald Radosh sees Lansing's Stockholm decision as strengthening the Allied right while weakening the very segment of the left that sought to promote the president's war aims: "The ban on Socialist participation at the Stockholm Conference had backfired." Another historian, Robert D. Warth, notes that the Bolsheviks, who had denounced the whole idea from the very first, gained from Allied refusal to allow even their patriotic Socialists to explore peace terms. Within Russia, the Menshevik and the Social Revolutionary factions, who had heretofore dominated the Petrograd Soviet and thus the course of the revolution, suffered irreparable loss of prestige. In September, a remnant of the conference did meet, issuing a manifesto calling for a negotiated peace, a league of nations, and the independence of subjugated European nationalities.[15]

In the spring and summer of 1917, the Socialist Party held numerous mass meetings and parades opposing U.S. participation in the war, focusing in particular upon conscription. In so doing, it often encountered vigilante action. On July 1 in Boston, soldiers and sailors, with bayonets fixed, broke up a Socialist parade and wrecked party headquarters. Twenty thousand people were involved in the melee. Party supporters carried banners declaring, "We demand Peace!" and "The United States Government Has Ordered 200,000 Coffins for Our Boys." In September, the Justice Department raided the offices of the Chicago *American Socialist*.[16]

In mid-July, Kate Richards O'Hare, formerly the party's national secretary, addressed a small crowd in Bowman, North Dakota. She claimed that "the women of the United States who didn't resist the taking of their sons in the army were nothing more or less than brood sows, to raise children to get into the army and be made into fertilizer." The war, she continued, was not being fought to make democracy safe but to enrich bankers and munitions makers. A U.S. District Court in Bismarck sentenced her to five years in the Missouri State Penitentiary; she served less than a year.[17]

Several liberals opposed such harassment. Pro-war socialist Frank Bohn warned, "Police intervention will merely fan the flame of opposition." *Nation* publisher Oswald Garrison Villard wrote Tumulty, denying he was personally a Socialist but claiming that Victor Berger, whose Milwaukee newspaper faced suppression, had a right to his views. Moreover, Villard noted, Socialist doctrine was currently supreme in half a dozen European countries. In mid-October, Colonel House warned Wilson that "no matter how much we deplore the attitude of the socialists as to the war, yet more harm may easily be done by repression." He forwarded a letter written to him by journalist Walter Lippmann, who observed that such respected figures as philosopher John Dewey feared such wartime censorship.[18]

The Socialist cause received fresh prominence in the New York City mayoral race of the fall of 1917, when Morris Hillquit became a much publicized party candidate. The Russian-born Hillquit was an attorney active in defending trade unions, particularly among garment workers. He was also an adept theoretician, writing a major history of American socialism. A reformist coalition of the Fusion and City parties supported incumbent John Purroy Mitchel ("the Boy Mayor"), a strong reformer and nominal Republican backed by the business community, the "good government" elements, and most of the city's powerful newspapers. At one mass meeting in front of City Hall, Mitchel's endorsers included Theodore Roosevelt; Charles Evans Hughes, former Supreme Court justice and 1916 presidential candidate; and Henry Morgenthau, Wilson's former ambassador to Turkey. Also in the mayor's ranks were William Howard Taft; 1904 Democratic presidential candidate Alton B. Parker; and 1916 Democratic gubernatorial candidate Samuel Seabury.[19]

The Democratic regulars, popularly known as Tammany Hall, supported John Francis ("Red Mike") Hylan, Brooklyn court judge and former fireman and engineer on the "elevated." One city newspaper judged Hylan so naive that it found him a man of "marvelous mental density."[20] More important was Hylan's backing by the Hearst press, of which Red Mike was its instrument. The Republican standard-bearer, William Mason Bennett, had been a Progressive; he lacked any organization and did practically no campaigning.

In July, when Hillquit received the Socialist Party nomination, the New York branch took a militantly anticonscription stance: "We most emphatically protest at this manner of forcing love of country upon the people and of compelling them to fight against their wills." In his acceptance speech made in late September, he proclaimed, "We are for peace. . . . Not warfare and terrorism, but Socialism and social justice will make the world safe for democracy." Early in October, he denied that Socialists favored immediate withdrawal from the war; rather, they wanted the United States to make the first move in ending hostilities. Opposing "German peace" or a "Kaiser peace," he claimed that his triumph would serve as "a mortal blow to autocracy in Germany and in all other countries." When a heckler asked Hillquit if he backed Wilson's policies, he replied, "I stand behind the President when I honestly believe that he is right, and only then. I stand behind the people all the time." He admitted that he would not buy Liberty Bonds, adding he would do nothing to "advance the war." Debs wrote him concerning the campaign, "I wish I could be there to fight it too."[21]

Because his stance on the war attracted a variety of New Yorkers, Hillquit's support far exceeded Socialist Party membership. During the second week of October alone, the party scheduled from 125 to 150 meetings every night. At the contest's height, Madison Square Garden hosted at least a half dozen Hillquit rallies, each filled to its capacity of 15,000.

Hillquit's stance also drew bitter opposition. Oscar Straus, Taft's secretary of commerce and labor, called his position treasonable. The *New York Times* found him "a seditionary. . . . To vote for him is to stab our soldiers and sailors in the back." Reformist rabbi Stephen Wise warned that a Mitchel defeat would turn Gotham into "the American suburb of Berlin." The Reverend Henry van Dyke pledged himself to hang any mayoral candidate who opposed U.S. belligerency. Such pro-war Socialists as Walling, Russell, Ghent, and Simons signed a statement accusing Hillquit of giving "needless aid and comfort to the enemies of democracy the world over." In a front-page headline with obvious anti-Semitic implications, the *New York Sun* said "Hillquit Was Once H-i-l-l-k-o-w-i-t-z." When Theodore Roosevelt branded Hillquit "the Hun inside our gates," the Socialist candidate recipro-cated by calling TR "the most serious menace to American democ-racy," one who "wants a war to make the world markets safe for our surplus products."[22]

The more moderate Hylan, too, was accused of disloyalty. He spoke little, usually criticizing Mitchel's administration and vaguely denouncing predatory interests. The *New York Times* attacked Hylan's Irish American backing, writing that "among his friends and spon-sors are notorious disloyalists, the conspirators against our associate in the war, Great Britain." Late in the campaign, incumbent Mitchel accused "Red Mike" in 1915 of acting as honorary vice chairman of the Friends of Peace, a group seeking a munitions embargo and thereby harming the Allies. Hylan replied that his name had been used with-out permission.[23]

Wilson refused to intervene in the race. In early October, jour-nalist Walter Lippmann warned the president that Mitchel's opponents represented "all the pro-German, anti-British, antiwar sentiment there is in the city." The November vote, he continued, should not appear as a test of the nation's war sentiment. Yet, on October 29, Wilson wrote Commerce Secretary William C. Redfield, saying he would not take part in the New York mayoral campaign. He claimed to have lost con-fidence in the New York mayor, promising to give his reason later. (He never did.) House referred in his diary to Wilson's "personal dislike" of Mitchel, a quality taken to a degree that was "not creditable to him." The president wrote Attorney General Gregory, arguing that con-demning Hillquit for his Liberty Loan opposition would only turn him into a martyr. Ironically, Wilson's secretary, Joseph Tumulty, backed Hylan, having a penchant for party regularity and being close to Tammany leaders Al Smith (president of New York's board of al-dermen) and Brooklyn boss John H. McCooey.[24]

In the end Hylan easily won the election, receiving 297,292 votes, almost half the total and the largest plurality for mayor yet achieved.

Mitchel came in second with 149,307, but Hillquit was a close third, receiving 142,178, which is 21.7 percent of the vote, about five times as much as any previous Socialist running for the office. He carried twelve of the city's assembly districts to Mitchel's eight. Moreover, New Yorkers elected ten Socialist assemblymen, seven aldermen, and a municipal court justice.

Reasons for Hylan's victory are complex. Theodore Roosevelt stressed that Mitchel lacked the common touch, being "too much with the Vanderbilts and in night restaurants where he danced." The *New York Times*, however, was undoubtedly correct in finding opposition to the war definitely a factor. So, too, did the *New Republic*, noting that an important body of opinion would not passively acquiesce in "the dictators of the majority."[25]

Historian Seward W. Livermore writes that Mitchel's Fusion movement had originally received strong administration backing, but that the mayor had turned the White House against him by supporting Hughes in 1916 and by lapsing into reactionary Park Avenue Republicanism. Possibly, Livermore muses, Tammany's congressional delegation threatened to oppose the war effort unless Wilson remained aloof from the conflict. At any rate, the Democratic leadership ordered all federal officeholders to ignore the incumbent. Another scholar, James Weinstein, argues that Mitchel ignored his own reformist record to push the war effort, losing support while playing into the hands of the Socialists.[26]

Socialists did well in other northern cities, polling more than a third in Chicago, 44 percent in Dayton, close to 34 percent in Toledo, 25+ percent in Buffalo, 19+ percent in Cleveland, and nearly 12 percent in Cincinnati. Healthy showings were also made in Boston, Rochester, Syracuse, Albany, Dayton, Utica, and Bridgeport. Pointing to such election results, Hearst's *New York American* remarked that the party's growth marked a most significant turn of events.[27] Never again would the party be so successful.

By December 1917, one significant voice, the *New Appeal* (formerly the *Appeal to Reason*), underwent something of a conversion. Editor Louis Kopelin endorsed Wilson's espousal of a democratic peace as he started to support the "war of defense" against Prussian militarism. Ever the optimist, he wrote that the war was creating revolution: "Socialism was never surer than now."[28]

About this time, Meyer London was slowly shifting his position. Born in a Polish province, the son of a Yiddish anarchist journalist, London—like Hillquit—had been a lawyer for East Side garment workers before becoming their congressman in 1914. He voted against the declaration of war, conscription, and the Espionage Act, but nonetheless backed military appropriations and gave passive assent to a $7 billion bond issue. During Hillquit's mayoral campaign, London told a rally, "The war cannot end until every inch of territory occupied in 1914 has been restored and returned." In February 1918, he remained sufficiently radical for Representative Martin Dies (D-Tex.) to link him with Lenin and Trotsky in "the blighting shadow of Bolsheviki socialism." By August, however, London told the House of Representatives that he regarded Wilson "more highly than any living man in American political life." A month later, he renounced the St. Louis manifesto, finding it divisive, and began participating in war bond rallies.[29]

The party itself continued to push its peace program. Opposing demands for total victory over the Central Powers, Hillquit feared "that if the bitter-end policy is persisted in, the end will be bitter indeed for the peoples of all lands." In February 1918, the party's national executive committee, a body that included Hillquit and Berger, endorsed U.S. recognition of the Bolshevik government that had recently taken control of Russia. In addition, it sought adoption of Lenin's peace program, based upon immediate cessation of hostilities without indemnities or annexation of territory. Otherwise, though its language was utopian, its position smacked strongly of Wilsonianism: universal disarmament, equality of trade conditions, the evacuation of occupied territory, reparations drawn from an international fund, self-determination of all nations and disputed territories, unrestricted freedom to travel over land and sea, an effective international peace-keeping organization, and the protection of the rights of "the weaker people (including the natives in the colonies)." Calling for immediate peace negotiations, the executive committee stressed, "We emphatically deny that it is necessary for the people of the United States to spill their blood and waste their treasure, in order to rearrange the map of Europe."[30]

Among the broader public, the party remained unpopular. In January 1918, authorities in Mitchell, South Dakota, prevented a state party convention from nominating a slate of candidates. In mid-March, a federal grand jury in Chicago indicted a number of party leaders, including its executive secretary, the editor of the *American Socialist*, the head of the Young People's Socialist League, and Wisconsin party leader Victor Berger. Within the year, Judge Kenesaw Mountain Landis had sentenced them to prison. In April, a federal court in Minneapolis condemned J. O. Bentall, Minnesota party gubernatorial candidate, to five years in prison for allegedly encouraging a young man to resist the draft.[31]

In June, a federal court in Kansas City gave Rose Pastor Stokes a ten-year term. A Russian-Jewish immigrant who had begun her working life as a cigar maker in Cleveland, she had married "the Socialist millionaire" J. G. Phelps Stokes. Though at first, like her husband, she had been a "pro-war" Socialist opposed to German militarism, by January 1918 she had adopted the party's antiwar position. She had written the editor of the *Kansas City Star* that "no government which is for the profiteers can also be for the people, and I am for the people, while the Government is for the profiteers." Earlier she had said that U.S. soldiers would some day learn that "they were not fighting for democracy but for the protection and safeguarding of Morgan's millions."[32]

Wilson approved of this "very just" sentence, while Colonel Harvey's *War Weekly* accused Mrs. Stokes of favoring her former oppressors over the nation that had given her asylum. Conversely, the *New Republic* asserted that the sentence fueled Germany's charge that American freedom and democracy were shams. Her husband sought to affirm her patriotism, arguing that both he and his wife supported Wilson's prosecution of the war.[33]

Given such repression, national membership fell drastically. The party's national committee, meeting in May 1918, decided against holding a convention or sponsoring a referendum. In August, a conference of state secretaries and party officials met in Chicago. Despite considerable confusion over policy, the body retained its adherence to the St. Louis proclamation. Praising Russia for having "cast aside the false idols of secret diplomacy and imperialism," it called the Bolshevik regime "a government of the workers, by the workers and for the workers." By the end of the war, Socialists estimated that violence and intimidation had reduced the number of chapters from 5,000 to 3,500.[34]

Soon after the war ended, the party experienced severe schism over events in Russia.

The most prominent instance of repression took place on June 16, 1918, in Canton, Ohio, when Eugene Debs, three times the party's presidential candidate, was arrested. For months Debs had been inactive, plagued by an unstable family life and having experienced a major physical collapse in mid-1917. The conviction of Kate Richards O'Hare, however, had aroused his indignation, and he made no secret of his intent to defy the Espionage Act.

In his two-hour address at a picnic before a thousand people attending the state party convention, he defended the IWW, embraced the Bolshevik Revolution, and backed political prisoners. The United States, he said, was not fighting to save democracy; rather it was involved in a greedy struggle for profit. He offered the ringing words, "When I rise it will be with the ranks and not from the ranks." At one point, he remarked, "We frankly admit that we *are* disloyalists and traitors to the real traitors to this nation." In the audience were stenographers from the U.S. attorney for the Northern District of Ohio, Edwin S. Wertz, who sent a copy of the speech to the Justice Department. Though Attorney General Thomas Gregory found the case against Debs dubious, Wertz sought prosecution. Two weeks later a federal grand jury charged the Socialist leader with violating the 1917 espionage and 1918 sedition laws.[35]

Debs's trial took place in early September in Cleveland. Seeking martyrdom, he refused to allow his lawyers to mount a defense. Rather, once the prosecution finished its case, he spoke for two hours. Instead of focusing upon the legality of the legislation, he admitted to obstructing the war effort and pleaded "guilty to the charge" of supporting the Bolshevik regime. He called his jailed comrades courageous, condemned capitalistic exploitation (singling out war profiteers in particular), and claimed the mantle of such prominent dissenters as Thomas Paine, John Adams, and several major abolitionists, not to mention Jesus and Socrates. Judge David Westenhaver, unmoved by his arguments, sentenced the Socialist leader to ten years in prison. Before he pronounced the sentence, Debs reached the height of his eloquence: "While there is a lower class, I am in it, while there is a criminal element I am of it, and while there is a soul in prison, I am not free." Though comparing John D. Rockefeller Sr.'s income of $60 million per year to wages of those living in penury, he ended with a touch of optimism, "for the cross is bending, the midnight is passing," and the present order could not endure. He did, however, concede that the judge had been "masterfully and scrupulously fair."[36]

When it came to radical dissent, the Socialists were not alone. Within the ranks of labor, no group was more subject to attack than the IWW. Founded in 1905, it differed from the American Federation of Labor, an association of craft unions, by seeking to organize all workers, irrespective of skill, into "One Big Union." Influenced by European theories of anarcho-syndicalism and endorsing sabotage and the general strike, the IWW took a distinctly revolutionary tone. Its preamble began: "The working class and the employing class have nothing in common. . . . Between these two classes a struggle must go on until the workers of the world organize as a class, take possession of the earth and the machinery of production and abolish the wage system."[37]

As an organization, the IWW opposed the war as an instrument of national policy and barred army enlistees from membership: "General Sherman said: 'War is Hell!' Don't go to hell in order to give the capitalists a bigger slice of heaven."[38] About 95 percent of its membership, however, registered with the Selective Service. Once the United States entered the conflict, the general executive board followed the lead of secretary-treasurer and de facto leader William ("Big Bill") Haywood, who found it "futile and foolish" to take any stand on U.S. participation in the war.

By 1917, "the Wobblies" listed about 60,000 dues-paying members. They were particularly active in the lumber industry of Washington State, the copper mines of Arizona, and fruit farms in Washington and California. Hence, their activities much affected enterprises associated with the war effort. Timber was essential for the construction of barracks, ships, and airplanes, copper for weapons and battlefield communication, food for civilians, troops, and the European Allies.

In the spring, the IWW began conducting major strikes, beginning with lumberjacks in the Northwest. Here the hours were long, pay low, camp life miserable. A three-month walkout involved fifty thousand workers, crippling the industry. On June 8, 1917, a disaster at the

Speculator copper mine, just outside Butte, Montana, killed 164 laborers. Three days later, the IWW led a strike, seeking recognition of the union and an end to blacklisting its members.

In late June, a major strike took place in Bisbee, Arizona, where the Phelps-Dodge Corporation produced 38 percent of the nation's copper. More than half the 4,700 workers at the Copper Queen mine walked out, production there reaching a near standstill. On July 12, two thousand vigilantes led by Sheriff Harry Wheeler, an ex-Rough Rider, rounded up 1,200 men, a mixture of IWW members and local sympathizers. First driven into concentration camps, the recalcitrant strikers were then herded into twenty-seven cattle cars, after which they were abandoned for three days without food, water, and shelter in the village of Hermanas, New Mexico. The refugees found temporary housing in an army camp in Columbus, New Mexico, but remained under military guard through the end of September.

Wilson publicly cabled Arizona governor Thomas Campbell, warning of "the great danger of citizens taking the law into their own hands." Union leader Haywood responded to Wilson with a threat, claiming that he had declared a general strike of metal miners in Michigan. Were the Bisbee strikers not returned home, miners in Minnesota and harvest workers in the Dakotas would also lay down their tools. In all, a quarter of a million men would be recruited. Now in a quandary, an indignant Wilson consulted his namesake and secretary of labor, William B. Wilson, who in turn asked Attorney General Gregory for advice. Labor Secretary Wilson accused Haywood of seeking "to intimidate the government by embarrassing it in its preparation for defense," in particular in its need for iron, coal, and copper. Gregory took no action against either Sheriff Wheeler or the vigilantes, seeing no federal issue involved. Vice President Thomas A. Marshall urged the mob to continue its intimidation until every last IWW member was hanged.[39]

A handful of prominent Americans opposed this treatment, among them George Creel and Lincoln Steffens. The *Nation* warned against creating martyrs by jailing IWW leaders unjustly. Senator Borah cautioned against mob rule. The *New York Times* found the Bisbee sheriff "on the right track" but claimed that "inhumanity is worse than the I.W.W." Journalist Ray Stannard Baker compared the IWW to primitive Christianity: "In its methods it may often be wrong, but in the great democratic ideals it is striving for it is sound and true, as I firmly believe." Harvard law professor Felix Frankfurter, secretary to the President's Mediation Commission that investigated the matter, found the Bisbee deportation "wholly without authority in law, either state or federal."[40]

In response, Henry Cabot Lodge accused Frankfurter of absolving criminals while condemning "the good citizens who have been the victims." Theodore Roosevelt, too, rebuked Frankfurter: "You are engaged in excusing men precisely like the Bolsheviki, who are murderers and encouragers of murder." The archrightist *Los Angeles Times* editorialized, "The citizens of Cochise county, Arizona, have written a lesson that the whole of America would do well to copy."[41]

On the night of August 1, 1917, in Butte, Montana, six men seized IWW organizer Frank Little, who was asleep in the Independent Miners' Union Hall. The posse brought him to a railroad trestle on the city's outskirts and hanged him. Historians Meirion and Susie Harries write that Little "looked the stereotype of a hobo agitator—part Indian, tall, spare, one-eyed, and beat-up." He was crippled by rheumatism and his broken leg was set in a plaster cast.[42] A member of the IWW executive board, Little had long been organizing lumberjacks, metal miners, and harvest binders; he was the board's only member expressing outright opposition to the war.

Rhetoric was fierce, particularly among senators from the West, as they sought ever-tighter legislation. In August 1917, Washington State's Miles Poindexter urged military force, claiming that IWW speakers "advocate murder" and "openly advocate destruction of property." Montana's Henry L. Myers referred to "incendiary and inflammatory talk," and Utah's William King called the IWW "a treasonable organization."[43]

Despite lack of any supporting evidence, certain opinion leaders kept asserting that the IWW was an agent of Berlin. Newspapers suggested Germany financed the strike at Butte. Senator Sherman accused the IWW of promoting a German military attack via Mexico. To Senator Henry F. Ashurst (D-Ariz.), its initials stood for "Imperial Wilhelm's Warriors."[44]

All this time, federal, state, and local authorities were seeking to break up the organization. Once the United States declared war, Minnesota and Idaho passed criminal syndicalism laws, effectively outlawing membership. In one state after another, officials ranging from sheriffs to governors to committees of national defense and vigilante groups went into action. Postal authorities suppressed IWW literature, maintaining that it tended to incite "arson, murder, or assassination." Wartime legislation caused several leading IWW newspapers to lose second-class mailing privileges. By July 1918, federal troops patrolled mining regions in Arizona and Montana, farms in eastern Washington, and timber areas in western Washington and Oregon. On September 5, Justice Department agents raided IWW offices in thirty-three cities, including Portland, Seattle, Minneapolis, Duluth, Milwaukee, and Detroit. More than five tons of material were seized.

Over the ensuing months, further additional roundups, arrests, intimidation, and violence took place, both by government officials and private citizens. In November, "the Knights of Liberty" tarred and feathered seventeen IWW members near Tulsa. In January 1918, U.S. Army major Omar Bradley occupied Butte, his troops fixing rifles and bayonets at strikers threatening the powerful Anaconda mining firm.[45]

In late September 1917, a Chicago grand jury, backed by the nation's press, indicted 166 leaders, including Haywood. Among the charges were delaying production and transportation of war supplies, interfering with the right of contract, and opposing conscription, recruitment, and the war itself. The trial began in April 1918 and lasted through August, an extremely long period for a criminal trial. In his conclusion, prosecutor Frank K. Nebeker found the IWW undermining America's political and economic structure, aiding Germany to accomplish this goal. Defense attorney George F. Vanderveer responded that only 3 of the 521 strikes called since April 1917 involved the IWW; all others were launched by AFL unions.

The Department of Justice lacked the evidence to convict most IWW defendants. By the common law of conspiracy, however, the government could hold all members of a group guilty for the actions of one. Though such administration figures as Tumulty, Colonel House, and secretaries Newton Baker and William B. Wilson wanted the charges dismissed, the president remained silent. Certain intellectuals called for a fair trial, among them philosopher John Dewey and economist Thorstein Veblen. In the end, it took the jury less than an hour to find the ninety-eight leaders guilty. The average sentence was eight years, yet Judge Kenesaw Mountain Landis awarded Haywood twenty. Haywood continued to appeal until 1921, when he escaped to Russia.

Conceding the administration's total disregard for civil liberties, historians H. C. Peterson and Gilbert C. Fite view the IWW leadership as poorly educated and politically naive, not up to the challenges engendered by the war. Years of persecution made the organization recalcitrant and combative, engaging in abusive language and frightening employers. Similarly, IWW historian Melvyn Dubofsky finds the Bill of Rights at stake. He observes, however, that IWW strikes had curtailed lumber and copper production, making it necessary for the federal government to act decisively against the union. Even had Haywood and other leaders remained free, Dubofsky maintains, the IWW would have inevitably faced decline, for any effort to transform American workers into a revolutionary vanguard was bound to fail. By continually making allusions to the general strike, Dubofsky writes, the IWW ended up lacking both concrete means and concrete goals.[46]

Another radical organization found itself subject to accusations of disloyalty. In 1915, North Dakotan Arthur C. Townley launched the Nonpartisan League (NPL). A former Socialist organizer, Townley had been fired by the state party for recruiting so many members that the leaders could not handle the massive enrollments. Composed primarily of Great Plains farmers who had experienced years of crop failure and low prices, the NPL attacked the grain combines, milling firms, and major railroads. Its platform demanded state ownership of terminal elevators, flour mills, stockyards, packing houses, storage plants, and coal mines. It sought a rural credit bank, hail insurance for storms, tax exemptions for farm improvements, and nationalization of telephone, telegraph, and railroads. Writes historian Daniel Bell, "True, most of the backstage operators were or had been well-known socialists. But its appeal and strength were populist; it was literally and figuratively straight corn."[47]

In February 1917, the NPL listed thirty thousand members. Active throughout the Middle West and Great Plains, it was particularly strong in North Dakota, where it captured the governorship, the legislature, and almost every state office. By 1919, the state's NPL had pushed through bills reducing farm taxes and freight rates while creating a hail insurance law and a state-owned grain elevator and flour mill complex.

Before April 1917, the NPL strongly opposed entry into the conflict. When in February the United States had broken relations with Germany, NPL governor Lynn J. Frazier stressed, "North Dakota is not in favor of war." Organizer Townley told an audience in St. Paul, Minnesota: "Let capital throw its resources into the war game unselfishly and the 100,000 of the Northwest will throw their resources and their blood, if necessary, into the game just as enthusiastically."[48]

Once the United States entered the war, NPL endorsement was at first guarded. When in April 1917, the first Liberty Loan campaign was announced, the NPL quietly campaigned against it. In mid-August, the North Dakota NPL released a platform declaring that the war was rooted in "the adroit rulers of warring nations for control of the world's markets. Rival groups of monopolists are playing a deadly game for commercial supremacy." It called upon the United States to issue an "immediate public declaration of peace terms without annexations of territory, indemnities, contributions or interference with the right of any nation to live and manage its own affairs."[49]

In July, NPL foes accused Townley of contrasting "big bellied, red-necked plutocrats" to U.S. troops "having their legs shot off, their arms shot off, their chests ripped open, their eyes torn out." Although the NPL denied the statement, it was widely accepted. Several months later, Townley did say of American corporation leaders that one might "get a German helmet, place it on THEIR head, and YOU SEE THE KAISER HIMSELF." Also in July, the organization's newspaper, the *Nonpartisan Leader*, continued calling for domestic reform, advocating government operation of the railroads, major utilities, and coal and oil resources.[50]

That month, North Dakota citizens elected NPL member John M. Baer to the U.S. House of Representatives. In a special election, Baer defeated standard-bearers of both major parties and carried almost every county in his district. A thirty-year-old civil engineer who had been a *Leader* cartoonist and postmaster of the village of Beach, Baer endorsed all-out prosecution of the war. At the same time, he wanted conscription of wealth at home, a foreign policy based on open diplomacy, and a statement of war aims. Noting that Britain had just gained a million square miles in Africa, he asked, "While we are fighting German Imperialism, shall we fight to support British Imperialism?"[51]

Attacks on the NPL were vehement. The *Boston Transcript* suggested that it was nothing more than "a sorry combination of old-time grangerism, socialism, I.W.W.-ism, and a form of pacifism with a distinctly German basis." One member of the Minnesota Committee of Public Safety, a Minneapolis district judge, told the U.S. Senate, "Where we made a mistake is in not establishing a firing squad in the first days of the war." Theodore Roosevelt was particularly strident, accusing the NPL in September 1918 of seeking to establish Bolshevism in the United States. He found Townley ranking with "Messrs. Lenine and Trotsky."[52]

Not surprisingly, the NPL experienced repeated intimidation. Accused of treason, its leaders faced incarceration, physical assault, and tarring and feathering. In some Minnesota counties, local officials locked up NPL speakers on sight. In Nebraska, sheriffs arbitrarily jailed members. In July 1917, an NPL organizer, who claimed that the war was fought on behalf of "the moneyed interests and Wall Street," faced a two-year prison term in Leavenworth. August saw another speaker, Minnesota state manager Joseph Gilbert, receiving a year's sentence for supposedly saying the United States was stampeded into the war "to pull England's chestnuts out of the fire." (In 1920, the U.S. Supreme Court upheld the conviction on the grounds that states had the right to prevent obstruction of national policies.) By March 1918, nineteen out of Minnesota's eighty-seven counties had banned NPL meetings. In 1918 and again in 1919, Townley was tried for having hindered enlistment. Flimsy evidence did not prevent him from receiving a ninety-day sentence.[53]

Yet the NPL was already proclaiming its patriotism. Sponsoring a Producers and Consumers Conference in St. Paul in September 1917, it declared: "We pledge our lives, our fortunes, and our sacred honor to our country and our flag in this, OUR WAR." By early 1918, the NPL had endorsed Wilson at every turn, with both speakers and the *Nonpartisan Leader* echoing his views. In February, Congressman Baer wrote the president: "Will you use us? We have an enthusiastic desire to use our influence in any way that you or any Governmental Department may suggest." In March, the NPL's *Minnesota Leader* called Liberty Loans "the best investment in the world today." In boasting of NPL support for the loans, Townley told the Senate Military Affairs Committee, "We do not want to stand before the country and the world branded as traitors."[54]

In spring of 1918, the Minnesota NPL chose Charles A. Lindbergh Sr., father of the future famous aviator, as gubernatorial candidate. Just a year before, the former Republican congressman had written a 220-page volume titled *Why Is Your Country at War and What Happens to You After the War, and Related Subjects*. In addition to his usual attacks on "special privilege" and Wall Street interests, he blamed U.S. involvement in the war on "speculative interests" who had provoked incidents on the high seas out of sheer greed. The *Bismarck Tribune* called Lindbergh "a sort of Gopher Bolshevik" at the very time he experienced shotgun fire and temporary arrest. Though he carried thirty counties, he lost the Republican primary by almost 50,000 votes. Ernest Lundeen of Minneapolis, the one incumbent Republican congressman receiving NPL endorsement, was also defeated in the same primary. Townley ascribed Lindbergh's defeat to "big business, with a kept press and chest of gold." In August, Bernard Baruch offered Lindbergh an appointment to his War Industries Board (WIB), but public outcry forced the Minnesotan's resignation. Creel was outraged, writing Wilson that Lindbergh and his associates were "your loyal supporters."[55]

Several Wilson appointees were friendly towards the NPL. In November 1917, George Creel brought Townley to Washington, where he met with Wilson and pledged the loyalty of western farmers. "Despite attacks," Creel wrote the NPL in March 1918, "I believe intensely in the loyalty of the Nonpartisan League. I have done all in my power to protect it from unfair assaults." Carl S. Vrooman, assistant secretary of agriculture, saw the NPL as "the only movement which will save the United States from revolution."[56]

Wilson himself kept the NPL at arm's length. In February 1918, he wrote Creel that the NPL activities were in many respects questionable, its leaders self-serving and untrustworthy. Yet on that very day, he corresponded with Congressman Baer, appreciating "the work of the sort you outline" because it contributed to "the universal cause." Obviously, Wilson appreciated the NPL's encroachment on Republican strongholds of Minnesota, North Dakota, Nebraska, and Montana. When Townley wrote Wilson in mid-March, saying 45,000 NPL farmers endorsed the president's war aims, Wilson confided to Tumulty that he still mistrusted both the NPL and its president. "We had better pull away from them," he soon told Creel. In April, reformer William Kent wrote Wilson, accusing the Minnesota Council of Public Safety of "high-handed persecution" of the NPL. The president simply replied, "It is a situation which will have to work itself out, much as I should like to take a hand in working it out." Two months later, Wilson mellowed, telling Attorney General Gregory that the NPL included people of dubious loyalty but that the organization had consistently and effectively aided the war effort.[57]

Unlike the other radical groups, the NPL was at the height of its power at the end of the war. In the 1918 elections it retained control of North Dakota. Frazier was easily reelected governor as the NPL kept full control of the legislature and added two North Dakota seats in the U.S. House.

The People's Council of America for Democracy and Peace was even more controversial than the NPL. It was launched on May 30–31, 1917, at a rally in New York's Madison Square Garden, its fundamental objective being an immediate negotiated peace. At the very first session, at least 400 delegates endorsed Russian demands of no annexations and no indemnities, called for self-determination of all peoples, opposed the government onslaught on free speech and assembly, and denounced the recent conscription act. Because authorities deemed the assembly at best suspect, more than four hundred armed patrolmen massed on surrounding street corners while police trucks equipped with searchlights drove through the area.[58]

For two days, one speaker after another assailed U.S. participation in the war. The presiding officer, Manhattan rabbi Judah Magnes, asked whether the goal "safe for democracy" referred to Germany alone, to all the Central Powers, to Japan's holdings, or to Allied domination of India, Morocco, Persia, and Ireland. Morris Hillquit cautioned, "We cannot force democracy upon hostile countries by force of arms." James Maurer, the Socialist president of the Pennsylvania Federation of Labor, accused American capitalists of spurring their nation into the conflict. Milwaukee Socialist leader Victor Berger condemned the business community for profiting from the war, warning of riots from coast to coast. International law expert William Isaac Hull of Swarthmore College feared that secret agreements might commit the United States to another conflict.[59]

Impetus for the People's Council came from Louis Lochner, secretary of the 1915 Ford peace ship expedition and a spearhead of the Emergency Peace Federation, which had been organized early in 1917. The PCA possessed a strong Socialist base, being particularly vibrant among the Jewish needle trades unions in New York City, where it boasted 284 branches representing 900,000 workers. It perceived itself modeled upon the Petrograd Soviet, a rival to Russia's provisional government, though not yet dominated by Bolsheviks. Within two months, it claimed 2 million members and had held mass meetings in New York, Philadelphia, Chicago, San Francisco, and Los Angeles. In addition, the organizing committee established branches in those cities and in Seattle and Salt Lake City.

The PCA was soon attacked. Stanford president Ray Lyman Wilbur warned his predecessor, David Starr Jordan, who had agreed to serve as temporary treasurer, that the organization was "distinctly unpatriotic." Wilbur particularly mistrusted Lochner, believing he was serving Germany. The AFL's Gompers remarked, "The Kaiser is greatly cheered by the reports he gets of the People's Council activities." To the *New York Times*, the PCA was "one of the long succession of societies of German propaganda and anti-American purposes." Columbia international law professor Ellery C. Stowell wrote a PCA officer that he would rather sever his right hand than join the association. Former Socialist John Spargo claimed that Germany's leaders, meeting at Potsdam, formulated its program. Even Lillian Wald, pacifist and settlement house leader, feared that the PCA represented "impulsive radicalism," not the "reflective thought of those opposed to war."[60]

Within the Wilson administration, there existed much suspicion. Postmaster General Burleson saw the PCA "doing much harm to the Government" and so warned Wilson. In August, Post Office solicitor William H. Lamar warned his chief that PCA backers, who ranged from "the extreme anarchist type to the Women's Peace Party," sought "to paralyze the activities of the Government in this war." Creel privately called the PCA "pro-German and disloyal."[61]

Wilson, however, balked at repressive moves, telling his cabinet in mid-August that it remained better to "let them show their impotence" than to suppress them, that is, "as long as they keep within the law." Two weeks later, Wilson dismissed the group as "eminent crooks and others who have sense in normal times."[62]

Matters came to a head in late August, when the PCA sought to hold a national convention in Minneapolis. Such a meeting could strengthen the larger urban chapters, unite the smaller councils emerging in the Middle West, and—so pro-war leaders feared—hinder the war effort by fostering nationwide strikes, anticonscription activity, and infiltration of the mainstream labor movement. When Minnesota governor Joseph Burnquist boasted that he would not allow any "anti-American" meeting to take place in his state, city business leaders denied the PCA a meeting hall. The organization then sought to meet in Fargo, North Dakota. State governor Lynn Frazier welcomed the group, but officials there, too, were hostile. When the PCA hoped to gather in Milwaukee, Wisconsin governor Emanuel Philipp wired the sheriff to refuse permission.

On August 30, Lochner and his co-workers were sitting in the lobby of the local hotel in Hudson, Wisconsin, just across the St. Croix River from Minneapolis. Suddenly they were confronting a mob of about a thousand bearing rope and noose and shouting, "Kill the Copperheads" and "String up the Kaiserites." The dissidents were able to escape.[63]

A day later, Chicago mayor William Hale ("Big Bill") Thompson permitted the PCA to hire his city's West Side Auditorium. In so doing, Thompson had defied his fellow Republican, Illinois governor Frank Lowden, who had forbidden the assembly. For the next two days, three hundred people heard Rabbi Magnes call for immediate negotiations with the Germans, asking, "Why not meet now?" Chicago congressman William Mason blasted Lowden: "I'm interested now more in free speech in Illinois than in what one European country shall pay another in indemnities." Former senator John Works (R-Calif.) sought a referendum on the draft and the immediate withdrawal of U.S. troops just arriving in France. The body adopted a platform reiterating its call for universal disarmament, conscription repeal, clearly defined war aims, and peace without conquest, annexation, or indemnities. Within three hours after adjournment, Lowden sent four companies of National Guard troops from Springfield to break up what he called a "treasonable conspiracy." The Chicago city council censured Thompson, the local press attacked him, and federal and state grand juries investigated him.[64]

Wilson supported such repression. In September, an obscure journal published in Washington, D.C., *The People's Counselor*, offered certain stock radical arguments (e.g., the war was illegal, being perpetuated by an international "money power" and fought only to make the world safe for plutocracy). Sponsored by the treasurer of the Chicago People's Council, it drew Wilson's wrath, the president asking Attorney General Gregory if such documents "do not form a sufficient basis for a trial for treason. There are many instances of this sort and one conviction would probably scotch a great many snakes." Such utterances, he argued, could easily lead to an indictment.[65]

In late October, one PCA speaker, the Reverend Herbert Bigelow of the People's Church of Cincinnati, was scheduled to address a socialist meeting in Newport, Kentucky, just across the Ohio River. The minister was gagged, handcuffed, thrust into a waiting auto, and received twelve lashes to his neck. By and large, the New York press ignored the matter. The *Evening Sun*, however, found the clergyman "less sinned against than sinning" while the *Herald* claimed that he was lucky to get off with "a good hiding."[66] All members of Congress were silent.

Newton D. Baker, a personal friend of Bigelow, publicly called the treatment "brutal and cowardly." The secretary of war brought the matter to Wilson's attention and asked Attorney General Gregory to investigate, but the matter went no further. On November 12, Wilson, in addressing the AFL convention in Buffalo, attacked in general "the mob spirit . . . displaying itself here and there in this country. I have no sympathy with what some men are saying, but I have no sympathy with the men who take their punishment into their own hands."[67] Neither Bigelow nor the incident was mentioned.

By October, the matter of PCA membership became an issue among the Columbia University faculty. At the 1917 commencement ceremonies, President Nicholas Murray Butler had put his faculty on warning: "What had been tolerated before became intolerable now. What had been wrongheadedness is now sedition." On the first of the month, the university trustees dismissed two faculty members over the conscription issue. Henry Wadsworth Longfellow Dana, assistant professor of English and comparative literature, was an active member of the PCA and of the Collegiate Anti-Militarism League. Similarly, the renowned scholar James McKeen Cattell, professor of psychology, had written several members of Congress opposing the sending of conscripts "to fight in Europe against their will." As a result of the joint dismissal, historian Charles A. Beard, himself pro-war, resigned his professorship, calling the trustees "reactionary and visionless in politics and medieval in religion." With little dissent, however, the press approved Butler's action.[68]

If by the fall of 1917, the PCA was the nation's most visible supporter of immediate peace, it was already becoming a spent force. Funds remained low, failing to reach $700 by October. Several mainstays, such as PCA organizer and feminist leader Crystal Eastman, dropped out. When Hillquit resigned as chairman to run for mayor of New York, he was replaced by Scott Nearing, a radical economist successively fired from the University of Pennsylvania and the University of Toledo. No sooner in office, Nearing engaged in a power struggle with executive secretary Lochner.[69]

Historian Frank L. Grubbs Jr. finds the PCA's main problem, however, in its image. The press, the Wilson administration, and the Gompers wing of American labor successfully branded it as a mouthpiece of German propaganda. The Socialists within the PCA, according to Rabbi Wise, were "not of the parlor or the drawing-room variety, but of the basement and cellar type, who, like their German colleagues, from the beginning of the war have served the interests of Germany."[70] After the Bolshevik revolution of November 1917, foes called the PCA communist.

The organization did nothing to counter this image. In February 1918, a month after Lenin had abolished the Constituent Assembly, Nearing told a PCA conference that Russia was teaching America "how to set the pace for free speech and democracy." "The Russian people are in the lead, and we must humbly follow." Magnes remarked, "I admit to be a real Bolshevik." Unlike the Socialist Party, the PCA preached control of industry by local soviets. By 1918, writes historian Michael Kazin, the organization had become little more than "cheerleader for the Bolsheviks" rather than "a place where anti-warriors of different stripes could gather."[71]

Little wonder the harassment continued. In November 1917, for example, sixty officers of the Duluth police force stormed a PCA meeting, arresting Nearing and holding him without bail. By April 1918, Lochner complained that mail censorship was so severe he could scarcely post a single letter. In October he shut the PCA down. After the war, the organization had a brief revival but disbanded during the postwar Red Scare of 1919–20.[72]

Obviously, vigilante societies, state and local groups of opportunistic and misled legislators, the postmaster general and attorney general—not to mention ordinary citizens—all sought to squelch dissenters. Historians place different emphases on the role of Woodrow Wilson, some accusing him of at best tacitly encouraging the hysteria, others finding him engaged in a rearguard action against extreme harassment.[73]

Despite the differences in emphases among the various scholars, one thing is certain: the president of the United States bore no small responsibility for the atmosphere of hysteria. The situation is particularly ironic given Wilson's later famous interview with Frank Cobb, crusading editor of the New York *World*, several weeks before the nation went to war. Once the country entered the conflict, he feared, "the spirit of ruthless brutality will enter into every fiber of our national life, infecting Congress, the courts, the policeman on the beat, the man in the street." The Constitution, not to mention freedom of speech and assembly, could not survive the ordeal, because it required "illiberalism at home to reinforce the men at the front."[74]

In private, the president occasionally expressed misgivings concerning specific acts of intolerance in particular and the climate of opinion in general. He undoubtedly realized that even calling for toleration of unpopular voices, be they scorned ethnic groups or political radicals, would enable critics to link him to subversive elements. Yet the president's powers of persuasion were considerable.

Furthermore, had he chosen more responsible administrators, he could have turned the Justice and Post Office Departments into his allies. Wilson had often written on the importance of leadership as the crucial element in attaining national goals. The warm reception given to his "peace without victory" speech, his war message, and—a year later—to his "Fourteen Points" address increased his awareness of his oratorical skills. Certainly, the president and cabinet alone could not stem the repressive tide, but undoubtedly some of it could have been curbed. The effort was simply not made. To argue that other leaders (e.g., Theodore Roosevelt, Elihu Root) would have been more intolerant is to beg the question. If intolerance was a problem, the president of the United States did not find it a major one.

Such repression was strongly affected by two major revolutions, both taking place in Russia in 1917. These upheavals would sorely try all the Allied powers and eventually cause commitment of U.S. ground troops to such far-flung shores as Archangel and Vladivostok.

EIGHT
"LIVING ON A VOLCANO"

Russia Amid Revolution

BOTH THE VIGILANTES AND THE DISSENTERS IN THE UNITED States were strongly affected by events that took place thousands of miles away in the Russian capital of Petrograd, recently St. Petersburg. There, early in March 1917, strikes and riots broke out, troops mutinied, and Tsar Nicholas II abdicated his throne. On the 12th, a committee of the Duma, the Russian parliament of more than five hundred seats, created a provisional government. Prince George E. Lvov, chairman of the Union of Zemstvos (local elected councils) and municipalities, became prime minister. Paul Milyukov, a professor of Russian history and leader of the Cadet Party (Constitutional Democrats), served as foreign minister. Alexander Kerensky of the Socialist Revolutionary Party, just thirty-six years old, was chosen as minister of justice, even though before the war he had been twice imprisoned for radical activities. The United States immediately recognized the new government, with England, France, and Italy soon following.

On the same day, the Council of Workers' and Soldiers' Deputies, informally called the Petrograd Soviet and originally numbering 250 members, was formed. Similar soviets were organized throughout Russia, reaching 1,400 by October. From the outset, the Petrograd Soviet rivaled the authority of the Duma, steadily gaining authority at the expense of Russia's formal rulers. In a sense, the provisional government exercised formal authority but possessed limited power; the Petrograd Soviet lacked legal legitimacy but found itself exercising much informal control. In the nation as a whole, all centralized authority was disintegrating, as local towns and regions engaged in de facto secession from the national state. "Russia, in short," writes historian Orlando Figes, "was being Balkanized."[1]

As far as war aims were concerned, Foreign Minister Milyukov pledged Russian adherence to the secret treaty made with the Allies in March 1915, whereby Britain and France promised his nation Constantinople and the Turkish Straits. In hostile hands, these "doors to our home," Milyukov warned, threatened his nation's coast and the Mediterranean Sea and severed Russia's grain trade with the West. Taking the opposite position, on April 4 the executive committee of the Petrograd Soviet laid down the "Petrograd Formula" of three major demands for remaining in the conflict: self-determination, no annexations, and no indemnities. It promised to join with socialists of other nations in refusing "to serve as an instrument of violence and conquest in the hands of kings, landlords, and bankers."[2]

Many Americans heartily welcomed the March revolution, with editors, politicians, labor leaders, and state legislatures all voicing approval. In his war message of April 2, 1917, President Wilson called the new Russia "a fit partner for a League of Honour." The nation, he maintained, was "known by those who knew it best to have been always in fact democratic at heart, in all the vital habits of her thought, in all the intimate relations of her people that spoke their natural instinct, their habitual attitude toward life." Indeed, the recent Russian autocracy, that is, the Romanov dynasty, "was not in fact Russian in origin, character, or purpose." Secretary of State Robert Lansing felt similarly: "The great Russian people have joined the powerful democracies who are struggling against autocracy."[3]

Just after the United States entered the war, Wilson extended a $100 million credit to Russia. Before Washington would make any further move, however, it sought much more information concerning the nation's stability and morale, in particular its willingness to continue the war effort. When, early in April, Lansing suggested sending a fact-finding mission, the president strongly concurred.[4]

On April 25, the administration announced that seventy-two-year-old Elihu Root would bear the formidable title "ambassador extraordinary of the United States of America on Special Mission to Russia." Root had served William McKinley and Theodore Roosevelt as secretary of war, after which he became TR's secretary of state and in 1909 senator from New York. When Treasury Secretary McAdoo brought up his name in a cabinet meeting, Lansing heartily agreed. Root's appointment revealed an obvious attempt at bipartisanship—he was a staunch Old Guard Republican. Privately he shared the contempt for the president held by his close friends Theodore Roosevelt and Henry Cabot Lodge.[5]

The rest of the Root mission was extremely diverse. Charles R. Crane, a Chicago plumbing magnate, long held a personal interest in Russian affairs, even establishing a lectureship in Slavic Studies at the University of Chicago. Another Chicagoan, Cyrus H. McCormick, headed International Harvester, a firm that had done extensive business there. Pro-war socialist Charles Edward Russell could supposedly appeal to Russia's radicals. It was hoped that seventy-nine-year-old James Duncan, a Scottish-born granite-cutter and American Federation of Labor vice president, would draw working-class support. Samuel Bertron was a Wall Street banker who stressed better trade relations. Prominent Methodist layman John R. Mott headed many ecumenical agencies, including the World Alliance of Young Men's Christian Associations (YMCA) and the World Student Christian Federation.[6]

A few members of the mission were military figures. Colonel William V. Judson, army engineer and protégé of Postmaster General Burleson, had served as a military observer during the Russo–Japanese War. Rear Admiral James H. Glennon, an ordnance expert, had commanded navy yards in New York and Washington. Major General Hugh L. Scott, army chief of staff, could well have been chosen to ease his retirement from the service, as he had shown himself too inept to direct the massive U.S. mobilization. Colonel T. Bentley Mott, personally close to Root, had twice served as military attaché in Paris. In Vladivostok, war correspondent Stanley Washburn, who had covered the region since the Russo–Japanese War, joined them as secretary. No one involved in the original mission spoke Russian or had more than a superficial knowledge of that nation.

On May 14, the Root mission left Washington, reaching Seattle on the 20th and arriving at Vladivostok on June 3. In his first conference onboard the aged navy cruiser, the USS *Buffalo*, Root outlined the mission's three objectives: express the deep sympathy of the United States towards Russia's new republic, ascertain the nation's financial needs, and avoid the appearance of a strong nation dictating to a weaker one. Lansing cabled Ambassador David R. Francis that the commission was prepared to confer the best ways and means "*to bring about effective cooperation between the two governments* in the prosecution of the war against the German autocracy," which he called "the gravest menace to all democratic governments (in the world)."[7]

From Vladivostok the group began its trip to Petrograd, often traveling on the imperial train of former Tsar Nicholas II. At every stop, the delegation made speeches. Of one of the villages that he visited, Root said privately, "I am a firm believer in democracy, but I do not like filth." Reaching Petrograd on June 13, the Americans were housed at the Winter Palace, which General Scott deemed a "damp, gloomy structure."[8]

Two days later, Root told the provisional government's Council of Ministers, "We see Russia as a whole, as one mighty, striving, aspiring democracy." At the same time, he warned, "The triumph of German arms will mean the death of liberty in Russia." Privately, he cabled Washington:

> Conditions here critical. General St. Petersburg opinion very pessimistic; industrial and financial conditions bad; Provisional Government seems secure; no visible agitation against it at present. . . . Please say to the President that we have found here an infant class in the art of being free containing one hundred and seventy million people and they need to be supplied with kindergarten material; they are sincere, kindly, good people but confused and dazed.[9]

Concerning the "kindergarten" remark, Charles Edward Russell confided to his diary, "Pray God that remark does not get out or our usefulness is done for here."[10]

All members of the mission addressed the Russians frequently, Root speaking as often as four times a day. In a pep talk to the Petrograd Soviet, labor leader Duncan stressed the importance of two- and three-hour shifts and a six-day workweek in essential industries.[11] The visit aroused no great popular interest and was practically ignored by the Russian press. A two-day visit to Moscow and less than twenty-four hours at Mogilev, headquarters of the general staff, produced little. Pleas to Washington for supplies, propaganda work, and $100,000 for recreation camps to improve army morale lacked immediate response. On July 9, the mission left Petrograd for Vladivostok, from which it headed back to the United States. Root was sanguine about the results of his journey, writing both his wife and Lansing that the mission had strengthened the provisional government and improved the morale of the people and the army. Upon his return, he told the press that he saw "no organic or incurable malady in the Russian democracy."[12]

In two brief reports submitted to Lansing, the group stressed Russia's needs. Financially the nation faced bankruptcy. Production was half the normal output. The country experienced a transportation bottleneck because 40 percent of its locomotives needed extensive repair. Yet the commission was astonishingly upbeat. Substantial aid was necessary, but "we have little doubt that they [the Russians] will be able to establish and maintain successfully free self-government on a great scale." If such a development could not be "accomplished in a day, . . . they are moving now with a rapidity which is quite extraordinary." Russia's leading general, Alexei Brusilov, "has great influence with the soldiers as a brilliant and successful military leader," but the commission did fear that his army might actually dissolve. "Just now America, as no other nation, holds the key to the situation."[13]

Privately some commission members expressed doubts. The day after General Scott arrived in Petrograd, he wrote his wife, "There is no real force in the Gov't—the army is run by town meeting votes of soldiers who do not obey their officers." Socialist Charles Edward Russell confided to his diary that the masses were "sick of the war" (he the lone delegate of the Root mission who observed this).[14]

On August 8, the Root Commission met for two hours with a surprisingly ill-at-ease Wilson, who appeared only interested in its recommendations for propaganda. It talked more extensively with Lansing, who wrote in his diary, "I was astounded at their optimism." The secretary of state expressed considerable skepticism concerning Kerensky, believing that the Russian leader had conceded too much to Petrograd's radical element. Noting the evolution of the French Revolution of 1789, he remarked, "In my judgment the demoralized state of affairs will grow worse and worse until some dominant personality arises to end it all." Meanwhile, the United States should prepare for the time when Russia would no longer be a military factor in the war.[15]

Wilson did act on a subsequent report drafted by John R. Mott and Charles Edward Russell, who recommended the establishment of a $5.5 million propaganda agency in Petrograd. The president turned the document over to George Creel, who radically reduced the project in size and budget. Creel appointed journalist and CPI associate chairman Edgar Sisson to direct publicity activities, but the emissary only arrived in Russia on November 25, 1917, several weeks after the Bolsheviks had seized power.

Other than this mild overture, Wilson lost all interest in his own commission. Writing a decade later, Root was acid: "Wilson didn't want to accomplish anything. It was a grand-stand play. He wanted to show his sympathy for the Russian Revolution. When we delivered his message and made our speeches, he was satisfied; that's all he wanted."[16]

Most historians are extremely critical of the mission, stressing such factors as naive arrogance and an effort to counter the Petrograd Soviet's war aims. Alton Earl Ingram, who has made a special study of the enterprise, comments, "It is difficult to understand how the group could have remained in the Russian capital for almost one month and yet have received such a distorted view of the realities of the situation." By limiting its contacts to conservative elites, the mission falsely reported that the provisional government was stable and that ordinary Russians thoroughly embraced continuation of the war. Only Charles Edward Russell deliberately sought out the Petrograd Soviet, yet even he did not mention its role in his own report. It would have been better, argues Ingram, to have had no mission at all.[17]

Ingram is right. It would have been wiser for U.S. leaders to confess ignorance of a terribly complicated situation than to mislead their own countrymen and ultimately themselves.

Another such venture, this one designed to rescue Russia's failing railroad system, also ended in failure. Inefficiency, lack of equipment, and an outmoded administrative system threatened the entire network with collapse. Particularly crucial was the Trans-Siberian Railway, which spanned 4,700 miles from Vladivostok to the Ural Mountains and which by the late spring of 1917 had practically ceased to function. Because the Central Powers had cut most of Russia off from its allies, the Trans-Siberian became increasingly critical in forcing Germany to remain fighting on two fronts. Due, however, to congestion all along the track, at most 120 cars left Vladivostok daily; 750,000 tons of material, ranging from cotton to barbed wire, clogged the city's docks, vacant lots, and adjacent hills.

In early June 1917, a commission of five American experts arrived in Vladivostok, led by John F. Stevens, who had been general manager of the Great Northern Railroad and chief engineer for the construction of the Panama Canal. Its task: a complete survey of all Russian railways, with appropriate recommendations to the Russian government. For thirteen days, the group traveled by rail to Petrograd, after which it inspected the railways of European Russia. During its journey, the mission observed discontent, idleness, and insubordination everywhere.

In mid-August, Wilson approved Stevens's commitment of 2,500 locomotives and 40,000 freight cars, but he warned against further promises. On November 1, three thousand railway engineers left the United States for Russia, followed seventeen days later by about three hundred officers and skilled mechanics slated to serve as instructors. Colonel George Emerson, general manager of the Great Northern Railway, headed the second group. While the first group was en route, the Bolshevik Revolution broke out, forcing the mission to retreat from Vladivostok to Japan. Stevens, furious over the matter, cabled Lansing from Nagasaki: "We should all go back shortly with a man-of-war and 5,000 troops. It is time to put the fear of God into these people." Some engineers ended up working for the Chinese Eastern Railroad, part of the Trans-Siberian line, which served as a de facto Russian colony within Manchu territory. As with the Root mission, that of Stevens proved abortive.[18]

On May 16, the provisional government created a new cabinet called the First Coalition. Prince Lvov remained prime minister, but Milyukov was replaced as foreign minister by Mikhail I. Tereshchenko, a young Ukrainian sugar magnate who totally lacked diplomatic experience. Kerensky became minister of war. With the shift in ministry came one in official war aims, for Tereshchenko publicly endorsed a peace that "aims neither at domination over other peoples, nor a seizure of their national patrimony, nor a taking by force of foreign territories, a peace without annexations or indemnities." At the same time, he warned that immediate publication of the secret treaties would be "equivalent to a rupture with the Allies and will result in the isolation of Russia."[19]

The U.S. Treasury indicated its approval of the First Coalition by extending a $100 million loan. On May 26, in a special message to Russia, Wilson himself sought to encourage the provisional government, proclaiming that the United States was fighting "for the liberation of peoples everywhere from the aggressions of autocratic force."[20]

On July 1, the situation in Russia took a radical turn. Its army, commanded by General Brusilov, launched a major attack along a twenty-mile front in Galicia. For the first time in three years, it seemed to possess sufficient resources to embark upon a campaign. Initially, Russian forces, which outnumbered their enemies almost three to one, appeared on the verge of a major victory. War Minister Kerensky proclaimed, "Today is the great triumph of the revolution. . . . The Russian revolutionary army with colossal enthusiasm assumed the offensive." Even the Petrograd Soviet endorsed the move.[21]

Some prominent Americans could not conceal their enthusiasm. Theodore Roosevelt wrote Prince Lvov, "We hail the advent of Russia to a foremost place among the free peoples of mankind." On his way home from Russia, Elihu Root addressed troops in Perm, a city close to the Urals: "God sent a great man to be your leader in Kerensky, and under his leadership, under his appeals to the soldiers at the front, discipline has been restored."[22]

David Rowland Francis, U.S. ambassador to Petrograd, cabled Washington concerning a "decisive victory for Russian forces on southeast, 9,000 prisoners taken. Outlook for Government more encouraging than for weeks past." Francis had received his appointment on strictly political grounds. A leading Missouri Democrat, he had served in turn as mayor of St. Louis, governor, and Grover Cleveland's secretary of the interior. Both arrogant and naive, he showed himself ill-suited to the task at hand. A British agent, R. H. Bruce Lockhart, confided in his diary, "Old Francis doesn't know a Left Social Revolutionary from a potato." Not exactly exuding modesty, Francis wrote of his arrival in Petrograd in spring 1916: "I needed all the self-confidence born of my experience." Only William V. Judson, now a general and chief of the U.S. Military Mission in Petrograd, dissented from the general optimism, writing his wife that the Russians were tired of fighting.[23]

The Allies would pay dearly for encouraging Brusilov. By July 14, 1917, the Russian offensive stalled. Four days later, the Germans counterattacked. The majority of the czar's troops fled in panic. From Rumania to the Baltic, the breakdown spread. In the process, the Russians lost 14 percent of their forces. The provisional government had been dealt a fatal blow, one that led directly to a summer crisis that in turn would create the Bolshevik Revolution. Forming the Second Coalition, Alexander Kerensky replaced Prince Lvov as prime minister and continued as war minister. Power continued to shift to the Petrograd Soviet.

Throughout late July and all August, Americans suddenly became aware that Russia was in crisis. The *Outlook* considered the Russian defeat also an American one. The *New Republic* denied that the Russian army could be considered an organized force. Senator Borah warned that if Kerensky fell, a "million American boys . . . will find graves upon European soil."[24]

In Washington, Lansing thought that U.S. policy should be based on the hypothesis that Russia would "go from bad to worse." Colonel House considered U.S. intervention, suggesting that Wilson send troops by way of the Pacific: "They would have open warfare instead of trench warfare, and would be a steadying force to the Russians. I do not think we can devote too much attention to the Russian situation, for if that fails our troubles will be great and many." It was more important, he said, to have Russia become "a virile republic" than to beat Germany "to her knees." Otherwise, Berlin might be dominating it both politically and economically. However, Acting Chief of Staff Tasker H. Bliss warned that such a scheme would force the United States to reexamine its entire role on the western front. Besides, it could not transport a large force across the Pacific in time to rescue the Russians.[25]

A few leading Americans remained optimistic. Ambassador Francis predicted that the Russian army "will fight like lions." The *New York Times* hinted at the desirability of a Kerensky dictatorship, for he had shown "marvelous power as a leader and inspirer of men." Elihu Root reassured Henry Cabot Lodge that Russia would not make peace. Although the "Council of Peasants and Soviets" controlled the army, Root remarked that Kerensky "possessed unusual force and great intensity." On August 24, Wilson wrote to a national political conference that Kerensky had convened in Moscow, expressing "confidence in the ultimate triumph of ideals of democracy and self-government within and without." He promised "renewed assurance of every material and moral assistance." The administration backed Wilson's words with a new $100 million credit to cover military contracts.[26]

Early in August, a new diplomatic element entered the picture as the American Red Cross Commission to Russia arrived in Petrograd. This commission had been created to distribute food, clothing, and medical supplies, but it played the far more important role of establishing informal links with Russia's more liberal pro-war elements, doing so in order to bolster the eastern front. Members were not on the Red Cross payroll nor did the organization pay the project's expenses. The mission stood under the personal direction of Red Cross chairman Henry P. Davison, a partner in the banking firm of J. P. Morgan. Wrote historian Leonid I. Strakhovsky in 1961, "Never before or since has the insignia of the Red Cross been used for such a blatantly political purpose."[27]

Although Dr. Frank G. Billings, a Chicago specialist in infectious diseases, nominally headed the mission, it was actually directed by William Boyce Thompson, financier, copper magnate, and operator on the New York Stock Exchange. While in Russia, the flamboyant Thompson lived in Petrograd's best hotel, was driven in a French limousine, and kept a wolfhound in tow. In order to keep Russia in the war, he sought to spread the fear that a German victory would restore the grand dukes, feudal landlords, and plutocratic industrialists to power: "We've got to interpret the holding of the front and the defeat of Germany in terms of saving the revolution." In order to raise the morale of Russian troops amid Bolshevik peace agitation, he personally gave a million dollars to establish a printing plant, several news bureaus, and a host of newspapers. When, however, Thompson suggested that Washington contribute $3 million a month for such activity, Wilson supposedly replied, "Has he gone crazy?"[28]

Second in command was Raymond Robins, who—in the early days of the Bolshevik Revolution—saw more Soviet leaders than did any other. A man of aquiline features, he reassembled—as the unofficial British agent H. Bruce Lockhart noted—"an Indian chief with a Bible for his tomahawk." Coal miner in Tennessee and Colorado, manager of a phosphate company in Florida, gold prospector in the Klondike, Congregationalist minister in Alaska, settlement house superintendent in Chicago, chairman of the Bull Moose Convention of 1916—Robins's résumé included all of these roles. Historian George F. Kennan aptly describes him as a figure out of a Jack London novel, "an orator, an actor, and a sentimentalist, but with it all a man of great force of character, exceptional physical and intellectual vigor, and unquestionable idealism." Yet Kennan finds Robins's strength also his weakness: the emissary lacked historical perspective on Russia and his tactlessness alienated the U.S. diplomatic corps.[29]

Because the wartime Red Cross was part of the armed forces, Thompson was designated a colonel, Robins a lieutenant colonel. All forty members of the commission held officer's rank. (Americans in Petrograd dubbed them the "Haytian army," for they lacked privates!)[30] Because the mission soon overlapped with the U.S. embassy, Francis opposed it, but eventually he felt forced to use it as an informal liaison.

By the beginning of September 1917, however, Russia experienced its greatest peril since Napoleon stood at its gates a century before. On the 3rd, Riga fell to the Germans, leaving Petrograd open to attack. Six days later, Russia's new supreme commander, Lavr Kornilov, dispatched a cavalry corps to Petrograd as the first step towards rescuing the provisional government from the influence of the city's soviet. The rebellion was soon suppressed. Certainly pessimism prevailed everywhere. In late September, Judson exclaimed, "We are living on a volcano." AEF commander John J. Pershing told General Hugh Scott, "The Russian situation today is probably the most serious obstacle to our success. Unless they can pull themselves together and make some sort of showing, there is nothing to prevent a large number of German divisions from coming to the western front." Early in October, Ambassador Francis cabled Washington: "Numerous outbreaks, some outrages, many defiances of authority, frequent acts of insubordination, have marked the progress of revolution," a situation not surprising in a primitive country where the masses, "kindhearted with good impulses," were superstitious and required guidance.[31]

Only on October 8, after three weeks of disorder, was Kerensky able to form a Third Coalition. Of sixteen ministers, ten were socialists. He also proclaimed Russia a republic and freed such Bolshevik prisoners as Leon Trotsky, then possibly better known to the outside world than Vladimir Ilyich Ulyanov, aka Lenin. Kennan writes, "To accept the armed aid of the Bolsheviki was, under the circumstances, to entrust oneself to the protection of a boa constrictor."[32] Unable to control events, Kerensky increasingly experienced delusions of grandeur while becoming increasingly isolated, indecisive, and addicted to morphine and cocaine. The nation itself remained briefly at a standstill, with workers on strike, peasants seizing land, and soldiers refusing to fight. Since March a million soldiers had deserted. Regime change was only a matter of time.

In mid-October, the U.S. Treasury Department betrayed its lack of realism, extending a further $50 million loan and soon promising $325 million more. On October 24, in ordering the CPI administrator Edgar G. Sisson to Russia, Wilson told him that the United States was ready to render such aid as "lies in our power," warning against "officious intrusion or meddling." Sisson was entrusted with the task of establishing such propaganda mechanisms as cinema, lectures, and a war cable.[33]

By now, however, lines of authority among Americans in Petrograd had become blurred. The president never established clear jurisdiction between such figures as the CPI's Sisson, Ambassador Francis, and Red Cross officials Thompson and Robins, a circumstance that did not bode well for the future.

The Russia policy had manifested extreme ineptitude and lack of perception. Though Washington obviously recognized the importance of maintaining the eastern front, its policies involved far too little far too late. Yet, even as loans, supplies, food, and mechanisms of propaganda were supplied, the Russian people were still determined to leave the war. No amount of Allied support could change that fact. A far more radical revolution was in store, as the United States was suddenly confronted with a far greater challenge.

The Bolshevik Revolution took place on the night of November 6–7, 1917. Soldiers of the Petrograd garrison, the workers' Red Guards, and sailors from the Kronstadt naval base seized government buildings, telephone exchanges, railroad stations, and electric power plants. When the warship *Aurora* turned its guns on the Winter Palace, where the skeleton provisional government was installed, there was hardly a person remaining to defend it. The takeover had little effect on much of the population. Many Petrograd citizens remained oblivious to the events, one commentator reporting that the transfer of power caused less disturbance than a strike of streetcar workers. Within days, Alexander Kerensky fled to Britain. Ambassador Francis tersely cabled Washington, "Bolsheviki appear to have control of everything here." When, in just a week, other Red Guards occupied Moscow's Kremlin, U.S. Consul Maddin Summers reported firsthand, "All relatively quiet."[34]

On the 7th, the Bolshevik-dominated Second All-Russian Congress of Soviets approved the change, pronouncing the provisional government defunct. It established a Council of People's Commissars, with V. I. Lenin as chairman and Leon Trotsky as commissar for foreign affairs. Trotsky was so confident of imminent worldwide revolution that he boasted, "I shall issue a few revolutionary proclamations to the peoples and then shut up shop." The All-Russian Congress passed Lenin's "Decree on Peace," a manifesto that called upon the peoples of all nations at war to negotiate a "an immediate democratic peace" in which no belligerent would receive indemnities or annex territory. All secret treaties would be abolished.[35] Within three months, he predicted, there would be self-determination of peoples and a Europe-wide armistice. An impending global revolution was assumed.

Trotsky at once began publishing Russia's secret treaties with the Allies in Bolshevik organs *Pravda* and *Izvestia*. Among the West's big-city dailies, only Britain's *Manchester Guardian* and Oswald Garrison Villard's *New York Evening Post* printed them in full. On the 25th, the *New York Times*, in an editorial titled "Outside the Pale," accused the Bolsheviks of engaging in "an act of dishonor"; the Russian nation had broken its word.[36] In most Allied countries, these clandestine agreements remained virtually ignored until after the war.

Initially the American press expressed little alarm over the Bolshevik takeover, predicting an early collapse of the "rebellion." The New York *World* saw no chance for immediate peace because Russia possessed no government with the authority to speak for the people or army.[37]

Soon, however, elements of the public expressed anxiety. Making a pointed analogy to the French Revolution, the December 29 issue of the *Literary Digest* carried an article titled "Russia under the Terror." To ex-president Taft, the followers of Lenin and Trotsky were simply "mad." By early December, many of the nation's newspapers had sought "immediate action" to resume the Russian front. Actual suggestions, however, were scattered and vague.[38]

At one point, Wilson implied that the Bolsheviks were tools of the Germans. On November 12, in speaking of the "fatuous . . . dreamers in Russia" to an AFL convention in Buffalo, the president warned, "Any body of free men that compounds with the present German government is compounding for its own destruction." Yet, on the following day, he wrote a Florida congressman: "I have not lost faith in the Russian outcome by any means. Russia, like France in a past century, will no doubt have to go through deep waters but she will come out upon firm land on the other side and her great people, for they are a great people, will in my opinion take their proper place in the world."[39]

On November 18, Foreign Commissar Trotsky addressed the Central Committee of the Soviet. Obviously miffed at Wilson's AFL remarks, he claimed that the president had entered the war because American "finance capital" sought to guarantee delivery of its war exports. Within two weeks, Wilson told his cabinet that Lenin and Trotsky sounded like "opera bouffe," for even a child would realize Germany would destroy any chance for the democracy the Russians desired.[40]

In late November, the State Department learned that rebellious Cossacks in southern Russia, wanting to continue the war, desired both help and recognition. "Too chaotic to act yet," Wilson responded. In his annual message of December 4, 1917, he claimed that Russia's progress towards "ordered and stable government of free men" had experienced "sad reverses," its population having been "poisoned by the very same falsehoods that have kept the German people in the dark." If the Allies had specified more altruistic war aims, the president implied, the Bolshevik revolution would not have taken place.[41]

In mid-December, after meeting with the president, House cabled Sir William Wiseman, intelligence official and informal liaison between the president and the British War Cabinet. The colonel declared that Wilson found it essential to help finance Polish and Cossack troops willing to fight Germany. The president had no power to use U.S. government funds directly but could launder the money through France and Britain. He would, however, leave the initiative to both countries.[42]

Secretary of State Lansing, too, sought surreptitious intervention. Writing Wilson directly on December 10, the secretary feared that the loss of the Russian front would prolong the war two to three years; the only hope lay in covert payments to a military dictatorship headed by Aleksey Maksimovich Kaledin, a Cossack general (or *ataman*), who led an anti-Bolshevik regime in the Don region. Within two days, the president expressed his "entire approval." Although no funds were ever made available, the proposal reveals that the United States did not in principle oppose such subsidies. The secretary of state would also appear cautious, telling the cabinet the next day, "Civil war possible. Everything now too chaotic to make any move."[43]

Soon another American initiative occurred. On December 15, Consul General Maddin Summers, acting without authorization, dispatched De Witt Clinton Poole, soon to be his successor at Moscow, to approach Kaledin and General Mikhail Alekseyev. Alekseyev had been chief of the general staff under the provisional government and was now helping lead counterrevolutionary White armies in the Don region. Summers's wife was the daughter of a Russian noble who had lost a considerable estate in the recent revolution. Not surprisingly, he saw Bolshevism as synonymous with ruin. By the end of the month, he wrote the State Department: "The Russia we welcome as a democratic nation" lay in the southern, non-Bolshevik part of the nation. Historians differ on the significance of these outlays, with Kennan dismissing the effort and David S. Foglesong stressing the covert nature of this activity.[44]

In early December, an exhausted Russia entered into a preliminary armistice with Germany. Soon informal negotiations were underway. Lansing wrote a personal memorandum in which he not only opposed recognizing Lenin's government but offered a sweeping indictment of the entire Bolshevik movement. Accusing the revolutionists of being anarchists, not socialists, he warned: "They are avowedly opposed to every government on earth; they openly propose to excite revolutions in all countries against existing governments; they are as hostile to democracy as they are to autocracy. . . . the Russian 'Terror' will far surpass in brutality and destruction of life and property the Terror of the French Revolution."

The secretary predicted "one of the most terrible tragedies in human history." "Russia will swim in blood, a prey to lawlessness and violence." Predicting that the new Petrograd regime lacked the means to retain power, he claimed that it would experience civil war, dividing itself into several distinct states that "the ruthless Germans" might dominate. By early January 1918, Lansing was writing Wilson that the nation remained "a despotic oligarchy as menacing to liberty as any absolute monarchy on earth."[45]

By mid-December, William Boyce Thompson left Russia, informing a host of people—ranging from British prime minister Lloyd George to the Rocky Mountain Club of New York City—that most Bolsheviks were "kindly, earnest men" who could be won over to the Allied side. Wilson refused to see him and Lansing called him "a crank," but House found himself in partial agreement, while Creel expressed enthusiasm. Oswald Villard's *New York Evening Post*, the Hearst press, and Senators William J. Stone and Robert L. Owen (D-Okla.) endorsed his pleadings, but the vigilante-minded National Civic Federation saw them embodying "Bolshevism, I.W.W'ism and Anarchism."[46]

Red Cross colonel Raymond Robins remained, in his own words, the only U.S. official permitted to be in contact with "the *de facto* government that has complete control over three fourths of Russian territory and more than five sixths of the bayonets of the Russian people." Washington perceived him purely as a listening post, even as he gained increasing access to Lenin and Trotsky. Finding Bolshevik and German cultures incompatible, Robins predicted the breakdown of peace talks. Lenin, he foresaw, would seek assistance from the Allies. Robins was nothing if not colorful. He called Trotsky "a four kind son of a bitch, but the greatest Jew since Christ. If the German General Staff bought Trotsky, they bought a lemon."[47]

On December 23, Lords Alfred Milner and Robert Cecil of the British War Cabinet, together with French premier Georges Clemenceau and foreign minister Stephen Pichon, endorsed contact with such "semi-autonomous provinces" as the Ukraine, Finland, Rumania, Siberia, the Caucasus, and the Cossack area. These regions would counterbalance "the treachery of the Russians in opening peace negotiations with our enemies." At the same time, "unofficial agents" should establish contact with the Bolsheviks. Except for a provision "bribing" the Persians, Wilson found the agenda sensible. Hence, the president perceived unofficial contacts with the Bolsheviks and covert aid to their foes as both in America's self-interest.[48]

Wilson was most aware of Russia's predicament when, on January 8, 1918, he delivered his famous address on the Fourteen Points. Conveying an entirely different tone from that of his November AFL address, he now claimed the Russian people would not abandon, "either in principle or in action," "their conception of what is right, what is humane and honorable for them to accept." Indeed, they had expressed themselves "with a frankness, a largeness of view, a generosity of spirit, and a universal human empathy which must challenge the admiration of every friend of mankind; and they have refused to compound their ideals or desert others that they themselves may be safe." Hence he hoped that "some way may be opened whereby we may be privileged to assist the people of Russia to attain their utmost hope of liberty and ordered peace." Point Six of the Fourteen Points called for "evacuation of all Russian territory," together with a settlement that would secure "an unhampered and unembarrassed opportunity for the independent determination of her own political development and national policy." Holding out the hope of "assistance of every kind that she may need and may herself desire," Wilson declared that the treatment the Western powers accorded Russia would serve as "the acid test of their good will."[49]

The Creel Committee printed nearly 2.5 million copies of the Fourteen Points speech in Russian. By and large, the Bolsheviks welcomed the address, Lenin personally telling Robins that he considered it "a potential agency promoting peace." *Izvestia*, the official

Bolshevik daily, called the speech a "a great victory" for "a democratic peace." *Pravda*, however, downplayed it, saying it merely represented the views of American capital and was delivered solely to curb the ambitions of Britain and Japan. The Red response undoubtedly marked the high point of Soviet–U.S. relations during the first years of Bolshevik rule.[50]

Within the United States, Wilson's Russian remarks received general approval. Senators Borah, John W. Weeks (R-Mass.), and John Walter Smith (D-Md.) all claimed his comments would be welcomed there. "Had Russia known these war-aims a few weeks ago," asserted Nonpartisan League congressman John M. Baer, "she might still have been in the fray." Colonel Harvey's *War Weekly*, usually a vehement Wilson critic, found the president observing "the plight of a great mass of human beings groping out of darkness." Scott Nearing of the radical People's Council declared, "The president has put into perfect English the splendid economic and social ideals of the New Russia." Lansing sought to curb any euphoria, sending Wilson a memorandum asserting that only when "undoubted proofs of the will of the Russian people are manifested" should the United States recognize the new government.[51]

All this time, the Hearst chain appeared solidly in Lenin's camp. Just a day before Wilson spoke, the *New York American* claimed that the Bolsheviks had "come nearer to Mr. Wilson's high ideals of peace than any other of the European nations." On February 3, the newspaper carried a column by "Nicolas Lenine" predicting that Bolshevism would spread throughout the world. Subsequent issues featured Trotsky's own account of his escape from Siberia and a sympathetic account of the revolution by journalist Louise Bryant. In early March, the publishing magnate called for outright recognition, finding the Soviet regime the most democratic government in Europe. Columnist Arthur Brisbane compared any German occupation of Russia to the conquests of Alexander the Great, Julius Caesar, and William the Conqueror. Eventually, he claimed, the occupied peoples triumphed over their invaders.[52]

On March 3, 1918, in the face of renewed German invasion, the Bolshevik negotiators signed the Treaty of Brest-Litovsk in order to exit the war. By its terms, Russia lost 44 percent of its population, about 62 million people. It yielded one-quarter of its territory (roughly 1.2 million square miles), 50 percent of its industrial holdings, and 90 percent of its coal. As a European power, Russia was reduced to the status of seventeenth-century Muscovy, a principality that simply centered around Moscow. Germany not only neutralized Russia but dominated Eastern Europe through client states stretching from the Baltic to the Black Sea. As historian David R. Woodward notes, Berlin gained more control of the former Russian Empire than Hitler would achieve at the height of his invasion.[53] Three hundred years of tsarist conquest had been dissolved in one day. The Bolshevik government in Petrograd, however, still had to ratify the agreement.

Even before the Bolshevik capitulation, U.S. reaction to the Bolshevik regime was becoming decidedly negative. In early February, the *Literary Digest* reported, "Leaderless troops are helpless, so the Bolsheviki have proceeded to the massacre of every officer in sight." Particularly horrific was the senseless massacre of hundreds of Russian naval officers at Kronstadt and at Black Sea ports. Once news arrived of the Brest-Litovsk Treaty, Russia met with almost universal condemnation. Harvey's *War Weekly* accused German conspirators of successfully financing "Comrade Trotsky's enterprise" through a Stockholm bank. Taft called Russia "a mass of babbling protoplasm," run by "whispering traitors" who were "gold-bricked by William of Hohenzollern and his Potsdam gang." Claiming to feel "contempt and abhorrence" for Russian capitulation, Theodore Roosevelt wrote his son Kermit that for centuries the Russians had most cruelly persecuted the Jews and now "the Jew leadership in Russia has been a real nemesis for the Russians." The more moderate New York *World* wrote, "Trotzky and Lenine have done their best by the Kaiser, whether actuated by money, or lust for power, or the insanity of class hatred."[54] Surprisingly ignored was a crucial event that took place in mid-January: the Bolshevik dispersion at bayonet point of the Constituent Assembly, a body designed to establish a constitutional government.

A few other voices were more accepting of Brest-Litovsk. The *New Republic* predicted that because the Bolshevik government would either be transformed or superseded, the West must not treat it as a deserter; its democracy held the key to the peace of Europe and consequently the world. The Hearst chain blamed the Bolshevik surrender on treachery at home and apathy abroad, particularly among the proletariat of the belligerents. Congressman Meyer London asked that Russia be granted allowances: "Can you improve a ship when it is struggling not to be wrecked?" The Socialist *New Appeal* accused the Allies of committing a "criminal blunder" by not responding to Russia's demand for democratic war aims, but it assailed Lenin and Trotsky for demobilizing their army before peace had been made. To George Sylvester Viereck, Germany's effort to rule unwilling subjects made it even more vulnerable than Austria. Russia "will redeem herself like Prussia after Tilsit," when in 1807 the defeated German state had been forced to make many concessions to Napoleon.[55]

Trotsky still harbored some hopes that Russia could hold out against the Germans. When, on March 8, U.S. military attaché Colonel James A. Ruggles and his assistant, Captain E. Francis Riggs, visited him, the Bolshevik leader sought Allied assistance, especially from the United States. The British considered offering aid, but France, Italy, and Japan balked. Colonel House and Ambassador Francis thought such help worth consideration, Francis telling Consul Summers that the Bolsheviks were "the only power in Russia which can offer any resistance whatever to the German advance. . . . When my house is on fire I don't ask the quality of the water used to extinguish the flame."[56]

On March 11, Wilson sent an extremely brief public message of friendship to the Fourth All-Russia Congress of Soviets, assembled to debate ratification of the treaty. The United States, the president asserted, was in no position to render direct and effective aid. Yet he sought to "assure the people of Russia through the congress that it avail itself of every opportunity to secure for Russia once more complete sovereignty and independence in her own affairs and full restoration to her great role in the life of Europe and the modern world. The whole heart of the people of the United States is with the people of Russia in the attempt to free themselves forever from autocratic government and become the master of their own life."[57]

The president may well have been less concerned with preventing ratification of the treaty than with keeping the Allies, especially Japan, out of Siberia, a region on which they already had their eyes.[58] As will be shown, pressure on him to approve Japanese intervention was already mounting.

Wilson's message to the Soviet Congress received domestic support across the political spectrum. To the *New Republic*, the president was giving Russian morale a needed boost amid the hostility of every power in Europe and Asia. Harvey's *War Weekly* felt similarly, adding that the United States should help determine Russia's direction. Viereck's *American Weekly* called Wilson's "rescue" of Russia "the supreme event of the week." Senator Lawrence Sherman struck a dissonant note, accusing the president of encouraging a government "founded and administered in repudiation, in confiscation, in wholesale murder."[59]

Four days later, the Soviet Congress responded to the president in a most insulting manner, ignoring Wilson by addressing directly "the laboring and exploited classes of the United States." It held to the "firm belief that the happy time is not far distant when the laboring classes of all countries will throw off the yoke of capitalism and will establish a socialistic state of society, which alone is capable of securing just and lasting peace as well as the culture and well-being of all laboring classes." A leading Bolshevik, Gregory Zinoviev, is said to have boasted, "We slapped the President of the United States in the face."[60] Certainly the insult could not have been more obvious.

Raymond Robins still hoped that the Bolsheviks would not sign the treaty. On March 5, Trotsky had told Robins that if the Allies offered economic cooperation and military support, he would withdraw Russian troops from both Petrograd and Moscow to Ekaterinburg, a city close to nine hundred miles east of Moscow. There he would regroup Russian forces and fight the Germans. He gave Robins several hypothetical questions—if his nation repudiated Brest-Litovsk and remained in the war,

1. Is the Soviet government assured of U.S., British, and French support?
2. How soon could supplies and transportation facilities be provided and under what terms?
3. In what way would U.S. assistance be expressed?

He also asked what measures the Allies, especially the United States, would take to prevent "a Japanese invasion in our Far East and assure uninterrupted connection with Russia via Trans-Siberian Railway." Further, he asked about possible British assistance by way of Murmansk and Archangel. Just to make sure that the Western powers did not think that Russia would reverse domestic course, he stressed that internal and foreign policy remained "directed by principles of international Socialism." Colonel Ruggles, William Judson's successor as military attaché, did not dispatch the message until two weeks later, by which time Brest-Litovsk had been ratified. In March 1919, Robins told a Senate subcommittee that U.S. bitter anti-Bolshevism was to blame for declining Trotsky's offer.[61]

Historians still differ over the feasibility of Trotsky's veiled proposals. Donald E. Davis and Eugene P. Trani stress their contingent nature, with far too many "ifs" for comfort: *if* the peace were broken, *if* the offensive were renewed, *if* Japan occupied Vladivostok and seized the Trans-Siberian Railway, *if* the United States could assure British aid through Murmansk and Archangel. The authors suspect that Trotsky might have been playing his own double game with Lenin, ensuring the continuation of his "no war, no peace" policy and ending any possibility of an agreement with Germany. Little wonder scholars have long debated the matter.[62]

It took several weeks for Russia's government to ratify the treaty. Only on March 16, after two days of debate, did the Soviet Congress approve the agreement, this just after Lenin harangued the body for two and a half hours on the futility of further resistance. The vote tallied 784 for concurrence, 261 opposed, and 115 not voting. The German Reichstag gave its approval within a week.

By signing the treaty, Lenin had undoubtedly saved the Soviet regime. Several facts about the agreement are often overlooked. Russia was not saddled with reparations. The territories seized did not desire Russian rule, much less Bolshevik domination. In turn, the Reds had never controlled these territories. The new border was considerably more favorable to Russia than the one imposed by the Allies after the Russian civil war ended in 1920. Similarly, only a small portion of the territory removed from Russia was directly annexed to Germany. Instead Brest-Litovsk gave birth to a separate Ukraine, a Transcaucasian Republic, and the precursors of the modern Baltic states. Most important of all, neither side entered into the agreement in good faith, both being determined to evade it as much as possible. Some fighting continued.[63]

Understandably, the Allies were both frightened and furious. Within two days after the signing, the Allied prime ministers and foreign ministers, with the United States abstaining, issued a joint declaration disavowing Brest-Litovsk. The agreement, they maintained, incarnated the "political crimes . . . committed against the Russian people." In Petrograd, Ambassador Francis warned that the treaty could make Russia virtually a German province. He pledged U.S. assistance to any element that would offer "sincere and organized resistance to the German invasion." The Bolsheviks themselves were far from pleased, *Pravda* branding it a peace of "masked indemnities, veiled annexations, and complete betrayal of self-determination."[64]

Despite Soviet ratification of the Brest-Litovsk Treaty, Trotsky—now the regime's war commissar—still sought U.S. support. Fearful that the peace would not hold, on March 18 he asked Robins if U.S. Army officers could train and equip their Soviet counterparts. He also sought railroad experts who could command his nation's entire system. Robins supported the proposals, receiving backing from Francis and the embassy's military attachés. Lansing rejected the notion, suspecting that Germany had secretly drafted the plan to divert Entente forces from the western front.[65]

Despite Brest-Litovsk, the Central Powers kept advancing. On March 7, the Germans and Austrians attacked in the Ukraine, with Kiev, Odessa, and Kharkov occupied by early April. In mid-March an apprehensive Lenin moved the capital from Petrograd to Moscow. On April 24, in addressing the Moscow Soviet, he declared, "We may be crushed at any moment."[66] A month later, German forces landed in Finland, soon taking Helsingfors (later Helsinki) and Viborg. Germany then turned its eyes to the Crimea, seizing Sevastopol on May 1. By then it had captured most of the Russian fleet.

Trotsky again sought Allied aid. In mid-March, as we will discuss, he told the U.S. military attaché that he approved of the Entente landings then taking place in Murmansk. Moreover, the war commissar claimed that the sheer presence of Allied officers would encourage their Russian counterparts to return to military service.[67]

In mid-April, Ambassador Robins pleaded with Francis, claiming that the Russian government was making daily requests for railroad personnel, army instructors, agricultural machinery, technical experts, and manufactures. He usually met with failure, but he did engage in several successful negotiations. American advisers helped organize the railroads. The United States bought sizable quantities of Russian platinum. The National City Bank was permitted to continue operations. Lenin exempted International Harvester, Singer Corporation, and Westinghouse Air Brake Company from Soviet decrees nationalizing all industry.[68]

Robins, however, could only do so much, for the State Department and the Red Cross soon recalled him "for consultation." Francis believed that the informal negotiator had outlived his usefulness, usurping authority and status that should be accorded to Francis alone. Moscow consul Maddin Summers suspected the Red Cross official of actually being a Soviet agent. Back in February, Wilson himself had written Lansing, "It is very annoying to have this man Robins, in whom I have no confidence whatever, acting as political adviser in Russia and sending his advice to private individuals." Robins simply mused to his wife, "I am the best hated and best liked man among the foreign leaders here."[69]

Leaving Russia on May 14, Robins carried a long proposal from Lenin embodying plans for major Soviet–U.S. economic cooperation. The United States would supply electrical, mining, and railroad equipment in return for Russian oil, manganese, platinum, and furs. Ever the romantic, Robins wrote Lenin less than three weeks before departure, "Your prophetic insight and genius of leadership have enabled the Soviet Power to become consolidated throughout Russia and I am confident that this new creative organ of the democratic life of mankind will inspire and advance the cause of liberty throughout the world." Lenin responded by predicting that "proletarian democracy" would crush "the imperialist-capitalist systems in the New and Old Worlds."[70]

When he was returning to the United States, Robins had his luggage searched for compromising links to local Bolsheviks. He found the White House door closed. He did meet with Lansing. However, the State Department itself was not much friendlier. Nonetheless, he was able to communicate his essential message—that U.S. economic and military aid would soften Bolshevik rigidity—to such progressives as William E. Borah, Hiram Johnson, Newton Baker, and even Theodore Roosevelt.[71]

As the Bolsheviks were ratifying Brest-Litovsk, the American press continued to cast Bolshevik rule in extremely negative terms. In late March, the *Literary Digest* noted reports that in Petrograd former generals and admirals had become street cleaners and railroad porters; ladies in fur coats sold newspapers on street corners. More significantly, "In many Russian towns the streets run red with the blood of the *bourgeoisie*, murdered by soldiers and sailors who long ago lost interest in the more dangerous occupation of killing Germans."[72]

A few prominent Americans still dissented. In April, Hearst's *New York American* opposed denunciations of the Bolsheviks, claiming the Russians could do more for democracy by maintaining it within their borders than by continuing in a futile war. The *New Republic* saw the Bolshevik social and political programs as "wholly unsound." It did, however, call for patience in dealing with Soviet "excesses," particularly as the French and British had undermined the Kerensky government by making impossible demands. A month later, Socialist Morris Hillquit told a labor audience that the Bolshevik regime was standing "in the vanguard of social progress, in the hands, all through top to bottom, of the people themselves, of the working class, the peasants."[73]

On May 18, 1918, speaking at New York's Metropolitan Opera House on behalf of the Red Cross, Wilson brought up the Brest-Litovsk agreement as a major argument against any peace bid by the Central Powers: "Every proposal with regard to accommodation in the West involves a reservation with regard to the East. Now, as far as I am concerned, I intend to stand by Russia as well as France." Although these remarks met with particular applause, the statement was decidedly unclear, with Russian rightists envisioning a full-scale military expedition and those on the left implying that it meant resisting both Allied and German intervention.[74]

The president was equally vague in his Fourth of July speech at Mount Vernon, Virginia, where he simply referred to the "unorganized and helpless" Russians standing opposed to "masters of many armies." In private, Wilson was more candid, telling Colonel House, "I have been sweating blood over the question of what is right and feasible (*possible*) to do in Russia." Finding the problem going "to pieces like quicksilver under my touch," he placed his hopes on economic assistance and, as we will develop, Czech forces fighting in Siberia.[75]

By June, the U.S. embassy had become so anti-Bolshevik that it engaged in covert activity. Ambassador Francis met with varied dissidents, ranging from industrialists to Social Revolutionaries, a large radical agrarian party. More important, he authorized espionage throughout western Russia and permitted Felix Cole, consul in Archangel, to finance counterrevolutionary organizations in the north. In August, the secret police, called the Cheka, arrested an American businessman, Xenophon Kalamatiano, for engaging in espionage. Military intelligence, payment receipts, and a cipher code were all discovered — within his cane![76]

July 1918 marked Bolshevik Russia at its nadir, facing a situation comparable to early winter 1941, when Wehrmacht troops were at the outskirts of Moscow. The government stood politically isolated, being surrounded by hostile armies, lacking sufficient forces to protect itself, and experiencing both famine and armed revolt. On the last day of August, a disgruntled Social Revolutionary attempted to assassinate Lenin, contributing to a series of strokes that eventually killed him.

On August 17, Germany and the Bolsheviks supplemented the Brest-Litovsk accord with a fresh agreement. By its terms, Berlin forced the Soviet regime to pay $1.46 billion in indemnities. It formally severed what are now Estonia and Latvia from Russian territory, thereby assuring German domination of the Baltic. It forced Lenin's regime to recognize the "independence" of Georgia, by now a German protectorate. The Soviet government promised to supply Germany with at least 25 percent of any oil produced in Baku.

Reports from within Russia remained most pessimistic. In mid-September, Consul DeWitt Clinton Poole reported from Moscow, "Massacre of Russian citizens by Bolshevik government continues. . . . More than 1,000 people have been shot in retaliation for attempt on Lenin." In Washington, Secretary Lansing was particularly apprehensive, writing Elihu Root that there existed "two great evils at work in the world of today, Absolutism, the power of which is waning, and Bolshevism, the power of which is increasing. We have seen the hideous consequences of Bolshevik rule in Russia. . . . The possibility of a proletariat despotism over Central Europe is terrible to contemplate."[77]

In the United States, the Bolsheviks received more condemnation than ever. Late in September, Wilson issued a public statement attacking Soviet "barbarism." The lead story in the September 21 issue of the *Literary Digest* bore the headline, "Red Russia as Our Foe."[78]

It was amid this environment that what became known as the "Sisson papers" were released. By the time the Soviets had signed the Brest-Litovsk Treaty, important figures in the U.S. embassy believed they possessed documentary proof that the Bolshevik leaders were receiving German subsidies. Early in February 1918, Robins had given the CPI's Edgar Sisson English translations of documents presumably drafted by Germany's General Staff, finance ministry, Reichbank, and other government offices. The material indicated that even before war had broken out in 1914, Berlin had paid Bolshevik leaders to help sabotage the Entente. Once Lenin, Trotsky, and their compatriots returned to Russia in 1917, the Germans extended financial aid. A Polish-born journalist in Petrograd, Anton Martynovich Ossendowski, had supposedly acquired this evidence, which in January 1918 had been published in Don Cossack newspapers. Robins, who did not reveal his source, himself considered them forgeries and in fact severed personal relations with Creel's representative over the matter.[79]

On February 9, Francis cabled the first series of these documents to the State Department, finding in them evidence that "disruption of Russia is but one move in plan of Germany to sow disorganization in Entente countries." Paying $25,000 for the supposed evidence, Sisson believed he possessed one of the greatest scoops in the history of journalism. Within two weeks, he wired Lansing, testifying to the documents' authenticity. Upon returning to the United States in early May, he turned them over to Creel, who found them revealing "the most amazing record of double-dealing and corruption." Lansing opposed their publication, claiming they would imperil the life of U.S. consul Poole and jeopardize the already precarious position of Allied representatives. Sisson snapped back, "A story that has been in newspaper offices of the country for 24 hours cannot be suppressed by normal means." Lansing, Frank L. Polk (counselor to the State Department), and Basil Miles, who directed Russian affairs in the department, all doubted their veracity. Colonel House feared that their release would signify "a virtual declaration of war upon the Bolsheviki Government." Wilson conceded this observation but felt "thoroughly satisfied."[80]

Beginning on September 15, the Creel Committee released all sixty-eight documents to the press. Certain opinion leaders had their suspicions of Soviet perfidy confirmed. To ex-president Taft, the papers revealed Lenin and Trotsky as "mere tools" of the German high command. The *Outlook* called both men enemy agents, noting that one document revealed that 50 million gold rubles had been transferred through Stockholm to the People's Commissars. Many newspapers affirmed their validity, the *New York Tribune* claiming that the two Russian leaders had given "a new touch of foulness to treason."[81]

British experts, however, considered them fraudulent. So did several Americans. The *Nation* referred to "bare-faced forgeries." Santeri Nuorteva, a Bolshevik who headed the Finnish Information Bureau in New York, claimed it was impossible to transfer 25 million dollars to Russia without making a visible dent in the gold market. The *New York Evening Post* posited that Germany's General Staff must have possessed remarkable insight, as the documents referred to events in Russia that had not yet occurred. Creel countered by accusing the newspaper of giving "aid and comfort to the enemies of the United States."[82]

Creel's Committee on Public Information, however, felt sufficiently threatened to seek scholarly endorsement. It received such legitimation from two prominent scholars. J. Franklin Jameson edited the *American Historical Review* and directed the Department of Historical Research at the Carnegie Institution. Samuel Harper held a professorship of Russian language and institutions at the University of Chicago; he had also served as special adviser to Ambassador Francis. After examining the proof sheets of the CPI pamphlet "The German–Bolshevik Conspiracy," which reproduced the documents, the two scholars claimed "no hesitation" in affirming their "genuineness or authenticity." In his introduction, Sisson showed himself even more extreme, denying that the Bolshevik government was genuinely Russian. It was, in fact, "a German government acting solely in the interests of Germany and betraying the Russian people . . . for the benefit of the Imperial German Government alone." The CPI printed more than 130,000 copies.[83]

In retrospect, Kennan finds it difficult to think that anyone would have taken the documents seriously. To do so would mean believing the impossible: (1) the Brest-Litovsk negotiations were completely fraudulent; (2) Germany controlled elections to the Bolshevik Central

Executive Committee; (3) its officials would casually list their own agents in routine dispatches in the midst of war; (4) the Bolsheviks were totally subservient to Berlin at the very time the Red Army was resisting German advances. Technically, similar problems existed. Would German officials sign their names in Cyrillic rather than use the Latin alphabet standard in their homeland? And would Germans date their documents according to the Russian Julian calendar, not the Western Gregorian one?[84]

Admittedly, before the November revolution, the Bolsheviks had received clandestine German subsidies, though modest amounts in relation to the party's needs. Never at any time, however, did their leaders act as secret agents carrying out orders from Berlin. After the November upheaval, no reason for such payments existed, as the Russian army was already disintegrating. Releasing the Sisson documents, as historian Christopher Lasch notes, created "a delusion of the most dangerous sort," namely, that the Bolsheviks remained a mere German tool. Hence, Washington assumed that once Berlin was defeated, the regime of Lenin and Trotsky would itself disappear. Therefore, direct intervention in Russia really did not constitute intervention at all; it simply served as another measure in the war against Germany.[85]

By October 1918, Wilson was comparing his Russian policy to his Mexican one. In both cases he was "letting them work out their own salvation, even though they wallow in anarchy for a while. I visualize it like this: A lot of impossible folk, fighting among themselves. You cannot do business with them, so you shut them all up in a room and lock the door and tell them that when they have settled matters among themselves you will unlock the door and do business."[86]

The president's wish was never fulfilled. Rather, the United States had betrayed the same ignorance it had displayed during the provisional government. Wilson's faith in the ultimate triumph of a vague entity he saw as "the Russian people" revealed the height of naïveté, as if an ideal could create its own reality. Admittedly, Colonel Robins's negotiations with Bolshevik leaders always bore little chance of success and were outdated within two weeks after they took place. Delegating such a marginal figure as Robins on missions to "feel out" the Bolsheviks, much less to receive proposals involving maintaining the Allied coalition, reveals that Ambassador Francis was hopelessly out of his depth. The tacit approval of Wilson and Lansing shows they could not have given much thought to the matter. The ultimate error of the Americans, indeed of the Allies as a whole, was to insist that a besieged Russia remain in a war that could only lead to its ruin. Many American voices deplored Bolshevik brutality, with the Hearst chain being the most notable exception. Few, however, had well-thought-out plans for toppling the regime. The Sisson papers were simply the logical culmination of months of U.S. misperception concerning the Reds as Berlin's puppets.

One can well note, however, that major American encounters with Russia had long ceased to center on Petrograd and Moscow. Rather, they took place on the White Sea and on the western coast of the Sea of Japan.

President Woodrow Wilson. Library of Congress, Prints & Photographs Division, photograph by Harris & Ewing, LC-DIG-hec-08253.

Colonel Edward Mandell House. Library of Congress, Prints & Photographs Division, LC-DIG-ggbain-20681.

Secretary of State
Robert Lansing.
Library of Congress,
Prints & Photographs
Division,
LC-USZ62-30260.

Secretary of the Navy
Josephus Daniels.
Library of Congress,
Prints & Photographs
Division,
LC-USZ62-36747.

Secretary of War Newton Diehl Baker. Library of Congress, Prints & Photographs Division, LC-DIG-ggbain-21073.

Postmaster General Albert Sidney Burleson. Library of Congress, Prints & Photographs Division, LC-DIG-ggbain-11438.

George Creel, chairman, Committee on Public Information. Library of Congress, Prints & Photographs Division, photograph by Harris & Ewing, LC-DIG-hec-08314.

General John J. Pershing, commander in chief, American Expeditionary Force. Library of Congress, Prints & Photographs Division, Theodor Horydczak Collection, LC-H823-1534.

General Peyton March, army chief of staff, 1918. Library of Congress, Prints & Photographs Division, LC-DIG-ggbain-26904.

General Hunter Liggett, commander, U.S. First Army, 1918. Library of Congress, Prints & Photographs Division, LC-DIG-ggbain-16581.

General Robert Lee
Bullard, commander,
U.S. Second Army, 1918.
Library of Congress,
Prints & Photographs
Division,
LC-USZ62-135378.

General Tasker Bliss,
chief of staff, 1917;
U.S. Representative,
Supreme War Council,
1918. Library of
Congress, Prints &
Photographs Division,
photograph by
Harris & Ewing,
LC-USZ62-36188.

James G. Harbord, Pershing's
chief of staff, 1917–18;
commander, Services of
Supply, 1918. Library
of Congress, Prints &
Photographs Division,
LC-USZ62-34654.

Admiral William Sowden
Sims, commander of Naval
Operations in European
Waters. Library of Congress,
Prints & Photographs
Division, photograph
by Harris & Ewing,
LC-DIG-hec-29841.

General William Judson, chief of American Military Mission in Russia. Library of Congress, Prints & Photographs Division, LC-DIG-ggbain-26095.

General William S. Graves, AEF commander in Siberia. Library of Congress, Prints & Photographs Division, LC-USZ62-122346.

Field Marshal Paul von Hindenburg, Kaiser Wilhelm II, and Field Marshal Erich Ludendorff. Library of Congress, Prints & Photographs Division, LC-USZ62-42297.

Former president Theodore Roosevelt. Library of Congress, Prints & Photographs Division, LC-DIG-ppmsca-35640.

Former president William Howard Taft. Library of Congress, Prints & Photographs Division, LC-USZC2-6279.

Elihu Root, head of Special Diplomatic Mission to Russia, 1917. Library of Congress, Prints & Photographs Division, photograph by Harris & Ewing, LC-DIG-hec-15214.

David Rowland Francis, ambassador to Russia. Library of Congress, Prints & Photographs Division, LC-USZ62-71967.

Colonel Raymond Robins, American Red Cross Mission to Russia. Library of Congress, Prints & Photographs Division, LC-DIG-ggbain-21748.

Archangel, Red Cross operations. Library of Congress, Prints & Photographs
Division, American National Red Cross Collection, LC-DIG-anrc-10311.

Vladivostok. Library
of Congress, Prints &
Photographs Division,
LC-DIG-ggbain-28204.

George Harvey, editor and
publisher, *North American
Review* and its *War Weekly*.
Library of Congress, Prints
& Photographs Division,
photograph by Harris &
Ewing LC-DIG-hec-04905.

William Randolph Hearst,
newspaper publisher.
Library of Congress,
Prints & Photographs
Division,
LC-DIG-ggbain-26519.

Walter Lippmann,
journalist; secretary,
the Inquiry. Library
of Congress, Prints &
Photographs Division,
photograph by
Harris & Ewing,
LC-DIG-hec-21695.

Lyman Abbott, editor, the *Outlook*. Library of Congress, Prints & Photographs Division, LC-DIG-ggbain-12831.

George Sylvester Viereck, editor and publisher, *Viereck's: The American Weekly* and *Viereck's: The American Monthly*. Library of Congress, Prints & Photographs Division, LC-DIG-ggbain-18562.

Socialist Party leader Eugene Victor Debs. Library of Congress, Prints & Photographs Division, LC-USZ62-29452.

Morris Hillquit, Socialist Party candidate for mayor of New York City, 1917. Library of Congress, Prints & Photographs Division, LC-DIG-ggbain-18322.

Max Eastman, editor,
the *Masses.* Library
of Congress, Prints &
Photographs Division,
Arnold Genthe
Collection,
LC-G432-1374.

Senator Henry Cabot
Lodge. Library of
Congress, Prints &
Photographs Division,
LC-USZ62-36185.

Senator Robert Marion La Follette. Library of Congress, Prints & Photographs Division, Arnold Genthe Collection, LC-DIG-agc-7a05840.

Representative Meyer London. Library of Congress, Prints & Photographs Division, LC-DIG-ggbain-07395.

Senator George Chamberlain. Library of Congress, Prints & Photographs Division, photograph by Harris & Ewing, LC-DIG-hec-03921.

Ferdinand Foch, commander in chief, Allied forces; George Clemenceau, premier of France; David Lloyd George, prime minister of Great Britain; Vittorio Orlando, prime minister of Italy; Baron Sidney Sonnino, foreign minister of Italy. Library of Congress, Prints & Photographs Division, LC-DIG-ggbain-28374.

Arthur Balfour, foreign secretary, Great Britain. Library of Congress, Prints & Photographs Division, LC-DIG-ggbain-23518.

Leon Trotsky, commissar for foreign affairs, Bolshevik Russia. Library of Congress, Prints & Photographs Division, LC-DIG-ggbain-28899.

Pope Benedict XV.
Library of Congress,
Prints & Photographs
Division,
LC-DIG-ggbain-17666.

Lord Lansdowne.
Library of Congress,
Prints & Photographs
Division,
LC-DIG-ggbain-02830.

Prince Max of Baden,
German chancellor,
October–November 1918.
Library of Congress,
Prints & Photographs
Division,
LC-DIG-ggbain-29141.

Wilhelm Solf,
German foreign secretary,
October–December 1918.
Library of Congress,
Prints & Photographs
Division,
LC-DIG-ggbain-25655.

Cantigny. Library of
Congress, Prints &
Photographs Division,
American National
Red Cross Collection,
LC-DIG-anrc-14290.

Belleau Wood.
Library of
Congress, Prints &
Photographs Division,
LC-DIG-stereo-1s04227.

Montfaucon. Library of Congress, Prints & Photographs Division, LC-DIG-stereo-1s04242.

St. Mihiel. Library of Congress, Prints & Photographs Division, LC-USZ62-37484.

NINE
"WALKING ON EGGS"

The Decision to Intervene

FEARFUL OVER THE LOSS OF THE RUSSIAN FRONT, THE
United States sent troops to two regions of Russia: Archangel
in June 1918 and Siberia in August. Although the commitment
originally centered on protecting large quantities of military
supplies, U.S. forces soon became entangled in much wider
matters.

Initially, the focus was on Murmansk. Located just
within the Arctic Circle, Murmansk was relatively ice-free
in winter, thanks to the Gulf Stream's sweep around northern
Scandinavia. In 1917, it was essentially a frontier town, complete with log cabins, wooden barracks, unpaved streets, and
the absence of a sewage system. Moderate socialists, not Bolsheviks, governed its soviet and cooperated with the British
naval force stationed there.

Archangel, too, became increasingly prominent. Even
though three hundred miles southeast of Murmansk, the city
was ice-bound for six months. Yet, protected by the Duna
Gulf, it remained the only significant port on the White
Sea. Serving as administrative and commercial center for
all of northern Russia, normally its population tallied fifty

thousand. In wartime, however, a flood of refugees had caused the city to double in size and at the same time impoverished it.

Because it was a strategic entrepôt, it is hardly surprising that more than 160,000 tons of Allied war materials, worth millions of dollars and designated for the Russian front, lay stockpiled there, including huge amounts of aluminum, antimony, copper, and lead. Once the Bolshevik Revolution took place, the British feared that these supplies would be used against them on the western front.[1] Lenin's government had not paid for these materials and renounced all foreign debts when it gained power.

In February 1918, the Bolsheviks had gained a majority on the Archangel Soviet and peacefully secured power throughout the city. By mid-spring, the German threat became real, particularly when the Bolshevik "Reds," acting under German pressure, ceded the Petsamo area, just west of Murmansk, to Finnish anti-Bolshevik "Whites."

On March 1, War Commissar Leon Trotsky, afraid that the Germans would soon conquer Petrograd, cabled the Murmansk Soviet, *"You must accept any and all assistance from the Allied missions* and use every means to obstruct the advance of the plunderers."[2] The cable was at best obsolete a few hours after it was sent, for the German threat proved most transitory. The dispatch was never specifically canceled, however, and in time became the basis for close cooperation between the Murmansk Soviet and Allied naval authorities stationed there. Inside of a week, 130 British marines landed. By June, British major general F. C. Poole commanded 1,200 British troops, 1,500 Serbs, a few hundred French, and three British warships.

The Allies kept pressing for U.S. participation. In early June 1918, the Supreme War Council (SWC) recommended the Russian Arctic ports. It would supply six battalions of U.S., British, French, and Italian troops plus one unit of the Czech Legion, then engaged in massive activity along the Trans-Siberian Railroad. The SWC, established in November 1917 to coordinate inter-Allied cooperation, was composed of heads of government and military representatives. The United States was represented by former chief of staff Tasker Bliss; it did not appoint a political representative because it sought to avoid such matters as war aims and territorial claims. The SWC warned that Germany, which already dominated Finland, could convert Murmansk into a first-rate submarine base, making Allied sea access to Archangel impossible. Were, however, the Allies to occupy both cities, the flanks of their armies would be protected and linking with anti-German forces in Siberia might be possible.[3]

Early in July, the SWC again stressed the need to occupy the northern ports, pointing to bridgeheads "from which forces can eventually advance rapidly to the center of Russia," thereby joining forces with an Allied presence in Siberia. This time General Poole spoke in terms of six Allied battalions, three of them American, fortified by 100,000 Russian troops anxious to fight the Germans. The Allied military expedition might "proceed inland with considerable American forces."[4]

Some in the U.S. military harbored misgivings. Chief of Staff Peyton March, stressing the need to remain focused on the western front, referred to Archangel and Murmansk as presenting "the greatest difficulty," Murmansk alone tying up a hundred thousand tons of American shipping. He could not find a single military man in Washington who favored major commitments there. Tasker Bliss concurred with the SWC appeal but wanted the U.S. role strictly limited to protecting Allied war supplies; U.S. forces, Bliss maintained, should never operate in Russia's interior to protect the "special interests" of other powers.[5]

Particularly outspoken was Felix Cole, U.S. consul at Archangel, who cabled Ambassador Francis: "Intervention will begin on a small scale, but with each step forward will grow in scope and in its demands for ships, men, money, and materials." Holding Archangel meant dominating the railroad there, which in turn necessitated an expedition into the interior, with the accompanying responsibility of maintaining all communication and transportation. He warned that "every foreign invasion that has gone deep into Russia has been swallowed up."[6]

Other Americans supported the SWC position. Pershing deemed the Archangel venture "wise." Ambassador Francis sought intervention, stressing the threat of German penetration, the need to protect the Murmansk base, and the urgency of guarding military stores. He quoted a high Bolshevik official, who called his government a "corpse that no one had the courage to bury."[7]

Secretary of State Lansing simply remarked that he far preferred a U.S. commitment to the White Sea area to one over Vladivostok. He told this to British ambassador Lord Reading (Rufus Daniel Isaacs), expressing his fear of Japanese penetration of eastern Russia by referring obliquely to the "racial difficulty" existing in Siberia. Only the remote area of northern Russia, he argued, held any military advantage for the Allies. Lansing also made the dubious claim that Trotsky still favored Allied intervention in the northern region.[8]

Wilson envisioned a limited undertaking in northern Russia. Because U.S. troops had not yet been engaged in full-scale fighting on the western front, he had been increasingly pressured to show a military presence to Germany's east. Furthermore, he remained skeptical concerning any commitment to Siberia, something the Allies very much wanted. He may also have feared that Germany's Baltic Division might seize the Allied weapons stored there, even if evidence for such an action was lacking. Here in the White Sea lay his chance to prove to the Allies that the United States was a genuinely participating partner in the grand coalition.[9]

Yet the president always remained cautious. On April 8, 1918, when the U.S. Navy sent the USS *Olympia*, Admiral George Dewey's old flagship, to Murmansk, Wilson stressed to Navy Secretary Daniels that "more important objects," that is, the western front, must not be sacrificed. Action must be limited to protecting the Allied stores and interests. On May 28, he was most prudent concerning the transferring of U.S. troops from France to northern Russia. Cabling General Bliss, the president stressed that such a move needed "the sure sympathy of the Russian people"; Wilson would not attempt "any restoration of the ancient regime."[10] On June 11, 150 marines landed at Murmansk, making it the first time U.S. troops were ever on Russian soil.

In a significant *aide-mémoire* (a written summary of a diplomatic communication) dated July 16, Wilson claimed that the United States opposed any British plans to use Archangel or Murmansk to penetrate Russia's interior. Rather, it committed itself only to guard military supplies supposedly stored at Kola, an unimportant village at the head of the Murmansk inlet, and to "make it safe for Russian forces to come together in organized bodies in the north." The Allies, the president said, contemplated no interference in Russia's internal affairs, but merely "such aid as shall be acceptable to the Russians in the organization of their own self-defence."[11] In the following days, against the opposition of Secretary of War Baker and Chief of Staff March, Wilson acceded to Britain's request for three full battalions and three companies of engineers.

By the end of July, Bolshevik foreign commissar Georgi V. Chicherin warned U.S. consul De Witt Clinton Poole that any foreign ship seeking to dock at a White Sea port would face Russian fire. Yet, when the Soviet government ordered the Murmansk Soviet to insist upon Allied evacuation, it refused to do so, thereby becoming what historian George F. Kennan calls "an anti-Soviet Soviet." In return, the Allies entered into a formal agreement with the local soviet recognizing its de facto authority for the entire region.[12] A clash was now inevitable.

On August 2, General F. C. Poole's 1,500 troops sailed into Archangel, linking themselves to a group of rebels who had just staged a successful uprising and established "The Provisional Government of Northern Russia." Ambassador Francis, stopping at the city before being evacuated to London, cabled the State Department: "If Allied forces were not here Bolsheviki would drive into Arctic Ocean all new government officials and supporters not caught and shot."[13]

Lenin's backers, however, remained on the outskirts of the city, surrounding the overextended troops. The only Americans present were fifty sailors. Chicherin protested against the city's occupation, accusing the Allies of killing Bolshevik Party members without any declaration of war. As part of the supplementary treaty to Brest-Litovsk signed late in August, a provision specified that "Russia will at once employ all the means at her disposal to expel the Entente forces from North Russian territory in observance of her neutrality." In return, Germany guaranteed that Finland would not attack Russia and particularly would not threaten Petrograd.[14]

On September 5, about 1:00 p.m. on a cold and rainy afternoon, 4,500 members of the U.S. 339th Infantry arrived at Archangel. They were known as "Detroit's Own," most of the draftees hailing from Michigan. They served under the British flag, were commanded by British officers, and were fitted out with British uniforms and old Russian rifles. They had originally been slated for Murmansk, but the British commander, concerned about instability there, rerouted them. Their assignment: protect munition stores, provide for Allied diplomats leaving Russia, and prevent the Germans from establishing a submarine base. Because of influenza and malnutrition caused by poor British rations, funerals were held every afternoon, caskets stacked four to five to a covered wagon. They found themselves confronting what historian W. Bruce Lincoln calls "some of the roughest terrain and most inhospitable climate to be found anywhere in the Western world."[15]

Immediately new responsibilities were assumed. Because the British believed that Lenin's regime served as Germany's puppet, they sought to replace it with one that would continue fighting on the eastern front. General Poole thought he had the perfect strategy. By seizing villages and towns on the Dvina River, Allied forces would eventually link up with a powerful Czech Legion that controlled much of Siberia. The joint force would then unite with a hundred thousand "friendly Russians" anxious to resume the struggle against Germany. The combined troops would traverse the 500 miles to Petrograd, even to Moscow. From there, they would seek to reconstruct an eastern front. No one suspected the degree of Bolshevik resistance.

Hence the British ordered the Yanks into combat situations, thereby making them belligerents in an extensive civil war. The intervention took on a life of its own, perpetuating itself by expanding initial goals. One U.S. battalion engaged in a 300-mile push up the Dvina River towards Kotlas, a junction of the Trans-Siberian Railroad. Another battalion journeyed down a 300-mile-long railroad line to capture the city of Vologda. A third remained quartered in local barracks. The Bolsheviks had already looted the supplies at Murmansk and moved them inland.

Neither Ambassador Francis nor the U.S. commander, Colonel George Stewart, protested against this exploitation of doughboys, much less questioned the wisdom of such plans. Historian James Carl Nelson finds the British scheme "hubris of the highest order." Even a limited defensive campaign would stretch Allied resources. To think that a handful of British and U.S. troops could be spread over the vast acreage of northern Russia was downright bizarre, particularly because by late 1918 the Bolshevik army numbered 600,000. Any dream of an offensive in the interior, much less one involving thousands of Allied troops and hordes of anti-Bolshevik Russians in revolt, strains credulity. Besides, the region itself held relatively little value, only possessing a population of 500,000, its undernourished peasants severed from food produced in the hinterland.[16]

The U.S. presence gave British general Poole confidence to back the overthrow of Archangel's leader, an aging populist named Nicholas Chaikovski, who headed the local Social Revolutionary Party and who claimed authority from the fallen Constituent Assembly. A genuine eccentric, during the 1870s Chaikovski had lived in Independence, Kansas, where he had attempted to create his own religious sect. Because he showed himself singularly inept as an administrator and military coordinator, on the night of September 5, a former tsarist naval officer, whose cover name was George Chaplin, took advantage of the newly arrived Americans to stage a coup. His band kidnapped Chaikovski's entire government, exiling it to a monastery on a frigid island while he assumed control. The local garrison and the industrial workers balked, triggering a general strike. For at least one day, U.S. troops operated Archangel's street cars. Largely because of the influence of Ambassador Francis, who immediately convened the Allied ambassadors, the Chaikovski government was restored and Chaplin exiled to a remote area of the province.

U.S. officials were most upset. Within two days, Tasker Bliss, writing from Paris, cabled Chief of Staff Peyton March: "I have always supposed that an invasion of Russian [*sic*] was repugnant to the intentions of the United States." The United States had "never contemplated nor recommended" General Poole's campaign. Besides, "it was up to him to obey his instructions and confine himself to the defense of the Arctic ports." Ambassador Francis feared that the British commander's authoritarian posture and mistrust of the Russian population would impair U.S. policy. Secretary of State Lansing sent word to London, threatening withdrawal unless Poole ended his high-handed methods. The SWC sought to rein in the Allied forces, demanding that operations be restricted until liaison with a major Czech force in western Siberia could be truly assured.[17]

The U.S. forces named themselves the "Polar Bear Expedition." Many arrived already ill with influenza, which was emerging as a pandemic, and were immediately hospitalized. By September 15, troops stationed near the village of Tiagra were under Bolshevik attack. All during the fall, these soldiers experienced sporadic casualties. Late in the season, temperatures sunk to well below zero, snow drifts reaching one's thigh. One Polar Bear later wrote, "'Guard duty at Archangel' was aiming now to be a real war, on a small scale but intensive."[18]

Wilson became apprehensive. On September 26, he wrote Lansing that the United States must insist that all Allied military efforts in northern Russia be limited to the guarding of ports and to "as much of the country round about them as may develop threatening conditions." Lansing immediately cabled Ambassador Walter Hines Page in London: "No more American troops will be sent to the northern ports." Francis balked, still seeking more U.S. forces, who would use Archangel and Murmansk to expedite the capture of Petrograd and Moscow. A hundred thousand men, he predicted, could perform the task. Were the Bolsheviks not suppressed, Austria might fall to revolution, a scenario that would in turn threaten "all countries."[19]

Local conditions remained unstable. Chaikovski's government soon disintegrated, leaving the British in control. In mid-October, London replaced General Poole with William E. Ironside, who later commanded the Imperial General Staff when World War II broke out. Archangel's workers, however, remained hostile, the peasantry apathetic, and many Russian troops went over to the Bolsheviks.

Admittedly, U.S. troops engaged in their most intensive combat with Bolshevik forces after the November 11, 1918, armistice. Yet only in June and July 1919, half a year afterward, did U.S. troops leave northern Russia. Wilson felt forced to wait until the White Sea unfroze. In February 1920, Bolshevik troops entered Archangel and Murmansk. By then, more than two hundred Americans had died, usually of injuries, accidents, or disease.

The United States, as Kennan aptly notes, handled the entire venture most ineptly. Wilson did not admonish the British, who held full command over U.S. forces with one exception: Britain could not legally define the uses to which these men would be put. When, however, the U.S. troops greatly exceeded the scope of their mission, the Wilson administration did not withdraw them, thus opening the United States up to the Soviet accusation of armed interference in its domestic affairs. Believing that his words were sufficient, Wilson, writes Kennan, assumed that he merely had "to give the general political line on a given question and things would then flow automatically, without further attention on his part to what he had said." Ironically, there were no military stores at Kola to protect. The only supplies had been stored in Archangel, several hundred miles away. Wilson's wider aim of bringing Russian forces together as a unified body revealed either an exaggerated fear of German activity in the area or a reluctance to recognize the full bitterness of Russia's developing civil war. For its part, London flagrantly ignored the limitations the president set on the use of U.S. troops. Kennan writes that many British regarded Americans as "stupid children," to be "wheedled into doing things they were not expected either to desire or to understand."[20]

One could develop this indictment even further. The Wilson administration, obviously embarrassed over relative lack of participation on the western front, was putting doughboys in harm's way because of decisions made almost casually. Certainly the president's follow-through remained far from ideal, leading to cynicism among U.S. forces.

If intervention on the White Sea ended up a disastrous fiasco, based on incorrect evaluations, U.S. intervention in Siberia revealed total ineptitude—and on a much larger scale. It would be difficult, if not impossible, to find a situation that was more muddled. The amorphous nature of the U.S. commitment and the vagueness of its rationale made the situation infinitely more difficult.

Northern Russia was not the only place where the Allies focused on war stores. Vladivostok housed four times the amount held at Archangel. By the time of the November revolution, tonnage reached more than 800,000. Included were high explosives, shells, barbed wire, phosphate, metals, food, and raw materials. Mountains of cotton bales were stockpiled, as were millions of rounds of ammunition, steel rails adequate to build a third track from Vladivostok to Petrograd, and sufficient barbed wire to enclose all Siberia. Goods worth between $750 million and $1 billion were involved.

Railroads complicated matters. Admittedly, the construction of the Trans-Siberian route had been an engineering miracle. It was the longest rail route in the world, stretching 5,700 miles. As the Stevens mission of 1917 had discovered, the Trans-Siberian's dilapidated condition had turned Vladivostok into a tremendous bottleneck. Along much of the Trans-Siberian, moderate democrats vied with Social Revolutionaries for control.

Japan played a crucial role in any Siberian involvement, as seen by its penetration of Manchuria. Traditionally, Manchuria was very much a part of China, which in reality remained too weak to exercise sovereignty. China's officially recognized government of dictator Yuan Shih-k'ai centered in Peking (now Beijing) even if a rebel regime led by Sun Yat-sen had established itself in Canton. In addition, local warlords exercised extensive authority. Japan controlled southern Manchuria, including its main artery, the South Manchurian Railroad. The island nation dominated the Peking government, ruled until 1916 by Yuan Shih-k'ai, and cast envious eyes upon northern Manchuria and eastern Siberia.

Not surprisingly, the United States sought to solidify relations with Japan. In early November 1917, notes were exchanged between Secretary Lansing and Viscount Ishii Kukujiro, special envoy to Washington and former foreign minister. Nothing if not ambiguous, these notes gave lip service to Chinese territorial sovereignty and the Open Door policy, but maintained that "Japan has special interests in China, particularly in that part to which her possessions are contiguous."[21]

Whereas the United States was seeking to reach a détente with Japan, acting in the hopes of restraining its activity on the Asian mainland, the European Allies had an entirely different focus. They desired to mobilize all anti-German elements in eastern Russia and hence reopen a major front. Even before the Bolshevik Revolution, the Entente had considered landing an expeditionary force in Siberia. Since Japan was both part of the Allies and obviously the closest power to eastern Russia, it appeared the most logical nation to send troops.

There was even more at stake, for each of the Allies had other goals. The Japanese wanted to strengthen their position on the Asian continent. The French sought to overthrow the Bolshevik regime, thereby salvaging investments in the Siberian and Manchurian railroads. The British desired a new channel to the Middle Eastern theater so as to check any German-Turkish advance there.

Within a month of the Bolshevik Revolution, the Allies began to eye Siberia. In mid-December 1917, the French publicly demanded Allied troops there. The military representatives to the SWC, with the exception of the American Tasker Bliss, called for supporting "by all means in our power" any group in Eastern Europe that would continue the war. Unless the Bolsheviks were stopped, Russia would start shipping oil and wheat to Germany. Needed was direct communication with "our friends in Russia," either by way of Vladivostok and the Trans-Siberian Railway or by Turkey. By January 1, 1918, the British War Cabinet recommended intervention in Vladivostok by an inter-Allied force composed primarily of Japanese troops but possessing token British and U.S. representation.[22]

In mid-January, the Japanese had sent four warships to Vladivostok and the British one. On the18th, Navy Secretary Daniels wrote in his diary, "Is Japan trying to get a foothold in Russia? Shall we send a ship to V [Vladivostok] or trust Japan alone? Delicate question. No solution reached."[23] On March 1, the USS *Brooklyn* arrived to join the Japanese and British vessels already anchored there. Their object: to prevent covert Bolshevik power from becoming overt.

Wilson was in a quandary over the entire matter, wavering frequently. In mid-January, he wrote Lansing that the United States should look upon Japanese activity "with distinct disapproval." On March 1, the president feared that once within Russia, Japan would never withdraw. However, he continued, the United States could not serve as a counterforce because it lacked the ships needed to send troops and matériel over so huge a distance. Besides, such intervention would cost the United States its "moral position." "Let Japan take the blame and the responsibility," the president told his cabinet. On the same day, however, he wrote an aide-mémoire in which he claimed no objection to any Japanese request to intervene, expressing confidence that Nippon's only purpose was saving Siberia from "the invasion of the armies and intrigues of Germany." Nonetheless, four days later, Wilson spoke of restraining Japan, writing the Japanese government that intervention might well play into Germany's hands.[24] Although historians differ on the reasons for Wilson's reluctance, it remains clear that his instincts were usually on the side of caution.[25]

Wilson's advisers were most concerned about Japanese activity. State Department counselor Frank L. Polk believed it would unite all Russian factions against the Western powers. Colonel House found that no military advantage could compensate for the racial antagonism created among Europe's Slavs. Food Administrator Herbert Hoover feared that a Japanese presence would simply unite the Russians behind Lenin. Given the hatred of Russians towards Nippon, it might take Japan's army ten years to subdue Germany. In the end, Japan would demand all Siberia as a reward.[26]

William C. Bullitt, chief of the State Department's Bureau of Central European Information, offered an extensive memorandum on the subject, claiming that indifference to Japanese intervention would put the United States on a par with Pontius Pilate. The Germans, he observed, were 2,500 miles from Vladivostok and posed no threat. Conversely, were the United States to protest a Japanese incursion publicly, the French and British governments would likely fall over the issue, being replaced by more liberal regimes. "In Russia to-day there are the rudiments of a government of the people, by the people and for the people," Bullitt wrote.[27]

In early March, Ambassador Francis warned that Japanese invasion would generate sufficient anger to turn Russia into a German province. Most U.S. representatives in the Far East placed great stock in the ruthless Grigori Semenov, whose 10,000-man army was fighting Bolsheviks on the Manchurian frontier. Wilson himself expressed curiosity concerning "several nuclei of self-governing authority that seem to be springing up in Siberia. It would afford me a great deal of satisfaction to get behind the most nearly representative of them if it can indeed draw leadership and control to itself."[28]

By mid-March, the American press differed over Japanese intervention. Some journals were opposed. The *Springfield Republican* saw a parallel to the recent U.S. fiasco in Mexico. Not surprisingly, William Randolph Hearst condemned such action. Finding a "Renaissance" among the Japanese, Chinese, and Indians, he warned, "Another great wave of yellow men, bent on submerging the world, will sweep out of Asia." If Japan invaded Siberia, the United States should "remove our ships and troops from Europe and transfer them to Asia" so as to block this move.[29]

By then, however, some U.S. opinion-makers endorsed Japan's entry into Siberia. The *New York Times* harbored no more objection to Japanese troops than to those of Western powers that had intervened in the Boxer Rebellion less than twenty years earlier. Colonel Harvey's *War Weekly* feared a "Hunnish" occupation of Siberia: "The Japanese are not Germans. They are civilized." Similarly, the *Outlook* claimed that only Japan could prevent Germany from conquering the world. Senator Miles Poindexter, in endorsing intervention, remarked that Japan "must find food for her people, room for her increasing population, somewhere on the face of the earth." By April, *Current Opinion* noted that any hostile American sentiment towards Japan had been dissipated.[30]

On April 4, 1918, events took an entirely new turn when several armed men wearing Russian uniforms entered a Japanese shop in Vladivostok, demanded money, and upon refusal killed three Japanese. On the next day, five hundred Japanese troops landed in the city. The British did likewise, ordering fifty men to guard their consulate. Probably Japan's orders were given by the local naval commander, Admiral Kato Kanji, not by the government in Tokyo.

During the spring, a new element was added to the Siberian equation that greatly complicated an already complex situation. Two divisions of the Czechoslovakian Corps, often called the Czech Legion, were formed. They were primarily composed of defectors from the Austro-Hungarian army. The disintegration of Russia's forces, particularly after the Bolshevik Revolution, had suddenly made the Czechs the strongest armed unit in the land. Originally part of the Russian army, in December 1917 the Czecho-Slovak National Council had placed them under French high command. By 1918, at least 40,000 to 50,000 troops were involved and possibly more. First stationed around Kiev, where they guarded war stores, they sought to reach Vladivostok, where they could be evacuated by sea and eventually fight on the western front.

By the second week in May, Czech forces, along with Russian anticommunist allies, occupied the Trans-Siberian Railway from a point west of Samara on the Volga to somewhat west of Irkutsk. Because the towns along the railroad were administrative centers, the Czechs — along with anti-Bolshevik Russian groups — occupied most of the 2,500-mile stretch east of the Urals. By the month's end, the Czechs were fighting Soviet armies all along the railroad line. In June, they took part in establishing an anti-Bolshevik regime at Omsk that claimed to speak for all Siberia.

If the Czech Legion, by controlling the Trans-Siberian, dominated a distance roughly equal to that of New York to Reno, there was less to its presence than meets the eye. Historian Betty Miller Unterberger points out that the inexperienced Czech leaders had negotiated clumsily with the Bolsheviks and displayed a morbid fear of the Germans.

Unprincipled young officers engaged in purposeless adventurism. The troops appeared quite willing to remain in Russia to fight both Germans and Bolsheviks, believing that the Allies would reciprocate by backing the establishment of an independent Czechoslovak republic.[31]

On June 29, the Allies seized Vladivostok from the Bolsheviks, 15,000 Czech troops taking the lead. The British and Japanese landed armed parties in the morning, the Chinese in the afternoon, and a small detachment of U.S. marines, sent to guard the consulate, in the evening. At that point, the Vladivostok Czechs appealed to the Allies to back their efforts to open the Trans-Siberian Railway and to reestablish contact with their fellow troops in central Siberia and the Urals.

Wilson's hand was being forced. All the American representatives in Russia, Siberia, and China sought intervention, as did the Far Eastern Division of the State Department and Consul Poole in Moscow. Further delay, reported Francis in late May, was dangerous. General Pershing endorsed "prompt favorable action." At the same time, Paul Reinsch, U.S. minister to China, cabled Washington from Peking, warning that Siberia would be under German control unless immediate action were taken. Conversely, with "only slight countenance and support," the Czechs could control the entire region.[32]

Interventionists kept pressing their case. A *Literary Digest* press survey dated June 1, 1918, noted that most editors sought a joint U.S.– Japanese expedition but differed over whether it should cooperate with the Bolsheviks. Taft sought 200,000 U.S. troops, entering Russia by both Vladivostok and Archangel. TR was more modest, suggesting U.S., British, and Japanese armies of 30,000 men each. He would even back Lenin or Trotsky if their armies fought the Germans! Harvey's *War Weekly* called for an army corps, led by TR or Leonard Wood, that would cooperate with Japan.[33]

Some senators were outspoken. William H. King submitted a resolution endorsing a military expedition that would include U.S., Chinese, and Japanese troops. Poindexter envisioned a coalition army in which 2 million Japanese would serve as the mainstay of an Allied coalition. James Hamilton Lewis warned that if Germany overran Siberia, it would invade the Aleutians, seize Alaska, and threaten the United States proper. "We must," said Lawrence Sherman, "trust Japan."[34]

Occasionally liberals offered a note of caution. The *New Republic* opposed the United States acting as "conquerors" over half of Russia. The *Nation* accused the Allies of assuming that "the Russian masses are hordes of savages who can be driven at will by a masterful hand."[35]

In mid-June, Wilson had hoped to skirt any dilemma by suggesting that Herbert Hoover be sent to Vladivostok as director of a "Russian Relief Commission." Colonel House was enthusiastic. After meeting with the food administrator, however, he wrote in his diary, "I have never known a man with a less sympathetic personality. If I were running Hoover for President I would keep him at home, and let him talk to the people entirely through the press."[36]

The president, however, waited in vain for any invitation from Lenin's government. Wilson developed second thoughts about any Hoover mission, finding that Hoover was irreplaceable at home, lacked the needed temperament, and projected a "capitalistic" image to the Bolsheviks. Kennan suspects that Hoover would, of necessity, have taken the entire Russian matter out of Wilson's hands.[37]

Yet the Allies were wearing down the Wilson administration. So, too, was fear of independent Japanese intervention, concern over the fate of the Czech Legion, and the belief that the Bolsheviks were arming Austro-Hungarian prisoners to fight the Allies. By mid-June 1918, the Germans were within forty miles of Paris. Therefore, any action that could divert German attention eastward appeared warranted. British foreign secretary Balfour warned on June 20 that without Allied intervention in Siberia, Germany would achieve world domination.[38]

On July 2, the SWC saw Allied intervention directed by Americans as "an urgent and imperative necessity." A Siberian invasion, it believed, would stimulate a national uprising inside Russia against German occupation, shorten the war by reconstituting the eastern front, prevent Russia's isolation from western Europe, deny Berlin essential supplies, and assist the Czech forces. On the following day, the SWC warned: "The Czechs are in danger of being cut off. The Bolsheviki are down and out. We must intervene to save the Czechs and to gain easy possession of Siberia."[39]

The SWC note was not only contradictory but dead wrong. As Unterberger notes, the Czechs were in no danger and the Bolsheviks were powerless. Hence, intervention was unnecessary. Wilson accused the SWC of proposing "such impractical things to be done immediately that he often wondered whether he was crazy or whether they were." He still feared that intervention would restore "the old regime."[40]

Two days after the SWC issued its note, Lansing urged that the United States and the Allies supply troops to the Czechs, stressing "a moral obligation to save these men from our common enemies, if we are able to do so." In Lansing's vision, observes historian David S. Foglesong, the Allies would arm 15,000 Czechs at Vladivostok, who would supposedly link with 50,000 compatriots west of Irkutsk. The combined force could defeat Red Guards and former prisoners of war in the Trans-Baikal region and secure control of the Trans-Siberian Railroad. Furthermore, if non-Bolshevik forces sought aid in combating Soviet forces west of the Urals, the Czech and Allied forces might remain there.[41]

By now, Wilson saw no choice. On the evening of July 6, the president conferred with his secretaries of state, war, and navy plus Chief of Staff Peyton C. March and Chief of Naval Operations William S. Benson. He read from a condensed version of an aide-mémoire whose full text would be drafted eleven days later. The large forces sought by France and Britain would, the document claimed, simply add to the present confusion, injuring rather than aiding the war against Germany. Even if such troops could effectively deliver an attack from the east, they would "be merely a method of making use of Russia, not a method of serving it." Military action was only admissible to "help the Czecho-Slovaks consolidate their forces and get into successful cooperation with their Slavic kinsmen and to steady any efforts at self-government or self-defense in which the Russians themselves may be willing to accept assistance." Be the locale Vladivostok, Murmansk, or Archangel, U.S. and Allied troops could only be legitimately employed to guard military stores, which may subsequently be needed by Russian forces, and to "render such aid as may be acceptable to the Russians in the organization of their own self-defense."

In a somewhat disingenuous passage, Wilson denied that any of these conclusions "is meant to wear the least colour of criticism of what other governments associated against Germany may think it wise to undertake." The United States had no wish, "even by implication, to seek limits to the action or to define the policies of its Associates." Also suggested was a commission of "merchants, agricultural exports, labour advisers, Red Cross representatives" and YMCA workers to spread "useful information" and render "educational help of a modest sort."[42]

In his summary of the meeting, Secretary Lansing noted a consensus that went beyond the memorandum. It was conceded that no eastern front could be created, even if a large Japanese force was recruited. Nor was any advance west of Irkutsk feasible. The United States would simply join Japan in each sending seven thousand troops to guard the Czech line of communication proceeding towards Irkutsk. During the conversation, General March was the lone participant to doubt whether Japan would limit itself to seven thousand men. Wilson replied, "Well, we will have to take that chance."[43]

Wilson had several audiences in mind. He sought to assure the Russians that the United States would not use intervention to exploit them. In referring, however, to their efforts at "self-defense," he implied an anti-Bolshevik purpose. The president was indicating to the Allies he would not support any imperialistic schemes, casting his eye particularly on the Japanese. The emphasis on rescuing the Czechs conveyed an altruism designed to allay domestic critics.[44]

Scholars have been devastating in their critiques. The president had decided without consulting a single ally, much less coordinating with the Entente. In a sense, the memo claimed that intervention was counterproductive, then sought to rationalize it. Wilson showed no knowledge of conditions within Siberia and greatly underestimated the number of troops needed to protect the Czechs. To center one's entire rationale on the Czech Legion appears either spurious or naive.[45] Certainly, Wilson was under enormous Allied pressure, particularly as the AEF was not yet playing a leading role on the western front. One might well argue that he had to respond positively in some form. The document, however, does him little credit.

On July 6, the day Wilson first presented the confidential aide-mémoire to his advisers, Navy Secretary Daniels ordered Admiral Austin Knight, commander in chief of the U.S. Asiatic Fleet, to "utilize the force at your disposal." Knight's ship *Brooklyn* was already in Vladivostok harbor. At the same time, the admiral had to avoid "any action tending to offend Russian sentiment or to become involved in any political question."[46]

Lloyd George was understandably furious over the aide-mémoire. In his eyes, Wilson had engaged in months of dangerous vacillation, then had taken it upon himself unilaterally to fix the terms of the intervention. The president was provoking the Bolsheviks without offering sufficient means to overthrow them. Fourteen hundred men, remarked the prime minister, was better than nothing but was surely insufficient. He compared Wilson's "half-fledged" acceptance of the SWC's plea to William E. Gladstone's failure to relieve General Charles George "Chinese" Gordon at Khartoum in 1885! In an effort to end the bloody stalemate on the western front, the British prime minister had suggested pouring 2.5 million Japanese into Siberia.[47]

Within three weeks, Japan responded. On July 24, Ishii Kukujiro, now ambassador to the United States, told Frank Polk, then acting secretary of state, that Japan could not confine itself to the 7,000 troops the president had specified in his aide-mémoire. Ishii's government did not intend to send large numbers of soldiers, but the number was too small to protect the Czech rear. Ishii spoke in terms of 12,000 men, which would compose a division. Even this number depended on the amount of Bolshevik resistance and an indeterminate number of Austrian and German prisoners, whom the Bolsheviks permitted to bear small arms to guard their own camps. An enclosed memorandum used the vaguest of language: "suitable forces," "a certain number of troops," a possible additional "detachment" along the Siberian railroad, the "special position of Japan" in the region, a desire to "act in harmony with the Allies," that is, the British and French.[48]

Washington had been put on guard. As Colonel House noted, the next day Wilson "fretted" over Japan's attitude. Had the president known his confidant's own attitude, he would have been even more upset, for House told Brigadier General Alfred Knox, chief of the British military mission to Siberia, that he should "tell the Japs that the main thing was that they should go in and go in quickly." Wilson wrote Daniels that the Japanese were trying to alter his entire Vladivostok policy.[49]

Japan soon tipped its hand. On August 2, Viscount Ishii simply informed Lansing that his nation was sending "suitable forces" to Vladivostok. His reason: the Central Powers were consolidating their hold on Russia, extending their activities to its Far Eastern possessions, and interfering with the passage of Czech troops across Siberia. Once the rescue mission was accomplished, Japanese troops would withdraw, leaving Russia's political and military sovereignty unimpaired. On the following day, Ishii told Polk that Tokyo accepted Wilson's proposals but, if necessary, reserved the right to send reinforcements "to Vladivostok or elsewhere." There might not be time for consultation, but Japan would never send more than ten to twelve thousand troops.[50]

Also on August 2, Acting Secretary of State Polk, having learned that Bolsheviks had gained control of Vladivostok's duma and mayor's office, cabled the U.S. consul there. The United States, he wrote, sympathized with those "patriotic groups" seeking "restoration of order and the welfare of the population," wording that obviously excluded the Bolsheviks. The United States was not, however, prepared to assist any particular movement or group.[51] Again, the Wilson administration was showing caution.

More important, on the very same day, Major General William S. Graves, stationed at Palo Alto, California, received a coded message from Washington telling him to travel immediately to Kansas City. Graves had been decorated for heroism during the 1903 Philippine insurrection and was assigned to the General Staff. There Newton Baker handed him a sealed envelope containing orders sending him to Siberia. Because Graves's train was late, the two men could only confer for a few minutes in the city's railroad station. Baker merely remarked, "This contains the policy of the United States in Russia which you are to follow. Watch your step; you will be walking on eggs loaded with dynamite. God bless you and good-bye." When Graves returned to his hotel, he opened the envelope, which simply contained Wilson's aide-mémoire of mid-July. It was only Wilson's personal appeal that kept Baker from resigning over the matter. He later wrote that the episode was "nonsense from the beginning" and marked the only real disagreement he ever had with the president.[52]

The State Department immediately backed the Graves mission, releasing a paraphrase of the aide-mémoire that stressed its limited nature: simply guarding military stores. It made public the original aim of steadying Russian efforts at "self-government or self-defense" while pledging no interference in internal affairs. The public version introduced the Czech Legion as the primary motive for intervention. For the first time, the United States spoke of "the armed Austrian and German prisoners of war who are attacking them," hence giving the false impression that the POWs served as part of the German and Austrian armies. Kennan finds that the stress upon German and Austrian prisoners of war was a "grievous distortion," particularly as few such Germans were in eastern Siberia. Fewer than one-tenth of these prisoners were Germans; most came from the Hapsburg Empire and did not speak German. At the same time, Wilson ignored the entire presence of the Bolsheviks, who were the Czechs' real enemy.[53]

American newspapers usually welcomed the State Department announcement, finding in it a means to reintegrate Russia with the Allies. Most papers accepted the fiction that the Bolsheviks were uninvolved; differences usually emerging over the scope, size, and timing of the expedition. Hearst columnist Arthur Brisbane, in endorsing Wilson's move, sought greater commitment, writing that 2 million well-armed, well-trained Japanese, together with 5 or 6 million fearless, hard-fighting Chinese, would go through the land "like a sharp knife through cheese." Possibly these Japanese could reach Berlin before the Western forces did. The *North American Review* saw the intervention leading to Russia's "salvation" and "rebirth."[54]

Some liberals predictably expressed caution. The *Nation* feared "a most perilous undertaking." Unless the Western powers understood "our unselfish intentions, it may turn out that we have done the very thing we are seeking to prevent—turned Russia over to the Germans." The *New Republic* surmised that the dangers of escalation would threaten both democracy and the Allied cause.[55]

Scholars aptly point to the folly of the entire enterprise. The orders were obsolete at the time they were issued. U.S. presence simply added to the already existing chaos. Graves remained ignorant of the forces with which he would have to deal. The polyglot nature of the occupying troops made his mission, amorphous to begin with, absolutely impossible. At no point were the Czechs in danger from German prisoners. Rather, they controlled much of Siberia. Furthermore, they were not heading towards Vladivostok but rather moving ever westward.[56]

August 3, the day of Graves's orders, also marked the day Allied troops began landing at Vladivostok. First the British and French arrived, then Japanese, and, within two weeks, nine thousand U.S. doughboys. Graves, who arrived on September 3, later wrote, "The fact that we were not troubled by custom inspectors and quarantine officials was my first initiation into a country without a Government."[57]

Wilson's apprehension concerning massive Japanese forces was well founded, for Graves's first report disclosed the presence of sixty thousand Japanese. A later account indicated seventy-two thousand, ten times the number Wilson had envisaged. The Japanese also dispatched an entire division of 1,200 men to the Chinese Eastern Railway zone, thereby dominating much of Manchuria. In mid-October, Tokyo was quite blunt about the whole matter, telling London it did not seek to restore Russia as a great power and was pursuing its own agenda in Siberia.[58]

By the time U.S. troops reached Vladivostok, eastern Siberia and Manchuria lay in utter confusion, with power divided among many nationalities: Czechs, Bolshevik Russians, Japanese, and Chinese. In all, thousands of soldiers and civilians, speaking more than a dozen languages, milled about, with no single person or institution taking responsibility. Although the Czechs had overthrown the Bolshevik regime in Vladivostok as in much of Siberia, they had not replaced it with any organized administration, government thereby being limited to a few tsarist officials. Two Russian generals were also active. Grigori Semenov, a Cossack from the Trans-Baikal, was dictator of Chita in lower Siberia. Known only for his cruelty, he enjoyed hijacking American trains passing through Chita. Ivan Kalmykov, *hetman* (military commander) of the Ussuri Cossacks, murdered political opponents with his own hands. The Japanese financed both men.

Needless to say, both Graves and his troops were confused about their mission, having been given no instructions concerning it. He did all he could to remain aloof from the various Siberian factions. Historian W. Bruce Lincoln observes that Graves's tenacity, personal integrity, and raw courage minimized damage to U.S. interests. When the general learned one of his men had arrested a Russian for simply being a Bolshevik, he issued the following order: "The United States is not at war with the Bolsheviki or any other faction of Russia. You have no orders to arrest Bolsheviks or anybody else unless they disturb the peace of the community, attack the people or the Allied soldiers. The United States is not here to fight Russia or any group or faction in Russia."[59]

By the first week of September, rail connections between eastern and western Siberia were set up, thus permitting all Czechs to reach Vladivostok, from where supposedly they would travel to France. However, being briefly in power as far east as Kazan, Orenburg, and Samara, the Czechs preferred participating in Russia's civil war to being shipped to the western front. In reality, however, the situation was highly unstable, with the vastly overextended Czechs menaced on all sides by the month's end.

Some Americans were most enthusiastic. Interior Secretary Franklin K. Lane perceived "the greatest romance" in "the advance of the Czecho-Slavs across five thousand miles of Russian Asia, — an army on foreign territory, without a government, holding not a foot of land, who are recognized as a nation!" Henry Cabot Lodge, comparing the Czech accomplishment to that described in Xenophon's *Anabasis*, found "nothing like it in all the past except the famous march of the 10,000 Greeks." Harvey's *War Weekly* described the Czechs as "opening up a way into the very heart of Great Russia itself."[60]

The two major liberal journals again raised questions. The *Nation* feared that given Russian suspicions of intervention, another setback lay in the offing, one similar to the Allied defeat in the Dardanelles in 1915. Asked the *New Republic*: "Just what do we wish in the matter of the Czecho-Slovaks?" Should they be granted "unmolested" exit? Or should they be allowed to remain where they are so as to interfere in the very Russian domestic affairs that the United States was pledged to avoid?[61]

The Wilson administration was certainly displeased with the entire Siberian situation. As early as August 20, 1918, the president had maintained that the United States was unable to increase the number of troops there. He opposed U.S. units proceeding west of Irkutsk to relieve the Czechs; rather, Graves's troops should remain in eastern Siberia, there to fight "hostile forces" along the Amur River and the Lake Baikal region. The Japanese, Wilson complained in early September, were "fighting on their own plan."[62] To Washington, the creation of any eastern front remained totally impractical.

From Paris, General Bliss reported, "The Allies think that having made a beginning in Russia and having put the foot in the crack of the door the whole body must follow." It was one thing, he continued, to keep the Czechs from being wiped out, quite another to aid them in establishing their own government inside Russia. Lansing sought modest provisions for Siberia's population but claimed military intervention would merely add to Russia's "present sad confusion." He balked at a French bid to coordinate U.S. doughboys with Allied forces in both Siberia and northern Russia, telling Ambassador Jusserand that the United States maintained "strict impartiality as between contending political parties." Cooperation would "be as unnecessary as it is undesirable." He confessed to Wilson in late September, "The more I consider the matter the more perplexing and distressing it becomes."[63]

U.S. reticence again revealed itself when in mid-month an All-Russian Provisional Government convened at Ufa, located in the southern Ural region. The product of a merger between various ad hoc anti-Bolshevik regimes, it was ruled by a five-man directory and appointed Aleksandr Kolchak, an able admiral but inept administrator, war minister. The regime repudiated the Brest-Litovsk Treaty, sought to continue the war with Germany, and pledged protection of private and foreign capital. Soon moving eastward to Omsk, it remained a shadow affair, marked by intrigue and mutual distrust. In early November, Ernst L. Harris, U.S. consul general at Irkutsk in southern Siberia, reported, "There has been no spontaneous enthusiastic uprising on the part of the people, especially the intelligent classes, to put their country in order and keep it from Bolshevism."[64] The United States neither recognized it nor gave it informal support.

Late in September, General Graves sought to establish a base at Omsk, 2,500 miles from Vladivostok. Roland S. Morris, U.S. ambassador to Japan, strongly endorsed the idea, arguing from Vladivostok that the move would give needed support to Czechs in the Volga region, solidify protection of the Trans-Siberian Railroad, and raise morale throughout the region. Wilson strongly rejected this advice, finding such an effort impossible. Allied efforts in either Siberia or the Volga area, replied Lansing to Morris, were neither "practical or based upon sound reason or good military judgment." Ambassador Jusserand feared a massacre in the region, telling Wilson, "This blood will be on your head, not ours, and it will be a grave responsibility to have caused these deaths."[65] The president remained unmoved.

Czech morale immediately plummeted. The Czechs felt the Allies had betrayed them, for they had counted on massive U.S. and Allied assistance. What had just been an effective fighting force suddenly deteriorated.[66]

At the time of the November 11 armistice, Japan had sent seventy thousand men to Siberia, all under direct control of its general staff in Tokyo. There was no longer any question who dominated the region. Within two weeks, General Graves wrote War Secretary Newton Baker: "I think some blood will be shed when troops move out but the longer we stay the greater will be the bloodshed when Allied troops do go." The United States, he continued, was "helping establish a form of autocratic government which the people of Siberia will not stand for." Baker felt somewhat similarly, writing Wilson that the American presence only abetted Japan's long-term ambitions for a sphere of influence. Bolshevism's attraction mystified him, "but I have a feeling that if the Russians do like it, they are entitled to have it."[67]

Before the November 11 armistice, U.S. forces were only involved in two minor skirmishes against Bolshevik forces. Preceding Graves's arrival, a Japanese general had convinced a small U.S. advance detachment just sent from the Philippines to fight against supposed German and Austrian prisoners. The doughboys fired no shots. A second brief engagement took place in early September when U.S. soldiers, along with Japanese and Chinese counterparts, guarded the Suchan coal mines seventy-five miles west of Vladivostok. The mines supplied fuel for the eastern part of the Trans-Siberian Railway.

Historians differ widely as to the entire rationale behind the Siberian venture. Among the suggested motives are rescuing the Czech Legion (Wilson's own rationale), fear that the Japanese would assume total control, restoring the eastern front, pressure from Britain and France, the desire to contain Bolshevism, and the result of "mission creep," whereby limited initial operations give way to unintended long-range commitments.[68]

Such interpretations reveal the difficulty of presenting any analysis that would remain comprehensive or definitive. The most knowledgeable officials, including Lansing, gave little credence to the supposed threat of armed German prisoners; Wilson himself did not mention them in his initial position paper, the July 17 aide-mémoire. The stress upon the president's fear of Japan might be exaggerated, at least before August 1918. Note that the president excluded Britain and France, but not Japan, from his initial intervention plan. As far as Allied pressure goes, one might argue that Wilson's reaction reflected far more exasperation than acquiescence. Had Wilson really focused on the Czech Legion, he would have ordered sufficient means to evacuate them from Siberia or have convinced the Allies to make rescue efforts. It appears ludicrous to send 14,000 U.S. and Japanese soldiers in order to rescue 70,000 Czechs.

Several historians have challenged any anti-Bolshevik thrust to Wilson's policy. Adam Tooze stresses that the Allies neither feared revolution nor anticipated the Cold War. Rather they envisioned what became reality in the foretaste of summer of 1941, when the Wehrmacht threatened to extend Hitler's empire throughout Russia. Carl J. Richard argues that although Wilson disliked the Bolsheviks, he loathed the leaders of imperial Germany. The overthrow of Lenin's government was simply one more step towards the greater goal of overthrowing the kaiser's state. The president suspected such overtures as Trotsky had made to Raymond Robins for two reasons. First, he doubted Petrograd's capability to sustain an armed struggle against the troops of Erich Ludendorff. Second, he feared that the Red Army would turn its strength primarily against anti-Bolshevik Russians, thereby forcing the vast majority of the population into the arms of the Germans. The president never diverted many troops from the western front, almost half of those ordered to Siberia coming from the Philippines. He did not use a single ship scheduled to cross the Atlantic.[69]

In all, there probably was no single motive for sending U.S. troops into play. Weighing all the factors remains difficult and subjective. It is still doubtful whether Wilson could have continually resisted both the foreign and domestic pressure, including that of his immediate advisers. Once General Graves's troops had embarked, the president can be faulted for his lack of clarity. As in the case of Archangel, U.S. forces were left with the vaguest of aims. And Baker's remarks to Graves, concerning "walking on eggs loaded with dynamite," appear most apt.

To Wilson, Siberia was simply an unpleasant diversion. Certainly, the entire Russian venture had contributed nothing to the war effort. A far more important matter lay at hand. From the time he entered the conflict, he was forced to wrestle with the war aims of both friend and foe and, more important, to develop his own. Just why was the war being fought?

TEN
WRESTLING WITH WAR AIMS, 1917

FOR THE ALLIES, THE YEAR 1917 WAS GRIM INDEED. UNTIL convoys were instituted, the German submarine campaign was quite successful. Not only had the British offensives at Arras and Passchendaele failed, but in late May, German planes bombed Folkestone, England, killing ninety-five people. Within six weeks, fifty-seven more died when another air strike hit London. General Robert Georges Nivelle's defeat in the Aisne in the spring led to such utter despair that dozens of French divisions mutinied in May.

In July, German and Austrian troops repulsed Alexei Brusilov's offensive, leading to the collapse of the entire eastern front and the disintegration of the Russian army. This massive Allied setback was equaled only by Italy's defeat that fall at Caporetto, a small town on the Isonzo River, where German and Austro-Hungarian forces had achieved a major breakthrough. Though British and French divisions came to Italy's rescue by establishing a new defense behind the Piave River, its cabinet fell, its factories lacked coal, and 340,000 troops became casualties. The nation's morale had collapsed. After dining with Lloyd George, Colonel House predicted in mid-November, "Venice will fall." Just one month later, Wilson's confidant found both Italy and Greece such a drag on the Allied war effort that he believed Britain would have been better off fighting alone. Waging its own war, he claimed, it could have seized Germany's colonies and driven its commerce from the seas with far less loss of life.[1]

Such setbacks, however, did not lead the Allies to unify their efforts. Though the Allies had fought for three years, their troops on the western front still lacked unified command. Decisions concerning the coordination of forces and supplies were made independently. In mid-July, Brigadier General James G. Harbord, AEF chief of staff and Pershing's chief subordinate, had confided to his diary: "Our Allies seem to hate each other." Only on November 7 did representatives of the British, French, and Italian governments establish a Supreme War Council. Even this body confined itself to such policy matters as coordination of resources. It had not yet developed an overall strategy.[2]

Through the war, several prominent Americans saw North America itself in danger. Were Germany to defeat the Allies, warned Elihu Root, the kaiser would take possession of Canada, thereby threatening the northern border. Such a situation, warned Interior Secretary Franklin K. Lane, would lead to 5 million Americans under arms and a military budget taking up to 40 percent of every man's income. "Who wants to live in such a country?" he asked. "The devil is in the saddle and we must pull him down, or else he will rule the world."[3]

As was the case before the United States entered the conflict, in 1917 some Americans feared actual invasion. The National Chamber of Commerce warned that a variety of circumstances—the collapse of Russia, defeat of the British fleet, starvation of the Allied population, reversals on the western front, continuation of the submarine menace—could result in German troops landing on U.S. shores. Secretary of State Lansing, speaking at Madison Barracks, New York, in July, asked, "Would not this country, with its enormous wealth, arouse the cupidity of an impoverished, though triumphant, Germany?" Slightly over two months later, Senator Frederick Hale (R-Me.) predicted that a victorious Germany would inevitably seek to overrun the United States, just as it had Belgium, Poland, and Serbia.[4]

Even were the United States not directly threatened, there existed a tremendous sense of futility. In July, the Hearst press predicted that the Central Powers had sufficient strength to fight ten more years. During the same month, Ambassador Page feared that the Germans would return Alsace-Lorraine and restore Belgium and France in exchange for dominating the eastern part of the European continent, a condition that could only result in another war. Were the Allies to kill five thousand Germans a day for three hundred days a year, it would take four years to obliterate their army. In early November, Page wrote an associate:

> This infernal thing drags its slow length along so that we cannot see even a day ahead, not to say even a week, or a year. If any man here allowed the horrors of it to dwell on his mind he would go mad. . . . There is hardly a country on the Continent where people are not literally starving to death and in many of them by hundreds of thousands; and this state of things is going to continue for a good many years after the war.[5]

The Allies seldom spoke optimistically. In early September, British prime minister Lloyd George wrote Wilson: "Every nation in Europe is becoming exhausted. The desire for peace in some quarters is becoming almost irresistible." Just over a month earlier, Jan Christian Smuts of the British War Cabinet had predicted an even darker future: "The *nadir* of our fortunes has by no means been reached."[6]

The French made it all too clear that they were only interested in holding a defensive position, not surprising since a million of their troops had died since 1914. The usually optimistic Pershing reported to War Secretary Baker in July, "The fact is that France is very tired of this war."[7] Cabinets shifted quickly, with that of Aristide Briand being replaced in March 1917 by that of Alexandre Ribot. In September, Ribot in turn was succeeded by Paul Painlevé, who then gave way in November to Georges Clemenceau. Fall brought even more pessimism.

Admittedly, conditions within the Central Powers were far from ideal. In April 1917, 300,000 workers went on strike in Berlin. By summer, Germany was experiencing shortages of everything from clothing to food. At the end of the year, its death rate had risen 32 percent above that of 1913, with young children experiencing fatalities at the same rate as adults. In July, Georg Michaelis, a colorless and obscure Prussian civil servant, replaced Theobald von Bethmann Hollweg as chancellor. The German military had found that Bethmann Hollweg lacked the needed zeal for the conflict. That October, Michaelis was followed in turn by Count Georg von Hertling, minister president of Bavaria and a leader of the Roman Catholic center party (Zentrumspartei). Like his predecessors, Hertling proved too weak to challenge the General Staff.

The army of Austria-Hungary was exhausted, its peace-minded civilian population lacking essential food and fuel. Such shortages led to a breakdown in transportation with accompanying strikes and mutinies. Germany's ambassador to Vienna reported, "This Monarchy is lurching on the edge of an abyss."[8] The Ottoman Empire was literally disintegrating, losing Baghdad in March, Gaza in November, Jerusalem in December.

When the United States entered the conflict, France and Britain first hoped it would concentrate on finance and shipping, for both powers assumed that the doughboys would arrive too late to play a significant role. Almost immediately, however, they increased their demands. In mid-April, British foreign secretary Arthur Balfour led a special diplomatic mission to the United States, as did René Viviani, France's prime minister. Accompanying Viviani was General Joseph Joffre, who was held in high esteem for repulsing Germany's initial offensive on the Marne River in September 1914. After his initial victories, however, Joffre had suffered one military defeat after another, and hence in December 1916 was removed from field command. Although he was "kicked upstairs," he was awarded the rank of field marshal and proved himself most useful for ceremonial functions.

Initially, Wilson was hesitant concerning the Balfour/Viviani mission, finding it possessing "manifest dangers," for it could create the impression that the United States was merely Britain's "assistant." Realizing, however, that his nation had suddenly become a major belligerent, the president decided that personal contact could be useful.[9] Hence both Balfour and Viviani were heartily welcomed, addressing Congress and touring the nation. The real business was conducted behind closed doors. Acting under instructions of the War Cabinet, the British delegation arrived with an extensive shopping list: continued American financial support, rapid expansion of tonnage (not surprising given the massive U-boat toll), a token force of regulars sent immediately to the western front, and the eventual transport of half a million regular troops to France, there to be amalgamated into British divisions.

On April 28, House met privately with Balfour over war aims. With the map of Europe spread out before them, the two men defined the ideal peace. They concurred on the restoration of France, Belgium, and Serbia, and the awarding of Alsace and Lorraine to France. Austria must give Bosnia and Herzegovina to Serbia, which in turn should restore to Bulgaria a part of Macedonia recently taken in the Second Balkan War. Rumania should receive small parts of Russia and Hungary that its nationals inhabited. Both leaders thought that Austria should reorganize itself into three states, one alternative being its division into Bohemia, Hungary, and Austria proper. Furthermore, they agreed that Constantinople (now Istanbul) should be internationalized. House suggested "a restored and rejuvenated Poland," "big enough and potential enough to serve as a buffer state between Germany and Russia." Balfour objected, claiming that an independent Poland would make it more difficult for Russia to come, if necessary, to France's rescue. Colonel House did warn that awarding Danzig to Poland would "leave an Alsace and Lorraine to rankle and fester for further trouble." The part of the conversation that involved secret Allied treaties contained political dynamite. Balfour conceded the existence of confidential pledges that, in his own words, divided up "the bearskin before the bear was killed."[10]

In the "Constantinople Agreements" of March 1915, Britain and France had promised Russia expansion to the south, a matter over which they had fought the tsarist empire in the Crimea less than a century before. In an exchange of notes among foreign ministers, Russia was awarded eastern Thrace and two islands in the Aegean. More important, Russia would control Constantinople, the Bosporus, and the Dardanelles. France would annex Syria and parts of Palestine and Cilicia, which is a part of Armenia.

By the terms of the treaty of London, initiated in April 1915 by Britain, France, and Russia, Italy promised to declare war against the Central Powers. In return it would receive Trieste; the Istrian peninsula;

the Dalmatian coast, including its offshore islands; and Trentino and the Tyrol, both facing its northern border. As Balfour confessed to House, Italy received "pretty much what she demanded." Within a month, it declared war on Austria-Hungary.

In February 1916, the British and French cabinets parceled much of the Ottoman Empire between them. Sir Mark Sykes, chief British adviser on Middle Eastern policy, and François Georges Picot, former French consul general in Beirut, negotiated the agreement. France received direct supervision of Lebanon and indirect control of Syria. Britain was given straight-out authority over Mesopotamia (now Iraq) from Baghdad to the Persian Gulf and a poorly defined jurisdiction of the territory stretching from east of Palestine to the Persian border.

At the April 28 meeting, House told Balfour he found such secret arrangements "all bad," creating "a breeding place for future war." He also warned against regarding Germany as a permanent enemy, as such a view would "confuse our reasoning" and lead to "mistakes." He suspected that it might not be possible to punish those responsible for the war and that the major empires of the Central Powers might ultimately remain intact.[11]

Two days later, when House and Balfour were joined by Wilson, the foreign secretary promised the president copies of the secret agreements. Though this might have been the time when Wilson could have exercised some leverage over Allied war aims, he refused to make an issue of the matter, believing that the maintenance of transatlantic ties took priority. On May 18, Balfour sent him copies, but Wilson biographer Arthur S. Link writes that the president probably filed the treaties away without reading them. Link further states that the president soon became aware of many of the general terms because the main provisions of the Treaty of London were revealed in the *New York Times*.[12] In November 1917, the Bolshevik press published Russia's secret treaties with the Allies, which two months later were reproduced in full in the *New York Evening Post*, which in turn gave publishing rights to nine other national newspapers.

Balfour and Viviani had every reason to be pleased with their visit. Their nations were assured of U.S. financial and material aid and the promise of cooperation in staving off the U-boat threat. An entire U.S. Army division was pledged to serve on the western front.

Wilson did stress U.S. diplomatic and military independence, insisting that the United States participate in the alliance as an "Associated Power," not as a full-fledged member of the "Allies." Privately, on April 14 he told a visiting member of the British Parliament that he intended to remain "detached from the Allies," particularly as he opposed recent pronouncements concerning the breakup of the Austro-Hungarian Empire. He also took issue with the Paris economic pact of June 1916, an understanding by which the Entente had sought to continue its economic war against the Central Powers once the fighting ended. Instead of a sweeping victory, Wilson desired "a negotiated settlement, whenever that was possible," with the United States "at the back of the settlement, a permanent guarantee of future peace."[13]

In short, Wilson had not yet repudiated his position of "peace without victory" as articulated before Congress on January 22, 1917, several months before the country entered the war. Indeed, in his April 2 war message, he had made explicit that he still had "the same things that I had in mind" in his previous address, that is, to "vindicate the principles of peace and justice in the life of the world as against selfish and autocratic power."[14] Certainly there lay the implication that the United States could withdraw from the struggle once it had achieved its own objectives.

The president could not have been comforted by the remarks of Lord Robert Cecil, who spoke for his government to the House of Commons on May 16, before Balfour had left the United States. Cecil denied any notion of "imperialistic conquest or aggrandizement," but would not rule out territorial changes affecting the Near East, Africa, Poland, Alsace-Lorraine, and *Italia irredenta*, which was the common term for Italy's territorial claims.[15]

By the end of June, Britain's David Lloyd George had presented his nation's public terms. Speaking on the 29th at Glasgow's St. Andrew's Hall and soon afterwards at Dundee, the prime minister sought the restoration of Belgium, the ceding of Alsace-Lorraine to France, and an independent Poland. Mesopotamia and Palestine, he continued, could never be returned to Turkey. The fate of German colonies would be settled at a peace conference that would give priority to the "wishes, desires and interests of the peoples themselves." Negotiations could only take place with "a free government of Germany," not one dominated by "the aggressive and arrogant spirit of Prussian militarism."[16]

The speech aroused diverse reactions in the United States. The Hearst press, for example, argued that such terms would make Britain "the undisputed dominant Power of the world," giving it control of the entire Near and Middle East. No people could henceforth trade overseas without its assent. Conversely, a truly genuine settlement must be based upon "a return to the status quo ante." The *New Republic*, however, expressed gratitude that the prime minister no longer expressly insisted on military victory, did not claim Mesopotamia for the British Empire, and distinguished between Bethmann Hollweg's government and the Junker class.[17]

At first, Wilson's own peace terms were decidedly vague. In his April war message, the president began by claiming that the mere existence of imperial Germany, a "natural foe to liberty," in itself threatened the world's democracies. In contrast, the United States would be fighting for "the ultimate peace of the world," "the liberation of its peoples, the German peoples included," and the "rights of nations great and small and the privilege of men everywhere to choose their way of life and of obedience." The world, he maintained, must be made "safe for democracy," a phrase still misunderstood. Wilson was not saying that the conflict was being fought on behalf of democracy. Rather, he was asserting the postwar world should involve an international order where democracy would be a viable option, able to be practiced without hindrance. He called for a "a steadfast concert for peace," manifested in "a partnership of democratic nations," yet he expressed himself in extremely general terms, such as "a league of honor, a partnership of opinion." He assured the world that the United States sought no spoils. To use Wilson's language, "no conquest," "no dominion," "no indemnities," "no material compensation." American blood, he concluded, was being shed on behalf of "a universal dominion of right by such a concert of free peoples as shall bring peace and safety to all nations and make the world itself at last free."[18] Most of Congress and the press warmly received the address.

In his "Appeal to the American People" of April 15 and his speech dedicating a Red Cross building in Washington, D.C., on May 12, Wilson again stressed that the country sought no profit or advantage but was fighting because its very principles were at stake. The president came closer to defining his goals ten days later in his message to Russia's provisional government, a document released to the press after several weeks. In an obvious effort to counteract strong sentiment for an immediate peace, he told the Russians that the United States was "fighting for liberty, the self-government, and undictated development of all peoples," tenets that must permeate "every feature of the settlement." The Germans, to the contrary, were weaving "a net of intrigue directed against nothing less than the peace and liberty of the world." He hinted at the need for an international league, saying that "the free peoples of the world" needed to "draw together in some common covenant." Because it was the status quo ante that led to the conflict, "wrongs already done" must be undone.[19]

When in late May, Wilson's cabinet met, it noted that Lord Robert Cecil and Alexandre Ribot, both French premier and foreign minister, had declared that France would continue fighting until Alsace-Lorraine was restored. Though all members agreed that this war aim was most unfortunate, the president remarked, "We are in an alliance or agreement and I have not permitted myself to think of plans & policies when war ends. We trust our allies but make no alliances & this country will be ready to see the right settlement is made when all sit at the table."[20]

When, on June 14, 1917, the president delivered his Flag Day address to about a thousand people at Sylvan Theater in Washington, D.C., he was far more strident, almost portraying Berlin in conspiratorial terms: "The war was begun by the military masters of Germany, who proved to be also the masters of Austria-Hungary. . . . They have regarded the smaller states, in particular, and the peoples who could be overwhelmed by force, as their natural tools and instruments of domination." Such intrigues included

> filling the thrones of Balkan states with German princes, putting German officers at the service of Turkey to drill her armies and make interest with her government, developing plans of sedition and rebellion in India and Egypt, setting their fires in Persia. The demands made by Austria upon Servia were a mere simple step in a plan which compassed Europe and Asia, from Berlin to Bagdad. . . . Their plan was to throw a broad belt of German military power and political control across the very centre of Europe and beyond the Mediterranean into the heart of Asia.

"Czechs, Magyars, Croats, Roumanians, Turks, Armenians, — the proud states of Bohemia and Hungary, the stout little commonwealths of the Balkans, the indomitable Turks, the subtile peoples of the East" — all would be subject to German domination. Hence the conflict was essentially "a People's War for freedom and self-government amongst all the nations of the world, a war to make the world safe for the peoples who live upon it and have made it their own." Woe, he added, "be to that man or group of men that seeks to stand in our way in this day of high resolution."[21]

At best Wilson was distorting history by placing so much war guilt on Germany and by implying that the other Central Powers were controlled by Berlin. As late as December 1916, so historian David R. Woodward notes, Wilson himself had pressed for a compromise peace that would have left the Central Powers controlling the heart of Europe and penetrating into Asia, thus being able to resume the war if they so desired. Another scholar, Lloyd E. Ambrosius, argues that had Germany been as dangerous as Wilson maintained, the president should not have waited two years to alert his countrymen. Less than a year before, Wilson had specifically denied that any single nation caused the war. "Nothing in particular started it," he told the Women's Club of Cincinnati in October 1916, "but everything in general."[22]

Wilson was also giving credence to an increasingly popular concept in Allied circles, that of *Mitteleuropa*. In 1915, German Progressive Party leader Friedrich Neumann wrote a book bearing that title. Neumann advocated a voluntary Central European economic federation centering on the German and Austro-Hungarian empires and including most of the region's small states and nationalities. Once, however, Germany began to win massive victories in the East, the concept took on a somewhat different meaning, involving German colonization of the Balkans and Near East. In a series of books and in articles in the *Atlantic Monthly*, sensationalist French publicist André Chéradame reached a wide American audience in propounding a German imperialist conspiracy at least two decades in the making.[23]

In a special edition of the Flag Day speech, the Creel Committee used the trappings of scholarship in an effort to argue that Germany had engaged in subversive activities even before the war had broken out. Pan-Germans sought to annex much of Europe, including Denmark. The effort to revive the Socialist International merely subverted the Allied cause. Germany's Social Democratic Party in reality served as "the cat's paw of the military authorities."[24] The pamphlet was published in eight languages and had a circulation of more than 6 million.

Colonel House privately found Wilson's Flag Day address containing "all errors of speech" but, ever obsequious, wrote Wilson that it had "stirred" him more than anything the president had ever done. American press reaction was generally favorable. The usually critical *New York Tribune*, which had found "too much transcendentalism" in Wilson's past orations, praised this one, warning that a successful Germany would "fasten her military yoke upon us."[25]

There was some dissent. George Sylvester Viereck conceded that German aggressions on the high seas justified U.S. entry into the war. Nevertheless, because the United States, Britain, Russia, France, and their allies were "the great landlords of the earth," owning practically its entire surface, the Teutonic powers had every reason to covet new territory. Social critic Randolph Bourne claimed that the speech marked "the collapse of American policy," finding the president substituting political annihilation of the Central Powers for his initial goal of a negotiated peace. The *New Republic* wrote, "The hesitation which the American people may feel about the war will never be removed by the inculcation of fear."[26]

The speech sought more to rally the American public than to reveal the president's genuine attitude. Biographer John Milton Cooper Jr. finds Wilson's private thoughts following "a more twisted path." In July, the president told Colonel House:

> England and France *have not the same views with regard to peace that we have* by any means. When the war is over we can force them to our way of thinking, because by that time they will, among other things, be financially in our hands, but we cannot force them now, and any attempt to speak for them or to speak our common mind would bring on disagreements which would inevitably come to the surface in public and rob the whole thing of its effect. . . . If there is to be an interchange of views at all, it ought to be between us and the liberals in Germany, with no one else brought in.[27]

By the spring of 1917, Germany had four main objectives: (1) keep its allies in the war; (2) bleed the Entente on the western front; (3) wage U-boat campaigns to starve the British; and (4) defeat Russia, thereby securing its rich grain lands while freeing troops to fight in the west. In late April, when its top leaders met at military headquarters at Kreuznach, Paul von Hindenburg, chief of the general staff, drafted his nation's most extravagant war aims to date. Germany would annex Luxembourg, the French iron ore basin on Briey-Longwy, and the Belgian armament center at Liège. It would control Belgium itself until it was ready to make a permanent alliance. It would seize Estonia, Lithuania, and eastern Poland; the rest of Poland would fall under Berlin's "predominance." Possessing such a substantial buffer zone, Germany could menace Paris, the Thames estuary, and Petrograd. These aims were approved by Kaiser Wilhelm II and initialed by Chancellor Bethmann Hollweg. The chancellor did qualify his support by declaring such conditions could only be realized if Germany emerged totally victorious. On May 15, Bethmann Hollweg, a genius at equivocation, told his nation's upper house, the Bundesrat, that he sought a peace with Russia that would leave "no sting and no discord."[28]

Because, however, of military stalemate in the west and economic hardship at home, peace sentiment was growing within Germany. On July 19, under the prompting of Matthias Erzberger, leader of the Zentrumspartei, the lower house, named the Reichstag, passed a peace resolution by a vote of 212 to 126. It endorsed a settlement based upon "mutual understanding and lasting reconciliation among the nations." In such an arrangement, there would be no "forced acquisitions" of territory or economic subjugation. Other goals included an end to blockades, freedom of the seas, and the creation of "international juridical organizations." As long, however, as the Allies sought conquest, Germans would "stand as one man" in continuing the war. Chancellor Georg Michaelis, in office for only five days, stressed that Germany would cede no land of its own.[29]

Two days later, Lloyd George, speaking in Queen's Hall, London, responded to the German proposal: "I see a sham independence for Belgium, a sham democracy for Germany, a sham peace for Europe." When, late that month, Ramsay MacDonald, Labor member of the House of Commons, introduced a resolution endorsing the Reichstag resolution, he was voted down 148–19.[30]

Within the United States, the German resolution was debated. Senate Democratic whip J. Hamilton Lewis found it "a righteous and appropriate hour for us seriously to consider the bid that Germany made for peace." Senator William King countered that German dreams equaled those of ancient Rome and Charlemagne. If necessary, said Senator Porter McCumber, the United States would fight for a generation to defeat Prussia.[31]

Such negative responses were echoed in the much of the press. The *North American Review*, dismissing the Reichstag as "a debating society," called its resolution a mere reaffirmation of Germany's desire to "put her yoke upon the neck of the world." Germany, it claimed, was in the hands of "the hair-brained Crown Prince, the satanic Ludendorff and the bully Hindenburg." The far more liberal *Nation*, noting that Michaelis had remarked that he would offer his own independent interpretation of the resolution, was reminded of "Andrew Jackson undertaking to enforce the Constitution only as he interpreted it." To the pro-administration New York *World*, Germany was still propounding "the peace of the gunman."[32]

The American Union Against Militarism, composed of such reformers as settlement worker Lillian Wald and editor Max Eastman, called for accepting the Reichstag's offer. Conceding that the legislature was not truly representative of the German people, the AUAM nonetheless claimed that a positive response would strengthen a peace-minded population against its ruling autocracy. Viereck's *American Weekly* claimed Michaelis sought "an immediate peace with honor without loss of territorial integrity in any part of the world." The Hearst press accused both Michaelis and Lloyd George of "schoolboy talk," imploring the United States to call a conference of the belligerents. In a signed editorial, Hearst himself endorsed a peace without indemnities or annexations, arguing that it would free Belgium and France from German occupation.[33]

By now certain voices were pressing both Wilson and the Allies to offer peace terms. On July 26, Senator William E. Borah, claiming that the Central Powers were winning the war, decried talk concerning "the future of Constantinople and the Bagdad railway," "the rehabilitation of certain nations of Europe," "the redistribution of European territory," and "the establishment of democracy in Europe." Instead, the United States should support Russia's opposition to indemnities and annexations and fight for purely American principles and goals. In August, Socialist congressman Meyer London introduced a resolution calling for an interparliamentary conference to discuss peace terms; Senator La Follette presented one asking for a restatement of Allied conditions. Senator Lawrence Sherman sponsored a resolution calling upon the president to confer with Allied representatives. The meeting would draft a peace agenda consisting of arms limitation, restoration of invaded territory, rejection of indemnities, and freedom of the seas.[34]

Early in August, the *New Republic* offered a rationale for German behavior:

> Suppose the United States had had for years as its northern neighbor not Canada, but Imperial Russia, autocratically ruled and in command of several hundred millions of population. Suppose Mexico were a highly civilized and powerful state like France, eager to recapture from us Texas and California. Suppose an island as near to us as Cuba were our greatest commercial rival and had the largest navy in the world. Suppose we had instead of thousands of miles of coast on two oceans, a few hundred miles on one, and a congeries of Balkan States between us and the other. . . . Can anyone doubt that our own junkers would have advocated annexations . . . as a means of making our future military and economic position more secure?[35]

Wilson directly addressed Senator Lewis's call to respond to the Reichstag resolution, personally telling him on August 6 that the time for negotiation was not ripe but that he would act at the appropriate moment. Several days later, he informed officers of the Atlantic Fleet that the United States was fighting "not only for ourselves, but everybody else that loves liberty under God's heaven, and, therefore, we are in some peculiar sense the trustees of liberty."[36]

At this point, the Vatican put in its own peace bid. On the Feast of the Assumption, August 15, 1917, Pope Benedict XV released a full-scale list of proposals drafted just two weeks earlier. Appealing for an end to the "useless massacre," he endorsed reduction of armaments, arbitration of international questions, freedom of the seas, renunciation of reparations, and evacuation and reciprocal restitution of occupied territory. Belgium, France, and the German colonies in Africa were specifically mentioned. Peaceful discussion of territorial problems would take into account "the aspirations of the population." A "spirit of equity and justice" must guide such questions as Alsace-Lorraine, "the old Kingdom of Poland," Armenia, and the Balkan states. All belligerents should cancel claims for damages inflicted.[37]

The proposal emerged from preliminary explorations. In May, papal diplomat Eugenio Pacelli, later to become Pope Pius XII, had been sent to Munich as nuncio to explore Germany's terms. In July, he presented Benedict's seven-point memorandum to Foreign Secretary Arthur Zimmermann; it later became the basis of the pontiff's August plea. The pope, fearing the growing influence of the annexationist German General Staff, wanted to act quickly. As noted by historian John J. Snell, the plan contained many basic principles of Wilson's, whose mediation moves the Vatican had favored. The complete restoration of Belgium would help satisfy the war-weary British leaders. The pope thought he could count on the support of Roman Catholic leaders within the belligerent nations and, because his schema incorporated many demands of European socialists, might win their backing.[38]

Responses among the belligerents varied. Georg Michaelis, now German chancellor, first claimed that the papal message "corresponds generally with our own view," but he expressed "reserve with regard to details." In an official reply several weeks later, Berlin welcomed the effort, claiming it would support every proposal compatible with its "vital interest." Speaking personally, Kaiser Wilhelm II claimed to give the overture his "whole-hearted support," yet simply spoke vaguely of "uninhibited competition with nations enjoying equal rights and equal esteem." Vienna initially accepted withdrawal from occupied territories but also wanted to include British evacuation of Gibraltar, Malta, and the Suez Canal. In its official response, timed with Germany's announcement, the Hapsburg Empire stressed freedom of the seas. Charles I, emperor of Austria and king of Hungary, was slightly more concrete than Wilhelm, claiming he was ready to negotiate for compulsory arbitration and mutual disarmament.[39]

Allied responses were predictably hostile. Balfour found both restoration and reparation necessary; guarantees were needed against any "repetition of the horrors." Lloyd George offered an indirect reply, stressing eventual Allied victory. French foreign minister Jules Cambon suspected that the pope specifically sought to aid Austria and to strengthen both his own power and that of the Roman Catholic Church. Prominent French legislator Clemenceau referred to the "boche Pope," while Italian foreign minister Baron Georgio Sidney Sonnino considered Benedict's proposal "a fine nothing." Serbian prime minister Nikola Pašić attacked the pope for ignoring the real victims of the war, that is, the Czechs, Slovaks, and most Yugoslavs. Czech leaders Thomas Masaryk and Eduard Beneš called the pope the agent of Count Ottokar Czernin, Austria's foreign minister.[40]

Within the United States, senators debated the appeal. "Coming from the Vatican," remarked J. Hamilton Lewis, "the whole world must listen." William Alden Smith (R-Mich.) wanted to give the proposals some weight, noting that "all peace-loving peoples" sought to end the conflict. Asle Gronna hoped for a honorable peace that would cost no further "slaughter of American lives."[41]

More senators, however, expressed opposition. John Sharp Williams declared that Germany must first withdraw its armies from Belgium and Serbia. To William King, only a military victory could resolve the fate of Alsace-Lorraine. Germany, warned Henry Ashurst, must begin by restoring all conquered countries and pay an indemnity for "her wild career of blood and devastation." John K. Shields (D-Tenn.) wanted Germany "brought to her knees."[42]

Hearst papers pushed one single message: "The European Belligerents Must Either Accept the Pope's Proposal of Negotiations or Face Warfare and Almost Certain Destruction." The pope's suggestions, they argued, should be submitted to referenda in all the belligerent powers. Because Russia was on the verge of still another revolution and Italy was experiencing hardship, the newspaper chain predicted parlays within several months.[43]

Arguing to the contrary, the *New York Times* spoke for far more of the American press in opposing the papal initiative. By proposing immediate restoration of all enemy territory, Benedict left untouched the all-important conditions of peace, which included the return of Italy's and France's "lost provinces."[44]

The Socialist press asserted that Benedict was echoing its own views. Ex-congressman Victor Berger argued that "nothing short of a

Socialist revolution in the European countries, including Germany and France, can stop this war; the Pope can not." Pro-war Socialist Charles Edward Russell conceded that Benedict was driven by "the most humane of motives." He warned, however, that the proposal did not provide for the return of German colonies, thereby enabling Berlin to resume a "grasping policy of colonization" that would lead to a more terrible war within two decades. The German American press was usually skeptical, finding that the pontiff lacked the influence to play a major role. Viereck proved an exception. Putting Benedict on the cover of his *American Weekly*, he saw the pope's views identical to Wilson's policy of "peace without victory."[45]

Austria's role was occasionally highlighted. *Nation* editor Simeon Strunsky discerned its government behind the papal move while concluding that Benedict's terms leaned more to the Allies than to the Germans. The *New Republic*, too, perceived the proposals rooted in the governments of the Central Powers. It would not, however, dismiss them, for the papal tenets recognized the principles of nationality and left Alsace-Lorraine open to compromise. The magazine called for negotiations: "The German government could not accept the terms proposed by the Pope without an acknowledgment of practical defeat."[46]

Religious journals manifested a Roman Catholic–Protestant split. To the Jesuit weekly *America*, any nation refusing to heed Benedict's call "writes itself down not as a vindicator of justice, but as a monster lustful of men's blood." Yet the *Outlook*, edited by reformist Protestant minister Lyman Abbott, accused the pope of believing in religious and political absolutism and hence was sympathetic to the Hohenzollerns. Moreover, his natural sympathies lay with Austria, "the one great ultramontane government left in the civilized world."[47]

Immediately upon learning of the papal bid, Colonel House suggested Wilson respond positively. Fearing Teutonic victory in the East, he found it more important that Russia "weld itself into a virile republic than Germany be beaten to her knees." If its provisional government succumbed to further "internal disorder," Berlin would dominate it politically and economically. Conversely, if Russia proved itself a sustainable democracy, in time the Reich would be forced to establish a representative government at home. Restoring a status quo ante bellum would permit the Entente to "emancipate" Austria from

Prussia. If Turkey was sustained as an independent nation and Constantinople and the Straits internationalized, the thorny question of Allied partition of Asia Minor could be avoided. House added that the war, which he saw as already unpopular at home, would become even more disliked as time went on. A settlement made during the oncoming winter would place the United States at the apex of its power.[48]

In his initial response to Colonel House, Wilson expressed suspicion of Benedict's plan. He claimed that no belligerent accepted the pontiff's terms, that one could not take the word of Germany's "morally bankrupt" government, and that a return to the status quo ante would leave the world in the same precarious condition it had been before 1914. House in turn replied that only the president could enforce peace terms of "liberalism and justice." The Allies were weak, the Germans even weaker. Russia's March revolution had put "the fear of God" into the hearts of German "imperialists," who were continuing the war because the Allies intimated territorial dismemberment and economic collapse. In his diary, House wrote that Wilson would make "a colossal blunder if he treats the note lightly and shuts the door abruptly."[49]

The president's reluctance to reply received strong reinforcement from Lansing, who stressed that the pope sought above all the preservation of the Hapsburg Empire, "the main support of the Vatican for half a century." The pontiff, Lansing noted, favored restoration of Belgium and Poland's Catholic monarchy but remained silent concerning Turkey and the restoration of the Balkan states, even of Serbia's former possessions. A day later, Lansing called the papal plan extremely one-sided: it condoned the harshness meted out to Serbia and Montenegro, the suffering of Rumania, the failure to compensate devastated northern France, and the damage German submarines were causing merchant vessels.[50]

By then, however, Wilson had decided to reply directly to the Vatican. On August 27, he released a public letter to the pontiff, not consulting the Allies beforehand. After thanking Benedict for his "humane and generous motives," the president denied that the present German government would support the pope's proposals. Berlin had "secretly planned to dominate the world" and had "swept a whole continent within the tide of blood," including "the blood of innocent women and children also and of the helpless poor." He repeated the distinction made in his war message between Germany's rulers and its people, who were controlled by a "ruthless master" and "who have themselves suffered all things in this war, which they did not choose." No peace could be made based on "punitive damages, the dismemberment of empires, the establishment of selfish and exclusive leagues," but only on "justice and fairness and the common rights of mankind." Needed were German guarantees concerning disarmament, arbitration, territorial adjustments, and the reconstitution of small nations.[51]

The president had skillfully dissociated himself from the territorial aims of the Allies while encouraging liberals in all the warring countries. Wilson biographer Link posits that had Germany's civilian leaders taken control from its military and sought a peace conference, the president would have eagerly responded, even making a separate agreement if necessary. Wilson felt sufficiently confident to fear no rupture with the Allies, placing tremendous faith in his ability to marshal world opinion behind a generous settlement.[52]

Within the United States, Wilson's reply met with almost universal accord, the *Literary Digest* noting surprising unanimity. The pro-Wilson New York *World* called the note "a new Emancipation Proclamation" for the German people themselves. Always given to superlatives, House wrote Wilson that it was "the most remarkable document ever written." To Ambassador Page, the White House response served as the best contribution the United States had thus far made to the war effort. Even the anti-Wilson *New York Tribune* hoped that it would lead the German people to liberate themselves, thus paving the way for a negotiated peace.[53]

Praise also came from those who stressed negotiation. The Hearst press saw no essential difference between the pope's formula and those of Wilson and the Russians. All desired a settlement without indemnities or annexation, not continuation of a war based upon territorial acquisition. The news chain specifically opposed granting Mesopotamia, Syria, Palestine, and Germany's African colonies to Britain; dividing German and Austrian territory; and allocating concessions in China among other Allies. "Without firing a shot in battle," it soon added, "the United States has won the greatest and most momentous victory ever won in the history of mankind."[54]

Socialists, too, expressed enthusiasm. The *Appeal to Reason* endorsed Wilson's opposition to punitive damages and dismemberment of empires; Meyer London predicted that Wilson's message would cause the conflict itself to "break down."[55]

Though Bernard Ridder, publisher of the *New Yorker Staats-Zeitung*, sought to rally German Americans behind Wilson's statement, some of his kinsmen remained critical. To *Issues and Events*, Wilson had composed "the most pre-eminently sane and statesmanlike note which has appeared," but the weekly found the reply too accusatory in tone. The German people, it claimed, would probably interpret it as an effort from an outside power to dictate their form of government, adding that even Germany's Socialists desired the monarchy. Viereck's *American Weekly* carried a story by Hearst's pro-German correspondent William Bayard Hale, who maintained that Wilson's response would only strengthen the resistance of the German people, for they saw themselves encircled by a league of enemies bent on crushing them. How, queried Viereck, could Wilson ask Germans to emancipate themselves from their government if at home he suppresses the People's Council, persecutes the Socialist Party, excludes radical publications from the mails, and denies free speech?[56]

Historians differ as to the president's wisdom, several finding it establishing Wilson as the ideological leader of the Allies, others seeing it as unclear and naive.[57] Given Hindenburg's war aims as presented to Germany's leaders in April, Wilson was undoubtedly correct in finding Germany obstinate as far as substantive terms were concerned. Wilson was continuing, however, to engage in conspiratorial rhetoric without offering any real follow-through of his own.

In late September, German chancellor Michaelis addressed the Reichstag. He claimed the United States was resorting to "unheard-of terrorism" to awaken a "war spirit which is lacking." Concerning war aims, "any open declaration of this kind could only have a disturbing effect and would injure German interests; it would not bring peace nearer but would have a tendency to prolong war." Wilson's effort to sow discord between the German people and government was hopeless.[58]

Wilson's response had little effect on the Allies. Admittedly some leading Englishmen endorsed the president's message. Lord Robert

Cecil cabled Colonel House: "We greatly admire the note and it has been received with much satisfaction by our press." The day it appeared, former foreign secretary Sir Edward Grey said Wilson's messages "fill me with satisfaction."[59]

The colonel soon learned just how comprehensive British war aims remained. In November, House was in London as Wilson's representative to an Inter-Allied Conference scheduled to meet soon in Paris. Conversing with Lloyd George, House discovered that the British sought Germany's African colonies, an independent Arabia under British control, an independent Armenia, the internationalization of the Dardanelles, and a new Zionist state in Palestine under either British or U.S. supervision. "It is strange," House mused, "that so brilliant a man could [on occasion] talk such nonsense."[60] Not surprisingly, France kept holding out for Alsace-Lorraine, Italy for enforcing the Treaty of London.

In mid-November, addressing the American Federation of Labor convention in Buffalo, Wilson again claimed that Germany had started the war. Moreover, he observed, Berlin totally dominated Europe from Austria-Hungary to Asia Minor and was "determined that the political power of the world shall belong to her." The president, however, felt confident about the ultimate triumph of his aims. Referring to Bolshevik peace bids ("the dreamers in Russia"), he told the delegates, "What I am opposed to is not the feeling of the pacifists, but their stupidity. My heart is with them, but my mind has a contempt for them. I want peace, but I know how to get it, and they do not."[61]

In December, House wrote Wilson from Paris, where he sought an Allied resolution repudiating any war fought for aggression or indemnity. Wilson cabled his full support: "Our people and Congress will not fight for any selfish aim on the part of any belligerent, with the possible exception of Alsace-Lorraine, least of all for divisions of territory such as have been contemplated in Asia Minor."[62]

If Wilson was still speaking in generalized terms, his chief and most visible foe, Theodore Roosevelt, began presenting some concrete war aims of his own. In October, he published *Foes of Our Own Household*, wherein he asserted that Britain and Japan should keep the colonies they had conquered. Poland should be made independent, with Galicia and Posen included and with boundaries reaching to the

Baltic. A Greater Bohemia should be formed, composed of Czechs, Moravians, and Slovaks. All Yugoslavs should be gathered in one state. The Turks should be ousted from Europe, Constantinople being "a free commonwealth of the Straits" or given to "democratic Russia." Arabia should be an independent Moslem state. Probably Armenia should be independent. Also on his agenda was the return of northern Schleswig to the Danes; full autonomy to Lithuania and Finland; Irish home rule within the empire; the awarding of Alsace-Lorraine to France and Rumanian Hungary to Rumania; the return of Italian ports held by Austria; the restoration and indemnification of Belgium; and full protection of the Syrians—Christians, Druses, and Moslems alike.[63] Wilson had by no means been so concrete.

Another highly publicized bid for immediate peace negotiations came on November 29 from Henry C. K. Petty-Fitzmaurice, the fifth Marquis of Lansdowne, who published an open letter in the *London Daily Telegraph*. Leader of the Conservative Party in the House of Lords, Lord Lansdowne embodied the British establishment in his own person, having been successively governor-general of Canada, viceroy of India, and war secretary. As foreign secretary from 1900 to 1905, he negotiated crucial alliances with France and Japan. He had lost two sons in the current conflict.

In his missive, he argued that continuation of the war would ruin the civilized world. It would also lead to another conflict, more deadly than the current one. Calling for an Allied declaration of war aims, he stressed that the Entente should proclaim that it would not annihilate Germany, impose an unpopular form of government upon it, or deny it a place among the world's "great commercial communities." Rather, the Allies should forgo all efforts at retaliation or reparation. To replace the existing international order, he envisioned one based upon compulsory arbitration backed by military coercion.[64]

In Britain, liberal, left, and pacifist elements offered Lansdowne their support. Former prime minister Herbert Asquith defended the effort to clarify British war aims. Lord Robert Cecil claimed he did not find the letter's substance objectionable. Lloyd George, however, feared that the letter would make any declaration on war aims more difficult, as it might convey a "wrong impression." Chancellor of the Exchequer Andrew Bonar Law called Lansdowne's bid "a national misfortune." The prominent British publisher Lord Northcliffe remarked, "I spent half an hour trying to find out what Lansdowne meant in his letter, and came to the conclusion that the old gentleman was suffering from paranoia."[65]

American reactions were predictable. Theodore Roosevelt claimed Lansdowne would "leave oppressed peoples under the yoke of Austria, Turkey, and Bulgaria" and place "the liberty-loving nations of mankind at the ultimate mercy of the triumphant militarism and capitalism of the German autocracy." Taft called the letter "the right thing at the wrong time," vaguely adding that it could be misconstrued. A surprising response came from the anti-Wilson *New York Sun*, which praised the Briton for stressing the need for Allied war aims, something that could trigger a German desire for peace.[66]

Both critics and supporters noted Lansdowne's aristocratic background. Viereck's *American Weekly* called him "the brain of Great Britain," one who foresaw "a world-wide cataclysm that will dwarf the French Revolution." Journalist Ray Stannard Baker, visiting Europe as special agent for the State Department, described the British leader as representing "old rich aristocrats and captains of industry who see their wealth and power dribbling away in income taxes." The *Outlook* found him "a tory of the tories," who in France would be an imperialist, in Germany a Junker.[67]

When, on December 4, 1917, Wilson delivered his State of the Union address to Congress, his focus was not on any peace agenda but on a call for a declaration of war against the Hapsburg Empire. That nation, he declared, was "not her own mistress but simply the vassal of the German Government." Even, however, as he used the language of belligerency, he added that "we do not wish in any way to impair or to rearrange the Austro-Hungarian Empire. It is no affair of ours what they do with their own life, either industrially or politically." Concerning the Balkan peninsula and the Turkish Empire, he simply sought to secure for those people "the right and opportunity to make their own lives safe." Both Bulgaria and the Ottoman Empire remained "tools" of Germany. Nevertheless, since they were not yet standing in "the direct path of our necessary action," it was unnecessary to make war against them.[68]

Since April, the Wilson administration had sought to remain at peace with Austria-Hungary, hoping it could be weaned from Germany. On May 1, Lansing assured Count Adam Tarnowski, the ambassador-designate to the United States, that when the "entire miserable business" ended, "Austria will not have a merciless enemy in America." As late as November 1917, the foreign ministers of Britain, France, and Italy, fearing that Russia would soon leave the war, asked Colonel House to explore peace terms with Vienna.[69]

To break with Austria would not be easy. Wilson's April war message had stressed entrance into the conflict as a defensive measure against Germany. Although he specifically noted that Austria-Hungary had endorsed Germany's submarine warfare against American ships, he continued that the Hapsburg Empire had not itself engaged in it.[70] Because the War Department sought to limit U.S. military activity to the western front, support for besieged Italy, engaged in bloody conflict with Austria, must be purely symbolic. Indeed, the only U.S. military aid to Italy came a few weeks later in the form of an ambulance corps.

Nonetheless, sentiment for war against Austria was increasing. By November, Roosevelt sought the breakup of both Austria and Turkey, stressing "liberty for the subject races in both countries." Both entities, he maintained, were not "nations" but "racial tyrannies." To the *Outlook*, Austria served as "the gateway through which Prussia must pass to the goal of Pan-Germany." That month, the *New York Times* noted widespread sentiment for war against all the Central Powers. Austrian submarines, it claimed, operated against American merchant vessels, its ports sheltered these U-boats, and its soldiers fought alongside German troops in Italy. War would justify legal measures against Austrian, Bulgarian, and Turkish spies and against foreign dynamiters operating within the United States. On November 26, Senate Democratic whip J. Hamilton Lewis and William J. Stone, chairman of the Senate Foreign Relations Committee, sought war against Austria, Bulgaria, and Turkey, though Lewis opposed Italian plans for seizing Hapsburg territory. In writing Wilson, Lansing conceded that "we have not a very strong case against Austria as far as hostile acts are concerned." He did fear subversion from "a very considerable body of Austrian subjects in this country."[71]

Wilson consulted no one about his decision. Historian Betty Miller Unterberger sees the Bolshevik Revolution, the Italian disaster at Caporetto, and U.S. participation on the SWC (where all the other participants had long been at war with Austria) all playing a role.[72]

Some congressional leaders regretted that Wilson excluded Turkey and Bulgaria in his fresh war message. Seeking hostilities against all three powers, Speaker of the House Champ Clark commented, "It is ridiculous to fight one half of the enemy and not the other half." Henry Flood (D-Va.) accused Austria of sinking two American ships, one in April, another in November. If the war ended, said Representative Clarence Miller, with the Turks still massacring Christians, it would have been fought in vain. He continued, "We must not forget that every friend of Germany is our foe." Senator Lodge thought, "It would be difficult to find in history a meaner or baser figure than the present sovereign of Bulgaria." He suspected King Ferdinand of conspiring to have his leading political rival murdered! Nonetheless, he called for deferring war against the two powers so as to save the president embarrassment.[73]

At least one congressman defended Wilson's decision to focus upon Austria alone. Henry Flood argued that the United States had spent $20 million in support of missionary and educational institutions in Turkey. Besides, despite the military alliance with Germany, Flood claimed that the Turks had always remained suspicious of Berlin. He quoted the Bulgarian minister to the United States, who denied that his nation would fight outside its own territory.[74]

When on December 7 votes were tallied, the Senate unanimously backed Wilson, debating for less than an hour. La Follette, who was caught in the Capitol subway and thereby missed the vote, claimed he would only have supported the declaration on one condition: the United States would refuse to be bound by any Allied agreement to deprive any nation of territory. With the exception of Meyer London and Ernest Lundeen, the entire House supported the move. Dissenter London called himself "a teetotaler," refusing to take "the first intoxicating drink." In response, Percy Quin labeled the Socialist congressman an "adjunct of the Kaiser," who espoused "flannel-mouthed anarchy." Wilson signed the resolution the same day.[75]

In a sense, had Wilson sought to weaken the polyglot Hapsburg Empire, his move was counterproductive. As noted by Unterberger, its official press immediately used the war message to discourage its subject nationalities from seeking independence. Wilson long feared that raising the specter of dismemberment would inhibit possible negotiations with the Hapsburg monarchy. Therefore, he leaned towards supporting the creation of a federation within the monarchy, not dividing the empire into independent states.[76]

Much else in the president's annual message was quite predictable and typically Wilsonian: the need for victory with "every power and resource we possess"; negotiation only with "properly accredited representatives" of the German people; liberation of both Eastern and Western Europe from "the Prussian menace"; a peace based on "generosity and justice, to the exclusion of all selfish claims to advantage even on the part of the victors"; repudiation of "any such covenants of selfishness and compromise as were entered into at the Congress of Vienna"; the preservation of Germany's independence and "peaceful enterprise"; the need to educate the Russians as to the Allies' liberal war aims. Ending his address by referring to the war's "just and holy cause," he exhorted: "The hand of God is laid upon the nations. He will show them favor, I devoutly believe, only if they rise to the clear heights of his own justice and mercy."[77]

The speech received almost unanimous approval. The chamber and galleries frequently rose and burst into applause. Hundreds of dailies endorsed his position. Even Roosevelt claimed that Wilson had set forth "in admirable language" the nation's "firm resolve" for total victory. The Hearst press called it "one of the best state papers of the times." "I am on your side," wrote Louis Kopelin, editor of the Socialist *Appeal to Reason*.[78]

Among the Allies, there was strong endorsement. *Current Opinion* noted that British statesmen were competing in efforts to imitate Wilson. Lansdowne saw the speech resembling his own views. Colonel House, then in Paris, reported a favorable reception in France. Austria's foreign minister, Count Ottokar Czernin, though obviously not welcoming war with the United States, expressed gratitude that Wilson did not seek to dismantle his empire. The German press was predictably hostile.[79]

Amid the euphoria at home and abroad, the *New Republic* warned against misconstruing the president. Wilson did not envision, as Allied leaders surmised, a decisive military victory as essential to his war aims; total defeat of the enemy remained optional. The Allies had already made clear it had rejected the president's peace agenda.[80]

As historian David Stevenson notes, during 1917 the increasingly vocal Wilson had played a surprisingly small role in Allied policymaking. Yet without significant U.S. aid, Stevenson argues, Britain, France, and Italy would most likely have been forced to compromise with the Germans. Wilson not only supplied economic, maritime, and psychological support; he backed them diplomatically by rejecting the Stockholm conference and papal peace note. By the end of the year, he had rejected the status quo ante; U.S. power would be applied to prevent any such outcome.[81]

American financial support was particularly crucial. In late June, the British Treasury faced bankruptcy, only being rescued when early in April, U.S. treasury secretary McAdoo authorized $200 million to Britain and France, the first of many massive loans. By the end of the war, the United States had lent $7.3 billion to the Allies.

Already the president was realizing the crucial need to articulate a far more detailed vision of his postwar order. It was becoming increasingly difficult to rally war sentiment in the increasingly exhausted Allied countries. Lenin and Trotsky, just catapulted to power, embodied an ecumenical appeal with their indictments of the "imperialist war" and an inevitable world revolution. Wilson found himself forced to meet this challenge.

ELEVEN
WILSON'S PEACE OFFENSIVE, 1918

IF, FOR THE ALLIES, 1917 HAD BEEN THEIR WORST YEAR, FOR the Central Powers it was the best one. On major fronts of the war—western, Russian, and Italian—the Entente confronted either stalemate or defeat. In December, Colonel Harvey's *North American Review* confessed, "This is the darkest moment since the battle of the Marne." As winter was approaching, even the United States appeared crippled, experiencing clogged railroads and a massive coal shortage. In January 1918, Senator Porter McCumber predicted it would take 7 million U.S. troops to defeat the Germans. Just a month later, Interior Secretary Franklin K. Lane forecast two more years of conflict; British press mogul Lord Northcliffe envisioned four to eight. By March 1918, journalist Ray Stannard Baker reported from London that Britain was close to starvation.[1]

One warning was particularly alarming. In February, pro-war Socialist William English Walling wrote that the continuing appeal of Russian Bolshevism, with its call to end the conflict, could lead to an international revolutionary strike, beginning in Italy or France, spreading to Britain, and reaching such U.S. cities as Chicago, New York, and

San Francisco. Even if, he continued, Germany alone was affected and its current government overturned, the Reichstag Socialists would not surrender the spoils of war or Berlin's domination over the old Russian Empire. Secretary of State Robert Lansing found Walling's analysis "helpful and sound," warning that "disorder and anarchy" were more dangerous than "intelligent despotism."[2]

For months the president had seen the need to articulate his vision of the postwar world order. In early September 1917, Wilson asked Colonel House to gather a group of specialists. Their assignment: to examine dispassionately the claims of the varied belligerent nations so that the United States could formulate its own position. House immediately responded with great enthusiasm. Yet in private he was concerned about the sheer magnitude of the task and found that he would be usurping the prerogative of the State Department. Lansing claimed to harbor no objection, however, and drew up a memorandum suggesting topics that this task force should cover. Of primary concern were boundaries between countries, a problem that often centered on the claims of conflicting nationalities in hotly contested areas. Examples included Alsace-Lorraine, Schleswig-Holstein, the Danzig region, and Macedonia. Should, the secretary of state asked, existing colonies remain unchecked, "without a limitation as to the character of the government, commercial freedom, and economic opportunity to other nations?"[3]

The group's research director, James T. Shotwell, a Columbia University historian, suggested naming the task force the "Inquiry." Its sheer blandness would provide a "blind to the general public, but would serve to identify it among the initiated."[4] The body eventually numbered about 150 scholars who created at least 1,200 maps and submitted 2,000 separate reports, some several hundred pages each. Until that point, it was the largest group of scholars ever assembled in government service. It was also very much of an "old boy's network," more than half of its leading members having ties to Harvard, Yale, Princeton, Columbia, and the University of Chicago. Representatives from southern and middle western institutions were often notable by their absence.

Ever the manipulator, House appointed his brother-in-law to head this team. Admittedly, Sidney Mezes possessed formal academic qualifications—a Harvard doctorate, past presidency of the University of Texas, current presidency of the City College of New York. However, the man lacked organizational skills and was ignorant concerning international relations; his specialty was the philosophy of religion. By August 1918, the Inquiry's de facto leader was Isaiah Bowman, director of the American Geographical Society, whose Manhattan offices served as Inquiry headquarters. Because Bowman specialized in Latin America, a disproportionate share of its funds was allocated to a cartographical study of a region bearing little relationship to peacemaking. Certain members possessed genuine skill, among them Shotwell, an excellent administrator; treasurer David Hunter Miller, accomplished in drafting legal memoranda; and journalist Walter Lippmann, instrumental in drawing up the territorial provisions of Wilson's Fourteen Points. House, absorbed in wider matters of diplomacy, offered little supervision.

In early November, Director Mezes presented an agenda that was nothing if not comprehensive. The research body should seek a peace fair to all, that is, one designed to prevent "planting the seeds of jealousy and discontent," which could only breed "fresh wars." It should explore postwar reconstruction, international business and law, proposals for an association of nations, and the problems of "suppressed, oppressed and backward peoples." Wilson personally stressed the need to honor "the just claims" of such larger states as Russia, Austria, and Germany regarding the main routes of commerce and the world's raw materials.[5]

In some ways, there was less to the Inquiry than met the eye. Many of the studies involved special pleading. Much research drew upon data easily available in secondary sources. Crucial topics, such as socialism, remained untouched. Few participants had been trained in the areas they would research. For example, of the four scholars assigned to cover Italy and Austria-Hungary, only two could qualify as experts. As Inquiry historian Lawrence E. Gelfand notes, "Youth and lack of specific qualifications characterized the men and women who worked on the Inquiry." In fairness to the staff, American universities had long focused on diplomatic history and international law; they usually neglected a world beyond Europe and the Americas. Yet, if the Wilson administration ignored the Inquiry's studies on Russia, Africa, and the Pacific Islands, it drew upon those on Europe and on international organization.[6] There is no evidence that the president himself read most of its reports.

In December 1917, House left Paris without being able to convince Allied leaders to abandon their imperialistic war aims. Meeting with Wilson on the 18th, he learned in just fifteen minutes of conversation on the topic that the president sought "to formulate the war aims of the United States." "I never knew a man who did things so casually," he confided to his diary.[7]

Finally, the Inquiry was given a concrete task. It went to work immediately. Within four days, it drafted a preliminary memorandum signed by Mezes, Lippmann, and Miller. In offering findings that would soon lie at the crux of the president's Fourteen Points, the authors noted a universal longing for peace, a popular sense that "the old diplomacy" was bankrupt, major expectations for a league of nations, and fear of "social revolution all over the world." Only "revolutionary measures about property" could solve the ascending toll of war debts. The United States would "show the way" to British and French liberals, who would follow the president's "liberal diplomatic offensive, because they would find in that offensive an invaluable support for their internal domestic troubles." Moreover, such a stance would "assure the administration the support of that great mass of the American people who desire an idealistic solution," doing "more than any other thing to create in this country the sort of public opinion that the President needs in order to carry through the program he has outlined."

The three authors sought the breakup of what was often called *Mittleuropa*, that is, German control of East Central Europe. One step involved the increased democratization of Germany. Reform of the Prussian franchise was needed, as it was heavily skewed in favor of the wealthier classes. Also needed was the granting of greater representation to southern and eastern Germany and to the large cities of Prussia, areas where the pro-peace Progressive, Center, and Social Democratic Parties were strongest. Germany's fear of exclusion from the world's markets and raw materials could both threaten and lure it into "a vision of world cooperation." Noting the unrest among the Czechs and South Slavs, the memo said: *"Our policy must therefore consist first in stirring up of nationalist discontent, and then in refusing to accept*

*the extreme logic of this discontent, which would be the dismember-
ment of Austria-Hungary.*[8] This memorandum, revised on January 2,
1918, was given by House to Wilson two days later.

Ironically, it was Lloyd George, not Wilson, who took the first
initiative in advancing liberal war aims, doing so in a way that did
not please the president. Addressing the Trades Union Congress on
January 5, the prime minister outlined goals that could well be called
Wilsonian. He spoke with the full approval of the War Cabinet and
relied heavily upon a draft written by Lord Robert Cecil, then acting
foreign secretary, and Jan Christian Smuts, former general in the Boer
army and a member of the War Cabinet. Lloyd George denied that
Britain was seeking to destroy Germany, Austria-Hungary, or Turkey.
Nor would it alter Germany's imperial form of government. He desired restoration and reparation for Belgium, Serbia, Montenegro, and
restoration of occupied portions of France, Italy, and Rumania. In regard to Alsace-Lorraine, he stood by the French demand for "a reconsideration of the great wrong of 1871," the year of France's defeat by
Prussia. He was most circumspect concerning territories of Russia
occupied by German troops. If the new Bolshevik regime negotiated
separately with Berlin, the Allies had "no means of intervening to arrest the catastrophe which is assuredly befalling their country." He
noted Count Czernin's remarks of December 23, in which the Austrian foreign minister denied that the Central Powers sought to rob
any nation of its political independence. Lloyd George found such
language far too loose, arguing that such states could still be subject to
crippling interference.

Turning to the status of the Hapsburg Empire, Lloyd George
sought to "square the circle." He denied that Britain sought its dissolution. At the same time, he endorsed "genuine self-government on
true democratic principles" for those subject "nationalities who have
long desired it." Similarly, he urged the satisfaction of "the legitimate
claims of the Italians for union with those of their own race and
tongue," adding that he desired that "justice be done" to Rumanians
in their "legitimate aspirations." He spoke of an independent Poland
composed of "all genuinely Polish elements." The British government
did not "challenge the maintenance of the Turkish empire in the home-
lands of the Turkish race with its capital at Constantinople," including

"the rich lands of Asia Minor and Thrace which are predominantly Turkish." Arabia, Mesopotamia, Syria, and Palestine, however, were "entitled to a recognition of their separate national conditions." After denouncing German treatment of its African subjects, he sought "a conference whose decision must have primary regard to the wishes and interests of the native inhabitants of such colonies." He endorsed "some international organization" that would "limit the burden of armaments and diminish the probability of war." In general, there must be a territorial settlement based on the right of "self-determination," which he defined as "the consent of the governed." Making an indirect reference to at best weakening the secret treaties, he implied that in light of Russia's collapse, he would be "perfectly ready to discuss them with our Allies."[9]

The prime minister was responding to several concerns. In late December, the British Labor Party had published a "Memorandum on War Aims." It declared that the war could only be continued if fought on the basis "that the world may henceforth be made safe for democracy." Needed was a league of nations, so "that there should be henceforth on earth no more war." Lloyd George realized that any Bolshevik foothold among British workingmen would seriously undermine the war effort, particularly as his nation was experiencing a manpower shortage. The recent Second Battle of Passchendaele had cost Britain 217,000 casualties, giving Lloyd George impetus to halt the conflict before Germany's expected spring offensive. On January 22, 1918, Field Marshal Douglas Haig doubted whether Britain could gain by continuing the conflict for another year, at which time "America would get a great pull over us." Historian David R. Woodward maintains that the prime minister sought to keep alive the possibility of a compromise peace, even at the expense of abandoning Russia. Irrespective of Lloyd George's motives, German chancellor Georg von Hertling denied that the speech, which implied his nation was guilty of "all sorts of crimes," conveyed "a serious will for peace."[10]

In the United States, the address was warmly received. William Jennings Bryan wrote, "The dove leaves the ark when the belligerents begin to exchange views as to terms of peace." Ex-president Taft claimed the United States would gladly make peace on the prime minister's terms. The *Nation* expressed relief that the Allies were no longer talking of freeing Czechs and Slovaks from foreign domination. Nor was Lloyd George speaking, as he had in September 1916, of delivering a "knockout blow." Socialist Morris Hillquit found the speech encouraging to "all friends of a speedy, general and democratic peace," even if he wished for clearer limitations upon Italian claims and feared that condemnation of colonial brutality applied only to Germany. Viereck's *American Weekly* praised Lloyd George's vague language concerning Alsace-Lorraine and silence concerning the status of Danzig, a major seaport coveted by the Poles.[11]

There remained some critics. The Hearst press attacked Lloyd George for overemphasizing territorial matters while neglecting topics relating to international justice, liberty, and popular rights. Senator La Follette interpreted the speech as evidence that the Allies sought to gain "great advantages" at the expense of the rest of the world. The German American weekly *Issues and Events* accused the British prime minister of seeking dismemberment of the Central Powers. As far as honoring the wishes of Germany's African subjects, would anyone treat similarly "the Moro headhunters of the Philippines, and the Sioux, Apaches and Comanches of Minnesota, the Dakotas, Arizona and other States"?[12]

The attention given to Lloyd George's address depressed Wilson, who saw himself preempted by the prime minister's agenda. On the very day of the prime minister's speech, House convinced the president to proceed with his own plan to address Congress three days later. Wilson's remarks, predicted House, would "so smother the Lloyd George speech that it would be forgotten and that the President would once more become the spokesman for the Entente, and, indeed, for the liberals of the world."[13] The two men conferred alone on the text for the next two days. Certainly no member of the cabinet or of the State Department, much less any of the Allies, was consulted.

When Wilson addressed Congress on January 8, 1918, he began by pointing to the role played by the Central Powers in their recently severed negotiations with the Bolsheviks. Whereas the Russians were bargaining "in earnest," their antagonists sought to "keep every foot of territory their armed forces had occupied, — every province, every city, every point of vantage, — as a permanent addition to their territories and their power." Nonetheless, as noted, he hoped "to assist the people of Russia to attain their utmost hope of liberty and ordered peace." He praised "the admirable candor" and "admirable spirit" embodied in Lloyd George's recent speech, adding, "There is no confusion of counsel among the adversaries of the Central Powers, no uncertainty of principle, no vagueness of detail."

Then followed his famous Fourteen Points.

I. *"Open covenants of peace, openly arrived at, after which there shall be no private international understandings of any kind but diplomacy shall proceed always frankly and in the public view."* Wilson was expressing his belief that the war was primarily caused by the secret alliance system. He assumed that no people anywhere would sanction the type of agreements that, he believed, had drawn an entire continent into conflict over an assassination in a disputed Balkan province. Just two months after he delivered this major address, he wrote Lansing, claiming that he did not oppose "private discussion of delicate matters" but that all resulting agreements "should be open, above-board, and explicit."[14]

II. *"Absolute freedom of navigation upon the seas, outside territorial waters, alike in peace and in war, except as the seas may be closed in whole or in part by international action for the enforcement of international covenants."* Here Wilson was seeking absolute protection of the maritime rights exercised by neutral nations against their violation by unrestricted U-boat warfare. He did not involve himself in the subtleties of blockading and cruiser rules.

III. *"The removal, so far as possible, of all economic barriers and the establishment of an equality of trade conditions among all the nations consenting to the peace and associating themselves for its maintenance."* This point is based on the premise that economic autarchy helped breed the rivalries that led to war.

IV. *"Adequate guarantees given and taken that national armaments will be reduced to the lowest point consistent with domestic safety."*

V. *"A free, open-minded, and absolutely impartial adjustment of all colonial claims, based on a strict observance of the principle that in determining all such questions of sovereignty the interests of the populations concerned must have equal weight with the equitable claims of the government whose title is to be determined."* The president was aware in general terms of the Allied secret treaties parceling out parts of the Ottoman and Hapsburg Empires. In contrast to his assumptions concerning European possessions, Wilson took at best a paternalistic tone towards the non-West, explicitly giving the colonial power "equal weight" with subject populations.

The next nine points treated territorial matters.

VI. *"The evacuation of all Russian territory and such a settlement of all questions affecting Russia as will secure the best and freest cooperation of the other nations of the world in obtaining for her an unhampered and unembarrassed opportunity for the independent determination of her own political development and national policy and assure her of a sincere welcome into the society of free nations under institutions of her own choosing; and more than a welcome, assistance of every kind that she may need and may herself desire. The treatment accorded Russia by her sister nations in the months to come will be the acid test of their good will, of their comprehension of her needs as distinguished from their own interests and of their intelligent and unselfish sympathy."* Far from challenging the Bolshevik leaders, Wilson here was tacitly envisioning them as potential partners in a democratic peace.

VII. *"Belgium, the whole world will agree, must be evacuated and restored, without any attempt to limit the sovereignty which she enjoys with all other free nations. . . ."* One should observe that if Germany paid for Belgium's restoration, it would be acknowledging de facto guilt for launching the war. "Restoration" itself remained undefined.

VIII. *"All French territory should be freed and invaded portions restored, and the wrong done to France by Prussia in 1871 in the matter of Alsace-Lorraine, which has unsettled the peace of the world for nearly fifty years, should be righted, in order that peace may once more be made secure in the interests of all."* Note that the language was deliberately phrased to avoid making the return of Alsace-Lorraine a primary U.S. objective. The Wilson administration did deem its return highly desirable, perhaps essential to French economic recovery. The Inquiry had reported that any joint plebiscite would indicate a strong preference for German sovereignty. It found that should the two provinces be polled separately, Lorraine (except for Metz) was likely to identify with France, lower Alsace with Germany. In

December, Wilson had told his cabinet he sought a plebiscite for the disputed provinces.[15]

IX. *"A readjustment of the frontiers of Italy should be effected along clearly recognizable lines of nationality."* The Inquiry had been more specific, as its memorandum on the topic concretely saw no justification for Italy's wider Adriatic claims, much less what was promised in the 1915 Treaty of London. It warned that once established on that coast, Italy would advance into the Yugoslav hinterland, extending its imperialistic influence into the Balkans. Wilson himself was excluding Italy's claims, as specified in the Treaty of London, to German-speaking Tyrol.[16]

X. *"The peoples of Austria-Hungary, whose place among the nations we wish to see safeguarded and assured, should be accorded the freest opportunity of autonomous development."* The Inquiry had sought concrete assurances that no dismemberment was intended. Historian Victor S. Mamatey notes the ambiguity of Wilson's phrasing, permitting everyone to read into it what one wished.[17]

XI. *"Rumania, Serbia, and Montenegro should be evacuated; occupied territories restored; Serbia accorded free and secure access to the sea and the relations of the several Balkan states to one another determined by friendly counsel along historically established lines of allegiance and nationality; and international guarantees of the political and economic independence and territorial integrity of the several Balkan states should be entered into."* Given the overlay of many of the nationalities within the Balkans, clear "lines of allegiance and nationality" were impossible.

XII. *"The Turkish portion of the present Ottoman Empire should be assured a secure sovereignty, but the other nationalities which are now under Turkish rule should be assured an undoubted security of life and an absolutely unmolested opportunity of autonomous development and the Dardanelles should be permanently opened as a free passage to the ships and commerce of all nations under international guarantees."* The Inquiry had specifically mentioned autonomous status for Armenia and "protection" by unspecified "civilized nations" for Palestine, Syria, Mesopotamia, and Arabia. Wilson hereby challenged the 1916 Sykes–Picot agreement dividing much of the Middle East.[18]

XIII. *"An independent Polish state should be erected which should include the territories inhabited by indisputably Polish populations, which should be assured a free and secure access to the sea, and whose political and economic independence and territorial integrity should be guaranteed by international covenant."* Wilson was ignoring border areas, which often had mixed populations, and the fact that access to the sea necessitated incorporation of non-Polish nationalities.

XIV. *"A general association of nations must be formed under specific covenants for the purpose of affording mutual guarantees of political independence and territorial integrity to great and small states alike."* Such language was nothing if not vague. In May 1916, speaking before the League to Enforce Peace, Wilson had endorsed a postwar organization devoted to freedom of the seas and the territorial integrity of its members. His "peace without victory" speech, delivered in January 1917, spoke of "formal and solemn adherence to a League for Peace." In March 1917, Wilson had told French ambassador Jules Jusserand that such an association should evolve gradually, beginning with "an entente" focusing upon such matters as arbitration. That August, in speaking again with Jusserand, he referred to a "machinery and practice of cooperation" that would "naturally spring up." November found him telling a Swiss political scientist that such a league should be more a matter of "moral persuasion" than of "political organization." In the words of historian Thomas J. Knock, Wilson at this point saw a league as a compass, not the final destination.[19]

In what biographer Arthur S. Link calls an implicit point as important as the previous ones he listed, Wilson denied any effort either to injure Germany or to block "her legitimate influence or power." The president ended with a typical Wilsonian flourish, pledging that Americans stood "ready to devote their lives, their honor, and everything that they possess" to support "the principle of justice to all peoples and nationalities, and their right to live on equal terms of liberty and safety with one another, whether they be strong or weak."[20]

The Fourteen Points centered on several goals. Wilson sought to arouse Germany's population against its military leaders. He aimed at breaking negotiations between the Bolsheviks and the Germans and, if possible, wooing the Russians back to the Allies. Here the president failed.

More successful was another aim: to meet the challenge of Bolshevik diplomacy. Lenin had stressed an immediate peace that would inevitably be followed by a proletarian revolution within the warring nations. The president indirectly admonished the Entente for engaging in such annexationist diplomacy as found in the Treaty of London with Italy. At the same time, by presenting more altruistic war aims, he instilled new life into the war-weary Allied peoples. In the process, he established himself as the leader of liberals throughout all the Entente nations. Ultimately he was able to foment dissension with the German and Austro-Hungarian Empires by offering a peace that appeared reasonable.

Congress reacted with enthusiasm. Wilson's comments concerning Alsace-Lorraine, the Lloyd George speech, and Russia met with particular approval. Many members used superlatives, Old Guard Republican congressman Joe Cannon wishing it could "be read to every man, woman and child." To Senator James Hamilton Lewis, the message "will bring us nearer to peace than we have been since the declaration of war began." With his genius for creative vocabulary, Warren Harding remarked, "It ought to better conserve our people in this war." The often critical Henry Cabot Lodge privately confessed that Wilson had delivered "a good speech as to terms," but he found the aims too utopian and, given the military stalemate, untimely proposed. William E. Borah introduced a resolution that would abolish Senate consideration of secret treaties, claiming he was backing the president; almost immediately the Senate adopted a version of his proposal.[21]

Several senators differed with certain points. Reed Smoot feared that Point Three would eliminate all tariffs. La Follette warned that Wilson would commit the United States to years of warfare in order to remedy ancient grievances. By such reasoning, the international community might call upon the United States to right the wrongs of the Mexican War and resolve its own race problem. Britain could be compelled to atone for the wrongs of the Boer War and grant independence to Ireland.[22]

The U.S. House of Representatives, too, harbored minor dissent. Wilson's speech "means ten years more of war," warned Fred Britten, "because the President closed all the doors to peace." William Mason reminded his colleagues that Alsace-Lorraine had been German before the time of the American Revolution and that Serbia was the nation that had "lit the match that set the world afire." "Shall we let our children go cold and hungry, our people ground to death by taxation," he asked, so Britain could keep its conquests? "Shall we fill European graves with American youths" in order for Japan to retain Germany's Pacific colonies?[23]

There was hardly an element of the American left that did not hail Wilson's address. Now assured that the United States was fighting to abolish the "old diplomacy" of power politics, prominent liberals and those possessing pacifist leanings enthusiastically backed the president's newly revealed agenda. Muckraking publisher S. S. McClure saw the address as "one of the greatest and noblest documents in American history," possibly equal to the Monroe Doctrine. The executive board of the Woman's Peace Party, chaired by reformer Jane Addams, hailed the speech as offering "the fundamental bases of the new world-order." The *Nation* called the president's principles "a sort of Grand Charter for the liberty and democracy of the ages to come." Socialist leader Eugene V. Debs said the points "deserve the unqualified approval of everyone believing in the rule of the people." *Masses* editor Max Eastman quipped that Wilson might now be ready to "come round and join the Socialist Party. I should take the risk of accepting him as a member."[24]

Some on the left stressed similarities between the president and the Bolsheviks. Meyer London claimed that their peace terms were almost identical, then called upon Wilson to lead a postwar international alliance dedicated to preserving peace. People's Council leader Scott Nearing declared, "The president has put into perfect English the splendid economic and social ideals of the New Russia."[25]

Voices often critical of the president praised the speech. The *Outlook* referred to Wilson's "great address." To the *New York Tribune*, it was "a second emancipation proclamation," looking towards the liberation of nationalities subject to the empires of the Central Powers. George Harvey's *War Weekly* called it "a veritable masterpiece." Theodore Roosevelt put his own spin on the message, seeing it as a reassertion of "our duty to stand with the allies to the end and to fight until we have achieved complete victory."[26]

Thanks to a powerful Marconi transmitter in New Jersey, George Creel arranged to have the address heard around the world. His Committee on Public Information distributed 4 million copies overseas. According to Creel's account, Germany's General Staff established the death penalty for those possessing it but the edict was not enforced; a million copies were printed in German. As observed, Lenin welcomed the speech, as did the Bolshevik journal *Izvestia*.[27]

In a close reading of the text, George Sylvester Viereck observed that Wilson used the auxiliary verb "must" for restoring Belgium, ending secret diplomacy, and guaranteeing the independence of all nations, great and small. The president, however, employed "should" for the return of "Elsass-Lothringen," cession of Prussian territory to Poland, the defining of the Italian frontier, the creation of an independent Polish state with access to the sea, and readjustments on the Italian frontier and in Austria-Hungary, Turkey, and the Balkans. He concluded: "Peace is knocking at the door, albeit the door is closed." Viereck's ardent ally, the *Gaelic American*, commented, "Irish citizens, we stand by Wilson."[28]

Significant dissent came from Robert Lansing, who confided to his diary that the principle of "self-determination" could not be applied to the "savages" inhabiting the German colonies or to the "longstanding and complex situation in the Balkans." Conversely, Lansing found domination of the Dalmatian coast and even Albania essential to Italian security. The wording of Point Ten in particular disturbed him, as he accurately predicted that its fulfillment necessitated the creation of new states—Polish, Czech, Yugoslav, and possibly Ruthenian—carved out of the Hapsburg Empire. In a note to Wilson just two days after the speech, Lansing added that only separation of Austria from Hungary could end German domination of Europe.[29]

Arguing from the right, former assistant attorney general James M. Beck declared that the United States itself had challenged freedom of the seas during its own civil war. Moreover, the United States had long violated the principle of self-determination, evidenced by its treatment of the southern Confederacy, Florida, Louisiana, California, Alaska, the Philippine Islands, and Puerto Rico.[30]

Strong support emerged within Britain. At a mass meeting at Edinburgh, Foreign Secretary Balfour called the speech a "magnificent pronouncement." Lloyd George expressed personal gratitude, finding Wilson's policies well aligned with his own. The prime minister did harbor reservations concerning freedom of the seas, asking the Trades Union Conference meeting in London whether it meant "freedom from submarines" or rather "starvation for this country." Lord Northcliffe's *Times* argued that the speech did not take "certain hard realities" into consideration: "Some of the proposals Mr. Wilson puts forward assume that the reign of righteousness upon the earth is already within our reach."[31]

AEF commander John J. Pershing and William G. Sharp, U.S. ambassador to France, reported a warm reception in Paris, particularly concerning Wilson's remarks about Alsace-Lorraine. French foreign minister Stephen Pichon endorsed the statements of both Wilson and Lloyd George. Prime Minister Clemenceau betrayed far more caution, simply adhering to his adage, "I prosecute the war." Sentiment in Italy was guarded, its press fearing abandonment of Italy's claim to the eastern Adriatic. Similarly, both Czechs and Slovaks were deeply disappointed that the address did not endorse their outright independence.[32]

Not surprisingly, Germany voiced opposition. Linked to Russia's own proposals of "no annexations, no indemnities," Wilson's manifesto might cause German and Austrian troops to defect. The government remained firm for prosecuting the war, with even the Socialist *Vorwärts* questioning Wilson's sincerity. The *Kölnische Zeitung* spoke for much of the press: "Under the false label of Society of Nations, Anglo-American world domination would be permanently reestablished and central Europe would be as poor and powerless as after the Thirty Years' War."[33]

On January 24, Count Hertling, speaking to the Reichstag main committee, took up each of the Fourteen Points in turn. He concurred with the more general tenets, that is, those concerning disarmament, open diplomacy, the ending of economic barriers, and a league of nations. He claimed to accept freedom of the seas, which—he maintained—must include removal of British naval bases at Gibraltar, Malta, Hong Kong, Aden, and the Falkland Islands. At the same time, he balked at the more concrete items. Evacuation of Belgian and French territory would have to be negotiated. Moreover, he rejected outright provisions regarding Alsace-Lorraine ("purely German territory"), the "integrity of Turkey" (read Ottoman Empire), and the restoration of German colonies. The fate of Poland, Russia, and Austria-Hungary only concerned these countries and Germany. Knowing that his nation was occupying strategic parts of western Russia and was preparing for a spring offensive, he concluded by saying, "Our military situation was never so favorable as at present. Let the Entente bring new proposals."[34]

Chancellor Hertling had made Germany's position clear. There would be no unconditional restoration of Belgian sovereignty, something crucial for Wilson. Berlin would not discuss Eastern Europe in general and Poland and Alsace-Lorraine in particular. Agreement with Wilson's proposals was limited solely to matters of abstract principle.

Austria, however, remained war-weary, with Vienna torn by a general strike triggered by a reduction in its flour ration. *Saturday Evening Post* correspondent Carl Ackerman reported from Bern, Switzerland, regarding the Dual Monarchy: "If there is not peace, or a great military victory, there will be a revolution."[35]

Hence the Hapsburg Empire gave Wilson's proposals a warmer reception. Speaking to Austria's Reichrath Committee on Foreign Affairs on the same day as Hertling addressed the Reichstag, Foreign Minister Count Ottokar Czernin claimed to have felt strengthened by Wilson's "peace offer," which he saw as similar to the stance of his own government. Indeed, an exchange of ideas between the two nations might pave the way for more general parlays. He backed open covenants, freedom of the seas, general disarmament, a league of nations, and an independent Poland. He boasted concerning Russia that "we are proving with deeds that we are ready to create a friendly, neighborly relationship." He balked at any proposals concerning Italy, Serbia, Rumania, and Montenegro, refusing "to make one-sided concessions to our enemies."[36]

Colonel House thought Hertling's and Czernin's differing replies to Wilson foreshadowed a schism between Germany and Austria-Hungary, something "more successful than we dared to hope." Historian Victor S. Mamatey claims that Czernin wished Wilson and Lloyd George would induce France and Italy to renounce their claims, allowing the Austrian diplomat in turn to push for German evacuation of Belgium and France.[37]

Historians offer mixed sentiment concerning the Fourteen Points. Some praise Wilson's tenets as articulate and noble, indeed the means by which peace could have been achieved. To other scholars, they were too vague and inarticulate, the president's remarks concerning Russia, the Balkans, and the Hapsburg Empire deemed especially naive.[38]

On February 2, Wilson received a communiqué from the Allied Supreme War Council (SWC) that pointed to the Central Powers' annexationist demands at Brest-Litovsk and their freshly disclosed "plans of conquest and spoliation." The Allied meeting did not submit its own peace terms but rather called for prosecuting the war "with the utmost vigor." Writing from London, Ambassador Page backed the SWC, predicting that although the war would be long, most Britons believed that "Germany now must be whipped to a finish." House called the SWC statement "a monumental blunder" that only served to undercut the president's peace efforts and unite the enemy coalition behind their governments. Wilson accused the Allies of "infinite stupidity," showing "a genius for making blunders of the most serious kind."[39]

Within two weeks, in an address to a joint session of Congress on February 11, 1918, Wilson responded directly to Hertling's and Czernin's speeches, comparing the German chancellor's "vague and confusing" tone to the Austrian foreign minister's "very friendly" one. Czernin, he said, "seems to see the fundamental elements of peace with clear eyes and does not seek to obscure them," as observed by his stance on Poland and, so Wilson claimed, on nationalistic aspirations within the Hapsburg Empire. German policy, to the contrary, he found governed by a "military and annexationist party," who would return to the *realpolitik* manifested at the 1815 Congress of Vienna.

Not repeating his more concrete Fourteen Points, Wilson offered four new abstract ones. First, each part of the final settlement must be based on "the essential justice of that particular case." Second, "peoples and provinces are not to be bartered about from sovereignty to sovereignty as if they were mere chattels and pawns in a game, even the great game, now forever discredited, of the balance of power." Third, every territorial settlement needed to be made in "the interest and for the benefit of the populations concerned." Fourth, "all well defined national aspirations shall be accorded the utmost satisfaction that can be accorded them without introducing new or perpetuating old elements of discord and antagonism." He stressed the tentative nature of the Fourteen Points, calling them a "provisional sketch of principles" and conceding they might not be "the best or the most enduring." Using Lloyd George's term "self-determination" for the first time, the president found in it "an imperative principle of action." Wilson was again taking an implicit slap at the secret treaties. He was no longer stressing any conspiracy by Germany's "military masters" but Berlin's general disregarding of "the rights of small nations and of nationalities."[40]

As usual, the address met with strong congressional approval. Colonel House did observe, "They applauded some of the points, but they were not enthusiastic. He was talking over their heads and but few of them knew what it was all about or what his purpose was in addressing them again at this time." In the Senate, Hiram Johnson expressed pleasure that the Fourteen Points appeared to have been modified. Warren Harding claimed that no one could disagree with the president's presentation. Thomas P. Gore, long a foe of Wilson's foreign policy, saw it opening the way to negotiations. Congressman Edward W. Pou called it "the most encouraging indication of peace that has appeared."[41]

The press was just as euphoric, the New York *World* finding the speech "the highest statesmanship" that had emerged from the entire war. To the *New Republic*, the address embodied "the most conclusive document that the war has produced," adding that the Central Powers were not required to surrender a single claim before the convening of a general conference. The pro-German *Issues and Events* saw it as the most significant move yet made on "the international chessboard."[42]

A few disapproved. James M. Beck attacked Wilson's "four exceedingly vague formulas" and called punitive justice a "sacred cause." The *North American Review* went so far as to defend the secret treaties, arguing that nothing else could be expected.[43]

Much of the British, French, and Italian press hailed the address. Lord Lansdowne contended that Wilson's four principles provided the basis for preliminary negotiations. Lloyd George, however, feared that Wilson might state conditions that Britain could not accept. Speaking for the British dominions, Jan Christian Smuts warned against "entrusting our interests to the United States."[44]

Surprisingly, some reports within Germany indicated favorable reaction. On February 25, however, Hertling claimed to accept Wilson's new Four Points, but then accused the Allies of coveting lands of the Central Powers. He saw a league of nations as "an aim devoutly to be wished" but not yet attainable. Though the "thoroughly imperialistic" Britain talked of self-determination, it drew its own line concerning India, Egypt, or Ireland: "Our war aims from the beginning were the defense of the fatherland, the maintenance of our territorial integrity, and the freedom of economic development." Even in the East, he argued, German military operations were defensive, in no way aimed at conquest.[45]

Hertling's speech quickly drew American responses. Several in Congress were hopeful. Congressman James Slayden, once president of the American Peace Society, claimed that because the leaders of Britain, Germany, and Austria all accepted Wilson's four principles, progress was being made. Representative Edward L. Hamilton (R-Mich.) predicted that Germany would negotiate on "some non-nebulous terms."[46]

Others challenged such views. Senate whip Lewis accused Hertling of refusing to relinquish territory and of seeking to "keep the back door to the Baltic." Congressman George Graham (R-Pa.) pointed to German action in Russia as evidence of "utter insincerity," as did former president Taft. Colonel Harvey's *War Weekly* claimed the cynicism of Hertling's terms would even make Bismarck blush! In Britain, Balfour offered a quick rebuff, declaring that a preliminary understanding must precede any negotiation.[47]

By his reference to "self-determination" and "well defined national aspirations," so historians note, Wilson opened himself to endless international controversy. Trygve Throntviet sees the president irresponsibly laying traps for himself by confusing ethnonationalism with self-government. Margaret MacMillan observes that at the time only Poland could be considered a well-defined nation. Especially in Central Europe, where there existed a rich mixture of religions, languages, and cultures, possibilities for dividing up peoples were unending. In fact, about half the population of any area could be considered as members of one national minority or another. If self-determination involved the holding of plebiscites, which Wilson had not mentioned, there remained the entire question of whether suffrage extended to women or to those who had personally moved into a disputed territory.[48]

Late in February, Austrian emperor Charles wrote Alfonso XIII, asking the king of Spain to forward a message to Wilson. Claiming that he concurred with Wilson's new Four Points, Charles saw them serving as the basis for a general peace conference. He favored the complete restoration of Belgium and maintained that such matters as Italy's claims, Serbia's access to the sea, and unification of all Bulgarians would be on any peace agenda. In response, Wilson asked Alfonso to be concrete concerning Balkan rivalries, concessions to Italy, the fate of the Adriatic coast, and "the national aspirations of the Slavic peoples." Early in April, Austria's Czernin told the Vienna City Council that he found the president's four principles a suitable basis for a general peace, with only the issue of Alsace-Lorraine preventing an accord with France.[49]

Despite its December 1917 declaration of war, the Wilson administration was still pursuing informal contact with the Hapsburg Empire. In early February 1918, George D. Herron met several times with Heinrich Lammasch outside Bern. Herron was a Congregationalist minister, a Socialist, and a Wilson devotee. Lammasch belonged to the Austrian House of Lords and was one of the world's leading authorities on arbitration; he sought to turn Austria-Hungary into a federal republic. Lammasch stressed a renewed peace with the United States, the "integration and separate development" of the empire's minorities, and release from "Prussian hegemony." Reporting to the U.S. embassy in Bern, Herron found the Austrian diplomat's stance falling far short of Wilson's vision. Upon learning from Wilson of Lammasch's proposals, Balfour called them "the old slavery under a new name."[50]

Early in April, Clemenceau released a letter from Charles to French president Raymond Poincaré. The communication was transmitted in Paris through Charles's brother-in-law, Prince Sixtus of Bourbon-Parma, who was a French national. Emperor Charles would support the restoration of Belgium, the reestablishment of Serbia with access to the Adriatic, and—most important of all—France's "just claims regarding Alsace-Lorraine." In return Austria would withdraw from the war.[51] With a German onslaught approaching Paris, Clemenceau could not reveal the fact that he had sought peace with the Austrians.

Berlin, learning of the Herron–Lammasch conversations, ordered Vienna to disown its informal emissary. The Austrian government frantically denied the authenticity of this quite genuine proposal. On April 14, Czernin resigned, replaced by the equally ineffective Baron Istvan Burian, a Hungarian who had been the empire's finance minister. Austria became more closely tied to Germany than ever. A day later, Emperor Charles turned total control over his troops to the German high command. All Austrian soldiers now served under German officers. The once mighty Hapsburg Empire was becoming a German vassal.

Reverend Herron wrote Hugh Wilson, secretary of the U.S. legation at Bern, observing that Clemenceau's attack on the Sixtus letter had "delivered Charles and his Empire, bound and helpless, into the arms of the beast we are all fighting." In late May, Wilson found it "a thousand pities" that the French premier had released the letter. Though unsympathetic personally to Charles, President Wilson realized that Clemenceau had permanently "rivetted" the Austrians to the Germans. Secretary Lansing concurred, calling the premier's move "the most astounding stupidity, for which no sufficient excuse can be made."[52]

By April 6, when Wilson next addressed the matter of war aims, the Germans had launched their spring campaign in which General Erich Ludendorff directed the greatest western offensive of the war. The Treaty of Brest-Litovsk and a preliminary peace with Rumania in March had given Berlin control of most of Eastern Europe and the Balkans. Speaking to a crowd of fifteen thousand in Baltimore on the anniversary of the U.S. entry into the conflict, the president claimed that Germany initially sought to wield authority over the new Baltic nations, all Slavic peoples, and "all the lands that Turkey had dominated and misruled." Ultimately Germany's military, "who are her real rulers," desired "an empire as hostile to the Americas as to the Europe which it will overawe,—an empire which will ultimately master Persia, India, and the peoples of the Far East." Wilson insisted he was ready to discuss a fair and just treaty anytime, but Brest-Litovsk showed that there was no mistaking where the Germans stood: "There is, therefore, but one response possible from us: Force, Force to the utmost, Force without stint or limit, the righteous and triumphant Force which shall make Right the law of the world and cast down every selfish dominion down in the dust."[53]

Though Wilson might well have realized that he had been a prisoner of his own rhetoric, his fundamental message was clear enough: peace now depended on victory, not negotiation. By at least hinting at a Carthaginian settlement, the president more than ever had to restrain the ambitions of his allies. Biographer Link, in noting Wilson's quandary, sees that the president had little choice. Once the German High Command sought total victory on the western front, there could be no bargaining. Historian Klaus Schwabe observes that Berlin would have interpreted any concession as a sign of weakness.[54]

The nation's press heartily approved the April 6 speech. Harvey's *War Weekly* undoubtedly offered the view of some Wilson critics in saying, "Now, if we can only hold him to it!" Overseas, reactions were hardly surprising. London and Paris welcomed the address; Berlin condemned it. Balfour found the moment "particularly opportune" to remind Germany of the United States' intent to pursue the conflict until the Reich's "militarism" was defeated.[55]

Admittedly, the president backtracked a bit two days later when he renounced "the language of braggadocio," repudiated any desire to "march triumphantly into Berlin," and denied "fighting for democracy except for the peoples that want democracy." "Nobody," he continued, "has the right to get anything out of this war," for "no injustice furnishes a basis for permanent peace." He added that no people, "great or little," should be compelled to live under conditions they did not willingly accept. These remarks, however, were addressed to about thirty correspondents representing foreign newspapers and remained confidential.[56]

Wilson's next opportunity to present his peace agenda came on May 18, when he spoke at a Red Cross fund drive held in New York's Metropolitan Opera House. He repeated the need to "win the war" and attacked Germany's program of "conquest and exploitation." Yet he appeared to retreat a bit from the Baltimore speech, again holding out some hope for negotiation. If the Central Powers wished peace, he remarked, "let them come forward through accredited representatives and lay their terms on the table. We have laid ours, and they know what they are."[57]

By late May, Wilson's vision of "autonomous development" for subject nationalities within the Hapsburg monarchy had become a chimera. From April 8 to 11, the Congress of the Oppressed Austrian Peoples took place in Rome. Czech, Yugoslav, Polish, Italian, and Rumanian representatives proclaimed the right of self-determination, stressing the need to fight against the Hapsburg Empire. Edward Beneš, general secretary of the Czecho-Slovak National Council, pointed to Czech armed forces in France and Russia as providing proof that a Czechoslovak state already existed.

On May 29, Secretary Lansing announced a major turning point in U.S. policy. He publicly proclaimed that "the nationalistic aspirations of the Czecho-Slovaks and Jugo-Slavs for freedom have the earnest sympathy of this Government." On the following day, Wilson reluctantly sanctioned Lansing's declaration. In conversing with Sir William Wiseman, he told the British liaison that since there existed no chance of making a separate peace with Austria, he "saw no other way." In late June, Wilson wrote Lansing, "We can no longer respect or regard the integrity of the artificial Austrian Empire."[58] By mid-August 1918, all the major Allies had recognized the independence of Czechoslovakia, the United States following early in September.

The president again offered war aims at Mount Vernon, Virginia, speaking on the Fourth of July. He outlined four principles that differed somewhat from those he presented on February 11. The war's settlement, he asserted, must be final and must rest upon four principles: (1) "the destruction of every arbitrary power anywhere" or "its reduction to virtual impotence"; (2) "the settlement of every question . . . upon the basis of the free acceptance of that settlement by the people immediately concerned"; (3) "the consent of all nations to be governed . . . by the same principles of honour and respect for the common law of civilized society that govern individual citizens of all modern states"; (4) "the establishment of an organization of peace which shall make it certain that the combined power of free nations will . . . serve to make peace and justice the more secure," this achieved by "affording a definite tribunal to which all must submit and by which every international readjustment that cannot be amicably agreed upon by the peoples directly concerned must be sanctioned."

Such "great ends" could not be realized through high-level intrigues, "with their projects for balances of power and of national opportunity"; they must spring from "the thinking peoples of the world desire, with their longing hope for justice and for social freedom and opportunity." Needed was "the reign of law, based upon the consent of the governed and sustained by the organized opinion of mankind."

Again reverting to the absolutist language of his Baltimore speech, he proclaimed: "The Past and the Present are in deadly grapple and the peoples of the world are being done to death between them. There can be but one issue. The settlement must be final. There can be no compromise. No half-way decision would be tolerable. No half-way decision is conceivable."[59]

The address drew little if any dissent. Hearst's *New York American* favorably compared Wilson's "statesmanship" to Theodore Roosevelt's desire, voiced in Passaic, New Jersey, to rearrange Europe's national boundaries. The *Nation* was more censorious, saying the president should have used words of magnanimity, not advocating a policy of "war to destruction's end."[60]

Even voices often critical of Wilson endorsed his speech. The *Outlook* claimed it should be read more than once by every true American. Harvey's *War Weekly* called it "one of the most impressive utterances that ever fell from the lips or pen of an American statesman"; the address "will rank as among the most finished and momentous in our history." On the other side of the ideological spectrum, Viereck's *American Weekly* labeled it "the Magna Charta of Nations."[61]

Overseas, Lloyd George responded that Germany could "have peace tomorrow" if it accepted Wilson's conditions. The German press found little to criticize in Wilson's words but claimed they were not supported by action.[62]

On July 11, Georg von Hertling accused Wilson of seeking a war of annihilation; Hertling himself endorsed the peace terms proposed by Pope Benedict XV. The German chancellor told the Reichstag that Germany had no intention of keeping Belgium after the war; it merely meant to use it as a pawn in future negotiations. Hertling maintained, however, that Germany's own territory was inviolate and that his nation deserved the opportunity for economic expansion. Only a week earlier, however, the High Command had decided that Belgium would be divided into two states, united only by a personal union and linked to Germany by special tariff and railroad arrangements.[63]

Five days later, Austro-Hungarian foreign minister Istvan Burian publicly praised Wilson's address, referring directly to the president's new four principles and asserting that his nation was prepared to discuss everything except the fate of its own country. He did, however, offer major qualifications. Although he claimed that only territorial aims separated the belligerents, he found Allied demands regarding Alsace-Lorraine, Trieste, the Trentino, and the German colonies insurmountable.[64]

Historians question both the substance and tone of Wilson's remarks. The president was backtracking from the Fourteen Points and the four additional ones of February 11 into what historian John Milton Cooper Jr. calls a retreat into generalities and a "whiff of uplift." Richard Striner finds talk of settling all questions democratically "extravagant to the point of becoming almost childish." Lloyd E. Ambrosius accuses Wilson of avoiding hard questions concerning his ideal international community and taking refuge in repeating vague principles.[65]

Certainly, since January, the president had retreated from his Fourteen Points address, both in tone and specificity. His retreat, however, was quite understandable, for since March the Allies had been imperiled by General Ludendorff's waves of offensives. Obviously the matter of detailed peace conditions could wait.

Furthermore, all of Wilson's words could mean nothing unless U.S. troops played a major role on the battlefield. When the United States first entered the war, few realized the obstacles to successful mobilization and the length of time it would take before an American Expeditionary Force saw combat.

TWELVE
THE MATTER OF PREPARATION

TO ACCOMPLISH WILSON'S PEACE AIMS, BE THEY AMORPHOUS or concrete, U.S. troops needed to play a major role in defeating the Germans. Yet the United States was abysmally unprepared.

Until the 1910s, Civil War veterans dominated the officer corps. Beginning with the rank of major, the aging brass had entered the service before the Spanish–American War. The General Staff was so small that only forty-one members were on duty when the 1914 conflagration broke out. Chief of Staff Hugh L. Scott had fought Indians on the western plains and Moros in the Philippine jungles, but in 1917 he was deaf and prone to fall asleep in his chair. His successor that October, Tasker Bliss, was superbly educated and read classical languages as a hobby. He had been military attaché in Spain when the Spanish–American War broke out, served in the invasion of Puerto Rico, was collector of customs during the U.S. occupation of Cuba, and had headed the Army War College. He was, however, an equally weak administrator, overwhelmed by his position and unable to exercise the needed control. It was still undetermined whether the army chief of staff was slated to command an entire army or simply advise the president and secretary of war.

Within the army, bureau chiefs reigned supreme over their fiefdoms. Admittedly, all were competent in their own sphere (ordnance, corps of engineers, etc.), but until the winter of 1917–18 no one could rein them in. Historian Robert H. Ferrell compares the War Department to the Near East after the death of Alexander the Great, when a huge empire was subdivided.[1]

Newton Diehl Baker, secretary of war and former mayor of Cleveland, took office totally ignorant of military matters. He was a short, shy-looking man of pacifist leanings, who, in the words of historian Donald Smythe, appeared as if "he ought to be teaching Latin in some girls' academy." He once said he had never even played with tin soldiers. In 1915, Baker had opposed the preparedness movement, but once in office he endorsed peacetime military training camps and created an army flying corps. Though articulate and well educated, he turned major decisions over to the military and waited two crucial years before reorganizing the War Department's antiquated structure. Wilson knew him from the early 1890s when they had shared the same boardinghouse in Baltimore while studying at Johns Hopkins University. The president respected him more than any other cabinet member.[2]

At first, Baker was somewhat ineffective. A believer in nineteenth-century liberalism and states' rights, he harbored suspicions of federal power. In chairing the Council of National Defense, he opposed the creation of a powerful War Industries Board and gave the bureau chiefs far too much autonomy. Publisher George Harvey, in noting Baker's safe journey overseas on an inspection trip, claimed that German U-boats would never attack a man who ran the War Department so inefficiently.[3] Only in the spring of 1918 was the secretary able to create a competent War Department. He did grow in the office, ably supervising the first successful military draft in U.S. history and—unlike Colonel House—never undercut President Wilson. He disappointed fellow liberals by ignoring the rights of conscientious objectors and by remaining silent during the administration's assault on civil liberties.

Once conscription became law, 72 percent of the army consisted of draftees. Many were poorly educated, three out of ten being totally illiterate or so poorly schooled as to misunderstand simple written examinations. One survey revealed that just under 18 percent had been to high school and fewer than 6 percent had seen the inside of a college classroom. Many had no idea of what Germany or the kaiser were.

Even in June 1917, weeks after Congress had passed conscription, some doubted whether any American Expeditionary Force lay in the offing. By the end of March, the War College Division had claimed that it would take more than two years before the United States could supply the Allies with anything beyond naval and economic aid. When one of Baker's aides, Major Palmer E. Pierce, appeared before the Senate Finance Committee, he pleaded for a $ 3 billion appropriation, the sum being necessary to bankroll the needed matériel—clothing, cots, food, blankets, medical supplies, horses, trucks, mules, artillery, rifles, pistols, and gas masks. The United States, Pierce went on, might have to maintain an army in Europe. Chairman Thomas S. Martin (D-Va.) was stunned: "Good Lord! You're aren't going to send soldiers over there, are you?"[4]

Baker chose John Joseph Pershing as AEF commander. The secretary had first preferred Major General Frederick Funston, who had captured the Filipino rebel leader Emilio Aguinaldo, but the former national guardsman had died shortly before the United States entered the war. Pershing had served in Cuba during the Spanish–American War and been governor of Moro Province in the Philippines. He so impressed Theodore Roosevelt that in 1906 the president promoted him from captain to brigadier general. Certainly, being the son-in-law of Francis Warren (R-Wyo.), chairman of the Senate Military Affairs Committee, did not hurt his career. He only gained national visibility two years later, however, when Wilson appointed him to lead the Punitive Expedition into Mexico against Pancho Villa. He was the only U.S. officer who had commanded a large body of troops in practically two decades.

Pershing certainly looked the part. The general stood tall and straight, possessing a square jaw, firm chin, sandy hair, heavy eyebrows, and trim mustache. Though he could smile if he wanted, his manner was aloof, his expression forbidding. Inspiring confidence more than affection, he conveyed an air of moral superiority, stark ambition, cold-bloodedness, discomfort with peers, and the desire to dominate. Such traits did serve him well when confronting the top brass of the Allies, men whose egos matched his own.

On May 8, Baker wrote Wilson, informing him that he had chosen Pershing as AEF commander. It was made clear to the general that U.S. forces must be preserved as a separate and distinct fighting unit, not one integrated with Allied troops. The secretary later claimed he told Pershing: "I will give you only two orders—one to go to France and the other to come home. In the meantime your authority in France will be supreme."[5] When in Europe Pershing held out against what was called "amalgamation" with Allied forces, he was simply following orders.

Wilson, always focusing on diplomacy, seldom intervened in military matters. On May 26, 1917, he officially appointed Pershing AEF commander, yet they conferred only once before the general left for France. In their conversation, they neither discussed the war nor the U.S. role in it. Unlike the other Allied generals, Pershing even operated independently of his own general staff in Washington. War correspondent Frederick Palmer wrote, "A dictatorship had been created for Pershing the day that he sailed. In our world in France his nod was law. No American in all history had ever been delegated such power." Military historians David R. Woodward and Edward M. Coffman accuse the president of surrendering his own role as commander in chief to the general, Coffman branding Pershing "America's proconsul in Europe."[6]

Pershing in turn chose James Guthrie Harbord ("the ablest officer I know") as his chief of staff. A graduate of Kansas State Agricultural College, Harbord had enlisted as a private in the Spanish–American War but did not see combat. He gained his reputation while serving ten years as a colonel in the Philippine Constabulary.[7]

Pershing landed at Liverpool on June 8, 1917, with a party of 191 officers and men, arriving on the SS *Baltic* through submarine-infested waters, Later that month, U.S. troops arrived in France in earnest, as 14,000 doughboys of the First Division disembarked at Saint-Nazaire. More than half were fresh to the army, having received minimal training and lacking familiarity with their weapons. Lower-ranking officers were usually green themselves, as the regulars remained in the states to assist in training.

When in mid-month, an AEF battalion arrived in Paris, it received a tumultuous welcome from war-weary Frenchmen who lined the route of their automobile procession from the Gare du Nord to the Hôtel de Crillon. When he visited Picpus Cemetery, one of Pershing's colonels, known for his oratorical skills, declared, "Lafayette, we are here." The only way this remark could get past the censors was to ascribe the famed epithet to Pershing himself. Harbord claimed his boss could have been elected king of France. Pershing biographer Frank E. Vandiver finds the general's initial status in France somewhere between President Poincaré and Louis XIV! General Philippe Pétain, the defender of Verdun, told Pershing, "I hope it is not too late."[8]

From the time he arrived in Europe, Pershing envisioned participation in Lorraine as the AEF's primary focus. British and Belgian forces were positioned on the left wing of the broad Allied front to protect the channel ports, the French massed in the center to guard Paris. Thanks to Pershing's scheme, American supplies could be routed south of the channel ports and Paris, hence less exposed to possible German attack. Relatively uncongested, Lorraine had seen relatively little action, offering places for unimpeded training called "safe zones."

In Pershing's thinking, within two years U.S. troops would advance towards the enemy stronghold at Metz, seizing steel plants, iron ore, and a crucial German trunk railway bringing matériel to the front. The General Staff told Secretary of War Baker that U.S. forces were located at "the nearest, quickest, and safest point from which to attack the enemy." "Success here will have a direct bearing on the primary objective of the Germans, which is the crushing of France." From there, the United States could launch "our great air campaign" against the U-boat bases and "the vitals of Germany."[9]

Pershing's field of operation was far from ideal. Historian Allan Millett notes that extensive fortifications between the Ardennes and Vosges Mountains protected an area resting in German hands for thirty-five years. Since the Germans never considered Lorraine a major theater of operations, the critical railroad so emphasized by Pershing turned west at Thionville, well beyond Metz, thereby requiring a far more extensive drive. Furthermore, Millett points out, Pershing exaggerated the resources of the area. The Saar, for example, produced only about 10 percent of Germany's coal and iron. Hence, the Allies could legitimately question whether Pershing offered any unique prospect for victory. The basic challenge remained: to destroy the ability of the German army to retain territory west of the Rhine River.[10]

Almost immediately, the Allies objected to U.S. inflexibility regarding troop integration. The Allies did not want a large, well-trained army that would fight—eventually. They sought a large number of small units that could immediately replenish their own ranks. Amalgamation had the advantage of instantly linking with an existing Allied military system, not establishing a totally new American one. In 1917, the Entente perceived Pershing's insistence upon a totally independent command necessitating a delay of two years before his forces engaged the enemy.

During the Balfour–Viviani mission of April 1917, the two statesmen not only spoke of the morale effect of immediate U.S. participation; they openly complained that the United States would not feel part of the war until it was "well bloodied." Needed, as General Bliss paraphrased their feeling, was "a large casualty list telegraphed home" that would "stir our fighting blood." General Sir William Robertson, chief of the Imperial General Staff, told Field Marshal Sir Douglas Haig, "It would be a good thing to get some Americans killed and so get the country to take a real interest in the war."[11]

From the time the AEF set foot in Europe, the French and British kept pressuring it to replenish depleted French battalions, with U.S. troops serving under French officers. In mid-August, Harbord, now a brigadier general, confided to his diary that "even our peace-loving people would hardly stand that sort of participation." Pershing will not be forced "to put his troops in the line in driblets, a regiment here, a battalion there, a little artillery somewhere else, instead of giving him in time his own sector of the front line in which America may exert the power of her trained legions." Wilson concurred, telling his cabinet, "We will have an American army or none."[12] Integration of U.S. forces, so the administration reasoned, would wound American pride; offend anti-British Irish Americans; impose a foreign language, in this case French, upon green troops; and—most important of all—reduce leverage in crucial diplomatic negotiations on matters of war and peace.

In early December, Lloyd George made his own amalgamation pitch, calling for mixing half-trained U.S. companies and battalions with Allied troops possessing several years combat experience. Pershing replied that no people possessing "a grain of national pride" would send their own men to build up a foreign army. Colonel House concurred, writing on a return trip from Europe, "If once we merge with them we will probably never emerge." Baker sought to take a conciliatory tone, cabling Pershing that responding to any "critical situation" took precedence over the autonomy of U.S. forces. By the end of the month, French president Raymond Poincaré had written Wilson directly, pointing to "the sad events in Russia," and pleading, "The fate of the war may depend on the conditions in which your valiant troops will be engaged on the battle front." Wilson responded evasively, simply replying that he was "anxious to do the best and most effective thing."[13]

The Allies received strong support from General Leonard Wood, former U.S. chief of staff, who was in Europe on an inspection tour. A highly partisan Republican and close ally of Theodore Roosevelt, the most popular general in the United States was a man whose ego was matched only by his tactlessness. Wood told Marshal Joffre on December 31 that U.S. units should immediately be placed in the front line next to Allied units. About three weeks later, he suggested to Pétain that half of U.S. artillery officers be trained by French units. At one dinner, he referred to Wilson as "that rabbit."[14] Needless to say, Wood's career was suddenly behind him, for by June 1918 the administration had forced him to sit out the rest of the war commanding a training camp in Kansas that drilled farm boys.

The debates over the best use of the AEF were somewhat moot. Independent or integrated, the doughboys remained ill-equipped for fighting. By September 1917, American war correspondents attempted to report that U.S. troops lacked the needed training for combat and that the military bureaucracy in Europe was incompetent. Without proper clothing, housing, and heat, U.S. troops were becoming ill. All such information was censored.[15]

In a speech that month in Chicago, Theodore Roosevelt pointed to the lack of field guns and airplanes. At Camp Grant, just outside of Rockford, Illinois, he found roughly one training rifle available for every three men. It would, he predicted, take a year before the U.S. armed forces equaled those of Portugal. Complaining that the War Department adopted the British Enfield rifle without providing the proper ammunition, TR attacked Major General William Crozier, the chief of ordnance, who had claimed that army camps possessed sufficient weapons for drills, that a six-month delay in supplying rifles was "perfectly endurable," and that any soldier ready for Europe would be outfitted with a rifle. TR accused the general of working at the pace of two figures of ancient history, Assyrian monarch Tiglath-Pileser and Egyptian pharaoh Necho II! In mid-December, he reported, "Our troops in France have received thousands of coffins, but an insufficient number of shoes." By the end of the month, he was writing of having personally witnessed "cannon" made of wood and thousands of men drilling with broomsticks instead of machine guns, riding barrels instead of horses.[16]

TR was not exaggerating. U.S. barracks and hospitals could lack heating. Sanitation and plumbing facilities were often inadequate, and thus some camps were difficult to drain. An unusually severe winter took a heavy toll on military camps, the freezing temperatures reaching as far south as Florida and Texas. Every army post reported deaths caused by disease. At Kansas's Camp Funston, for instance, 922 cases of influenza were reported in November 1917; 2,480 in March 1918.

November saw the Wilson administration descend into damage control. After touring camps in the South, Baker—who had not kept the public informed as to the true situation—had claimed that health conditions were satisfactory. The medical corps concurred. In his December 4, 1917, State of the Union address, Wilson referred to "the criticism and the clamor of the noisily thoughtless and troublesome," whom, he claimed, did not speak for the nation. "They do not touch the heart of anything. They may safely be left to strut their uneasy hour and be forgotten." It took Baker two more weeks before he released a report by Major General William C. Gorgas, widely known for his successful battle against yellow fever in the Panama Canal Zone. After inspecting four army camps, Gorgas reported that recruits lived in overcrowded tents and wore summer uniforms in winter weather.[17] Until April 1918, troops overseas lacked sufficient gas masks and the AEF provided at best sparse training in chemical warfare. In late December 1917, Wilson nationalized the railroads, designating Treasury Secretary McAdoo director general, so as to accelerate the shipment of war materials.

By the year's end, war manufacturing appeared painfully slow. The Shipping Board had yet to deliver a vessel. Army troop craft were operating at half capacity. Not a single plane had flown in the sky. Of the twelve hundred 75-mm guns ordered, only thirty-three had been produced.

From the outset, Congress had sought to control military policy. Within a week after Wilson had delivered his April war message, Senator John Weeks and Representative Martin Madden offered resolutions to create a Joint Committee on the Conduct of the War. The bipartisan committee would "study the problems arising out of the war, confer with the president and department heads, and periodically report its findings to the Congress." This body could subpoena witnesses at the highest level, including generals and cabinet secretaries.[18] Wilson, fully aware of the damage a similar committee inflicted upon Abraham Lincoln's administration, persuaded the Democratic-controlled Senate Rules Committee to bury the measure but the president was on warning.

In late December 1917, the Senate Military Affairs Committee held hearings that resulted in the gravest challenge yet to Wilson's control of the war effort. After touring field camps in France in November, Congressmen Clarence B. Miller and Porter H. Dale (R-Vt.) reported U.S. soldiers as lacking rifles, blankets, and clothing. The most powerful congressional voice came from Congressman Medill McCormick (R-Ill.), co-publisher of the *Chicago Tribune*, who had visited both the western and Italian fronts. He reported that the French and British could no longer supply U.S. forces from their own stocks. In fact, without 25,000 more cannon, they could lose the war.[19]

Every witness passed the blame elsewhere. Army ordnance chief Crozier indicted Congress for delaying war appropriations, manufacturers for charging excessively and postponing production until plants were funded, and Secretary Baker for allowing the shortage of small arms and for being unable to deliver a single machine gun overseas. Quartermaster General Henry G. Sharpe accused Chief of Staff Bliss of interfering with his bureau. Particularly damning testimony came from Major General Edwin Greble, commander of Camp Bowie in Fort Worth, Texas, who cited sixteen deaths per day and national guardsmen lacking winter clothing. He told the committee that his pleas to the War Department went unanswered.[20] In the midst of such highly defensive testimony, Baker "kicked [Crozier] upstairs" by appointing him to a newly created War Council and severing him from the Ordnance Department.

In January 1918, a particularly savage blizzard hit the Northeast, tying up transportation to such a degree that thousands of plants were closed in New York City alone. Railroad cars were backed up miles from the Atlantic ports. Hundreds of ships were immobilized. As fuel ran low, with coal particularly scarce, steel production slowed down and people either froze to death or died of pneumonia.

Fuel Administrator Harry Garfield, son of the twentieth president, prominent Cleveland businessman, and later president of Williams College, took draconian action. In order to free transportation for coal supplies, he ordered his agency to close down almost all factories east of the Mississippi for a week, effective midnight January 18, and for a specified number of Mondays thereafter.

The result: universal outrage. Within a day, the Senate voted 50 to 19 to delay the order, with 22 Democrats siding with their Republican colleagues. Only parliamentary maneuvering kept the House from voting on a similar measure. The pro-Wilson New York *World* called the edict "a wild experiment in economic lunacy worthy of a Bolshevik government," while its editor, Frank Cobb, phoned Wilson to plead for the thousands surviving on daily wages and lacking any savings. Colonel House privately remarked that he had never heard such a storm of protest, adding that he did not think Wilson had created an effective war organization. The president stoutly defended the order, writing Bernard Baruch, commissioner for raw materials of the War Industries Board, that he deplored people who "wince and cry when they are a little bit hurt." Less candid with the public, he simply told the press that the nation was "upon a war footing" and hence Americans should "observe the same sort of discipline that might be involved in the actual conflict itself." Fortunately for the nation, the situation rapidly improved, for coal began to move into the cities and shipping resumed to Europe within the week. Nonetheless, for the president the damage had been done.[21]

Now the eyes of all were on the secretary of war. Critics offered the slogan, "We need a butcher, not a Baker." Colonel House suggested that Wilson replace him with Interior Secretary Franklin K. Lane. Obviously no Democratic newspapers would claim, as Theodore Roosevelt did, that Baker's appointment was the greatest service Wilson could ever make to the kaiser. Their criticism, nonetheless, was almost as unrestrained as the Republican press. Historian Seward W. Livermore writes that had Congress been able to devise some means short of impeachment, Baker would have been removed. In mid-January, the war secretary offered to resign but the president would not permit it.[22]

Beginning on January 10 and for two days thereafter, Baker testified before the Senate Military Affairs Committee, answering hundreds of questions. He conceded the shortages of clothing, weapons, and equipment, but claimed that all such problems had been remedied. He explicitly denied that any U.S. soldier needing a rifle lacked one and argued that matériel was being procured as rapidly as possible. Death rates from disease were lower among U.S. troops than among civilians. A substantial, prepared force was already in place in France. Offering a barrage of statistics, he boasted that "no army of similar size in the history of the world has ever been raised, equipped, or trained so quickly."[23]

Senator George E. Chamberlain, chairman of the Senate Military Affairs Committee, was skeptical. A sturdily built, short man, who sported pince-nez glasses and a white mustache, he physically and politically resembled Theodore Roosevelt. Chamberlain was a progressive Democrat from Oregon who had been a district attorney, then state governor. He usually backed Wilson's policies, yet he possessed the temperament of a maverick. He had first expressed irritation when Baker and Chief of Staff Bliss rejected his alternative strategy for the AEF, for he sought to abandon assaults on the western front in favor of penetrating the Balkans, a strategy also favored by Lloyd George.

By mid-January 1918, Senator Chamberlain had introduced two measures. One would establish a department of munitions similar to the unit created in Britain in 1915 and originally headed by Lloyd

George. The other would provide for a war cabinet of "three distinguished citizens of demonstrated executive ability" appointed by the president and confirmed by the Senate; the new body would totally control the war effort under the sole direction of the president. Obviously, Baker and Navy Secretary Daniels would be sidelined and Wilson himself deprived of directing mobilization. The president responded immediately, arguing that overseas such munitions ministries had proven disappointing and that general "re-coordination" of the war effort would merely cause more delay.[24]

Chamberlain had just begun his crusade. On January 19, he addressed 1,900 people at a joint luncheon of the National Security League and the American Defense Society presided over by Elihu Root. In words quoted approvingly throughout the nation's press, he proclaimed: "The military establishment of America has fallen down; there is no use to be optimistic about a thing that does not exist; it also stopped functioning. Why? Because of inefficiency in every bureau and in every department of the Government of the United States." Wilson again responded, declaring that Chamberlain's allegations were "an astonishingly and absolutely unjustifiable distortion of the truth." Baker remained "one of the ablest officials I have ever known." The president told his cabinet that the Republicans sought a governing body controlled by "representatives of privilege." Hence, the board envisioned by the Oregon senator would not be established until he, Wilson, "was dead." The creator of the New Freedom, with its strong antimonopolistic thrust, was not about to establish an "economic general staff" that could fix prices, rationalize industries, and control markets.[25]

Senate Republicans backed Chamberlain. In a debate held on January 21, Lodge stressed that his party had supported all war measures proposed by the president but that shortages of sugar and coal, and conditions in the training camps, made investigation necessary. The far more polemical Boies Penrose accused Wilson of filling war offices with incompetent Democrats, asserted that Fuel Administrator Garfield had never seen the inside of a coal mine, and called Colonel House "some kind of mysterious traveler," whose expenses were paid from "a contingent fund." Known for his caustic personality, Penrose remarked that Colonel House's military genius obviously equaled that of Napoleon or Caesar![26]

One of the strongest volleys came from a member of Wilson's own party, Senator Gilbert Hitchcock. A man as opinionated as he was conceited, the Nebraska newspaper publisher had crossed swords with Wilson before the country had entered the war, often voicing pro-German views. Even after Germany had declared unrestricted submarine warfare, Hitchcock sought an arms embargo.

In early February 1918, Hitchcock accused the nation's mobilization system of being so organized as to guarantee inefficiency, even finding Baker out of touch with his own War Department. The senator claimed that Wilson remained ignorant of the true situation and as isolated as a monarch surrounded by courtiers. Twenty pairs of shoes had been ordered for every man in the army, yet the sizes were often far too small. Troops still lacked woolen breeches and blouses. "Tens of thousands of men" lacked overcoats.[27]

Senate Democrats did their best to counter such charges. John Sharp Williams accused administration critics of playing the "German game" of "muckraking" the administration. He accused Wilson's critics of maneuvering Crozier's removal from the Ordnance Department, whereas the general obviously knew more than they did. James Reed conceded serious defects in the mobilization program but asserted that any military machine that put 1.5 million men into the field within eight months was no failure. Kentucky's Ollie James, known for his oratory, gave a two-hour philippic, saying of Wilson, "Do not badger him. Do not heckle him. Do not annoy him. He will make the journey safely over this ocean of blood and peril."[28]

Among the House Democrats, there were similar sentiments. Carter Glass of Virginia found Chamberlain's accusations "wild and foolish," the utterances of a "theatrical public man." Illinois's William Mason cried out, "For God's sake let's quit fighting each other and fight the Kaiser."[29]

For the most part, participants in the debate took predictable positions. George Creel denied that a single life had been lost by negligence. The Hearst press claimed Senator Chamberlain was obligated to give Wilson sufficient time to carry out his policies. The *New Republic* called Chamberlain's war council proposal "crude, ill considered and indefensible"; it recommended instead a daily meeting of department chiefs with the president. Conversely, the *Outlook* accused the administration of acting as if it were attempting "to run a

British war tank with a motor built for a Ford runaround." Theodore Roosevelt went to Washington in order to expedite the creation of Chamberlain's war cabinet. Telling one person he was "going after the man in the White House," he wrote another that he would now be close to the helm of government.[30]

Some reactions, however, were surprising. The *New York Times*, usually sympathetic to Wilson, saw the American people losing faith in the War Department. Colonel Harvey's *War Weekly* called Chamberlain's specific proposal beyond "the scope of reason or common sense" while nonetheless seeking a bill giving the president "the concentrated assistance" he so badly needed. William Howard Taft wrote that any new council could end up serving as a "mere speaking-tube" for the president. Taking a moderate position, he found the truth lying between Baker's "rosy" picture and Chamberlain's charges.[31]

Chamberlain struck back. On January 24, he spoke to a packed gallery in the Senate for three hours, reading from letters of grief-stricken parents describing death from disease and exposure in the training camps. His colleagues had heard him deliver this general indictment before but he now held Baker directly responsible for these tragedies. William Kirby offered a brief rebuttal, absolving the military hospitals of any negligence.[32]

Four days later, Baker again testified before Chamberlain's committee, parrying hostile questions from critics for four and a half hours. The secretary offered a detailed defense concerning such matters as food, housing, and clothing. Soon the United States would have 500,000 troops in France and another 1.5. million by year's end. He could not refrain from claiming that years before it had been Leonard Wood, a highly partisan Roosevelt backer, who as chief of staff had chosen the camp sites that proved the most unsanitary. He concluded with the words, "Has any army in history ever, since the beginning of time, been so raised and cared for as this army has been? Can the picture be duplicated?" Chamberlain told Baker, "The committee has been much impressed."[33]

Despite Baker's more able effort this time, his critics continued their barrage. Roosevelt challenged the secretary by reporting that a major general had told him in October that his training camp possessed 100 rifles for 20,000 men. TR privately wrote his son Kermit that both Baker and Wilson should be impeached. Hitchcock referred to "camp hospitals without drainage," "sick men without nurses." In early February, Baker was again summoned before the Military Affairs Committee, there subject to outright harassment by Senators Weeks and James W. Wadsworth Jr. (R–N.Y.).[34]

Not all reaction was negative. The Hearst press carried an editorial titled "The Splendid Achievement of the War Department Deserves Praise." When Baker arrived in France in March, Lieutenant Colonel George S. Patton, who commanded a tank brigade, said of him, "He is a little rat, but very smart."[35]

Chamberlain's efforts to create a special war cabinet never came up to a vote. Informal polling of the Senate showed only twenty-seven members in favor. Public support for Wilson, pressure from the White House, and the illnesses of Roosevelt and Chamberlain resulted in the legislation being pigeonholed.[36]

In reality, the fault, as noted by historian David R. Woodward, lay in the Army Reorganization Bill of 1916, which had created a strictly peacetime structure. The prominent liberal Oswald Garrison Villard aptly wrote in the *Nation* that to expect that rearmament "could all be done in six months, without errors of judgment or mistakes of policy, is to demand the impossible. We are living in extraordinary times, but not in days of magic." At the same time, as Baker's biographer Daniel R. Beaver notes, Baker had only partially sensed the tremendous strain to which the War Department would be subjected.[37]

Already the administration was making substantial changes. In mid-January, it reorganized the department's procurement and, to avoid duplication, demanded the purchasing agencies of the army, navy, and Shipping Board clear orders through the Council of National Defense. Wilson also made the highly efficient Edward Stettinius, a J. P. Morgan partner, surveyor of supplies; the man soon became second assistant secretary of war. In addition, press censorship concerning the defense effort was relaxed.

The next month saw the much respected George W. Goethals become director of procurement and transport, thus breaking the power of the inept Quartermaster Department. In March, Wilson named Bernard M. Baruch to chair an upgraded War Industries Board. The able Wall Street broker, though often lacking formal powers, used his informal influence to establish priorities, set production quotas, and determine wages and prices. With Baruch acting as "economic dictator" and the WIB serving as the government's most powerful agency, order was finally brought into the mobilization effort and criticism practically ceased.

At the same time, Baker pulled Major General Peyton March out of France, where he had commanded Pershing's artillery, making him acting army chief of staff. March received the full title in May. He replaced chaos with order, ruthlessly disregarding age, rank, and seniority to find the most able officers possible. He reformed military intelligence; created an air service, a tank corps, and chemical services; and eliminated distinctions between the regular army, national guard, and draftees. The first man to appear at the War Department in the morning, he could remain until 1 a.m. Ever cutting through red tape, he pledged, "I propose to get men to France if they have to swim." Baruch aptly called him "the right man in the right place." Even the often critical *War Weekly* found him "a man in sympathy with the virile elements of the universe."[38]

Such efficiency came with a price, for March possessed the negative skill of fighting everyone in sight. Newton Baker later described him as "arrogant, harsh, dictatorial and opinionated . . . riding roughshod over everyone." He fought with Pershing over matters ranging from promotion prerogatives to the wearing of the Sam Browne belt (a waste of good leather, said March).[39] Fear that March might select Goethals to reorganize Pershing's supply system forced the AEF commander to reorganize his own faltering supply system. In late July 1918, Pershing appointed his chief of staff, General James G. Harbord, to head the Services of Supply, a responsibility that Harbord performed well. Always the essential matter at issue, and both March and Pershing knew it, was just who was to plan, develop, and most of all execute the entire army program. Wilson and Baker never really resolved the matter.

Wilson's major response to Chamberlain's proposals, however, took place on February 1, when Wilson rallied leading Democratic senators to promote fresh legislation drafted by the War Department. The bill gave the president practically unlimited authority to reorganize the executive branch and authorized him to redistribute functions among varied agencies. Admittedly, the Lever Act of August 1917 had already given the president sweeping authority over production, manufacture, and distribution of foodstuffs, fuel, fertilizers, and farm implements. Nonetheless, in light of the controversy over the current snags in production and over Baker's performance, Wilson wisely saw that more was needed to reassure the public. To introduce the bill, he chose Lee S. Overman, chairman of the powerful Senate Rules Committee, who had staunchly supported New Freedom domestic legislation.

Republicans fought the legislation vigorously, managing to keep it bottled in the Judiciary Committee for several weeks. Only when William E. Borah, Knute Nelson, and LeBaron Colt (R-R.I.) switched allegiance did the bill reach the Senate floor. Once debate began, Senator Lawrence Sherman took the opportunity to accuse Wilson of surrounding himself with a "bunch of economic fakers and howling dervishes," "firebrands and pestilent fiends of sedition." He described Baker, who as Cleveland's mayor had fostered municipal operation of his city's streetcars, as "half a pacifist and the other half Socialist." Finding Overman's bill "utterly unconstitutional," Frank Brandegee claimed that the president had "the country by the throat." He personally did not intend to be like "a little white poodle dog or a spaniel running from the Capitol to the White House with a ball in my mouth."[40]

On April 28, the Senate passed Overman's bill 63–13, with 21 Republicans backing the administration. Ohio senator Harding protested against a forthcoming "dictatorship," even though less than a year before he had sought just such powers for the president. Brandegee caustically offered an amendment providing that "any power, constitutional or not, [that] has been inadvertently omitted in this bill" has been "hereby granted in full." Surprisingly enough, Colonel Harvey's *War Weekly* endorsed the legislation, believing it would clear bureaucratic tangles. On May 14, the House voted in favor 295–2 and six days later Wilson signed the measure.[41] Now there was no question that the president had authority to direct the nation's resources.

If public concern over matters of training and supply finally became somewhat resolved, major problems in both areas still existed through the rest of the war. One matter remained particularly glaring, that of aircraft. Aviation itself was only fourteen years old when the United States entered the conflict. At the time, the infant Air Service was a neglected part of the Army Signal Corps. In May 1917, the AEF possessed fifty-five planes and twenty-six qualified pilots.

In June, Baker had promised the manufacture of 100,000 planes and the training of 6,000 pilots, claiming that American airmen might turn the tide of the war. By October, Interior Secretary Franklin K. Lane spoke in terms of only 22,000 planes. At the end of the year, the United States had yet to send a single "winged crusader" to Europe and still lacked the necessary plants, engineers, machinery, and trained personnel. Production had been turned over to automobile manufacturers inexperienced in mass production of aircraft. Factory workers did not possess needed skills. Faulty construction of the obsolete De Havilland DH-4 training aircraft cost the lives of many pilots. Lieutenant Colonel Billy Mitchell, who commanded all U.S. air units on the front line, later wrote, "Flyers at the front were generally afraid of this plane."[42]

In November 1917, Gutzon Borglum offered to investigate the matter. A prominent sculptor who later was responsible for the carved faces on Mount Rushmore, Borglum was an amateur air enthusiast. Planes he designed never left the drawing board but he sensed a personal kinship to Leonardo da Vinci. He convinced Baker, a personal friend, of his qualifications in aircraft production, at which point Wilson asked him to "discover the facts in this business."[43]

Borglum submitted his preliminary report to the president in January 1918, blaming the production snag on greedy auto producers under government contract. Wilson forwarded the document on to Baker: "There may be something worthy of our consideration, and suggestions worthy to be adopted." Replying immediately, Baker accused Borglum of making wild statements.[44]

Baker himself drew further attacks by claiming in mid-February that the first American-built "battleplanes" were en route to France. On March 25, General Leonard Wood, just back from France, testified before the Senate Military Affairs Committee, declaring that U.S. troops could not ward off air attacks in their own battle sector. German planes flew so low that the doughboys had to fight them off with pistols.[45]

That very day, in what the *New York Times* called the bitterest Senate debate of the war, Lodge claimed that the American front in France was not defended by a single combat plane. Moreover, only two ships had been built. Harry S. New (R-Ind.) cited official figures to show that only thirty-seven planes would be ready for service by July. Overman responded that such attacks were singularly inappropriate. Referring to General Ludendorff's recently launched offensive, which imperiled the entire western front, he berated his Republican colleagues for injuring the nation's morale during "the saddest hour of our history during the war."[46]

On April 10, the majority report of the Military Affairs Committee demanded that the air program be taken out of the hands of the Signal Corps, where it was lodged, and placed under a single presidential appointee. Four Democrats, including Chamberlain and Hitchcock, concurred with five Republicans in stressing the flaws in the De Havilland craft and the mass-produced Liberty engine. A minority report, signed by three Wilson loyalists, defended the Signal Corps, stressing the innumerable production obstacles and claiming that Americans could be "justly proud" of its record.[47]

In mid-April, Wilson abruptly severed relations with Borglum: "I merely gave you the right to look into the matter of your own volition." The president denied ever making him "an official investigator."[48] He also fired auto manufacturer Howard E. Coffin, chairman of the aircraft production board, and Major General George O. Squier, chief of the Signal Corps. On May 3, John D. Ryan, president of the Anaconda Copper Mining Company, became director of aircraft production.

Borglum, who considered himself shabbily treated, would not be silenced. In late April, he told the *New York Times* that nearly a billion dollars had been lost in "colossal profiteering." He was frequently cited when the Senate called for a thorough investigation. On May 2, several senators—Hitchcock, Miles Poindexter, and Philander Knox (R-Pa.) among them—spoke in terms of launching a criminal investigation. Brandegee accused Baker of outright lying concerning the merits of the Liberty engine. When asked about Borglum's qualifications for investigating the aircraft industry, the Connecticut senator had recently snapped, "The president selected him and, therefore, I think he didn't have any such qualifications." William King remarked that a government officer told him someone "ought to be shot" for the failure to supply "flying machines." Wilson commented privately, "Borglum is sure to make an ass out of himself when he tries to make good." Baker gave Attorney General Gregory a military intelligence report alleging that Borglum had a large financial stake in an aircraft company that had been denied a government contract.[49]

In an effort to put matters to rest, on May 12, Charles Evans Hughes agreed to investigate the aircraft industry. Formally, he was merely acting on behalf of the Department of Justice. In reality he was given comprehensive fact-finding power. Hughes had been governor of New York, a Supreme Court justice, and the Republican nominee for president in 1916. He had originally made his reputation as special counsel of the New York State legislature investigating gas, electric, and insurance firms. Colonel House suggested the appointment to ward off Chamberlain's resolution for an official investigation, fearing the senators would "splash all the mud around that they can." Wilson realized the wisdom of appointing Hughes but had a low opinion of the man. Just three months before, he had written the chairman of the Interstate Commerce Commission, "I hope with all my heart that Charles E. Hughes will never be connected in any way with affairs down here, he proved himself so absolutely false in the last campaign."[50]

The appointment met with wide press approval. Even Lodge conceded that Wilson had done "a very astute thing." Hughes was reluctant to undertake this most unpleasant assignment but saw it as his duty.[51]

Hughes's hearings were held behind closed doors so as to avoid embarrassing the war effort or disclosing military secrets. They lasted five months and involved 280 witnesses who gave 17,000 pages of testimony. When, on October 31, 1918, the report was made public, it conceded bureaucratic ineptitude, but no major corruption. The past few months, the account went on, marked great improvement, thanks to Ryan's reorganization of the Aircraft Division. It blamed General Squier for initial delays and recommended court-martialing a colonel who headed the Signal Corps's equipment division. The Liberty engine, the document claimed, performed better than any of its international rivals.[52]

Wilson and Baker had handled the entire matter poorly. Borglum was totally out of his depth but justly felt that Wilson had undercut him. Part of the problem, as historian David R. Woodward notes, was with Pershing and his staff. One month they would order fighters, bombers, and observation planes in certain quantities. The next month they would cancel them, yet in still another month they would reorder the same models in completely different quantity.[53]

In all the nations at war, the public followed adoringly the exploits of the air "aces," those pilots who shot down enemy planes or balloons. Yet, though air war promised glamor, a remnant of chivalry amid massive brutality, it played little role in the winning the conflict. Moreover, until the end of the conflict, AEF aviators flew French and British aircraft.

Fortunately for U.S. forces overseas, the United States and the Allies had long entered into a tacit agreement. The Yanks would send men; the factories of France and Britain would provide artillery, horses, mules, airplanes, automatic weapons, and tanks. The French not only trained 80 percent of the AEF, but doughboys used their artillery, airplanes, and machine guns. British ships transported many U.S. units. Lacking direct authority over the War and Navy Departments, the Wilson administration was unable to coordinate military purchases.

During the whole of 1918, as Pershing conceded, "We were literally beggars as to every important weapon, except the rifle." Statistics bear the general out. Only one-third of the AEF automatic rifles were made at home. Of 6,287 AEF airplanes available on Armistice Day, only 1,216 were of American manufacture; most were of a type branded "Flaming Coffins." Few if any tanks or the 155-mm howitzers used by the doughboys were made in the United States. The same condition held true for 75-mm guns. Except for shrapnel, little American-produced artillery ammunition reached the front.[54]

When it comes to preparation, the Wilson administration deserves criticism. Admittedly, massive troop training and conversion to wartime production would be a difficult task under the best of circumstances. Understandably, too, such a situation lends itself to political posturing. Secretary Baker, though, was inordinately slow in gaining control of the War Department at the time when speed was crucial.

Senators Chamberlain and Hitchcock, both Democrats, raised genuine issues concerning governmental competence. Fortunately, Wilson took sufficient hold of the situation to push through the Overman bill and to empower such competent administrators as Baruch.

The fighting in Europe, however, would not wait upon quarreling senators and bureaucratic infighting. U.S. troops were finally being put to the test.

THIRTEEN
CHECKING LUDENDORFF

THE WINTER OF 1917-18 WAS MARKED BY AN OMINOUS stalemate with relatively little activity on the western front. Only in early November 1917, eight months after the United States entered the war, did doughboys suffer their first deaths. These troops were stationed near Somerviller, slightly southeast of Nancy, France. This "quiet sector" had seen little action and remained ideal for training and "seasoning." On the evening of the 3nd, more than two hundred Germans charged a platoon of U.S. Company F, 16th Regiment, leaving one soldier shot dead, another with his throat slit, and a third with a crushed skull. Five were wounded, twelve captured. In midmonth, Major General Robert L. Bullard, who commanded the First Division, wrote in his diary, "So far as we are concerned, the war is practically lost." "Alas, I think we came *too late*."[1]

Both sides of the conflict realized that Germany would launch a massive offensive in the spring of 1918. Berlin's U-boat campaign had failed and the British blockade was creating severe shortages. First Quartermaster General Erich Ludendorff, de facto commander of the German army, realized the critical importance of delivering a crippling blow before, as he said, "America can throw strong forces into the scale." Similarly, Philippe Pétain told his French troops that superiority depended on "large units" of U.S. forces.[2] The defeat of Russia and the Italian collapse at Caporetto had permitted Ludendorff to shift troops to the western front, giving his army an edge of 191 divisions to the Allied 178.

Hence, the British and French pressed even harder for immediate amalgamation of the arriving U.S. forces. In January 1918, when War Secretary Baker prodded Pershing concerning the "critical situation" on the western front, the general denied that the situation warranted such a move. He gave the usual reasons. Putting his companies and battalions into Allied divisions under foreign commanders would cause U.S. troops to lose their "national identity," creating morale problems overseas and at home. Sudden integration would disrupt the Allies' own preparation. A different type of training would confuse the green U.S. forces. He soon added that the country's postwar position would be stronger if its army played "a distinct and definite part."[3]

By the end of the month, Pershing supplied other rationales. Political opponents of the Wilson administration would challenge the president's conduct of the war, something in fact already under way. Within the United States, German propagandists would stir up antiwar opinion. Black Jack noted that Britain had seldom sought to amalgamate troops of its own empire, that is, those from Australia, Canada, and India. Nor had France attempted to integrate Senegalese, Moroccans, and other colonial forces. The heavy casualties accumulated by Allied forces in three-plus years of trench warfare offered no reassurance of Allied competence. Pershing noted that even French general Joffre had admitted that only after sustaining 10,000 to 15,000 casualties could an infantry general really become competent. If Americans "went in," the general told Colonel House," very few of them would ever come out."[4]

Baker was briefly converted, informing the French ambassador that once AEF soldiers were handed over to Allied command, it would be reluctant to return them. When Pershing heard that London was preparing an offensive in Palestine so as to knock out Turkey, he doubted whether Britain really feared a crisis on the western front. Moreover, in private, French general Joseph Joffre, British field commander Sir Douglas Haig, and the British War Cabinet all denied that any German attack would succeed.[5]

The Allied estimate of Pershing and his troops remained low. On January 12, General Sir William Robertson, chief of the Imperial General Staff, called U.S. increasing strength "a weak reed to lean upon," telling Haig that Pershing had "no grasp of the task in front of him." Haig in turn wrote in his diary that the Yanks "were criticizing their Government because there seemed to be no results to show for the money which America has been spending! No troops in the field, no aeroplanes, no guns, no nothing yet in fact!" The French grumbled, "We expected to see two million cowboys throw themselves upon the Boches and we see only a few thousand workers building warehouses." They could not help noting that the Americans were apathetic concerning supply and liaison, ordered impossible artillery barrages, and failed to place their machine guns in advantageous positions. By February, only 236 U.S. troops had been killed in action. Both Haig and Pétain feared that it would take more than a year before independent AEF divisions could serve on the front line.[6]

Pershing blamed much of his supply slowdown on the French and the U.S. War Department, noting that the Ordnance Department would send over spittoons, lawn mowers, and window shades when ammunition, boots, and winter clothing were needed. The real blame, as the general's biographer Donald Smythe notes, lay far more with the man himself, as his headquarters at Chaumont remained overstaffed and top-heavy.[7]

By mid-January, Robertson told Pershing that he found conditions on the western front most serious. In fact, the small number of British troops available for combat would be so exhausted that they would lack the strength to be gainfully employed once the war ended. Pershing yielded slightly on January 16, 1918, mentioning short-term assistance to meet the emergency. He offered temporary amalgamation for training purposes, but the gesture was an empty one: once instructed, the doughboys would return to their own commanders. He did lend twelve battalions of his four "colored regiments" to the French. These African American troops were absorbed into French divisions and wore the French uniform; they performed most ably.

Former chief of staff Tasker Bliss, sent to Europe as U.S. representative to the Supreme War Council, backed the Allied amalgamation request. As he wrote Baker late in January, "If we do not make the greatest sacrifices *now* and, as a result, a great disaster should come, we will never forgive ourselves nor will the world forgive us. . . . We have no time to lose."[8]

Some historians find a case for the Allied plea, stressing an obvious need for men. Donald Smythe notes that the Entente had the staffing essential for divisions, corps, and field armies; it lacked only the men to fill the units. Conversely, U.S. forces possessed the troops but fell short in staff. Complete U.S. divisions would take five times as long to transport and even longer to train. Thus, if amalgamation were adopted, raw recruits would be instructed better and quicker alongside seasoned fighters. The current tonnage bottleneck would be alleviated, for the United States would not need massive matériel or the support troops that made up about 45 percent of the AEF. Once "bloodied" and proficient, the doughboys could return to their own units. Too much postponement and the war could be lost. Impervious to the need for priority shipments of infantry and machine-gun units, Pershing was, in Smythe's words, "like a man playing Russian roulette. He lived through it, but he was lucky he didn't blow his head off."[9]

Several other scholars concur. David F. Trask thinks that amalgamation might have hastened the armistice. The quarrel did not result in disaster but certainly enhanced tension in inter-Allied circles. Even, writes Richard Striner, if one concedes the need for a distinct U.S. chain of command and for protecting American soldiers from such commanders as Haig, Pershing appeared callous and Wilson, who always backed the general, "the worst kind of prima donna."[10]

Other scholars defend Pershing, emphasizing matters of morale and long-range U.S. plans. David R. Woodward finds it difficult to argue with the general, approvingly quoting him as later saying, "no people with a grain of national pride would consent to furnish men to build up the army of another nation." John S. D. Eisenhower asserts that Pershing's effort to retain a single army was necessary, particularly given all U.S. operational plans for a gigantic push in 1919.[11]

On March 21, 1918, slightly before dawn, Germany launched the largest single offensive yet in the war. Writing in 1931, Winston Churchill called it "without exception the greatest onslaught in the history of the world." In what Germany deemed Operation Michael, named after Germany's patron saint, Ludendorff triggered a surprise attack, focusing upon a twelve-mile sector between Arras and St. Quentin,

France. The French had concentrated on reinforcing the ridge at Chemin des Dames, the British on protecting the channel ports. Thus neither power expected the onslaught to take place where it did. Germany's recent defeat of Russia had released half a million of its troops for the western front. For a brief moment, the Allies were outnumbered. Ludendorff had told his commanders several months before, "Our overall position requires the earliest possible blow . . . before the Americans can throw strong forces into the scales."[12]

The 6,000-gun preliminary artillery barrage was so massive that it dwarfed all those launched in World War II. Within five hours, the Germans had fired 3.5 million shells. Seventy-six elite German divisions fell upon British lieutenant general Sir Hubert Gough's already weakened Fifth Army, which was soon destroyed. Entire British units either surrendered or retreated. A massive fog, continuing intermittently for three days, favored the attackers. Storm troops (the "assault divisions") infiltrated enemy lines, followed by heavy machine guns and field artillery, succeeded in turn by heavily equipped units (the "trench divisions") to mop up the strong points. The aim: to separate most of the British army from the French. If the British Expeditionary Force (BEF) was isolated, the French army protecting Paris would be so exposed that capitulation would be inevitable.

Within three days, the Germans had crossed the Somme River, in the process regaining territory that the British has captured at huge sacrifice in 1916. March 24–26 marked Britain's worst days of this first major engagement. Its forces became increasingly separated from French ones, the BEF fleeing northeast towards the channel ports. On the 26th, Pétain told French premier Clemenceau, "The Germans will defeat the British in the open country; after that they will defeat us."[13]

As Paris suffered bombardment, London experienced a state of panic. On March 23, Lloyd George had informed British publisher Lord Riddle, "The news is very bad. I fear it means disaster." On the same day, Foreign Secretary Balfour instructed Ambassador Reading to tell President Wilson: "Send over infantry as fast as possible." Pleading for the brigading of U.S. troops with British and French ones, he warned, "If America delays it may be too late." As he placed his hand on Reading's shoulder, the president responded, "I'll do my damnedest." Not wanting to bolster Wilson's domestic critics, Lloyd George issued a public statement on April 1 declaring that the president had done everything possible to assist the Allies. Privately, however, he was most impatient, writing Ambassador Reading that Allied chances depended on the prompt appearance of U.S. forces. The difference of even a week, he feared, could win or lose a battle.[14]

Amid the congressional queries concerning War Department incompetence, some Americans voiced a sense of urgency. James Beck saw "the future of mankind for decades" hanging in the balance. Ex-president Taft accused his countrymen of living in a fool's paradise: "The war has been remote to us." The *Outlook* warned that Allied defeat would force the Yanks into a desperate dilemma: fighting "Teutonic invaders" on our own shores or making "a slavish peace with the Prussian conquerors" involving huge indemnities and possibly humiliating annexations. The *Nation* was slightly more optimistic, claiming that if Paris fell, the British and Americans would still dominate the seas. The *New Republic*, though acknowledging the British retreat, denied that overall the western line had been broken.[15]

The Allied military expressed skepticism concerning any U.S. commitment. Meeting on March 27, the SWC issued Joint Note 18, calling "in principle" for the rushing of U.S. units to serve with Allied corps and divisions. It did concede the temporary nature of such orders, pledging their eventual return to the U.S. Army. Preference, the note stressed, must be given to infantry and machine-gunners. Implicit was the suspending of artillery and technical units needed to create an independent AEF. Haig commented, "I hope the Yankees will not disappoint us in this. They have seldom done anything yet which they have promised." Clemenceau later recalled that it was "heart-rending . . . to see our men being mown down unceasingly while . . . large bodies of American troops remained idle, within earshot of the guns. . . . Pershing, with his tight-lipped smile, kept putting things off." The battlefields, the French premier continued, "had already drunk the best blood of France."[16] In Allied eyes, the general was giving the Germans a needed breathing space.

Both General Bliss and Secretary Baker, then in Europe inspecting U.S. facilities, sided with the SWC. Pershing still balked, denying that this emergency should force any change of plans. On March 28, he did pledge to French general Ferdinand Foch, just made supreme commander of the Allied forces: "At this moment there are no other questions but of fighting. Infantry, artillery, aviation, all that we have are yours; use them as you wish. More will come, in numbers equal to requirements. I have come especially to tell you that the American people will be proud to take part in the greatest battle of history."[17]

Yet, in practice, the general's offer meant little. The U.S. 1st Division, though ordered from Lorraine to the front in Picardy, arrived too late to be needed. The 2nd Division simply extended its front. The 26th and 42nd merely relieved French divisions in quiet sectors.

On April 5, Ludendorff suspended Operation Michael. German troops had outpaced their support system. Because the kaiser's army possessed few trucks, soldiers carried supplies on their backs. Underfed horses and mules lacked the strength to pull their guns forward. The absence of light tanks prevented rapid pursuit. Ludendorff possessed a good eye for battlefield tactics but did not have an overall strategic vision. By March 23, he had settled on the objective of Amiens, realizing that it was the linchpin of the major railroad system between northern France and Paris. But the German Second Army delayed in order to forage, losing precious time, and on April 4 it halted.

On April 9, at 9 a.m., Germany launched its second major offensive, Operation Georgette, this time against twelve miles of British lines on the Lys River in Flanders. Ludendorff commented, "We shall simply tear open a hole and the rest will follow. That is the way we did it in Russia." The Germans stormed Messines Ridge in Belgium and took Armentières, France, the first day, opening a wide breach. On April 11, Haig, again caught by surprise, issued a desperate Order of the Day: "Every position must be held to the last man: there must be no retirement. With our backs to the wall and believing in the justice of our cause, each of us must fight on to the end."[18] By now Ludendorff's forces were within fifteen miles of Allied ports along the English Channel.

Colonel House called for immediately using every American available, noting that the British compared the situation to the crucial Battle of Verdun in 1916. Furthermore, he feared that German success would lead to "denunciations from such as Roosevelt, Wood and their kind." Wilson, however, was distressed by Britain's continual demands for amalgamation. According to Navy Secretary Daniels's notes, the president told his cabinet on April 15, "Fear I will come out of the war hating English."[19]

On April 20, U.S. troops experienced their heaviest engagement thus far. At 5 a.m., at Seicheprey, almost three thousand Germans ("Hindenberg's Traveling Circus") overwhelmed the Yanks, resulting in 699 AEF casualties. Pershing accused his troops of sitting "quietly in trenches during a heavy fog" and allowing "a surprise attack to be sprung" upon them. Such "inexcusable" conduct would not be "tolerated." Historian David R. Woodward finds the general's accusation unfair, for two of his companies had fought valiantly against a force six times its size. Ironically the American press deigned Seicheprey a success. Lloyd George remarked, "This kind of result . . . is bound to occur on an enormous scale if a large amateur United States Army is built up without the guidance of more experienced General Officers."[20]

During Germany's second offensive, the British assumed that the United States would transport 120,000 infantry and machine gun units per month for four months and would brigade these forces with French or British troops. In meeting with a British general just before Germany's April strike, Pershing denied any such understanding, saying only that 60,000 troops were pledged, and this only for the month. On April 21, in what became known as the "Baker–Reading agreement," the secretary of war promised 680,000 men from April through July, though specific assignments remained with Pershing.

Three days later in London, while meeting with Alfred Milner, who had just become British war secretary, Pershing had the agreement modified. Infantry and machine-gunners would not be the only troops shipped, and the arrangement would only hold true for May. Black Jack had again outmaneuvered both Washington and the Allies. Foch and Clemenceau were particularly furious, for Britain alone would be lent U.S. troops. By the time U.S. forces arrived in mass, Foch wasted no time in warning Pershing that Britain would be pushed into the sea, the French driven behind the Loire River. Pershing again responded that in a true emergency, U.S. troops were always available.[21]

Germany's second assault ended on April 29. The termination marked a turning point in morale. Ludendorff's troops, depressed and exhausted, had only advanced twelve miles and saw no further prospect of breaking Allied lines. Infantry continued to outdistance artillery and supplies. Many a bulge in the enemy front could be turned into a vulnerable salient difficult to defend. German casualties numbered about 110,000, about equal to those of the Allies. Although the British army suffered exhaustion, Allied rail communication remained intact, their ports open. Historian Woodward compares the German commander to a tired boxer, behind on points, swinging wildly for a knockout punch before American reinforcements overwhelmed him. Ludendorff had lost more than a quarter of a million men, while Berlin's General Staff kept 1.5 million troops in occupied Russia.[22]

On May 1, the SWC met at Abbeville. Pershing accused the Allies of pressing the Americans, whom — he claimed — needed nine weeks of trench training to fight immediately in their units. Allied generals responded that the emergency justified throwing even partially trained men into battle. When an exasperated Foch asked, "You are willing to risk our being driven back to the Loire?," Pershing replied, "Yes, I am willing to take the risk. Moreover, the time may come when the American Army will have to stand the brunt of this war and it is not wise to fritter away our resources in this manner." Black Jack stormed out of the meeting. Haig found the U.S. commander "very obstinate" and "stupid," lacking the necessary troops for a self-contained American army while not realizing the urgency of the situation. Were the United States not able to offer immediate aid, remarked Lloyd George, France and Britain might have to yield, fighting to the last man, while the U.S. Army "would have to stop without putting into line more men than little Belgium." A British soldier wrote home sardonically of a U.S. Army "of three millions, fully equipped, each man, with a hair mattress, a hot-water bottle, a gramophone, and a medicine chest, which they tell us will get to Berlin and 'cook the goose' of the Kaiser."[23]

Within the month, the Germans attempted their third offensive, code name Blücher after one of the great Prussian generals of the Napoleonic Wars. On May 27, Ludendorff intended to make a feint against the French along Chemin des Dames, an area where the French least expected attack. It sought to reach the Soissons–Rheims line, then to attack on both flanks to secure Compiègne and Rheims. The Germans then would strike such a crushing blow against the British that they would be driven into the sea. Utilizing twenty-five divisions, Ludendorff moved so rapidly that his advance was the greatest the war had seen since 1914. The German Empire stood at its greatest extent, dominating Europe from the Ukraine and Baku to northern France.

Ludendorff advanced twelve miles the first day, capturing Soissons the second. In a countermove made on May 28, nearly four thousand U.S. troops quickly took the village of Cantigny, an observation post for German artillery on the Somme River. Thirty-five minutes was all the engagement took. The next day the Germans launched a brutal counterattack. AEF forces lacked the heavy guns needed to halt the seventy-two-hour artillery barrage. Although Ludendorff's assault was soon repulsed, the cost involved 199 American lives, 652 wounded, 200 gassed, and 126 missing, a high price for a crossroads so minor it does not appear on many maps.

At home Americans were boastful, the press offering eulogistic accounts. Major General Robert Lee Bullard found it "a demonstration to the world of what was to be expected of the Americans." "Our troops behaved splendidly," Pershing wrote later.[24]

The Cantigny operation remains debatable. Those historians praising the move stress its immediate success and boost to morale. Critics emphasize the cost expended for such a trivial gain.[25]

By May 30, the Germans had reached the Marne River and were only thirty-seven miles from Paris, where the population could hear their guns. A million people began to leave the city. In a humiliating and disorganized retreat, 60,000 French troops were taken prisoner, 650 heavy artillery captured. The French government started packing for Bordeaux. Military writer Frederick Palmer called the German strike "the most complete, overwhelming and masterly surprise in the history of the western front, if not the war." American aid was deemed more crucial than ever.[26]

That very day, Pétain visited Pershing, asking him for U.S. troops to help hold the French line in the region of Château-Thierry. The AEF commander agreed to commit 56,000 U.S. troops, who would serve under French command. Foch was still not satisfied. On the next day, when the SWC met at Versailles, Pershing told him that previous concessions had already set back his efforts to create a balanced integrated army. Foch again asked Pershing if he would risk France's being driven back to the Loire River. When Black Jack still answered affirmatively, Lloyd George threatened to take the matter up with President Wilson. Pershing snapped that the president would back him, then stomped out of the meeting.[27]

On June 2, Pershing told the SWC that Wilson should be urged to send massive numbers of infantry and machine-gunners immediately, even if untrained, to prevent defeat. At the prompting of Colonel House, the premiers of France, Britain, and Italy wrote the president collectively, warning that 162 Allied divisions faced 200 German ones. Clemenceau, Lloyd George, and Italian premier Vittorio Orlando sought 100 U.S. divisions at the rate of 300,000 men per month, a request that would have resulted in the call-up of 4 million American males. House, March, and Baker wanted Pershing off the SWC, arguing that the general was overburdened. Jan Christian Smuts of the British War Cabinet told Lloyd George that he personally would gladly take charge of the entire U.S. army! He wrote the prime minister, "Pershing is very commonplace, without real war experience, and already overwhelmed by the initial difficulties of a job too big for him."[28]

The president had recently told British liaison William Wiseman that if necessary, he would order Pershing to step aside. He implied nonetheless that dismissing the general would be unnecessary, for he thought that during the summer the Allies alone could hold back the German onslaught.[29]

Doughboys would again see action, however, for on June 6 General Harbord ordered AEF troops to capture a hunting preserve called Belleau Wood. Only a square mile in area and ten kilometers from Château-Thierry, it was a defender's dream, abounding in forest, ravines, and massive boulders—all offering perfect cover. Barbed wire, sharpshooter pits, heavy mortars, artillery, and machine-gun emplacements made its capture extremely difficult. Before reaching the wood itself, one had to advance through waist-high wheat fields under heavy machine-gun fire. To ensure the element of surprise, the AEF did not first engage in an artillery barrage.

Historian Frank Freidel calls the engagement "almost a miniature Verdun." When a retreating French major warned a U.S. captain to withdraw, the American responded, "Retreat, hell!! We just got here." One noncom yelled, "Come on, you sons of bitches! Do you want to live forever?"[30]

Over the next three weeks, in a seesaw battle, sections of the wood changed hands seven times. One private referred to "days of hell." This half a square mile involved fighting so intense that reinforcements, food, and medical supplies were unavailable. Bodies lay where they fell. Soldiers living on "monkey meat"—a greasy Madagascar corned beef—scavenged food from corpses. At times brigade, regimental, and battalion commanders did not know the location of their men. Arriving in the middle of the battle, U.S. Marine major general John A. Lejeune denied that "the reckless courage of the foot soldier with his rifle and bayonet" could overcome well-protected machine guns lodged in rocky nests. Only on July 1 was Belleau Wood safely in American hands.[31]

By the end of the battle, the United States had suffered 4,600 casualties. Losses as a percentage equaled those of Gettysburg, Chickamauga, and the entire Anglo-American invasion force on the D-Day invasion. In twenty-four hours alone, the Marine Corps took more than a thousand casualties, losing half of its force and suffering the costliest day of its history until the Battle of Tarawa in World War II.

Americans, however, reveled in positive news accounts, spearheaded by the *Chicago Tribune*'s Floyd Gibbons, who lost an eye in the battle. Claiming that the doughboys had stopped the German thrust on the Marne, Gibbons wrote of the Yanks stepping "into the breach to save the democracy of the world." Melville Stone, manager of the Associated Press, boasted that the marines had saved Paris.[32]

Correspondents who wrote critical commentary had their stories censored or entirely suppressed. The *New York Times*'s Edwin James found his cable killed when he reported that the army lacked essential ammunition, gas, and airplanes. The same held true for the *New York Tribune*'s Heywood Broun, who pointed to the need for clothing, equipment, and housing.[33]

Historians disagree about the entire enterprise. As with Cantigny, some scholars find the price far too high. Others see the attack as crucial in stemming the German tide that threatened Paris.[34] Certainly, one must concede that the doughboys lacked needed artillery protection, a problem that continued throughout the war.

(Despite the controversy over Belleau Wood, U.S. troops did fight brilliantly on July 1 when two battalions overran Vaux, a town between Belleau Wood and Château-Thierry. The town was built of stone, so every house could serve as a fort. In a nearly perfect attack, a heavy artillery bombardment permitted the infantry to overrun Vaux in twenty minutes. Only forty-six Americans were killed.)

By June 6, Operation Blücher had failed. Again Ludendorff had become the victim of his own success. Though the general had advanced forty miles and established a foothold on the Marne, his narrow salient on the Aisne experienced continual artillery fire. His troops lacked needed rest. His forces faced increasing supply problems, being ninety miles from his railroads. As earlier, he had sacrificed valuable resources without gaining his objectives. "In truth," wrote a German chief of staff, "the brilliant offensive had petered out."[35]

Nevertheless, three days later, Ludendorff launched a fourth offensive, code name Gneisenau after another hero of the Napoleonic struggles. This strike aimed again at French lines stretching from Soissons and Rheims. On June 17, Foch requested that Pershing hand over five U.S. divisions remaining with the British, claiming that his countrymen were asking, "Where are the Americans, and what are they doing?" As usual, Pershing balked, but one more time pledging that in a true emergency he would do whatever was needed.[36]

In a cable to Colonel House two days later, Black Jack exclaimed, "The Allies are done for and the only thing that will hold them (specially France) in the war will be the assurance that we have force enough to assume the initiative." The United States alone would win the war in 1919 or there would be no victory. Believing that Americans would do twice as much concentrated in large units under their own leader, within a month Pershing cabled Baker, "The fact is our officers and men are far and away superior to the tired Europeans." House in turn had written Wilson that if the Allies could maintain their morale until fall, the war would be "largely won."[37]

Such assurances did not stop Baker from urging Pershing on July 7 to launch an immediate offensive, saying he wanted the general to have the honor of beating the Germans. American "energy and dash" would "put a new face on the situation on the Western Front."[38]

Pershing, though, was taking no chances. He had requested a hundred divisions totaling 5 million men, a number almost as large as the combined Allied and German armies. At the time fewer than a million doughboys were stationed in France. Although the general's request far exceeded the nation's shipping capacity, it took the General Staff until September to turn him down.

Though Ludendorff could not sustain this fourth attack, on July 15 he tried a fifth one, beginning with a massive artillery bombardment just after midnight. The Germans called it *Friedensturm*, or "peace offensive"; to the West it was the Second Battle of the Marne. The Germans pitted fifty-two divisions against thirty-four Allied ones, nine of which were American. Ludendorff continued his grand strategy of drawing Allied reserves into France so that his powerful forces in Flanders could drive the isolated British into the sea. He also sought to enlarge his salient, the "Marne pocket." As the Allies ably exploited defense in depth and many German troops were experiencing battle fatigue, the assault became stymied east of Rheims. His forces had crossed the Marne, but he otherwise made little progress. Within four days Ludendorff called off the offensive, realizing that his slight gains had not been worth the high cost. The general was becoming increasingly rattled, having taken only three days off in four years and losing his beloved stepson in Operation Michael.

Soon it would be the Allies' turn to undertake a massive offensive. The competence of the AEF would again be tested—with the stakes much higher.

FOURTEEN
TOWARDS ALLIED VICTORY

ON JULY 18, 1918, THE ALLIES STARTED THEIR OWN OFFENSIVE, one that marked the decisive turning point of the war. By now considerably superior in numbers, they sought to take advantage of Germany's weakness, not allowing them to regroup, as they struck between the Meuse and Aisne Rivers. Six days later, Foch issued his famous memorandum: "The Allied Armies have reached the turning point of the road. The moment has come to abandon the general defensive attitude and to pass to the offensive."[1] Caught by surprise, Ludendorff's forces lost the initiative. Their effort at achieving victory before major AEF participation had failed.

Pershing immediately issued orders, to go into effect on August 10, creating the U.S. First Army. At Soissons, which marked a major reversal in German fortunes, doughboys participated in the general Allied onslaught. On August 4, however, waves of troops rushed forward, only to be mowed down by German machine-gunners. Marching in formation across open terrain, they presented the Germans with an artilleryman's dream. An observer engaged in understatement in reporting that "the officers and men were too reckless."[2] AEF forces were still fighting the way the Allies had first fought in 1914.

When, on August 8, British, Australian, and Canadian troops attacked at Amiens, Germany suffered its greatest defeat to date, one so
severe that Ludendorff called it his army's "black day." Whole bodies
of men, he recalled, had surrendered to the enemy. Wilhelm II declared, "The war must be concluded."³

Despite the fact that the major activity remained in the northern
Belgian sector, Pershing insisted on an independent U.S. action at St.
Mihiel, a huge triangle jutting into Allied lines. Foch called St. Mihiel
a "hernia."⁴ A jump-off point for a German attack on Verdun to the
west or Nancy to the east, it protected Metz and the Briey iron mines.

Fearful that the AEF might run short of troops, on August 31, the
U.S. Congress expanded conscription age limits to include all men between eighteen and forty-five. The Senate passed the bill unanimously,
the House 336 to 2.⁵ Southern Democrats had sought to defer the
drafting of boys eighteen to nineteen until those older had been tapped;
their effort failed 191 to 146.

On September 2, Foch finally conceded to Pershing, allowing for
an AEF attack on St. Mihiel. He did, however, insist upon one extremely important qualification: once U.S. troops had secured their
objective, within two weeks they must move their forces to a twenty-
four-mile sector between the Meuse River and the Argonne Forest,
there to prepare for a joint attack towards the railroad hub of Sedan.
The town had proven crucial to Germany's entire defense system on
the western front because the railroad carried half of the supplies and
troops stationed in Belgium and occupied France.

In the meantime, the doughboys were about to engage in their first
major operation, but in some ways it was far from being an independent one. As with the rest of the AEF effort, the Allies supplied all
cannon, shell, and tanks. Only half the gun crews were American.
Pétain lent the U.S. forces four French infantry divisions. In a sense,
one saw amalgamation in reverse.

September 12 marked the U.S. First Army's offensive at St. Mihiel.
U.S. thrusts from opposing sides of the salient came together, pinching
thousands of enemy troops. The 304th Tank Brigade, commanded
by George Patton, drew its first blood. Colonel Billy Mitchell commanded the skies, having been lent 1,500 Allied aircraft. Within four
days, 550,000 U.S. and 110,000 French troops took 13,251 prisoners

and 466 guns, recovering 200 square miles in the process. Yank casualties were quite light: 4,100 killed, 5,000 wounded. Not even the massing of the Union Army in 1864 compared with this offensive. Pershing now controlled the railroad between Nancy and the west, thereby eliminating a threat to the rear of the Allied forces.

Success, however, came a bit too easily, making the doughboys overconfident. The First Army had outnumbered the Germans eight to one, guaranteeing success. The AEF had flung its enormous force on the backs of an army retreating to a less vulnerable and shorter line.

There were already signs of impending trouble. The enemy had withdrawn in orderly fashion, escaping before the pincers closed. U.S. discipline was lax, logistics faulty. Artillery and infantry lacked coordination. Ground troops fired at U.S.-piloted planes. German prisoners were pilfered, animals misused, and commanders remained too far from the front to maintain control. Road maintenance was a disaster; traffic jammed. One unit of farm boys were woefully unprepared, experiencing only one day of preliminary rifle instruction and two days on the rifle range. If the Germans had committed themselves to an all-out defense, stalled AEF units would have been slaughtered. Historian Geoffrey Wawro writes, "The stable door had been left open too long; the horse was backing out as quickly as he could." Pershing biographer Donald Smythe makes a disturbing observation: "Far from being impressed by the American effort, many felt that it revealed serious deficiencies which boded ill for the future."[6]

Both Brigadier General Douglas MacArthur, commander of the 42nd, or "Rainbow," Division, and Colonel George C. Marshall, Pershing's chief of operations, recommended driving on to Metz immediately. The argued that the Hindenburg Line, named for Germany's most popular general, was largely undefended. Not only was Metz a critical German fortress and transportation hub; it protected the iron ore fields of Lorraine, by far the most important in Europe. Pershing quickly refused, realizing that his troops were largely untested and underfed. He wrote in his memoirs that such a move would have delayed the far more substantial Meuse-Argonne operation. Moreover, Major General Hunter Liggett, commander of the First Corps, realized that U.S. forces did not possess the well-oiled, coordinated machine necessary for the operation.[7]

One could question the entire St. Mihiel engagement. The Allies considered the area a mere sideshow, for eastern France remained the least vital sector on the western front. The decision precluded using the best U.S. troops for far more important engagements west of the Meuse. For the rest of the war, the AEF suffered from Pershing's decision. Yet the easy victory in their first major engagement did help boost the morale of unseasoned troops. Furthermore, had the Germans retained the St. Mihiel bulge, they could constantly threaten Verdun, distracting U.S. forces as they attacked in the Meuse–Argonne area.

Now Pershing had to pay the heavy price for the bargain he had made with Foch, as he was obligated to shift the bulk of his forces from St. Mihiel to the Meuse–Argonne sector. George Marshall, who directed the operation, had only ten days to move at least 300,000 men sixty miles over miserable roads. To retain the element of surprise, the operation had to take place in darkness. Because the army lacked the needed hay and oats, it lost almost half its horses, forcing many troops to walk. Far too much was being asked of relatively green forces.

On September 26, 1918, at 5:30 a.m., Pershing launched the first phase of the Meuse–Argonne offensive, a campaign that lasted until the armistice. Its aim: to cut the German rail lines near Sedan that supplied all its troops in Flanders. Its forty-seven days marked the most prolonged single engagement in U.S. history—and the deadliest. More than a million AEF troops were involved and about 100,000 French soldiers, known as *poilus* ("hairy ones"). Again, one saw reverse amalgamation at work. The United States suffered 117,000 casualties while inflicting 100,000 on the enemy. The operation cost twice as many deaths as there would be twenty-seven years later at Okinawa.

Foch's orders called for U.S. forces to capture the German trench line of Kriemhilde Stellung within a day. The line, which served as Germany's main defense in the area, was named after a Norse heroine celebrated in the operas of Richard Wagner. The German barriers were enveloped by mist and shielded by barbed wire and mortar bombs, so victory appeared by no means certain.

At first the U.S. offensive went well. Within two days, AEF forces had captured a German line of defense at Montfaucon Hill, the "Mount of the Falcon," which dominated the entire region from the Meuse River to beyond the Argonne chain. Soon, however, this forward thrust came to a halt, pinned down by German guns that appeared everywhere—the Argonne, the Meuse Heights, and most of the high ground in between. There had been just enough delay for the Germans to bring up reserves. Furthermore, the no-man's-land, heavily shelled since 1914, made U.S. artillery support difficult. By September 29, the First Army was paralyzed, experiencing what Sir Frederick Maurice, who had directed military operations in the British War Office, called the worst traffic jam of the war.[8]

From September 30 to October 3, communication and logistics were so bad that the entire U.S. Army felt forced to pause, thereby ending the first phase of the campaign. A day later, Pershing launched the second phase, which lasted the rest of the month and proved far less successful. A quarter of a million AEF assault troops were packed into a space twelve miles wide and infested with German machine guns. Some marine battalions had lost half their officers. The Germans used the time to replenish their forces. Within days, entire divisions would wear out, forcing Pershing to throw in new ones. The severe fighting involved innumerable cases of hand-to-hand combat. In one week, doughboys suffered 75,000 combat casualties, among the worst figures tallied by any army on the western front. A single regiment lost more than a thousand men, 50 percent of its assault forces. The event marked the most casualties suffered in a single day. One veteran later compared the situation to pins falling down in a bowling alley. Another remarked, "The poor boys were getting slaughtered as fast as sheep could go up a plank." At one point, Pershing himself broke down, burying his head in his hands and crying out the name of his late wife, who had died in a fire in 1915: "Frankie . . . Frankie . . . My God, sometimes I don't know how I can go on."[9]

On October 2, units of the 77th Division had reached a designated objective but found themselves severed from Allied lines, surrounded by German machine-gunners, and lacking food and medical attention. Within two days, rations were used up. Two battalions were almost wiped out trying to reach them, and attempts at rescue by air had failed. The American press turned their plight into the biggest story of the war, even if the troops were never really lost. Although they were rescued on October 8, the toll had been heavy: 191 survivors of an original 670.

On October 6, the day the "Lost Battalion" was rescued, Corporal Alvin York became America's most famous hero of the war. According to U.S. (but not German) accounts, the former conscientious objector from Tennessee single-handedly captured 132 Germans, killed 25 enemy soldiers, and took about 35 machine-gun units. At first he received little attention, but accounts published in April 1919 made the now "Sergeant York" renowned.[10]

In examining the stalemate, certain factors must be noted. Almost everywhere, the attacking U.S. troops found the terrain a nightmare. Correspondent Frederick Palmer, now a lieutenant colonel with the Signal Corps, referred to "a most wicked task." General Liggett called the Battle of the Wilderness, where Grant had fought Lee in 1864, a park by comparison. "Machine guns," he wrote, "lurked like copperheads." Brigadier General Hugh Drum, chief of staff of the First Army, recalled it as the most ideal defense he had ever seen.[11] Woods were so thick that no unit could retain contact with those on its flanks. The terrain possessed steep ridges and deep ravines. Such high ground gave the Germans the opportunity to study most of the battlefield. Given the accuracy of their artillery, the sector was a virtual shooting gallery, with the ability to maneuver absolutely impossible.

The Germans had created defensive positions reaching an average depth of thirteen miles. Taking advantage of every hill and clump of rocks, they installed a vast complex of trenches, mine fields, machine-gun nests, pill boxes, tank traps, and acres of barbed wire, all supported by a network of roads, air coverage, and narrow-gauge railways. At first only five undermanned German divisions defended the area, but five reserve divisions were brought up quickly.

AEF troops were often unprepared. Because the troops used in the St. Mihiel engagement could not reach the Meuse–Argonne area in time for the initial attack, many untrained forces had to be used. Two-thirds of the divisions had no battle experience. More than half of one division, the 79th, had been in uniform for only four months, leading historian Edward M. Coffman to ask why such inexperienced troops were permitted to participate in crucial operations. To compound U.S. weakness, the AEF lacked sufficient officers to command such masses.[12] In some ways, the American experience resembled the European armies in the early period of the war.

Logistics proved to be a nightmare. The First Army possessed only half the trucks it needed. Adding to the difficulties, the AEF lost thousands of critical horse-drawn wagons. Frequent rain created impassible mud, weighing down already heavy uniforms and making the movement of needed provisions almost impossible. Advances were all uphill, through patches of heavily wooded country. Only three roads existed to resupply U.S. troops. One administrative breakdown led to another. Some units took days to organize themselves; others were so confused that they were mauled by German counterattacks.

Weapons left much to be desired. Tanks, so crucial in wiping out machine-gun nests, lingered behind, clogging up roads. Lacking artillery support, they drew so much fire that soldiers abandoned these tanks to German troops, who dropped grenades through their hatches. AEF planners rejected light howitzers in favor of heavy French 75-mm and 155-mm guns, a situation that improved firepower but limited one's ability to keep up with advancing infantry.

Scarcity remained a major problem. At one point, divisions were ordered to economize with ammunition. Pershing and Harbord blamed the War Department for deficiencies in the supply chain, but the nation lacked the shipping to transport the troops and equipment needed.

In October 1918, a worldwide influenza epidemic had reached the AEF, with 16,000 cases being reported the first week. It was called the "Spanish flu," but it probably began at Camp Funston, Kansas. At one time or another, a quarter of the entire U.S. Army came down with the disease, 40 percent of sailors were struck, and 38,000 doughboys lost their lives, some on the very troop ships transporting them to Europe. Worldwide, between 40 and 50 million people were wiped out, more than half a million Americans. Though at first Ludendorff thought that the pandemic might rescue his retreating armies, the virus soon struck German forces too, so much so that the general blamed it for the failure of his 1918 offensives.[13]

Most crucial of all, U.S. fighting tactics often exposed AEF forces to needless fire. Pershing later wrote that he found it "reasonable to count on the vigor and the aggressive spirit of our troops to make up in a measure for their inexperience."[14] Doughboys attacked in bunches, giving machine-gunners the ability to mow down an entire platoon in one sweep. Repeating the mistakes of St. Mihiel, troops would advance without needed artillery support. Soldiers would run up to barbed wire, not knowing how to pass through it, and end up slaughtered.

AEF men failed to cover their flanks as they advanced, so they found themselves surrounded, fighting enemy troops to their own rear.

The U.S. Army had long shown a singular inability to adopt to mechanized warfare. Historian Richard S. Faulkner aptly called the AEF a "rifle-centric" organization.[15] Between 1914 and 1917, the *Infantry Journal* kept stressing the role of rifle and bayonet. One author wrote, "In real war infantry is supreme . . . it is the infantry which conquers the field, which conducts the battle and in the end decides its destinies." Similarly the *Field Service Regulations* claimed that lightly armed riflemen decided "the ultimate issue of combat."[16] The curriculum at Fort Leavenworth neglected instruction in artillery, machine guns, aircraft, and automobiles. The Army War College emphasized nineteenth-century offensive and maneuver tactics, continually drawing upon Civil War engagements. Training of recruits did not go much beyond close-order parade drill and practice with rifle and bayonet, but few face-to-face encounters ever took place on the western front. Early contingents were trained with the obsolete Krag–Jørgenson rifle. Coordination of infantry and artillery was seldom taught, even though artillery counted for 80 percent of the war's casualties. At first, even in the front trenches, troops would not wear helmets and did not take gas drills seriously.

Pershing must assume some responsibility. The general's strength lay in organization, not tactics. Admittedly he had made his reputation in engagements where the infantry had usually ruled supreme against weaker enemies—campaigns against Plains Indians, Spaniards in Cuba, Philippine Moros, Pancho Villa's guerillas. But he was almost obtuse in failing to adjust to the realities of the western front. He even wrote in his war memoirs that war "must be won by driving the enemy into the open and engaging him in a war of movement." Admittedly there was some logic to his thinking. He had seen four years of trench warfare as having proved futile, sacrificing millions of casualties while moving battle lines little more than ten miles in either direction. "We were right," he continued, "both in emphasizing training for open warfare and insisting upon proficiency in the use of the rifle."[17] Yet historians are correctly critical of Pershing's focus on "open warfare."[18]

Foch, fully aware that he had numerical superiority, had envisioned all of his armies advancing simultaneously, moving so quickly that the Germans would have no time to recoup. British and French offensives proved successful, driving the Germans into Flanders and crashing the formidable Hindenburg Line. By September 30, the British had reached the outskirts of Cambrai.

Elsewhere, Germany was in trouble. Bulgaria surrendered on September 29. Both the Austro-Hungarian and Ottoman Empires were collapsing, Damascus being taken on October 1 and Beirut on the 6th. On October 1, Ludendorff told the General Staff that victory was out of the question: the Allies would soon gain "a *great* victory, a *breakthrough in grand style.*"[19]

By now Pershing felt forced to reorganize the AEF, unburdening himself of some heavy responsibilities. On October 12, he handed over a trimmed-down First Army of fourteen divisions and 390,000 men to Major General Hunter Liggett, who was ordered to crack the Kriemhilde Line, seize the Meuse Heights, and drive on to Sedan. Liggett's sixty years and massive frame (he arrived in France with his own chef) belied his military acuity. He grasped the nature of mechanized war in a way that Pershing never could, so much so that historian Geoffrey Wawro calls him the best U.S. general of the war.[20] Unlike Pershing, who was bleeding the AEF white, Liggett realized that his depleted army needed several more weeks of training before engaging in combat. He successfully resisted his superior's pressure to attack, thereby saving many of his troops' lives and proving much more successful as a commander.

Pershing also created a Second Army of five divisions and 176,000 men, entrusting it to Lieutenant General Robert Lee Bullard. The lean, tough Alabaman lacked brilliance but possessed common sense and the needed élan. Bullard's task was to attack eastward to the Moselle River, pushing on to Metz, Thionville, and the Briey mines. Ironically, the Second Army saw little action, holding a defensive sector in Lorraine and only besieging Metz two days before the armistice. Pershing now named himself commander of the entire "Group of American Armies," hence equal in prerogative to Haig and Pétain and subordinate only to Foch. Only then was a comprehensive plan created for a major AEF attack scheduled for November 1.

It did not take the Allies long to express their impatience with the AEF. When, on September 30, Newton Baker met with Lloyd George in London, the prime minister told him that Pershing's force was "perfectly useless, and the shipping devoted to bringing it over utterly wasted." Baker called Lloyd George's bluff: "I shall cable immediately to Washington to cease sending troops on British ships, which may then be released at once." Foch soon found himself "very disappointed" with the AEF, accusing it of "marking time." Meeting with Pershing just a week later, the French commander remarked that the Allies were making "very marked progress on all fronts except [for] the Americans" and again demanded an advance: "No more promises! Results!" Pershing retorted that no troops in the world could have done better under the circumstances. He blamed the difficult terrain and the tenacious German resistance. Foch cut him off: "Results are the only thing to judge by. . . . If an attack is well planned and well executed, it succeeds . . .; if it is not . . . there is no advance."[21]

Pershing balked at such criticism. Although an attack by his Third Corps on October 12 generated 10,000 U.S. casualties, he would not suspend operations. To do so would be to admit that his vision of an independent army had been an erroneous one. Never known for his modesty, he told a staff officer that once doughboys dominated the battlefield, Foch should be replaced by an American. There is no doubt whom he had in mind.

On October 14, troops under the direct command of Douglas MacArthur captured Côte de Châtillon, thereby creating a breach in the Kriemhilde Stellung. In three horrendous days of intense combat, the U.S. forces lost 4,000 men. Overall it had taken three weeks and 100,000 casualties to achieve what Pershing's staff had thought they could do in a single day. Pershing wrote in his diary, "Hope for better results tomorrow. There is no particular reason for this hope except that if we keep pounding, the Germans will be obliged to give way."[22]

Now, however, the U.S. offensive ground to a near standstill. For nearly two weeks, Pershing could only advance several hundred yards per day, while the French and British, traversing easier terrain, were able to move much more swiftly. Nonetheless, the slowness was certainly justified, given the exhaustion of his troops.

Clemenceau, writing Foch on October 21, referred to Pershing's "invincible obstinacy." "Our worthy American allies, who thirst to get into action and who are unanimously acknowledged to be great soldiers, have been marking time ever since their forward jump on the first day; and in spite of heavy losses, they have failed to conquer the ground assigned them as their objective. Nobody can maintain that these fine troops are unusable; they are merely being unused." If Pershing remained obstinate, it would be "high time to tell President Wilson the truth and the whole truth concerning the situation." This time Foch defended the Americans, noting their heavy losses at St. Mihiel and in the more recent Meuse–Argonne struggle "over particularly difficult terrain and in the face of serious resistance by the enemy." Haig remained unconvinced, declaring that it would take a year before the U.S. First Army proved itself an effective fighting force. Clemenceau complained again on October 27, telling Colonel House that Pershing was not making the progress he should.[23]

By the beginning of November, the defeat of Germany was never in doubt, but the last week and a half of the war had its own share of surprises—and in some cases of military incompetence. There remained little reason for the casualties resulting from irresponsible decisions made by generals who by now should have been well-seasoned in the hazards of the western front.

Success finally came to U.S. forces on November 1, when Pershing resumed his offensive and broke through the German lines, thus beginning the third and final phase of the Meuse-Argonne offensive. Six days later, the U.S. army crossed the Meuse River, surging towards the vital railroad center at Sedan. The attack began with a massive barrage involving poison gas, high explosives, and machine guns. By evening the AEF had driven five miles into the German lines, forcing the enemy to retreat from the Argonne. Now the doughboys advanced an average of two miles per day on a fourteen-mile front, utilizing a crucial edge in manpower. Certain division commanders—Robert Lee Bullard, Charles P. Summerall, and marine general John A. Lejeune—had wisely abandoned doctrines of "open warfare," adapting themselves to mechanized combat. Though fighting was as fierce as ever and many casualties resulted, the end of the conflict was clearly in sight.

Again, though, Pershing overreached himself, this time not in seeking a drive to Berlin but rather authorizing the capture of Sedan, where in 1870 Prussia had humiliated the French. Foch had placed Sedan in the zone of his own Fourth Army, so the U.S. commander would have deprived the French of the honor involved in taking possession. Possibly Pershing sought to prove American superiority, particularly as the French brass had long accused the AEF of dragging its feet. James G. Harbord, the general closest to him, saw the American request akin to French general Jean-Baptiste Donatien de Vimeur, Comte de Rochambeau, in 1781 seeking permission to elbow George Washington "out of the reviewing stand at Yorktown."[24]

So as to meet Pershing's desire to have the honor of beating the French to Sedan, General Summerall pushed his First Division to surpass all rivals. Acting as if the war depended on what in reality was essentially an unnecessary operation, he told his men: "I don't expect to see you again. But that doesn't matter. You have the honor of a definite success—give yourself to that."[25]

Brigadier General Frank Parker, seeking credit for the operation, moved his men from the center of the American sector to its left, thereby cutting off other U.S. forces. U.S. commanders crossed into each other's fields of fire and those of the French. Major General Joseph Dickman gave the order on November 6: "Sedan must be reached and taken tonight, even if the last man and officer drops in his tracks." As one officer later commented: "Someone was glory hunting. An army officer is dangerous when he begins to be a glory hunter."[26]

The inevitable occurred. Communications were disrupted and traffic jammed, creating chaos everywhere. One U.S. patrol "captured" brigade commander Douglas MacArthur, whose garb was singularly unorthodox (he was sporting a bright scarf and floppy hat), marching him off at gunpoint! The flamboyant general, suspected of being a German officer, at least pretended to be bemused. First Army commander Hunter Liggett, who found the operation the worst tactical "atrocity" he had seen during the war, was able to halt the operation.[27] Ironically, neither the French nor the Americans captured Sedan before the war ended.

No historian praises this effort. An enemy counterattack, writes David R. Woodward, could have created catastrophe.[28] The scholars are right. There remains no excuse for this operation.

Throughout all the fighting and delays, President Wilson sought to end the conflict. Perhaps predictably, the varied peace terms he advanced met with much controversy—and led to bitter opposition at home.

FIFTEEN
FINAL NEGOTIATIONS
WITH THE GERMANS

BY MID-JULY 1918, WHEN THE ALLIES OPENED THEIR OFFENSIVE
on the western front, the Central Powers were becoming increasingly less confident of victory. A month earlier, Erich
Ludendorff, Germany's de facto dictator, had written Chancellor Georg von Hertling that "diplomatic action must ac-
company the military," thereby admitting that arms alone
could no longer win the war.[1]

German civilian morale was terrible. An emergence of
the flu pandemic was affecting both soldiers and civilians.
Coal, gas, and clothing were scarce. Wages were not keeping
up with rapidly rising prices and rents. Outright salary re-
ductions, combined with increased working hours, led to
an increasing number of strikes. By September, every third
week was a meatless one, the cost of butter and milk was
rising, and cotton for clothing and munitions was in increasingly short supply. Life within the Hapsburg Empire was
becoming even worse than within Germany, as Austria was
facing actual starvation.

Once the Central Powers experienced the full onslaught
of the Allied armies, they began to present concrete peace

terms. On September 12, Frederick von Payer, Germany's vice chancellor, spoke in Stuttgart. He denied that Germany could reestablish the old order within Russia, much less return Poland or Finland. Treaties Berlin had made with Russia, the Ukraine, and Rumania—giving Germany a huge sphere of influence—must remain intact. All captured German colonies must be handed back. As soon as peace was restored, Germany could evacuate Belgium while retaining economic ties. In short, the Reich would keep its eastern conquests but give up its western ones. Payer did endorse such Wilsonian goals as a league of nations, international arbitration courts, and mutual disarmament. Under his conditions, Alsace-Lorraine would remain German. He conceded that the participation of U.S. troops on the front meant "a heavy and ever-increasing burden for us."[2]

On the 16th, the American press reported an Austrian proposal. Vienna suggested an informal nonbinding parley of specially appointed envoys who would meet in a neutral country. Wilson responded tersely, answering within twenty-five minutes after officially receiving the note and declaring that the United States had already made its conditions plain. The Allies concurred.[3]

The president's rejection received strong support from the press and congressional leaders. Even Socialist congressman Meyer London, usually quite dovish, stressed that Germany must first renounce "all spoils gained by the sword." "The Greeks bearing gifts were hardly more to be suspected than the Austrians proffering peace," remarked the *Boston News Bureau.*[4]

A few dissented from Wilson's stance. Colonel House found the president unwise to speak without consulting the Allies, particularly as he was simultaneously promoting a world league that would be based on close economic and political ties with them. Wilson, House went on, was alienating "semi-pacifist, socialist, and advanced labor groups." About a week later, House confessed in his diary that Wilson lacked any notion of how to deal with the Austro-Hungarian Empire, much less have an idea of what its postwar boundaries should be: "Generally, he [Wilson] thought the League of Nations should settle many such problems and smooth over insuperable difficulties." Almost alone among American newspapers, the *New York Times* claimed the Allies could honorably accept Austria's bid in the confident belief that it would lead to ending the war.[5]

Prominent Americans were already offering their own terms. On August 23, Henry Cabot Lodge addressed the Senate, speaking for the first time in his capacity as party leader. Having earned one of the first PhDs ever granted from Harvard University, where he studied medieval history under Henry Adams, Lodge combined deep erudition with the arrogance of a Boston Brahmin. The Massachusetts Republican had long detested Wilson, privately referring to him as "a mean soul" and "a lily-livered skunk."[6]

Differences with the president, however, far surpassed personality. In regard to domestic policy, Lodge saw the administration's price-fixing and excess-profits tax as being too harsh on business. When his son-in-law, Congressman Augustus P. Gardner, died of pneumonia in a military training camp, he blamed Wilson for the loss.

The two men also parted ways on foreign policy. Lodge saw a clearly defined conception of national interest taking priority over global universalism and international moral obligations. Therefore, he found himself having much more in common with European leaders than with his own president. To Lodge, wartime foreign policy should involve attaching the United States to a revived Concert of Europe and containing Germany in a cordon sanitaire. Congress, not the president, should take the initiative in such matters. Increasingly the physical security of the Allies became his preoccupation.

Yet, in his August 23 speech, delivered after consulting with party leaders, Lodge offered a program that in some ways overlapped with Wilson's Fourteen Points. He desired restoration of Alsace and Lorraine to France; the return of all areas where the "Italian race" is predominant, including Trieste; an independent Serbia and Rumania; a "secure" Greece; independent statehood for "Jugo-Slavs," "Czech-Slovaks," and Poles; restoration of Russian territory ceded at Brest-Litovsk; Constantinople turned into a free port; Palestine removed from Turkish rule; and safety for the Christians of Syria and for Armenians. Omitted, though, were such broader Wilson tenets as freedom of the seas, reduction of armaments, the lowering of economic barriers, and a league of nations. Claiming it was impossible to annihilate the German people, much less change the government of that nation, he raised some probing questions concerning Wilsonianism: "We intend to make the world safe for democracy. But what exactly do we mean by democracy?" He ended up opposing any compromise "peace of bargain, of give and take, and of arrangement," seeking instead a settlement dictated by the Allies.[7]

Lodge's speech met with a mixed reception. Colonel House privately accused him of advancing such rigid terms that he was inadvertently helping to preserve the German military machine. Hearst's *New York American* objected to creating small and feeble states in Central Europe, finding them easy prey to German domination. The *New Republic* accused the senator of ignoring sensitive issues existing between any liberated states, citing in particular Dalmatia, Saloniki, the Ionian islands, and a small region in the southern Balkans called the Banat of Temesvár.[8]

Conversely, the Lodge speech received strong support among many Republicans. The *Outlook* claimed that the oration expressed the conviction of the nation. Theodore Roosevelt put it on a par with addresses by Henry Clay, Daniel Webster, John C. Calhoun, and Thomas Hart Benton. On September 6, Roosevelt himself publicly offered a set of proposals somewhat similar to those of Lodge, adding the return of northern Schleswig to Denmark, a consideration of Lithuania's claims, Palestine as a Jewish state, and home rule for Ireland within the British Empire.[9]

At least one Democrat praised Lodge's address. Senator Hitchcock, chairman of the Senate Foreign Relations Committee, backed Lodge's plea that any discussion of peace terms must wait upon German surrender. The *New York Times* claimed that Lodge spoke for all Americans.[10]

On September 27, opening the campaign for the Fourth Liberty Loan, Wilson addressed three thousand volunteers gathered at New York's Metropolitan Opera House. Wilson asserted that the treaties imposed on the Russians at Brest-Litovsk proved that the Central Powers could not be trusted. So did the conditions imposed at Bucharest, where the Rumanians were forced to cede the highly contested region of Dobrudja to Bulgaria and Carpathian mountain passes to Austria-Hungary. Germany had yet to "redeem her character."

In order to have a just settlement, Wilson continued, five points must be observed: (1) "impartial justice" that played "no favourites"; (2) no special interest incongruous with the common interests of all; (3) no special "leagues or alliances or general covenants and understandings"; (4) "no special, selfish economic combinations"; and (5) publicity for all international agreements. He stressed the need for a league of nations that would serve as "an indispensable instrumentality . . . necessary to guarantee the peace." Anticipating isolationist opposition, he maintained that the new international body would not violate George Washington's warning against "entangling alliances," for this "general alliance" would avoid "entanglements" while still advancing "common understandings and the maintenance of common rights." A careful reading of this address shows that it attacked Allied policy while indicating increasing rigidity towards the Central Powers.[11]

The American press and Congress received the speech enthusiastically. They usually ignored the president's Five Points while hailing his unwillingness to negotiate with the current leaders of the Central Powers. Even Harvey's *War Weekly* heaped praise, claiming that Wilson had outdone himself. The *Nation* was almost alone in catching its wider implications, saying that such reactionary Allied leaders as Italian foreign minister Sidney Sonnino, British press mogul Lord Northcliffe, and British War Cabinet members Lord Alfred Milner and Lord George Nathaniel Curzon should take warning. It was the last Wilson speech to reflect a domestic consensus. The Allied governments offered polite responses.[12]

Though Wilson's address claimed that a league of nations was "indispensable," until recently he had given little concrete thought to this topic. His previous language had usually referred to "a concert of nations," a "feasible association of nations," and a "concert of power." Even after the United States entered the war, he studiously avoided any cooperation with the League to Enforce Peace (LEP), a major internationalist organization headed by William Howard Taft. In March 1918, he told Theodore Marburg, vice chairman of the LEP and former minister to Belgium, that he found it unwise to discuss a league to enforce peace because "all sorts of jealousies" would surface. Over the summer, he scrutinized a detailed British report drafted by jurist Sir Walter Phillimore and commissioned by the cabinet; it closely resembled that of the LEP in its stress on arbitration. After examining versions by Colonel House and Inquiry staffer David Hunter Miller, on September 7 he drew up a proposal for a league in which the

"Contracting Powers unite in guaranteeing to each other political independence and territorial integrity."[13] In mid-month, Wilson was still speaking in the most general of generalities. He had not laid the needed groundwork for what he saw as the linchpin of his peace agenda.

By now the Central Powers were experiencing outright defeat on the battlefield. On September 29, Ludendorff told a council of German leaders that an immediate armistice was necessary. The general sought a respite that would enable Germany to establish a strong defensive line, enabling it to negotiate from strength. He hoped the Reich would be able to accept a Wilsonian agreement in the West while still keeping Alsace. In the East, it could retain its free hand. Foreign Secretary Paul von Hintze reported that Austria-Hungary was ready to collapse, Turkey was an increasing burden, and that Bulgaria was about to surrender. Germany's fleet was of little use, remaining bottled up in harbor since its repulse in the 1916 Battle of Jutland. Discussion was conducted on the principle, as Hintze later wrote, that "every hour of delay is dangerous." Wilson, he suggested, should be asked to call a peace conference on the basis of his espoused principles. At a second conference held that very day, Wilhelm II approved the armistice bid.[14]

On October 3, the moderate Bavarian monarchist Maximilian of Baden, known commonly as Max, became Germany's new chancellor, replacing the inept Georg von Hertling. Cousin to the emperor, Max had been president of his principality's upper house. Though a strong monarchist, he favored liberal peace terms. Heading a coalition of Socialists, Liberals, and the Catholic Center Party, Prince Max promised internal reforms that pointed towards the conversion of Germany into a constitutional monarchy. Paul von Hindenburg, acting as chief of the general staff, wrote Max immediately, speaking for both Ludendorff and himself. He declared that defeats on the western and Macedonian front had made victory impossible. Hence, Germany must instantly request an armistice. Ironically, Germany's civilian government wanted to keep on fighting, but Ludendorff insisted.[15]

In his inaugural speech to the Reichstag delivered two days later, Max offered the full restoration of Belgium, negotiations concerning reparations, and the establishment of representative bodies in Lithuania and Poland while remaining silent concerning Alsace-Lorraine. He claimed that Wilson's proclamations stood in accord with "general ideas" cherished by Germany's new government and by "the overwhelming majority" of its people. In a public note to Wilson released on October 6, he asserted that his government had accepted the Fourteen Points and the president's subsequent pronouncements as "a basis" for an armistice. Privately, Max opposed his own proclamation, calling it "ineffective" and "dangerous"; the world would regard it as "an admission of German defeat." He was, however, overruled by Ludendorff and Hindenburg.[16]

Austria-Hungary fully backed Max's overture. Moreover, Emperor Charles, obviously responding to Wilson's demands, promised local autonomy for each subject nationality within his empire. Wilson had recently told Colonel House he had no idea what should be done with the Hapsburg Empire or with any fragmented parts, and he sought to leave the matter to the new League of Nations.[17]

If the saying in Berlin was "Max equals Pax," the Allies were taking no chances. Lloyd George, Clemenceau, and Orlando, meeting in Paris on October 7, laid down what they expected from Germany: cessation of submarine warfare; total withdrawal from France, Belgium, Luxembourg, and Italy; retirement behind the Rhine; and evacuation of Alsace-Lorraine, Trentino, Istria, Serbia, Montenegro, the Caucasus, and all territory belonging to Russia and Rumania before the war. Attacking Wilson's unilateral diplomacy, the French premier remarked, "He wishes to remain isolated and superior. He is Jupiter." Within a day, Allied military and naval representatives added to these demands, insisting that the present blockade remain in place and that the German fortresses of Metz, Thionville, Strasbourg, Neuf-Brisach, and Lille be surrendered. So, too, the fortified island of Heligoland in the North Sea.[18]

The American press expressed strong hostility to Max's note. The New York *World* saw Max revealing that Berlin knew it was "whipped." The *Boston Herald* referred to Germany's "empty talk." The *Pittsburgh Dispatch* pointed to Russia's experience as evidence that the Reich would not respect any armistice. To the *San Francisco Chronicle*, "Kaiserism" was again reverting to deception. The *New York Times* editorial was titled "No Peace with the Hohenzollerns."[19]

In the Senate, the language was particularly strong, with not one member advocating an armistice. Porter McCumber introduced a resolution demanding the disbanding of Germany's armies, the return of Alsace-Lorraine, and reparations for destroyed cities and villages. James Reed asked how anyone could talk peace with the Germans while they were "carrying on war in a manner more atrocious" than the Sioux or the "savages of South Africa." Henry F. Ashurst corrected him, replying that the Sioux never treated a treaty as a "scrap of paper"! Lodge wanted Germany to return Alsace-Lorraine, gained during the Franco-Prussian War, and Silesia, originally seized by Frederick the Great. Miles Poindexter hoped to execute those "murderers and robbers who have laid waste Belgium and France"; he also called for court-martialing the kaiser. Frank Brandegee hoped Germany's opponents would leave a "trail of fire and blood from the Rhine to Berlin."[20]

Wilson became increasingly apprehensive concerning American sentiment. He privately found his countrymen too vengeful, possessing "a dangerous attitude and not one calculated to have us conclude the wisest sort of peace." His secretary, Joseph Tumulty, later recalled Wilson saying, "The gentlemen in the Army who talk about going to Berlin and taking it by force are foolish. It would cost a million American lives to accomplish it."[21]

The president's reply to Max, which can be called his "First Note," was harsh, for it really asked Germany to acknowledge defeat. On October 8, Americans learned that Wilson would "not feel at liberty to propose a cessation of arms" to the Allies so long as the armies of the Central Powers remained on their soil. The president asked if Chancellor Max was "speaking merely for the constituted authorities of the Empire who have so far conducted the war." He also queried if Germany had really accepted the Fourteen Points and his subsequent pronouncements as a basis for negotiation.[22]

Meeting in Paris, Allied leaders had mixed reactions to Wilson's note. Because the First Note stressed evacuation of occupied territory, Clemenceau called it an "excellent document." Lloyd George, however, had recently said that "once an armistice was declared we should never be able to start the war again." German evacuation from enemy territory, it was feared, could merely allow Ludendorff's forces time to regroup. Armistice terms must be fixed after consultation with military experts, particularly Marshal Foch. First Lord of the Admiralty Sir Eric Geddes was quite blunt: "To get us all to talk of peace is just what Germany wants."[23] As far as the Fourteen Points were concerned, the prime ministers voiced neither agreement nor opposition.

Colonel House feared public reaction, writing in his diary that Wilson did not realize "how war mad our people have become." Lansing referred to an "intense feeling, which approaches fanaticism." The secretary of state also had another concern very much on his mind, an anxiety concerning Bolshevism that he had voiced as early as December 1917. In a private letter, he wrote, "Bolshevism is raising its abominable head, and a Germany crushed might become prey to that hideous movement. If it did, Europe might become a seething mass of anarchy." This ideology, he claimed, was even gaining a foothold in the United States. By October 16, Wilson, too, had told British envoy Sir William Wiseman, "The spirit of the Bolsheviki is lurking everywhere and there is no more fertile soil than war-weariness. . . . If we humiliate the German people and drive them too far, we shall destroy all form of government, and Bolshevism will take its place."[24]

Congress offered a mixed response. Warren Harding noted, "Those who commended President Wilson because he kept us out of war will most severely condemn him now if he gets out of it too soon." Lodge expressed strong disappointment that the president was negotiating at all, adding that allowing Germany to withdraw from Belgium and northern France would simply enable it to replenish its armies. Remarked Senator William Kirby, "We are organized to whip hell out of Germany and I think we had better do it before we quit." To Senator Christie Benet (D-S.C.), "the only way to treat an outlaw is to disarm and then handcuff him." TR publicly accused Wilson of "treacherous diplomacy."[25]

Wilson did draw some support. William E. Borah praised the president for clarifying a most involved situation. Congressman Robert Thomas found the note reflecting "the very highest statesmanship." To Senator Fernifold Simmons (D-N.C.), Wilson's approach embodied the only way to deal with the matter. Senator Key Pittman accused Lodge of seeking nothing but "war for victory, revenge and advantage," while the program of the president means "war for victory, justice and everlasting peace."[26]

The press was equally divided. The *Chicago Tribune*, often a Wilson critic, praised the president's masterly skill. The *St. Paul Pioneer*

Press concurred: "The Hun Government has been outmaneuvered." To the *New York Globe*, the president proved himself worthy of "Talleyrand in his best days." The *Boston Transcript*, however, was reminded of Wilson's "sterile" note-sending during the *Lusitania* crisis; the *Memphis Commercial Appeal* condemned negotiating at all with "a murderer." The *Outlook* thought Wilson's note vague, subject to varied interpretations; the war must be pursued to Berlin.[27]

On October 8, the SWC declared that any armistice was essentially a military accord requiring experts to fix the conditions. Evacuation of invaded territory per se involved no guarantee against renewed German hostilities. The U.S. delegate to the SWC, General Tasker Bliss, balked, refusing to sign the document. He wrote Baker that the Allies were telling Germany, "We will not treat with you on the terms of President Wilson's fourteen propositions or on any other terms. Surrender, and we will then do as we please." Victory, Bliss continued, should not result in "the abolition of *German* militarism while leaving *European* militarism as rampant as ever."[28]

Conditions within Germany kept worsening. The nation experienced a financial crisis, with banks failing and the value of stocks declining. Railroad transportation was curtailed, the population advised to travel only if necessary. The flu epidemic reached ten thousand Germans by mid-October, resulting in the closing of many schools.

American anger only heightened when, on October 11, the press reported that two German torpedoes had sunk the British mail carrier *Leinster* in the Irish Sea. Among the 176 lives lost were several Americans. The twenty-two-year-old submarine captain had given no warning.

On the same day, Americans learned that U-boats had sunk the Japanese liner *Hirano Maru* in the same waters. Of 400 passengers, only 20 were saved. The U.S. destroyer *Sterett* attempted rescue efforts, but enemy fire drove it away. The *New York Times*, accusing the Germans of being involved in the sheer love of murder, titled its editorial "Ferocity Asks for Peace."[29]

Because of these sinkings, the timing of Germany's public reply to Wilson's initial foray could not have been more inopportune. On October 12, Berlin's new foreign secretary, Wilhelm Solf, declared that his government was ready for an armistice, suggesting a joint commission to make necessary arrangements. Chancellor Max, he claimed, was backed by "the great majority of the Reichstag" and spoke "in the name of the German Government and of the German people." He accepted the peace terms Wilson had laid down in his various speeches and assumed that the president spoke for the Allies.[30]

Meeting with his cabinet two days after Germany's second note was issued, Wilson denied that any armistice could be reached until Berlin pledged itself to sink no more passenger ships and kill no more civilians. He added that it must accept the stipulation made in the president's 1918 Fourth of July address, which called for ending its autocratic government. Yet, abhorring vindictive terms, he did not seek, as House noted, "to have the Allied armies ravage Germany as Germany has ravaged the countries she has invaded."[31]

The Allies remained far from pleased. Lloyd George saw the Entente "in a devil of a mess," for Wilson had "promised" the Germans an armistice. Fearing a "sham or humbugging peace," the prime minister called Wilson's conditions "inadequate." Foch warned Pershing that the Germans were merely playing for time, hoping to regroup their armies.[32]

Wilson never made it clear he was speaking only for himself, in the process misleading the Germans. Historian Charles E. Neu notes, however, that Wilson did have some leverage. Lloyd George and Clemenceau realized that rejecting an armistice and prolonging the war into 1919 would only put the United States in a more commanding position.[33]

The American press voiced only hostility to the German bid, the *Literary Digest* reporting: "Nothing less that the deposition of the House of Hohenzollern will satisfy the American people." In a signed editorial, William Randolph Hearst warned against leaving "this cruel, calculating, criminal autocracy in the saddle." The *New York Tribune* responded with "death to the Kaiser." The *Richmond Times-Dispatch* saw Germany never more dangerous than in defeat. Journalist David Lawrence wrote Wilson that over time American war propaganda had turned the kaiser, who might be a mere figurehead, into a national obsession.[34]

A few newspapers gave Germany a slight benefit of the doubt. The *St. Louis Republic* trusted the president to decide whether Foreign

Secretary Solf was offering "a sham or an honest step toward peace." The *Albany Argus* suspected that Berlin's note might signify unconditional surrender and the end of the war.[35]

The Senate remained suspicious. Indiana's Harry S. New, chairman of the Republican National Committee, saw the United States "in more danger of a diplomatic defeat than we are from armed attack." Thomas P. Gore suspected "the same old face behind a mask." Accepting Berlin's note, warned Lodge, meant losing the war, for Germany would bide its time and strike again. Albert Cummins vaguely proposed "capital punishment" for Germany but conceded that "many innocent German people will suffer."[36]

By this time, the Fourteen Points themselves became increasingly subject to debate. Senator Miles Poindexter declared that an armistice based on these tenets signified outright German victory. His colleague Philander Knox claimed that presidents lacked the authority to define any war aims, be they wise or foolish, as Congress alone was empowered in this regard. Taft found the points so vague that hostilities could be renewed. In late October, the Republican Congressional Campaign Committee released three campaign bulletins charging that Point Three committed the United States to free trade.[37]

Theodore Roosevelt was particularly adamant. The loss of his son Quentin, an aviator who died in combat that July, undoubtedly embittered the ex-president even more, for he called upon the Senate to engage in downright repudiation of the Fourteen Points. In mid-October, he claimed that some points "may mean anything or nothing," having "a merely theoretical value"; others were "absolutely mischievous." Freedom of the seas, "if accepted in the German sense, involved a surrender to the German plan of murder." The proposed disarmament "would leave us at the mercy of any foreign power that chose to regard the plan as a 'scrap of paper.'" Autonomy, rather than independence, for the "oppressed races" of Austria and Turkey involved "a base betrayal" of "Czechoslovaks," Armenians, and other smaller Allies. Little wonder, he told a rally of 5,000 people at New York's Carnegie Hall late that month, the Fourteen Points had been welcomed "by Germany and by all the pro-Germans on this side of the water, especially the Germanized Socialists and by the Bolshevists of every grade." As far as the proposed League of Nations went, TR "gravely" doubted "whether a more silly or more mischievous plan was ever proposed by a great nation." Roosevelt did endorse an association of nations as an "addition to preparing our own strength for our own defense." Privately he confessed he was using a mere "platonic expression" to appease Taft's League to Enforce Peace.[38]

TR's close friend, Henry Cabot Lodge, concurred. A real league of nations, he claimed, already existed "in the glorious present alliance of the many powers with whom we are now fighting." Far better to cultivate this existing body rather than to create a new one that envisions "a world state" or "a great catalogue of unnatural self-restraints."[39]

The Fourteen Points, so welcomed eight months earlier, still had their defenders. Senator Porter McCumber called them "great doctrines," "the foundation upon which to build the structure of a lasting peace." Senator Henry Ashurst aptly asked why Wilson's critics had long been "ominously silent" concerning the president's tenets, only expressing opposition at "this very grave hour."[40]

Ashurst was concerned enough over the increasing hostility towards Wilson to meet with the president on October 14. The Arizona senator stressed that the Senate, press, and people expected total capitulation. By negotiating with the Germans, Wilson was "signing away with the pen much of the advantage that our valorous soldiers won with the sword." Referring to the Fourteen Points and demands made in subsequent speeches, the president replied that the people should remember the conditions the Germans must meet. Wilson had threatened that if he was destroyed because of his conciliatory peace terms, he would read poetry the rest of his life! Ashurst snapped that the president would have to "read it in a cellar to escape the cyclone of the people's wrath." Wilson later recalled that he replied, "Senator, it would relieve a great many people of anxiety if they did not start with the assumption that I am a damned fool. . . . Had you rather have the Kaiser or the Bolsheviks?"[41]

On the day he met with Ashurst, Wilson publicly issued his "Second Note" to Germany, far more severe in tone. Responding to Solf's communiqué delivered two days before, he offered a strong indictment. He accused Germany of offering peace proposals while its submarines were sinking passenger ships and lifeboats. Furthermore, the president accurately noted that its troops left a wake of "wanton destruction" in their withdrawal from Flanders and France. "Cities and villages, if not destroyed, are being stripped of all they contain," often including "their very inhabitants." The president was clearly pointing to the burning and pillaging of such cities as Cambrai, Laon, and Lens. Noting the deportation of Belgian civilians to work in war industries, he accused Berlin of engaging in "acts of inhumanity, spoliation, and desolation." Neither the United States or the Allies would consider an armistice "so long as the armed forces of Germany continue the illegal and inhumane practices which they still persist in." Such arrangements, Wilson went on, must "come by the action of the German people themselves."

In the most important sentences of the entire dispatch, Wilson wrote that all evacuation and armistice conditions "must be left to the judgment and advice of the military advisers of the Government of the United States and the Allied governments." Needed were "absolutely satisfactory safeguards and guarantees of the maintenance of the present military supremacy of the armies of the United States and of the Allies in the field."[42] The point was made clear: there would be no mixed commission supervising Germany's evacuation from Belgium and France. The only acceptable peace was one guaranteeing the present supremacy of the Allied armies and the AEF. Again, Wilson had not consulted with the Allies.

Whether Wilson realized it or not, turning armistice details over to the generals assured airtight guarantees of military supremacy while compromising his own peace agenda. The *New Republic* saw Wilson implying that if the Germans wished to be consulted about their own fate, they would first have to overthrow their own government. Historian John M. Blum writes that while the president may not have explicitly called for the kaiser's overthrow, his notes certainly implied this.[43]

Before news of Wilson's Second Note reached the Senate, Lodge had offered a resolution demanding unconditional surrender. Charles S. Thomas (D-Colo.) countered with one endorsing Wilson's peace tenets. Ashurst, just returned from his conference with Wilson, denied that the president would counter the moves of Generals Foch, Haig, and Pershing. James A. Reed accused Germany of having premeditated the war for fifty years, then committing the greatest crime in world history, but he denied that Wilson would "fritter away the fruits" of the conflict. Mississippi's John Sharp Williams envisioned a ruined Prussian and Austrian autocracy, not a totally devastated Germany: "It would give my heart no gratification to burn a single German village or to retaliate for the death of Belgian women by killing German women."[44]

Once Wilson's note was released, the senators burst into applause, then united in praising it. Senator Morris Sheppard called it one of "the greatest documents of world history." Lodge declared himself "genuinely pleased that the President takes the ground he does," if privately he took credit for Wilson's sudden stiffening. Poindexter pronounced it "refreshing," Reed called it "the voice of America." Harding claimed it showed "the real spirit." To Hitchcock, the president had "removed all doubts" as to the wisdom of his course. Fernifold Simmons found Wilson's terms not far from unconditional surrender. To Atlee Pomerene (D-Ohio), "We will now see whether the peace eggs laid by Prince Max hatch out a peace dove or a serpent."[45]

Other opinion leaders felt similarly. Noting that Wilson had declined an armistice, Taft expressed "a deep sign of relief." Many newspapers praised the Second Note. The *Omaha World-Herald* found the president speaking "with wisdom, with greatness, with power." The New York *World* praised the president for sweeping away "foolish fears" fostered by "unscrupulous politicians." Hearst's *New York American* claimed that in seeking the banishment of the Hohenzollerns, Wilson voiced the nation's overwhelming sentiment. To the *Charleston News and Courier*, the president had thrown "à flaming torch into the enemy's camp."[46]

Yet several newspapers faulted Wilson for acting far too slowly. The *Boston Herald* called his note inconclusive, "not the utterance of a man of action." The *New York Herald* maintained that he should have sent his missive a week earlier.[47]

The Allies welcomed the Second Note's uncompromising tone but remained disappointed at Wilson's continued monopolization of the negotiations. The U.S. chargé in London reported that the Entente expressed "grave doubts" as to whether the Fourteen Points sufficiently met their demands. They found some points downright detrimental, namely, those dealing with freedom of the seas, economic barriers, colonial claims, and the Ottoman Empire. British field marshal Sir Henry Wilson, chief of the Imperial General Staff, claimed that the War Cabinet considered the president involved in "a disgraceful usurpation of power."[48]

In Germany, Wilson's note aroused absolute fury. Upon receiving the note, Wilhelm II said to his aide, "Read it! It aims directly at the overthrow of my house, at the complete overthrow of monarchy." Chancellor Max called it a "frightful document." Ludendorff responded: "We should say to the enemy: Win such terms by fighting for them." "Wilson gave us nothing," he later recalled, as the president did not even tell Germany whether the Entente favored the Fourteen Points.[49]

Moreover, Ludendorff, who had favored an armistice, suddenly realized the implications of its execution. Telling Berlin's civilian government on October 17 that Wilson's terms were meant "to put us out of the fight," Ludendorff sought "an orderly evacuation," which would give him "a respite of at least two or three months," and allow him, if necessary, to resume hostilities. The civilian government balked, regarding his request as another sign of his emotional instability. On that very day, German newspapers published an official notification: the armies had been ordered to cease all devastation "unless absolutely forced to follow this course by the military situation for defensive reasons."[50]

For a brief moment, attention shifted to Austria-Hungary. On October 16, Emperor Charles issued a manifesto titled "To My Loyal Austrian Peoples": "Following the desires of her peoples Austria must become a federated state in which every race will form its own state commonwealth in the districts inhabited by it."[51] The declaration, however, offered too little, too late. Winning over neither Wilson nor the subject nationalities, it simply accelerated the empire's dissolution. A day later, Hungary separated from Austria. The day after that the Czechs seized Prague, denouncing mere home rule.

Wilson made clear to Austria-Hungary that Point Ten of the Fourteen Points, centering on "autonomous development" of the peoples within Austria-Hungary, no longer held true. On October 7, Vienna had requested an armistice based on the president's own pronouncements. Twelve days later, the president openly refused the entreaty. He publicly recognized "the belligerency of the Czecho-Slovak forces operating in Siberia" and claimed he would deal with the Czecho-Slovak National Council "as with an independent national authority." He had also recognized "in the fullest manner the justice of the national aspirations of the Jugo-Slavic peoples." Only the subject peoples involved could judge what satisfied their aspirations. With the Czecho-Slovak National Council formally declaring independence, the *Washington Post* called Wilson's reply "the death-knell of the Hapsburg Empire." Czech leader Thomas Masaryk used the term "death sentence." Wilson had recently assured the French that he opposed any merger of Austria and Hungary. He also turned down another alternative. Were German Austria to merge with Germany proper, so Wilson feared, a "great central Roman-Catholic nation" would be established "under control of the Papacy." On October 12, Eduard Beneš, general secretary of the National Council, proclaimed the establishment of the Czechoslovak provisional government in Paris.[52]

Soon Czechs, Germans, Ruthenians, Poles, and Yugoslavs within the empire were forming local administrative parliaments. By the end of October, 208 members of the Reichsrat, representing the German-speaking parts of the empire, met in Vienna to form a German-based Austrian state, after several months choosing Social Democrat Karl Renner as its first chancellor. In mid-November, a Hungarian republic was formed.

On October 20, Solf publicly wrote Wilson again. The foreign secretary pledged that Germany would evacuate occupied territories prior to entering into any armistice. He left arrangements to "the judgment of the military advisers" and "the actual standard of power on both sides in the field." His government hoped that Wilson would "approve of no demand which would be irreconcilable with the honor of the German people." He protested against the accusations of inhumanity, asserting that German soldiers were under orders to spare private property and protect the populace: "Where transgressions occur in spite of these instructions, the guilty are being punished." Arguing that the German navy had never intentionally destroyed lifeboats carrying passengers, he suggested a neutral commission to "clear up" the facts. He told the president that Berlin had sent orders to all submarine commanders forbidding the torpedoing of passenger ships, without—for technical reasons—being able to guarantee that these orders would reach every single U-boat at sea.

Solf continued by writing that the new government, composed of leaders of major political parties, had been "formed in complete accord with the wishes of the representation of the people based on the equal, universal, secret, direct franchise." The permanence of the new system was safeguarded "by the unshakable determination of the German people, whose vast majority stands behind these reforms and demands their energetic continuance." Hence, Germany's offer of peace and an armistice came from a government "free from any arbitrary or irresponsible influence." Journalist Mark Sullivan later paraphrased the note: "Yes, Germany was saying, we are now a democracy like the United States, just what you, Mr. Wilson, wanted us to be."[53]

The German note caused consternation among the Allies. Foch accused Berlin of setting a trap, adding that it was undesirable for Wilson to serve as any kind of arbiter. British leaders, too, feared that the president would continue negotiations without consulting them.[54]

On the following day, Wilson, Lansing, Baker, Daniels, and General March discussed the German note. They decided that Germany was acting in good faith and had accepted Wilson's demands. Yet Daniels commented in his diary, "Public sentiment here wants blood."[55]

On October 22, when the cabinet met for two hours, consensus emerged on only one matter: the American people sought a harsh peace. Treasury Secretary McAdoo feared that the United States was bankrupting itself: "The expenditures are frightful, and I do not know where we can get the means without wrecking ourselves." Agriculture Secretary David F. Houston asked Wilson if Germany had approached the United States alone in hopes of more lenient terms. At first, the president replied that his conditions reflected "Lloyd George and Allied sentiment." Later in the meeting, however, he conceded that Clemenceau and Italy were silent on the matter. He also found it possible that Germany saw the United States as the only "reasonable" nation involved. Indeed, he declared that it was the Allies who needed to be coerced, for they were "getting to a point where they were reaching out for more than they should have in justice." Wilson again expressed concern about the advent of Bolshevism in Europe, suggesting that Germany's kaiser be retained as a check on its rise to power and as preserving some vestiges of order in his nation.[56]

Senate leaders found Berlin's latest note unsatisfactory. Not surprisingly Poindexter claimed that any response by Wilson should be met by impeachment; he introduced a resolution making such negotiations unlawful. Were Solf "a direct descendant of both Mephistopheles and Machiavelli," Ashurst remarked, "he could not have done better—or worse." Borah called the reply "a sham" and Solf "a liar." Lodge saw it as a "clumsy trap, awkwardly put, to involve us in diplomatic discussions—of all things to be avoided at this moment." Charles Thomas denied believing in a "deathbed repentance." To Congressman Simeon Fess (R-Ohio), Germany sought to postpone conflict until it was able to "crush the world." Senator Hitchcock felt inclined to accept the German response at face value, but still wanted the war prosecuted.[57]

Few in the press reacted positively, the *San Diego Union* simply saying, "It won't do." To the *Philadelphia Inquirer*, it was "mere bosh"; to the *St. Louis Globe-Democrat*, "wholly hypocritical." The *Raleigh News and Observer* was slightly more moderate, expressing gratification that the note reflected a major advance over Germany's previous communications.[58]

When, on October 23, Wilson met with his top war advisers, he revealed his acute awareness of his nation's belligerent sentiment and the imminent congressional elections. He called public opinion "as much a fact as a mountain and must be considered." He predicted that after forty-eight hours of trauma, however, "the people would quit being hysterical & become reasonable & prefer getting what they are fighting for now than to fight on to Berlin & keep up the war."[59]

Wilson publicly responded to Germany on the same day with his "Third Note." He began by asserting that Germany's ministers, "who speak for the majority of the Reichstag and for an overwhelming majority of the German people," had "unreservedly" accepted the peace terms laid down in his previous notes. The Reich had also explicitly promised adherence to "humane rules of civilized warfare." Therefore, he "cannot decline to lay the matter of an armistice before the Allies." If the Allies agreed to his previously stated "terms and principles" and if they deemed such an armistice acceptable "from the military point of view," their army staffs would recommend terms. Such an armistice must give the United States and the Entente "unrestricted power" to enforce any agreement, hence making German renewal of hostilities impossible. To put the matter bluntly, though Wilson was not this explicit, there remained little doubt that Foch, Pétain, Haig, and Pershing would impose the military terms upon a defeated nation.

Germany's note of October 22 indicated the country would make significant constitutional changes, but Wilson continued, "the principle of a government responsible to the German people has not yet been fully worked out." "The power of the King of Prussia to control the policy of the Empire," he continued, "is unimpaired." Therefore, "the nations of the world do not and cannot trust the word of those who have hitherto been the master of Germany policy." The United States could not deal with "any but the veritable representatives of the German people." Journalist Sullivan later put Wilson's message to Germany aptly: "I don't believe you."[60]

Britain's reaction was mixed. Lloyd George differed less with its contents than with Wilson again taking the initiative unilaterally: "We have borne the heat of the burden of the day and we are entitled to be consulted." Sir Henry Wilson of the General Staff wrote, "Everyone angry and contemptuous of Wilson. A vain ignorant weak ASS." The War Cabinet noted the president's silence concerning Alsace-Lorraine and the German fleet. As historian Gregor Dallas observes, few Britons were fighting for the democratization of Germany.[61]

The German military balked, with Hindenburg and the ever-fluctuating Ludendorff immediately cabling the army to call Wilson's note "unacceptable to us soldiers." Resistance must be continued "with every means at our command." Wilhelm II complained, "With every note more is demanded." The monarch found the president an "impudent lout," his note "unadulterated Bolshevism."[62]

Colonel House opposed the message, privately claiming that Wilson's "long and effusive discussion" could stiffen German resistance, welding its people behind their military leaders. Writing in his diary, he accused the president of taking "a reckless and unnecessary gamble. It might cost him the leadership of the Peace Negotiations, for it is conceivable that the Germans may approach some of the Entente Powers, believing that Wilson is the more difficult to deal with." Now back in London, House told General Haig that the president should simply have passed Germany's armistice request on to the Allies.[63]

The two former presidents split over the matter. Taft saw the president getting increasingly closer to unconditional surrender and finally recognizing the Allied role in peacemaking. In a cable to Lodge that he made public, Roosevelt proclaimed, "Let us dictate peace by the hammering guns and not chat about peace to the accompaniment of the clicking of typewriters."[64]

Congressional sentiment remained divided. Several senators sought to brush away Wilson's effort at negotiations and to insist upon unconditional surrender. Lodge continued to deplore any exchange of notes with the Germans, particularly as the Allies were winning on the battlefield. Poindexter doubted whether Britain or France would agree to any negotiated peace. If one encouraged revolution inside Germany, feared Hitchcock, "nobody will have the power to make final arrangements." Democrats generally defended the president, Senator William King calling the note "a diplomatic triumph" that would hasten popular rule in Germany.[65]

Press reaction was similarly bifurcated. Hearst's *New York American* claimed that Wilson's Third Note would be admired for generations. Whereas "extremists" sought a peace of extermination, "millions of plain people" yearned for a Wilsonian peace. The *New Republic* asserted that Wilson held out "a just peace, if a harsh one." The president could well have saved many lives. Charles W. Eliot, Harvard's president emeritus, accused the Republican opposition of acting in an "irresponsible and passionate manner." What will happen in peacetime, he asked, when they must face more complicated issues centering on complicated geographical, racial, and commercial matters.[66]

Nonetheless, the *Literary Digest* noted the tremendous press hostility towards retaining the Hohenzollern dynasty. If Secretary of State Lansing had endorsed discriminating between Central Europe's "military dictators" and the people who served them, American editors proposed trying the kaiser, exiling him either to St. Helena or to castles in Scandinavian lands. The *Philadelphia Public Ledger* suggested mutilation, crucifixion, or gassing him to death. The *North American Review* was quite blunt: "The people are as bad as the Kaiser and must be thus treated." Berlin must undergo occupation until all indemnities are paid, even if the Allies possessed it for a hundred years.[67]

Conversely, the *Nation* maintained that Germany would probably not be able to fulfill Wilson's demands for many months; in the meantime, the president was yielding to the "bitter-enders." It approvingly quoted the New York *World*, usually an ardent defender of Wilson, which asked, "How many of the Americans who are shouting for 'unconditional surrender' know the meaning of the words they use?" It also cited an authority who claimed that carrying the war to Berlin would involve three more years of fighting and the loss of millions of lives.[68]

Historians differ over the wisdom of Wilson's message. Some praise the president for continuing to stress his own terms. Others see it as too ambiguous, for one did not know just what type of German regime he would accept.[69] Given that Wilson was acting independently of the Allies, it would have been difficult for him to be more concrete.

All throughout these exchanges with Wilson, Germany was democratizing itself. Unknown to Wilson or the Allied leaders, much less the populations they represented, the kaiser had long exercised little power. Far from being "the beast of Berlin," he was serving as a mere figurehead.

On October 28, 1918, Germany instituted major constitutional reforms. The chancellor was now dependent on the confidence of the Reichstag, which would henceforth direct foreign and military affairs. The army came under civilian control. The legal status of the emperor was now that of a constitutional monarch. In short, the Germany of Bismarck's day had ended. Yet during the crucial weeks of October, the Reichstag seldom met, assembling only on October 5 to hear Max proclaim the new government, and then on the 22nd and the 29th. Such a gap in the exercise of power was already proving most costly.

Just after receiving Wilson's Third Note, Ludendorff and Hindenburg issued a proclamation to their troops. Seeking an immediate cease-fire on existing battle lines, the two generals called Wilson's Third Note "a demand for unconditional surrender" and hence "unacceptable to us soldiers." The army must "continue our resistance with all our strength."[70]

Meeting with Vice Chancellor Friedrich von Payer (Max was ill) on the 25th, the two generals claimed that they could hold the western front through the winter. France, they continued, lacked coal and faced internal disorders. Payer saw little chance of continuing the struggle, forcing Ludendorff's dismissal. Two days later, Solf replied to Wilson, cabling that peace negotiations were being conducted by "a government of the people." Germany awaited armistice proposals as "the final step toward a peace of justice, as described by the President in his pronouncements."[71]

Historian Gary Armstrong raises a crucial issue. Had Wilson definitely signaled that Germany had changed sufficiently enough to make a peace agreement, the chaotic revolution that took place there in November could possibly have been avoided. A reformed monarchy, rather than the weak republican regime, might have signed both the armistice and subsequent peace treaty. Were the rapid and total collapse of Germany avoided, the United States would possess greater leverage over the Allies at Paris. Armstrong concedes that given the stance of the Allies and majority of the American public, chances for such a solution were still slim.[72]

Instead, on October 30, sailors began a mutiny at Kiel and Wilhelmshaven, having heard a report that the German fleet had been ordered to make a quixotic mad dash to engage the British fleet in the North Sea. The nation as a whole appeared on the very eve of civil war. Turkey capitulated on the same day, British general Edmund Allenby having destroyed its army at Megiddo a month earlier. The Entente now possessed access to the Bosporus and Dardanelles and was permitted to occupy all strategic points.

The exchange of notes was over. By late October 1918, as Germany's foes saw victory within their grasp, U.S. policymaking was no longer centered in Washington but in Paris, where Colonel House had set out on the most important mission of his career.

SIXTEEN
THE COLONEL'S LAST MISSION

ON THE EVENING OF OCTOBER 14, 1918, WILSON APPOINTED Colonel House as his personal representative to the Supreme War Council. Now that the Allies were winning on the western front, the president deemed it essential that they back him on the crucial matter of peace terms. He had negotiated with Germany on the basis of the Fourteen Points and had gained German acceptance to an astonishing degree. He still needed to convey to the enemy that the Entente would accede to these provisions. Wilson could not cross the seas himself at such a time in the war effort, particularly as he faced a crucial congressional election. Therefore, he instinctively relied on the man who was ideologically and personally closest to him.

House appreciated the wide discretion awarded him, writing in his diary: "The President certainly gives me the broadest powers. It virtually puts me in his place in Europe. . . . I am going on one of the most important missions any ever undertook, and yet there is no word of direction, advice or discussion between us. He knows that our minds run parellel [*sic*], and he also knows where they diverge. I will follow his bent rather than my own."

As House was leaving, Wilson told him, "I have not given you any instructions because I feel you will know what to do." They even arranged a secret code, although the British were able to crack it within days after transmission. House added that Wilson "has his weaknesses, his prejudices, and his limitations like other men, but all in all, Woodrow Wilson will probably go down in history as the great figure of his time, and I hope, of all time."[1]

By now, House stood second only to Wilson as the most powerful person in the United States. His short stature and slight frame, together with a diffident personality (one critic nicknamed him "Colonel Mouse"), belied his adeptness in influencing the president. He exhibited a sense of sympathy to all he encountered, so much so that journalist Walter Lippmann referred to him as "the Human Intercessor, the Comforter, the Virgin Mary." His personality was marked by shameless flattery, a burning ambition, an overreaching ego, and a penchant for intrigue. House had played a crucial role in selecting the president's cabinet, defining Wilson's peace terms, and representing him abroad. The fact that he held no public office gave him the ability to maneuver amid bureaucratic interstices that seasoned diplomats could only envy. He studiously kept a low profile, receiving a minimum of press coverage. Though he privately differed with Wilson on numerous matters, the president trusted him implicitly. He supposedly said of his deputy, "His thoughts and mine are one. If I were in his place, I would do just as he suggested." At one point, however, he claimed that House's mind was "not of the first class. He is a counselor, not a statesman."[2]

It was, however, in the role of statesman that House again traveled to Europe, engaging in what his biographer Charles E. Neu calls "the most difficult diplomatic challenge of his career."[3] Despite Wilson's confidence in him, House's negotiating record had not been strong. His ineptitude had been particularly revealed in February 1916, when he reported back to Wilson that British foreign secretary Sir Edward Grey had committed his nation to a wide-sweeping agreement: the United States would enter the war were Germany to decline a peace conference proposed by the Allies. By the middle of the year, London had made it quite clear that it had no interest in any such arrangement, making House look foolish indeed. When Wilson issued a peace note that December, House undercut him by assuring Sir Horace Plunkett, chairman of the Irish convention and home rule advocate, that the administration's pro-British policies had not changed.

In May 1917, House had proposed a secret alliance between the United States and Britain to contain Japan. The U.S. Navy would rely upon British capital ships, such as cruisers, in return for its concentrating on destroyers. The British Foreign Office balked, fearing that Japan might be so offended that it would join the Central Powers.[4]

Colonel House did share Wilson's general outlook. He opposed Russian ambitions and also the concrete demands of Italy, Serbia, and Rumania. He preferred making a separate peace with the dual monarchy of Austria-Hungary, but at the same time he encouraged the nationalistic aspirations of the Poles. As the war continued, he became increasingly less sympathetic to French claims to Alsace-Lorraine. At the same time, he always sought to cooperate with the British and French governments, seeing the sacrifice of parochial interests as necessary to preserve the entire coalition. He wanted to head the U.S. delegation to the postarmistice general peace conference, undoubtedly preferring to keep Wilson at home.[5]

House surely realized he possessed some leverage. Financially, the entire Allied war effort was based on American credit. Only U.S. support prevented the collapse of the pound sterling on the international exchange market. The United States was supplying one-sixth of all artillery shells, 60 percent of raw copper, 100 percent of smokeless powder and sulfuric acid. Furthermore, U.S. aid would remain crucial in the immediate postwar period.[6]

As historian David R. Woodward stresses, the British realized that militarily they were at their maximum strength; they could do no more. Moreover, their French ally was even weaker. Hence Lloyd George was not about to torpedo the peace process, prolong the war, and create an irreparable schism with Washington, provided, of course, that the British Empire's postwar position was protected.[7]

Yet, as House traveled to Europe, the Allies had not publicly endorsed the Fourteen Points. Neither they nor the United States had prepared specific armistice terms, much less examined how those terms would relate to a comprehensive postwar peace. Though Lloyd George's Trades Union speech of January 5, 1918, had closely resembled Wilson's far more famous address delivered three days later, all Allied leaders harbored strong suspicions of at least some of the president's provisions. Their anxiety had not been helped by Pershing's opposition to amalgamating his troops, the months of delay in committing U.S. forces to combat, Wilson's continued proclamation of war aims unilaterally, and the president's go-it-alone approach in negotiating with the Germans. Furthermore, the Allies were losing close to 5 million men in this struggle, the Americans so far only 114,000. French premier Georges Clemenceau remarked, "God gave us his Ten Commandments and we broke them. Wilson gave us his Fourteen Points — we shall see."[8]

Arriving at Brest, France, House reached Paris on October 26. He reported to Wilson that he found both Clemenceau and Allied commander Foch confident that Germany was already beaten. Therefore, the two men reasoned, Berlin would accept any terms offered. British general Sir Douglas Haig differed, arguing that Germany possessed the military resources to hold out against total capitulation. Within a day, House cabled Wilson that "too much success or security on the part of the Allies will make a genuine peace settlement exceedingly difficult if not impossible." He told British intelligence liaison Sir William Wiseman and Ambassador Reading that the nations of the world would no more submit to Britain's "complete domination of the seas" than to Germany's "domination of the land." If challenged, the United States would create an army and navy greater than Britain's.[9]

Knowing that victory was in sight, House feared an outcome as dishonorable as Germany's own pledge not to violate Belgian neutrality. He fully realized that Germany had begun negotiations on the basis of the Fourteen Points. Moreover, he believed that the Allies had already tentatively accepted them. Aside from selected Inquiry staffers, who worked on particular items, House had been the only top administration official influential in drafting the final text of these points. Even Secretary of State Robert Lansing had not been consulted.

House must have anticipated trouble. Just before he began negotiating, he commissioned two members of his delegation to draft a nine-page memorandum on the Fourteen Points that would clarify any ambiguous meaning. Chosen were journalists Frank Cobb and Walter Lippmann, the latter a prominent Inquiry staffer who was in part responsible for originally framing the Points.

The first part of the "Cobb–Lippmann" memorandum, as it was called, concerned Wilson's general provisions. Their interpretation of the points permitted confidential negotiations on "delicate matters," granted a nation sufficient armament to protect it against invasion, limited colonial claims to Germany's former colonies, and tied freedom of the seas to a league of nations. The second section, covering territorial settlements, included independence for Poles, Finns, Lithuanians, Letts, and possibly Ukrainians; French sovereignty over all Alsace-Lorraine; Italian rule over northern Trentino, populated by Germans; Trieste and Fiume as free ports; protection of minorities within the dissolving Austro-Hungarian Empire; Serbia's access to the sea; Rumanian acquisition of Dobrudja, Bessarabia, and probably Transylvania; an independent Armenia under the aegis of a protecting power; "special international control" for Greek-speaking islands off Turkey's west coast; and Britain serving as a mandatory power for Arabia, Mesopotamia, and "the Palestine."[10]

Cobb–Lippmann made explicit previous modifications Wilson himself had specified during the past several months. Implicit was approval of the promises France and Britain had made with Italy in 1915 and the 1916 Sykes–Pikot agreement that had parceled out much of the Middle East. House drew upon Cobb–Lippmann on October 29, reading its provisions out loud to the Allied leaders the first day he negotiated with them.[11]

If House thought that Cobb–Lippmann would serve as a clear articulation of Wilson's views, he was very much mistaken. The president immediately wired House: "Analysis of fourteen points satisfactory interpretation of principles involved but details of application mentioned should be regarded as merely illustrative suggestions and reserved for peace conference. Admission of inchoate nationalities to peace-conference most undesirable."[12]

This message did not make House's task any easier. It was, however, highly naive to assume that a memorandum drafted within twenty-four hours by two members of House's delegation would represent Wilson's latest thinking on some of the most complex problems that Europe had ever faced. Lippmann had already alienated Wilson by arguing that the administration had failed to educate public opinion concerning the character of the peace.[13]

On the first day of negotiation, October 29, House emphasized the need to act before civil disorder overtook Eastern Europe. Lloyd George concurred: Britain itself might face unrest and "anything" might happen in France. At the same time, House learned just how rigid the Allied leaders could be. Both Lloyd George and Clemenceau told him that Wilson had never consulted them concerning the Fourteen Points. The French premier and Italian foreign minister Sidney Sonnino opposed any league of nations. When House threatened that the United States might withdraw from the war altogether, making a separate peace, Lloyd George replied that Britain would single-handedly continue the conflict rather than agree to Point Two. Freedom of the seas, he argued, would deprive his nation of the power of blockade, long its primary weapon in wartime. House retorted that postwar British interference with American trade might find the United States siding with John Bull's enemies. He privately told Lloyd George that the United States would respond to such rigidity by embarking upon the greatest naval program the world had yet seen! As far as the other thirteen points were concerned, House found the British prime minister "sufficiently elastic to enable us to put our own interpretation upon them."[14]

As for an armistice, House discovered that British war secretary Milner and Generals Tasker Bliss and Douglas Haig favored moderate terms. Clemenceau held out for the harsher provisions of General Foch, even if the supreme Allied commander himself warned against excessive demands on Germany's navy. The French premier accused Pershing of poor generalship because the AEF had not kept pace with the other armies.[15]

When House informed Wilson of the Allied reaction, the president balked. "It is the fourteen points that Germany has accepted," he snapped, cabling House, "I am ready to repudiate any selfish programme openly, but assume that the Allies cannot honorably turn the present discussions into a peace conference without me."[16]

Not surprisingly, negotiations on the next day, October 30, did not start well. House entered the meeting under the assumption that he would publicly break with the Allies unless they accepted the Fourteen Points. "The French," House reported to Wilson, "are inclined not to accept your terms." The president promptly cabled back that he could not consent to any negotiations that did not include either freedom of the seas or a league of nations. If necessary, he would make his concern public.[17]

Nonetheless all ended harmoniously, in large measure because House gave way on crucial matters. First, he concurred with a draft signed by the Allied leaders asserting that Point Two regarding the seas was "open to various interpretations." Therefore, its final resolution awaited an impending peace conference. Hence, the main stumbling block to British—and thereby Allied—approval of the Fourteen Points was removed. Second, he concurred with Lloyd George's insistence that Germany must pay compensation "for all damage done to the civilian population of the Allies, and their property by land, by sea, and from the air." No precise definition was given to the terms "all damage" and "civilian populations" or what might be implied. Such a provision went beyond Point Seven, which only referred to Belgium's "restoration," and to Point Eight, which spoke of "restoring" the occupied portion of France. Third, he accepted French demands for occupying the Rhineland. Both he and Lloyd George warned Clemenceau that extreme demands on Germany could risk revolution throughout Europe, but the premier claimed he would lose his majority in the Chamber of Deputies if France did not occupy the east bank of the Rhine.[18]

Lloyd George also conveyed his desires concerning Germany's colonies. German Southwest Africa should be awarded to the South African Federation; German Pacific islands to Australia. Britain would assume a protectorate over Mesopotamia and possibly Palestine. Arabia would become autonomous. France might be given a sphere of influence in Syria. The United States should become trustee for German East Africa, where the rulers had treated the "natives" inhumanely. "The British," House reported to Wilson, "would like us to accept something so that they might more freely take what they desire." The prime minister hoped that the Allies should in general "thresh out their differences" before a three-week peace conference began.[19]

On the very same day, October 30, as House was participating in the most sensitive of part of his negotiations, Pershing was complicating things immeasurably. At a meeting held five days earlier at Senlis, twenty-five miles north of Paris, with Foch, Pétain, and Haig,

Pershing outlined armistice terms that differed little from those of Foch. He sought evacuation of Belgium and France within thirty days, Allied occupation of Alsace-Lorraine and of crucial beachheads east of the Rhine, and the surrender of all rolling stock and of U-boats and their bases. Two days later, War Secretary Baker cabled Pershing that Wilson was relying on his military commander's "counsel and advice" concerning armistice conditions. Nevertheless, the president desired only German evacuation of enemy territory; he doubted the wisdom of occupying Alsace-Lorraine and the eastern side of the Rhine. "The terms of the armistice," Wilson wrote, "should be rigid enough to secure us against the renewal of hostilities by Germany but not humiliating beyond that necessity." More stringent conditions "would throw the advantage to the military party in Germany."[20] In short, Wilson desired an armistice that would leave the Reich's ground forces intact but render them incapable of resuming offensive operations.

Suddenly, on October 30, Pershing was raising the ante. Wilson's terms, he believed, were far too weak. Though he had yet to distinguish himself in the Meuse–Argonne offensive, he cabled Secretary Baker, declaring that anything short of German surrender depended upon imposing stringent peace conditions. Without informing Wilson, Baker, or House, Black Jack also expressed his sentiments to the SWC. Although stricken with the flu and writing from a sickbed, he was directly challenging Wilson's directions. In sharp contrast to his position just five days previously, he now claimed that an armistice would "revivify the low spirits of the German Army and enable it to reorganize and resist later on."[21] In short, Pershing wanted—in his own words—"unconditional surrender." Hence, while House was entering into conversations with Allied leaders, Pershing was attempting to make a crucial policy decision entirely on his own, in the process engaging himself in blatant insubordination.

Not surprisingly, Wilson and Baker were enraged, the secretary writing a stinging reprimand. Chief of Staff Peyton March expressed both amazement and distress. Tasker Bliss compared Pershing's policy to that of ancient Rome. The United States was saying: "No, we haven't killed enough of you, there are some towns we want to burn." House and Lloyd George both used the term "politics," a reference to a possible presidential bid by Pershing in 1920. Even Clemenceau found the general "theatrical." The French premier had just gained House's approval for what he had most sought, occupation of the Rhineland. Furthermore, lenient reparation conditions had been ruled out. Pershing's proposal was unnecessary, for Foch was already demanding stringent terms. House wrote Wilson that no Allied commander had ever submitted such a document without clearing it with the civilian authorities. The Allied leaders, not fond of Pershing to begin with, realized that he did not speak for Wilson. Was Pershing, asks historian David R. Woodward, about to become Wilson's George B. McClellan, the general who challenged Lincoln's authority during the Civil War?[22]

On October 31, Foch—in a communication formally addressed to Colonel House—responded to Pershing most candidly: "I am not waging war for the sake of waging war. If I obtain through the Armistice the conditions that we wish to impose on Germany, I am satisfied. Once this object is attained, nobody has the right to shed one more drop of blood."[23]

Moreover, the Allied armies were war-weary, having experienced grueling battles over four years with horrendous loss of life. They still did not see the United States as possessing a first-rate combat force. For their part, doughboys in France, severely bloodied in the Meuse–Argonne campaign, would not have welcomed continuing a conflict that their civilian leaders deemed unnecessary.

House deftly conveyed Wilson's opposition to Pershing, thereby avoiding turning the general into a martyr. Early in November, Pershing did apologize to House for not consulting him before sending his proposal to the SWC. Writing in 1931, however, he did not regret his call for unconditional surrender. Under such terms, the German army would have been virtually treated as "paroled prisoners of war," something that would have served as "a greater deterrent against possible German aggression."[24]

Historian John S. D. Eisenhower concurs with Pershing, claiming that had the German army been crushed and all its territory occupied, "the Second World War might never have occurred." Eisenhower does concede that Allied public opinion would have balked at further fighting. Margaret MacMillan writes that the Allies should have marched triumphantly into Berlin, just as the Germans had done in Paris in 1871. As a result of the armistice terms, most Germans never experienced defeat firsthand.[25] One can only counter that an exhausted Europe, often experiencing internal strife, would not tolerate any bloodshed that could be avoided. To invade Germany, much less attempt to occupy it, would have proven an incredibly difficult operation, beneficial only to the revolutions already sweeping over much of Central Europe.

October 31 saw House in an optimistic mood. He cabled Wilson:

> If you will give me a free hand in dealing with these immediate negotiations, I can assure you that nothing will be done to embarrass you or to compromise any of your peace principles. You will have as free a hand after the Armistice is signed as you now have. It is exceedingly important that nothing be said or done at this time which may in any way halt the Armistice which will save so many thousands of lives. Negotiations are now proceeding satisfactorily.[26]

Wilson simply replied, "I am proud of the way you are handling the situation." He balked, however, at Lloyd George's suggestion that the Western powers should "thresh out their differences" before the major conference met. The president was still dissatisfied with British rigidity concerning freedom of the seas, even if—to use biographer John Milton Cooper Jr.'s metaphor—he ended up believing that half a loaf was better than none.[27]

When on November 1, the SWC discussed military aspects of the armistice, Lloyd George and Haig opposed Foch's demand for bridgeheads on the east bank of the Rhine, as Allied forces would be relatively close to Frankfurt. House played little role in the debate but leaned towards Foch and Clemenceau. Historian Bullitt Lowry finds House flying in the face of Wilson's opposition to Rhineland occupation, House believing that French support of the Fourteen Points was worth the price. Lowry also stresses the major concession concerning reparations, in particular a provision that "any future claims or demands on the part of the Allies remain unaffected." This apparently innocent phrasing would plague the U.S. delegation at the Paris peace conference of 1919 as it led to exorbitant Allied demands that jeopardized the success of the entire meeting.[28]

On November 3, House boasted of having a "red letter day," as Lloyd George claimed he would interpret freedom of the seas "in the light of the new conditions which have arisen by reason of the war."[29] By now the Allied leaders had accepted what later became known as the Pre-armistice Agreement—with its approval of most all of the Fourteen Points, including a league of nations. They also concurred to the principle of reparations, even if they did not specify the amount to be exacted. What had begun as the drafting of armistice terms had resulted in a severe preliminary peace.

November 3 also marked Austria's agreement to an armistice with the Allies, effective the following day. Not only had Austrian armies been defeated on the Italian front, but Vienna was experiencing starvation. Terms included complete demobilization of its armies, withdrawal of troops fighting alongside the Germans, surrender of its fleet and half its military equipment, and Allied occupation of strategic points. These conditions were sufficiently severe for Clemenceau to comment, "We have left the breeches of the Emperor and nothing else." The Austrians had sought to end the war on the basis of the Fourteen Points, but House wanted to have them accepted only when the Allies had agreed upon armistice terms for Germany.[30] The Hungarian parliament had already declared complete independence from Austria. By the end of the year both nations would become republics.

The remaining Paris meetings were anticlimactic. Even on November 4, however, Wilson cabled House, threatening to "build up the strongest navy our resources permit." On the following day, House telegraphed Wilson their cause had "won a great diplomatic victory," for the Allies had accepted the president's terms in the face of "a hostile and influential junta" within the United States and an unsympathetic Entente overseas. In London, however, Lloyd George told the Imperial War Cabinet that he had refused to accept Point Two and that the vagueness of the Fourteen Points did not threaten his nation's interests.[31]

Wilson thought he had gained a great victory, telling his cabinet on November 5 that the Paris conferees had agreed to the Fourteen Points with reservations limited to freedom of the seas and the nature of Belgian and French restoration. Interior Secretary Franklin K. Lane claimed that the president was "certainly in splendid humor and in good trim—not worried a bit. And why should he be, for the world is at his feet, eating out of his hand! No Caesar ever had such a triumph."[32]

Several historians praise House's diplomacy, claiming that the Allied leaders had made significant concessions.[33] There is, however, much to criticize concerning the entire mission. Arthur S. Link notes that House had gained at best only a "shadow victory," the Allies a "substantive" one. Charles E. Neu sees House stumbling on French demands for reparations and security against German attack. As Cooper stresses, the Germans accepted Wilson's principles as stated, but the Allies saw them as filtered through House via Cobb–Lippmann, a circumstance that created a fatal flaw in the final peace agreement. One does not necessarily have to adopt Inga Floto's claim that House had "lost his head" to be critical.[34]

House was by no means more qualified as a diplomat to engage in this mission than he had been in previous ones. He was overly captivated by Clemenceau's personality, prejudged the attitude of the Allies, and felt increasingly frustrated in his personal dealings with Wilson. Both he and the president kept pressing freedom of the seas, not appreciating how crucial naval blockades were to British security. They permitted loose language concerning reparations, one of the great stumbling blocks of postwar negotiations. They appeared oblivious to the fact that Foch's military conditions precluded any Wilsonian peace, particularly given the rapidity of Germany's collapse.

If House bears primary responsibility for the sloppiness of the negotiations, which appeared to lack any agenda, Wilson also failed in crucial aspects. He did not give House specific instructions, particularly concerning the most sensitive matters, even dismissing the Cobb–Lippmann memorandum as "merely illustrative suggestions." He should have been much clearer in his interpretation of his often ambiguous Fourteen Points. He took little advantage of radio contact and cable technology at his disposal, giving House far too much leeway.

The president had a concern just as immediate, namely, a congressional election that he hoped would serve as a public endorsement of his peace agenda.

SEVENTEEN
"NOT ORDINARY TIMES"

The 1918 Elections

THE CONGRESSIONAL ELECTION OF 1918 WAS PARTICULARLY critical, one of the most significant in U.S. history. It was not a presidential race, but nothing less than the survival of a Wilsonian peace was at stake, particularly as the war was coming to an end and Allied victory was clearly in sight. Were the Republican Party to control Congress, the president's foreign policy agenda would be jeopardized. The Senate Foreign Relations Committee would determine the form in which any peace treaty would be presented to the full body, which would then vote on its acceptance. Indeed, given the belligerent tone of prominent Republican critics while he was negotiating with the Germans, Wilson would be severely handicapped before any peace conference was convened.

Wilson sought to give the demeanor of being nonpartisan as far as waging war was concerned. On May 27, 1918, in addressing the Congress concerning a tax bill, he told the legislators, "Politics is adjourned. The elections will go to those who think least of it." Only in a conversation held four and a half months later did the president clarify just what he meant. He conceded that it was impossible to disregard politics altogether. Yet "any one, in the midst of war, who took some step for political advantage rather than a step destined purely for war purposes, was disloyal to his country."[1]

The president, however, was already acting in a most partisan manner, as revealed by his behavior in a Wisconsin senatorial race. On October 21, 1917, Senator Paul O. Husting (D) had died of gunshot wounds suffered in a hunting accident. By mid-March 1918, Governor Emanuel Phillip had called for a special election. After a tight primary race, the Republicans chose Representative Irvine L. Lenroot as their candidate. The Democrats picked Joseph Davies, a prominent Wilson backer who had resigned as chairman of the new Federal Trade Commission to run. The Socialist Party, strong in Milwaukee and among German Americans throughout the state, supported the Austrian-born Victor Berger, editor and publisher of the *Milwaukee Leader* and former congressman.

Wilson entered the fray almost immediately. In a public letter to Davies, the president directly attacked Lenroot's prewar antipreparedness record while finding Davies a man of "true loyalty and genuine Americanism." In backing the Democratic cause, Vice President Thomas Riley Marshall told an audience in Madison, "Your state is under suspicion." Indeed, the vice president accused Lenroot of attracting the "sewage" of "disloyal" voters. Senator John Sharp Williams echoed such sentiments, claiming Lenroot had been "lukewarmly attached to America and the Allies."[2]

In the special election held on April 2, Lenroot won by a plurality of 15,000-plus. Davies had pulled the largest support of any Democrat yet save Wilson, but it was not enough. Socialist Berger did surprisingly well, carrying close to 100,000 votes and capturing twelve counties, including Milwaukee. Wisconsin's La Follette, too, was a loser, as he had deemed Lenroot a renegade from his state machine.

Wilson, as historian David M. Kennedy observes, had not only lost a Senate seat. He had sacrificed much of the aura of nonpartisanship that is among the greatest political assets of a sitting president, especially in wartime. He had literally invited the Republicans, until then at least partly restrained by the war emergency, to battle against him far more openly. By placing the issue on the ground of loyalty to administration war measures, he exposed himself to the plausible Republican claim that they had supported the president's wartime measures more steadfastly than many of his own party.³ Conversely, the president undoubtedly believed he had no choice in backing such a loyal follower.

Wilson's next blunder took place on June 13, when he convinced Henry Ford to run for the Senate on the Democratic ticket. "You are the only man in Michigan," the president said, "who can be elected and help bring about the peace you so much desire."⁴ The idea was first promoted by Josephus Daniels, who sought a replacement for retiring Republican incumbent William Alden Smith. The navy secretary hoped to enter Ford in both the Democratic and Republican primaries, something then permissible under Michigan law, in the hopes that he would win both nominations and run unopposed in the general election.

During the campaign, Ford delivered no public speeches and made no pronouncements. Most Democrats throughout the country were decidedly unenthusiastic; Wilson aide Joe Tumulty called him "a cause of great embarrassment." Historian Kennedy notes that the nomination "was positive proof that the President was desperate, perhaps, suggested some, even unhinged."⁵

The Republicans pounced on Ford's record. Colonel Harvey's *War Weekly* declared that the auto manufacturer was "not a true American; he is an 'internationalist'; a man without a country; a Pacifist; a Profiteer; a breaker of pledges; a cheat and a liar." Theodore Roosevelt relished quoting Ford's remark about flying American flags over his own factory: "I don't believe in the flag. When the war is over these flags shall come down, never to go up again." Memories of his quixotic peace ship, an effort to end the war in 1915, were soon raised. To the *Nation*, a weekly often far more dovish than TR, "Mr. Ford's mental equipment is of the poorest for the high office he seeks. He has the guilelessness of a child and the political ignorance of a small schoolboy." By September even Wilson harbored some misgivings, writing Daniels of his concern that Ford's son, Edsel, had been exempted from the draft.⁶

In late August, Truman H. Newberry won the Republican primary by nearly 50,000 votes, leaving Ford to run only on the Democratic ticket. A multimillionaire industrialist, Newberry had seen action off the Cuban coast in the Spanish–American War as a navy lieutenant. He had served as Roosevelt's assistant secretary of the navy for three years, then briefly as secretary. In the November election,

Newberry defeated Ford by the narrow margin of 220,000 to 212,000. Given Ford's lack of qualifications, the result had been surprisingly close. Newberry's huge monetary contributions exceeded limits set in Michigan's campaign law and in 1922, after much controversy, he gave up his seat.

Wilson had somewhat better success in purging the Democratic Party of congressional opponents whose base was in the South, a one-party region. In Dixie, the primaries, not the November election, determined who was sent to Congress. Most southern politicians had embraced the president's war measures, in part undoubtedly to erase the stain of "treason" bestowed after the Civil War. Some recalcitrant members, such as Claude Kitchin, House majority leader and chairman of the Ways and Means Committee, were so powerful that Wilson deemed it unwise to challenge them.

In several primaries, however, the president did intervene, often with success. In the process, he helped turn the region from serving as a bastion of anti-interventionism to being the one most committed to internationalism. He endorsed Nathaniel B. Dial, a wealthy conservative banker from Charleston, for the Senate seat in South Carolina. Dial's rival, former governor Coleman L. Blease, had commented that on Judgment Day "every American citizen who is killed in this war, off of American soil, will be charged against the President of the United States and the members of the Congress."[7] In the late August primary, Dial trounced Blease by 21,000 votes.

Wilson was also successful in two Texas congressional races. Both Jeff McLemore of Houston, elected at large, and James Slayden of San Antonio had long opposed Wilson's foreign policy. In the July primary, McLemore, subject to redistricting, only polled 2,000 out of 21,000 votes in his race. Speaking to the House in September, he blamed his defeat on a "prejudiced, a perjured, and a paid press" controlled by banker J. P. Morgan. Also in July, Slayden dropped out of his race, Wilson having cabled a San Antonio publisher that the congressman had withheld needed support. Postmaster General Burleson had drafted Wilson's letter, his own son-in-law being a candidate. Since Slayden had been a relatively mild Wilson critic, the president soon regretted his blunder, particularly because in November the Republicans won the district.[8]

James K. Vardaman (D), senator from Mississippi, was another Wilson target. An archracist who voted progressive on economic issues, he was, in the words of historian Seward W. Livermore, "a rabble rouser of incredible virtuosity, impressive even in a region noted for high-level performance in that art."[9] Vardaman was extreme enough to be one of the six senators who voted against U.S. entry into the war, so the president backed Pat Harrison, an administration supporter. Campaigning against Vardaman's war record, Harrison won the August 31 primary 56,000 to 44,000.

Georgia harbored a demagogue as equally impassioned as Vardaman: Thomas Edward Watson, always known as Tom Watson. The editor of a weekly magazine, the *Jeffersonian*, Watson accused Wilson of pulling his nation into war on behalf of Morgan banks and the "steel trust," called conscription unconstitutional, and ridiculed the president's war aims: "The world must be made safe for democracy even though none is left in these United States." In a congressional primary, the president supported Congressman Carl Vinson of Milledgeville, a staunch advocate of military preparedness, who accused Watson of "seditious utterances" in his "disloyal incendiary publications."[10] Although Vinson defeated Watson in the House race, the result was surprisingly close, with each candidate carrying six counties.

The president had an easier time with another Georgian, Senator Thomas Hardwick. Although Hardwick reluctantly voted for the war resolution, he opposed selective service, the Espionage Act, and legislation regulating food, fuel, and railroads. Wilson endorsed William J. Harris, former chairman of the Federal Trade Commission, who won the Democratic nomination.

Wilson did experience several setbacks. He opposed Tennessee senator John K. Shields, a conservative Democrat, who had fought the president over patronage, not foreign policy. Early in August, the senator easily won his state's primary over his rival, the pro-Wilson governor Tom C. Rye. Similarly, Alabama representative George Huddleston won 60 percent of the votes cast in the mid-August primary and remained in the House until 1937.

Several voices found Wilson's purges most unwise. The Democratic press deplored Wilson's attack on Slayden, whom it saw as a party loyalist, particularly as the president had endorsed such a strong antiwar figure as Henry Ford. The pro-administration New York *World* accused the president of taking "unnecessary risks" in contesting the powerful Vardaman. Colonel Harvey's *War Weekly* asserted that Wilson should have pointed to the Mississippi senator's "lack of patriotism," not arrogantly speak of opposition to "my administration."[11]

The *Nation* quoted Wilson as refusing to intervene in West Virginia because he abhorred "even so much as the appearance of an effort to pick and prefer a candidate." Remarked the liberal weekly, "Consistency is plainly not a hobgoblin of the Presidential mind."[12] The journal was right. The president's obvious vicissitudes had weakened his position.

All this time, Republicans were far from inactive. In February 1918, the Grand Old Party chose Will Hays as party chairman. Genial, energetic, and politically savvy, he had served as state chairman in Indiana. He opposed New Freedom legislation ("the present socialistic tendency in our government") while enthusiastically supporting the war effort. In fact, he accused the Democrats of accepting "any kind of a compromise" with Germany if such a move would keep them in power. Conversely, Hays claimed that "every Republican vote cast is another nail in the Kaiser's coffin; every Republican congressman elected is another stone piled on his tomb." By late October, he was accusing Wilson of giving Germany "the fruits of a victory greater than she should win by a hundred years of fighting."[13] In dealing with a party still split into Taft and Roosevelt factions, Hays served as the ideal unifier, backed by party leaders of both wings, as reflected by such diverse figures as progressive William E. Borah and Old Guardsmen Reed Smoot and Boies Penrose.

In mid-July, Lodge, Roosevelt, Elihu Root, and Taft all called for the election of a Republican Congress, arguing that their party had supported Wilson's war measures with greater devotion than his own Democrats. The claim was a common one within party ranks. Back in March, Smoot told his Senate colleagues that the president's appointments were partisan "from first to last." Though Democratic senators William J. Stone and J. Hamilton Lewis had pointed to such administration Republicans as Fuel Administrator Harry A. Garfield and a host of military personnel, their opponents were hardly assuaged. The pro-Wilson *New Republic* admitted that Wilson had appointed Republicans only to strictly subordinate positions, refusing to share even minor responsibility for the management of the war.[14]

As the AEF became increasingly involved in combat overseas, particularly in the Meuse–Argonne campaign, prominent Republicans portrayed their party as the single entity holding back compromise peace with Germany. Ohio representative Simeon Fess, in accepting the chairmanship of the National Congressional Committee early in September, declared that Republican control of the next Congress would guard against an "inconclusive peace." The *New Republic* responded quickly: "Peace in a world of unrelated national states merely through the exemplary punishment of Germany; prosperity at home through the abrogation of war emergency legislation; that in a nutshell is the Republican creed."[15]

In some instances, the war effort compromised traditional loyalties. In April 1918, Colonel Harvey's conservative *War Weekly* sought reelection of almost all Congress's present members: "The Hun is at the gate; the Republic is in peril; freedom is at stake; civilization and humanity tremble in the balance; America must save the cause." Republican victory, it warned, would make James R. Mann, who opposed Wilson's foreign policy before the war, Speaker of the House. Moreover, the party as a whole would not yet gain real power, for major appropriations would be completed before it took control in March. Mann himself struck a different tone, declaring two months later that "in war there is no partisanship. We stand as a united country and a united people, unwilling to let bickerings at home affect our determination to win abroad."[16]

The National Security League struck a similar note when it intervened in the elections. In May, honorary president Elihu Root attempted to set the tone. Addressing the group's annual convention held at New York's Metropolitan Opera House, he called upon members of all parties to stand by the Wilson administration. Any candidate "must have a loyal heart or it is treason to send him to Congress." The NSL mailed a chart of eight "acid test" measures to 1,800 newspapers. Not surprisingly, a legislator could be attacked for voting against the declaration of war on April 6, 1917, and the Kahn amendment to the army bill, which sought to restore the War Department's original provisions for conscription. Other listed offenses, however, took place in 1916, some a year before the United States entered the war. These included warning Americans against traveling on armed merchant craft belonging to belligerent nations, opposition to the authorization of several more battleships, voting against increasing the regular army to 178,000 and later to 250,000, and turning down a federally controlled volunteer force that would have abolished the state-dominated militia. Charles D. Orth, a hemp manufacturer who served as the organization's executive secretary, designed the list. Ironically, Root became critical of such activity, believing it subjected the NSL to attacks of "New York" interference in local matters. He could not, however, dissuade the organization.[17]

By NSL criteria, only forty-seven congressmen made its "Roll of Honor." Of these, forty-five hailed from eastern states and only three were Democrats. The NSL was particularly effective in primaries, where the great majority of its opponents were defeated. Certain Wisconsin Republicans fell victim, as did Democrats from Ohio, Colorado, and Missouri.

Critics responded that the NSL ignored the 119 war measures enacted by Congress since the United States entered the conflict. Furthermore, only two of the eight "acid test" bills had been subject to a straight yes-or-no vote; the others involved complicated parliamentary maneuvers that did not accurately reflect the legislator's final position. The NSL snapped that it was Congress's own fault for conducting its business in an incomprehensible manner. Jeff McLemore accused the NSL of being financed by "war profiteers." Socialist Meyer London felt similarly, attacking the "National Obscurity League" and saying that "every self-respecting Representative should rejoice at being repudiated by that crowd."[18] After the general election, a special House committee investigated the organization, finding that it violated the Corrupt Practices Act of 1910 by failing to file a list of contributors and expenses with the clerk of the House.

Less prominent in this regard was the League for National Unity (LNU), an organization that opposed "voices of dissension and sedition," particularly targeting proponents of negotiation with "any irresponsible and autocratic dynasty." Theodore N. Vail, president of the American Telephone and Telegraph Company, served as chairman. Former assistant attorney general James Beck headed the executive committee. Vice chairmen included AFL leader Samuel Gompers; George Pope, president of the National Association of Manufacturers; Cardinal James Gibbons of Baltimore, the country's leading Roman Catholic prelate; Frank Mason North, president of the Federal Council of Churches; and Charles Barrett, president of the Farmers' Educational and Cooperative Union.[19]

In February 1918, Wilson endorsed the organization, expressing appreciation for its efforts "to swing the whole force of the nation behind the constitutional authorities now conducting the war." That June, the LNU sponsored a petition of five hundred prominent citizens calling for the defeat of all "disloyal candidates," irrespective of party. Signers included Charles Evans Hughes; women suffrage leader Carrie Chapman Catt; and diplomat Henry Morgenthau. Inactive compared to the NSL, the group saw its role as setting a tone rather than engaging in actual political warfare.[20]

By October, the rhetoric became more heated than ever. In mid-month, Congressman Tom Heflin told fellow House members that "every halfhearted American and every German sympathizer" would be voting Republican. Arizona senator Henry F. Ashurst warned that an opposition Congress would "give aid and comfort to the enemy."[21]

The Republicans were quick to respond. On October 31, Taft and TR issued a joint appeal, warning that Wilson's exchange of notes with Germany "has caused a deep concern among our people," for Berlin might secure "a peace around a council table, instead of a sentence from a court."[22]

Wilson increasingly feared that the congressional elections would jeopardize his peace program. As he said to financier Thomas Lamont on October 4, a Republican victory would indicate to the Allied peoples that he had been repudiated, with the "sort of peace" upon which he had set his heart suddenly vanishing. After consulting with Homer Cummings, Democratic national chairman, and Vance McCormick, chairman of the party's National Campaign Committee, on October 25 the president issued an appeal to his countrymen, asking them to return only Democrats to both houses of Congress. Though denying that "any political party is paramount in matters of patriotism," he maintained nonetheless that "the nation should give its undivided support to the government under a unified leadership." He continued:

The leaders in the minority of the present Congress have unques-
tionably been prowar, but they have been anti-administration. At
almost every turn, since we entered the war, they have sought to
take the choice of policy and the conduct of the war out of my
hands and put it under the control of instrumentalities of their
own choosing. This is no time for divided counsel or for divided
leadership. Unity of command is as necessary now in civil action
as upon the field of battle.

Most significant of all, the return of a Republican majority to
either house would "certainly be interpreted on the other side of the
water as a repudiation of my leadership." He concluded that ordinarily
he would never make such an appeal, "but these are not ordinary
times."[23] He did not elaborate upon this comment.

For months Wilson had been smarting under Republican attacks,
particularly those centering on his peace agenda and extensive negotiations with the Germans. On the very day Wilson made his appeal,
Roosevelt proclaimed that adoption of the Fourteen Points would
"represent not the unconditional surrender of Germany but the con-
ditional surrender of the United States."[24] In particular, the president
feared Henry Cabot Lodge chairing the Senate Foreign Relations
Committee. The president was also responding to pleas from local candidates, who were undoubtedly disappointed when in September he
canceled a Liberty Loan tour of the West.

Within the Wilson camp, there was strong dissent. The nation,
claimed Interior Secretary Lane, believed that the president had "low-
ered himself." Even before it had been released, Wilson's wife, Edith,
found his plea undignified. Colonel House used the terms "needless
venture," "great gamble," "political error." The president, he maintained, should have simply asked Americans to reelect members who
supported U.S. war aims "regardless of party."[25]

The Republicans immediately produced a rejoinder. Lodge,
Simeon Fess, Reed Smoot (chairman of the party's senatorial committee), and Massachusetts congressman Frederick H. Gillett (ranking
minority member) released a biting statement. Wilson, it claimed, conceded that Republicans were "loyal enough to fight," to "take up great
loans and pay enormous taxes," and to "furnish important men at no
salary to some of the great war boards in Washington." Nonetheless,

he did not find them loyal enough to be trusted with "any share in the government of the country or legislation for it." House Republicans, the manifesto continued, cast more supportive votes on crucial war bills than had the Democrats. Similarly, their Senate counterparts voted 72 percent in favor of such crucial legislation as compared to the Democrats 67 percent. With a Republican victory, the strongly pro-draft Julius Kahn would replace the anticonscription Hubert S. Dent Jr. on the Military Affairs Committee. Such administration critics as Claude Kitchin and Champ Clark would be ousted as chairman of the House Ways and Means Committee and as House Speaker, respectively. Above all it stressed, "This is not the President's personal war."[26]

Some Republicans expressed themselves in more impassioned terms. Columbia University president Nicholas Murray Butler, GOP vice presidential candidate in 1912, saw "political profiteering" at work. Will Hays called Wilson's message an insult to every loyal Republican in the nation. To Taft, Wilson was really saying, "Unless you give me uncontrolled power, you repudiate me and my leadership before the world." Harvey's *War Weekly* labeled the message "a menace to all mankind," titling its editorial on the subject "God Save the Republic!" The liberal *Nation* magazine accused Wilson of playing a dangerous game and playing it badly: "The golden haze has largely vanished and the politician stands revealed."[27]

Some private comments were even more biting. Roosevelt expressed private gratification that the president had "come out in the open": "I fear Judas most when he can cloak his activities behind a treacherous make-believe of non-partisanship." Lodge wrote, "The President has thrown off the mask. The only test of loyalty is loyalty to one man no matter what he says."[28]

Wilson had his defenders. The Hearst press gloried in the president's "courage" and "frankness." The *New Republic* praised his "courageous and salutary political utterance." The *New York Times* recalled that after the Union had won the Battle of Gettysburg, it had continued to support Lincoln, thereby repudiating "a division of leadership and of counsel in Washington."[29]

Democrats asserted that Wilson was only following Republican precedent. During the 1898 congressional campaign, so Tumulty observed, Colonel Theodore Roosevelt himself made a partisan plea. In running for governor of New York, TR had argued that "the nations of Europe" would view a refusal to sustain President McKinley as rejecting both the Spanish–American War itself and efforts of the U.S. peace commission to secure its fruits. At this time, Lodge, too, had warned that a Democratic victory would mean repudiating the results of the conflict.[30]

Two days before the election of 1918, the highly respected Herbert Hoover, until then a markedly nonpartisan figure, publicly endorsed "a solid front and a sustained leadership" under Wilson's direction. Hoover biographer George H. Nash writes that the food administrator probably wanted to strengthen Wilson's hand at a critical moment in history. The "master of emergencies," Nash continues, may also have feared losing power if he did not rally to the president's side.[31]

Republicans reacted to Hoover with bitterness. Simeon Fess accused him of "prostitution of official station"; he hinted that the next session of Congress would investigate Hoover's Food Administration. To TR, Hoover had shown himself "in a very contemptible light."[32]

Historians differ over the wisdom of Wilson's appeal, some find the president foolish in attacking the loyalty of his political opponents. Defenders posit that the statement might actually have boosted his party in some races, saving some Democrats and preventing worse defeats.[33] John Milton Cooper Jr. observes that the political rhetoric in 1918 was so intense that the effect of Wilson's broadside was probably exaggerated; at times opposition to the president already bordered on hatred.[34]

It is hard to fathom, however, why Wilson took such a risk. He surely would have realized that the Republicans would maintain that their patriotism was being questioned. Precedents concerning the Spanish–American War, a brief skirmish in comparison to the current conflict, offered little parallel to the exhausting struggle in which the United States was currently involved. Moreover, as *Current Opinion* pointed out, probably no president had ever before made an appeal "so frankly and exclusively personal."[35]

Above all, by turning a congressional election, almost always decided on local issues, into a referendum on his foreign policy, Wilson had shown a lack of fundamental understanding of how U.S. politics works. Such a deficiency is surprising for someone who had devoted much of his career to studying just how the U.S. government functioned. He created the very situation he hoped to avoid: a perception in Europe that his foreign policy had been repudiated. In short, Wilson had gambled—and lost.

On November 5, the Republicans captured both houses of Congress. They won control of the Senate 49–47, and in many states the margin of victory was equally slim. Had the Democrats gained just one more Senate seat, the vice president could have broken any tie, thereby allowing them to retain the chairmanships of the major committees.

The House of Representatives now had 239 Republicans, 193 Democrats, and 5 members of minor parties. Fifty-one seats had changed hands and the Republicans controlled the body for the first time since 1910. The GOP popular vote in the House exceeded that of the Democrats by 2 million, a huge figure for a midterm election. Democrats did upset Republicans in New York, where Al Smith became governor, and in Massachusetts, where David I. Walsh defeated Senate incumbent John Weeks. Both results reveal the rising role of ethnics with the Democratic Party, in this case, the increasing prominence of Irish Americans.

The Socialists, the party the most critical of the war effort, experienced mixed results. In Wisconsin, Victor Berger recovered his congressional seat; the party elected twenty-two state legislators, a gain of nine. Socialists were also elected to the Minnesota legislature and acquired some local offices in several other states. In New York City, Morris Hillquit lost a House bid. Congressional candidate Fiorello La Guardia, running on an interparty Fusion ticket, had just served as a combat AEF aviator in Italy. He had called Hillquit "part of the German army" and had asked of his radical opponent Scott Nearing, "What is his regiment?" Meyer London failed in his reelection bid to Congress, facing opposition from a united Democratic and Republican candidate, left-wing Socialists who found him too moderate, and Jews critical of his opposition to Zionism and lack of religious orthodoxy. In some major races, Socialist ballots disappeared, were destroyed, or disqualified under suspicious circumstances.[36] In North Dakota, the Non-Partisan League won all three branches of the state government, with Lynn Frazier reelected governor. By early 1919, the NPL's power was at its zenith, enlisting more than 200,000 members in thirteen states.

The Republicans were jubilant. Taft wrote a relative, "The news is too good to be true." George Harvey's *War Weekly* referred to ending Wilson's "usurpation of powers." Lodge expressed himself similarly, writing British historian Sir George Otto Trevelyan, "The people did not mean to have a dictatorship or an autocracy." He found the results the greatest defeat an incumbent president had ever received.[37]

To Theodore Roosevelt, the election marked "much more a victory for straight Americanism than for Republicanism." He ascribed the victory to the GOP's stance on unconditional surrender. Privately, he called for his party to be composed of "sane but thoroughgoing progressives," for the "Romanov attitude" of "mere standpatism" spelled disaster.[38]

Both TR and Lodge immediately used the election to undercut the president in matters that they would have deemed treasonous had the situation been reversed. Roosevelt wrote British foreign secretary Balfour that the Republicans stood "for absolute loyalty to France and England in the peace negotiations" and did not adhere to Wilson's "interpretation" of freedom of the seas. Lodge visited the British and French embassies, informing them that their governments should not adopt Wilson's policies towards Germany.[39]

Arguing from the left, the *Nation* accused Wilson of failing to cultivate a liberal base, executing a blundering policy towards Russia, and yielding to Allied demands concerning punitive damages and freedom of the seas. The *New Republic* found the American people voting "in the dark." The nation remained unprepared to cope with the very revolutionary changes resulting from "its own acts and the convulsions of the world."[40]

The pro-Wilson Hearst chain was officially silent after the election. Within a week, however, it turned the editorial pages over to an unidentified "Jeffersonian Democrat" who began by praising the administration for having just concluded "quickly, efficiently, successfully and economically the greatest war in the history of the world." The author, however, noted "a great deal of flagrant, wanton, unnecessary and ignorant interference with the fundamental rights and liberties of the press and the people and the business institutions of the United States. . . . There has developed a certain air of autocracy, a certain atmosphere of arbitrary, irresponsible power, and the people have become fearful of this dynastic autocratic tendency."[41]

Democratic chairman Homer Cummings ascribed his party's defeat to three major factors. First, the Republicans spent lavishly. Second, Democratic congressional leaders possessed a parochial outlook, particularly those House southerners who had opposed the draft. Third, Wilson's October 25 appeal to the people was misrepresented, the GOP claiming it attacked the patriotism of the Republicans who had loyally supported the war effort. He quoted Taft, who wrote on November 7, "It was unfortunate for the President and his party that his opening note to Germany and the correspondence alarmed the people, lest he might make a peace by negotiations." Cummings added concerning the imminent Allied victory, "Had the good news from Europe broken a little earlier, it would have constituted a most complete refutation of these charges and have satisfied the public mind."[42]

There were other explanations. The *New York Times* found the Republican capture of the House quite normal in years when the presidency was not an issue. It was, however, surprised by the Senate results. Interior Secretary Lane noted that "the feeling in the North and West was strong that the South in some way was being preferred."[43]

Though privately distressed, the president tried to appear optimistic. In February 1919, Wilson told the Democratic National Committee that he was "not in the least discouraged" by the results. Any party that carries out a "great and constructive program" was "sure to bring out a reaction," for "a great many definite interests" were touched "in a way that distressed them." William Jennings Bryan spoke against pessimism, writing that the presidential veto would put the new Republican majority on the defensive.[44]

One must note that Wilson never possessed a powerful political base. Since the election of McKinley in 1896, the United States had normally been Republican. Wilson won the presidency in 1912 only because Republican ranks were split between the Old Guard Taft wing and Bull Moose supporters of TR. In 1916, he retained the White House by a narrow margin, winning traditionally midwestern and Great Plains states where progressivism was strong. In the 1917–1919 Congress, each major party possessed 215 votes in the House, and it was four third-party members who swung the body to the president. In short, his base was already contracting. Moreover, in mid-term congressional elections, the dominant party usually loses seats.

Until 1918 Wilson had led a fragile coalition of South and West. In this tenuous alliance, however, the presidency, cabinet, and Congress were all dominated by southerners. Sectionalism could remain something of an issue, as when Illinois congressman William E. Mason remarked, "No Republican ever fired on the American flag."[45]

Certainly the Far and Middle West were outraged that the Democratic administration had never put a price ceiling on southern cotton but had levied one on Plains State wheat. Hence, by 1918, cotton was 400 percent above prewar levels but that of wheat only 109 percent. In July, the president, responding to urban pressures and fearful of further inflation, vetoed a bill that would have raised the price of wheat from $2.20 to $2.50 a bushel. By this single act, he lost the western agricultural vote. Three million farmers were affected, twenty-one seats lost. Had the administration fixed the price of cotton at thirty cents a pound, so posits historian Seward W. Livermore, the entire industry would have been stabilized, flagrant profiteering in textiles would have been eliminated, and the wheat states somewhat assuaged.[46]

Many women were alienated by southern opposition to female suffrage, the Dixie Democrats being motivated by the fear that Black women would be enfranchised. Conversely, African American migration to the North increased Republican registration. Throughout the nation, high prices and wartime shortages of food and fuel took their toll. The Congress gained a reputation for obstruction and demagoguery, with more than one Republican pointing to Claude Kitchin's proposals to "soak-the-rich." Many German Americans resented the war itself, much less the "Hun" label so frequently applied to their overseas kinsmen. Irish Americans opposed being aligned with Britain. Arguably, given the circumstances, the Democrats did better than could be expected.

Historian Thomas J. Knock stresses that Wilson had failed to nurture the coalition that constituted his winning majority in 1916. Taking for granted the support he had gained, the president did little to keep the support of progressive internationalists. The *New Republic*, for example, accused him of deliberately discouraging discussion of his "great plan" to bring "a healing peace to Europe." George Creel wrote Wilson, "All the radical, or liberal friends of your anti-imperialist war policy were either silenced or intimidated." "There was no voice left to argue for your sort of peace." Similarly, *Nation* publisher Oswald Garrison Villard addressed Tumulty: "I am dismayed by the defeat, because you in the White House have not built up a liberal party and have permitted Burleson and Gregory to scatter and intimidate such liberal forces as have existed."[47]

Despite Republican claims, historians deny that the election was a referendum on foreign policy. The public, argues Seward W. Livermore, did not share the president's passion for world affairs. As Michael Kazin notes, far more House members who voted against the war declaration were returned than were defeated. Selig Adler finds no state in which either the Fourteen Points or the embryonic League of Nations were important issues. In Senate races where these issues had been broached, the margin was close, the Republicans tallying 3.3 million to the Democrats 3.2 million. Thomas A. Bailey notes, "The average voter was not concerned with remaking the world but with electing a man that would look after the local interests of, say, the Nineteenth Illinois District. . . . The rank and file of the electorate did not have the remotest idea that their vote would have any bearing upon the subsequent defeat of the Treaty of Versailles." If, as John Milton Cooper Jr. observes, the electorate had been as war-mad as many people believed, the opposition party would have scored an even greater win. Excluding the South, most races were close.[48]

All of these factors undoubtedly played a role in the Democratic defeat, the agrarian issue quite possibly being the most important one. Wilson's politicizing of his foreign policy, as reflected in his October 25 appeal, turned a setback into a severe defeat.

Meanwhile, military victory was close at hand.

EIGHTEEN
ARMISTICE

THE WAR'S END WAS AT HAND. THE FINAL U.S. NOTE TO Germany, sent by Secretary of State Lansing and dated November 5, offered Allied acceptance of the Fourteen Points as the basis for peace, adding the qualification that freedom of the seas was "open to various interpretations." It also included Allied insistence upon the evacuation of invaded territories and an item crucial to postwar negotiations: German compensation for "all damage done to the civilian population of the Allies and their property."[1]

German intelligence realized that within about a week, the Allies were planning a huge mobilization, mainly with U.S. troops, that would push through Lorraine and break into the Saar, thereby cutting off entire armies. It feared the advance of U.S. forces north of Verdun and across the Rhine. Already on October 31 a successful Allied offensive was taking place all along the western front.

On November 6, the German chancellor, Prince Max, decided that the war must be ended immediately. On the following evening, a delegation, led by Center Party leader Matthias Erzberger, crossed the front lines to meet Foch in a railroad siding in Compiègne Forest just forty miles from Paris. Negotiations were held in the personal railroad coach of Napoleon III, whom the Germans had defeated at Sedan in 1870.

Erzberger sought an immediate cease-fire, informing the French that keeping the Reich's armies intact could prevent a Bolshevik invasion of Europe. Field Marshal Foch would not budge, replying that fighting would not end until after an armistice had been signed. He gave the Germans a seventy-two-hour deadline to meet his terms. Conditions included the evacuation of Belgium, Luxembourg, and France, including Alsace-Lorraine, within fourteen days; Allied occupation of the western bank of the Rhine; creation of three bridgeheads across the Rhine at Coblenz, Mainz, and Cologne; surrender of railroad equipment; withdrawal of all German troops in the east behind Germany's 1914 frontiers; internment of the German battle fleet; and "reparation for damages done" in Belgium and northern France. 5,000 cannon, 25,000 machine guns, 3,000 trench mortars, 1,700 planes, 75 warships, and all submarines were to be surrendered. So, too, were transportation facilities, which included 5,000 locomotives and 10,000 trucks. Even though Germany was close to famine, a blockade would remain.[2] Such terms made it impossible for Germany to resume the conflict. In the meanwhile, Foch was taking no chances. On the following day, unaware of Germany's sorry state, he warned Pershing that the enemy might be deceiving the Allies. Hence, hostilities must continue until he commanded otherwise.[3]

Though nothing had been finalized, Henry B. Wilson, commander of U.S. naval forces in France, located in Brest, told Roy Howard, president and general manager of the United Press, that the war's end was imminent. No mere desk journalist, Howard sought to be a genuine war correspondent. The admiral had received the news from the U.S. naval attaché to the embassy in Paris or from a French official. Howard cabled New York that an armistice had been signed on November 7 at 11 a.m. and hostilities had ceased at 2 p.m. He added that U.S. troops had taken Sedan. His message reached the United States, where it was 11:20 a.m., November 7, causing a wave of celebration throughout the nation. Schools canceled classes, factories closed, and spontaneous parades took place. Americans celebrated, in the words of Navy Secretary Daniels, "as if Thanksgiving Day, Memorial Day, Labor Day, and Christmas had been rolled into one."[4] Similar celebrations took place from Paris to Havana to Sydney.

By 5 p.m. on the 7th, Secretary Lansing felt forced to release a statement that no armistice had been signed. "The heart went out of the excitement," recalled journalist Mark Sullivan. The *New York Tribune* called the incident "one of the famous fakes of history." The rumor appears to have originated with the Paris office of French army intelligence. Howard later claimed that anyone with the slightest claim to being a reporter would have acted exactly as he did.[5]

By now all Germany was experiencing anarchy. After the Kiel mutiny in late October, 100,000 seamen in other ports soon rebelled. A popular uprising in Munich led to the proclamation of a republic in Bavaria. Rebellions followed quickly—Hanover, Cologne, Brunswick, Leipzig, Magdeburg, Stuttgart. Almost everywhere, revolutionaries controlled important rail centers and supply depots. On November 9, Wilhelm II reluctantly abdicated, fleeing to the Netherlands. Socialist leader Philip Scheidemann proclaimed a German republic. A day later, Hapsburg emperor Charles relinquished his throne. Two days later, Austria announced that it had become a republic.

On November 9, Foch, even knowing that an armistice was at hand, called for an acceleration of the Allied advance. U.S. Second Army general Robert Lee Bullard, equally aware that peace appeared imminent, responded by ordering his troops to keep moving forward.

As biographer Arthur S. Link notes, this unexpected collapse undermined the president's own desire for a negotiated peace. Wilson had hoped that German military power would remain strong enough to check the wider ambitions of France and Britain. Such a circumstance was now impossible. Historian Klaus Schwabe argues that the president would have been satisfied had Germany been allowed to form a parliamentary monarchy. In October, Schwabe continues, the United States had misjudged the very real opportunities for saving lives, for Germany was creating a liberal regime. Now it was too late.[6]

As noted, despite the revolutionary conditions in Germany and Austria, General Charles P. Summerall told the commanders of the 2nd Division that he sought a bridgehead on the Rhine's east bank by the next morning. Marines braved cold and rain to cross a footbridge swept by German machine-gun fire. Writes historian Thomas Fleming, "It was little short of a massacre."[7]

(This decision did little to hinder Summerall's subsequent career. From 1921 to 1924, he commanded the army's Hawaii Department, where he engaged in a running feud with the controversial air power advocate, Billy Mitchell. From 1927 to 1931, he was army chief of staff. From 1931 to 1953, he served as president of the Citadel, a state-supported military college in Charlestown, South Carolina.)

The last day of the war saw unnecessary casualties. On November 11, all the belligerents gave orders to fight until the very last minute. Each side feared the other would renege on the armistice. Zeal, rigidity, and love of glory combined with hopes for a better strategic position and postwar political advantage. Indeed, Pershing instructed General Hunter Liggett to mount a general attack. At 6:25 a.m. on the 11th, Liggett heard the news that the armistice had just been signed and countermanded his own orders. By then, though, frontline units were beyond reach. Hence, on that day alone, the western front experienced almost 11,000 U.S. casualties, including 2,738 dead, more than G.I. casualties on D-Day. The new *Harvey's Weekly*, edited by Wilson's bitter foe George Harvey, aptly remarked, "Hundreds of lives were wantonly sacrificed to no military purpose whatever."[8] The journal was really a continuation of the *North American Review*'s *War Weekly*, which usually attacked the president for his "soft" policies.

It was on the eleventh hour of the eleventh day of the eleventh month Paris time that the armistice went into effect. The German army was given fourteen days to evacuate all occupied territory and the three crucial military bridgeheads on the left bank of the Rhine. The new German government believed that it was signing on the basis of the Fourteen Points, not writing a blank check to the Allies. Had Germany been faced with a demand for outright unconditional surrender, so argues historian Harry R. Rudin, the war would not have ended in 1918. Legally, as historian Richard S. Faulkner notes, the armistice was merely a cease-fire in a war that officially remained ongoing.[9]

The Allies were more than willing to avoid any march to Berlin. After the Battle of Verdun in 1916, France was a spent force, severely depleted in manpower. Britain was facing a wave of strikes, a shortage of coal, a major flu epidemic, brewing crisis in Ireland, and lack of army replacements. Had the war continued, historian Stanley Weintraub predicts that the conflict could possibly have lasted until spring 1919. It would have been fought in the face of ferocious German resistance fighting on native soil, often by U.S. troops whose generals were often not sufficiently imaginative to cope with newer ways of war. Hugh S. Johnson, now a general and director of purchase and supply, later claimed that had the war gone on two more months, the AEF would have experienced catastrophic shortages. "I think it was the finger of God that saved this government from the most terrible cataclysm that ever overtook the nation."[10]

Wilson released a statement to the press: "A supreme moment of history has come. The eyes of the people have been opened and they see. The hand of God is laid upon the nations. He will show them favour, I devoutly believe, only if they rise to the clear heights of His own justice and mercy."[11]

In a terse armistice proclamation, he boasted, "Everything for which America fought for has been accomplished." Colonel House echoed these sentiments, cabling Wilson, "Autocracy is dead." Agriculture Secretary David Houston compared the event to Alexander's defeat of Persia, the fall of Rome, the breakup of feudalism, and the French Revolution.[12]

The false alarm of November 7 did not prevent full-scale celebrating four days later. In Newport News, Virginia, servicemen broke windows and wrecked streetcars. In Hartford, ten thousand citizens took two hours to pass the reviewing stand. In Chicago, Mayor William Hale Thompson kept all saloons open. In Boston, the 160-year-old State House bell tolled in jubilation. In Washington, D.C., fifty-nine bonfires lit the Ellipse between the White House and the Potomac River. In New York, soldiers and sailors waved signs, "No more beans! No more camouflaged coffee! No more monkey stew!" Five thousand shipbuilders, clad in work clothes and tools, held a banner reading, "We are the layers-out who laid the Kaiser out!"[13] Everywhere images of the German emperor were entombed, put to the fire, or faced the hangman's noose.

That very afternoon of the 11th, Wilson addressed the Congress. Most of his thirty-five-minute speech centered on a detailed presentation of the armistice terms, but he had barely reached the second clause when he was greeted by spontaneous applause. Showing how the provisions made it impossible for Germany to renew the conflict, he claimed that the victors were united in "the common purpose" of establishing a peace based upon "disinterested justice," one that would "satisfy and protect the weak as well as to accord their just rights to the strong." Warning of revolution within the Central Powers, he called for feeding their populations. The Russian experience, he went on, showed that "excesses accomplish nothing."[14]

Congress received the speech warmly. Congressman Pat Harrison called the address "a second Declaration of Independence—independence for the world, a Magna Charta for oppressed peoples in every clime." To Senator Claude Swanson (D-Va.), Wilson was "the world's greatest elder." Senator Porter McCumber called it the greatest of the president's messages. Even La Follette applauded once, at the point when Wilson remarked that the war had come to an end.[15]

The armistice provisions, too, were welcomed. "The wolf-like nations," said Senator Willard Saulsbury (D-Del.), "have been caught and chained." To Congressman Claude Kitchin, "The terms could not have been better." Senators Peter Gerry (D-R.I.) and Boies Penrose both saw the conditions as embodying unconditional surrender, but Senator Henry L. Myers, espousing a minority view, wanted more German territory seized.[16]

The two major liberal weeklies differed in their reactions. The *New Republic* rejoiced that "democracy is momentarily supreme," going forth "with its faith in itself renewed." The *Nation*, however, warned that the presence of occupation troops on German soil appeared as "the negation of the principles of democracy and self-determination."[17]

Although Pershing's generalship obviously had its limitations, it was clear that it had been U.S. forces that had turned the balance in favor of the Allies. When the Ludendorff offensive was launched in March 1918, the Germans held a preponderance of about 400,000 men on the western front. By November, thanks to the infusion of 2 million doughboys, the Allies held a 600,000-troop edge. Furthermore, U.S. Treasury loans, shipping, wheat, and oil made a crucial difference in the eventual victory, particularly as they came into play at the time of French army mutinies, Italian defeat, and Russian withdrawal from the war.

Historian Robert H. Ferrell surmises that had the Germans understood in January 1917 what sort of demonic force they were loosing, they never would have ordered their submarines to sink American craft. Rather, they would have quickly made peace with Britain and France on whatever terms they could. John S. D. Eisenhower observes that without the AEF, the kaiser's Germany would have dominated continental Europe. In time, the United States would have found it difficult to avoid eventual confrontation with Berlin.[18]

Throughout most of the war, of course, the Allies—not the United States—bore the brunt. Losses had been most uneven. The Germans and Russians each lost 2 million men; France and Austria-Hungary 1 million each; Britain, 700,000; and Italy, 460,000. In contrast, the United States suffered 117,000 deaths, most occurring in the last six weeks of the conflict and making October 1918 the bloodiest month in the nation's military history. The Americans never endured the years of brutal trench warfare, usually fighting during the conflict's closing weeks. Over half died in a single battle, the Meuse–Argonne. AEF casualties for the entire war tallied less than such single battles as the Somme or Verdun. The French shot 51 out of every 100 artillery shells fired, the British 43, and the Americans just 6. By now the United States had mobilized more than 4 million men. Because, however, the armistice took place so suddenly, many of those forces never got closer to France than Camp Upton on Long Island.[19]

As far as the war at sea goes, it was the British navy that enforced the blockade and eliminated the submarine menace. On the western front, the AEF supplied only 10 percent of the victors' air power. In terms of matériel, the AEF depended on the Allies for tanks, high-explosive shells, and—for most of the war—automatic weapons. Almost half of the doughboys were transported to Europe on British ships.[20]

Several weeks before the armistice was signed, journalist Ray Stannard Baker, serving as the State Department's special representative in Europe, was apprehensive as to what the president would confront in the days ahead. Finding not a single European leader in accord with Wilson's program, Baker asked of the president, "Wilson has yet to prove his greatness. . . . Can he 'put it over'?"[21] The president was again facing the question he had encountered when the United States entered the conflict: Would the final result be worth the sacrifice? There was little reason for optimism.

CONCLUSION

THE STORY OF U.S. INVOLVEMENT IN WORLD WAR I IS IN many ways the story of Woodrow Wilson. The president determined overall policy, set the context of national debate, and served as the public face of the United States overseas. In filling these roles, in many ways he acted as the conscience of the country, articulating the nation's ideals with extreme eloquence and perception. Only in the case of Abraham Lincoln did Wilson find his match. Until the final weeks of the war, he gauged public opinion with uncanny accuracy while appealing to "the better angels of our nature."

Equally important, Wilson's war aims showed far more foresight than those of the Allies. He foreswore anything that hinted of a Carthaginian peace. He was certainly unrealistic in his belief that "the people" everywhere, in contrast to "their rulers," shared his democratic ideals, but he realized that any war worth fighting must have as its goal something loftier than territorial conquest. Such a conflict must be "a Peoples' War, a war for freedom and justice and self-government amongst all the nations of the world, a war to make the world safe for the peoples who live upon it and have made it their own."[1] His vision energized liberal and left elements throughout the entire world. In the United States, his peace agenda appealed to those Socialists who had broken from the national party in protest against its absolutist antiwar position. In time, the president even drew support from the leading Socialist weekly, the *Appeal to Reason.*

One might find Wilson's belief that a league of nations could resolve major tensions highly naive, but his vision of world organization embodied a great advance over the prewar status quo. The old balance-of-power system had proved itself unworkable, creating neither justice nor international stability but rather an international tinder box that blew up disastrously in 1914. Better, in the words of historian David F. Trask, to stress "peaceful reform than militant violence—purification rather than purgation."[2] There were, of course, problems with Wilson's league of nations proposal: he was extremely vague concerning its structure, devoted little time to reflection on the matter, and failed to enlist such allies as William Howard Taft's League to Enforce Peace, a well-organized and well-financed body that had devoted considerable study to the subject. By focusing entirely on self-determination and collective security, he neglected problems concerning any underlying international equilibrium.

The president's noble rhetoric, however, could in itself be a source of entrapment. *New Republic* editor Herbert Croly once remarked that the president wrote for "nothing shorter than a millennium," adding that Wilson made "even the most concrete things seem like abstractions."[3] Admittedly the phrase "safe for democracy" was usually misunderstood as imposing democracy upon peoples who were at best reluctant. But even some of his more specific phrases— "absolute freedom of navigation upon the seas," "the freest opportunity of autonomous development" for "the peoples of Austria-Hungary"—could be infuriatingly vague, particularly when the time came to translate them into concrete, substantive proposals. At times he appeared to assume that the rhetoric itself would create the reality.

Moreover, Wilson undercut his own Fourteen Points just a month after he delivered them, telling Congress in February 1918 that they were a "provisional sketch of principles" that might not be "the best or the most enduring." By July 1918, the president offered four "great ends" of the war that were nothing if not amorphous. During conversations with Clemenceau and Lloyd George in October 1918, Colonel House sought to give the points more specificity by having Frank Cobb and Walter Lippmann offer a commentary. Wilson undercut him by calling their analysis "merely illustrative suggestions" that should not be discussed until the peace conference. Admittedly, the president realized there were definite limits to quarrelling with the Allies over a war that had yet to be won, particularly as he appeared to be "dragging" concerning White Sea and Siberian expeditions and also opposing amalgamation of AEF forces with those of the Allies. Given the buildup of the Allies by the Creel Committee, Wilson could little afford to express deep-rooted differences openly. Moreover, he would risk domestic support in the process. He was very much engaged in a balancing act.

Wilson's dichotomy of a degenerate Old World and a revitalized New World could border on Manicheanism. In 1910, he had proclaimed that the United States had been founded to bring "liberty to mankind"; he never abandoned this goal. Addressing teachers in 1918, the president claimed that "it was the high logic of events and the providence of God" that the United States "should thus meet in battle to determine whether the new democracy or the old autocracy shall govern the world."[4] Although such entities as the British Empire found no direct threat in his rhetoric, realizing just how strong an Anglophile he was, such language still could not help but appear grating.

During the crucial exchange of notes with the Germans in October 1918, Wilson correctly feared his countrymen's desire for unconditional surrender, much less the occasional talk of hanging the kaiser and pursuing the German army all the way to Berlin. He probably remained unaware, however, of his own responsibility for such sentiment—he had far too often put the struggle in the most simplistic of terms. To Wilson, differentiating between the German "people," of whom he spoke kindly, and their "rulers" might appear quite lucid, but it only strengthened the ordinary Teuton's desire to continue fighting. Until close to the war's end, Germans perceived themselves fighting to defend their homeland, not engaging in crass imperialism. Wilson remained slow in comprehending the radical nature of the last-minute political changes within the Reich: increased revolutionary activity caused undue delays in establishing an armistice.

When it came to administration, few leaders were more conscientious. Wilson ran an administration relatively free of graft. His tax policies, which included a progressive income tax, sought equitable distribution of sacrifice. Not a man to avoid detail, he personally wrote all his speeches and handled all important diplomatic correspondence. He maintained daily oversight of all military operations, reading General Bliss's daily reports from the Supreme War Council while leaving matters of tactics and strategy to the professionals.[5] The president was quick to realize that once the United States entered the war, its troops would have to fight overseas. The president took a particular interest in naval matters, instituting convoys in the face of British suspicion and shifting production from battleships to destroyers, a more useful craft for this particular conflict.

All this does not mean that the president's manner of governance was flawless. Both Colonel House and British emissary Sir William Wiseman correctly complained that Wilson failed to delegate responsibility, the president allowing himself to become absorbed in trivia. Teamwork was not his strength. Moreover, the president neglected sharing his global views with foreign leaders, an attitude for which he would later pay dearly. After all, it was their armies that had borne the burden for most of the war.[6]

During the last year of the conflict, Wilson's political sagacity left him. The man who successfully engineered a host of progressive legislation through Congress—tariff revision, laws regulating corporations, a ban on child labor, the creation of the Federal Reserve—committed one blunder after another. His endorsement of Joseph Davies in Wisconsin severely detracted from the image of one who stood above the political fray. His backing of Henry Ford in Michigan was, to say the least, bizarre. His claim that the European powers would deem the election of a Republican majority a repudiation of his leadership was nothing short of disastrous, weakening his bargaining position overseas when he needed to maximize support.

In some highly significant ways, George Creel's Committee on Public Information (CPI) did the president no favors. The CPI was most skillful in promoting U.S. war aims, but its simplistic approach—particularly in personally demonizing the kaiser as Germany's despotic dictator—soon led to demands for unconditional surrender, thereby making Wilson's negotiations with the Germans in late 1918 far more difficult. In a sense, the president stood victimized by his own propaganda machine. He in turn did little to communicate international complexities to the electorate.

Add to this the postponement of crucial matters. From the moment the United States entered the war, it held serious leverage over the Allies. Indeed, Wilson might well have been able to make acceptance of his broad agenda the condition for U.S. belligerency. The United States could supply an apparently unlimited number of troops. It maintained a severe financial hold on the Allies while serving as the major supplier of food and raw materials. Without such support, in fact, the Allies would probably have been forced to sue for peace, particularly after Russia left the war. Wilson could have made his peace conditions more concrete at any time, rather than wait until October 1918, when Allied victory was already imminent. By allowing the Supreme War Council, headed by General Foch, to determine the conditions of the cease-fire, Wilson inadvertently assured that Germany would not experience a true armistice. Rather, it was to face military occupation of its crucial defensive positions and in time be saddled with huge reparations.

Wilson showed himself at best an indifferent judge of talent. Because he feared that Interior Secretary Franklin K. Lane had leaked cabinet discussions, he brought little of substance before that body. Navy Secretary Josephus Daniels was instrumental in creating one of the world's great military machines. However, the general caliber of ambassadors remained mediocre, with the possible exception of Walter Page, who was so outspokenly pro-British that Wilson ignored him. Converting from peacetime to wartime production inevitably would result in snags, but the appointment of sculptor Gutzon Borglum to investigate aircraft production bordered on the ludicrous.

War Secretary Newton Diehl Baker's record was mixed. He ably supervised the necessary shipping of troops and supplies overseas. Under his aegis, draft boards registered 9.5 million men with minimal resistance. He showed himself, however, far too hesitant in grasping the full implications of total war, particularly in regard to aviation. It took the crippling blizzard of 1917–18 to get the administration to put industrial production on a genuine wartime footing.

Two cases stand out. Colonel House's limitations had been evident since the abortive "House–Grey memorandum" of February 1916, under which the United States would presumably join the Allies as a full-scale belligerent if certain conditions had been met. By the end of 1917, House betrayed sufficient arrogance to maintain privately that he alone, and certainly not Wilson, possessed the qualities needed to conduct war and make peace.[7] His negotiations in October 1918 with Clemenceau and Lloyd George confused shadow with substance, permitting the papering over of major differences just as an armistice was approaching.

Secretary of State Lansing had severely undercut Wilson in December 1916 when the president was making a peace initiative. The president privately declared in September 1917 that the secretary was "so stupid" that he might "commit some serious blunder." However, he kept Lansing on.[8] At best the secretary served as a glorified clerk while putting Wilson's abstract ideas into the prose of diplomacy. Yet Lansing's knowledge of global conditions, if based alone on the daily dispatches crossing his desk, could have proven invaluable. So would have his energy, legal acumen, and administrative ability. When he was given free rein, he could show himself quite competent. If his agreement with Japan's Viscount Ishii skirted over major differences concerning the Asian continent, it postponed tensions with Japan at a time when a common front was absolutely necessary.

Wilson's approach to the war effort was too partisan. Admittedly, he appointed Elihu Root to head the Russian mission, Charles Evans Hughes to investigate the aircraft industry, and Taft to lead the Labor War Board, but such appointments were far below the abilities of those men. The same holds true for the "dollar-a-year" administrators, those GOP business leaders who filled various bureaucratic slots but never affected major policies. On sheer partisan grounds, the president turned down the appointment of international lawyer Charles W. Warren to the judge advocate's office and Henry L. Stimson, Taft's secretary of war, to the London embassy.

The U.S. military bore its share of responsibility for the nation's inadequate mobilization, a situation that continued well after the country had entered the conflict. Until Peyton March became acting chief of staff in March 1918, the War Department remained better suited to fighting Native Americans on the Great Plains than engaging in a brutal mechanized conflict. Training conditions often proved miserable, with enlisted men lacking proper clothing and weapons. During its entire period of engagement, the AEF found itself dependent upon Allied artillery, aircraft, and machine guns. Pershing's focus on Metz as his major goal was misplaced. So was his belief in the bayonet, rifle, and frontal assault, even if he reflected an attitude that had long permeated the entire U.S. military. If such generals as Hunter Leggett and John Lejeune could learn from their experiences at such places as Belleau Wood, so could the man soon titled general of the armies.

The entire Russian policy remained a complete fiasco and a most destructive one at that. The Root mission misread Russia's pathetic condition, deceiving both the mission itself and the American public. When the provisional government, led by Alexander Kerensky, sought to democratize Russian war aims, stressing a peace without annexations, it received no American support. U.S. personnel lacked coordination, with the embassy, the Red Cross mission, and the Creel Committee all going in radically different directions. The Bolshevik Revolution of November 1917 caught the United States completely unawares. From the forged Sisson papers, claiming that Lenin and his comrades were in the pay of Germany, to the disastrous interventions in Archangel and Siberia, the United States committed one blunder after another. To his credit, Wilson resisted sending troops to Siberia until foreign and domestic pressure became insuperable. The major problem lay in a fallacious assumption shared by the United States and the Allies alike, namely, that Russia could ever be reconstituted as an effective fighting force.

It is hardly surprising that the United States would fall prey to censorship and wartime hysteria, for such was the case in all belligerent nations. What is remarkable is how quickly the harassment took place. Months before a single doughboy lost his life in combat, journals were banned and meetings broken up. In placid times, Americans could celebrate the virtues of the melting pot, but the war proved that any existing consensus was indeed fragile. Progressivism could always be a double-edged sword, with its continued stress upon enforced morality. If sweatshops could be outlawed, so could antiwar meetings. The reformist state that progressives fostered had created the machinery by which to conduct a veritable crusade against dissent. The fact that Lenin's peace program embodied an immediate settlement, one without annexations or reparations, enabled nationalist crusaders to link antiwar sentiment to political radicalism, an attitude reflected in the suppression of the Socialist Party, the People's Council, and the

Industrial Workers of the World. It must be noted that the bulwark of such patriotic leagues as the National Security League and the American Defense Society lay with such figures as former secretary of state Elihu Root, Harvard historian Albert Bushnell Hart, and financier Cornelius Vanderbilt III, in short, the very core of the nation's establishment.

The president's record on civil liberties remains a lasting blemish on his record. If the Wilson administration was not responsible for outrageous excesses, it did little to curb them. In his Flag Day address of June 14, 1917, the president warned that Germany "has many spokesmen here, in places high and low." Though these people did not engage in actual sedition, they sought to undermine the government with "false professions of loyalty."[9] Wilson signed the Espionage, Trading with the Enemy, and Sedition Acts without comment. He overtly supported repression of a journal of the People's Council and endorsed the jailing of Socialists Rose Pastor Stokes and Eugene Debs. Though at times holding reservations concerning the Post Office Department's withdrawal of mailing privileges essential to a journal's survival, Wilson never reined in his postmaster general, Albert Sidney Burleson, one of several Colonel House protégés in the cabinet, who had been a minor Texas politician. As with all who held his office, Burleson's major role was handling patronage; he was totally out of his depth in dealing with dissenting views. Wilson might request restraint, but ultimately he seldom balked at any of Burleson's actions. In fact, in October 1918, having just saved the liberal *Nation* from the postmaster general's onslaught, he sought to withdraw mailing privileges from George Harvey's rightist *War Weekly*.

Ironically, certain targets were already in decline. The Socialist Party had been losing members since the height of its power in 1912. Its surprisingly strong showings in the 1917 mayoral elections could be interpreted more as a protest vote on the war than as reflecting increased commitment to the party's doctrine. The party would never recover from the defection of pro-war Socialists in 1917. Moreover, it underwent a major split over the Russian Revolution just after the war ended. Similarly, the IWW's growth would have been at best limited — war or no war, it offered the vaguest of social visions.

Occasionally Wilson himself took a more moderate stance. His December 1917 State of the Union address called for tolerating heterodox views. His administration frowned on the National Security League and the American Defense Society. Nevertheless, even if the president always harbored suspicions of the mass-based American Protective League, he never disavowed the summer 1918 slacker raids that even such conservatives as Albert Fall and Reed Smoot could not stomach. And though he privately expressed frustration with the absurdity of banning German music and performers, he issued no public statement on the matter. He did oppose the deportations of IWW workers in Bisbee, Arizona. In November 1917, after the beating of a Cincinnati minister scheduled to speak to a socialist group, Wilson publicly condemned "the mob spirit," but he did not refer to any specific incident. In June 1918, he privately predicted that governments would have to control "everything that everybody needs and uses," mentioning the railroads, coal mines, oil fields, water power, and "the lighting facilities." He once told British ambassador Spring Rice that he could only take actions that would be supported by "the great majority" of Americans, thereby revealing that he prioritized unity over principle.[10]

One could argue that Wilson could no more control the hysteria of World War I than could President Harry S. Truman have squelched the McCarthyism of the early 1950s. Certainly, in comparison to such leaders as Elihu Root, Henry Cabot Lodge, or William Howard Taft, Wilson does not come out badly. Historian John Milton Cooper Jr. notes that the administration headed off total censorship and martial law, both advocated by Theodore Roosevelt. Scholars Arthur S. Link and John Whitclay Chambers II find Wilson seeking to limit harassment from state, local, and private sources.[11] Still in all, the president was at best weak on the entire matter.

The war did not mark Theodore Roosevelt's finest hour. Vitriolic towards the president well before the country entered the war, throughout he viciously attacked such "foes of our own household" as German Americans and conscientious objectors. Not the least of his targets was Wilson himself, whom TR found the worst president ever elected.[12] Roosevelt's ill health, triggered in part from his experience with near death on the Amazon River in 1913, undoubtedly strengthened the negative aspects of his personality, making him almost irrational in his advocacy of "100% Americanism." The same could be said of Roosevelt's leading protégé, General Leonard Wood, who took every opportunity to undercut the administration.

Even given all of Wilson's faults, it is hard to find a viable rival who could have been a more effective wartime leader. None could articulate the nation's ideals so ably. The ailing and bitter Roosevelt served as the most polarizing of individuals, conducting a personal vendetta against the president. Taft possessed almost negative charisma, besides advocating a foreign policy increasingly based upon unconditional surrender. Charles Evans Hughes, a man equally lacking in magnetism, lacked foreign policy experience and showed no particular interest in warfare and diplomacy. By 1917, William Jennings Bryan, always singularly inept as a diplomat, was a spent force. Within a year Robert La Follette would find his own Senate seat in jeopardy. Henry Cabot Lodge was certainly knowledgeable about international affairs. His speech of August 28, 1918, differed little in detail from Wilson's own agenda regarding such matters as the fate of Alsace-Lorraine and the evacuation of Russian territory. He opposed, however, even the hint of negotiation with the Central Powers and saw the linchpin of the postwar order in maintaining the wartime coalition of Britain, France, and the United States

It is with a sense of tragedy that one concludes an account of the war, particularly when noting the lack of response to the varied peace overtures made in 1917. Because neither the Central Powers nor the Allies would yield on long-held war aims, the July Reichstag resolution, Pope Benedict XV's appeal of August, and Lord Lansdowne's open letter written that November remained stillborn. Berlin and Vienna felt too strong to make any compromise settlement; London and Paris saw themselves as too weak. Obviously, Allied victory was far preferable to Allied defeat, something that could well mean German domination of western Eurasia, even control of Europe to the English Channel. The price, however, remained extremely high, as the victors would soon learn.

NOTES

Introduction

1. WW, War Message, Apr. 2, 1917, *PWW*, 41:527; WW, *NYT*, Apr. 16, 1917, 1; WW, Flag Day address, June 14, 1917, *PWW*, 42:504; WW, speech, *NYT*, May 28, 1918, 1, 6.

2. Justus D. Doenecke, *Nothing Less Than War: A New History of America's Entry into World War I* (Lexington: University Press of Kentucky, 2011).

ONE   Raising an Army

1. *NYT*, July 21, 1918, 1, 2; New York *Evening World*, July 21, 1917, 1, 2.

2. Robert H. Ferrell, *Woodrow Wilson and World War I, 1917–1921* (New York: Harper & Row, 1985), 14; David R. Woodward, *The American Army and the First World War* (New York: Cambridge University Press, 2014), 1.

3. Late in 1916, assuming that the United States would soon become a belligerent, Captain Edward Davis, U.S. military attaché in Greece, advocated sending half a million men to the Balkans. French general Maurice Sarrail, Allied commander in chief on the Balkan front, strongly backed the proposal. Combined with diplomacy, the move supposedly might force Bulgaria to surrender immediately, thereby prompting the collapse of Austria-Hungary and Turkey. The plan received little backing. In late March 1917, Major General Joseph E. Kuhn, commandant of the U.S. Army War College, stressed the difficulties of establishing an independent Macedonia front. The scheme would take more than ten months to fulfill and use up half of America's shipping. Yet even that November the administration was discussing such a strategy. See Woodward, *American Army*, 85–87.

4. THB to Hugh L. Scott, Mar. 31, 1917, in Frederick S. Calhoun, *Power and Principle: Armed Intervention in Wilsonian Foreign Policy* (Kent, Ohio: Kent State University Press, 1986), 170.

5. EMH to WW, Mar. 19, 1917, *PWW*, 41:429; McAdoo, in W. B. Fowler, *British–American Relations: The Role of Sir William Wiseman* (Princeton, N.J.: Princeton University Press, 1969), 26.

6. Fiorello La Guardia, *The Making of an Insurgent: An Autobiography* (Philadelphia: Lippincott, 1948), 140.

7. Lloyd George quoted in John J. Pershing, *My Experiences in the World War* (New York: Frederick A. Stokes, 1931), 1:75.

8. WW, War Message, Apr. 2, 1917, *PWW*, 41: 522; Baker, *NYT*, Apr. 6, 1917, 1, 3.

9. Gompers, *Labor Advocate* (Cincinnati), April 28, 1917, 7; David Levering Lewis, *W. E. B. Du Bois, 1869–1919* (New York: Henry Holt, 1993), 530–31; mayors, *CR*, Apr. 23, 1917, 939; preparedness societies, *NYT*, Apr. 23, 1917, 3; "Volunteers, Conscription, and Democracy," *LD* 54 (Apr. 21, 1917): 1148.

10. *NYTr*, Apr. 10, 1917, 1; Edward William Pou to WW, Apr. 11, 1917, *PWW*, 42:42; House poll, in Alex Mathews Arnett, *Claude Kitchin and the Wilson War Policies* (Boston: Little Brown, 1937), 246.

11. Crosser, *CR*, Apr. 6, 1917, 1186.

12. John Whiteclay Chambers II, *To Raise an Army: The Draft Comes to Modern America* (New York: Free Press, 1987), 154–55.

13. *CR*: Kellogg, Apr. 27, 1917, 1318; Myers, Apr. 26, 1917, 1169; Heflin, 1266.

14. *CR*: McArthur, Apr. 26, 1917, 1283; Fall, Apr. 27, 1917, 1308.

15. *CR*: Lenroot, Apr. 24, 1917, 1050; Lever, Apr. 26, 1917, 1211; Johnson, 1236; McKeown, 1196.

16. *CR*: on taxation and other matters, Congressman Lindley Hadley (R-Wash.), Apr. 26, 1287, and Congressman John C. Linthicum (D-Md.), Apr. 27, 1917, 1230; Miller, 1289. Creel, in David M. Kennedy, *Over Here: The First World War and American Society* (New York: Oxford University Press, 1980), 145n2.

17. *CR*: Jones, Apr. 27, 1917, 1296; Johnson, Apr. 28, 1917, 1481.

18. Chamberlain, *NYT*, Apr. 20, 1917, 3. *CR*: Smith, Apr. 27, 1917, 1386; Kahn, 1375; Williams, Apr. 28, 1917, 1490.

19. *CR*: Heflin, Apr. 26, 1918, 1228; Williams, Apr. 28, 1917, 1441.

20. *CR*: La Follette, Apr. 27, 1918, 1355–56 (quotation at 1363).

21. *CR*: Slayden, Apr, 26, 1917, 1188; Helm, Apr. 27, 1917, 1412.

22. Church, *CR*, Apr, 26, 1917, 1245.

23. *CR*: Sherwood, Apr. 26, 1917, 1205; Hardwick, Apr. 27, 1917, 1319; London, Apr. 25, 1917, 1146.

24. *CR*: Emerson, Apr. 25, 1917, 1138; Wise, Apr. 26, 1917, 1211.

25. *CR*: Byrnes, Apr. 25, 1917, 1098; Clark, 1120; Smith, Apr. 27, 1917, 1386.

26. *CR*: Morin, Apr. 26, 1917, 1272; Kirby, Apr. 28, 1917, 1489; Bacon, Apr. 26, 1917, 1276.

27. *CR*: Sherman, Apr. 26, 1917, 1156; Anthony, Apr. 24, 1917, 1041; Shouse, April 27, 1917, 1420; Huddleston, Apr. 25, 1917, 1094.

28. *CR*: Sisson, Apr. 26, 1917, 1220; Claypool, Apr. 27, 1917, 1421; Hardwick, 1421; Thomas, Apr. 26, 1917, 1222.

29. *CR*: Garrett, Apr. 25, 1917, 1119; Reed, 1072, 1084.

30. *CR*: Browne, Apr. 27, 1917, 1419–20; Wise, Apr. 26, 1917, 1208; Reed, Apr. 25, 1917, 1081.

31. Vardaman, *Vicksburg Herald*, Apr. 7, 1917, 4; Heflin, *CR*, Apr. 26, 1917, 1227–28.

32. Barkley and Adamson, *CR*, Apr. 26, 1917, 1228.

33. Chambers, *To Raise an Army*, 165–66; House vote, *CR*, Apr. 28, 1917, 1555, 1557.

34. Senate vote, *CR*, Apr. 28, 1917, 1500–1501; HCL to Sturgis Bigelow, Apr. 30, 1917, HCLP.

35. Senate vote, *CR*, Apr. 28, 1917, 1493. House vote, Apr. 27, 1917, 1387.

36. TR, *Norton County* (Kans.) *News*, Oct. 28, 1904, 6; TR to Jean Jules Jusserand, February 16, 1917, *LTR*, 8:1152 and note 1; TR to Frederic Collin Walcott, Mar. 7, 1917, *LTR*, 8:1160.

37. TR to NDB, Feb. 2, 1917, *LTR*, 8:1149; Mar. 19, 1917, 1164; Mar. 23, 1917, 1166. Philip C. Jessup, *Elihu Root* (New York: Dodd, Mead, 1938), 2:327.

38. NDB to TR, Feb. 7, 1917, *LTR*, 8:1151n1; Joseph P. Tumulty, *Woodrow Wilson as I Knew Him* (Garden City, N.Y.: Doubleday, Page, 1921), 288; TR to John Callan O'Laughlin, Apr. 13, 1917, *LTR*, 8:1173; TR, speech at Cooper Union, *NYT*, Nov. 4, 1916, 4.

39. NDB to TR, Apr. 13, 1917, *PWW*, 42:56–57; Alvin Johnson, *Pioneer's Progress: An Autobiography* (New York: Viking, 1952), 253.

40. John Milton Cooper Jr., *Woodrow Wilson: A Biography* (New York: Knopf, 2009), 394–95; Cooper, *The Warrior and the Priest: Woodrow Wilson and Theodore Roosevelt* (Cambridge, Mass.: Harvard University Press, 1983), 325–26; Chambers, *To Raise an Army*, 138.

41. THB, in David R. Woodward, *American Army*, 92; Bridges, in Edmund Morris, *Colonel Roosevelt* (New York: Random House, 2010), 492–93.

42. TR to Chamberlain and Dent, *NYT*, Apr. 16, 1917, 1; Harding, *CR*, Apr. 28, 1917, 1437.

43. Wood, in Seward W. Livermore, *Woodrow Wilson and the War Congress, 1916–1918* (Seattle: University of Washington Press, 1966), 19; McCoy, in TR to NDB, Feb. 7, 1917, *LTR*, 8:1151; Stimson, in J. Lee Thompson, *Never Call Retreat: Theodore Roosevelt and the Great War* (New York: Palgrave Macmillan, 2013), 166; Tumulty, *Wilson*, 286.

44. Borah and J. Baker, in C. H. Cramer, *Newton D. Baker: A Biography* (Cleveland: World, 1961), 110; Eisenhower, in Richard Striner, *Woodrow Wilson and World War I: A Burden Too Great to Bear* (Lanham, Md.: Rowman & Littlefield, 2014), 257n98; Sunday, *NYT*, May 2, 1917, 7.

45. *NYA*, May 12, 1917, 20; Gardner, *CR*, Apr. 27, 1917, 1381–82.

46. *CR*: Mason, Apr. 26, 1917, 1190; Chandler, May 12, 1917, 2206; Vare, Apr. 26, 1194; Cannon, May 12, 1917, 2214.

47. Lewis L. Gould, *Chief Executive to Chief Justice: Taft betwixt the White House and the Supreme Court* (Lawrence: University Press of Kansas, 2014), 88; Connally, *CR*, May 12, 1917, 2213; Stone, *CR*, May 17, 1917, 2451; "The Call to Arms," *NAR* 205 (May 1917): 646.

48. *NYT*, Apr. 28, 1917, 12; New York *World*, in "T.R.'s Plan to Beard the Kaiser," *LD* 54 (Apr. 28, 1917): 1242; Leiter, *CR*, Apr. 27, 1917, 1323.

49. *NYT*, May 11, 1917, 1; May 12, 1917, 1.

50. CR: Anthony, May 12, 1917, 2201; Quin, 2211; Caldwell, 2208; Gardner, 2203.

51. Vote, *CR*, May 12, 1917, 2215; Chambers, *To Raise an Army*, 169.

52. Thomas Fleming, *The Illusion of Victory: America in World War I* (New York: Basic Books, 2003), 91; House vote, *NYT*, May 17, 1917, 1; Senate vote, *CR*, May 17, 1917, 2457; TR to Anna Roosevelt Cowles, May 17, 1917, *LTR*, 8:1192.

53. WW, statement, May 18, 1917, *PWW*, 42:324–25; TR to WW, May 18, 1917, *PWW*, 42:324; WW to TR, May 19, 1917, *PWW*, 42:346; Donald Smythe, *Pershing: General of the Armies* (Bloomington: Indiana University Press, 1986), 9.

54. TR to NDB, April 23, 1917, *LTR*, 8:1180; public statement, *NYT*, May 21, 1917, 2; Livermore, *Woodrow Wilson and the War Congress*, 20.

55. Joffre, in Thompson, *Never Call Retreat*, 183; Clemenceau, *NYT*, May 28, 1917, 1; TR to Georges Clemenceau, June 6, 1917, *LTR*, 8:1201.

56. Striner, *Wilson*, 110, 257n98; David R. Woodward, *Trial by Friendship: Anglo–American Relations, 1917–1918* (Lexington: University Press of Kentucky, 1993), 50; Kennedy, *Over Here*, 149.

57. Conversation between WW and Joffre, May 2, 1917, *PWW*, 42:187; WW to NDB, May 3, 1917, *PWW*, 42:202.

58. WW, proclamation, *NYT*, May 19, 1917, 1; Peyton C. March, *The Nation at War* (Garden City, N.Y.: Doubleday, Doran, 1932), 235; Morris, *Colonel Roosevelt*, 494.

59. Dowell, in Fred Davis Baldwin, "The American Enlisted Man in World War I" (PhD diss., Princeton University, 1964), 9.

60. Goldman, in "Our Anticonscription Enemies," *LD* 54 (June 2, 1917): 1686; New York meeting, *Washington Herald*, May 19, 1917, 1; *ATR*, May 12, 1917, 2; Joan Maria Jensen, "The American Protective League, 1917–1919" (PhD diss., University of California, Los Angeles, 1962), 39; H. C. Peterson and Gilbert C. Fite, *Opponents of War, 1917–1918* (Madison: University of Wisconsin Press, 1957), 24.

61. WW, *Washington Evening Star*, June 5, 1917, 1; *New York Telegram*, in "How the United States Goes to War," *CO* 63 (July 1917): 2.

62. Baldwin, "American Enlisted Man," 12, 22–23; NDB to WW, May 1, 1917, *PWW*, 42:180.

63. Crowder, in Meirion Harries and Susie Harries, *The Last Days of Innocence: America at War, 1917–1918* (New York: Random House, 1997), 97; Crowder, in Ronald Schaffer, *America in the Great War: The Rise of the War Welfare State* (New York: Oxford University Press, 1991), 177.

64. WW to Joseph Tumulty, July 30, 1917, *PWW*, 43:318.

65. James R. Green, *Grass Roots Socialism: Radical Movements in the Southwest, 1895–1943* (Baton Rouge: Louisiana State University Press, 1978), 359–61; quotation at 359.

66. Lundeen and Mason polls, see Robert L. Hachey, "Dissent in the Upper Middle West during the First World War" (PhD diss., Marquette University, 1993), 128; Mason, *CR*, June 19, 1917, 3850; *DD*, June 15, 1917, *PWW*, 42:526; Hastings, *NYT*, June 20, 1917, 10.

67. Gore, *CR*, Aug. 18, 1917, 6146; *NYT*, Aug. 19, 1917, 3.

68. *CR*: Hardwick, Sept. 7, 1917, 6742; Williams, 6744; Nelson, 6733; voting, 6740–41.

69. Norris, *CR*, Apr. 4, 1917, 214.

70. Chambers, *To Raise an Army*, 171.

TWO   The Naval War

1. John Keegan, *The First World War* (New York: Knopf, 1999), 332; Pétain, in Charles E. Neu, *Colonel House: A Biography of Woodrow Wilson's Silent Partner* (New York: Oxford University Press, 2015), 310.

2. "With the Military Experts," *VTAW* 6 (May 2, 1917): 217; "America First," *VTAW* 6 (Apr. 25, 1917): 205.

3. Britten, *CR*, May 4, 1917, 1820; Gronna, *I&E* 6 (June 30, 1917): 369.

4. HCL to George Otto Trevelyan, Apr. 7, 1917, HCLP; "The Call to Arms," *NAR* 205 (May 1917): 645–46; Simonds, *NYTr*, May 6, 1917, 23; Beck, *NYT*, July 21, 1917, 5.

5. Roosevelt, *Washington Evening Star*, June 2, 1917, 2; WHP to Frank N. Doubleday, May 3, 1917, in Burton J. Hendrick, *The Life and Letters of Walter Hines Page* (Garden City, N.Y.: Doubleday, Page, 1922), 2:242; NDB, *NYA*, May 28, 1917, 4; EMH, June 30, 1917, in Charles Seymour, ed., *The Intimate Papers of Colonel House* (Boston: Houghton Mifflin, 1926–28), 3:10; James G. Harbord, *Leaves from a War Diary* (New York: Dodd, Mead, 1925), 50; JJP to NDB, July 9, 1917, *PWW*, 43:461.

6. Balfour, in Neu, *Colonel House*, 309; Northcliffe, in Seymour, ed., *Intimate Papers of Colonel House*, 3:97; WHP to RL, June 27, 1917, *FR, 1917, Supp. 2, The World War* (Washington, D.C.: Government Printing Office, 1932), 1:532.

7. JJP to NDB, July 9, 1917, *PWW*, 43:263; Maurice Francis Eagan to RL, Apr. 17, 1917, *FR, 1917, Supp.* 2, 1:29; Ira Nelson Morris to RL, Apr. 23, 1917, *FR, 1917, Supp.* 2, 1:37.

8. Holtzendorff and Ludendorff, in Holger H. Herwig and David S. Trask, "The Failure of Imperial Germany's Undersea Offensive," *Historian* 33 (August 1971): 612–13.

9. Jellicoe, in Frank Freidel, *Over There: The Story of America's First Great Overseas Crusade* (Boston: Little Brown, 1964), 29.

10. Roosevelt, *NYT*, Dec. 17, 1914, 9.

11. General Board, in Kenneth J. Hagen, *The People's Navy: The Making of American Sea Power* (New York: Free Press, 1991), 254.

12. Frank Freidel, *Franklin D. Roosevelt*, Vol. 1, *The Apprenticeship* (Boston: Little Brown, 1952), 307; Edward M. Coffman, *The War to End All Wars: The Military Experience in World War I* (Lexington: University Press of Kentucky, 1968), 90.

13. Benson, in Harries and Harries, *Last Days of Innocence*, 216–17.

14. Sims, *NYT*, Dec. 18, 1910, 1.

15. *American Chronicle: The Autobiography of Ray Stannard Baker* (New York: Scribner's, 1945), 324–25.

16. Sims to Daniels, Apr. 14, 1917, in Josephus Daniels, *The Wilson Era*, Vol. 2, *Years of War and After, 1917–1923* (Chapel Hill: University of North Carolina Press, 1946), 69; Sims to Daniels, Apr. 21, 1917, *PWW*, 42:121; Sims to Daniels, July 7, 1917, in Ray Stannard Baker, *Woodrow Wilson: Life and*

Letters (New York: Scribner's, 1927–39), 7:151; Sims to William V. Pratt, July 3, 1917, in David F. Trask, *Captains & Cabinets: Anglo–American Naval Relations, 1917–1918* (Columbia: University of Missouri Press, 1972), 90.

17. WHP to RL, Apr. 28, 1917, *FR, 1917, Supp. 2*, 1:46; WHP to RL, June 20, 1917, *FR, 1917, Supp. 2*, 1:107; naval headquarters, in Mark Sullivan, *Our Times*, Vol. 5, *Over Here, 1914–1918* (New York: Scribner's, 1933), 389n2.

18. WW to Sims, July 3, 1917, *PWW*, 43:80; WW, speech aboard the USS *Pennsylvania*, *PWW*, Aug. 11, 1917, 43:430.

19. Rathenau and Bethmann Hollweg, in Herwig and Trask, "Failure," 619–20.

20. D. F. Trask, "Woodrow Wilson and the Reconciliation of Force and Diplomacy, 1917–1918," *Naval War College Review* 27 (Jan.-Feb. 1975): 28.

21. Franklin Roosevelt, in Kathleen Dalton, *Theodore Roosevelt: A Strenuous Life* (New York: Knopf, 2002), 502; U-boats, *NYT*, July 22, 1918, 1, 6; HCL, in Joseph L. Morrison, *Josephus Daniels: The Small-d Democrat* (Chapel Hill: University of North Carolina Press, 1966), 100–101.

22. Edward J. Sheehy, "United States Navy," in *The United States in the First World War: An Encyclopedia*, ed. Anne Cipriano Venzon (New York: Garland, 1995), 751; Trask, *Captains & Cabinets*, 363.

23. McAdoo to Law, June 30, 1917, in Fowler, *British–American Relations*, 43; Spring Rice to Balfour, Oct. 25, 1917, in Herwig and Trask, "Failure," 623.

24. Geddes, in Fowler, *British–American Relations*, 218–19; "A Memorandum by Sir Eric Geddes," November 7, 1918, *PWW*, 51:633–34; House, in Trask, *Captains & Cabinets*, 350.

25. General Board, Sept. 10, 1918, *PWW*, 51:345n1; WW, in Hagen, *People's Navy*, 257.

THREE   Mr. Creel Administers a Committee

1. Wilson, *NYT*, Apr. 16, 1917, 1; Gompers, *New York Sun*, Apr. 9, 1917, 1; Bryan to WW, *Wichita Weekly Eagle*, Apr. 13, 1917, 1; Louis W. Koenig, *Bryan: A Political Biography of William Jennings Bryan* (New York: Putnam, 1971), 570; Root, *NYT*, Apr. 10, 1917, 3; Calder, *NYT*, Apr. 10, 1917, 3; Harding, *NYT*, Aug. 12, 1917, VI:1.

2. Untermyer, *NYA*, Apr. 7, 1917, 7; Cohalan, *NYA*, Apr. 9, 1917, 16; *VTAW* 6 (Apr. 18, 1917): cover; NAACP, in Fleming, *Illusion of Victory*, 108.

3. Federal Council, *CR*, Appendix, May 25, 1917, 241; Gibbons, *NYT*, Apr. 6, 1917, 10; Cochran, in John Edward Cuddy, *Irish-America and National Isolationism* (New York: Arno Press, 1976), 141; Sunday, *NYT*, Feb. 19, 1918, 11.

4. Root, *NYT*, Aug. 16, 1917, 1; Harvard professor Dermot Mac-Murrough, *Akron Beacon Journal*, Sept. 13, 1917, 2; McAdoo, *Charlotte Observer*, Sept. 23, 1917, 4; Gregory, *NYT*, Nov. 21, 1917, 3.

5. Philip Marshall Brown, "War's Intellectual Anarchism" (book review), *NYT*, Dec. 2, 1917, 78; Perry, *Yale Review* 7 (April 1918): 670.

6. Bryan, *Commoner* 17 (Aug. 1917): 1; "Dealing with Sedition," *O* 116 (Aug. 1, 1917): 506.

7. Williams, *CR*, Sept. 7, 1917, 6746; Lewis, *SFE*, Sept. 26, 1917, 1; Harding, *NYT*, Mar. 4, 1918, 11; Kahn, *NYT*, Mar. 25, 1918, 8.

8. Cobb, August 26, 1917, in John L. Heaton, ed., *Cobb of "The World": A Leader in Liberalism* (New York: Dutton, 1924), 325; petition and reply, *NYT*, May 6, 1917, 1.

9. Lillian D. Wald, Crystal Eastman, Roger Baldwin, and L. Hollingsworth Wood to WW, Aug. 10, 1917, plus enclosed memo of Aug. 13, 1917 to WW, *PWW*, 43:421–24.

10. Harbord, *Leaves*, 50; press reports, in H. C. Peterson, *Propaganda for War: The Campaign against American Neutrality, 1914–1917* (Norman: University of Oklahoma Press, 1939), 323; Kenyon, in *DD*, Aug. 24, 1917, 195; WHT, "A Test of Patriotism," Nov. 1, 1917, in James F. Vivian, ed., *William Howard Taft: Collected Editorials, 1917–1921* (Westport, Ct.: Greenwood, 1990), 2; Steffens memo, ca. Dec. 28, 1917, *PWW*, 45:381; George Creel, *Rebel at Large: Recollections of Fifty Crowded Years* (New York: Putnam, 1947), 157. For American ignorance of war objectives, see Arthur S. Link, *American Epoch: A History of the United States since the 1890's*, 2nd. ed. (New York: Knopf, 1963), 192; and John Milton Cooper Jr., *Pivotal Decades: The United States, 1900–1920* (New York: Norton, 1990), 268.

11. Unidentified journalist, in Fleming, *Illusion of Victory*, 93.

12. Reporter, remarks on Lodge, in Stephen L. Vaughn, *Holding Fast the Inner Lines: Democracy, Nationalism, and the Committee on Public Information* (Chapel Hill: University of North Carolina Press, 1970), 21–22; Walton E. Bean, "George Creel and His Critics" (PhD diss., University of California, Berkeley, 1941), 10; remarks on Johnson, in Sullivan, *Our Times*, 5:438; regarding Harvey, Nock, Pinchot, in Bean, "Creel," 10, 255–56; Sullivan, in Creel, *Rebel at Large*, 161.

13. Creel on censorship, in Creel, *Rebel at Large*, 156; on policy, Vaughn, *Holding Fast*, 17–18; on salesmanship, in George Creel, *How We*

Advertised America (New York: Harper, 1920), 4, 5; Baker, foreword, in ibid., xiii.

14. Carol A. Gruber, *Mars and Minerva: World War I and the Uses of the Higher Learning in America* (Baton Rouge: Louisiana State University Press, 1975), 139; Vaughn, *Holding Fast*, 238.

15. Lane, in Vaughn, *Holding Fast*, 85; Vaughn comment, 24; historian Cushing Strout on progressivism, 337n14.

16. Corwin, in Vaughn, *Holding Fast*, 54; Commons, 56; Creel, 248n85; Ford, 59.

17. Lane, Bates in Vaughn, *Holding Fast*, 44; Sherman, 47; Becker, 48, 115.

18. WW, Creel, in Vaughn, *Holding Fast*, 235 (emphasis Creel).

19. Spying, censorship, in James R. Mock and Cedric Larson, *Words That Won the War: The Story of the Committee of Public Information, 1917–1919* (Princeton, N.J.: Princeton University Press, 1939), 64–65 (illustration); Vaughn, *Holding Fast*, 228–29.

20. *War Cyclopedia*, in George T. Blakey, *Historians on the Home Front: American Propagandists for the Great War* (Lexington: University Press of Kentucky, 1970), 51.

21. Notestein, in Vaughn, *Holding Fast*, 69.

22. John S. B. Tadlock, in Vaughn, *Holding Fast*, 88 (map at 89); script, in William R. Walker, "'Only the Heretics are Burning': Democracy and Repression in World War I America" (PhD diss., University of Wisconsin, 2008), 63; Moran, in Blakey, *Historians*, 47.

23. Atrocity posters, in Vaughn, *Holding Fast*, 157–58.

24. African Americans, in Vaughn, *Holding Fast*, 124, 207.

25. American history, in Vaughn, *Holding Fast*, 90–95; Perkins quotation at 91.

26. Gompers, *St. Joseph* (Mo.) *Union-Observer*, Aug. 31, 1917, 24; Creel, in Frank L. Grubbs Jr., *The Struggle for Labor Loyalty: Gompers, the A.F. of L., and the Pacifists, 1917–1920* (Durham, N.C.: Duke University Press, 1968), 44.

27. AALD, *NYT*, Sept. 7, 1917, 3; Vaughn, *Holding Fast*, 56–57.

28. Kent Kreuter and Gretchen Kreuter, *An American Dissenter: The Life of Algie Simons, 1870–1950* (Lexington: University of Kentucky Press, 1969), 187.

29. Ronald Radosh, *American Labor and United States Foreign Policy* (New York: Knopf, 1969), 70–71.

30. Creel, *Rebel at Large*, 159.

31. Daniels, *NYT*, July 4, 1917, 1; Penrose, *NYT*, July 10, 1917, 1, and *CR*, July 24, 1917, 5419; Walsh, *CR*, July 10, 1917, 4923.

32. James, *CR*, July 24, 1917, 5422; Gleaves, *Washington Post*, Aug. 2, 1917, 1, 4.

33. Creel, in Sullivan, *Our Times*, 5:436.

34. *NARWW* 1 (Feb. 9, 1918): 7; Creel, *How We Advertised America*, 447.

35. Watson, *CR*, Apr. 4, 1918, 4567–69 (includes Creel editorials); Borah, 4567.

36. Creel, *NYT*, Apr. 9, 1918, 13.

37. Longworth, *NYT*, Apr. 10, 1918, 8; Madden, *CR*, Apr. 9, 1918, 4856; Sherman, *CR*, Apr. 23, 1918, 5489; *NYT*, Apr. 11, 1918, 12; *NYA*, Apr. 26, 1918, 26.

38. Creel, *New York Tribune*, May 13, 1918, 1.

39. George B. LaBarre to WW, May 14, 1918, *PWW*, 48:11, 12n2; Pou, in Daniels, *Wilson Era*, 2:228; Kitchin, *CR*, May 13, 1918, 6469; Garrett, *NYT*, May 18, 1918, 8; "We Exonerate Mr. Creel," *NARWW* 1 (Apr. 27, 1918): 4.

40. Creel to Pou, *NYT*, May 18, 1918, 8; Creel, *How We Advertised America*, 61.

41. WW, in *DD*, Apr. 12, 1918, 298–99; Creel, "Woodrow Wilson, the Man Behind the President," *Saturday Evening Post* 203 (Mar. 28, 1931): 40.

42. Cannon, in Creel, *How We Advertised America*, 64; McCumber, *CR*, June 3, 1918, 7289; House action, *NYT*, June 18, 1918, 7; Byrnes, *CR*, June 17, 1918, 7914.

43. Creel, *How We Advertised America*, 451; Bean, "Creel," 216.

44. Ford, in Blakey, *Historians*, 91; Van Tyne memo, *CR*, Sept. 17, 1918, 10379–81; Lodge and Reed, Aug. 17, 1918, 10378.

45. Vaughn, *Holding Fast*, 216, 234, 238; on Ford, 40, 279n79, 281n97.

46. Bean, "Creel," 262, 265; Mock and Larson, *Words That Won the War*, 6, 12.

47. Cooper, *Pivotal Decades*, 296.

FOUR Legislating Unity

1. *NYT*, Apr. 11, 1917, 1, 2.

2. Cabinet, in *DD*, Apr. 6, 1917, 130.

3. *CR*: Borah, Apr. 18, 1917, 779; Lodge, 781; Brandegee, Johnson, 784.

4. Smith, *NYT*, Apr. 20, 1917, 15; Clark, *CR*, May 2, 1917, 1716; London, *CR*, May 4, 1917, 1824.

5. *Los Angeles Times*, May 9, 1917, 1; *NYA*, Apr. 9, 1917, 16; *NYTr*, May 23, 1917, 8; *NYT*, Apr. 19, 1917, 14.

6. Arthur Brisbane to WW, Apr. 20, 1917, *PWW*, 42:107–8; WW to Arthur Brisbane, Apr. 25, 1917, *PWW*, 42:129.

7. Overman, *NYT*, Apr. 19, 1917, 15. *CR*: Nelson, Apr. 19, 1917, 838; Fall, 842; Stone, May 11, 1917, 2102; Webb, May 31, 1917, 3132.

8. "War and a Free Press," *O* 116 (May 9, 1917): 56; New York *World*, in *NYT*, May 24, 1917, 2.

9. House vote, *CR*, May 4, 1917, 1841; Burleson, *PWW*, 42:247n1; WW, in *NYT*, May 5, 1917, 1; Senate vote, *CR*, May 14, 1917, 2270–71.

10. WW to Webb, *NYT*, May 23, 1917, 1; WW to Frank Cobb, May 23, 1917, *PWW*, 42:376.

11. House vote, *CR*, May 31, 1917, 3144–45.

12. Kennedy, *Over Here*, 26; Livermore, *Woodrow Wilson and the War Congress*, 37; Ernest Freeberg, *Democracy's Prisoner: Eugene V. Debs, the Great War, and the Right to Dissent* (Cambridge, Mass.: Harvard University Press, 2008), 49.

13. Burleson, in Donald Johnson, *The Challenge to American Freedoms: World War I and the Rise of the American Civil Liberties Union* (Lexington: University of Kentucky Press, 1963), 56–57 (Johnson's italics).

14. Burleson on Morgan, in Thomas J. Knock, *To End All Wars: Woodrow Wilson and the Quest for a New World Order* (New York: Oxford University Press, 1992), 135; EMH diary, February 11, 1918, *PWW*, 46:327; Thomas on Burleson, in Kennedy, *Over Here*, 76; Burleson to Thomas, in W. A. Swanberg, *Norman Thomas: The Last Idealist* (New York: Scribner's, 1976), 63; John Nevin Sayre to WW, Sept. 19, 1918, *PWW*, 51:77; Lamar, in Oswald Garrison Villard, *Fighting Years: Memoirs of a Liberal Editor* (New York: Harcourt, Brace, 1939), 357n2.

15. James Harvey Robinson, "The Threatened Eclipse of Free Speech," *Atlantic Monthly* 120 (November 1917): 818; *NR* 11 (July 21, 1917): 316; *NYA*, July 21, 1917, 18.

16. London, *CR*, July 10, 1917, 4931; Gordon J. Goldberg, *Meyer London: A Biography of the Socialist New York Congressman, 1871–1927* (Jefferson, N.C.: McFarland, 2013), 162; text of resolution, *CR*, July 31, 1917, 5634; Burleson to Bankhead, Aug. 21, 1917, in Johnson, *Challenge to American Freedoms*, 59.

17. Eastman et al. to WW, July 12, 1917, *PWW*, 43:165; Oswald Garrison Villard to Joseph Patrick Tumulty, July 20, 1917, *PWW*, 43:239–40; WW to Tumulty, 239; WW to Clarence Darrow, Aug. 9, 1917, *PWW*, 43:400; WW to Albert S. Burleson, Sept. 4, 1917, *PWW*, 44:147; WW to Max Eastman, Sept. 18, 1917, *PWW*, 44:210–11.

18. TR to Emory Speer, Sept. 4, 1917, *LTR*, 8:1235.

19. King, *CR*, Sept. 12, 1917, 7021; legislation, in *NYT*, Oct. 15, 1917, 6.

20. Burleson quoted in *I&E* 7 (October 6, 1917): 214; *Topeka Daily Capital*, Oct. 4, 1917, 4.

21. Norris, *CR*, Sept. 24, 1917, 7342; Cummins, 7348. Vardaman, *NYT*, Sept. 25, 1917, 7; NCLB, in L. Hollingsworth Wood et al. to WW, Sept. 26, 1917, *PWW*, 44:267–68; Villard to Tumulty, Sept. 26, 1917, *PWW*, 44:271; *I&E*, 7 (Oct. 6, 1917): 214.

22. London, *CR*, Oct. 6, 1917, 7909.

23. Walter Lippmann to EMH, Oct. 17, 1917, *PWW*, 44:394; EMH to WW, Oct.. 17, 1917, *PWW*, 44:393.

24. WW to Albert S. Burleson, Oct. 11, 1917, *PWW*, 44:358; WW to Grenville S. Macfarland, Oct. 18, 1917, *PWW*, 44:397; WW to Albert S. Burleson, Oct. 18, 1917, *PWW*, 44:397.

25. Herbert Croly to WW, Oct. 19, 1917, *PWW*, 44:408–10; WW to Herbert Croly, Oct. 22, 1917, *PWW*, 44:420; WW to George Creel, Oct. 27, 1917, 44:452; John Spargo to WW, Nov. 1, 1917, *PWW*, 44:492; WW to Joseph Tumulty, Nov. 2, 1917, *PWW*, 44:491; WW, annual message, Dec. 4, 1917, *PWW*, 45:195.

26. House vote, *CR*, March 4, 1918, 3004; Cox, Miller, 3003.

27. *CR*: Walsh, Apr. 4, 1918, 4559–60; Overman, 4562; Poindexter, Apr. 5, 1918, 4637, 4778; McKellar, Apr. 6, 1918, 4718; Watson, Apr. 4, 1918, 4568.

28. *CR*: Johnson, Apr. 24, 1918, 5544; Hardwick, Apr. 5, 1918, 4639; Reed, Apr. 4, 1918, 4573; Gore, Apr. 5, 4631; Vardaman, 4643; Sherman, Apr. 8, 1918, 4763.

29. Lodge, *CR*, Apr. 5, 1918, 4645, and Apr. 4, 1918, 4562; WHT, in Dalton, *Roosevelt*, 643n58.

30. TR, *Washington Post*, Apr. 6, 1918, 3; Stone, *CR*, Apr. 6, 1918, 4694; TR, *Atlanta Constitution*, May 8, 1918, 3; Cooper, *Warrior and Priest*, 329.

31. *CR*: Vote, Apr. 10, 1918, 4898; France, Apr. 24, 1918, 5542; John Lord O'Brian to Edwin Webb (Apr. 16, 1918), Apr. 24, 1918, 5542; Johnson, *NYT*, Apr. 28, 1918, 12; Fall, *CR*, Apr. 24, 1918, 5544.

32. *CR*: Senate vote, May 4, 1918, 6057; House vote, May 7, 1918, 6186–87; London, 6172; Quin, 6185.

33. Peterson and Fite, *Opponents of War*, 216.

34. NCLB, in Johnson, *Challenge to American Freedoms*, 71; *N* 106 (May 4, 1918): 558; *NR* 15 (May 18, 1918): 65.

35. Gregory, *Washington Herald*, May 31, 1918, 6; Thomas W. Gregory to WW, Aug. 21, 1918, *PWW*, 49:307; Striner, *Wilson*, 149.

36. List, in *New York Herald*, Sept. 1, 1918, 12; Lodge, *CR*, Sept. 17, 1918, 10378; second list, "More Condemned Books," *LD* 59 (Oct. 12, 1918): 27.

37. "The Airplane Scandal," *O* 120 (Sept. 4, 1918): 10; WW to Joseph Tumulty, Sept. 16, 1918, *PWW*, 51:15; "The One Thing Needful," *N* 107 (Sept. 14, 1918), 283.

38. New York *World*, in Knock, *To End All Wars*, 160; *NR* (Sept. 28, 1918): 240; "The Press Must Be Free," *NARWW* 1 (Oct. 5, 1918): 2; Pinchot, in Arthur A. Ekirch Jr., *Decline of American Liberalism* (New York: Longmans, Green, 1955), 230.

39. John Palmer Gavit to Joseph Tumulty, Oct. 25, 1918, *PWW*, 51:483; WW to Albert S. Burleson, Oct. 29, 1918, *PWW*, 483; Albert S. Burleson to WW, Oct. 30, 1918, *PWW*, 51:521.

40. Max Eastman, *Love and Revolution: My Journey through an Epoch* (New York: Random House, 1964), 31.

41. Ibid., 33, 37.

42. Ibid., 59.

43. Hand, *New York Tribune*, July 27, 1917, 16; George P. West, "A Talk with Mr. Burleson," *New York Public* 20 (Oct. 12, 1917): 986; Rogers, in Peterson and Fite, *Opponents of War*, 97.

44. Max Eastman, Amos Pinchot, John Reed to WW, July 12, 1917, *PWW*, 43:165; Albert S. Burleson to WW, July 16, 1917, *PWW*, 43:188; Baker, *Wilson*, 7:165n1; WW to Max Eastman, Sept. 18, 1917, *PWW*, 44:211.

45. *NR* 12 (Aug. 25, 1917): 86; Sinclair to WW, Oct. 30, 1917, *PWW*, 44:469.

46. *NYT*, Apr. 23, 1918, 9; Apr. 28, 1918, 5.

47. *NYT*, Oct. 4, 1918, 10; Oct. 5, 1918, 11; *New York Sun*, Oct. 6, 1918, 16.

48. WW to Lee Overman, Apr. 20, 1918, *PWW*, 47:381; WW to Anita McCormick Blaine, Apr. 22, 1918, *PWW*, 47:394.

FIVE   The Ramparts We Watch

1. Groups, in Peterson and Fite, *Opponents of War*, 18.

2. Creel, in Fleming, *Illusion of Victory*, 90.

3. For a general account, see John Carver Edwards, *Patriots in Pinstripe: Men of the National Security League* (Washington, D.C.: University Press of America, 1982).

4. McElroy, in *NYTr*, Apr. 15, 1918, 9; Hart, in Blakey, *Historians*, 62.

5. McElroy, in Blakey, *Historians*, 78; Creel, in Peterson and Fite, *Opponents of War*, 108.

6. Menken, *NYA*, June 18, 1918, 11; Hearst, *NYA*, June 29, 1918, 18.

7. Advisory board, in Edwards, *Patriots in Pinstripe*, 26; Thompson, *NYT*, Jan. 26, 1918, 9.

8. General stance, vigilante patrol, in Jensen, "The American Protective League," 77; loyalty categories, *Donaldsonville* (La.) *Chief*, Jan. 5, 1918, 1; pledge, *NYT*, Aug. 16, 1918, 6; Hornaday, in *I&E* 7 (Oct. 13, 1917): 230–31.

9. WW to William Kent, Sept. 30, 1918, *PWW*, 51:161; Creel, *Rebel at Large*, 196; TR, in Kathleen Dalton, *Roosevelt*, 649n131.

10. For a general account of the APL, see Joan M. Jensen, *The Price of Vigilance* (Chicago: Rand McNally, 1968), and her "American Protective League."

11. William Gibbs McAdoo to WW, May 15, 1917, in Jensen, *Price of Vigilance*, 43; McAdoo to Thomas W. Gregory, June 2, 1917, *PWW*, 42:441; McAdoo to WW, June 2, 1917, *PWW*, 42:448; Gregory to McAdoo, June 12, 1917, in Jensen, *Price of Vigilance*, 49–50.

12. WW to Gregory, June 4, 1917, *PWW*, 42:446; Gregory to McAdoo, June 12, 1917, *PWW*, 42:512–15; Kennedy, *Over Here*, 83.

13. Bielaski permission, in Jenson, "American Protective League," 43; *Chicago Tribune*, Aug. 25, 1917, 1.

14. Jensen, *Price of Vigilance*, 153–54; Jensen, "American Protective League," 125.

15. McAdoo to Gregory, Jan. 5, 1918, in Jensen, *Price of Vigilance*, 95.

16. Jensen, "American Protective League," 116; Emerson Hough, *The Web* (Chicago: Reilly and Lee, 1919), 372.

17. De Mille, in Jensen, *Price of Vigilance*, 141; Jehovah's Witnesses, 173–74; IWW, 126–28; German assets, 165.

18. Jensen, "American Protective League," 208–9.

19. *Chicago Tribune*, July 12, 1918, 1–2; July 13, 1918, 1.

20. *NYT*, Sept. 4, 1918, 1, 17; Jensen, *Price of Vigilance*, 208–9.

21. General opposition, in Christopher Capozzola, *Uncle Sam Wants You: World War I and the Making of the Modern American Citizen* (New York: Oxford University Press, 2008), 49; Johnson, *CR*, Sept. 5, 1918, 9978; Fall, *NYT*, Sept. 7, 1918, 4; Smoot, *CR*, Sept. 6, 1918, 10063; New York *World*, in *CR*, Sept. 5, 1918, 9976.

22. Jones, *NYT*, Sept. 7, 1918, 4; Poindexter, *New York Tribune*, Sept. 6, 1918, 5; Brisbane, *NYA*, Sept. 13, 1918, 16.

23. Gregory to WW, *PWW*, Sept. 9, 1918, 49:502.

24. Capozzola, *Uncle Sam Wants You*, 51–52.

25. Jensen, *Price of Vigilance*, 169; Kennedy, *Over Here*, 82.

26. Martial law, in Cooper, *Pivotal Decades*, 298; conscientious objectors, *St. Louis Post-Dispatch*, Sept. 25, 1918, 7; church services, *The Great*

Adventure, in *The Works of Theodore Roosevelt: National Edition* (New York: Scribner's, 1926), 19:301; Viereck, in TR to Ralph Montgomery Easley, June 5, 1917, *LTR*, 8:1207; *Staats-Zeiting* et al., in "Sinister Allies," *Oklahoma City Times*, Nov. 3, 1917, 10, and *N* 105 (Aug. 23, 1917): 210; imprisonment, *Washington Post*, Apr. 16, 1918, 3; pacifists, *Buffalo Evening News*, May 18, 1918, 13; hostile letters, in Dalton, *Roosevelt*, 643n63.

27. Foes, in Roosevelt, *Foes of Our Own Household*, in *Works*, 29:6; Cooper, *Warrior and Priest*, 326; czar remark, in *Washington Post*, Oct. 29, 1918, 1.

28. *Nation*, in Ralph Stout, ed., *Roosevelt in the Kansas City Star* (Boston: Houghton Mifflin, 1921), xliii.

29. TR, Fourth of July speech, *New York Sun*, July 5, 1917, 3; "Our Democracy on Trial," *I&E* 7 (July 14, 1917): 26.

30. *NYA*, Oct. 24, 1917, 18; May 27, 1918, 20; "moral traitor," Jan. 23, 1918, 16; cartoon, Jan. 25, 1918, 18.

31. Sherman, in "Why Mr. Roosevelt and the Rest of Us Are at War," *N* 105 (Nov. 15, 1917): 536; *Chicago Tribune*, Sept. 28, 1917, 6; *VTAW*, 6 (July 25, 1917): 418.

32. Daniels and Burleson, in *DD*, Oct. 5, 1917, 216; McAdoo, Nov. 2, 1917, in Livermore, *Woodrow Wilson and the War Congress*, 64.

33. Postal inspector, in Stout, *Roosevelt*, xli; Burleson, in *N* 105 (Nov. 29, 1917): 584; WW, ca. Dec. 18, 1917, *PWW*, 45:320; Ray Stannard Baker diary, Mar. 8, 1919, *PWW*, 55:467.

34. Stone, *CR*, Jan. 21, 1918, 1083; Lodge, 1088.

35. TR to Archibald Bulloch Roosevelt, Feb. 2, 1918, *LTR*, 8:1280.

36. Carnegie Hall, *NYT*, July 7, 1917, 1, 4; German Americans, TR, *Great Adventure*, in *Works*, 19:303, 309; Dalton, *Roosevelt*, 496.

37. Labor Day speech, *Emporia* (Kans.) *Gazette*, Sept. 6, 1917, 7; Ethel Roosevelt to Richard Denby, Dec. 12, 1917, and TR to Meyer Lissner, Mar. 26, 1918, in Dalton, *Roosevelt*, 493, 497. TR to William Allen White, Apr. 4, 1918, *LTR*, 8:1360.

38. Dalton, *Roosevelt*, 482; Cooper, *Warrior and Priest*, 327; TR, *Foes of Our Own Household*, in *Works*, 19:27.

SIX   Foes of Our Own Household

1. *After All: The Autobiography of Norman Angell* (New York: Farrar, Straus and Young, 1952), 200; Minnesota, in Walker, "Only Heretics," 77.

2. *NARWW* I (Jan. 5, 1918): 3; Kenyon, *CR*, Jan. 10, 1918, 755; Van Dyke quoted by Poindexter, *CR*, July 13, 1918, 9059; Atherton, in "Jeremiah's Warnings for To-Day," *LD* 58 (Aug. 31, 1918): 32; McElroy, *Wilmington* (N.C.) *Dispatch*, Oct. 28, 1917, 11.

3. Pershing, *New York Tribune*, July 11, 1918, 6; NDB, in *DD*, Oct. 16, 1918, 341.

4. Sunday invocation, *CR*, Jan. 10, 1918, 762; *NYT*, June 6, 1917, 18.

5. Memorandum, William English Walling, Sept. 3, 1917, *PWW*, 44:103.

6. Hurd, *NYT*, Mar. 31, 1918, 8; Young, *Ottawa* (Kans.) *Herald*, May 25, 1918, 8.

7. Creel, *How We Advertised America*, 170.

8. Editorial, *NYT*, July 8, 1917, 18; Tillman, *New York Sun*, July 6, 1917, 1; Gompers, *Harrisburg Evening News*, Nov. 17, 1917, 1; "The Kaiser's Secret Army Here," *LD* 55 (Dec. 1, 1917): 15; Adams, in Frederick C. Luebke, *Bonds of Loyalty: German-Americans and World War I* (DeKalb: Northern Illinois University Press, 1974), 267–68; Eaton, *New York Tribune*, Feb. 14, 1918, 3.

9. WW, war message, Apr. 22, 1917, *PWW*, 41:526.

10. WW, Flag Day address, June 14, 1917, *PWW*, 42:503; Michael Kazin, *War against War: The American Fight for Peace, 1914–1918* (New York: Simon & Schuster, 2017), 190.

11. Heflin, *CR*, Sept. 21, 1917, 7305, and *Washington Post*, Sept. 22, 1917, 1; congressional skirmish, *Washington Times*, Sept. 27, 1917, 1–2, and *NYT*, Sept. 28, 1917, 1; Heflin concession, *NYT*, Oct. 4, 1917, 12; House finding, *CR*, Oct. 6, 1917, 7906.

12. WW, *NYT*, Apr. 7, 1917, 1; Rathom, in Luebke, *Bonds of Loyalty*, 243; Simonds, in "The Kaiser's Secret Army Here," *LD* 55 (Dec. 1, 1917), 16.

13. Olds, "The Disloyalty of the German American Press, *Atlantic Monthly* 120 (July 1917): 138, 140; Hagedorn, "The Menace of the German-Language Press," *O* 116 (Aug. 15, 1917): 579; National Security League, in *NYT*, Aug. 6, 1917, 3.

14. Gregory to WW, July 22, 1917, *PWW*, 43:243; Burleson, in *DD*, Oct. 26, 1917, 227.

15. Lodge, Nelson, *CR*, Apr. 10, 1918, 4889; Harding, 4890; Borah, 4892.

16. Capozzola, *Uncle Sam Wants You*, 180.

17. Harding in London, *CR*, June 5, 1918, 7402–3; ADS, *New York Tribune*, Mar. 1, 1918, 9; "Enemy Speech Must Go," *NAR* 207 (June 1918): 811; ADS, in *NYT*, Mar. 18, 1918, 3.

18. Housekeeper, *DD*, Mar. 30,1917, 125; Leonidas C. Dyer to WW, July 30, 1917, *PWW*, 43:323–24; WW to Dyer, Aug. 1, 1917, *PWW*, 43:336; Aspinwall, in *DD*, Oct. 16, 1917, 227; WW to Tumulty, ca. Apr. 10, 1918, *PWW*, 47:311.

19. Hurd, *New York Tribune*, Apr. 3, 1918, 4; *Los Angeles Times*, June 18, 1918, 16; "Music and Patriotism," *O* 117 (Nov. 14, 1917), 407; Milwaukee, in Luebke, *Bonds of Loyalty*, 250.

20. *Chicago Tribune*, Apr. 29, 1917, 70; *N* 107 (July 6, 1918): 3.

21. Metropolitan Opera, *Boston Globe*, Nov. 3, 1917, 2; Mar. 15, 1918, 2. Kreisler, *Washington Evening Star*, Mar. 9, 1918, 2. For Muck, see Randy Roberts and Johnny Smith, *War Fever: Boston, Baseball, and America in the Shadow of the Great War* (New York: Basic Books, 2020), chaps. 2, 6, 8, 11, 21.

22. Otto H. Kahn to WW, Apr. 6, 1917, *PWW*, 42:7; WW to Tumulty, ca. Apr. 7, 1917, *PWW*, 42:8; Tumulty to Mrs. W. S. Jennings, Nov. 21, 1917, *PWW*, 46: 604, n2; WW to Leopold A. Stokowski, Aug. 20, 1918, *PWW*, 49:360.

23. Prager incident, *NYT*, Apr. 5, 1918, 4.

24. Gregory, *NYT*, Apr. 6, 1918, 15; Sherman, *St. Louis Globe-Democrat*, Apr. 9, 1918, 4, and *Munsey Evening Press*, Apr. 12, 1918, 2; *Washington Post*, Apr. 12, 1918, 6.

25. Trial, *New York Tribune*, June 2, 1918, 1, 18; Lowden, *Chicago Tribune*, June 4, 1918, 6; *NARWW* 1 (June 8, 1918): 11; Donald R. Hickey, "The Prager Affair," *Journal of the Illinois Historical Society* 62 (Summer 1969): 126; *NYT*, July 27, 1918, 8.

26. Walker, in *Honolulu Star-Bulletin*, Apr. 15, 1918, 8, and *San Francisco Chronicle*, May 12, 1918, 1; WW, Statement to the American People, July 26, 1918, *PWW*, 49:97.

27. Luebke, *Bonds of Loyalty*, 227, 229, 234.

28. Francke, *NYT*, Apr. 18, 1918, 12; Bernard Ridder to WW, Aug. 9, 1917, *PWW*, 43:410; *New Yorker Staats-Zeitung*, in *NYT*, Aug. 2, 1918, 4.

29. WW, *Washington Evening Star*, Aug. 10, 1918, 1.

30. Hermann Hagedorn, *Where Do You Stand? An Appeal to Americans of German Origin* (New York: Macmillan, 1918), 109, 68, 123.

31. Alliance, Luebke, *Bonds of Loyalty*, 231.

32. *Louisville Courier-Journal*, in *CO* 64 (Apr. 1918): 232; Senate committee, *NYTr*, Feb. 25, 1918, 14. Campbell, in *Pittsburgh Post-Gazette*, Mar. 1, 1918, 2; Ohlinger, *NYT*, Feb. 24, 1918, 1; disbanded, *NYT*, Apr. 13, 1918, 4; Senate, *NYT*, July 3, 1918, 8.

33. *Fort Wayne Sentinel*, Dec. 19, 1917, 3; Mock and Larsen, *Words That Won the War*, 216–18.

34. Rhodes, Carnegie, cover, *I&E*, May 12, 1917; "Voluntary Military Service Has Always Been a Failure," *I&E* 6 (May 12, 1917): 268; "Buy Liberty Loan!," *I&E* 6 (May 26, 1917): 287.

35. Phyllis Keller, *States of Belonging: German-American Intellectuals and the First World War* (Cambridge, Mass.: Harvard University Press, 1979), 157.

36. Rhodes, in Viereck, "America First and America Only," *VTAW* 6 (Apr. 11, 1917): 163; U-boats, *VTAW* 6 (May 9, 1917): 234.

37. Platform, in Viereck, "An Open Letter to Senator Poindexter," Oct. 2, 1917, *VTAW* 7 (Oct. 10, 1917): 190.

38. Candidate slate, *VTAW* 7 (Aug. 22, 1917): 58.

39. Keller, *States of Belonging*, 155–58.

40. Viereck, "Conscription and the German Americans," *VTAW* 6 (May 16, 1917): 250; Viereck, "German Americans as Soldiers of the Soil," *VTAW* 6 (May 30, 1917): 282; Viereck, "Do You Want an American Dreyfus Case?," *VTAW* 6 (June 4, 1917): 372; George Sylvester Viereck to David Starr Jordan, June 28, 1918, Box 81, the Papers of David Starr Jordan, Stanford University.

41. Britten, *CR*, June 25, 1917, 4257; *VTAW* 6 (July 11, 1917): 379–82; *VTAW* 7 (Nov. 14, 1917): 270; *New York Call*, in *VTAW* 6 (July 18, 1917): 396.

42. Bilbo, in *Stone County Enterprise* (Wiggins, Miss.), July 7, 1917, 1; Cox, in *Indianapolis News*, June 28, 1917, 6; WW burning, in Baker, *Wilson*, 7:171; Roosevelt, *Foes of Our Own Household*, in *Works*, 19:32.

43. Raids, in Keller, *States of Belonging*, 157; Poindexter, *VTAW* 7 (Oct. 10, 1917): 172; Poetry Society, *VTAW* 8 (July 10, 1918): 363; *VTAM* 10 (Mar. 1919): 20, and Keller, *States of Belonging*, 299n35; Authors' League, *VTAW* 8 (Aug. 7, 1918): 430; Mount Vernon, *New York Tribune*, Aug. 11, 1918, 16.

44. Loyalty pledge, United Irish-American Societies of New York, *NYT*, Apr. 23, 1917, 8; WW to RL, Apr. 10, 1917, *PWW*, 42:24; meeting with delegation, Jan. 10, 1918, *PWW*, 45:560; *DD*, Jan. 11, 1918, 265; WW, April 3, 1918, *PWW*, 47:228n2.

45. Petition, *CR*, Appendix, Apr. 30, 1917, 164; *NYA*, Mar. 15, 1918, 20; TR to George William Russell, Aug. 3, 1917, *LTR*, 8:1218; WHT, "England's Mistakes in Ireland," May 23, 1918, in Vivian, ed., *William Howard Taft*, 61–63.

46. *Gaelic American*, in *New York Sun*, Apr. 7, 1917, 6, and in *VTAW* 6 (May 9, 1917): 231; Devoy, *NYT*, Nov. 26, 1917, 15.

47. Cohalan, *NYT*, Sept. 23, 1917, 1, 6; varied journals, *NYT*, Jan. 23, 1918, 9.

48. *NYT*, May 20, 1918, 3.

49. Press opinion, "The Storm Raised by Conscription for Ireland," *CO* 64 (May 1918): 304; "The Sinn Fein Crisis," *NARWW* 1 (May 25, 1918): 5; *O* 120 (Sept. 4, 1918): 11–12.

50. *NYA*, June 10, 1917, editorial section, 1; *NYA*, Aug. 18, 1917, 16.

51. *SFE*, Apr. 12, 1917, 22; *Deutsches Journal*, in *CO* 65 (July 1918): 6; *NYA*, May 17, 1917, 18; *NYA*, June 24, 1917, pt. 2, 1; diplomat, *NYA*, June 17, 1917, 2; referendum, *NYA*, July 17, 1917, 18; Hearst, *SFE*, July 28, 1917, 2.

52. *NYA*, Apr. 24, 1917, 18; *NYA*, June 18, 1917, 16.

53. *NYTr*, Sept. 16, 1917, 1; David Nasaw, *The Chief: The Life of William Randolph Hearst* (Boston: Houghton Mifflin, 2000), 268; "Hearst and the Control of the Press," *N* 106 (June 15, 1918): 701.

54. Beck, *New York Sun*, Nov. 3, 1917, 5; Mitchel, *NYT*, Oct. 3, 1917, 1, 4; TR to Teddy Roosevelt Jr., Nov. 7, 1917, *LTR*, 8:1149; TR, *Brooklyn Eagle*, Oct. 31, 1917, 10.

55. Bolo, in Ben Proctor, *William Randolph Hearst*, Vol. 2, *The Later Years, 1911–1951* (New York: Oxford University Press, 2007), 61–62; Becker, *NYT*, Aug. 9, 1918, 20.

56. Mount Vernon, *NYT*, May 26, 1918, 20; Poughkeepsie, *NYTr*, May 31, 1918, 14; Albuquerque, in Proctor, *Hearst*, 66; national efforts, "The Case of Mr. Hearst and His Newspapers," *CO* 65 (July 1918): 5.

57. TR to Georges Clemenceau, Mar. 12, 1918, *LTR*, 8:1302.

58. On Daniels, *NYA*, June 14, 1917, 18; on McAdoo, *NYA*, May 28, 1918, 18; on Hurley, *NYA*, May 16, 1918, 22.

59. Grenville Macfarland to WW, Sept. 28, 1917, *PWW*, 44:275; *SFE*, Oct. 10, 1917, 18; *New York Tribune*, July 5, 1918, 14.

60. WW to Albert Sidney Burleson, Oct. 4, 1917, *PWW*, 44:302; Tumulty and Baker, "The Trail of German Propaganda in the American Press," *CO* 65 (Aug. 1918): 140–41.

61. Loyalty parade, Clark, in *VTAW* 8 (July 17, 1918): 383; Reed, *Buffalo Enquirer*, July 15, 1918, 2.

62. Brisbane, *SFE*, Sept. 6, 1918, 18; *NYA*, Sept. 14, 1918, 14.

63. *NYTr*, Sept. 21, 1918, 8.

64. Ian Mugridge, *The View from Xanadu: William Randolph Hearst and United States Foreign Policy* (Montreal: McGill-Queen's University Press, 1995), 114.

65. La Follette, *CR*, Aug. 11, 1917, 5956.

66. Van Tyne, *NYT*, Aug. 21, 1917, 8; *NR* 12 (Aug. 18, 1917): 58–59; "La Follette's Maneuvers for Peace," *O* 116 (Aug. 22, 1917): 602; Redfield, *NYT*, Aug. 23, 1917, 2.

67. Speech reported in *Minneapolis Star Tribune*, Sept. 21, 1917, 1; *Baltimore Sun*, Sept. 23, 1917, 8; denial, *NYT*, Sept. 24, 1917, 1.

68. Bryan, *NYT*, Oct. 6, 1917, 6; NSL, in Belle Case La Follette and Fola La Follette, *Robert M. La Follette, June 14, 1855–June 18, 1925* (New York: Macmillan, 1953), 2:777; ADS, *Washington Post*, Dec. 4, 1917, 2; other critics, *NYT*, Oct. 2, 1917, 6; Oct. 6, 1917, 6; Oct. 7, 1917, 19. TR, *SFE*, Sept. 27, 1917, 1; Russell, *Indianapolis News*, Sept. 24, 1917, 13; Taft, *LD* 15 (Oct. 6, 1917): 15; Butler, *Pittsburgh Post-Gazette*, Sept. 28, 1917, 1; WW to Joseph Tumulty, ca. Oct. 12, 1917, *PWW*, 44:365.

69. La Follette, *CR*, Oct. 6, 1917, 7878–86 (quotation at 7886).

70. Kellogg, *CR*, Oct. 6, 1917, 7887; Robinson, 7890–91; Fall, 7894; Vardaman, *Pittsburgh Post-Gazette*, Oct. 7, 1917, 6; Senate subcommittee, *St. Louis Post-Dispatch*, Oct. 6, 1917, 1.

71. Wisconsin senate, *NYT*, Feb. 26, 1918, 4; Huber, in "La Follette Condemned at Home," *LD* 57 (Mar. 23, 1918): 18; Wisconsin assembly, *NYT*, Mar. 9, 1918, 1, 4.

72. *VTAW*, 7 (Oct. 17, 1917): 186–87; Horace Kallen, "Politics, Profits, and Patriotism in Wisconsin," *N* 206 (Mar. 7, 1918): 258.

73. AP retraction, *NYT*, May 22, 1918, 9; *N* 106 (June 1, 1918): 637–38; Williams, *CR*, Jan. 16, 1919, 1525; tally at 1527.

SEVEN   The Anti-Radical Crusade

1. Stance of 1914, in Jack Ross, *The Socialist Party of America: A Complete History* (Lincoln, Neb.: Potomac Books, 2015), 157; Debs, in Freeberg, *Democracy's Prisoner*, 61; Hillquit, in Kazin, *War against War*, 213.

2. Majority report, *ATR*, Apr. 21, 1917, 1; referendum, *NYT*, July 8, 1917, 10; Nick Salvatore, *Eugene V. Debs: Citizen and Socialist* (Urbana: University of Illinois Press, 1982), 287.

3. Minority reports, *ATR*, Apr. 21, 1917, 1, 4.

4. Stokes, in Kenneth E. Hendrickson Jr., "The Pro-War Socialists, the Social Democratic League and the Ill-Fated Drive for Industrial Democracy in America, 1917–1920," *Labor History* 11 (June 1970): 308.

5. Walling, in "The Socialist as Patriot," *LD* 54 (June 16, 1917): 1837.

6. Simons, *CR*, May 11, 1917, 2090; Spargo, in Hachey, "Dissent in the Upper Middle West," 90; Benson, *Grand Forks* (N.D.) *Herald*, June 14, 1917, 6; Ghent, *California Outlook*, April 1917, 8; Walling, *Corvallis* (Ore.) *Gazette-Times*, July 5, 1917, 2; Russell, in John A. Thompson, *Reformers and War: American Progressive Publicists and the First World War* (New York: Cambridge University Press, 1987), 180; Gaylord, *CR*, May 11, 1917, 2089; Stokes, in Radosh, *American Labor*, 37.

7. Hendrickson, "Pro-War Socialists," 310–11.

8. Robert Dwight Reynolds Jr., "The Millionaire Socialists: J. G. Phelps Stokes and His Circle of Friends" (PhD diss., University of South Carolina, 1974); 277; Radosh, *American Labor*, 187, 213.

9. National Party platform, March 1918, *PWW*, 47:254n1; Walling, in Radosh, *American Labor*, 42–43.

10. *ATR*, Apr. 28, 1917, 1; *NYT*, May 25, 1917, 9.

11. *NYT*, Apr. 29, 1917, 17; May 10, 1917, 8.

12. Lansing refusal, *NYT*, May 24, 1917, 1; Hillquit, in Morris Hillquit, *Loose Leaves from a Busy Life* (New York: Macmillan, 1934), 157; RL to DRF, Apr. 12, *FR, 1917, Supplement 2*, 1:19; RL to Henry Cabot Lodge, May 28, 1917, HCLP; three radicals, Ira Morris to RL, June 22, 1917, *FR, 1917, Supplement 2*, 1:744.

13. Poem, in Kazin, *War against War*, 216.

14. Strunsky, "The Socialist Passports," *N* 104 (May 31, 1917): 650; *NR* 11 (June 2, 1917): 119; Walling, *NYT*, May 24, 1917, 1; *NYA*, May 18, 1917, 8; *VTAW* 7 (Aug. 22, 1917): 58.

15. Radosh, *American Labor*, 121; Robert D. Warth, *The Allies and the Russian Revolution: From the Fall of the Monarchy to the Peace of Brest-Litovsk* (Durham, N.C.: Duke University Press, 1954), 88; rump conference, in *N* 105 (Oct. 25, 1917): 469.

16. *Boston Globe*, July 2, 1917, 1–2; *Chicago Tribune*, Sept. 6, 1917, 1–2.

17. O'Hare, *Bismarck* (N.Dak.) *Tribune*, July 26, 1917, 8; Peterson and Fite, *Opponents of War*, 35–36.

18. Frank Bohn, "The Socialist Party and the War," *NYT*, Sept. 27, 1917, 12; Oswald Garrison Villard to Joseph Tumulty, Sept. 26, 1917, *PWW*, 44:272; EMH to WW, Oct. 17, 1917, *PWW*, 44:392–93; Walter Lippmann to EMH, Oct. 17, 1917, *PWW*, 44:393–94.

19. *NYT*, Nov. 2, 1917, 1, 2; "Hearst, Tammany, Mitchel, and America," *LD* 55 (Oct. 13, 1917): 11–13.

20. Newspaper quoted in W. A. Swanberg, *Citizen Hearst: A Biography of William Randolph Hearst* (New York: Scribner's, 1961), 310.

21. Anticonscription, in Peterson and Fite, *Opponents of War*, 31; acceptance speech, *NYT*, Sept. 24, 1917, 6; on withdrawal, Michael Bassett, "The American Socialist Party and the War," *Australian Journal of Politics and History* 11 (Dec. 1965–66): 281; "mortal blow," *NYT*, Oct. 23, 1917, 3; on Wilson, *NYT*, Oct. 30, 1917, 1; Liberty Bonds, in Hillquit, *Loose Leaves*, 190; Debs, in Grubbs, *Struggle for Labor Loyalty*, 84.

22. Straus, *NYT*, Nov. 2, 1917, 8; editorial, Nov. 3, 1917, 14. Wise, *Brooklyn Eagle*, Nov. 4, 1917, 4; Van Dyke, *NYT*, Nov. 2, 1917, 8; ex-socialists, *NYT*, Oct. 29, 1917, 4; *New York Sun*, Oct. 31, 1917, 1; Roosevelt, *NYTr*, Oct. 30, 1917, 1; Hillquit, *NYT*, Oct. 31, 1917, 5.

23. *NYT*, Oct. 30, 1917, 14; Nov. 1, 1917, 1.

24. Walter Lippmann to WW, Oct. 8, 1917, *PWW*, 44:334; WW to William C. Redfield, Oct. 29, 1917, *PWW*, 44:464; EMH diary, Dec. 30, 1917, *PWW*, 45:400; WW to Thomas W. Gregory, Oct. 19, 1917, *PWW*, 44:463. John Morton Blum, *Joe Tumulty and the Wilson Era* (Boston: Houghton Mifflin, 1951), 152.

25. TR to Teddy Roosevelt Jr., Nov. 7, 1917, *LTR*, 8:1250; *NYT*, Nov. 7, 1917, 12; *NR* 13 (Nov. 10, 1917): 31.

26. Livermore, *Woodrow Wilson and the War Congress*, 106; James Weinstein, *The Decline of Socialism in America, 1912–1925* (New York: Vintage, 1967), 150.

27. *NYA*, Nov. 19, 1917, 16.

28. *New Appeal*, Dec. 22, 1917, 1.

29. London on war aims, *NYT*, Oct. 22, 1917, 4; Dies, *CR*, Feb. 23, 1918, 2577; London on Wilson, *CR*, Aug. 27, 1918, 9604.

30. Hillquit, letter to *NR*, 13 (Dec. 1, 1917): 125; party executive committee, Feb. 9, 1918, the Papers of Ernest Lundeen, Hoover Institution on War, Revolution and Peace, box 224, folder 15.

31. South Dakota, in London, *CR*, Feb. 1, 1918, 1522; Chicago indictments, *NYTr*, Mar. 14, 1918, 6; Bentall, *St. Louis Star and Times*, Apr. 19, 1918, 2.

32. *NYTr*, Mar. 24, 1918, 8; Peterson and Fite, *Opponents of War*, 185.

33. WW to Thomas W. Gregory, June 14, 1918, *PWW*, 48:405; *NARWW* 1 (June 18, 1918): 11; *NR*, 15 (June 8, 1918): 158; husband, in Reynolds, "Millionaire Socialists," 305.

34. Bassett, "American Socialist Party and the War," 289; Weinstein, *Decline of Socialism*, 165–66; chapters, Freeberg, *Democracy's Prisoner*, 60.

35. Salvatore, *Debs*, 292–94 (quotation at 292); Freeberg, *Democracy's Prisoner*, 76–77 (quotation at 76; emphasis Debs).

36. Salvatore, *Debs*, 295; Freeberg, *Democracy's Prisoner*, 107.

37. IWW preamble, Peterson and Fite, *Opponents of War*, 49. Much material on this and the following paragraphs can be found in Harries and Harries, *Last Days of Innocence*, 183–89; Melvin Dubofsky, *We Shall Be All: A History of the Industrial Workers of the World* (Urbana: University of Illinois Press, 2000); and Patrick Renshaw, *The Wobblies: The Story of the IWW and Syndicalism in the United States*, new updated ed. (Chicago: Ivan R. Dee, 1999).

38. Harries and Harries, *Last Days of Innocence*, 203.

39. WW, *Arizona Republican*, July 14, 1917, 10; Haywood, *Bismarck Tribune*, July 31, 1917, 1; W. B. Wilson, in Hachey, "Dissent in the Upper

Middle West," 341; Gregory, in Harries and Harries, *Last Days of Innocence*, 188; Marshall, in Ross, *Socialist Party*, 188.

40. Creel, Steffens, Baker, in Thompson, *Reformers and War*, 223; *N* 105 (Aug. 23, 1917): 191; Borah, *CR*, March 21, 1918, 3821; *NYT*, July 14, 1917, 6; Frankfurter, in Harries and Harries, *Last Days of Innocence*, 188.

41. HCL to Felix Frankfurter, Dec. 19, 1917, HCLP; TR to Felix Frankfurter, Dec. 19, 1917, *LTR*, 8: 1264; *Los Angeles Times*, July 15, 1917, 18.

42. Harries and Harries, *Last Days of Innocence*, 188.

43. Poindexter, *CR*, Aug. 11, 1917, 5949; Myers, 5950; King, in Renshaw, *Wobblies*, 173.

44. Press, in Fleming, *Illusion of Victory*, 139; Sherman, *CR*, June 20, 1918, 8065; Ashurst, *CR*, Aug. 17, 1917, 6014.

45. Tulsa, *Washington Evening Star*, Nov. 10, 1917, 8; Bradley, in Harries and Harries, *Last Days of Innocence*, 288.

46. Peterson and Fite, *Opponents of War*, 49–50; Dubofsky, *We Shall Be All*, 228, 269.

47. Daniel Bell, "The Background and Development of Marxian Socialism in the United States," in *Socialism and American Life*, ed. Donald Drew Egbert and Stow Persons (Princeton, N.J.: Princeton University Press, 1952), 1:303.

48. Frazier, *NYT*, Feb. 4, 1917, 4; Townley, *Oregon Daily Journal*, Mar. 12, 1917, 5.

49. Platform, in *New Ulm* (Minn.) *Post*, Aug. 24, 1917, 10.

50. Townley later quoted in *Grand Forks* (N.Dak.) *Herald*, Mar. 22, 1919, 6; Townley, in Michael J. Lansing, *Insurgent Democracy: The Nonpartisan League in North American Politics* (Chicago: University of Chicago Press, 2015), 103; *Leader*, July 5, 1917, in Robert L. Morlan, *Political Prairie Fire: The Nonpartisan League, 1915–1922* (Minneapolis: University of Minnesota Press, 1955), 111.

51. Baer, *Appleton* (Wis.) *Post-Crescent*, Aug. 10, 1917, 4.

52. *Boston Transcript*, in "A New National Party," *LD* 55 (Aug. 11, 1917): 13; Judge John F. McGee, *Minneapolis Star Tribune*, Apr. 20, 1918, 1; TR to Stitzel X. Way, Nov. 1, 1917, *LTR*, 8: 1386; TR, Sept. 12, 1918, in Stout, *Roosevelt*, 214.

53. Minnesota, in Morlan, *Political Prairie Fire*, 166; organizer, in Peterson and Fite, *Opponents of War*, 65–66; Gilbert, in *St. Louis Post-Dispatch*, July 8, 1919, 3.

54. St. Paul conference, in Morlan, *Political Prairie Fire*, 143; John M. Baer to WW, Feb. 7, 1918, *PWW*, 46:270; *Minnesota Leader*, in Hachey, "Dissent in Upper Middle West," 204; Townley, *NYT*, May 2, 1918, 5.

55. The 1917 volume, in Bruce L. Larson, *Lindbergh of Minnesota: A Political Biography* (New York: Harcourt Brace Jovanovich, 1973), 212; *Bismarck Tribune*, June 6, 1918, 5; Townley, in *Jackson* (Mississippi) *Daily News*, July 16, 1918, 5; George Creel to WW, Sept. 12, 1918, *PWW*, 49:536.

56. Townley and Wilson, in Livermore, *Woodrow Wilson and the War Congress*, 154, and *Minneapolis Star Tribune*, Dec. 1, 1917, 6; Creel and Vrooman, in Morlan, *Political Prairie Fire*, 189.

57. *PWW*: WW to George Creel, Feb. 18, 1918, 46:369; WW to John M. Baer, Feb. 18, 1918, 46: 370; Arthur C. Townley to WW, Mar. 20, 1918, 47:87; WW to Joseph Tumulty, ca. Mar. 20, 1918, 47:88n1; William Kent to WW, Apr. 22, 1918, 47: 400; WW to William Kent, May 1, 1918, 47:475; WW to Thomas C. Gregory, June 12, 1918, 48:290.

58. *ATR*, June 16, 1917, 2; *NYT*, June 1, 1917, 1.

59. Magnes and Hillquit, in *ATR*, June 16, 1917, 2–3; Maurer, *NYT*, June 1, 1917, 2; Berger and Hull, in Grubbs, *Struggle for Labor Loyalty*, 30–31.

60. Ray Lyman Wilbur to David Starr Jordan, July 1, 1917; Wilbur to Jordan, July 24, 1917, box 82, Jordan Papers; Gompers, *NYT*, Aug. 11, 1917, 3; editorial, *NYT*, Aug. 11, 1917, 6; Stowell, *NYT*, Aug. 21, 1917, 8; Spargo quoted in *N* 105 (Aug. 23, 1917): 210; Lillian Wald to Crystal Eastman, Aug. 22, 1917, copy, box 19, Jordan Papers.

61. Albert S. Burleson to WW, Aug. 8, 1917, *PWW*, 43:397; William H. Lamar to Albert S. Burleson, Aug. 8, 1917, *PWW*, 43:395; Creel, in Peterson and Fite, *Opponents of War*, 76.

62. *DD*, Aug. 17, 1917, 192; Aug. 31, 1917, 199.

63. Hachey, "Dissent in Upper Middle West," 373–74.

64. *Chicago Tribune*, Sept. 3, 1917, 3; Sept. 4, 1917, 2. *NYT*, Sept. 3, 1917, 3; Arthur W. Thurner, "The Mayor, the Governor, and the People's Council," *Journal of the Illinois State Historical Society* 66 (Summer 1973): 135–36.

65. *People's Counselor*, in *Fort-Wayne Journal Gazette*, Sept. 14, 1917, 4; WW to Thomas E. Gregory, Sept. 25, 1917, *PWW*, 44:247.

66. *NYT*, Oct. 30, 1917, 3; newspapers cited in *NR* 13 (Nov. 10, 1917): 36.

67. NDB, in *Hartford Courant*, Nov. 30, 1917, 6; NDB to WW, Sept. 6, 1917, *PWW*, 44:157–58; and Daniel R. Beaver, *Newton D. Baker and the American War Effort, 1917–1919* (Lincoln: University of Nebraska Press, 1966), 236; WW, *NYT*, Nov. 13, 1917, 3.

68. Butler, *NYT*, June 7, 1917, 2; Dana and Cattell, in Michael Rosenthal, *Nicholas Miraculous: The Amazing Career of the Redoubtable Dr.*

Nicholas Murray Butler (New York: Farrar, Straus and Giroux, 2006), 234–36; Beard, *NYT*, October 9, 1917, 3; press opinion, "Stamping Out 'Sedition' in the Columbia Faculty," *CO* 63 (Nov. 1917): 294–96.

69. Grubbs, *Struggle for Labor Loyalty*, 81.

70. Ibid., 78; Wise, *NYT*, Sept. 24, 1917, 13.

71. Nearing, in *NYTr*, Feb. 17, 1918, 1, and Stephen J. Whitfield, *Scott Nearing: Apostle of American Radicalism* (New York: Columbia University Press, 1974), 92; Magnes, *NYT*, Feb. 18, 1918, 5; Kazin, *War against War*, 222.

72. Duluth, *NYT*, Nov. 13, 1917, 22; Grubbs, *Struggle for Labor Loyalty*, 127.

73. Richard Striner accuses Wilson of abdicating a crucial role as a wartime leader by failing to mitigate, control, or at least condemn the hysteria. He attributes Wilson's "small-mindedness, myopia, hypocrisy, and—why pull punches?—stupidity" to a "psychopathology," a mental decline evident as early as 1917 and in part created by stress (Striner, *Wilson*, 150–52). Trygve Thronviet, claiming that the president lost his moral and political bearings on the home front, sees Wilson lacking the strength "to drag a great, hesitating democracy onto the world stage without doing it violence." Possible reasons include the need to teach recalcitrant Americans "a lesson," inability to rein in overreaching subordinates, and preoccupation with his quest for "a democratically united world"; see Thronviet, *Power without Victory: Woodrow Wilson and the American Internationalist Experiment* (Chicago: University of Chicago Press, 2017), 215; Thomas J. Knock observes that Wilson never made "an impressive statement" concerning civil liberties, allowing Postmaster Burleson and Attorney General Gregory to become virtual arbiters of the First Amendment (Knock, *To End All Wars*, 134–35).

Other historians take a somewhat milder approach. Ronald Schaffer asserts that a Wilson more deeply committed to preserving free speech would have treated dissenters less harshly. Leniency, however, would have made him and his party more vulnerable to attacks from "reactionary chauvinists" and would have possibly increased opposition to the war; see Schaffer, *America in the Great War*, 30. John Milton Cooper Jr. calls the violations of civil liberties the "ugliest blot" on Wilson's presidency, but argues that some form of official repression was perhaps inevitable. Furthermore, writes Cooper, the administration headed off such extreme measures as total censorship and rule of martial law, both policies advocated by Theodore Roosevelt. He adds that some of Victor Berger's remarks bordered on praise of the Central Powers and that Eugene Debs made inflammatory statements in deliberate violation of the Espionage and Sedition Acts. Yet, observes Cooper, Wilson had to draw on popular passions so as to take action.

Though not taking overt action himself, he gave free rein to subordinates (Cooper, *Pivotal Decades*, 297–300; Cooper, *Wilson*, 400).

Arthur S. Link and John Whiteclay Chambers II go further in defending Wilson, claiming that the president sought to contain rampant chauvinism, frequently seeking to limit the harassment and repression stemming from state, local, and private sources; see Link and Chambers, "Woodrow Wilson as Commander in Chief," in *The United States Military under the Constitution of the United States, 1789–1989*, ed. Richard H. Kohn (New York: New York University Press, 1991), 335. Similarly, August Heckscher sees the public hysteria as lying beyond Wilson's control, but he admits that Wilson failed to hold Burleson and Gregory in check; see Heckscher, *Woodrow Wilson: A Biography* (New York: Scribner's, 1991), 452.

74. Cobb, "A Recollection," in Heaton, *Cobb*, 269–70.

EIGHT "Living on a Volcano"

1. Orlando Figes, *A People's Tragedy: A History of the Russian Revolution* (New York: Viking, 1996), 360.

2. Miliukov, in W. Bruce Lincoln, *Passage through Armageddon: The Russians in War and Revolution, 1914–1918* (New York: Simon and Schuster, 1986), 358–59; Petrograd Soviet, in Adam Tooze, *The Deluge: The Great War, America and the Remaking of the Global Order, 1916–1931* (New York: Viking, 2014), 71.

3. General opinion, in Peter G. Filene, *Americans and the Soviet Experiment, 1917–1933* (Chapel Hill: University of North Carolina Press, 1967), 11; "The Foe at Russia's Gate," *LD 54* (April 7, 1917): 971; WW, war message, Apr. 2, 1917, *PWW*, 41:524; RL to DRF, Apr. 6, 1917, *FR, 1918, Russia*, 1:20–21.

4. WW to RL, Apr. 12, 1917, *PWW*, 42:43.

5. McAdoo, Lansing, in Daniels, *Wilson Era*, 2:57; HCL to TR, May 26, 1917, HCLP.

6. Much of this and subsequent paragraphs is drawn from Alton Earl Ingram, "The Root Mission in Russia" (PhD diss., Louisiana State University, 1970).

7. Root, in Ingram, "Root Mission," 104; RL to DRF, May 18, 1917, *PWW*, 42:368 (emphasis his).

8. Root, in Jessup, *Root*, 2:361; Scott, in Robert Edward Barnett, "Frustrated Partnership: Russia's Relations with Great Britain, France, and the United States during World War I" (PhD diss., Texas Tech University, 1990), 191.

9. Root, in *Danville* (Pa.) *News*, June 18, 1917, 2; Root to RL, June 17, 1918, *FR, 1918, Russia*, 1:121–22.

10. Russell, in Robert Miraldi, *The Pen Is Mightier: The Muckraking Life of Charles Edward Russell* (New York: Palgrave Macmillan, 2003), 250.

11. Duncan, in Radosh, *American Labor*, 88.

12. Root, in Jessup, *Root*, 2:367; Root to RL, July 10, 1917, *FR, 1918, Russia*, 1:129; *New York Sun*, July 11, 1917, 2.

13. Root mission reports, July 10, 1917, *FR, 1918, Russia*, 1:131–53; quotations at 143–44, 153.

14. Scott, in Ingram, "Root Mission," 193, and Russell, diary entry, June 19, 1917, in ibid., 232.

15. *War Memoirs of Robert Lansing, Secretary of State* (Indianapolis: Bobbs-Merrill, 1921), 337–38.

16. Root, Sept. 16, 1930, in Jessup, *Elihu Root*, 2:356.

17. Ingram, "Root Mission," 302–16; quotation at 310–11. Peter G. Filene indicts the commission for misleading the American public, thereby increasing its bewilderment and frustration when Russia continued to decay (Filene, *Americans and the Soviet Experiment*, 19). George Schild observes that Wilson was not seeking genuine advice but rather reaffirmation of his belief in the survival of Russian democracy; see Schild, *Between Ideology and Realpolitik: Woodrow Wilson and the Russian Revolution, 1917–1921* (Westport, Conn.: Greenwood, 1995), 33. Leonid I. Strakhovsky sees the group's stress on propaganda as equaling "a suggestion of pouring a spoonful of syrup to extinguish a blazing fire"; see Strakhovsky, *American Opinion about Russia* (Toronto: University of Toronto Press, 1961), 18. To Christopher Lasch, the mission was "America's answer to Stockholm," the effort of certain European Socialists to explore peace terms. Washington deliberately sought to "throw cold water" on the Soviet's campaign to revise war aims; see Lasch, *The American Liberals and the Russian Revolution* (New York: Columbia University Press, 1962), 42. Donald E. Davis and Eugene P. Trani fault Wilson for not relying on genuine experts and orthodox diplomatic channels instead of establishing an ad hoc mission led by a Republican leader, who in some sense was his rival; see Davis and Trani, *The First Cold War: The Legacy of Woodrow Wilson in U.S.–Soviet Relations* (Columbia: University of Missouri Press, 2002), 57. George F. Kennan indicts the mission for being a destructive distraction to a Russian government that neither wanted nor needed it; the country was already in the process of disintegration. Root himself, Kennan writes, lacked enthusiasm and conveyed a smug and patronizing attitude; see Kennan, *Russia Leaves the War* (New York: Princeton University Press, 1956), 21.

18. WW to RL, Aug. 14, 1917, *FR-LP*, 2:342; John F. Stevens to RL, Dec. 20, 1917, *FR, 1918, Russia*, 3:213.

19. Tereshchenko, statement of May 19 to Russian press, in DRF to RL, May 21, 1917, *FR, 1918, Russia*, 1:75–76.

20. WW, May 26 message in *NYT*, June 10, 1917, 1.

21. Kerensky, in Warth, *Allies and Russian Revolution*, 112.

22. TR to Prince Lvov, July 10, 1917, *LTR*, 8:1212; Root, in Barnett, "Frustrated Partnership," 231.

23. DRF to RL, July 2, 1917, *FR, 1918, Russia*, 1:99; Lockhart cited in Harper Barnes, *Standing on a Volcano: The Life and Times of David Rowland Francis* (St. Louis: Missouri State Historical Society Press, 2001), 335; David R. Francis, *Russia from the American Embassy, April 1916–November 1918* (New York: Scribner's, 1921), 3; William V. Judson to Alice Judson, July 12, 1917, in Neil V. Salzman, ed., *Russia in War and Revolution: General William V. Judson's Accounts from Petrograd, 1917–1918* (Kent, Ohio: Kent State University Press, 1998), 39.

24. "Our Disaster in Russia," *O* 116 (Aug. 1, 1917): 494; "Justice to Russia," *NR* 12 (Aug. 4, 1917): 6; Borah, *NYT*, July 27, 1917, 1.

25. Lansing, in Davis and Trani, *First Cold War*, 54; EMH to WW, July 23, 1917, *PWW*, 43:249; EMH to WW, Aug. 15, 1917, *PWW*, 43:471; Frederick Palmer, *Bliss, Peacemaker: The Life and Letters of General Tasker Howard Bliss* (New York: Dodd, Mead, 1934), 169.

26. Francis quoted in Judson report to PCM, June 18, 1919, in Barnes, *Standing on a Volcano*, 256; *NYT*, July 24, 1917, 10; Root, in HCL to Sturgis Bigelow, Aug. 25, 1917, HCLP; WW to National Political Conference, Aug. 24, 1917, *PWW*, 44:38.

27. Strakhovsky, *American Opinion about Russia*, 20.

28. Hermann Hagedorn, *The Magnate: William Bryce Thompson and His Time (1869–1930)* (New York: John Day, 1935), 203, 219.

29. H. Bruce Lockhart, *British Agent* (New York: Putnam, 1933), 220; George Kennan, *Russia and the West under Lenin and Stalin* (Boston: Little Brown, 1961), 52; Kennan, *Russia Leaves the War*, 63–64.

30. The Haitian army was supposedly full of high-ranking officers that not a member of the army held the rank of private. Everyone was a general or colonel, or some other high rank.

31. Judson to War College staff, Sept. 28, 1917, in Salzman, *Russia in War and Revolution*, 91; JJP to Hugh L. Scott, Oct. 1, 1917, in Calhoun, *Power and Principle*, 192; DRF to RL, Oct. 4, 1917, *FR, 1918, Russia*, 1:202–3.

32. Kennan, *Russia and the West*, 28.

33. WW to Edgar Grant Sisson, Oct. 24, 1917, *PWW*, 44:435–36.

34. Hagedorn, *The Magnate*, 240; DRF to RL, Nov. 7, 1918, *FR, 1918, Russia*, 1:224–25; and Summers to RL, Nov. 8, 1918, 226.

35. Trotsky, in Figes, *People's Tragedy*, 537; decree on peace, *Brooklyn Eagle*, Nov. 8, 1917, 1.

36. *NYT*, Nov. 25, 1917, 26.

37. Press, including New York *World*, "Bolsheviki at Russia's Throat," *LD* 55 (Nov. 17, 1917): 10.

38. "Russia under the Terror," *LD* 55 (Dec. 29, 1917): 24; WHT, "Nationalism and Opportunism," Nov. 23, 1917, in Vivian, ed., *William Howard Taft*, 7; "The Perils of a Bolshevik Peace," *LD* 55 (Dec. 8, 1917): 15.

39. WW, address to the American Federation of Labor, Nov. 12, 1917, *PWW*, 45:14; WW to Congressman Frank Clark (D-Fla.), Nov. 13, 1917, *PWW*, 45:39.

40. Trotsky, Nov. 18, 1917, in DRF to RL, Nov. 24, 1917, *PWW*, 45:119; WW, in *DD*, Nov. 27, 1917, 243.

41. *DD*, Nov. 30, 1917, 244; WW, annual message, Dec. 4, 1917, *PWW*, 45:199.

42. EMH to Sir William Wiseman, Dec. 18, 1917, *PWW*, 45:322.

43. RL to WW, Dec. 10, 1917, *PWW*, 45:263–65; WW to RL, Dec. 12, 1917, *PWW*, 45:274; Lansing caution, *DD*, Dec. 11, 1917, 249.

44. Summers, in William Appleman Williams, *American–Russian Relations, 1781–1947* (New York: Holt, Rinehart and Winston, 1952), 113, 119–20; Kennan, *Russia Leaves the War*, 177–78; David S. Foglesong, *America's Secret War against Bolshevism: U.S. Intervention in the Russian Civil War, 1917–1920* (Chapel Hill: University of North Carolina Press, 1995), 77.

45. Lansing, Dec. 2, 1917, *War Memoirs*, 340–42; RL statement, Dec. 4, 1917, *PWW*, 45:205–7; RL to WW, Jan. 2, 1918, *PWW*, 45:427–30.

46. Thompson to WW plus memorandum, Jan. 3, 1918, *PWW*, 45:443; House diary, Jan. 2, 1918, EMHP; reactions, in Hagedorn, *The Magnate*, 266–67.

47. Robins to Elizabeth Robins, Dec. 20, 1917, in David W. McFadden, *Alternative Paths: Soviets and Americans, 1917–1920* (New York: Oxford University Press, 1993), 79; Robins's general views, 69; Robins on Trotsky, in Lockhart, *British Agent*, 222.

48. Memo, British Foreign Office, prepared for Milner and Cecil, in WW to RL, Jan. 1, 1918, *PWW*, 45:417–19.

49. WW, address to the Congress, Jan. 8, 1918, *PWW*, 45:536–37.

50. Creel Committee, in Warth, *Allies and the Russian Revolution*, 213; Robins on Lenin, in DRF to RL, Jan. 12, 1918, *FR, 1918, Russia*, 1:426;

Izvestia, in *NYT*, Jan. 14, 1917, 3; *Pravda*, in Salzman, *Russia in War and Revolution*, 216.

51. Borah, Weeks, Smith, *NYT*, Jan. 9, 1918, 2; Baer, *LD* 56 (Jan. 19, 1918): 12–13; *NARWW* 1 (Jan. 12, 1918): 1; Nearing, *LD* 16 (Jan. 19, 1918): 11. RL to WW, Jan. 10, 1918, *PWW*, 45:564.

52. *NYA*, Jan. 7, 1918, 24; Lenin, Feb. 3, 1918, *NYA*, II:1. Hearst, *SFE*, March 1, 1918, 20; Brisbane, *NYA*, Feb. 27, 1918, 20.

53. Woodward, *American Army*, 167.

54. "Slaughtering Russia's Officers," *LD* 56 (Feb. 9, 1918): 21; "Facing the Facts," *NARWW* 1 (Feb. 16, 1918): 4; WHT, *NYT*, Feb. 22, 1918, 4; TR to Kermit Roosevelt, Mar. 12, 1918, *LTR*, 8:1297; New York *World*, in "Russia at Germany's Mercy," *LD* 56 (Feb. 23, 1918): 16.

55. *NR* 14 (Feb. 16, 1918): 68; *SFE*, Mar. 14, 1918, 22; London, *CR*, Feb. 23, 1918, 2578; *New Appeal*, Mar. 9, 1918, 1; Viereck, *VTAW* 8 (Mar. 27, 1918): 126.

56. Ruggles, Riggs, in George F. Kennan, *The Decision to Intervene* (Princeton, N.J.: Princeton University Press, 1958), 112, and House, 128; Francis, in McFadden, *Alternative Paths*, 112.

57. WW message, *NYTr*, Mar. 12, 1918, 1.

58. Kennan, *Russia Leaves the War*, 373; Lawrence W. Martin, *Peace without Victory: Woodrow Wilson and the British Liberals* (New Haven, Conn.: Yale University Press, 1958), 167.

59. *NR* 14 (Mar. 16, 1918): 185; *NARWW* 1 (Mar. 16, 1918): 2; *VTAW* 8 (Mar. 20, 1918): 109; Sherman, *NYT*, Apr. 24, 1918, 13.

60. Soviet Congress, in Summers to RL, Mar. 15, 1918, *FR, 1918, Russia*, 1:399–400; Zinoviev, in Francis, *Russia from the American Embassy*, 230.

61. Trotsky, in Kennan, *Russia Leaves the War*, 496; DRF to RL, Mar. 12, 1918, *FR, 1918, Russia*, 1:398; Robins, *NYT*, Mar. 7, 1919, 18.

62. Davis and Trani, *First Cold War*, 112–13, 115. Robins's biographer Neil V. Salzman argues that Allied action could have delayed or altered the peace terms; see Salzman, *Reform and Revolution: The Life and Times of Raymond Robins* (Kent, Ohio: Kent State University Press, 1991), 247. David W. McFadden finds Trotsky's bid to Robins most credible, based upon the Russian leader's earlier entreaties for Western aid and his continued unwillingness to support the peace with Germany (McFadden, *Alternative Paths*, 72).

Some historians are more critical. W. Bruce Lincoln finds Robins as unbalanced on the one side as were his superiors on the other, for he never understood the depths of Bolshevik hatred for the capitalist West; see Lincoln, *Red Victory: A History of the Russian Civil War* (New York: Simon and Schuster, 1989), 168, 170. Peter G. Filene suggests that Trotsky's questions were hypothetical; he had never promised that his government would reject the treaty. Chances of Soviet resistance to the German army were indeed slim; the discussions were trivial in nature (Filene, *Americans and Soviet Experiment*, 30). Lloyd C. Gardner doubts whether the United States bungled a major opportunity to keep Russia in the war; evidence of U.S. opposition to Japanese intervention in Siberia or to British maneuvers in northern Russia's seaports was unlikely to change Lenin's mind; see Gardner, *Safe for Democracy: The Anglo-American Response to Revolution, 1913–1923* (New York: Oxford University Press, 1984), 175. Kennan calls the conversations "a tempest in a teapot," as chances of working through the Soviet government were very slender; see Kennan, *Russia and the West*, 60.

63. For this argument, see Kennan, *Russia Leaves the War*, 370–71; Kennan, *Russia and the West*, 41; Tooze, *Deluge*, 109.

64. WHP to RL, Mar. 25, 1918, *FR, 1918, Russia*, 1:438; Francis, statement of Mar. 16, 1918, in DRF to RL, Apr. 15, 1918, *FR, 1918, Russia*, 1:441; *Pravda*, in William Hard, *Raymond Robins' Own Story* (New York: Harper, 1920), 96.

65. Salzman, *Reform and Revolution*, 251–52, 265; McFadden, *Alternative Paths*, 74–75, 118–19; DRF to RL, Mar. 22, 1918, *FR, 1918, Russia*, 1:486; RL to DRF, Mar. 23, 1918, 486.

66. Lenin, in Maddin Summers to RL, Apr. 26, 1918, *FR, 1918, Russia*, 1:505.

67. Trotsky, in James A. Ruggles dispatch, Mar. 12, 1918, in RL to WW, Mar. 21, 1918, *PWW*, 47:141.

68. Robins to Francis, Apr. 18, 1918, in McFadden, *Alternative Paths*, 121, and Robins's arrangements, 118–19.

69. Kennan, *Decision to Intervene*, 181; WW to RL, Feb. 4, 1918, *PWW*, 46:232; Robins to Elizabeth Robins, Apr. 14, 1918, in Salzman, *Reform and Revolution*, 262.

70. Robins to Lenin, Apr. 25, 1918, in Barnes, *Standing on a Volcano*, 325.

71. Luggage, in McFadden, *Alternative Paths*, 160; progressives, in Williams, *American–Russian Relations*, 146–47.

72. "What Next in Russia?," *LD* 56 (March 30, 1918): 16.

73. *NYA*, Apr. 5, 1918, 24; "For and Against the Bolsheviki," *NR* 14 (Apr. 6, 1918): 280–81; Norma Fain Pratt, *Morris Hillquit: A Political History of an American Jewish Socialist* (Westport, Conn.: Greenwood, 1979), 136.

74. WW, address, May 18, 1918, *PWW*, 48:54; *NYT*, May 19, 1918, 1; reactions, in Foglesong, *America's Secret War*, 47–49, and Lasch, *American Liberals*, 103.

75. WW, address, July 4, 1918, *PWW*, 48:516; WW to EMH, July 8, 1918, *PWW*, 48:550 (emphasis Wilson's).

76. Barnes, *Standing on a Volcano*, 338–39; DRF to RL, June 11, 1918, *FR, 1918, Russia*, 1:560–61; DRF to Felix Cole, July 10, 1918, in Foglesong, *America's Secret War*, 114; Kalamatiano, 118.

77. Poole to RL, Sept. 9, 1918, *FR, 1918, Russia*, 1:668; Lansing memorandum, Oct. 28, 1918, in Klaus Schwabe, *Woodrow Wilson, Revolutionary Germany, and Peacemaking, 1918–1919: Missionary Diplomacy and the Realities of Power* (Chapel Hill: University of North Carolina Press, 1985), 76.

78. WW, *St. Louis Post-Dispatch*, Sept. 24, 1918, 14; "Red Russia as Our Foe," *LD* 58 (Sept. 21, 1918): 9.

79. George F. Kennan, "The Sisson Documents," *Journal of Modern History* 38 (June 1956): 130, 145–47.

80. DRF to RL, Feb. 9, 1918, *FR, 1918, Russia*, 1:371–78; Edgar Sisson, *One Hundred Red Days: A Personal Chronicle of the Bolshevik Revolution* (New Haven, Conn.: Yale University Press, 1931), 296; Creel, in Foglesong, *America's Secret War*, 196; RL to Sisson, Sept. 14, 1918, *FR-LP*, 2:384; Sisson to RL, 385; Polk and Miles, in McFadden, *Alternative Paths*, 169; EMH diary, Sept. 24, 1918, *PWW*, 51:104.

81. WHT, "Our Russian Policy," Sept. 26, 1918, in Vivian, ed., *William Howard Taft*, 93; "Lenine and Trotsky Paid German Agents," *O* 120 (Sept. 25, 1918): 118; general press, "Proof of Russia's Betrayal," *LD* 58 (Sept. 28, 1918): 16; *NYTr*, Sept. 22, 1918, 25.

82. Arthur Balfour to William Wiseman, Oct. 4, 1918, *PWW*, 51:246; *N* 107 (Sept. 28, 1918): 334; Nuorteva, *NYTr*, Oct. 5, 1918, 12; *New York Evening Post* and Creel, in Lasch, *American Liberals*, 114.

83. "The German–Bolshevik Conspiracy" (Washington, D.C.: Committee on Public Information, 1918), 3, 27.

84. Kennan, "Sisson Documents," 134, 139–40.

85. Lasch, *American Liberals*, 117; Christopher Lasch, "American Intervention in Russia: A Reinterpretation," *Political Science Quarterly* 77 (June 1962): 220.

86. Sir William Wiseman, interview with WW, Oct. 16, 1918, *PWW*, 51:350.

NINE "Walking on Eggs"

1. British anxiety, Coville A. De R. Barclay to Lansing, Mar. 4, 1918, *FR, 1918, Russia*, 1:391.

2. Trotsky, in Kennan, *Decision to Intervene*, 46 (emphasis Trotsky's).

3. Supreme War Council, Joint Note No. 31, "Allied Intervention at the White Sea Ports," June 3, 1918, *PWW*, 48:287n1.

4. THB to RL, NDB, PCM, July 5, 1918, *PWW*, 48:536–37.

5. March, *Nation at War*, 117; THB to RL, NDB, PCM, July 5, 1918, *PWW*, 48:536–37; Palmer, *Bliss*, 303.

6. Felix Cole to DRF, June 1, 1918, *FR, 1918, Russia*, 2:477–84; quotations at 477, 480.

7. JJP, in March, *Nation at War*, 134; Kennan, *Decision to Intervene*, 213; DRF to RL, June 6, 1918, *FR, 1918, Russia*, 1:553.

8. RL to WW, May 11, 1918, *PWW*, 48:605.

9. Calhoun, *Power and Principle*, 199; Eugene P. Trani, "Woodrow Wilson and the Decision to Intervene in Russia: A Reconsideration," *Journal of Modern History* 48 (Sept. 1976): 454–55; Woodward, *American Army*, 261.

10. WW to Josephus Daniels, Apr. 8, 1918, *PWW*, 47:290; Davis and Trani, *First Cold War*, 155; WW to THB, May 28, 1918, *PWW*, 48:182.

11. WW, aide-mémoire, July 16, 1918, *PWW*, 48:626.

12. Chicherin, in Foglesong, *America's Secret War*, 201; Kennan, *Russia and the West*, 75.

13. DRF to RL, Aug. 31, 1918, *FR, 1918, Russia*, 2:516.

14. Chicherin to DeWitt C. Poole Jr., August 5, 1918, *FR, 1918, Russia*, 1:659–60; supplementary treaty, in WHP to RL, Sept. 27, 1918, 1:600.

15. Lincoln, *Red Victory*, 182.

16. James Carl Nelson, *The Polar Bear Expedition: The Heroes of America's Forgotten Invasion of Russia, 1918–1919* (New York: William Morrow, 2019), 276.

17. THB to PCM, Sept. 7, 1918, *PWW*, 51:54; THB to T. Col. Bentley Mott, Sept. 7, 1918, cited in Betty Miller Unterberger, *The United States, Revolutionary Russia, and the Rise of Czechoslovakia* (Chapel Hill: University of North Carolina Press, 1989), 296; DRF to RL, Sept. 10, 1918, *FR, 1918, Russia*, 2:532; RL to WHP, Sept. 12, 1918, *FR, 1918, Russia*, 2:533–34; SWC in THB to RL, Sept. 14, 1918, *FR-LP*, 2:152.

18. Capt. Joel Roscoe Moore, in Nelson, *Polar Bear Expedition*, 44.

19. WW to RL, Sept. 26, 1918, *PWW*, 51:121. RL to WHP, Sept. 26, 1918, *FR, 1918, Russia*, 2:395; DRF to RL, Oct. 10, 1918, 2:555–56.

20. Kennan, *Decision to Intervene*, 419–21.

21. The contents were first specified in RL to Viscount Ishii, Oct. 20, 1917, *PWW*: 44:419–20.

22. French, Dec. 14, 1917, in John Albert White, *The Siberian Intervention* (Princeton, N.J.: Princeton University Press, 1950), 224; SWC, Joint Note No. 5, Dec. 23, 1917, in Calhoun, *Power and Principle*, 193; British War Cabinet in Balfour to Reading, Jan. 1, 1918, *PWW*, 45:420.

23. *DD*, Jan. 18, 1918, 269.

24. WW to RL, Jan. 20, 1918, *PWW*, 46:46; *DD*, March 1, 1918, 285; Franklin K. Lane to Albert S. Burleson, Mar. 1, 1918, in Lane and Wall, eds., *Letters of Franklin K. Lane*, 266; WW, aide-mémoire, Mar. 1, 1918, *PWW*, 46:498–99; WW, in Polk to Roland Sletor Morris, Mar. 5, 1918, *PWW*, 46:545.

25. David S. Foglesong claims that Wilson's reluctance stemmed less from liberal principles or moral qualms than from fear of the likely consequences. The president's vacillation showed he was not absolutely opposed to intervention per se but to excessively direct and offensive forms of interference (Foglesong, *America's Secret War*, 149). Arguing to the contrary, Kennan sees Wilson and his advisers remaining "undeviatingly high-minded" (Kennan, *Decision to Intervene*, 83). Donald E. Davis and Eugene P. Trani write that though Wilson opposed U.S. participation in Siberia in an aide-mémoire, he mistakenly opened the door to others, allowing the Japanese to squeeze in. The Allies, realizing his mistake would perforce involve U.S. intervention, redoubled their pressure on him (Davis and Trani, *First Cold War*, 126).

26. Frank L. Polk to Roland S. Morris, Jan. 20, 1918, *FR, 1918, Russia*, 2:31; EMH to WW, Feb. 2, 1918, *PWW*, 46:214–15; George H. Nash, *The Life of Herbert Hoover*, Vol. 3, *Master of Emergencies, 1917–1918* (New York: Norton, 1996), 464.

27. William C. Bullitt to Frank L. Polk, Mar. 2, 1918, *PWW*, 46:510–13; quotation at 513.

28. DRF to RL, Mar. 10, 1918, *FR, Russia, 1818*, 1:394–95; Semenov sentiment, in Foglesong, *America's Secret War*, 153; WW to RL, Apr. 18, 1918, *FR-LP*, 2:360.

29. Varied journals, *Springfield Republican*, in "Armed Japanese Intervention in Russia," *LD* 56 (Mar. 16, 1918), 14; *SFE*, Mar. 4, 1918, 18. Hearst, *NYA*, Mar. 8, 1918, 20; Hearst (quotation), Mar. 9, 1918, 18.

30. *NYT*, in "Armed Japanese Intervention in Russia," *LD* 56 (Mar. 16, 1918) 13; "Japan and Siberia," *NARWW* 1 (Mar. 9, 1918), 2; "Japan and Russia," *O* 118 (Mar. 20,1918): 440; Poindexter, *CR*, Mar. 26, 1918, 4063; "Japan's Proposed Entry into Siberia—An Invasion or a Rescue?," *CO* 64 (Apr. 1918): 233.

31. Unterberger, *Rise of Czechoslovakia*, 200, 212, 251.

32. Varied diplomats, in Unterberger, *Rise of Czechoslovakia*, 216, 217, 220; DRF to RL, May 29, 1918, *FR, Russia, 1918*, 2:180; JJP to NDB and PCM, June 14, 1918, in Woodward, *American Army*, 261; Reinsch to RL, May 30, 1918, *FR, 1918, Russia*, 2:181; June 5, 1918, 189; June 13, 1918, 206–7.

33. "Our Duty in Eastern Europe," *LD* 57 (June 1, 1918): 23; WHT, "Watchful Waiting Won't Save Russia," June 6, 1918, in Vivian, ed., *William*

Howard Taft, 66; TR, *Buffalo Evening News*, June 20, 1918, 3; TR to WHT, June 5, 1918, *LTR*, 8:1337; "To Stand by Russia," *NARWW* 1 (June 1, 1918): 12–13.

34. King, *CR*, June 10, 1918, 7557; Poindexter, *NYT*, June 9, 1918, 32; Lewis, *CR*, June 19, 1918, 7998; Sherman, *CR*, June 20, 1918, 8065.

35. "Intervention in Russia," *NR* 15 (June 1, 1918): 132; "How Not to Help Russia," *N* 106 (June 1, 1918): 640.

36. EMH diary, June 17, 1918, in Neu, *Colonel House*, 350.

37. Nash, *Hoover*, 3:467–68; Kennan, *Decision to Intervene*, 387.

38. Balfour to Reading, June 20, 1918, *PWW*, 48:379.

39. SWC, in Arthur Hugh Frazier to RL, July 2–3, 1918, *FR, Russia, 1918*, 2:241–45.

40. RL to WW, July 4, 1918, in Unterberger, *Rise of Czechoslovakia*, 237; WW on SWC, *DD*, July 9, 1918, 318.

41. Lansing, in Unterberger, *Rise of Czechoslovakia*, 236; Foglesong, *America's Secret War*, 160.

42. Wilson Siberian decision, *NYTr*, July 7, 1918, 1–2; memorandum to Allied governments embodying July 6, 1918, decision, July 17, 1918, *PWW*, 48:640–43.

43. RL, memo of White House Conference, July 6, in *FR, 1918, Russia*, 2:262; March, *Nation at War*, 126.

44. Motives, in Robert J. Maddox, *The Unknown War with Russia: Wilson's Siberian Intervention* (San Rafael, Calif.: Presidio, 1977), 53.

45. Carl J. Richard sees Wilson insufficiently suspicious of the Japanese; see Richard, *When the United States Invaded Russia: Woodrow Wilson's Siberian Disaster* (Lanham, Md.: Rowman & Littlefield, 2013), 27. Arthur Walworth claims the president's ambiguous and straddling statement made him vulnerable to accusations of meddling in Russia's internal affairs. At the same time, Wilson failed to provide liaison with Allied forces in Russia; see Walworth, *Woodrow Wilson: World Prophet*, 2nd ed. rev. (Baltimore: Penguin, 1965), 173. John Albert White notes that the term "consolidate their forces" could be interpreted as limiting activity to Vladivostok or extending it to the entire Volga front (White, *Siberian Intervention*, 231). David W. McFadden observes that Wilson made a strong argument as to why military intervention was unjustified, then explained why he deemed it necessary (McFadden, *Alternative Visions*, 357n146). Betty Miller Unterberger concedes that Wilson thought he could better restrain Japan by serving as part of an interventionist coalition than by remaining outside it. The number of troops he proposed for the rescue of 70,000 Czechs, however, was ludicrously small; see Unterberger, *America's Siberian Expedition, 1918–1920*:

A Study of National Policy (Durham, N.C.: Duke University Press, 1956), 88. Kennan finds Wilson conveying "the wildest and most alarmist image" of a threatened Siberia saved only by "the heroic Czechs." Official Washington permitted itself to be manipulated by the Czech Legion, Admiral Austin Knight (who commanded the U.S. Asiatic Fleet), the Japanese, French, the Russian Whites, and the Social Revolutionary leaders of the Siberian cooperative movement. Kennan asks: But to what end were the Czech forces to be consolidated? Was it to enable them to make their way to France? Or was it to enable them to participate in a Russian civil war (which, incidentally, at the time of Wilson's decision, they were already enthusiastically doing)? Furthermore, by failing to forewarn the French and British governments, Wilson had committed a flagrant discourtesy (Kennan, *Decision to Intervene*, 401–5).

46. Daniels, in Lansing memorandum, July 6, 1918, *FR, 1918, Russia*, 2:263–64.

47. Lloyd George, in Tooze, *Deluge*, 159–160; Woodward, *Trial by Friendship*, 180–81; Lloyd George to Reading, July 10, 1918, *PWW*, 48:587–88; on Japanese role, Edward M. Coffman, *The Hilt of the Sword: The Career of Peyton C. March* (Madison: University of Wisconsin Press, 1966), 97.

48. Ishii, in Polk to WW, July 24, 1918, *PWW*, 49:75–77.

49. EMH diary, July 25, 1918, *PWW*, 49:96; EMH, in Unterberger, *Rise of Czechoslovakia*, 274; WW to Daniels, Aug. 1, 1918, *PWW*, 49:149.

50. Ishii to RL, Aug. 2, 1918, *FR, 1918, Russia*, 2:324–25; Polk to WW, Aug. 3, 1918, *PWW*, 49:175–76.

51. Polk to John K. Caldwell, Aug. 2, 1918, *FR, 1918, Russia*, 2:323–24.

52. William S. Graves, *America's Siberian Adventure, 1918–1920* (New York: Jonathan Cape and Harrison Smith, 1931), 4; Baker resignation threat, in Beaver, *Baker*, 184.

53. Polk to Ishii and the press, Aug. 3, 1918, *FR, 1918, Russia*, 2:328–29; Kennan, *Decision to Intervene*, 402–3.

54. "Fiddling While Russia Burns," *LD* 58 (Aug. 10, 1918): 14; "Our First Step in Siberia," *LD* 58 (Aug. 17, 1918): 10; "New Forces in Russia," *LD* 58 (Aug. 24, 1918): 8; Lasch, *American Liberals*, 110–11; Brisbane, *NYA*, Aug. 8, 1918, 9; *NAR*, 208 (Sept. 1918): 340.

55. *N* 107 (Aug. 10, 1918): 135; *NR* 16 (Aug. 10, 1918): 30.

56. Historians find such orders irresponsible. Even at the time they were presented to Graves, writes Kennan, they were utterly inadequate, outdated, and, within two months, totally irrelevant (Kennan, *Decision to Intervene*, 414). By the time the United States took action, Unterberger notes, the Czechs had already been in possession of important points on the Trans-

Siberian Railway for some two months. Wilson had simply launched "one of the strangest adventures in American military history" (Unterberger, *America's Siberian Expedition*, 8, 88). Charles E. Neu sees Wilson only offering further confusion to a region where Bolshevik, Chinese, Czech, Japanese, and White Russian forces struggled for power (Neu, *Colonel House*, 351). Robert James Maddox observes that the very nature of the mission precluded real neutrality. Although General Graves made every effort to treat all factions impartially, his forces—which ended up guarding the lifeline between Vladivostok and Czech forces in the interior—functioned in practice as enemies of the Bolsheviks (Maddox, *Unknown War with Russia*, 62). Graves himself later stressed he had been given no information as to military or political circumstances within Russia (Graves, *America's Siberian Adventure*, 55). To John Albert White, Wilson's assurances concerning Russian self-governance "introduced one of the most gruesome and cruel episodes of the war, an episode which not only stimulated but which, in a very real sense, sustained the civil war in Eastern Siberia" (White, *Siberian Intervention*, 194). Christopher Lasch notes that the State Department openly acknowledged that the Czechs were not heading towards Vladivostok, their ostensible goal, but were in fact moving towards European Russia to aid kinsmen who were fighting there (Lasch, *American Liberals*, 109–10). Peter G. Filene points out that only a few thousand prisoners, mostly Austrians, were armed; they presented little danger (Filene, *Americans and Soviet Experiment*, 45). Carl J. Richard finds the stress on war prisoners a resort to "public war hysteria" (Richard, *When the United States Invaded Russia*, 21).

57. Graves, *America's Siberian Adventure*, 56.

58. March, *Nation at War*, 128; Japan, in Unterberger, *Rise of Czechoslovakia*, 312.

59. Lincoln, *Red Victory*, 187; Graves, in Unterberger, *America's Siberian Expedition*, 90.

60. Lane to William Marion Reddy, Sept. 13, 1918, in Lane and Wall, *Lane*, 293; Lodge, *CR*, Sept. 17, 1918, 10379; *NARWW*, 1 (Sept. 14, 1918): 10.

61. *N* 107 (Aug. 31, 1918): 213; *NR* 16 (Aug. 31, 1918): 120.

62. WW, in Lansing memorandum, Aug. 20, 1918, *FR, 1918, Russia*, 2:351; WW to RL, Sept. 2, 1918, *PWW*, 49:417.

63. THB to PCM, Sept. 3, 1918, *PWW*, 49:531–32; RL to Roland Sletor Morris, Sept. 9, 1918, *PWW*, 49:508; RL to Jusserand, Aug. 31, 1918, *FR, 1918, Russia*, 2:362; RL to WW, Sept. 24, 1918, *PWW*, 51:98.

64. Ufa government, in Ernest L. Harris to RL, Sept. 21, 1918, *FR, 1918, Russia*, 2:385; Harris to RL, Nov. 1, 1918, 420.

65. Roland S. Morris to RL, Sept. 23, 1918, *PWW*, 51:99–100; WW to RL, Sept. 26, 1918, *PWW*, 51:121; Lansing to Morris, Sept. 26, 1918, *FR, 1918, Russia*, 2:393; Jusserand to French Foreign Ministry, Sept. 28, 1918, *PWW*, 51:153.

66. Maddox, *Unknown War*, 65.

67. Graves, Nov. 22, 1918, in Gardner, *Safe for Democracy*, 195; NDB to WW, Nov. 27, 1918, *PWW*, 53:227–28.

68. Christopher Lasch stresses Wilson's own rationale, namely, that the Bolsheviks, working under Berlin's command, were arming German and Austrian prisoners of war to such a degree that they threatened all Siberia. Lasch muses that if it "seems preposterous that men in their right minds could have entertained such a illusion, the answer is that Wilson and his countrymen were not perhaps *in* their right minds" (Lasch, "American Intervention," 217–18, 223; emphasis Lasch's). Both John Albert White and Betty Miller Unterberger focus on the president's fear that the Japanese would seize the region outright, exercising total control. Once Tokyo indicated it would act independently, Washington's hand was forced, as it feared the closing of the Open Door (White, *Siberian Intervention*, 261–62; Unterberger, *America's Siberian Expedition*, 87–88). Arthur S. Link and George F. Kennan highlight the quixotic effort to rescue the Czech Legion. Kennan finds the Allies greatly exaggerating the possibility of German seizure of the war stores. Transporting this matériel to German forces in European Russia would have taken years, if not decades; see Link, *Woodrow Wilson: Revolution, War, and Peace* (Wheeling, Ill.: Harlan Davidson, 1979), 97; Kennan, *Russia and the West*, 101; Kennan, *Russia Leaves the War*, 285. John Milton Cooper Jr. sees Czech leader Thomas Masaryk, who met with Wilson on June 19, as the most influential voice reaching the president (Cooper, *Wilson*, 438–39). To Robert J. Maddox, Wilson envisioned reopening the eastern front as crucial, particularly in light of Germany's spring offensive (Maddox, *Unknown War*, 45–46). Davis and Trani focus on British and French pressure, which was most intense in the summer of 1918 (Davis and Trani, *First Cold War*, 148–49). William Appleman Williams stresses the desire to overthrow Bolshevism, noting in particular American rejection of Lenin's and Trotsky's overtures to Raymond Robins. In fact, Washington ended up being more ideologically dogmatic concerning overtures to hostile powers than was Moscow itself; see Williams, *American–Russian Relations*, chap. 6; Williams, "American Intervention in Russia, 1917–1920" (Part 2), *Studies on the Left* 4 (Winter 1964): 39–57. N. Gordon Levin Jr. finds the United States attempting to create a liberal and pro-Allied Russia in Siberia, in the process promoting an alternative to Russian Bolshevism and German

imperialism; see Levin, *Woodrow Wilson and World Politics: America's Response to War and Revolution* (New York: Oxford University Press, 1968), 87. Offering a more subtle interpretation, Foglesong, acknowledging Wilson's caution, highlights the discontent of U.S. diplomats with the radical agenda of the Social Revolutionaries, who dominated many local governments, and the desire for a military strong man that would "restore order" (Foglesong, *America's Secret War*, 177). Carl J. Richard finds in the expedition a classic example of "mission creep." He asserts that Wilson operated on what the president called "the shadow of a plan," one never fully formed or rationally thought out. Wilson acted under the illusion that Russians would rally around a foreign force (the Western powers) merely because it housed fellow Slavs (the Czechs) (Richard, *When the United States Invaded Russia*, 169–70). Much of the earlier literature is analyzed in Carl J. Richard, "'The Shadow of a Plan': The Rationale behind Wilson's 1918 Siberian Intervention," *Historian* 49 (Nov. 1986): 64–84.

69. Tooze, *Deluge*, 156–57; Richard, "Shadow," 77–78.

TEN   Wrestling with War Aims, 1917

1. EMH to WW, Nov. 14, 1917, *PWW*, 45:47; EMH, report, Dec. 15, 1917, *FR, 1917, Supp.* 2, 1:356.

2. Harbord, July 12, 1917, in Coffman, *War to End All Wars*, 130.

3. Jessup, *Root*, 2:325; Lane and Wall, *Lane*, 280.

4. Chamber of Commerce, *Washington Times*, June 6, 1917, 8; Lansing, *NYTr*, July 30, 1917, 2; Hale, *CR*, Oct. 5, 1917, 7827.

5. *SFE*, July 25, 1917, 20; WHP to Arthur W. Page, July 8, 1917, in Hendrick, *Page*, 2:292–93; WHP to Frank N. Doubleday, Nov. 9, 1917, in Hendrick, *Page*, 2:325.

6. David Lloyd George to WW, Sept. 3, 1917, *PWW*, 44:129; Smuts, Imperial War Cabinet, July 31, 1917, in Woodward, *Trial by Friendship*, 77 (emphasis Smuts).

7. JJP to NDB, July 9, 1917, *PWW*, 43:262.

8. Ambassador, in Neu, *Colonel House*, 339.

9. WW to EMH, Apr. 6, 1917, *PWW*, 41:553.

10. EMH diary, Apr. 28, 1917, *PWW*, 42:155–57.

11. Neu, *Colonel House*, 303.

12. EMH diary, Apr. 30, 1917, *PWW*, 42:172; Link, *Woodrow Wilson*, 78.

13. Memorandum by John Howard Whitehouse, Apr. 14, 1917, *PWW*, 42:65–66.

14. WW, war message, Apr. 2, 1917, *PWW*, 41:523.

15. Cecil, *NYT*, May 17, 1917, 1.

16. Lloyd George, *NYT*, June 30, 1917, 1, 2; *NYTr*, July 1, 1917, 3.

17. *NYA*, July 5, 1917, 16; July 24, 1917, 18. "Lloyd-George Looks Ahead," *NR* 11 (July 7, 1917), 260.

18. WW, war message, Apr. 2, 1917, *PWW*, 41:524–27.

19. WW, "Appeal to the American People," Apr. 15, 1917, *PWW*, 42:72; WW, Red Cross address, *NYT*, May 13, 1917, 2; "Message to the Provisional Government of Russia," May 22, 1917, *PWW*, 42:365–68.

20. *DD*, May 29, 1917, 159.

21. WW, Flag Day address, June 14, 1917, *PWW*, 42:499–504.

22. Woodward, *Trial By Friendship*, 59–60; Lloyd Ambrosius, *Wilsonian Statecraft: Theory and Practice of Liberal Internationalism during World War I* (Wilmington, Del.: Scholarly Resources, 1991), 103; WW, Oct. 26, 1916, *PWW*, 38:531–32.

23. André Chéradame, *The Pan-German Plot Unmasked* (New York: Charles Scribner's Sons, 1917); Chéradame, *The United States and Pangermanism* (New York: American Rights League, 1917); Chéradame, *Pan-Germany: The Disease and Cure* (Boston: Atlantic Monthly Press, 1917).

24. *How War Came to America* (pamphlet) (Washington, D.C.: Committee on Public Information, 1917), 1–29.

25. EMH diary, June 13, 1917, EMHP; EMH to WW, June 14, 1917, in Seymour, *Intimate Papers of Colonel House*, 3:137; press reaction, "What the United States Is Fighting For," *CO* 63 (July 1917): 6–7; *NYTr*, June 15, 1918, 8.

26. Viereck, "Wilson vs. Wilson," *VTAW* 6 (June 27, 1917): 351; Bourne, "The Collapse of American Strategy," in Carl Resek, ed., *The World of Randolph Bourne* (New York: E. P. Dutton, 1965), 31; "The Fighting Hope," *NR* 11 (June 23, 1917): 199.

27. Cooper, *Wilson*, 417; WW to EMH, July 21, 1917, *PWW*, 43:238 (emphasis Wilson's).

28. Hindenburg, in David L. Stevenson, *1917: War, Peace, and Revolution* (New York: Oxford University Press, 2017), 154; Bethmann Hollweg, *NYT*, May 16, 1917, 2.

29. Reichstag resolution, Michaelis, *NYT*, July 21, 1917, 1–2.

30. Lloyd George, *NYTr*, July 22, 1917, 1.

31. Lewis, *CR*, July 23, 1917, 5384; King, July 23, 1917, 5386; McCumber, Aug. 13, 1917, 6004.

32. "Unconditional Surrender: The Only Way," *NAR*, 206 (August 1917), 179, 181; *N* 105 (Aug. 30, 1917), 211; New York *World*, in *Baltimore Sun*, August 1, 1917, 5.

33. AUAM, *NYT*, July 30, 1917, 2; *VTAW* 6 (Aug. 1, 1917), 442; *NYA*, July 25, 1917, 18; Hearst, *NYA*, July 27, 1917, 16.

34. *CR*: Borah, July 26, 1917, 5495–97; London, Aug. 4, 1917, 5814; La Follette, Aug. 11, 1917, 5956–57; Sherman, Aug. 15, 1917, 6039–40.

35. "The Center of Strategy," *NR* 12 (Aug. 4, 1917): 4.

36. Lewis, Wilson, *NYT*, Aug. 7, 1917, 1; Wilson, address to officers of the Atlantic Fleet, Aug. 11, 1917, *PWW*, 43:429.

37. Papal proposal, in WHP to RL, Aug. 15, 1917, *PWW*, 43:482–85.

38. John L. Snell, "Benedict XV, Wilson, Michaelis, and German Socialism," *Catholic Historical Review* 37 (July 1951): 157.

39. Michaelis, *NYT*, Aug. 23, 1917, 1–2; German and Austrian official responses, *Brooklyn Eagle*, Sept. 22, 1917, 2; monarchs, *NYT*, Sept. 22, 1917, 1.

40. Balfour, in WHP to WW, Aug. 21, 1917, *PWW*, 44:24; Lloyd George, *NYT*, Aug. 17, 1917, 1; Campon, in William Graves Sharp to RL, Aug. 21, 1917, *PWW*, 44:25; Clemenceau, Sonnino, in Stevenson, *1917*, 253–54; Pašić, in Sharp to Lansing, Aug. 27, 1917, *FR, 1917, Supp.* 2: 1:180; Masaryk, Beneš, in Unterberger, *Rise of Czechoslovakia*, 55.

41. Lewis, *NYT*, Aug. 15, 1917, 2; Smith, Gronna, *NYA*, Aug. 17, 1917, 2.

42. Williams, King, Ashurst, *NYT*, Aug. 15, 1917, 2; Shields, *NYA*, Aug. 17, 1917, 1.

43. Editorial, *NYA*, Aug. 16, 1917, 18; Aug. 20, 1917, 16.

44. Editorial, *NYT*, Aug. 15, 1917, 8; general press opinion, "The Peace-Vision of the Vatican," *LD* 55 (Aug. 25, 1917): 11.

45. Socialist and German American voices, *LD* 55 (Aug. 25, 1917): 10–11; Russell, *NYT*, Aug. 15, 1917, 1; *VTAW* 7 (Aug. 29, 1917), 67.

46. Strunsky, "The Pope Acts," *N* 105 (Aug. 16, 1917): 166; *NR* 12 (Aug. 18, 1917): 57.

47. *America*, in "The Church View of the Pope's Peace Plea," *LD* 15 (Sept. 8, 1917): 32; "A Catholic on the Papal Note of Peace," *O* 117 (Sept. 19, 1917): 80.

48. EMH to WW, Aug. 15, 1917, *PWW*, 43:471.

49. WW to EMH, Aug. 16, 1917, *PWW*, 43:488; EMH to WW, Aug. 17, 1917, *PWW*, 43:508; House diary, Aug. 18, 1917, *PWW*, 43:521.

50. RL, memorandum, Aug. 19, 1917, *PWW*, 44:19; RL to WW, Aug. 20, 1917, *PWW*, 43:524.

51. WW to Pope Benedict XV, Aug. 27, 1917, *PWW*, 44:57–59.

52. Link, *Woodrow Wilson*, 79–80.

53. "'No Peace with Prussian Autocracy,'" *LD* 55 (Sept. 8, 1917): 11–13; New York *World*, in St. *Louis Post-Dispatch*, Aug. 29, 1917, 2; EMH to WW,

Sept. 4, 1917, *PWW*, 44:149; Page, in EMH to WW, Oct. 16, 1917, *PWW*, 44:390–91; *NYTr*, Aug. 30, 1917, 8.

54. *SFE*, July 6, 1917, 16; Sept. 24, 1917, 16.

55. *ATR*, Sept. 8, 1917, 1; London, *NYT*, Sept. 11, 1917, 3.

56. Ridder, in EMH, Sept. 19, 1917, EMHP; "The President's Reply to the Pope," *I&E* 7 (Sept. 8, 1917): 154–55. Hale, "The President and the German People," *VTAW* 7 (Sept. 12, 1917): 100; Viereck, "Put Yourself in His Place," 106.

57. Some historians are positive. Lloyd C. Gardner finds Wilson's reply masterful. The president had managed to leave the impression that, now more than ever, only the United States stood above the passions of the moment, just as it already stood above the Allies in the nature of its war aims (Gardner, *Safe for Democracy*, 145). Biographer John Milton Cooper Jr. observes that by walking a fine line between military resolve and generous peace terms, Wilson was establishing himself as the Allies' moral and ideological leader (Cooper, *Wilson*, 418).

Other scholars find drawbacks. David Stevenson notes Wilson's vagueness as to how Germany should behave (Stevenson, *1917*, 254). Lloyd E. Ambrosius perceives Wilson's reply as an example of his continued failure to coordinate ends and means. The president simply assumed that sheer words from Washington could exercise a decisive influence over events in Europe. America's righteous cause would automatically triumph in the wake of military victory; see Ambrosius, *Wilsonian Statecraft*, 105–6; Ambrosius, *Woodrow Wilson and the American Diplomatic Tradition: The Treaty Fight in Perspective* (New York: Cambridge University Press, 1987), 34.

58. Michaelis, in Marshall Langhorne to RL, Sept. 28, 1917, *FR, 1917, Supp. 2*, 1:215.

59. Cecil, Grey, in Seymour, *Intimate Papers of Colonel House*, 3:165.

60. Neu, *Colonel House*, 322.

61. WW, address to the American Federation of Labor, Nov. 12, 1917, *PWW*, 45:12–14.

62. EMH to WW, Nov. 30, 1917, *FR, 1917, Supp.* 2, 1:328; WW to EMH, Dec. 1, 1917, 331.

63. Roosevelt, *Foes of Our Own Household*, in *Works*, 19:10–11.

64. Lansdowne, *NYT*, Nov. 30, 1917, 1–2.

65. Asquith, *NYT*, Dec. 12, 1917, 1; Cecil and Lloyd George, in David R. Woodward, "The Origin and Intent of David Lloyd George's January 5 War Aims Speech," *Historian* 34 (Nov. 1971): 27–28; Law, *Manchester Guardian*, Dec. 1, 1918, 7–8; Northcliffe, in "Lord Lansdowne's Cry of Despair," *LD* 55 (Dec. 15, 1917): 14.

66. TR, *New York Sun*, Dec. 3, 1917, 3; WHT and editorial, 6.

67. *VTAW* 8 (Feb. 13, 1918): 31; Baker, in Thompson, *Reformers and War*, 193; "The President's Message: Peace by Victory," *O* 117 (Dec. 12, 1917): 593.

68. Wilson, annual message, Dec. 4, 1917, *PWW*, 45:197, 200.

69. Lansing, in Unterberger, *Rise of Czechoslovakia*, 52; House to WW, Nov. 28, 1917, *PWW*, 45:151.

70. WW, war message, Apr. 2, 1917, *PWW*, 41:525–26.

71. TR, *NYT*, Nov. 17, 1917, 1; TR, *NYT*, Dec. 9, 1917, 7; "Declare War on Austria!," *O* 117 (Nov. 14, 1917), 408; general observation of public, Lewis, Stone, *NYT*, Nov. 27, 1917, 1, 24; RL to WW, *FR-LP*, Nov. 20, 1917, 2:61.

72. Unterberger, *Rise of Czechoslovakia*, 65.

73. Clark, *NYT*, Dec. 5, 1917, 2; Flood, *CR*, Dec. 7, 1917, 85–86; Miller, *CR*, Dec. 6, 1917, 51; Lodge, *CR*, Dec. 7, 1917, 64–65.

74. Flood, *CR*, Dec. 6, 1917, 52.

75. Senate vote, *CR*, Dec. 7, 1917, 67–68; House vote, 99–100; La Follette, 68; London, 91; Quin, 98.

76. Unterberger, *Rise of Czechoslovakia*, 68.

77. Wilson, annual message, Dec. 4, 1917, *PWW*, 45:196–202.

78. Popular reaction, *NYT*, Dec. 5, 1917, 2; Roosevelt, *Chicago Tribune*, Dec. 6, 1917, 6; *NYA*, Dec. 6, 1917, 18; Kopelin, in "Our War-Aims—Victory and Justice," *LD* 55 (Dec. 15, 1917): 5.

79. *CO* 64 (Jan. 1918): 1; Lansdowne, in "Our War-Aims—Victory and Justice," *LD* 55 (Dec. 15, 1917): 6; EMH to WW, Dec. 7, 1917, *PWW*, 45:232; Czernin, German press, in *NR* 13 (Dec. 15, 1917): 160.

80. *NR* 13 (Dec. 15, 1917): 159.

81. Stevenson, *1917*, 270.

ELEVEN   Wilson's Peace Offensive, 1918

1. "Are We Losing the War?," *NAR* 206 (Dec. 1917): 832; McCumber, *CR*, Jan. 16, 1917, 879; Lane and Northcliffe, in Franklin K. Lane, Feb. 16, 1918, in Lane and Wall, *Lane*, 270; Baker, *Wilson*, 8:27.

2. Walling report, in Samuel Gompers to WW, Feb. 9, 1918, *PWW*, 46:310–13; RL to WW, Feb. 15, 1918, *PWW*, 46:349–50.

3. WW to EMH, Sept. 2, 1917, *PWW*, 44:120–21; EMH to WW, Sept. 4, 1917, *PWW*, 44:149; Neu, *Colonel House*, 314; RL, "Confidential Memorandum on Preparatory Work for the Peace Conference," Sept. 19, 1917, *PWW*, 44:217–19.

4. Shotwell, in Lawrence E. Gelfand, *The Inquiry: American Preparations for Peace, 1917–1919* (New Haven, Conn.: Yale University Press, 1963), 41.

5. S. E. Mezes to RL, Nov. 9, 1917, *FR, Paris Peace Conference, 1919*, 1:15–17; WW to S. E. Mezes, Nov. 12, 1917, *PWW*, 45:17.

6. Gelfand, *Inquiry*, 67.

7. EMH diary, Dec. 18, 1917, *PWW*, 45:323.

8. The Inquiry, "The Present Situation: The War and Peace Terms It Suggests," Jan. 4, 1918, *PWW*, 45:459–62 (emphasis original authors).

9. Lloyd George speech, *Times* of London, Jan. 7, 1918, 7–8.

10. Labor memorandum, in Arno J. Mayer, *Political Origins of the New Diplomacy* (New Haven, Conn.: Yale University Press, 1959), 316–21. Woodward, "Origin and Intent," 36; Haig, in ibid., 38–39; Hertling, *Times* of London, Jan. 26, 1918, 18.

11. Bryan, *Commoner* 13 (Jan. 1918): 1; WHT, "International Equity," Jan. 10, 1918, in Vivian, ed., *William Howard Taft*, 26; "War Aims That Aim at Peace," *N* 106 (Jan. 10, 1918): 30; Hillquit, *NYT*, Jan. 7, 1918, 2; *VTAW* 7 (Jan. 16, 1918): 414.

12. *NYA*, Jan. 7, 1918, 24; *La Follette's Magazine* 10 (Jan. 1918): 4; "Lloyd George's Dismemberment Speech," *I&E* 8 (Jan. 12, 1918): 26–27.

13. EMH diary, Jan. 9, 1918, *PWW*, 45:556–57.

14. WW to RL, Mar. 12, 1918, *PWW*, 46:606.

15. Gelfand, *Inquiry*, 141–43; WW, in *DD*, Dec. 4, 1917, 246.

16. Inquiry memorandum, Jan. 4, 1918, *PWW*, 45:469. See also Gelfand, *Inquiry*, 142–43.

17. Victor S. Mamatey, *The United States and East Central Europe, 1914–1918: A Study in Wilsonian Diplomacy and Propaganda* (Princeton, N.J.: Princeton University Press, 1957), 180; Gelfand, *Inquiry*, 143.

18. Gelfand, *Inquiry*, 146.

19. WW, address to the League to Enforce Peace, May 27, 1916, *PWW*, 37:113–16; Senate address, Jan. 22, 1917, *PWW*, 40:535; Jules Jusserand to French Foreign Ministry, Mar. 7, 1917, *PWW*, 41:356; WW views, in Frank L. Polk to Jules Jusserand, Aug. 3, 1917, *PWW*, 44:360; William E. Rappard, memorandum, Nov. 1, 1917, *PWW*, 44:484–90; Knock, *To End All Wars*, 127. For Wilson's entire Fourteen Points address, see address to a joint session of Congress, Jan. 8, 1918, *PWW*, 45:534–39.

20. Link, *Woodrow Wilson: Revolution, War, and Peace*, 83; WW, address to Congress, Jan. 8, 1918, *PWW*, 45:539.

21. General reaction (including Cannon), *NYT*, Jan. 9, 1918, 1, 2; Lewis, *NYA*, Jan. 9, 1918, 3; Harding, *St. Louis Globe-Democrat*, Jan. 9, 1918, 1;

HCL to William Sturgis Bigelow, Jan. 10, 1918, HCLP; John A. Garraty, *Henry Cabot Lodge: A Biography* (New York: Knopf, 1953), 340; Borah, *CR*, Jan. 9, 1918, 705, and *Washington Post*, Jan. 10, 1918, 2.

22. Smoot, *NYT*, Jan. 9, 1918, 2; La Follette, "Peace Terms," *La Follette's Magazine* 10 (Jan. 1918): 4.

23. Britten, *NYA*, Jan. 9, 1918, 3; Mason, *CR*, Feb. 7, 1918, 1828–30.

24. McClure letter, *NYT*, Jan. 11, 1918, 14; Woman's Peace Party, *NYT*, Jan. 13, 1918, 18; "The President's World Leadership," *N* 106 (Jan. 17, 1918): 54; Debs, in Kennedy, *Over Here*, 354; Eastman, in Kazin, *War against War*, 248.

25. London, *Chicago Tribune*, Jan. 12, 1918, 3; Nearing, in "America's Peace Ultimatum," *LD* 56 (Jan. 19, 1918): 11.

26. "The President's Great Address," *O* 118 (Jan. 16, 1918): 87; *NYTr*, Jan. 9, 1918, 12; *NARWW* 1 (Jan. 12, 1918): 1; TR, *Chicago Tribune*, Jan. 10, 1918, 2.

27. Creel, *How We Advertised America*, 289, 377; Robins on Lenin in DRF to RL, Jan. 12, 1918, *FR, 1918, Russia*, 1:426; *Izvestia*, in *NYT*, Jan. 14, 1917, 3.

28. Viereck, "Mr. Wilson's Fourteen Theses," *VTAW* 7 (Jan. 23, 1918): 430–31; *Gaelic American*, in Cuddy, "Irish-America," 156.

29. Lansing, in Ambrosius, *Wilsonian Statecraft*, 112; Ferrell, *Woodrow Wilson and World War I*, 263n14; Gelfand, *Inquiry*, 152; RL to WW, Jan. 10, 1918, in Lansing, *War Memoirs*, 261.

30. Beck, *NYT*, Mar. 3, 1918, 16.

31. Balfour, *NYT*, Jan. 11, 1918, 2; Lloyd George, in Sir Eric Drummond to Cecil Spring Rice, Jan. 12, 1918, *PWW*, 45:577; Lloyd George, *FR, 1918, Supp. 1*, 1:78; *Times* of London, Jan. 10, 1918, 7.

32. JJP to NDB, Jan. 14, 1918, *PWW*, 45:595; William G. Sharp to RL, Jan. 10, 1918, *FR, 1918, Supp. 1*, 1:19; Pichon, in Ambrosius, *Wilsonian Statecraft*, 111; Clemenceau, in Mayer, *Political Origins*, 384; Italy, in Thomas Nelson Page to RL, Jan. 18, 1918, *FR, 1918, Supp. 1*, 1:26; Czechs and Slovaks, in Unterberger, *Rise of Czechoslovakia*, 96–97, and Mamatey, *United States and East Central Europe*, 213–19.

33. German reaction, in Seymour, *Intimate Papers of Colonel House*, 3:347; *Kölnische Zeitung*, in John W. Garrett to RL, Jan. 11, 1918, *FR, 1918, Supp. 1*, 1:24.

34. Hertling, in John W. Garrett to Lansing, Jan. 24, 1918, FR, 1918, Supp. 1, 1:39–42.

35. Carl W. Ackerman to EMH, Feb. 4, 1918, *PWW*, 46:556.

36. Czernin, in Hugh Wilson to RL, Jan. 30, 1918, *FR, 1918, Supp. 1*, 1:54–59.

37. EMH diary, Jan. 29, 1918, *PWW*, 46:167; Mamatey, *United States and East Central Europe*, 195.

38. Arthur S. Link sees an appeal for peace "in the name of all that was high and holy in the Christian democratic tradition in order to give western civilization a second chance"; see Link, "Woodrow Wilson and Peace Moves," in *The Higher Realism of Woodrow Wilson and Other Essays* (Nashville: Vanderbilt University Press, 1971), 108. In the words of historian John Milton Cooper Jr., the president was putting "flesh on the skeleton of peace without victory." Wilson's agenda "could end the war without him and millions of others having to tread further down this grim and passion-racked path of waging war" (Cooper, *Wilson*, 424).

Thomas A. Bailey counters that the points were pitched too high. Germany would, he argues, have been defeated just as rapidly had Wilson been clearer, more reasonable, and more realistic. The points' vagueness led to mindless sloganeering, their meaning differing with each reader. The sheer loftiness was bound to create feelings of disillusionment among Wilson's own people, deception among the Allies, and betrayal among the Germans. Better to have had fewer points and have them more clearly defined. Moreover, people throughout the world thought the president was speaking for all the Allies: "The senior partner is ordinarily presumed to speak for the entire firm." The president should have merely restated Lloyd George's more idealistic aims; see Bailey, *Woodrow Wilson and the Lost Peace* (New York: Macmillan, 1945), 29–31; quotation at 30. Thomas Fleming calls Wilson's comments concerning Russia "rhetoric from never-never land," his comments concerning any unity of Allied policy a measure of his desperation (Fleming, *Illusion of Victory*, 177–78). Richard Striner claims that Wilson falsely assumed that such intermingled nationalities as those living in the Balkans or the Austro-Hungarian Empire could "be harmonized into perfectly neat, straightforward, and homogeneous politics, notwithstanding the sorts of divisions that result from conflicting religious or ethnic claims to the same land. The pages of history are bloody with assertions of rival nationality, assertions that could never be reconciled (in some cases) without carnage" (Striner, *Wilson*, 136).

39. WW to RL, Feb. 2, 1918, *PWW*, 46:234; WHP, memorandum, Feb. 10, 1918, in Hendrick, *Page*, 2:352–53; EMH to WW, Feb. 3, 1918, *PWW*, 46:221; WW to RL, Feb. 4, 1918, *PWW*, 46:233.

40. WW, address to joint session of Congress, Feb. 11, 1918, *PWW*, 46:318–24.

41. House, in Mamatey, *United States and East Central Europe*, 226n190; members of Congress, *NYT*, Feb. 12, 1918, 1–2; *NYA*, Feb. 12, 1918, 2.

42. New York *World*, other press response, in *NYA*, Feb. 12, 1918, 3; *NR* 14 (Feb. 16, 1918): 67; *I&E* 8 (Feb. 23, 1918): 120.

43. Beck, *NYT*, Mar. 3, 1918, 16; "Town Meeting Diplomacy," *NAR* 207 (February 1918): 182.

44. British press, *N* 106 (Feb. 21, 1918): 222; French press, in William G. Sharp, Feb. 14, 1918, *FR, 1918, Supp. 1*, 1:114; Italian press, in Thomas Nelson Page to RL, Feb. 13, 1918, *FR, 1918, Supp. 1*, 1:113; Lansdowne, *NYA*, Mar. 6, 1918, 22; Lloyd George and Smuts, in Woodward, *Trial by Friendship*, 154.

45. German reaction, in James McNally to RL, Feb. 19, 1918, *FR, 1918, Supp. 1*, 1:130; Hertling, in John W. Garrett to RL, Feb. 25, 1918, *FR, 1918, Supp. 1*, 1:135–38, and *PWW*, 46:498n1.

46. Slayden, Hamilton, *NYT*, Feb. 27, 1918, 2.

47. Lewis, Graham, *NYT*, Feb. 27, 1918, 2; WHT, "The Debate Should End," Feb. 28, 1918, in Vivian, ed., *William Howard Taft*, 39; *NARWW* 1 (Mar. 2, 1918): 1; Balfour, *NYTr*, Feb. 28, 1918, 1.

48. Throntveit, *Power without Victory*, 258; Margaret MacMillan, *Paris 1919: Six Months That Changed the World* (New York: Random House, 2001), 12.

49. Charles, in Alfonso XIII to WW, Feb. 25, 1918, *PWW*, 46:442; WW to Alfonso XIII, Feb. 28, 1918, *PWW*, 46:486–87; Czernin, *NYT*, Apr. 3, 1918, 3.

50. Mitchell Pirie Briggs, *George D. Herron and the European Settlement* (Stanford, Calif.: Stanford University Press, 1932), 78; Hugh Wilson to RL, Feb. 8, 1918, *FR, 1918, Supp. 1*, 1:82–105; Balfour to EMH, Feb. 27, 1918, *PWW*, 46:483.

51. Charles letter, *NYT*, Apr. 12, 1918, 1, 3.

52. Herron to Hugh Wilson, Apr. 13, 1918, in Unterberger, *Rise of Czechoslovakia*, 118; WW, in Wiseman to Drummond, May 30, 1918, *PWW*, 48:205; Lansing note, Apr. 12, 1918, in Lansing, *War Memoirs*, 265.

53. WW, Baltimore address, Apr. 6, 1918, *PWW*, 47:267–70.

54. Link, *Woodrow Wilson: Revolution, War, and Peace*, 85–86; Schwabe, *Woodrow Wilson, Revolutionary Germany, and Peacemaking*, 19, 417n52.

55. Press, in "We Accept the Kaiser's Challenge," *LD 57* (Apr. 20, 1918): 15; *NARWW* 1 (Apr. 13, 1918), 4; London, in WHP to RL, Apr. 10, 1918, *FR, 1918, Supp. 1*, 1:205; Paris, in William G. Sharp to RL, Apr. 8, 1918, 204; Berlin, in John W. Garrett to WW, Apr. 10, 1918, 206–9; Balfour, in Lord Reading to WW, Apr. 13, 1918, *PWW*, 47:334–35.

56. WW, remarks to foreign correspondents, Apr. 8, 1918, *PWW*, 47:287–88.

57. WW, Red Cross speech, May 18, 1918, *PWW*, 48:53–54.

58. RL, *NYT*, May 30, 1918, 3; William Wiseman to Eric Drummond, May 30, 1918, *PWW*, 48:206; WW to RL, June 26, 1918, *PWW*, 48:435.

59. WW, Mount Vernon address, July 4, 1918, *PWW*, 48:516–17.

60. *NYA*, July 17, 1918, 18; TR, *NYTr*, July 5, 1918, 14; "The President at Mount Vernon," *N* 107 (July 13, 1918): 31.

61. "The President Defines International Law," *O* 119 (July 17, 1918): 444; "The President Betters His Best," *NARWW* 1 (July 13, 1918): 3; "The President Wants a New Deal," *VTAW* 8 (July 17, 1918): 382.

62. Lloyd George, *NYT*, July 6, 1918, 1; German press, in Pleasant A. Stovell to RL, July 12, 1918, *FR, 1918, Supp. 1*, 1:287.

63. Hertling, *NYT*, July 14, 1918, 1, and John W. Garrett to RL, July 12, 1918, *FR, 1918, Supp. 1*, 1:284–85; High Command, July 2–3, 1918, in Harry R. Rudin, *Armistice 1918* (New Haven, Conn.: Yale University Press, 1944), 10.

64. Burian, in *NYT*, July 17, 1918, 1, 4; *N* 107 (July 20, 1918): 56.

65. Cooper, *Wilson*, 441; Striner, *Wilson*, 154; Ambrosius, *Woodrow Wilson and American Diplomatic Tradition*, 43.

TWELVE The Matter of Preparation

1. Ferrell, *Woodrow Wilson and World War I*, 24.

2. NDB, in Smythe, *Pershing*, 6–7; Cooper, *Wilson*, 396.

3. Harvey, in Cramer, *Newton D. Baker*, 132.

4. War College, in Coffman, *March*, 41; Martin, in Frederick Palmer, *Newton D. Baker: America at War* (New York: Dodd, Mead, 1931),1:120; 2:152.

5. Baker, in David F. Trask, *The AEF and Coalition Warmaking, 1917–1918* (Lawrence: University Press of Kansas, 1993), 12.

6. Woodward, *American Army*, 136, 259; Palmer, cited at 150; Coffman, *War to End All Wars*, 343.

7. Harbord, in Smythe, *Pershing*, 10.

8. Lafayette statement, in March, *Nation at War*, 221; Harbord, Pétain, in Harbord, *Leaves*, 85, 47; Frank E. Vandiver, *Black Jack: The Life and Times of John J. Pershing* (College Station: Texas A&M University Press, 1977), 2:718.

9. General staff, in Stevenson, *1917*, 389.

10. Alan R. Millett, "Over Where? The AEF and the American Strategy for Victory, 1917–1918," in *Against All Enemies: Interpretations of American*

Military History from Colonial Times to the Present, ed. Kenneth J. Hagen and William R. Roberts (Westport, Conn.: Greenwood, 1986), 239.

11. THB to NDB, May 25, 1917, *PWW*, 42:409–10; Robertson, in Woodward, *American Army*, 90.

12. Harbord, *Leaves*, 122; WW, in Daniels, *Wilson Era*, 2:163.

13. Pershing, *My Experiences*, 1:255; EMH, report, Dec. 15, 1917, *FR, 1917, Supp. 2*, 1:357; NDB to JJP, Dec. 18, 1917, in Woodward, *American Army*, 136; Poincaré to WW, Dec. 28, 1917, *PWW*, 45:372; WW to Poincaré, Jan. 8, 1918, *PWW*, 45:539.

14. Wood, in J. Lee Thompson, *Never Call Retreat: Theodore Roosevelt and the Great War* (New York: Palgrave Macmillan, 2013), 232.

15. Censorship, in Caitlin Marie Thérèse Jeffrey, "Journey through Unfamiliar Territory: American Reporters and the First World War" (PhD diss., University of California, Irvine, 2007), 42–43.

16. Crozier, *New York Times*, Sept. 29, 1917, 1; TR, *Chicago Tribune*, Sept. 27, 1917, 2; *New York Sun*, Dec. 18, 1917, 5; *Indianapolis Star*, Dec. 28, 1917, 6.

17. NDB, medical corps, in Livermore, *Woodrow Wilson and the War Congress*, 73; WW, annual message, Dec. 4, 1917, *PWW*, 45:195; Gorgas, *NYT*, Dec. 19, 1917, 1.

18. Weeks, *CR*, Apr. 9, 1917, 459; Madden, 497.

19. Miller, in *Collyer* (Kan.) *Advance*, Dec. 27, 1917, 1; Dale, in *Randolph* (Vt.) *Herald and News*, Dec. 27, 1917, 7; McCormick, in *Chicago Tribune*, Dec. 19, 1917, 3.

20. Crozier, *NYT*, Dec. 14, 1917, 1; Sharpe, in Beaver, *Baker*, 90; Greble, *Chicago Tribune*, Dec. 29, 1917, 1–2, and *Rochester Democrat and Chronicle*, Dec. 29, 1917, 1.

21. Senate vote, *CR*, Jan. 17, 1918, 936; New York *World*, in *SFE*, Jan. 18, 1918, 16; Frank Cobb to WW, Jan. 17, 1918, 8, *PWW*, 46:16; EMH diary, Jan. 17, 1918, *PWW*, 46:23; WW to Bernard Baruch, Jan. 19, 1918, *PWW*, 46:36; WW statement, *NYT*, Jan. 19, 1918, 1.

22. Slogan, in Jonathan Daniels, *The End of Innocence* (Philadelphia: Lippincott, 1954), 249; EMH diary, Jan. 9, 1918, *PWW*, 46:556; TR, *The Great Adventure*, in *Works*, 19:285; press views and analysis, in Livermore, *Woodrow Wilson and the War Congress*, 81; NDB resignation, in *DD*, Jan. 23, 1918, 165.

23. Livermore, *Woodrow Wilson and the War Congress*, 81; NDB, *NYT*, Jan. 11, 1918, 1, 3.

24. Chamberlain, *La Crosse* (Wis.) *Tribune*, Jan. 4, 1918, 1; *CR*, Jan. 22, 1918, 1146; WW to George E. Chamberlain, Jan. 11, 1918, *PWW*, 45:566.

25. Chamberlain, *NYT*, Jan. 20, 1918, 1, 14; public reaction, "Our Part in the War and the Way We Are Playing It," *CO* 64 (March 1918): 156; WW, press release, Jan. 21, 1918, *PWW*, 46:55–56; *DD*, Jan. 22, 1918, 271–72; economic general staff, Harries, *Last Days of Innocence*, 202.

26. Lodge, *CR*, Jan. 21, 1918, 1087–88; Penrose, 1090–91.

27. Hitchcock, *CR*, Feb. 4, 1918, 1607, 1615.

28. Williams, *CR*, Feb. 4, 1918, 1615; Reed, 1618; James, Feb. 14, 1918, 2103.

29. Glass, *CR*, Feb. 7, 1918, 1821; Mason, 1828.

30. Creel, *NYT*, Apr. 9, 1918, 13; *NYA*, Jan. 24, 1918, 18; *NR* 13 (Jan. 26, 1918), 357; "The President, the Congress, and the Country," *O* 118 (Feb. 6, 1918): 204; TR, in Livermore, *Woodrow Wilson and the War Congress*, 92.

31. *NYT*, Jan. 26, 1918, 12; *NARWW* 1 (Feb. 9, 1918): 2; WHT, "Truth Found between Extremes," Jan. 31, 1918, in Vivian, ed., *William Howard Taft*, 31–32.

32. Chamberlain, Kirby, *CR*, Jan. 24, 1918, 1196–1211.

33. NDB, *NYT*, January 29, 1918, 1–2, 8–10, and Beaver, *Baker*, 103; Chamberlain, in Palmer, *Baker*, 2:80.

34. TR, *NYTr*, Feb. 2, 1918, 4; TR to Kermit Roosevelt, Feb. 18, 1918, *LTR*, 8:1285; Hitchcock, *CR*, Feb. 4, 1918, 1607; Weeks, Wadsworth, *NYT*, Feb. 7, 1918, 1.

35. *NYA*, Apr. 24, 1918, 24; Patton, in Smythe, *Pershing*, 94.

36. Livermore, *Woodrow Wilson and the War Congress*, 100–101.

37. Woodward, *American Army*, 141; Villard, "The Investigation of the War Department," *N* 105 (Dec. 20, 1917): 680; Beaver, *Baker*, 108–9.

38. PCM, in Smythe, *Pershing*, 90; Baruch, in Coffman, *March*, 151; "A Good Appointment," *NARWW* 1 (Feb. 9, 1918): 7.

39. NDB, in Trask, *AEF and Coalition Warmaking*, 27; Sam Browne belt, in Brian Neumann, "A Question of Authority," *Journal of Military History* 73 (Oct. 2009): 1138–39.

40. Sherman, *CR*, Apr. 23, 1918, 5485, 5491; Brandegee, Apr. 25, 1918, 5607–8.

41. Harding, *CR*, Apr. 29, 1918, 5747; Brandegee, 5764; Senate vote, 5766; Harding, *NYT*, Aug. 12, 1917, magazine section, 1; "A Real Army— To Be or Not To Be," *NARWW* 1 (May 11, 1918): 2; House vote, *NYT*, May 15, 1918, 1.

42. NDB, *NYT*, June 18, 1917, 8; Lane, *Los Angeles Times*, Oct. 7, 1917, 5; Mitchell, in Harries and Harries, *Last Days of Innocence*, 200–201.

43. Gutzon Borglum to Joseph P. Tumulty, Nov. 14, 1917, *PWW*, 45:69–70; NDB to WW, Jan. 2, 1918, *PWW*, 45:426–27; WW to Borglum, Jan. 2, 1918, *PWW*, 45:427.

44. WW to NDB, Feb. 1, 1918, *PWW*, 46:206; NDB in Beaver, *Baker*, 163.

45. NDB, *Washington Post*, Feb. 22, 1918, 3; Wood, *NYT*, Mar. 26, 1918, 4.

46. *NYT*, Mar. 27, 1918, 1; Lodge, *CR*, Mar. 26, 1918, 4058; New, 4065; Overman, 4062.

47. *NYT*, Apr. 11, 1918, 1, 11.

48. WW to Borglum, Apr. 15, 1918, *PWW*, 47:344.

49. Borglum, *NYT*, Apr. 29, 1918, 13. Hitchcock, Knox, Poindexter, *CR*, May 2, 1918, 5929; Brandegee, 5925; Brandegee quotation, Apr. 29, 1918, 5741; King, May 2, 1918, 5929. WW to Joseph Tumulty, May 6, 1918, *PWW*, 47:588; NDB in Beaver, *Baker*, 164–65.

50. EMH to WW, May 9, 1918, *PWW*, 47:584; WW to Winthrop M. Daniels, Feb. 4, 1918, *PWW*, 46:238.

51. Press and Lodge, in Livermore, *Woodrow Wilson and the War Congress*, 132–33; Merlo J. Pusey, *Charles Evans Hughes* (New York: Macmillan, 1952), 1:375.

52. *NYTr*, Nov. 1, 1918, 1, 7.

53. Woodward, *American Army*, 299.

54. Smythe, *Pershing*, 233.

THIRTEEN   Checking Ludendorff

1. Bullard, in Coffman, *March*, 48 (emphasis Bullard).

2. Ludendorff, in John Keegan, *First World War*, 393–94; Pétain, in Freidel, *Over There*, 114.

3. Allied pressure, in NDB to JJP, Dec. 18, 1917, *PWW*, 45:328; NDB to WW, Jan. 3, 1918, *PWW*, 45:438; JJP to NDB, Jan. 17, 1918, in Trask, *AEF and Coalition Warmaking*, 39.

4. JJP to Henry Pinckney McCain, received Jan. 31, 1918, *PWW*, 46:197; Joffre, EMH, in Smythe, *Pershing*, 70–71.

5. NDB to WW, Jan. 3, 1918, *PWW*, 45:438; JJP, in Woodward, *American Army*, 138; Allied leaders, in Harries and Harries, *Last Days of Innocence*, 216.

6. Robertson, in Woodward, *American Army*, 139; Haig, 146; French attitudes, in Smythe, *Pershing*, 69, and Harries and Harries, *Last Days of Innocence*, 211; Haig and Pétain, in Trask, *AEF and Coalition Warmaking*, 40–41.

7. Pershing, *My Experiences*, 1:185; Smythe, *Pershing*, 82.

8. Palmer, *Bliss*, 240 (emphasis Bliss).

9. Smythe, *Pershing*, 69, 70, 76; quotation at 234–35.

10. David F. Trask, *The United States in the Supreme War Council: American War Aims and Inter-Allied War Strategy, 1917–1918* (Middletown, Conn.: Wesleyan University Press, 1961), 99; Striner, *Wilson*, 145–46.

11. Woodward, *American Army*, 168; John S. D. Eisenhower, *Yanks: The Epic Story of the American Army in World War I* (New York: Free Press, 2001), 295.

12. Winston S. Churchill, *The World Crisis, 1911–1918* (New York: Free Press, 2005; orig. 1931), 769; Ludendorff, in Hew Strachan, *The First World War: A New Illustrated History* (New York: Simon and Schuster, 2003), 283.

13. Pétain, in Trask, *AEF and Coalition Warmaking*, 49.

14. Lloyd George, in David R. Woodward, *Trial by Friendship*, 149; Balfour to Lord Reading, Mar. 23, 1918, *PWW*, 47:130–31; Wilson reply, in John S. D. Eisenhower, *Yanks*, 115; Lloyd George, in *NYT*, Apr. 2, 1918, 1; Lloyd George to Lord Reading, Apr. 2, 1918, *PWW*, 47:229.

15. Beck, *NYT*, Mar. 29, 1918, 11; WHT, "The Great Drive," Mar. 29, 1918, in Vivian, ed., *William Howard Taft*, 45; "Are We Too Late!," *O* 118 (Apr. 3, 1918): 525; "Stand Fast," *N* 106 (Mar. 28, 1918), 337; *NR* 14 (Mar. 30, 1918), 245.

16. SWC, in THB to Henry C. McCain, Mar. 23, 1918, *FR, 1918, Supp. 1*, 1:179; Haig, in Trask, *AEF and Coalition Warmaking*, 54; Clemenceau, in Smythe, *Pershing*, 101.

17. JJP, in Smythe, *Pershing*, 101.

18. Ludendorff, in Woodward, *American Army*, 210; Haig, in Baker, *Wilson*, 8:87.

19. EMH to WW, Apr. 9, 1918, *PWW*, 47:303; WW, in *DD*, Apr. 15, 1918, 299.

20. Pershing, in Woodward, *American Army*, 205; Lloyd George, in Trask, *AEF and Coalition Warmaking*, 59.

21. Fowler, *British–American Relations*, 145–46; Foch, in Pershing, *My Experiences*, 2:13.

22. Woodward, *American Army*, 236.

23. Smythe, *Pershing*, 115; Haig and British soldier, in Trask, *AEF and Coalition Warmaking*, 64; Lloyd George, in Pershing, *My Experiences*, 2:31.

24. Bullard, in Eisenhower, *Yanks*, 132; Pershing, *My Experiences*, 2:60.

25. Forrest C. Pogue stresses the positive morale factor both in France and at home; see Pogue, *George C. Marshall: Education of a General, 1880–1939* (New York: Viking, 1963), 165. Mark Ethan Grotelueschen argues that Cantigny proved that at least some AEF units could deliver a highly organized, well-executed blow and hold on to their gains; see Grotelueschen, *The AEF Way of War: The American Army and Combat in World War I* (New York: Cambridge University Press, 2007), 73. Geoffrey Wawro calls the en-

counter "an unqualified success"; see Wawro, *Sons of Freedom: The Forgotten Soldiers Who Defeated Germany in World War I* (New York: Basic Books, 2018), 157.

Other scholars are less enthusiastic. John S. D. Eisenhower suggests that the attack should have been canceled, as the engagement unnecessarily exposed U.S. troops (Eisenhower, *Yanks*, 127). Woodward claims that once the AEF lost French artillery and air support, it should have withdrawn from a hamlet possessing little tactical value and no strategic significance. Pershing had wasted American lives (Woodward, *American Army*, 231). At the very least, write Meirion and Susie Harries, the operation should have been postponed, for Ludendorff's third campaign showed this was no time to waste lives (Harries and Harries, *Last Days of Innocence*, 245). Donald Smythe finds it sad that fourteen months after entering the war, the total U.S. war effort consisted of capturing an obscure village: "The mountainous AEF had labored mightily and brought forth a mouse" (Smythe, *Pershing*, 129).

26. Palmer, *Bliss*, 268.

27. Smythe, *Pershing*, 135; Lloyd George, in Trask, *AEF and Coalition Warmaking*, 74–75.

28. JJP, in Beaver, *Baker*, 147–48; French, British, Italian prime ministers to WW, June 2, 1918, *PWW*, 48:226; House, March, and Baker, in Neumann, "A Question of Authority," 1131–32; Smuts, in Smythe, *Pershing*, 136.

29. William Wiseman to Eric Dummond, May 30, 1918, *PWW*, 48:205–6.

30. Freidel, *Over There*, 183; captain, in Wawro, *Sons of Freedom*, 166; noncom, in Woodward, *American Army*, 249.

31. Private, in Coffman, *War to End All Wars*, 219; Lejeune, in Trask, *AEF and Coalition Warmaking*, 71.

32. Gibbons, in Chris Dubbs, *American Journalists in the Great War: Rewriting the Rules of Reporting* (Lincoln: University of Nebraska Press, 2017), 225; Stone, in Josephus Daniels, *Wilson Era*, 2:150.

33. James, Broun, in Jeffrey, "Journey," 133n270.

34. Edward M. Coffman and Frank E. Vandiver write that militarily the objective was not worth the price. The infantry could have bypassed it, artillery and tanks neutralizing the area with a heavy gas barrage, thereby isolating the Germans and forcing their surrender (Coffman, *War to End All Wars*, 214–15; Vandiver, *Black Jack*, 2:897–98). John S. D. Eisenhower calls the assault "a tragedy, a useless slaughter of valiant, dedicated men for minimal gains" (Eisenhower, *Yanks*, 144). David R. Woodward places much blame on General Harbord, who continued to order assaults without artillery support (Woodward, *American Army*, 250). In fact, Robert H. Ferrell suggests that one tank in front of the advancing marines might have knocked out the German guns (Ferrell, *Woodrow Wilson and World War I*, 71–72).

Other historians are more positive. John Mosier concedes that the entire operation was tactically a fiasco from beginning to end but claims that it turned the tide. By stopping the general German advance, it saved France; see Mosier, *The Myth of the Great War: A New Military History of World War I* (New York: HarperCollins, 2001), 321–22. Geoffrey Wawro quotes German officers who later claimed that Belleau Wood kept Paris from falling. He goes so far as to argue that Pershing's stress on bayonet and rifle served the doughboys well. Artillery was loud and predictable, whereas the rifle offered the element of surprise (Wawro, *Sons of Freedom*, 175).

35. German chief of staff, in Woodward, *American Army*, 245.

36. Foch, JJP, June 17, 1918, in Smythe, *Pershing*, 145.

37. JJP to EMH, June 19, 1918, in Smythe, *Pershing*, 146; JJP to NDB, July 28, 1918, in Pershing, *My Experiences*, 2:188; EMH to WW, June 23, 1918, *PWW*, 48:400.

38. NDB to JJP, July 7, 1918, in Beaver, *Baker*, 183.

FOURTEEN Towards Allied Victory

1. Foch, in Daniels, *Wilson Era*, 2: 347.

2. Observer, in Grotelueschen, *AEF Way of War*, 101.

3. Erich von Ludendorff, *Ludendorff's Own Story, August 1914–November 1918* (New York: Harper & Bros., 1919), 2:326; Lamar Cecil, *Wilhelm II: Emperor and Exile, 1900–1941* (Chapel Hill: University of North Carolina Press, 1996), 273.

4. Foch, in Smythe, *Pershing*, 179.

5. House vote, *CR*, Aug. 24, 1918, 9506–7; Senate, *NYT*, Aug. 28, 1918, 1.

6. Wawro, *Sons of Freedom*, 271; Smythe, *Pershing*, 189.

7. MacArthur and Marshall, in Harries and Harries, *Last Days of Innocence*, 346; Pershing, *My Experiences*, 2:270; Liggett, in Mosier, *Myth of the Great War*, 332.

8. Maurice, in Smythe, *Pershing*, 200.

9. Veteran, in Wawro, *Sons of Freedom*, 353; "sheep" comment, in Freidel, *Over There*, 275; JJP, in Harries, *Last Days of Innocence*, 388.

10. See, for example, *La Grande* (Ore.) *Observer*, Apr. 13, 1919, 19; *Atlanta Constitution*, Apr. 25, 1919, 1.

11. Palmer, in Baker, *Wilson*, 8:426; Liggett, in Eisenhower, *Yanks*, 207; Drum, in Wawro, *Sons of Freedom*, 305.

12. Coffman, *War to End All Wars*, 305.

13. Jack McCallum, "Influenza Pandemic," in *The European Powers in the First World War: An Encyclopedia*, ed. Spencer C. Tucker (New York: Garland, 1996), 360.

14. Pershing, *My Experiences*, 2:293.

15. Richard S. Faulkner, *Pershing's Crusaders: The American Soldier in World War I* (Lawrence: University Press of Kansas, 2017), 215.

16. Military journals, in Grotelueschen, *AEF Way of War*, 17.

17. Pershing, *My Experiences* 1:152–53.

18. James W. Rainey claims that the general insisted upon "a tactical doctrine that was totally at odds with reality"; see Rainey, "Ambivalent Warfare: The Tactical Doctrine of the AEF in World War I," *Parameters* 123 (Sept. 1983): 43–44. Finding the general "a flawed commander," David F. Trask predicts that had the war continued into 1919, he might have fallen from grace (Trask, *AEF and Coalition Warmaking*, 175). David R. Woodward accuses Pershing of taking the stance of "training, experience, and doctrine be damned" (Woodward, *American Army*, 330).

For other examples of criticism, see T. Harry Williams, *The History of American Wars from Colonial Times to World War I* (New York: Knopf, 1981), 403; Smythe, *Pershing*, 235–37; Wawro, *Sons of Freedom*, 308, 374; Kennedy, *Over Here*, 204–5; Mary Sue Mander, "Pen and Sword: A Cultural History of the American War Correspondent, 1895–1945" (PhD diss., University of Illinois, 1979), 130–31. For more appreciative remarks, see Eisenhower, *Yanks*, 295; Mosier, *Myth of the Great War*, 306–7; Ferrell, *Woodrow Wilson and World War I*, 58.

19. Ludendorff, in Neu, *Colonel House*, 363 (emphasis Ludendorff).

20. Wawro, *Sons of Freedom*, 213.

21. NDB to Lloyd George, in Woodward, *American Army*, 322; Foch, in Smythe, *Pershing*, 203; Foch and JJP, Oct. 13, 1918, in Smythe, *Pershing*, 206.

22. JJP, in Grotelueschen, *AEF Way of War*, 56.

23. Clemenceau, Foch, in Trask, *AEF and Coalition Warmaking*, 145, and Clemenceau, in Baker, *Wilson*, 8:494–95; Haig, in Woodward, *American Army*, 362; Clemenceau, in EMH to WW, Oct. 27, 1918, *PWW*, 51:462.

24. Harbord, in Woodward, *American Army*, 369.

25. Summerall, in Stanley Weintraub, *A Stillness Heard Round the World: The End of the Great War: November 1918* (New York: Dutton, 1985), 95.

26. Dickman, in D. Clayton James, *The Years of MacArthur*, Vol. 1, *1880–1941* (Boston: Houghton Mifflin, 1970), 231; Lt. Col. Clarence R. Huebner, in Coffman, *War to End All Wars*, 353.

27. Smythe, *Pershing*, 228; James, *Years of MacArthur*, 1:233; Liggett, in Ferrell, *Woodrow Wilson and World War I*, 83.

28. Woodward, *American Army*, 370. Smythe, *Pershing*, 228, calls the move unworthy of any army. Kennedy, *Over Here*, 201, writes of "a military atrocity of the first order." Trask, *AEF and Coalition Warmaking*, 174, finds "an operational and political monstrosity."

FIFTEEN   Final Negotiations with the Germans

1. Ludendorff, June 8, 1918, in Harry R. Rudin, *Armistice*, 5.

2. Payer speech, Sept. 12, 1918, in Alexander Kirk to RL, Sept. 13, 1918, *FR, 1918, Supp. 1*, 1:304–6; *NYTr*, Sept. 13, 1918, 1.

3. Austrian proposal and press reaction, *NYTr*, Sept. 16, 1918, 1, 4; WW to RL, Sept. 16, 1918, *PWW*, 51:10–11 and note 1.

4. Press, in "Austria's Diplomatic Waterloo," *LD* 58 (Sept. 28, 1918): 14–16; Congressional leaders, Meyer London, *NYT*, Sept. 18, 1918, 2–3.

5. EMH diary, Sept. 16, 1918, *PWW*, 51:23; House to Wiseman, Sept. 17, 1918, in Fowler, *British–American Relations*, 221; House diary, Sept. 24, 1918, *PWW*, 51:106–7; editorial, *NYT*, Sept. 16, 1918, 10.

6. HCL to TR, Apr. 23, 1917, in Garraty, *Lodge*, 336; HCL to Sturgis Bigelow, June 9, 1917, HCLP.

7. HCL, *CR*, Aug. 23, 1918, 9392–94.

8. House, in Arthur M. Walworth, *America's Moment, 1918: American Diplomacy at the End of World War I* (New York: Knopf, 1977), 19n4; editorial, *NYA*, Aug. 29, 1918, 18; "War Aims and Party Politics," *NR* 16 (Aug. 31, 1918): 122.

9. "A Dictated Peace," *O* 120 (Sept. 4, 1919): 6; TR, *Washington Post*, Sept. 2, 1918, 2; TR, *NYT*, Sept. 7, 1918, 3.

10. Hitchcock, *NYT*, Aug. 28, 1918, 6; editorial, Aug. 26, 1918, 1.

11. WW, address at Metropolitan Opera House, Sept. 27, 1918, *PWW*, 51:129–31.

12. General reaction, Seymour, *Intimate Papers*, 4:71; "The President Speaks," *NARWW* 1 (Oct. 5, 1918): 3; "Clearing Skies and a Trumpet Call," *N* 107 (Oct. 5, 1918): 360.

13. WW to Theodore Marburg, Mar. 8, 1918, *PWW*, 46:572; enclosure, WW to House, Sept. 7, 1918, 49:467–71.

14. Conferences of September 29, 1918, in Rudin, *Armistice*, 50–52.

15. Hindenburg, in Koppel S. Pinson, *Modern Germany: Its History and Civilization*, 2nd. ed. (New York: Macmillan, 1966), 343.

16. Maximilian, *NYT*, Oct. 7, 1918, 1, 5, and *PWW*, 51:270n1; reluctance, in Rudin, *Armistice*, 76–79, 88.

17. Charles, in "Splitting Up Austria-Hungary," *LD* 59 (Nov. 2, 1918): 12; EMH diary, Sept. 24, 1918, *PWW*, 51:106–7.

18. Berlin saying, Ferrell, *Woodrow Wilson and World War I*, 130; Allied terms, in THB to NDB and PCM, Oct. 7, 1918, *PWW*, 51:261–62; Clemenceau, in Walworth, *America's Moment*, 21; military demands, in THB to RL, Oct. 8, 1918, *PWW*, 51:273–75.

19. Press, in Seymour, *Intimate Papers*, 4:76; *San Francisco Chronicle*, Oct. 7, 1918, 16; other press, in *NYT*, Oct. 7, 1918, 2; editorial, 12.

20. McCumber, *CR*, Oct. 7, 1918, 11162; Reed, Ashurst, 11158; Lodge, 11160; Poindexter, 11157; Brandegee, *NYT*, Oct. 8, 1918, 8.

21. Tumulty, *Wilson*, 311.

22. WW, First Note, *NYT*, Oct. 9, 1918, 1.

23. Clemenceau and Lloyd George, in Bullitt Lowry, *Armistice 1918* (Kent, Ohio: Kent State University Press, 1996), 23. Allied response, in Robert Cecil to British Embassy, Oct. 9, 1918, *PWW*, 51:288–89 and note 1; Geddes, Oct. 9, 1918, 51:317n3.

24. House, in Walworth, *America's Moment*, 19n4; Lansing, Oct. 12, 1918, in Inga Floto, *Colonel House in Paris: A Study of American Policy at the Paris Peace Conference 1919* (Princeton, N.J.: Princeton University Press, 1973), 277n101; Wiseman memorandum, Oct. 16, 1918, in Fowler, *American–British Relations*, 284.

25. Harding, *NYT*, Oct. 11, 1918, 9; Lodge, Kirby, Benet, *NYT*, Oct. 9, 1918, 1, 3; TR, *NYTr*, Oct. 14, 1918, 2.

26. Borah, Thomas, Simmons, *NYT*, Oct. 9, 1918, 1, 3; Pittman, *CR*, Oct. 10, 1918, 11167.

27. Press reaction, "The President's Reply and the People's Reply," *LD* 59 (Oct. 19, 1918): 7–10; *O* 120 (Oct. 16, 1918): 241.

28. SWC, in Walworth, *America's Moment*, 22; THB to NDB, Oct. 9, 1918, *PWW*, 51:430 (emphasis Bliss).

29. *NYT*, Oct. 12, 1918, 12.

30. Solf, *NYTr*, Oct. 13, 1918, 1.

31. *DD*, Oct. 14, 1918, 340; WW, in Seymour, *Intimate Papers of Colonel House*, 4:83.

32. John Grigg, *Lloyd George: War Leader, 1916–1918* (London: Penguin, 2002), 626; Lloyd George to Geddes, Oct. 12, 1918, in Trask, *Captains & Cabinets*, 308; Foch, Oct. 13, 1918, in Trask, *AEF and Coalition Warmaking*, 215n29.

33. Neu, *Colonel House*, 366.

34. "Passing Sentence on the Kaiser and His People," *LD* 59 (Oct. 26, 1918): 15, and *NYT*, Oct. 14, 1918, 3; Hearst, *NYA*, Oct. 14, 1918, 18; *NYTr*, Oct. 14, 1918, 10; *Richmond Times-Dispatch*, Oct. 13, 1918, 18; David Lawrence to WW, Oct. 13, 1918, *PWW*, 51:320.

35. Additional press reaction, *NYT*, Oct. 14, 1918, 3.

36. New, Gore, Lodge, *NYA*, Oct. 14, 1918, 3; Cummins, *CR*, Oct. 14, 1918, 11215.

37. Poindexter, *NYT*, Oct. 13, 1918, 3; Knox, *CR*, Oct. 28, 1918, 11485, 11488; WHT, "Wilson's Dialectic," Oct. 10, 1918, in Vivian, ed., *William Howard Taft*, 100; Republican releases, *CR*, Oct. 24, 1918, 11441.

38. TR, *Washington Evening Star*, Oct. 17, 1918, 21; TR, *SFE*, Oct. 29, 1918, 7; *NYT*, Oct. 29, 1918, 7; *Cincinnati Enquirer*, Oct. 31, 1918, 5; TR to Albert J. Beveridge, Oct. 31, 1918, *LTR*, 8:1385.

39. Lodge, *CR*, Oct. 28, 1918, 11487.

40. McCumber, *CR*, Oct. 10, 1918, 11190; Ashurst, Oct. 14, 1918, 11229.

41. Ashurst diary, Oct. 14, 1918, *PWW*, 51:339–40; Homer Cummings diary, Oct. 20, 1918, *PWW*, 51:391; *DD*, Oct. 21, 1918, 342–43.

42. WW, Second Note, *NYT*, Oct. 15, 1918, 1.

43. *NR* 16 (Oct. 19, 1918): 324; Blum, *Joe Tumulty*, 164.

44. Lodge resolution, *CR*, Oct. 14, 1918, 11214; Thomas, 11205; Reed, 11216; Ashurst, 11229; Williams, 11219.

45. Senators, *NYT*, Oct. 15, 1918, 2; Lodge to Sir George Otto Trevelyan, Oct. 18, 1918, HCLP.

46. WHT, "Wilson's Disguised Demand," Oct. 15, 1918, in Vivian, ed., *William Howard Taft*, 102; *NYA*, Oct. 18, 1918, 20; press, in *NYT*, Oct. 15, 1918, 3.

47. Additional press reaction, in *NYT*, Oct. 15, 1918, 3.

48. Irwin R. Laughlin to RL, Oct. 15, 1918, *FR, 1918, Supp. 1*, 1:365–66; Sir Henry Wilson, in Lowry, *Armistice*, 137–38.

49. Wilhelm II, Max, in Rudin, *Armistice*, 133–34; Ludendorff, in Lowry, *Armistice*, 37, and Ludendorff, *Ludendorff's Own Story*, 407.

50. Ludendorff, Oct. 17, 1918, in Seymour, *Intimate Papers of Colonel House*, 4:84–85; German declaration, *NYT*, Oct. 18, 1918, 1.

51. Charles manifesto, in Pleasant A. Stovall to RL, Oct. 18, 1918, *FR, 1918, Supp. 1*, 1:367–68, and New York *Evening World*, Oct. 18, 1918, 1.

52. Austrian and Wilson notes, *NYT*, Oct. 20, 1918, 1; *Washington Post*, Oct. 20, 1918, 27; Masaryk, in Baker, *Wilson*, 8: 492n1; WW, in Franklin K. Lane memorandum, Nov. 1, 1918, *PWW*, 51:548.

53. Germany's third note, *NYT*, Oct. 22, 1918, 1; Sullivan, *Our Times*, 5:509.

54. Rudin, *Armistice*, 167–68.

55. *DD*, Oct. 21, 1918, 342–43.

56. David F. Houston, *Eight Years with Wilson's Cabinet* (Garden City, N.Y.: Doubleday, Page, 1926), 1:309, 315–16; memorandum by Franklin K. Lane, Oct. 23, 1918, *PWW*, 51:414–15.

57. Poindexter, *NYT*, Oct. 22, 1918, 2; Poindexter, *CR*, Oct. 21, 1918, 11402; Ashurst, Borah, Thomas, Fess, *NYT*, Oct. 22, 1918, 1, 2; Lodge, *NYT*, Oct. 23, 1918, 2; Borah, Hitchcock, *NYA*, Oct. 22, 1918, 2.

58. Press, in *NYT*, Oct. 22, 1918, 3; *St. Louis Globe-Democrat*, Oct. 22, 1918, 10; *Raleigh News and Observer*, Oct. 22, 1918, 4.

59. *DD*, Oct. 23, 1918, 344.

60. WW, Third Note, *NYT*, Oct. 24, 1918, 1; Sullivan, *Our Times*, 5:509.

61. Walworth, *America's Moment*, 27; Gregor Dallas, *1918: War and Peace* (Woodstock, N.Y.: Overlook Press, 2001), 90.

62. Hindenburg to Ludendorff, Oct. 24, 1918, in Arthur Rosenberg, *The Birth of the German Republic* (London: Oxford University Press, 1931): 256; Cecil, *Wilhelm II*, 2:283.

63. House diary, Oct. 22, 1918, in Floto, *Colonel House in Paris*, 39–40; House to Haig, Oct. 26, 1918, in Walworth, *America's Moment*, 35.

64. WHT, "The Inevitable Surrender," Oct. 23, 1918, in Vivian, ed., *William Howard Taft*, 109; Roosevelt, *NYT*, Oct. 25, 1918, 2.

65. Lodge, Poindexter, Hitchcock, King, *NYT*, Oct. 24, 1918, 1–2.

66. *NYA*, Oct. 25, 1918, 18; *NYA*, Oct. 28, 1918, 18; *NR* 16 (Oct. 26, 1918): 357; "Why the President Did It," *NR* 17 (Nov. 2, 1918): 3; Charles W. Eliot, *NYT*, Oct. 31, 1918, 12.

67. "Passing Sentence on the Kaiser," *LD* 59 (Oct. 26, 1918): 14; "Germany Not Ready for an Allied Peace," *LD* 59 (Nov. 2, 1918): 7–9; Lansing, *NYTr*, Oct. 11, 1918, 5; *Philadelphia Public Ledger*, Oct. 11, 1918, 12; "The Perils of Peacemaking," *NAR* 208 (Nov. 1918): 648–49.

68. *N* 107 (Oct. 26, 1918): 473; "The Right Reply to Germany," 476; "The Way of Peace," 477.

69. Charles E. Neu calls Wilson's October 23 note a triumph for U.S. diplomacy: it drew Berlin into negotiations, induced sweeping changes within Germany, and hastened the end of the war (Neu, *Colonel House*, 367). David F. Trask finds Wilson's bilateral exchanges with the Germans brilliant, as they resulted in Germany's agreement to negotiate along the lines of Wilson's grand design (Trask, "Woodrow Wilson and the Reconciliation of Force and Diplomacy," 30). Klaus Schwabe claims that the president had skillfully fulfilled a number of aims: taking "the wind out of the sails"

of such jingoes as Lodge and Roosevelt; remaining true to his supporters on the left; retaining his position as arbiter of the anti-German coalition; and leaving to himself the option of whether or not to keep negotiating if the kaiser remained (Schwabe, *Woodrow Wilson, Revolutionary Germany, and Peacemaking*, 69–70). Bullitt Lowry notes that Wilson had managed to exclude the Allies from the negotiations until he gained complete German concurrence to the Fourteen Points (Lowry, *Armistice*, 41).

Wilson's response, though, also has its scholarly critics. Gary Armstrong sees the note making "shambles of logic," both declaring and denying at the same time that the German government represented its peoples in the bid for peace. Moreover, the American public misinterpreted the note as a demand for German surrender, a view met with no contradiction from the White House; see Armstrong, "The Domestic Politics of War Termination: The Political Struggle in the United States over the Armistice, 1918" (PhD diss., Georgetown University, 1994), 2:388–89. Harry R. Rudin notes Wilson's ambiguity concerning the status of the kaiser. Some passages in his notes and statements appeared to demand abdication; others seemed to accept a constitutional monarchy (Rudin, *Armistice*, 221).

70. Rudin, *Armistice*, 207–8.

71. Solf, in ibid., 213.

72. Armstrong, "Domestic Politics," 2:179, 198.

SIXTEEN The Colonel's Last Mission

1. EMH diary, entry of Oct. 15, 1918, *PWW*, 51:340–42.

2. "Colonel Mouse," *Hartford Courant*, July 8, 1916, 8; Walter Lippmann to Sidney E. Mezes, Sept. 5, 1918, in *Public Philosopher: Selected Letters of Walter Lippmann*, ed. John Morton Blum (New York: Ticknor & Fields, 1985), 95; WW, in Seymour, *Intimate Papers of Colonel House*, 1:114; WW to Edith Bolling Galt, Aug. 28, 1915, *PWW*, 34:352.

3. Neu, *Colonel House*, 368.

4. House plan, in Trask, *Captains & Cabinets*, chap. 3; Fowler, *British–American Relations*, 53n34.

5. For House's general views, see Mamatey, *United States and East Central Europe*, 83–84; Gelfand, *Inquiry*, 116. For peace conference, see Lowry, *Armistice*, 78.

6. Harries, *Last Days of Innocence*, 409.

7. Woodward, *Trial by Friendship*, 218.

8. Clemenceau, in Thomas A. Bailey, *A Diplomatic History of the American People*, 10th ed. (Englewood Cliffs, N.J.: Prentice-Hall, 1980), 608.

9. EMH to WW, Oct. 27, 1918, *PWW*, 51:462; EMH to WW, Oct., 28, 1918, *PWW*, 51:473; Rudin, *Armistice*, 182; House diary, Oct. 28, 1918, EMHP.

10. Cobb-Lippmann memorandum, in EMH to WW, Oct. 29, 1918, *PWW*, 51:495-504.

11. Stephen Bonsal, *Unfinished Business* (Garden City, N.Y.: Doubleday, Doran, 1944), 1.

12. WW to EMH, Oct. 30, 1918, *PWW*, 51:511.

13. Lippmann, in Throntviet, *Power without Victory*, 268.

14. EMH diary, Oct. 29, 1918, EMHP; Neu, *Colonel House*, 369; Fowler, *British–American Relations*, 223; EMH to WW, Oct. 30, 1918, *PWW*, 51:511-14; Seymour, *Intimate Papers of Colonel House*, 4:160-67.

15. EMH to WW, Oct. 27, 1918, *PWW*, 51:462; Foch, in Trask, *Captains & Cabinets*, 333.

16. WW to EMH, Oct. 29, 1918, *PWW*, 51:505.

17. EMH to WW, Oct. 30, 1918, *PWW*, 51:511; WW to EMH, Oct. 30, 1918, *PWW*, 51:513.

18. EMH to RL, Oct. 30, 1918, *PWW*, 51:515-16.

19. EMH to WW, Oct. 30, 1918, *PWW*, 51:514-15.

20. JJP memorandum, Oct. 26, 1918, *PWW*, 51:454-55; NDB to JJP, Oct. 27, 1918, *PWW*, 51:470-71; WW, in PCM to JJP, Oct. 27, 1918, *PWW*, 51:472.

21. JJP to NDB, Oct. 30, 1918, in Baker, *Wilson*, 8:532; JJP to SWC, Oct. 30, 1918, in Pershing, *My Experiences*, 2:367.

22. WW, NDB, in Woodward, *Trial by Friendship*, 213; PCM, in NDB to WW, Oct. 31, 1918, *PWW*, 51:525; THB, in Eisenhower, *Yanks*, 278-79; Clemenceau and Lloyd George, in EMH to WW, Oct. 31, 1918, *PWW*, 51:523; EMH diary, Oct. 30, 1918, EMHP; EMH to WW, Oct. 31, 1918, *PWW*, 51:523; McClellan analogy, in Woodward, *American Army*, 360.

23. Foch to Pershing, Oct. 31, 1918, in Smythe, *Pershing*, 222.

24. Pershing apology, in Trask, *AEF and Coalition Warmaking*, 157; Pershing, *My Experiences*, 2:369.

25. Eisenhower, *Yanks*, 291; MacMillan, *Paris 1919*, 158.

26. EMH to WW, Oct. 31, 1918, in Seymour, *Intimate Papers of Colonel House*, 4:174.

27. New, *Colonel House*, 371; Cooper, *Wilson*, 449.

28. Neu, *Colonel House*, 371; Seymour, *Intimate Papers of Colonel House*, 4:126; Lowry, 119.

29. EMH to WW, Nov. 3, 1918, *PWW*, 51:569.

30. Rudin, *Armistice*, 191, 275.

31. WW to EMH, Nov. 4, 1918, *PWW*, 51:575; EMH to WW, Nov. 5, 1918, *PWW*, 51:594; Lloyd George in Neu, *Colonel House*, 372.

32. Lane and Wall, *Lane*, 298.

33. Defenders of Colonel House include his first major biographer, Charles Seymour, who lauds him for winning "an explicit approval of Wilson's programme" (Seymour, *Intimate Papers of Colonel House*, 4:151). David F. Trask, *AEF and Coalition Warmaking*, 216n38, asserts that American gains far outweighed any losses; Thomas J. Knock, *To End All Wars*, 184, finds that given Allied fears of a German *levée en masse* and the domestic difficulties facing Wilson, House had not done badly. Bullitt Lowry, *Armistice*, 172, admits House's concessions regarding reparations, the Rhineland, freedom of the seas, and the application of the Fourteen Points to the Austro-Hungarian armistice. However, "No one was likely to have done much better" in winning "superficial Allied adherence to the Wilsonian program."

34. Link, *Woodrow Wilson: Revolution, War, and Peace*, 87; Neu, *Colonel House*, 372; Cooper, *Wilson*, 450; Floto, *Colonel House in Paris*, 60. For further criticism, see Link, "Foreword," to Floto, *Colonel House in Paris*, viii.

SEVENTEEN   "Not Ordinary Times"

1. WW speech, *NYT*, May 28, 1918, 6; memorandum of conversation by Thomas W. Lamont, Oct. 4, 1918, *PWW*, 51:224–25.

2. WW to Joseph E. Davies, Mar. 18, 1918, *PWW*, 47:52; Marshall, *Wisconsin State Journal*, Mar. 27, 1918, 1, and La Follette and La Follette, *Robert M. La Follette*, 2:871; Williams, *CR*, Mar. 27, 1918, 4133.

3. Kennedy, *Over Here*, 238.

4. Wilson meeting with Ford, June 13, 1918, in Livermore, *Woodrow Wilson and the War Congress*, 159.

5. Joseph P. Tumulty to WW, June 18, 1918, *PWW*, 48:347; Kennedy, *Over Here*, 238.

6. *NARWW* 1 (June 22, 1918): 2; TR, *St. Louis Post-Dispatch*, Aug. 20, 1918, 3; *N* 106 (June 29, 1918): 749; WW to Josephus Daniels, Sept. 6, 1918, *PWW*, 49:461.

7. For a full treatment of the southern purges, see Anthony Gaughan, "Woodrow Wilson and the Rise of Militant Internationalism in the South," *Journal of Southern History* 65 (Nov. 1999): 771–808. For Blease, see *NYT*, July 5, 1918, 10.

8. McLemore, *CR*, Sept. 11, 1918, 10217; WW to H. L. Beach, *San Antonio Light*, July 24, 1918, PWW, 49:73; Slayden, *NYTr*, July 26, 1918, 6; Cooper, *Wilson*, 435.

9. Livermore, *Woodrow Wilson and the War Congress*, 139.

10. C. Vann Woodward, *Tom Watson: Agrarian Rebel* (New York: Macmillan, 1938), 457, 462.

11. Democratic press, in Livermore, *Woodrow Wilson and the War Congress*, 163; "Down with Disloyalists!," *NARWW* 1 (Aug. 17, 1918): 1, which cites the New York *World*.

12. "In the Driftway," *N* 107 (Aug. 17, 1918): 170.

13. Hays, *Indianapolis Star*, Aug. 28, 1918, 6; *NYT*, Sept. 12, 1918, 9; *Rochester Democrat and Chronicle*, Oct. 18, 1918, 2.

14. HCL, TR, Root, WHT, in Knock, *To End All Wars*, 167. Smoot, *CR*, Mar. 27, 1918, 4138; Stone, *CR*, Jan. 21, 1918, 1084–85; Lewis, 1095. "Politics during War," *NR* 14 (Apr. 13, 1918): 309.

15. Fess, *NYTr*, Sept. 8, 1918, 11; "Politics during War," *NR* 16 (Sept. 14, 1918): 180.

16. "A Call to the Patriots of America," *NARWW* 1 (Apr. 13, 1918): 1; Mann, *CR*, May 8, 1918, 6218.

17. Root, *NYT*, May 9, 1918, 6. For a general account, see John Carver Edwards, "The Price of Political Innocence: The Role of the National Security League," *Military Affairs* 42 (Dec. 1978): 190–96.

18. NSL statement, in Livermore, *Woodrow Wilson and the War Congress*, 166–67; McLemore, in *CR*, Sept. 11, 1918, 10218; London, Aug. 27, 1918, 9604.

19. League for National Unity, *Chicago Tribune*, Oct. 9, 1917, 1–2.

20. WW to Theodore N. Vail, Feb. 4, 1918, in Baker, *Wilson*, 7:525–26; appeal, *Philadelphia Inquirer*, June 5, 1918, 10; "Only Loyal Congressmen Wanted," *LD* 57 (June 22, 1918): 12.

21. Heflin, *CR*, Oct. 17, 1918, 11325; Ashurst, 11315.

22. WHT, TR, in *NYT*, Nov. 1, 1918, 14.

23. Memorandum of conversation with Thomas W. Lamont, *PWW*, Oct. 4, 1918, 51:225; WW, "An Appeal for a Democratic Congress," Oct. 19, 1918, *PWW*, 51:381–82.

24. TR, *San Francisco Chronicle*, Oct. 25, 1918, 8.

25. Memorandum by Franklin K. Lane, Nov. 1, 1918, *PWW*, 51:548; Edith Wilson, in Cooper, *Wilson*, 446; EMH diary, Oct. 25, 1918, EMHP.

26. Republican leaders, *SFE*, Oct. 26, 1916, 5.

27. Butler, *NYT*, Oct. 26, 1918, 2; Hays, *NYT*, Oct. 28, 1918, 1, 3; WHT, "The President's Appeal," Oct. 25, 1918, in Vivian, ed., *William*

Howard Taft, 110; "God Save the Republic," *NARWW* 1 (Nov. 2, 1918): 1–2; "Woodrow Wilson, Politician," *N* 107 (Nov. 2, 1918): 503.

28. TR to HCL, Oct. 25, 1918, in *Selections from the Correspondence of Theodore Roosevelt and Henry Cabot Lodge, 1884–1918* (New York: Scribner's, 1925), 2:542; HCL to J. B. Bishop, Oct. 26, 1918, HCLP.

29. *NYA*, Oct. 28, 1918, 18; "Why the President Did It," *NR* 17 (Nov. 2, 1918): 3; *NYT*, Oct. 28, 1918, 10.

30. Tumulty, *SFE*, Oct. 28, 1918, 3; *Indianapolis News*, Oct. 28, 1918, 5; original speeches, TR, *Boston Globe*, Oct. 20, 1898, 1; Lodge, Oct. 7, 1898, 4.

31. Hoover to Frederic Coudert, *NYT*, Nov. 4, 1918, 8; Nash, *Hoover*, 3:425.

32. Fess, *NYT*, Nov. 5, 1918, 5; TR to Miles Poindexter, Nov. 18, 1918, *LTR*, 8:1396.

33. Arthur S. Link called the statement "an invitation to disaster": it outraged those Republicans who had made his war measures possible, threw the peace settlement into the arena of partisan discussion, and asked for a vote of confidence when Wilson should have known no such tally was possible in congressional elections (Link, *American Epoch*, 218). By declaring that a Democratic loss would be regarded as a repudiation of his leadership, argues Thomas A. Bailey, Wilson had "burned all his bridges behind him" (Bailey, *Woodrow Wilson and Lost Peace*, 67). Selig Adler finds Wilson's language ("my leadership," "your spokesman") badly chosen, as it slighted Republican support for his policies; see Adler, "The Congressional Election of 1918," *South Atlantic Quarterly* 36 (Oct. 1937): 457–58. Trygve Throntveit observes that Wilson had failed to recognize that the election would turn on wartime domestic issues, not on high international policy. Furthermore, Allied leaders would not weigh heavily any mandate from the American people, though they might be influenced by a rebuke of the administration (Throntveit, *Power without Victory*, 267).

Other scholars are more accepting of Wilson's statement. David M. Kennedy claims the plea might actually have helped some Democratic candidates, narrowing—for example—Henry Ford's margin in traditionally Republican Michigan by nearly 100,000 votes (Kennedy, *Over Here*, 241). Thomas J. Knock maintains that given party pressure on him, the president would have been equally damned had he stayed silent. Moreover, compared to the abusive rhetoric of his opponents, the president remained relatively restrained (Knock, *To End All Wars*, 179).

34. Cooper, *Wilson*, 446; John Milton Cooper Jr., *Breaking the Heart of the World: Woodrow Wilson and the Fight for the League of Nations* (New York: Cambridge University Press, 2001), 31n41.

35. "Has President Wilson Been Repudiated in the Recent Elections?," *CO* 65 (December 1918): 350.

36. La Guardia, *NYTr*, Oct. 29, 1918, 12, and Kazin, *War against War*, 273; Goldberg, "Meyer London," 480–508.

37. WHT, in Knock, *To End All Wars*, 184; "The President and the People," *NARWW* 1 (Nov. 9, 1918): 1; HCL to Sir George Otto Trevelyan, Nov. 19, 1918, HCLP; HCL to Andrew F. West, Nov. 14, 1918, HCLP.

38. TR, *NYT*, Nov. 7, 1918, 1; TR to Teddy Roosevelt Jr., Nov. 10, 1918, *LTR*, 8:1390.

39. TR to Arthur Balfour, Dec. 5, 1918, in *LTR*, 8:1415; Lodge, in Cooper, *Wilson*, 448.

40. "Choose Ye This Day," *N* 107 (Nov. 16, 1918): 573; *NR* 17 (Nov. 9, 1918): 26.

41. *SFE*, Nov. 14, 1918, 22.

42. Homer Cummings to WW, Nov. 7, 1918, *PWW*, 51:628–33.

43. *NYT*, Nov. 10, 1918, 37; Lane to James H. Hawley, Nov. 9, 1918, in Lane and Wall, *Lane*, 301.

44. WW, address to the Democratic National Committee, Feb. 28, 1919, *PWW*, 55:309; Bryan, "The Election of 1918," *Commoner* 18 (Nov. 1918): 2.

45. Mason, *CR*, Aug. 27, 1918, 9096.

46. Livermore, *Woodrow Wilson and the War Congress*, 243.

47. Knock, *To End All Wars*, 185; *NR* 17 (Nov. 9, 1918): 26; George Creel to WW, Nov. 8, 1918, *PWW*, 51:645–46; Oswald Garrison Villard to Joseph P. Tumulty, Nov. 8, 1918, *PWW*, 51:646.

48. Livermore, ed., *Woodrow Wilson and the War Congress*, 246; Kazin, *War against War*, 272; Adler, "Congressional Election," 461; Bailey, *Woodrow Wilson and Lost Peace*, 65; Cooper, *Wilson*, 447.

EIGHTEEN   Armistice

1. RL to Hans Sulzer, Nov. 5, 1918, *FR, 1918, Supp. 1*, 1:468–69.

2. Rudin, *Armistice*, 339; terms, Wawro, *Sons of Freedom*, 471; Weintraub, *Stillness Heard Round the World*, 54; and Martin Gilbert, *The First World War: A Complete History* (New York: Henry Holt, 1994), 500.

3. Foch to JJP, Nov. 7, 1918, Weintraub, *Stillness Heard Round the World*, 17.

4. Howard cable and Daniels remark, in Daniels, *Wilson Era*, 2:338–39.

5. Lansing, New York *Evening World*, Nov. 7, 1918, 1; Sullivan, *Our Times*, 5:513; *NYTr*, Nov. 8, 1918, 10; Patricia Beard, *Newsmaker: Roy W.*

Howard—The Mastermind behind the Scripps-Howard News Empire from the Gilded Age to the Atomic Age (Guilford, Conn.: Lyons Press, 2016): 80; French intelligence, Weintraub, *Stillness Heard Round the World*, 39.

6. Link, "Woodrow Wilson and Peace Moves," in Link, ed., *Higher Realism*, 108–9; Schwabe, *Woodrow Wilson, Revolutionary Germany, and Peacemaking*, 113.

7. Fleming, *Illusion of Victory*, 303.

8. "An Open Letter," *Harvey's Weekly* 2 (Feb. 8, 1919): 2.

9. Rudin, *Armistice*, 397; Faulkner, *Pershing's Crusaders*, 603.

10. Weintraub, *Stillness Heard Round the World*, 159; Johnson, in Woodward, *American Army*, 197–98.

11. WW statement, ca. Nov. 11, 1918, *PWW*, 53:34.

12. Wilson, *San Francisco Chronicle*, Nov. 12, 1918, 1; EMH to WW, Nov. 11, 1918, *PWW*, 53:24; Houston, *Eight Years*, 1:326.

13. Sullivan, *Our Times*, 5:520–22; *NYT*, Nov. 12, 1918, 1–2.

14. WW, address to Congress, Nov. 11, 1918, *PWW*, 53:34–43; *NYT*, Nov. 12, 1918, 1–2.

15. *NYT*, Nov. 12, 1918, 4.

16. Ibid.

17. "The Pivot of History," *NR* 17 (Nov. 16, 1918): 58–59; "The Armistice," *N* 107 (Nov. 23, 1918): 615.

18. Ferrell, *Woodrow Wilson and World War I*, 16; Eisenhower, *Yanks*, 297.

19. Wawro, *Sons of Freedom*, 482; Woodward, *American Army*, 377; Smythe, *Pershing*, 233; Faulkner, *Pershing's Crusaders*, 599, 606.

20. Woodward, *Trial by Friendship*, 216; Faulkner, *Pershing's Crusaders*, 166.

21. Baker, *Wilson*, 8:481.

Conclusion

1. WW, "A Flag Day Address," June 14, 1917, *PWW*, 42:503.

2. David F. Trask, "Woodrow Wilson and International Statecraft: A Modern Assessment," *Naval War College Review* 27 (Mar.-Apr. 1975): 63.

3. Croly, *New Republic* 2 (Mar. 27, 1915): 194.

4. WW, Oct. 28, 1910, *PWW*, 21:462; WW, address to teachers, June 28, 1918, *PWW*, 48:457.

5. David Lawrence, *The True Story of Woodrow Wilson* (New York: George H. Doran, 1924), 224–25.

6. EMH diary, Aug. 20, 1918, *PWW*, 49:294; William Wiseman to Lord Reading, Sept. 5, 1918, *PWW*, 49:454; Link and Chambers, "Woodrow Wilson as Commander in Chief," 320–21.

7. EMH diary, Dec. 11, 1917, EMHP.

8. WW, in EMH diary, Sept. 27, 1918, *PWW*, 51:144.

9. WW, "A Flag Day Address," June 14, 1917, *PWW*, 42:503.

10. WW on socialism, conversation of August 1919, in Stockton Axson, *"Brother Woodrow": A Memoir of Woodrow Wilson* (Princeton, N.J.: Princeton University Press, 1993), 198; Spring Rice to Balfour, Jan. 4, 1918, *PWW*, 45:455.

11. Cooper, *Pivotal Decades*, 297–98; Link and Chambers, "Woodrow Wilson as Commander in Chief," 335.

12. TR to Anna Roosevelt Cowles, May 17, 1917, *LTR*, 8:1192.

BIBLIOGRAPHIC ESSAY

Creating a comprehensive bibliographic essay for a subject as large as U.S. participation in World War I is well nigh an impossible task. Hence, of necessity, I have limited listings to those accounts I have personally found most helpful for this particular work.

By far the most extensive bibliography remains Thomas J. Knock's "The United States, World War I, and the Peace Settlement, 1914–1920," in *American Foreign Relations since 1600: A Guide to the Literature*, 2 vols., ed. Robert L. Beisner (Santa Barbara, Calif.: ABC Clio, 2003), 1:665–735, and James T. Controvich, *The United States in World War I: A Bibliographic Guide* (Lanham, Md.: Scarecrow, 2012). One should also note Dennis Showalter, "The United States in the Great War: A Historiography," *OAH Magazine of History* 17 (October 2002): 5–13; Lloyd E. Ambrosius, "Woodrow Wilson and World War I," in *A Companion to American Foreign Relations*, ed. Robert D. Schulzinger (Malden, Mass.: Blackwell, 2003), 149–67; Jennifer D. Keene, "The United States," in *A Companion to World War I*, ed. John Horne (Malden, Mass.: Wiley-Blackwell, 2010), 508–23; Keene, "Remembering the 'Forgotten War': Historiography on World War I," *Historian* 79 (Fall 2016), 439–68; Lloyd E. Ambrosius, "Woodrow Wilson and World War I," *Passport: The Society for Historians of American Foreign Relations Newsletter* 48 (April 2017): 31–42; and Justus D. Doenecke, "American Diplomacy, Politics, Military Strategy, and Opinion-Making, 1914–1918: Recent Research and Fresh Assignments," *Historian* 80 (Fall 2018): 509–32.

Anne Cipriano Venzon, ed., *The United States in the First World War: An Encyclopedia* (New York: Garland, 1995), and Spencer C.

Tucker, ed., *The European Powers in the First World War: An Encyclopedia* (New York: Garland, 1996), are excellent launching pads for studying the conflict.

Among the many excellent accounts of World War I, I have found certain works distinctively insightful: David Stevenson, *The First World War and International Politics* (New York: Oxford University Press, 1988); Martin Gilbert, *The First World War: A Complete History* (New York: Henry Holt, 1994); John Keegan, *The First World War* (New York: Knopf, 1999); Ian F. W. Beckett, *The Great War, 1914–1918* (New York: Longman, 2001); John Mosier, *The Myth of the Great War: A New Military History of World War I* (New York: HarperCollins, 2001); Hew Strachan, *The First World War: A New Illustrated History* (New York: Simon and Schuster, 2003); David Stevenson, *Cataclysm: The First World War as Political Tragedy* (New York: Basic Books, 2004); and Michael S. Neiberg, *Fighting the Great War: A Global History* (Cambridge, Mass.: Harvard University Press, 2005). David Stevenson, *1917: War, Peace, and Revolution* (New York: Oxford University Press, 2017), and Gregor Dallas, *1918: War and Peace* (Woodstock, N.Y.: Overlook Press, 2000), ably cover two critical years. For two accounts by famous participants, see Winston S. Churchill, *The World Crisis, 1911–1918* (New York: Free Press, 2005; orig. 1931), and Erich Ludendorff, *Ludendorff's Own Story, August 1914–November 1918*, 2 vols. (Harper & Bros., 1919). Holger H. Herwig and Neil M. Heyman, *Biographical Dictionary of World War I* (Westport, Conn.: Greenwood, 1982), deftly draw portraits of major figures.

Able general treatments of the United States during its wartime years, including the experience of the doughboy, are offered in David M. Kennedy, *Over Here: The First World War and American Society* (New York: Oxford University Press, 1980); Robert H. Ferrell, *Woodrow Wilson and World War I* (New York: Harper and Row, 1985); Ronald Schaffer, *America in the Great War: The Rise of the War Welfare State* (New York: Oxford University Press, 1991); Meirion Harries and Susie Harries, *The Last Days of Innocence: America at War, 1917–1918* (New York: Random House, 1997); Ronald H. Zieger, *America's Great War: World War I and the American Experience* (Lanham, Md.: Rowman & Littlefield, 2000); Thomas Fleming, *The*

Illusion of Victory: America in World War I (New York: Basic Books, 2003); and Garrett Peck, *The Great War in America* (New York: Pegasus, 2018). Adam Tooze, *The Deluge: The Great War, America, and the Remaking of the Global Order, 1916–1931* (New York: Viking, 2013), shows the emergence of U.S. economic dominance. Robert E. Hannighan, *The Great War and American Foreign Policy, 1914–24* (Philadelphia: University of Pennsylvania Press, 1017), is similar in nature, stressing that Wilson sought to prop up an international order that had long been dominated by London. Mark Sullivan, *Over Here, 1914–1918*, Vol. 5 of *Our Times* (New York: Scribner, 1926–35), is impressionistic but captures contemporary moods.

Scholars dealing with Wilson's wartime presidency must begin with volumes 41 to 53 of Arthur S. Link, et al., eds., *The Papers of Woodrow Wilson*, 69 vols. (Princeton, N.J.: Princeton University Press, 1966–93). Also indispensable are the U.S. State Department, *Papers Relating to the Foreign Relations of the United States, 1917–1918: Supplement: The World War* (Washington, D.C.: Government Printing Office, 1931–33); *Russia*, 3 vols. (1931); and *Lansing Papers*, Vol. 2 (1940).

Unfortunately, Arthur S. Link terminated his five-volume magisterial life of Woodrow Wilson with the president's war message of April 1917, when the United States entered the conflict. Many of Link's insights concerning Wilson as war leader are revealed in Link, *Higher Realism of Woodrow Wilson* (Nashville: Vanderbilt University Press, 1971), a series of previously published essays, and Link, *Woodrow Wilson: Revolution, War, and Peace* (Wheeling, Ill.: Harlan Davidson, 1979), a rewriting of Link, *Wilson The Diplomatist: A Look at His Major Foreign Policies* (Baltimore: Johns Hopkins University Press, 1957). Perceptive material is found in Link and John Whiteclay Chambers II, "Woodrow Wilson as Commander in Chief," in *The United States Military under the Constitution of the United States, 1789–1989*, ed. Richard H. Kohn (New York: New York University Press, 1991), 317–75, and in his general survey, Link, *American Epoch: A History of the United States Since the 1890s*, 2nd ed. (New York: Knopf, 1963); Link's informal reflections are revealed in an interview in John A. Garraty, *Interpreting American History: Conversations with Historians* (New York: Macmillan, 1970), 2:121–44. Link is usually supportive of Wilson, but he makes some negative observations.

His interpretation is critiqued in Robert D. Accinelli, "Confronting the Modern World: Woodrow Wilson and Harry S. Truman—Link's Case for Wilson the Diplomatist," *Reviews in American History* 9 (September 1981): 285–94.

There are several one-volume lives of the twenty-eighth president. By far the best is John Milton Cooper Jr., *Woodrow Wilson: A Biography* (New York: Knopf, 2009), a sympathetic account that promises to be definitive. Cooper, *Pivotal Decades: The United States, 1900–1920* (New York: Norton, 1990), and Cooper, *The Warrior and the Priest: Woodrow Wilson and Theodore Roosevelt* (Cambridge, Mass.: Harvard University Press, 1983), offer a wider context, the latter work finding Wilson as hardheaded as Theodore Roosevelt. Ray Stannard Baker, *Woodrow Wilson: Life and Letters*, Vol. 7, *War Leader, 1917–1918*, and Vol. 8, *Armistice, Mar. 1–Nov. 11, 1918* (New York: Scribner's, 1939), were once the leading works and still contain much of value. The works of Arthur Walworth empathize with their subject. Note Walworth, *Woodrow Wilson: World Prophet*, 2nd ed., rev. (Baltimore: Penguin, 1965), and Walworth, *America's Moment, 1918: American Diplomacy at the End of World War I* (New York: Norton, 1977). For other major biographies, see August Heckscher, *Woodrow Wilson: A Biography* (New York: Scribner, 1991), and A. Scott Berg, *Wilson* (New York: Putnam, 2014). Superior brief accounts include Kendrick A. Clements, *Woodrow Wilson: World Statesman*, rev. ed. (Chicago: Ivan R. Dee, 1999), John A. Thompson, *Woodrow Wilson* (London: Longman, 2002), and Patricia O'Toole, *The Moralist: Woodrow Wilson and the World He Made* (New York: Simon and Schuster, 2018).

Certain thematic works are most valuable. Edward H. Buehrig, *Woodrow Wilson and the Balance of Power* (Bloomington: Indiana University Press, 1955), defends Wilson against charges of naiveté. N. Gordon Levin Jr., *Woodrow Wilson and World Politics: America's Response to War and Revolution* (New York: Oxford University Press, 1968), sees Wilson seeking a middle way between traditionalist imperialism and revolutionary Bolshevism, if always adhering to the West's economic and political hegemony. Edwin A. Weinstein, *Woodrow Wilson: A Medical and Psychological Study* (Princeton, N.J.: Princeton University Press, 1981), shows how Wilson's wartime presidency became increasingly marked by fatigue, diminished emotional control, increased suspiciousness, and lapses in judgment and memory. Frederick S. Calhoun, *Power and Principle: Armed Intervention in Wilsonian Foreign Policy* (Kent, Ohio: Kent State University Press, 1986), stresses that Wilson found the use of force sometimes necessary, but he always sought to limit it. Kendrick A. Clements, *The Presidency of Woodrow Wilson* (Lawrence: University Press of Kansas, 1992), admires his subject's intelligence but concedes his rigidity and self-righteousness. Thomas J. Knock, *To End All Wars: Woodrow Wilson and the Quest for a New World Order* (New York: Oxford University Press, 1992), reveals how Wilson first attracted liberals, Socialists, and pacifists to his crusade but then failed to nurture this center-left coalition. Cara Lea Burnidge, *A Peaceful Conquest: Woodrow Wilson, Religion, and the New World Order* (Chicago: University of Chicago Press, 2016), describes a worldview that combined southern evangelicalism with social Christianity. Trygve Throntveit, *Power without Victory: Woodrow Wilson and the American International Experiment* (Chicago: University of Chicago Press, 2017), denies that Wilson sought to impose American-style democracy on other peoples, much less desire global economic hegemony. In a seminal study, John A. Thompson, "Wilsonianism: The Dynamics of a Conflicted Concept," *International Affairs* 86 (2010): 1–22, notes that only when the United States entered the war did Wilson argue that a peaceful world order required the extension of democracy.

Wilson has never been without critics. Thomas A. Bailey, *Woodrow Wilson and the Lost Peace* (New York: Macmillan, 1945), critiques the president's role in drafting the Fourteen Points and in the 1918 elections. John Morton Blum, *Woodrow Wilson and the Politics of Morality* (Boston: Little Brown, 1956), finds his subject far too rigid to be a discerning leader. Alexander L. George and Juliette L. George, *Woodrow Wilson and Colonel House: A Personality Study* (New York: John Day, 1956), attempt a psychoanalytical study, with mixed results. Ross A. Kennedy, *The Will to Believe: Woodrow Wilson, World War I, and America's Strategy for Peace and Security* (Kent, Ohio: Kent State University Press, 2009), faults the president, his critics among pacifists, and such "Atlanticists" as Theodore Roosevelt and Henry Cabot Lodge. Kennedy, "Woodrow Wilson, World War I, and an American Conception of National Security," *Diplomatic History* 25 (Winter 2001): 1–31, finds serious flaws in his leadership.

George F. Kennan, *American Diplomacy, 1900–1950* (Chicago: University of Chicago Press, 1951), played a major role in a "realist" critique of Wilson, something picked up at greater length in Robert Endicott Osgood, *Ideals and Self-Interest in America's Foreign Relations: The Great Transformation of the Twentieth Century* (Chicago: University of Chicago Press, 1953). Certain works by Lloyd E. Ambrosius—*Wilsonian Statecraft: Theory and Practice of Liberal Internationalism during World War I* (Wilmington, Del.: Scholarly Resources, 1991); *Woodrow Wilson and the American Democratic Tradition: The Treaty Fight in Perspective* (New York: Cambridge University Press, 1987); and *Woodrow Wilson and American Internationalism* (New York: Cambridge University Press, 2017)—drive the realist theme home. Richard Striner, *Woodrow Wilson and World War I: A Burden Too Great to Bear* (Lanham, Md.: Rowman & Littlefield, 2014), offers a blanket indictment of Wilson, portraying him as possessed by character flaws and involved in self-destruction.

Wilson's secretary of state contributed his own account in Robert Lansing, *War Memoirs of Robert Lansing, Secretary of State* (Indianapolis: Bobbs-Merrill, 1935), most noteworthy for its confirmation that Lansing was always strongly pro-Ally. Thomas H. Hartig, *Robert Lansing: An Interpretive Biography* (New York: Arno Press, 1982), stresses that the secretary well understood U.S. global interests. For the wartime activities of Lansing's predecessor at Foggy Bottom, see Louis W. Koenig, *Bryan: A Political Biography of William Jennings Bryan* (New York: Putnam, 1971), and Michael J. Kazin, *A Godly Hero: The Life of William Jennings Bryan* (New York: Knopf, 2006). State Department operations are traced in Walter Fulghum Bell, "American Embassies in Belligerent Europe, 1914–1986" (PhD diss., University of Iowa, 1983).

The president's leading confidant, Colonel House, has found his most thorough biographer in Charles E. Neu, *Colonel House: Woodrow Wilson's Silent Partner* (New York: Oxford University Press, 2015), a work more critical than Godfrey Hodgson, *Woodrow Wilson's Right Hand: The Life of Colonel Edward M. House* (New Haven, Conn.: Yale University Press, 2006). Inga Floto, *Colonel House in Paris: A Study of American Policy at the Paris Peace Conference 1919* (Princeton, N.J.: Princeton University Press, 1973), strongly negative, offers extensive coverage of the prearmistice negotiations held in the fall of 1918. The House papers (MS 466) are at Manuscripts and Archives, Yale University Library, New Haven, Connecticut, https://archives.yale.edu/repositories/12/resources/4566.

The often maligned Navy Secretary Josephus Daniels offers a memoir, Daniels, *The Wilson Era: Years of Peace, 1910–1917* (Chapel Hill: University of North Carolina Press, 1944). E. David Cronon, ed., *The Cabinet Diaries of Josephus Daniels* (Lincoln: University of Nebraska Press, 1963), is most valuable. Lee A. Craig, *Josephus Daniels: His Life and Times* (Chapel Hill: University of North Carolina Press, 2013), praises his subject for building one of history's greatest war machines. Daniels's son Jonathan gives an insider's account of wartime Washington in Jonathan Daniels, *The End of Innocence* (Philadelphia: Lippincott, 1954). Daniels's assistant secretary, FDR, is covered in Frank Freidel, *Franklin D. Roosevelt*, Vol. 1, *The Apprenticeship* (Boston: Little, Brown, 1952), and in Geoffrey C. Ward, *A First-Class Temperament: The Emergence of Franklin Roosevelt* (New York: Harper and Row, 1989).

For material on Wilson's best-known secretary of war, Newton Baker, see Frederick Palmer, *Newton D. Baker: America at War*, 2 vols. (New York: Dodd, Mead, 1931); C. H. Cramer, *Newton D. Baker: A Biography* (Cleveland: World, 1961); and the particularly thorough Daniel R. Beaver, *Newton D. Baker and the American War Effort, 1917–1919* (Lincoln: University of Nebraska Press, 1966). Beaver finds Baker becoming increasingly competent as secretary of war, but Douglas B. Craig, *Progressives at War: William G. McAdoo and Newton D. Baker, 1863–1941* (Baltimore: Johns Hopkins University Press, 2013), describes both the secretaries of the treasury and war as leaving much to be desired. Additional material on McAdoo is given in William G. McAdoo, *Crowded Years: The Reminiscences of William G. McAdoo* (Boston: Houghton Mifflin, 1931), and the favorable John J. Broesamle, *William Gibbs McAdoo: A Passion for Change, 1863–1917* (Port Washington, N.Y.: Kennikat, 1973).

Anne Wintermute Lane and Louise Herrick Wall, eds., *The Letters of Franklin K. Lane: Personal and Political* (Boston: Houghton Mifflin, 1922), and Keith W. Olson, *Biography of a Progressive: Franklin K. Lane* (Westport, Conn.: Greenwood, 1979), deal with Wilson's interior secretary. David F. Houston, *Eight Years with Wilson's Cabinet* (New York: Doubleday, Page, 1926), is a memoir by the president's secretary of agriculture. Needed is a full-scale study of Albert Sidney Burleson, the postmaster general who spearheaded suppression of dissenting journals. A start has been made with Donald Johnson, "Wilson, Burleson, and Censorship in the First World War," *Journal of Southern History* 28 (Feb. 1962): 46–58.

Other relevant memoirs include journalist David Lawrence, *The True Story of Woodrow Wilson* (New York: George H. Doran, 1924), and Wilson's press secretary, Joseph P. Tumulty, *Woodrow Wilson as I Know Him* (Garden City, N.Y.: Doubleday, Page, 1921), the latter work somewhat corrected by John M. Blum, *Joe Tumulty and the Wilson Era* (Boston: Houghton Mifflin, 1951). Food Administrator Herbert Hoover gives his own account in volume 1 of his memoirs, Hoover, *Years of Adventure, 1874–1920* (New York: Macmillan, 1951). George H. Nash, *The Life of Herbert Hoover*, Vol. 3, *Master of Emergencies, 1917–1918* (New York: Norton, 1983–96), is a model of thoroughness.

Certain works are particularly helpful on German wartime policy. The highly controversial Fritz Fischer, *Germany's Aims in the First World War* (New York: Norton, 1967), contains extremely valuable detail. More mainstream in its interpretation is Hans-Jürgen Schröder, *Confrontation and Cooperation: Germany and the United States in the Era of World War I, 1900–1924* (Providence, R.I.: Berg, 1993), and Holger H. Herwig, *The First World War: Germany and Austria-Hungary, 1914–1918* (New York: Arnold, 1997). See also Herwig, *Politics of Frustration: The United States in German Naval Planning, 1889–1941* (Boston: Little, Brown, 1976). Lamar Cecil, *Wilhelm II*, Vol. 2, *Emperor and Exile, 1900–1941* (Chapel Hill: University of North Carolina Press, 1996), is superior on the kaiser. For an unmatched view of German admiralty politics, see Walter Görlitz, ed., *The Kaiser and His Court: The Diaries, Note Books, and Letters of Admiral Georg von Müller, Chief of the Naval Cabinet, 1914–1918* (New York: Harcourt, Brace & World, 1964). Klaus Schwabe, *Woodrow Wilson, Revolutionary Germany, and Peacemaking, 1918–1919: Missionary Diplomacy and the Realities of Power* (Chapel Hill: University of North Carolina Press, 1985), stresses Wilson's increasing concern with a Bolshevized Germany. For the downfall of imperial Germany, see long-respected Arthur Rosenberg, *The Birth of the German Republic* (London: Oxford University Press, 1931).

British-American relations have been carefully scrutinized. John Grigg, *Lloyd George: War Leader, 1916–1918* (London: Allen Lane, 2002), is the definitive biography of the prime minister. For Britain's ambassador to Washington, note Stephen Gwynn, ed., *The Letters and Friendships of Sir Cecil Spring Rice: A Record*, Vol. 2 (Boston: Houghton Mifflin, 1929). Two studies of Spring Rice's counterpart in London, Walter Hines Page, criticize their subject: Ross Gregory, *Walter Hines Page: Ambassador to the Court of St. James's* (Lexington: University Press of Kentucky, 1970), and John Milton Cooper Jr., *Walter Hines Page: The Southerner as American, 1855–1918* (Chapel Hill: University of North Carolina Press, 1977). For the ambassador's own perspective, see Burton J. Hendrick, ed., *The Life and Letters of Walter H. Page*, 3 vols. (New York: Doubleday, Page, 1922–26). Britain's covert activities are described in Jennifer Luff, "The Anxiety of Influence: Foreign Intervention, U.S. Politics, and World War I," *Diplomatic History* 44 (Nov. 2020): 756–85.

Certain works cover wider relations between the two nations, among them Sterling J. Kernek, *Distractions of Peace during War: The Lloyd George Government's Reaction to Woodrow Wilson, December, 1916–November, 1918* (Philadelphia: American Philosophical Society, 1975), and David R. Woodward, *Trial by Friendship: Anglo–American Relations, 1917–1918* (Lexington: University Press of Kentucky, 1993). W. B. Fowler, *British–American Relations, 1917–1918: The Role of Sir William Wiseman* (Princeton, N.J.: Princeton University Press, 1969), gives an intimate look at London's chief "troubleshooter" in the United States and includes valuable correspondence. Laurence W. Martin, *Peace without Victory: Woodrow Wilson and the British Liberals* (New Haven, Conn.: Yale University Press, 1958), argues that British liberals significantly influenced Wilson's policies. Lloyd C. Gardner, *Safe for Democracy: The Anglo-American Response to Revolution, 1913–1923* (New York: Oxford University Press, 1984), sees both Wilson and Lloyd George waging war on behalf of an international structure that would maintain the peace but also allow the world to make necessary changes.

Most helpful on France are Jean-Jacques Becker, *The Great War and the French People* (Providence, R.I.: Berg, 1983), and Gregor Dallas, *At the Heart of the Tiger: Clemenceau and His World, 1841–1929* (New York: Carroll and Graf, 1973). For a view from the embassy in Paris, see *The War Memoirs of William Graves Sharp: American Ambassador to France, 1914–1919* (London: Constable, 1931).

Not surprisingly, Theodore Roosevelt has been the subject of considerable scholarship. One might begin with *The Days of Armageddon, 1914–1919*, Vol. 8 of *The Letters of Theodore Roosevelt*, ed. Elting E. Morison (Cambridge, Mass.: Harvard University Press, 1951–54). Among Roosevelt's own books during the war are *America and the World War*, *Fear God and Take Your Own Part*, *The Great Adventure*, and *Foes of Our Own Household*, all in volumes 18 and 19 of *The Works of Theodore Roosevelt: National Edition* (New York: Scribner's, 1926). For TR's syndicated newspaper columns, see Ralph Stout, ed., *Roosevelt in the "Kansas City Star"* (Boston: Houghton Mifflin, 1921).

Full-scale biographies of TR include William Henry Harbaugh, *Power and Responsibility: The Life and Times of Theodore Roosevelt* (New York: Farrar, Straus and Cudahy, 1961); Cooper, *Warrior and Priest*; H. W. Brands, *T. R.: The Last Romantic* (New York: Basic, 1997); and Kathleen Dalton, *Theodore Roosevelt: A Strenuous Life* (New York: Knopf, 2002). For focus on TR's later years, see Patricia O'Toole, *When Trumpets Call: Theodore Roosevelt after the White House* (New York: Simon and Schuster, 2005); Edmund Morris, *Colonel Roosevelt* (New York: Random House, 2010); and J. Lee Thompson, *Never Call Retreat: Theodore Roosevelt and the Great War* (New York: Palgrave Macmillan, 2014),

Henry Cabot Lodge: William C. Widenor, *Henry Cabot Lodge and the Search for an American Foreign Policy* (Berkeley: University of California Press, 1980), remains the best work on the ideology of the Massachusetts senator, but John A. Garraty, *Henry Cabot Lodge: A Biography* (New York: Knopf, 1953), is still extremely valuable. For various speeches, see Lodge, *War Addresses, 1915–1917* (Boston: Houghton Mifflin, 1917). Lodge, *The Senate and the League of Nations* (New York: Scribner, 1925), touches upon earlier periods. *Selections from the Correspondence of Theodore Roosevelt and Henry Cabot Lodge*, 2 vols. (New York: Scribner, 1925), reveals the strong friendship between the two men, even if there is no substitute for examining the Papers of Henry Cabot Lodge, Massachusetts Historical Society, Boston.

To understand the political partisanship of the wartime United States, one should begin with Seward W. Livermore, *Woodrow Wilson and the War Congress* (Seattle: University of Washington Press, 1966). Note also Richard Kenneth Horner, "The House at War: The House of Representatives during World War I, 1917–1919" (PhD diss., Louisiana State University, 1977).

The 1918 election campaign has been subject to much analysis. For coverage of Wilson's purge of recalcitrant southern legislators, consult Anthony Gaughan, "Woodrow Wilson and the Rise of Militant Interventionism in the South," *Journal of Southern History* 65 (Nov. 1999): 771–808. Also essential is Gary Armstrong, "The Domestic Politics of War Termination: The Political Struggle in the United States over the Armistice, 1918" (PhD diss., Georgetown University, 1994). Selig Adler, "The Congressional Election of 1918," *South Atlantic Quarterly* 36 (Oct. 1937): 447–65, stresses underlying economic issues.

Certain Democratic congressional leaders have been examined, but not nearly enough. Alex Mathews Arnett, *Claude Kitchin and the Wilson War Policies* (Boston: Little Brown, 1937), eulogizes Kitchin as a strong critic of Wilson's foreign policy. For a corrective, see the more dispassionate Homer Larry Ingle, "Pilgrimage to Reform: A Life of Claude Kitchin" (PhD diss., University of Wisconsin, 1967). Studies of other southern legislators include C. Vann Woodward, *Tom Watson: Agrarian Rebel* (New York: Macmillan, 1939); George Coleman Osborn, *John Sharp Williams: Planter-Statesman of the Deep South* (Baton Rouge: Louisiana State University Press, 1943); Dewey W. Grantham Jr., *Hoke Smith and the Politics of the New South* (Baton Rouge: Louisiana State University Press, 1958); and William F. Holmes, *The White Chief: James Kimble Vardaman* (Baton Rouge: Louisiana State University Press, 1970). Thomas W. Ryley, *Gilbert Hitchcock of Nebraska: Wilson's Floor Leader in the Fight for the Versailles Treaty* (Lewiston, N.Y.: Edwin Mellen, 1998), traces the evolution of a strong anti-interventionist. Ruth Warner Towne, *Senator William J. Stone and the Politics of Compromise* (Port Washington, N.Y.: Kennikat, 1979), portrays a loyal backer of Wilson's New Freedom fighting his overseas measures.

Republican insurgent congressional leaders have been given as much attention as the party's Old Guard. In Belle Case La Follette and Fola La Follette, *Robert M. La Follette, June 14, 1855–June 16, 1925*, 2 vols. (New York: Macmillan, 1953), the wife and daughter of the prominent Wisconsin dissenter, contribute a highly sympathetic account. Nancy C. Unger, *Fighting Bob La Follette: The Righteous Reformer* (Chapel Hill: University of North Carolina Press, 2000), offers a more analytical treatment. Richard Lowitt, *George W. Norris*, Vol. 2, *The Persistence of a Progressive, 1913–1933* (Urbana: University of Illinois Press, 1971), supplies needed background to *Fighting Liberal: The Autobiography of George W. Norris* (New York: Macmillan, 1945). Robert James Maddox, *William E. Borah and American Foreign Policy* (Baton Rouge: Louisiana State University Press, 1969), focuses upon an influential maverick.

Philip C. Jessup, *Elihu Root: 1905–1937* (New York: Dodd, Mead, 1938), details the career of a powerful Republican internationalist. Howard W. Allen, *Poindexter of Washington: A Study of Progressive Politics* (Carbondale: Southern Illinois University Press, 1981), reveals the hawkishness of an ardent Bull Mooser. Other works include Robert P. Wilkins, "Porter J. McCumber and World War I," *North Dakota History* 34 (Summer 1967): 192–207; Bruce L. Larson, [Charles A.] *Lindbergh of Minnesota: A Political Biography* (New York: Harcourt Brace Jovanovich, 1973); and Alan Boxerman, "[Julius] Kahn of California," *California Historical Quarterly* 55 (Winter 1976): 340–51.

Congressional memoirs include Henry Lee Myers, *The United States Senate: What Kind of Body?* (Philadelphia: Dorrance, 1939); Fiorello La Guardia, *The Making of an Insurgent: An Autobiography, 1882–1919* (Philadelphia: Lippincott, 1948); and George F. Sparks, ed., *A Many-Colored Toga: The Diary of Henry Fountain Ashurst* (Tucson: University of Arizona Press, 1962). Certain figures in Congress merit more intense investigation, among them Champ Clark, Clyde H. Tavenner, Augustus Gardner, George E. Chamberlain, Fred A. Britten, Philander C. Knox, Frank Brandegee, John W. Weeks, James Slayden, and Thomas Hardwick.

For overall views of the Republican Party and the Progressive Party, note Howard Scott Greenlee, "The Republican Party in Division and Reunion" (PhD diss., University of Chicago, 1950), and

James Oliver Robertson, *No Third Choice: Progressives in Republican Politics, 1916–1921* (New York: Garland, 1983). Works on Taft include Henry F. Pringle, *The Life and Times of William Howard Taft: A Biography*, Vol. 2 (New York: Farrar & Rinehart, 1939), and Lewis L. Gould, *Chief Executive to Chief Justice: Taft betwixt the White House and the Supreme Court* (Lawrence: University Press of Kansas, 2014). For Taft's newspaper column in the *Philadelphia Public Ledger*, which was occasionally syndicated, see James E. Vivian, ed., *William Howard Taft: Collected Editorials, 1917–1921* (Westport, Conn.: Praeger, 1990). Wilson's rival in the 1916 presidential election is covered in Merlo J. Pusey, *Charles Evans Hughes*, 2 vols. (New York: Macmillan, 1952).

Certain opinion leaders have received special attention. Of the many biographies of America's leading press czar, Ben Proctor, *William Randolph Hearst: The Later Years, 1911–1951* (New York: Oxford University, 2007), is outstanding. So is Ian Mugridge, *The View from Xanadu: William Randolph Hearst and United States Foreign Policy* (Montreal: McGill-Queens University Press, 1995). Other comprehensive works include W. A. Swanberg, *Citizen Hearst: A Biography of William Randolph Hearst* (New York: Scribner's, 1961), and David Nasaw, *The Chief: The Life of William Randolph Hearst* (Boston: Houghton Mifflin, 2000). There is no substitute for reading firsthand the *New York American* and the *San Francisco Examiner*. A life of Hearst's leading columnist by Oliver Carlson, *Brisbane: A Candid Biography* (New York: Stockpole, 1937), is woefully inadequate. For a man who later became a prominent rival of Hearst, see Patricia Beard, *Newsmaker: Roy W. Howard: The Mastermind behind the Scripps-Howard News Empire from the Gilded Age to the Atomic Age* (Guilford, Conn.: Lyons Press, 2016). A strong contrast to Hearst is found in major New York *World* editorials of Frank Cobb, reproduced in John L. Heaton, ed., *Cobb of "The World": A Leader in Liberalism* (New York: Dutton, 1924). Both Cobb and the highly influential *World* need examination.

John A. Thompson, *Reformers and War: American Progressive Publicists and the First World War* (New York: Cambridge University Press, 1967), reveals the dilemma experienced by many liberals. The *New Republic*'s editors are covered in Charles Forcey, *The Crossroads of Liberalism: Croly, Weyl, Lippmann, and the Progressive Era, 1900–1925* (New York: Oxford University Press, 1961); Ronald Steel, *Walter Lippmann and the American Century* (Boston: Little, Brown, 1980); and David W. Levy, *Herbert Croly of the New Republic: The Life and Thought of an American Progressive* (Princeton, N.J.: Princeton University Press, 1985). The publisher of the *Nation* and *New York Evening Post* is treated in Michael Wreszin, *Oswald Garrison Villard: Pacifist at War* (Bloomington: Indiana University Press, 1965), and Oswald Garrison Villard, *Fighting Years: Memoirs of a Liberal Editor* (New York: Harcourt, Brace, 1939). Since most of the *Nation*'s editorials are anonymous, Daniel C. Haskell performs an invaluable service by compiling *The Nation, Volumes 1–105: Indexes of Titles and Contributors* (New York: New York Public Library, 1951). Willis Fletcher Johnson, *George Harvey: "A Passionate Patriot"* (Boston: Houghton Mifflin, 1929), is the only work on the publisher of the *North American Review*; a far more detailed biography is needed. Ira V. Brown, *Lyman Abbott, Christian Evolutionist: A Study in Religious Liberalism* (Cambridge, Mass.: Harvard University Press, 1953), covers the editor of the *Outlook*. Carl Resek, ed., *The World of Randolph Bourne* (New York: E. P. Dutton, 1965), includes scathing criticism of Wilson's interventionism.

American socialism is subject to intense and often sympathetic study. Jack Ross, *The Socialist Party of America: A Complete History* (Lincoln, Neb.: Potomac Books, 2015), offers a new comprehensive work. For a classic critique, see Daniel Bell, "The Background and Development of Marxian Socialism in the United States," in *Socialism and American Life*, ed. Donald Drew Egbert and Stow Persons (Princeton, N.J.: Princeton University Press, 1952), 1:213–405. Both James Weinstein, *The Decline of Socialism in America, 1912–1925* (New York: Vintage, 1967), and Norman Binder, "American Socialism and the First World War" (PhD diss., New York University, 1970), offer much on party reaction to the Great War. See also Michael Bassett, "The American Socialist Party and the War," *Australian Journal of Politics and History* 11 (Dec. 1965–66): 277–91, and Sally M. Miller, "Socialist Party Decline and World War I: Bibliography and Interpretation," *Science and Society* 34 (Winter 1970): 398–411.

Studies of certain individual Socialists are most helpful. The party's frequent presidential candidate receives thorough treatment in

Nick Salvatore, *Eugene V. Debs: Citizen and Socialist* (Urbana: University of Illinois Press, 1982), but one must also consult Ernest Freeberg, *Democracy's Prisoner: Eugene V. Debs, the Great War, and the Right to Dissent* (Cambridge, Mass.: Harvard University Press, 2008). For work on Meyer London, the prominent congressman from New York's Lower East Side, note William Frieburger, "The Lone Socialist Vote: A Political Study of Meyer London" (PhD diss., University of Cincinnati, 1980), and Gordon J. Goldberg, *Meyer London: A Biography of the Socialist New York Congressman, 1871–1927* (Jefferson, N.C.: McFarland, 2013). New York party leader Morris Hillquit, *Loose Leaves from a Busy Life* (New York: Macmillan, 1934), offers an autobiography, yet one must also utilize Norma Fain Pratt, *Morris Hillquit: A Political History of an American Jewish Socialist* (Westport, Conn.; Greenwood, 1979). W. A. Swanberg, *Norman Thomas: The Last Idealist* (New York: Scribner's, 1976), gives the life of a budding party leader.

Masses editor Max Eastman wrote two autobiographies: *Enjoyment of Living* (New York: Harper, 1948), and *Love and Revolution: My Journey through an Epoch* (New York: Random House, 1964). Biographies include William L. O'Neill, *The Last Romantic: A Life of Max Eastman* (New York: Oxford University Press, 1978), and Christoph Irmscher, *Max Eastman: A Life* (New Haven, Conn.: Yale University Press, 2017). The IWW, labor's major opponent of the war, is covered in Patrick Renshaw, *The Wobblies: The Story of the IWW and Syndicalism in the United States*, new updated ed. (Chicago: Ivan R. Dee, 1999), and Melvin Dubofsky, *We Shall Be All: A History of the Industrial Workers of the World* (Urbana: University of Illinois Press, 2000).

For the literature on efforts to promote the war, see Richard L. Hughes, "Propaganda: Wilson and the Committee for Public Information," in Ross A. Kennedy, *A Companion to Woodrow Wilson* (Malden, Mass.: Wiley-Blackwell, 2013), 308–22. Stephen L. Vaughn, *Holding Fast the Inner Lines: Democracy, Nationalism, and the Committee on Public Information* (Chapel Hill: University of North Carolina Press, 1970), remains the major work on the Creel Committee. One still finds useful material in Walton E. Bean, "George Creel and His Critics" (PhD diss., University of California, Berkeley, 1941), and James R. Mock and Cedric Larson, *Words That Won the War: The*

Story of the Committee of Public Information, 1917–1919 (Princeton, N.J.: Princeton University Press, 1939). Creel, *How We Advertised America* (New York: Harper, 1920), and his autobiographical *Rebel at Large: Recollections of Fifty Crowded Years* (New York: Putnam, 1947), give his own story.

The role of pro-war scholars is ably portrayed in George T. Blakey, *Historians on the Home Front: American Propagandists for the Great War* (Lexington: University Press of Kentucky, 1970), and Carol A. Gruber, *Mars and Minerva: World War I and the Uses of the Higher Learning in America* (Baton Rouge: Louisiana State University Press, 1975). Michael Rosenthal, *Nicholas Miraculous: The Amazing Career of the Redoubtable Dr. Nicholas Murray Butler* (New York: Farrar, Straus and Giroux, 2006), covers Columbia University's firing of two antiwar faculty.

Various ethnic groups, particularly German Americans, have been closely scrutinized. The sensitive Frederick C. Luebke, *Bonds of Loyalty: German-Americans and World War I* (De Kalb: Northern Illinois University Press, 1974), offers thorough analysis. Karl J. R. Arndt and May E. Olsen, *German-American Newspapers and Periodicals, 1732–1955: History and Bibliography* (Heidelberg: Quelle & Myer, 1961), presents an extremely thorough listing. For a lynching of a German American, see Donald R. Hickey, "The Prager Affair," *Journal of the Illinois Historical Society* 62 (Summer 1969): 117–34. Extensive treatment of symphony conductor Karl Muck is found in Randy Roberts and Johnny Smith, *War Fever: Boston, Baseball, and America in the Shadow of the Great War* (New York: Basic Books, 2020). The latest comprehensive treatment is found in Zachary Smith, *Age of Fear: Othering and American Identity during World War I* (Baltimore: Johns Hopkins University Press, 2019).

Phyllis Keller, *States of Belonging: German-American Intellectuals and the First World War* (Cambridge, Mass.: Harvard University Press, 1979), gives perceptive portraits of Hugo Münsterberg, George Sylvester Viereck, and the Roosevelt partisan Hermann Hagedorn. Viereck is treated most responsibly in Neil M. Johnson, *George Sylvester Viereck: German-American Propagandist* (Urbana: University of Illinois Press, 1972). Elmer Gertz, *Odyssey of a Barbarian: The Biography of George Sylvester Viereck* (Buffalo: Prometheus Books,

1978), is really a personal memoir. One must, however, consult first-hand Viereck's *Fatherland*, Viereck's *New World*, and *Viereck's: The American Weekly* and *American Monthly*. For another strident German American voice, examine Frederick Franklin Schrader's *Issues and Events*. Hagedorn, *Where Do You Stand? An Appeal to Americans of German Origin* (New York: Macmillan, 1918), endorses the war.

For Irish counterparts, see John Edward Cuddy, *Irish-America and National Isolationism, 1914–1920* (New York: Arno Press, 1976), and John Patrick Buckley, "The New York Irish: Their View of American Foreign Policy, 1914–1921" (PhD diss., New York University, 1974).

The essential literature on domestic repression is presented in Kathleen Kennedy, "Civil Liberties," in Kennedy, *Companion to Woodrow Wilson*, 323–42. The general story is ably narrated in William R. Walker, "'Only the Heretics Are Burning': Democracy and Repression in World War I America" (PhD diss., University of Wisconsin, 2008). For detailed accounts of legislation, see Harry N. Scheiber, *The Wilson Administration and Civil Liberties, 1917–1921* (Ithaca, N.Y.: Cornell University Press, 1960).

Several preparedness organizations have found their historians. The nation's leading group is treated in Robert D. Ward, "The Origin and Activities of the National Security League, 1914–1919," *Mississippi Valley Historical Review* 47 (June 1960): 51–65; John Carver Edwards, "The Price of Political Innocence: The Role of the National Security League," *Military Affairs* 42 (Dec. 1978): 190–96, and Edwards, *Patriots in Pinstripe: Men of the National Security League* (Washington, D.C.: University Press of America, 1982). Edwards, "American Vigilantes and the Great War, 1916–1918," *Army Quarterly and Defence Journal* 106 (July 1976): 277–86, shows that there is more to be discovered on this group. Joan M. Jensen has produced two somewhat different studies on the same topic: "The American Protective League, 1917–1919" (PhD diss., University of California, Los Angeles, 1962), and *The Price of Vigilance* (Chicago: Rand McNally, 1968). APL staffer Emerson Hough wrote the official history, *The Web* (Chicago: Reilly and Lee, 1919). Needed are studies of the American Defense Society and the League for National Unity.

Efforts to rally American labor to the war effort are conveyed in Frank L. Grubbs Jr., *The Struggle for Labor Loyalty: Gompers, the*

A.F. of L., and the Pacifists, 1917–1920 (Durham, N.C.: Duke University, 1968), and Ronald Radosh, *American Labor and United States Foreign Policy* (New York: Knopf, 1969). Updated research is revealed in Elizabeth McKillen, *Making the World Safe for Workers: Labor, the Left, and Wilsonian Internationalism* (Urbana: University of Illinois Press, 2013). Works on former Socialists who backed U.S. intervention are Kent Kreuter and Gretchen Kreuter, *An American Dissenter: The Life of Algie Simons, 1870–1950* (Lexington: University of Kentucky Press, 1969); Robert Dwight Reynolds Jr., "The Millionaire Socialists: J. G. Phelps Stokes and His Circle of Friends" (PhD diss., University of South Carolina, 1974); Robert Miraldi, *The Pen Is Mightier: The Muckraking Career of Charles Edward Russell* (New York: Palgrave Macmillan, 2003); and Markku Ruotsila, *John Spargo and American Socialism* (New York: Palgrave Macmillan, 2006). Their collective effort is narrated in Kenneth E. Hendrickson Jr., "The Pro-War Socialists, the Social Democratic League and the Ill-Fated Drive for Industrial Democracy in America, 1917–1920," *Labor History* 11 (June 1970): 304–22. Administration overseas efforts are described in John Reinertson, "Colonel House, Woodrow Wilson and European Socialism, 1917–1919" (PhD diss., University of Wisconsin, 1971).

Major histories of wartime dissenters include H. C. Peterson and Gilbert C. Fite, *Opponents of War, 1917–1918* (Madison: University of Wisconsin Press, 1957), and Michael Kazin, *War against War: The American Fight for Peace, 1914–1918* (New York: Simon and Schuster, 2017). Christopher McNight Nichols, *Promise and Peril: America at the Dawn of a Global Age* (Cambridge, Mass.: Harvard University Press, 2011), places wartime critics in a wider framework of anti-interventionism.

The green corn rebellion is covered in James R. Green, *Grass Roots Socialism: Radical Movements in the Southwest, 1895–1943* (Baton Rouge: Louisiana State University Press, 1978). Robert L. Hachey, "Dissent in the Upper Middle West during the First World War" (PhD diss., Marquette University, 1993), treats such groups as the Nonpartisan League, itself the subject of Robert L. Morlan, *Political Prairie Fire: The Nonpartisan League, 1915–1922* (Minneapolis: University of Minnesota Press, 1955); Larry Remele, "The Tragedy of Idealism: The National Nonpartisan League and American Foreign

Policy, 1917–1919," *North Dakota Quarterly* 44 (Autumn 1974): 78–95; and Michael J. Lansing, *Insurgent Democracy: The Nonpartisan League in North American Politics* (Chicago: University of Chicago Press, 2015). Material on the NPL can be found in the Ernest Lundeen papers, Hoover Institution on War, Revolution and Peace, Stanford University. Donald Johnson, *The Challenge to American Freedoms: World War I and the Rise of the American Civil Liberties Union* (Lexington: University of Kentucky Press, 1963), traces how concern for conscientious objectors led to a much wider focus.

We still lack a full-scale study of the People's Council of America. F. L. Grubbs Jr., "The International Outlook of the People's Council of America," *Science and Society* 37 (Fall 1973): 336–42, describes some activity. Arthur W. Thurner, "The Mayor, the Governor, and the People's Council," *Journal of the Illinois State Historical Society* 66 (Summer 1973): 125–43, reveals efforts to squelch a national PCA meeting in Chicago. For material on two major PCA leaders, see Louis P. Lochner, *Always the Unexpected: A Book of Reminiscences* (New York: Macmillan, 1956), and Stephen J. Whitfield, *Scott Nearing: Apostle of American Radicalism* (New York: Columbia University Press, 1974).

Autobiographies of peace activists include Lillian D. Wald, *Windows on Henry Street* (Boston: Little, Brown, 1934), and David Starr Jordan, *The Days of a Man: Being Memories of a Naturalist, Teacher and Minor Prophet of Democracy*, Vol. 2 (New York: World Book, 1922). For Jordan, see also Edward McNall Burns, *David Starr Jordan: Prophet of Freedom* (Stanford, Calif.: Stanford University Press, 1953), and Luther William Spoehr, "Progress' Pilgrim: David Starr Jordan and the Circle of Reform, 1891–1931" (PhD diss., Stanford University, 1975). Jordan's papers at the Stanford University Library are a rich source on the PCA.

The very titles of Ray H. Abrams, *Preachers Present Arms* (New York: Round Table, 1933), and Richard M. Gamble, *The War for Righteousness: Progressive Christianity, the Great War, and the Rise of the Messianic Nation* (Wilmington, Del.: ISI Books, 2003), betray their perspective. Russell Samuel McMahan Jr., "The Protestant Churches during World War I: The Home Front, 1917, 1918" (PhD diss., St. Louis University, 1968), shows how the churches voluntarily became a government agency. John F. Piper Jr., *The American Churches in World War I* (Athens: Ohio University Press, 1985), sacrifices probing of ideological issues to stress institutional history. Jonathan H. Ebel, "'The Wreckage and All the Glory': Protestant America and the Legacy of the Great War," *Journal of Presbyterian History* 92 (Spring-Summer, 2014), 4–25, gives the rationale for pro-war sentiment. For a thorough study of one of American Protestantism's leading figures, a man who served on the Root Commission, see C. Howard Hopkins, *John R. Mott, 1865–1955: A Biography* (Grand Rapids: Eerdmans, 1979). A more in-depth examination, with special attention to denominational journals, is still much needed.

Connected is the subject of internationalism. Warren F. Kuehl has contributed two major works: *Seeking World Order: The United States and World Organization* (Nashville: Vanderbilt University Press, 1969), and *Hamilton Holt: Journalist, Internationalist, and Educator* (Gainesville: University of Florida Press, 1960), the latter a biography of the editor of the *Independent* magazine. Ruhl J. Bartlett, *The League to Enforce Peace* (Chapel Hill: University of North Carolina Press, 1944), remains definitive on the nation's leading internationalist body.

U.S. policy on Russia has received a tremendous amount of attention, summarized in David S. Foglesong, "Policies towards Russia and Intervention in the Russian Revolution," in Kennedy, *Companion to Woodrow Wilson*, 386–405. Other interpretive bibliographic accounts include Christopher Lasch, "American Intervention in Russia: A Reinterpretation," *Political Science Quarterly* 77 (June 1962): 205–23; Eugene P. Trani, "Woodrow Wilson and the Decision to Intervene in Russia: A Reconsideration," *Journal of Modern History* 48 (Sept. 1976): 440–61; and Carl J. Richard, "'The Shadow of a Plan': The Rationale behind Wilson's 1918 Siberian Intervention," *Historian* 49 (Nov. 1986): 64–84.

Among the general histories that cover Russia in 1918–19, I have found particularly helpful W. Bruce Lincoln, *Passage through Armageddon: The Russians in War and Revolution, 1914–1918* (New York: Simon and Schuster, 1986); Lincoln, *Red Victory: A History of the Russian Civil War* (New York: Simon and Schuster, 1989); and Orlando Figes, *A People's Tragedy: A History of the Russian Revolution* (New York: Viking, 1996).

Crucial to the study of Russian policy are the *Russia* volumes for 1917–18 in the *Foreign Relations* series. Also consult Neil V. Salzman, ed., *Russia in War and Revolution: General William V. Judson's Accounts from Petrograd, 1917–1918* (Kent, Ohio: Kent State University Press, 1998).

Early studies include William Appleman Williams, *American–Russian Relations, 1781–1947* (New York: Holt, Rinehart and Winston, 1952); Robert D. Warth, *The Allies and the Russian Revolution: From the Fall of the Monarchy to the Peace of Brest-Litovsk* (Durham, N.C.: Duke University Press, 1954); and Alton Earl Ingram, "The Root Mission in Russia" (PhD diss., Louisiana State University, 1970).

Because of their widespread influence, the works of George F. Kennan deserve special mention: "The Sisson Documents," *Journal of Modern History* 38 (June 1956): 130–54; *Russia Leaves the War* (New York: Princeton University Press, 1956); *The Decision to Intervene* (Princeton, N.J.: Princeton University Press, 1958); and *Russia and the West under Lenin and Stalin* (Boston: Little, Brown, 1961). Writing in part to refute Soviet claims concerning American involvement in Russia, Kennan triggered entire waves of fresh research.

Such scholarship includes Robert Edward Barnett, "Frustrated Partnership: Russia's Relations with Great Britain, France, and the United States during World War I" (PhD diss., Texas Tech University, 1990); David W. McFadden, *Alternative Paths: Soviets and Americans, 1917–1920* (New York: Oxford University Press, 1993); George Schild, *Between Ideology and Realpolitik: Woodrow Wilson and the Russian Revolution, 1917–1921* (Westport, Conn.: Greenwood, 1995); and Donald E. Davis and Eugene P. Trani, *The First Cold War: The Legacy of Woodrow Wilson in U.S.–Soviet Relations* (Columbia: University of Missouri Press, 2002).

For biographies of leading participants, see Hermann Hagedorn, *The Magnate: William Bryce Thompson and His Time (1869–1930)* (New York: John Day, 1935); Neil V. Salzman, *Reform and Revolution: The Life and Times of Raymond Robins* (Kent, Ohio: Kent State University Press, 1991); Salzman's study of General Judson; and Harper Barnes, *Standing on a Volcano: The Life and Times of David Rowland Francis* (St. Louis: Missouri State Historical Society Press, 2001). William Hard's *Raymond Robins' Own Story* (New York: Harper, 1920) deals entirely with Russia.

Certain autobiographies are pertinent. Note Edgar Sisson, *One Hundred Red Days: A Personal Chronicle of the Bolshevik Revolution* (New Haven, Conn.: Yale University Press, 1931); H. Bruce Lockhart, *British Agent* (New York: Putnam, 1933); and William S. Graves, *America's Siberian Adventure, 1918–1920* (New York: Jonathan Cape and Harrison Smith, 1931).

The U.S. interventions in Archangel and Siberia are discussed in John Albert White, *The Siberian Intervention* (Princeton, N.J.: Princeton University Press, 1950), 224; Betty Miller Unterberger, *America's Siberian Expedition, 1918–1920: A Study of National Policy* (Durham, N.C.: Duke University Press, 1956); William Appleman Williams, "American Intervention in Russia, 1917–1920" (Part 2), *Studies on the Left* 4 (Winter 1964): 39–57; Robert J. Maddox, *The Unknown War with Russia: Wilson's Siberian Intervention* (San Rafael, Calif.: Presidio, 1977); David S. Foglesong, *America's Secret War against Bolshevism: U.S. Intervention in the Russian Civil War, 1917–1920* (Chapel Hill: University of North Carolina Press, 1995); and Carl J. Richard, *When the United States Invaded Russia: Woodrow Wilson's Siberian Disaster* (Lanham, Md.: Rowman & Littlefield, 2013). James Carl Nelson, *The Polar Bear Expedition: The Heroes of America's Forgotten Invasion of Russia, 1918–1919* (New York: William Morrow, 2019), looks at the Archangel venture from the perspective of the foot soldier.

Public opinion is covered in Leonid I. Strakhovsky, *American Opinion about Russia* (Toronto: University of Toronto Press, 1961); Christopher Lasch, *The American Liberals and the Russian Revolution* (New York: Columbia University Press, 1962); and Peter G. Filene, *Americans and the Soviet Experiment, 1917–1933* (Chapel Hill: University of North Carolina Press, 1967).

Attention has long been given to the role of the Hapsburg Empire and its successor states. To peruse the literature, one should note M. B. B. Biskupski, "Wilson's Policies toward Eastern and Southeastern Europe, 1917–1919," in Kennedy, *Companion to Woodrow Wilson*, 406–25. For a comprehensive overview, see Victor S. Mamatey, *The United States and East Central Europe, 1914–1918: A Study in Wilsonian Diplomacy and Propaganda* (Princeton, N.J.: Princeton University Press, 1957). Betty Miller Unterberger, *The United States,*

Revolutionary Russia, and the Rise of Czechoslovakia (Chapel Hill: University of North Carolina Press, 1989), shows why the president sought to rescue in the Czech Legion that occupied Siberia. Nicole M. Phelps, *U.S.–Habsburg Relations from 1815 to the Paris Peace Conference: Sovereignty Transformed* (New York: Cambridge University Press, 2013), finds Wilson heavily responsible for the empire's breakup. Mitchell Pirie Briggs, *George D. Herron and the European Settlement* (Stanford, Calif.: Stanford University Press, 1932), narrates an effort at informal diplomacy by an American clergyman.

Much attention is given to the debate over U.S. war aims. John A. Thompson, "War Aims, 1917 to November 11, 1918," in Kennedy, *Companion to Woodrow Wilson*, 367–86, covers the literature. U.S. response to the August 1917 papal peace plea is treated in John L. Snell, "Benedict XV, Wilson, Michaelis, and German Socialism," *Catholic Historical Review* 37 (July 1951): 151–78. Lawrence E. Gelfand, *The Inquiry: American Preparations for Peace, 1917–1919* (New Haven, Conn.: Yale University Press, 1963), reveals Colonel House's attempt to create a "think tank" designed to research and recommend national goals. The theme of Wilson versus Lenin is given particular prominence in Arno J. Mayer, *Political Origins of the New Diplomacy* (New Haven, Conn.: Yale University Press, 1959). Margaret MacMillan, *Paris 1919: Six Months That Changed the World* (New York: Random House, 2001), is trenchant on the entire matter of self-determination and its origins.

Varied perspectives on entering the war are found in Arthur S. Link, *Wilson: Campaigns for Progressivism and Peace, 1916–1917* (Princeton, N.J.: Princeton University Press, 1965); Cooper, *Wilson*; Justus D. Doenecke, *Nothing Less Than War: A New History of America's Entry into World War I* (Lexington: University Press of Kentucky, 2011); and Michael S. Neiberg, *The Path to War: How the War Created Modern America* (New York: Oxford University Press, 2016).

For the background to conscription legislation, see John Whiteclay Chambers II, *To Raise an Army: The Draft Comes to Modern America* (New York: Free Press, 1987). The effect of military service is covered in Jennifer D. Keene, *Doughboys, the Great War, and the Remaking of America* (Baltimore: Johns Hopkins University Press, 2001), and Christopher Capozzola, *Uncle Sam Wants You: World*

War I and the Making of the Modern American Citizen (New York: Oxford University Press, 2008).

Of the many works on the American Expeditionary Force, I have found especially useful Edward M. Coffman, *The War to End All Wars: The American Military Experience in World War I* (Lexington: University Press of Kentucky, 1968); John S. D. Eisenhower, *Yanks: The Epic Story of the American Army in World War I* (New York: Free Press, 2001); Mark Ethan Grotelueschen, *The AEF Way of War: The American Army and Combat in World War I* (New York: Cambridge University Press, 2007); David R. Woodward, *The American Army and the First World War* (New York: Cambridge University Press, 2014); and Geoffrey Wawro, *Sons of Freedom: The Forgotten American Soldiers Who Defeated Germany in World War I* (New York: Basic Books, 2018). The massive Richard S. Faulkner, *Pershing's Crusaders: The American Soldier in World War I* (Lawrence: University Press of Kansas, 2017), discusses every aspect of doughboy life. One should not, however, neglect Fred Davis Baldwin, "The American Enlisted Man in World War I" (PhD diss., Princeton University, 1964), and Frank Freidel, *Over There: The Story of America's First Great Overseas Crusade* (Boston: Little Brown, 1964). T. Harry Williams, *The History of American Wars from Colonial Times to World War I* (New York: Knopf, 1981), offers a superior, if brief, analysis.

Not surprisingly, U.S. generals have received extensive treatment. Jack McCallum, "Wilson and His Commanders," in Kennedy, *Companion to Woodrow Wilson*, 426–41, ably offers a good guide to this topic. Frank E. Vandiver, *Black Jack: The Life and Times of John J. Pershing* (College Station: Texas A&M Press, 1977), is far less critical than Donald Smythe, *Pershing: General of the Armies* (Bloomington: Indiana University Press, 1986). John J. Pershing, *My Experiences in the World War*, 2 vols. (New York: Frederick A. Stokes, 1931), is marred by a running feud with Chief of Staff Peyton C. March, who seeks to rebuke him in March, *The Nation at War* (Garden City, N.Y.: Doubleday, Doran, 1932). For a defense of the chief of staff, see Edward M. Coffman, *The Hilt of the Sword: The Career of Peyton C. March* (Madison: University of Wisconsin Press, 1966). The famous Pershing–March rivalry is revisited in Brian Neumann, "A Question of Authority," *Journal of Military History* 73 (Oct. 2009): 1117–42. Frederick Palmer, *Bliss, Peacemaker: The Life and Letters of General*

Tasker Howard Bliss (New York: Dodd, Mead, 1934), covers the career of the U.S. representative to the Allied War Council. James J. Harbord, first Pershing's chief of staff, then his director of services of supply, wrote *Leaves from a War Diary* (New York: Dodd, Mead, 1925). Biographies of officers who later became prominent include Forrest C. Pogue, *George C. Marshall*, Vol. 1, *Education of a General, 1880–1939* (New York: Viking, 1963), and D. Clayton James, *The Years of Mac-Arthur*, Vol. 1, *1880–1941* (Boston: Houghton Mifflin, 1970). For studies of the general most outspoken in his contempt for Wilson, note the hostile account by Jack C. Lane, *Armed Progressive: General Leonard Wood* (San Rafael, Calif.: Presidio, 1978), and the somewhat more friendly one by Jack McCallum, *Leonard Wood: Rough Rider, Surgeon, Architect of American Imperialism* (New York: New York University Press, 2006).

David F. Trask's work is essential to understanding U.S. military relationships with the Allies. Among his seminal works are *The United States in the Supreme War Council: American War Aims and Inter-Allied Strategy, 1917–1918* (Middletown, Conn.: Wesleyan University Press, 1961); *Captains & Cabinets: Anglo-American Naval Relations, 1917–1918* (Columbia: University of Missouri Press, 1973); *The AEF and Coalition Warmaking, 1917–1918* (Lawrence: University Press of Kansas, 1993); "Woodrow Wilson and the Reconciliation of Force and Diplomacy," *Naval War College Review* 27 (Jan.-Feb. 1975): 23–68; and "Woodrow Wilson and International Statecraft: A Modern Assessment," *Naval War College Review* 27 (Mar.-Apr. 1975): 57–68.

For the debate over early deployment of U.S. troops, see Alan R. Millett, "Over Where? The AEF and the American Strategy for Victory, 1917–1918," in *Against All Enemies: Interpretations of American Military History from Colonial Times to the Present*, ed. Kenneth J. Hagen and William R. Roberts (Westport, Conn.: Greenwood, 1986), 235–56, and Ronald H. Spector, "'You're Not Going to Send Soldiers Over There Are You!': The American Search for an Alternative to The Western Front, 1916–1917," *Military Affairs* 36 (February 1972): 1–4. James W. Rainey, "Ambivalent Warfare: The Tactical Doctrine of the AEF in World War I," *Parameters* 123 (Sept. 1983): 34–46, critiques U.S. tactics.

The navy's supporting role in the Allied effort is succinctly covered in Edward J. Sheely, "United States Navy," in Venzon, ed., *United States in the First World War*, 745–51, a volume that also includes specialized articles on such topics as mines and the leading admirals. Kenneth J. Hagen, *The People's Navy: The Making of American Sea Power* (New York: Free Press, 1991), puts the naval war in a wider context. Trask, *Captains & Cabinets*, is indispensable. Admiral William H. Sims, *The Victory at Sea* (London: J. Murray, 1920), is autobiographical, while Elting Morison, *Admiral Sims and the Modern American Navy* (Boston: Houghton Mifflin, 1942), is obviously far more analytical. Mary Klachko with David F. Trask, *Admiral William Shepherd Benson, First Chief of Naval Operations* (Annapolis, Md.: Naval Institute Press, 1975), tells of an admiral much at odds with Sims. The Reich's abortive U-boat effort is covered in Philip K. Lundeberg, "The German Naval Critique of the U-Boat Campaign, 1915–1918," *Military Affairs* 27 (January 1964), 105–18, and Holger H. Herwig and David S. Trask, "The Failure of Imperial Germany's Undersea Offensive," *Historian* 33 (August 1971): 611–36.

For matters of war reporting and the accompanying censorship, see Emmet Crozier, *American Reporters on the Western Front, 1914–1918* (New York: Oxford University Press, 1959), and Chris Dubbs, *American Journalists in the Great War: Rewriting the Rules of Reporting* (Lincoln: University of Nebraska Press, 2017). One should note two dissertations: Mary Sue Mander, "Pen and Sword: A Cultural History of the American War Correspondent, 1895–1945" (PhD diss., University of Illinois, 1979), and Caitlin Marie Thérèse Jeffrey, "Journey through Unfamiliar Territory: American Reporters and the First World War" (PhD diss., University of California, Irvine, 2007). Bullitt Lowry, *Armistice 1918* (Kent, Ohio: Kent State University Press, 1996), uses major collections still closed when Harry R. Rudin, *Armistice 1918* (New Haven, Conn.: Yale University Press, 1944), published his book. Lowry, "Pershing and the Armistice," *Journal of American History* 55 (September 1968): 281–91, shows the general's abortive effort to continue the war. Stanley Weintraub, *A Stillness Heard Round the World: The End of the Great War: November 1918* (New York: Dutton, 1985), offers a lively account of the conflict's termination.

Many newspapers cited can be found at http://newspapers.com.

INDEX

Abbott, Lyman, 5, 81, 219. See also
    Outlook
Ackerman, Carl, 246
Adams, Samuel Hopkins, 51, 81,
    98, 111, 113
Adamson, William, 16
Addams, Jane, 47–48, 51. *See also*
    Woman's Peace Party
Adler, Selig, 357, 440n.33
African Americans: and Creel
    Committee, 54; and fear of
    Black troops, 16; and fear of
    popular uprising, 63; troops
    absorbed in French divisions,
    281; welcomed in Roosevelt
    regiment, 25. *See also* Du Bois,
    W. E. B.; Miller, Kelly; Na-
    tional Association for the Ad-
    vancement of Colored People
Aiken, Conrad, 107
aircraft: and Baker, 75–76, 258;
    Creel Committee's misleading
    reports concerning, 57; Hearst
    belief in, 110; investigation by
    Charles Evans Hughes, 276;
    investigation by Gutzon
    Borglum, 274–76, 277, 371;
    obsolete conditions of, 8; re-
    sponsibilities for scandal, 277;

shortage of, 265. *See also*
    Mitchell, William ("Billy") L.
Alekseyev, Mikhail, 161
Alfonso XIII (king of Spain), 249
Allenby, Edmund, 31, 327
Alsace-Lorraine: armistice terms,
    360; Austrian leaders on, 250,
    255; Benedict XV on, 217, 218;
    Cecil on, 208; claims of
    German predominance, 60,
    242; Cobb–Lippmann memo-
    randum on, 333; collective
    Allied leadership on, 311;
    French demands for, 211, 223,
    245; German leaders, 245, 246,
    306, 310; House and Balfour
    on, 207; House on, 331; the
    Inquiry on, 239–40; Lloyd
    George on, 235, 237; Lodge
    on, 307, 312, 376; McCumber
    resolution on, 312; Roosevelt
    on, 224; Wilson on, 239–40,
    242, 244, 336
amalgamation controversy, 260,
    262–63, 280–82, 332, 369. *See
    also* Ludendorff offensives
Ambrosius, Lloyd E., 212, 255,
    418n.57
America (journal), 219

471

American Alliance for Labor and Democracy (AALD), 55

American Defense Society (ADS): attack on Creel Committee, 57; backing conscription, 10, 15; blasting of La Follette, 115; Chamberlain addresses, 268; Creel opposition to, 84; on German language, 100; leadership and activity, 83–84; repression of civil liberties, 61, 94, 374; and Wilson administration, 375. *See also* Hurd, Richard M.

American Expeditionary Force (AEF). *See* Pershing, John Joseph: appointment as commander of American Expeditionary Force

American Federation of Labor (AFL), 10, 56, 131, 134. *See also* Gompers, Samuel; Wilson, Woodrow: American Federation of Labor address

American Geographical Society, 233

American Protective League (APL), 26, 84–90, 94, 97. *See also* slacker raids

American Red Cross Commission to Russia, 156–57, 373. *See also* Robins, Raymond; Thompson, William Boyce

American Rights League, 10, 81

American Socialist (Chicago), 123, 129

American Socialist and Labor Mission, 53

American Telephone and Telegraph Company, 48

American Truth Society, 109

American Union Against Militarism, 48, 70, 215

American Weekly: backing of La Follette, 116; backing of war effort, 46; on civil liberties, 222; endorsement of Stockholm Conference, 123; favoring Lansdowne peace plan, 225; favoring Michaelis peace plan, 215; favoring papal peace bid, 219; history of, 105–6; on Kermit Roosevelt, 92; Poindexter on, 107; praising Wilson's Mount Vernon speech, 254; seeking U.S. military restraint, 32; on Wilson reply to Benedict XV, 222

Amiens, 285; battle of, 294

Anaconda Copper Mining Company, 275

Angell, Norman, 95

Anthony, Daniel R., 15, 22

Antilles (U.S. ship), 42

Appeal to Reason: background of, 117; backing Wilson, 368; blaming war on capitalism, 121; endorsement of Wilson's reply to Benedict XV, 222; newspaper outlawed, 68; opposition to conscription, 25; *See also* Kopelin, Louis; *New Appeal*

Approaches to the Peace Settlement (Balch), 75

Arabia: Cobb–Lippmann memorandum on, 333; House on, 223; the Inquiry on, 240; Lloyd George on, 236, 335; Roosevelt on, 224

Archangel: background of, 177–78; Bolsheviks reentering, 184;

British arrive, 178; intervention debated, 178–80; occupation by U.S. infantry, 181–84; Soviets' objection to Allied intervention, 181; and Trotsky, 168; venture evaluated, 184–85, 373; and Wilson, 180–81, 184–85, 192, 369

Argonne Forest. *See* Meuse-Argonne campaign

Armenia: Benedict XV on, 217; Cobb–Lippmann memorandum on, 333; Constantinople Agreements on, 207; Hertling on, 245; the Inquiry on, 240; Lloyd George on, 223; Lodge on, 307; Theodore Roosevelt on, 224, 316; Wilson on, 212

Armstrong, Gary, 327, 435n.69

Army League, 21

Army Reorganization Act (1916), 271

Army War College. *See* War College, U.S. Army

Arras: British offensive (1917), 203; Ludendorff first offensive (1918), 282

Ashurst, Henry F.: attack on Industrial Workers of the World, 133; and 1918 congressional election of 1918, 349; offer of own peace terms, 218; and Wilson's October 1918 negotiations with the Germans, 312, 317, 318, 323

Asquith, Herbert, 224

Associated Press: on La Follette, 176; and Melville Stone, 290

Astor, Vincent, 82

Atherton, Gertrude, 81, 96

Atlantic Monthly, 99, 212

Austro-Hungarian Empire: armistice terms, 339; becoming German vassal, 260; empire dissolves, 301, 310, 320–21; House on, 219–20, 331; Lansing on, 244, 253; link to Benedict XV, 219; Lloyd George on, 235; Roosevelt on, 226, 316; starvation within, 206, 305; U.S. declaration of war upon, 225–27; and Wilson, 227–28, 233, 240, 253, 320–21. *See also* Benedict XV; Charles I; Czernin, Ottokar

Authors' League of America, 107–8

Babson, Roger W., 51

Bacon, Mark, 15

Bacon, Robert, 83

Baer, John M., 99, 136–37, 138, 164

Baghdad. *See* Berlin-to-Baghdad railroad

Bailey, Thomas A., 357, 422n.38, 440n.33

Baker, George F., 82

Baker, Newton Diehl: on amalgamation, 263, 280, 284; appointment of Peyton March as army chief of staff, 272; arrival in Paris, 271; attack by Senator Sherman, 273; background of, 8, 258; ban of certain books from army camps, 75; condemnation of Herbert Bigelow whipping, 142; controversy over aircraft, 75, 274, 275–76, 277, 371; controversy with Congress over mobilization shortages, 265, 267, 270–71, 273; and Creel Committee,

Baker, Newton Diehl (*cont.*)
50; defense of Hearst press,
113; draft preparation, 7, 10,
25; evaluation of, 4, 371; on
German atrocities, 96; on
making northern Russia commitment, 180, 192; opposition
to prosecution of Industrial
Workers of the World, 134;
opposition to Roosevelt
regiment, 18; ordering of
Graves to Siberia, 195, 200,
202; original opposition to
conscription, 9–10; and
Pershing, 260, 289, 291, 301–2,
336; responsibility for supply
incompetence, 277; role played
in general conscription debate,
11; seeking armistice, 322;
sober war prognosis, 32; on
training camp inadequacies,
264; on war censorship, 64
Baker, Ray Stannard: on Admiral
Sims, 36–37; on British hardship, 231; on dubious postwar
future, 365; on Industrial
Workers of the World, 132–33;
on Lord Lansdowne, 225; and
Meuse-Argonne campaign,
302; seeking amalgamation,
280; on Wilson-Roosevelt
feud, 92
Baker–Reading agreement, 286
Balch, Emily Greene, 75
Baldwin, Fred Davis, 26
Balfour, Arthur, 191, 207, 217–18,
244, 252
Balfour–Viviani Mission, 24, 33,
206–8, 262
Balkans, U.S. strategy proposal for,
8–9, 377n.3

Barrett, Charles, 349
Barton, Bruce, 81
Baruch, Bernard, 138, 271–72, 278
Bates, Catherine Lee, 52
Bean, Walton E., 49, 61
Beard, Charles A., 53, 143
Beaver, Daniel R., 271
Beck, James M.: attack on freedom
of the seas, 244; attack on
Hearst, 111; attack on Wilson's
Four Points speech, 248;
fearful of war outcome, 32;
and League for National
Unity, 348–49; on Ludendorff
offensive, 284
Becker, Albert, 107
Becker, Carl, 51, 53, 54
Beckman, Alexander, 75, 77
Belgium: and armistice conditions,
311, 360; Benedict XV on, 217,
220; Charles I on, 250;
Hertling on, 245, 246, 254;
Hindenburg on, 214; House
and Balfour on, 207; and
House October 1918 negoti-
ations in Paris, 335, 336; Lloyd
George on, 209, 239; Max of
Baden on, 320; Payer on, 306;
Roosevelt on, 224; Wilson
on, 239
Bell, Daniel, 135
Belleau Wood, battle of, 289–90,
429n.34
Belmont, Perry, 83
Benedict XV (pope), peace appeal,
106, 216–22, 376
Beneš, Eduard, 218, 253, 321
Benet, Christie, 313
Bennett, William Mason, 125
Benson, Allan Louis, 117, 119,
120, 121

Benson, William S., 36, 192

Bentall, J. O., 129

Berger, Victor: appearing to praise Central Powers, 401n.73; background of, 342; denouncement of war profiteering, 139–40; desire for Bolshevik regime recognized, 128; desire for Europe-wide socialist revolution, 218–19; indictment, 129; and 1918 congressional election, 342, 353; remaining with Socialist Party (1917), 120; rights defended by Villard, 124; and Stockholm conference, 122

Berlin-to-Baghdad railroad, 211, 215

Bernays, Edward, 51

Bernhardi, Friedrich, 53

Bertron, Samuel, 149

Bethmann Hollweg, Theobald von, 40, 206, 214

Bielaski, Bruce, 85, 86, 89

Bigelow, Herbert, 142

Bilbo, Theodore, 107

Billings, Frank G., 156

Bisbee, 1917 strike in, 131–33, 375

Bitter Cry of the Children, The (Spargo), 119

Blacks. See African Americans

Black Tom explosion (1916), 63, 96

Blease, Coleman, 344

Bliss, Tasker; accusation of interfering with Quartermaster Corps, 265; background of, 257; favoring amalgamation, 281–82, 284; on nature of German surrender, 314, 334; opposition to Balkan strategy, 267; opposition to intervene to rescue Russian provisional government, 155; opposition to northern Russia intervention, 179, 183; opposition to Siberia intervention, 186–87, 199; paraphrasing Balfour–Viviani mission, 262; on Pershing unconditional surrender policy, 336; seeing initial U.S. Army participation limited, 9; on Supreme War Council, 178. See also Supreme War Council

Blum, John Morton, 318

Bohn, Frank, 105, 121, 124

Bolo Pasha, Paul, 112

Bolshevism, fear of: Erzberger on, 360; Lansing on, 313; Roosevelt on, 93, 137; Walling on, 231; Wilson on, 313, 317, 322

Bonaparte, Charles J., 83

Borah, William E.: on Allied war aims, 215; backing Overman Act, 273; backing Will Hays as Republican chairman, 346; backing Wilson overture to Bolshevik Russia, 164; favoring Roosevelt regiment, 20; on German American press, 100; opposition to conscription, 20; opposition to Creel, 58; opposition to espionage bill, 64; opposition to secret treaties, indemnities, 242–43; supporting Kerensky regime, 155; on Wilson's negotiations with the Germans, 313, 323

Borglum, Gutzon, 274–76, 277, 371

Boudin, Louis, 118

Bourne, Randolph, 76, 121, 213

Bowman, Isaiah, 233

Boy-Ed, Karl, 112

Bradley, Omar, 134

Brandegee, Frank, 40, 64, 273, 275–76, 312

Brandeis, Louis, 112

Branting, Hjalmar, 122

Brest-Litovsk, treaty of: American and Allied reaction, 165–66, 169; Kolchak regime repudiation, 199; Lodge on, 307; supplementary agreement (August 1918), 171, 181; and Supreme War Council, 246–47; terms of, 164–65, 168, 251; Wilson on, 171, 251, 308

Briand, Aristide, 205

Bridges, George, 19

Briggs, Albert, 85, 89

Brisbane, Arthur, 65, 89, 113–14, 164, 196

Britten, Fred, 32, 98–99, 107, 242

Brooklyn (U.S. ship), 187, 193

Broun, Haywood, 51

Brown, Philip Marshall, 47

Browne, Edward E., 16

Brusilov, Alexei, 151, 154, 155, 203

Bryan, William Jennings: favoring curbs on free speech, 47; favoring Lloyd George's Trades Union Congress speech, 236; lack of influence, 376; and *Lusitania* controversy, 114–15; on 1918 congressional election, 355; pledging support of war effort, 45; quoted by Creel Committee, 53

Bryant, Louise, 164

Bucharest, Treaty of (1918), 308

Bulgaria: Charles I on, 249; House and Balfour on, 207; part of early U.S. invasion scheme,

377n.3; reported as ready to surrender, 310; surrenders to Allies, 301; Wilson on, 225

Bull (journal), 109

Bullard, Arthur, 49, 56

Bullard, Robert Lee, 279, 288, 301, 303, 361

Bullitt, William C., 188

Burgess, John W., 75

Burian, Istvan, 250–51, 254–55

Burleson, Albert Sidney: attack on German American press, 100; attack on *Masses*, 77–78; attack on People's Council of America, 140; background of, 67; calling some newspapers pro-German, 69; censorship role of, 3, 64, 68; defended by Wilson, 71; on Harvey's *War Weekly*, 76; on *Kansas City Star*, 92; lobbies for Espionage Act, 66; and Texas congressional race, 344; Villard on, 357; and Wilson, 374, 401n.73. *See also* Post Office Department

Burnquist, Joseph, 141

Butler, Nicholas Murray, 115, 142, 351

Byrnes, James F., 14, 59–60

Calder, William, 45

Caldwell, Charles P., 22

Cambon, Jules, 218

Camp, Walter, 82

Campbell, Henry C., 105

Cannon, Joseph, 11, 21, 59, 242

Cantigny, battle of (1918), 288, 428n.25

Caporetto, battle of (1917), 203, 226, 280

Carnegie, Andrew, 105
Carnegie Corporation, 82
Carnegie Institution, 174
Catt, Carrie Chapman, 349
Cattell, James McKeen, 143
Cavell, Edith, 108–9
Cecil, Robert: accepting of Lans-
    downe letter, 224; comments
    on French war aims, 211;
    contact with Russian prov-
    inces, 163; drafting Lloyd
    George Trades Union speech,
    235; giving British peace terms
    (May 1917), 209; praise for
    Wilson's reply to Benedict XV,
    223
censorship, U.S. military, 263, 271,
    290
Chaikovski, Nicholas, 183
Chamberlain, George E.: on air-
    craft flaws, 275, 276; back-
    ground of, 267; contribution
    recognized, 278; illness of, 271;
    investigation of mobilization
    efforts, 267–68, 269, 270, 272;
    pro-conscription, 11, 13;
    seeking death penalty for
    dissenters, 79
Chambers, John Whiteclay, II: on
    conscription alignment, 12;
    on Roosevelt regiment, 19, 22;
    on volunteer alternative, 29; on
    Wilson's civil liberties role,
    375, 401n.73
Chandler, Walter M., 20
Chaplin, George, 183
Cháradame, André, 212
Charles I (emperor of Austria; king
    of Hungary): letter to Poincaré
    giving peace terms, 250–51;
    promising local autonomy

with empire, 311; relinquishing
    of throne, 361; response to
    Benedict XV peace plea, 217;
    surrendering power to
    Germany, 251; writing Alfonso
    XIII on Wilson's peace
    program, 249
Château-Thierry, 289, 290. See also
    Belleau Wood, battle of
Châtillon, Côte de, 302
Chicago Tribune: on American
    Protective League, 86; on anti-
    German attitudes, 101; praise
    for Wilson's October 1918
    note, 313; on Theodore Roo-
    sevelt, 91. See also Gibbons,
    Floyd; McCormick, Medill
Chicherin, Georgi V., 181
China, 186, 221
Chinese Eastern Railway, 153,
    197
Choate, Joseph, 82
Church, Denver, 14
Churchill, Winston, 282
Clabaugh, Hinton, 85
Clan na Gael, 46. See also Gaelic
    American
Clark, Champ: on conscription,
    11, 14–15, 17; desire for war
    against all Central Powers,
    227; endorsement of Hearst,
    113; opposition to censorship,
    64; role as House speaker, 351
Claypool, Harold K., 15–16
Clemenceau, Georges: on Austrian
    surrender, 339; becoming
    prime minister, 205; endorse-
    ment of Roosevelt division, 23;
    favoring Russian breakaway
    regimes, 163; on Fourteen
    Points, 245, 332, 334; and

Clemenceau, Georges (*cont.*)
House October 1918 negotiations, 332, 334–35; opposition
to Benedict XV peace bid, 218;
on Pershing's unconditional
surrender terms, 336–37, 338;
reaction to Wilson's negotiations with Germany, 311, 312,
315; release of Sixtus letter,
250–51; seeing American army
as inert, 284, 289, 302–3
Cobb, Frank: on Garfield's fuel
order, 266; interview with
Wilson, 144; support for civil
liberties, 47; Wilson's choice to
head Committee on Public
Information, 49, 61
Cobb–Lippmann memorandum,
332–33, 340, 368–69
Cochran, Bourke, 46
Cochran, William, Jr., 121
Coffin, Howard E., 275
Coffman, Edward M.: on Belleau
Wood, 429n.34; on Josephus
Daniels, 35; on Meuse-
Argonne campaign, 298; on
Wilson-Pershing relationship,
260
Cohalan, Daniel F., 46, 106, 109
Cole, Felix, 172, 179
Collegiate Anti-Militarism League,
143
Colt, LeBaron, 273
Committee on Public Information
(CPI). *See* American Alliance
for Labor and Democracy;
Creel, George; Creel Com-
mittee; Friends of German
Democracy; Sisson, Edgar
Commoner, 47. *See also* Bryan,
William Jennings

Commons, John R., 52
Communism. *See* Bolshevism, fear
of
Congress of Oppressed Austrian
Peoples, 252–53
Connally, Tom, 21
conscription: age limit expanded
(August 1918), 294; congres-
sional debate, 10–24; drawing
of draftee numbers (July
1917), 7; legislation signed
(May 1918), 24; prewar plans
for, 8–9; Registration Day
(June 5, 1917), 26; Wilson's
War Message (April 1917), 10.
See also Roosevelt, Theodore:
and proposed division
Constantinople, 207, 220, 224, 235,
307
Constantinople Agreements
(March 1915), 148, 207
Cooper, John Milton, Jr.: on Creel
Committee, 61; on Fourteen
Points, 422n.38; on House
October 1918 negotiations in
Paris, 338, 340; on 1918 con-
gressional election, 352, 357;
on Roosevelt, 73, 91, 94; on
Roosevelt regiment, 18–19; on
Siberian venture, 414n.68; on
Wilson and civil liberties, 375,
401n.73; on Wilson's Flag Day
(June 14, 1917) speech, 213; on
Wilson's July 4, 1918, speech,
255; on Wilson's 1917 reply to
Benedict XV, 418n.57
Corwin, Edward, 52, 53
Council of National Defense, 113,
258, 271
Councils of Defense (state), 61, 79,
81, 88, 95, 115; Iowa, 97

Cox, James, 107

Cox, William E., 72

Cram, Ralph Adams, 112

Crane, Charles R., 149

Creel, George: accomplishments of, 2; attack on *Masses*, 78; attacks on, 3, 58–60; background of, 49; being chosen to head Committee on Public Information, 49–50; defense of Wilson's mobilization program, 269; favoring conscription, 13; favoring powerful presidency, 53; favoring William Boyce Thompson, 162; finding People's Council of America disloyal, 140; fostering propaganda in Russia, 152; grilling before House Appropriations Committee, 58; opposition to American Protective League, 88; opposition to Bisbee deportations, 132; opposition to National Security League, American Defense Society, 84; opposition to Vigilantes (organization), 82; promotion of Sisson documents, 173–74; recalling wartime hysteria, 87; seeing lack of war enthusiasm, 48; "slumming" remark about Congress, 58–59; telling Wilson that progressives alienated, 356–57; and Townley, 138

Creel Committee: and African Americans, 54; attacks on, 56–58; distribution of Sisson documents, 174; distribution of Wilson's Fourteen Points speech in Russia, 243–44; editing of Wilson's 1917 Flag Day speech, 212–13; evaluation of, 60–62, 370; ideological message of, 51–54; and labor, 55–56; origin of, 49–50; propaganda accomplishments of, 50–51; and Russian activity, 152, 158, 373; and Vigilantes (organization), 82. *See also* American Alliance for Labor and Democracy; Friends of German Democracy; Sisson, Edgar

Crisis (journal), 10

Croly, Herbert, 48, 71, 368. See also *New Republic*

Crosser, Robert, 12

Crowder, Enoch, 7, 25, 27

Crozier, William, 264, 265, 266, 269

Cummings, Homer, 349, 355

Cummins, Albert B., 69–70, 316

Curley, James, 10

Current Opinion: on Lansdowne speech, 228; on sentiment towards Japan, 189; on Wilson appeal (October 25, 1918), 352

Curzon, George Nathaniel, 309

Czech Legion: activity in Siberia, 189, 197, 198; activity in Vladivostok, 190, 197, 198; British vision for, 182; Ishii on, 195; Lansing on, 192; morale plummets, 200; nature of, 189; State Department on, 196; Supreme War Council on, 178, 191; Wilson aide-mémoire (July 6, 1918), 192–93; Wilson policy evaluated, 200–201, 411n.45, 412n.56, 414n.68

Czechoslovak National Council, 189, 253, 320–21

Czechs: achievement of self-government, 320–21; and Congress of Oppressed Austrian Peoples, 252–53; and Fourteen Points, 245; Lansing on, 244, 253; Lodge on, 307; Roosevelt on, 224, 316; Wilson on, 212

Czernin, Ottokar: accusation of manipulating Benedict XV, 218; backing Wilson speech (Feb. 11, 1918), 250; on Central Powers war aims (Dec. 23, 1918), 235; giving Austrian war aims (Jan. 24, 1918), 246; relieved by Wilson's 1917 Annual Message, 228; resignation as foreign minister, 250; Wilson on Czernin's war aims, 247

Dale, Porter H., 265
Dallas, Gregor, 324
Dalmatia, 208, 244
Dalton, Kathleen, 93–94
Dana, Henry Wadsworth Longfellow, 143
Daniels, Josephus: agreement with British on patrols, 36; background of, 35; on censorship, 64; consultation over Russia intervention, 192; and Creel Committee, 50, 57, 59; defended by Lodge, 40–41; evaluation of, 2, 371; finding Roosevelt's writings seditious, 92; on Japan's aims in Russia, 187; ordering of Admiral Knight to Siberia, 193; on phony December 7 armistice, 360; praised by Hearst press, 112–13; and Sims, 36, 37; suggestion of Henry Ford for Senate race, 343; on Wilson's negotiations with the Germans, 322

Danzig, 207, 237
Dardanelles, 240, 327
Darrow, Clarence, 53
Davies, Joseph, 342, 370
Davis, Donald E., 168, 403n.17, 410n.25, 414n.68
Davis, Edward, 377n.3
Davison, Henry P., 156
Debs, Eugene Victor: ailment of, as U.S. enters war, 118; and election of 1912, 117; endorsement of Fourteen Points, 243; opposition to war effort, 125; remaining loyal to Socialist Party, 120; trial for violating Espionage Act, 130–31, 401n.73. See also Socialist Party

De Havilland aircraft engine, 275
De Mille, Cecil B., 87
Denman, William, 43
Dent, Hubert S., 11, 17, 351
Deutsches Journal, 110
Devoy, John, 108–9
Dewey, John, 124, 134
Dial, Nathaniel B., 344
Dickman, Joseph, 304
Dies, Martin, Sr., 128
Doty, Madeline, 75
Dowell, Cassius M., 5
Drum, Hugh, 298
Du Bois, W. E. B., 10
Dubovsky, Melvin, 135
Duff, Alexander L., 38
Duncan, James, 149
Dyer, Leonidas, 101

Eastman, Crystal, 48, 143
Eastman, Max: and American Union Against Militarism, 215; defense of Socialist Party, 121; endorsement by Viereck, 106; endorsement of Wilson's Fourteen Points speech, 243; protest against censorship, 68; and suppression of the *Masses*, 76–79
East St. Louis, 1917 riots, 93
Eaton, Charles A., 98
Eddystone explosion (1917), 63, 85
Eisenhower, Dwight David, 20
Eisenhower, John S. D.: on amalgamation, 282; on Belleau Wood, 429n.34; on Cantigny, 428n.25; on overall role of AEF, 364; on Pershing generalship, 431n.18; on unconditional surrender, 337
Eliot, Charles W., 325
Emergency Fleet Corporation, 43
Emergency Peace Federation, 140
Emerson, George, 153
Emerson, Henry I., 14
England. *See* Great Britain
Erzberger, Mattias, 359–60
Espionage Act (1917): debate on, 64–66; and Debs, 130, 401n.73; enforcement of, 66–68; and German Americans, 95, 97; Gregory on, 75; and Jeremiah O'Leary, 109; and *Masses* indictment, 77; signing of, 66, 374; and Viereck, 107
Estonia, 172, 214
European War of 1914 (Burgess), 75
Everybody's Magazine, 98

Fairchild, Charles Stebbins, 84
Fall, Albert B.: favoring censorship, 65, 74; opposition to La Follette, 116; opposition to slacker raids, 89, 375; seeing German danger, 12
Farmer's Educational and Cooperative Union, 349
Fatherland, 105. *See also* Viereck, George Sylvester
Faulkner, Richard S., 300, 362
Fay, Sidney Bradshaw, 51, 53
Federal Council of Churches, 46, 349
Federal Reserve Board, 104
Ferdinand (king of Bulgaria), 227. *See also* Bulgaria
Ferrell, Robert H.: on 1917 condition of U.S. army, 8, 258; on U.S. potential force, 364
Fess, Simeon, 323, 347, 350, 352
Figes, Orlando, 148
Filene, Peter G., 403n.17, 406n.62, 412n.56
Finland: Cobb–Lippmann memorandum on, 333; and German-Russian supplementary treaty (Aug. 1918), 181; Germans conquering of, 169, 178; Milner and Pichon on, 163; Payer on, 306; Roosevelt on, 224; Whites's seizure of Petsamo area, 178
Fite, Gilbert C., 26, 74, 135
Fiume, 333
Flagg, James Montgomery, 51, 82
Fleming, Thomas, 22, 361, 422n.38
Flood, Henry, 227
Floto, Inga, 340
Foch, Ferdinand: and armistice conditions, 312, 323, 334, 337,

Foch, Ferdinand (*cont.*)
340, 371; continual frustration
with Pershing, 302; defense of
Americans against Clemen-
ceau, 303; fearing German
regrouping, 315, 322; and final
armistice negotiations, 360,
361; frustrated by Pershing
obstinacy during Ludendorff
offensive, 286, 287, 288, 291;
giving Pershing permission for
St. Mihiel attack, 294;
launching of Allied offensive,
293, 300–301; and Pershing
armistice terms, 335–36, 337;
receiving Pershing troop
pledge (Mar. 28, 1918), 284–85
Foes of Our Own Household, The
(Roosevelt), 91, 223
Foglesong, David S.: on Lansing's
Siberian vision, 192; on
Maddin Summers's initiative,
161; on U.S. suspicion of
Social Revolutionaries,
414n.68; on Wilson's reluctance in Siberia, 410n.25
Folkestone, 1917 bombing of, 203
Food Administration, 352. *See also*
Hoover, Herbert
Ford, Edsel, 343
Ford, Guy Stanton, 52, 60
Ford, Henry: 1915 peace ship of,
140, 343; 1918 senatorial race,
343–44, 346, 370, 440n.33
Four Minute Men, 51
Fourteen Points: Allied prime
ministers and, 313, 314, 319,
331–32; and armistice negoti-
ations, 359, 362; and Cobb–
Lippmann revisions, 332–33;
congressional suspicion of,

316; evaluation of speech,
246–47, 422n.38; Germany
negotiations on basis of, 311,
312, 332, 435n.69; Hiram
Johnson on modification, 248;
and House October 1918
negotiations in Paris, 334–35,
338–40, 438n.33; and Lodge,
307; and Max of Baden, 311,
312; and 1918 congressional
election, 357; Roosevelt
seeking repudiation of, 316–17,
350; speech (Jan. 8, 1918), 144,
163–64, 233, 237–46; undercut
by Wilson himself, 368–69;
Wilson seeing Austria-
Hungary provision outmoded,
320
Fox, Edward Lyell, 75
France: aims on Asian continent,
186; army mutiny, 31, 203, 364;
conditions within (1918), 362;
economic scarcity (spring
1917), 9; funds needed, 33; and
Hearst, 111, 112, 171; hostility
towards, 99, 171; leadership
shifts within, 205; loans to,
229; military setbacks (spring
1917), 31–32, 203; Wilson
suspicious of, 213, 285–86. *See
also* Supreme War Council;
and individual leaders;
military engagements
Francis, David Rowland: background of, 154–55; backing
of Sisson documents, 173;
and Brest-Litovsk, 169; on
Brusilov offensive, 154;
encouraging anti-Bolshevik
elements, 171–72; evaluation
of, 175–76, 275–76; and

northern Russia intervention, 179, 181, 182, 183, 184; noting of Bolshevik takeover, 159; remaining optimistic, 156; and Robins, 169–70; and Siberian intervention, 188, 190; and unclear diplomatic jurisdictions, 158

Franke, Kuno, 104

Frankfurter, Felix, 133

Frazier, Lynn, 136, 139, 141, 353

Freeberg, Ernest, 66

freedom of the seas: and armistice terms, 359; and Benedict XV peace bid, 216; Czernin on, 246; domestic opposition to, 244, 316, 354; and Fourteen Points, 238, 368; Hertling on, 245; and House October 1918 negotiations to Paris, 333, 334, 335, 338, 339, 340, 438n.33; and July 1917 Reichstag resolution, 214; Lloyd George on, 244; Lodge and, 307; and Wilson's League to Enforce Peace speech (May 1916), 241

Freeman's Journal, 109

Freidel, Frank, 289

Frick, Henry Clay, 82

Friends of German Democracy, 105

Friends of Irish Freedom, 109

Friends of Peace, 126

Funston, Frederick, 259

Gaelic American, 108, 109, 244

Gardner, Augustus, 20, 22, 307

Gardner, Lloyd C., 406n.62, 418n.57

Garfield, Harry, 266, 268, 346

Garrett, Daniel E., 16, 59

Gavit, John Palmer, 76

Gaylord, W. R., 120

Geddes, Eric, 44, 312–13

Gelfand, Lawrence E., 233

General Board, U.S. Navy, war plans of, 35

General Staff, U.S. Army: desired terms of draftee service, 17; early war plans, 8; opposition of immediate division to Europe, 24; on Pershing's troop request, 291; prewar condition of, 257–58; strategic plans in Europe, 261. See also Bliss, Tasker; March, Peyton

George V (king of England), 36

Georgia (Russian province), 172

Gerry, Peter, 364

German-American Handbook (Schrader), 75

German Americans: attack on press and language, 82, 84; background of, 3, 95–96; and congressional election of 1918, 358; and Creel Committee, 60; general attacks upon, 96–108; and Theodore Roosevelt, 23, 69, 90, 91, 93; and Trading with the Enemy Act, 69

Germany: Armstrong analysis of German surrender, 327; collapse, 361; establishment of republic, 326; hardships within (1917), 32, 33, 205–6; hardships within (1918), 305, 314; surrender terms, 360; Wilson on regime, 200–201, 210, 211–13, 214, 233, 251, 317–18, 323, 368. See also individual leaders; military engagements

Germany, colonies: Benedict XV on, 217, 219; Burian on, 255; Cobb–Lippmann memorandum, 333; Hearst favoring preserving, 221; Hertling on, 245; *Issues and Events* on, 237; Lansing on, 244; Lloyd George on, 209, 223, 236, 335; Nonpartisan League on, 136–37; Payer on, 306

Ghent, William G., 119, 120, 126

Gibbons, Floyd, 290

Gibbons, James, 46, 349

Gibson, Charles Dana, 82

Gilbert, Joseph, 137

Gillett, Frederick H., 350–51

Glass, Carter, 269

Gleaves, Albert, 57

Glennon, James, 149

Goethals, George W., 43, 271, 272

Goldman, Emma, 25, 77

Gompers, Samuel: and American Alliance for Labor and Democracy, 55; attack on People's Council of America, 140; backing war effort, 45; confrontation with Roosevelt over East Louis riots, 93; criticism by the *Nation*, 76; focus on labor protection, 55; and League of National Unity, 348; opposition to conscription, 10; warning against German infiltration, 97–98. *See also* American Federation of Labor

Gore, Thomas P., 17, 28–29, 73, 248, 316

Gorgas, William C., 264

Gough, Hubert, 31, 283

Graham, George, 249

Graves, William S., 195–96, 197–98, 412n.56

Great Britain: and Admiral Benson, 36; economic hardship (1917), 9, 33, 34; goals on Asian continent, 186; and Hearst, 64, 111, 171; hostility towards, 32, 91, 99, 108, 171, 195, 242; internal conditions (1918), 231, 331, 362; loans to, 33, 229; military setbacks (spring 1917), 31, 203; Wilson's negative attitude towards, 213, 285. *See also* Archangel; Murmansk; Supreme War Council; Vladivostok; *and individual leaders*; *military engagements*

Grebel, Edwin, 266

Greece, Lodge on, 307

Green Corn Rebellion, 27–28

Greene, Evarts B., 54

Gregory, Thomas: on American Protective League, 86, 87, 89; on Bisbee deportations, 132; on Debs indictment, 130; on dissenters, 46; on Espionage Act, 64, 74, 75; on German American press, 100; on Prager lynching, 102–3; Villard on, 357; and Wilson, 401n.73. *See also* Justice Department

Grey, Edward, 223. *See also* House, Edward Mandell: House-Grey memorandum

Griffith, D. W., 51

Gronna, Asle, 29, 32, 218

Grotelueschen, Mark Ethan, 428n.25

Grubbs, Frank L., Jr., 143

Gruber, Carol, 50

Hadley, Lindley, 378n.16

Hagedorn, Hermann, 99–100, 104

Haig, Douglas: favoring moderate peace terms, 334, 338; impatience concerning American forces, 281, 284, 287, 303; and Pershing armistice terms, 335; seeing Germany remaining strong (Oct. 1918), 332; setting armistice terms, 323; threat of Ludendorff offensive, 285; on war's outcome (Jan. 1918), 236, 280

Hale, Frederick, 204

Hale, William Bayard, 112, 222

Hamilton, Edward L., 249

Hand, Augustus, 78

Hand, Learned, 77, 78

Hapsburg Empire. See Austro-Hungarian Empire

Harbor, The (Poole), 120

Harbord, James G.: background of, 260; blaming War Department over supply chain, 299; on capturing Sedan, 304; on France's survival, 33; as head of Services of Supply, 272; on inter-Allied animosity, 204; opposition to amalgamation, 262; ordering of Belleau Wood attack, 288, 429n.34; on Pershing's image in France, 261; on public apathy, 48

Harding, Warren Gamaliel: endorsement of Fourteen Points speech, 242; endorsement of Wilson's (Four Points) speech (Feb. 11, 1918), 248; favoring presidential dictatorship, 45–46; on German American press, 100; opposition to

Overman Act, 273; proposal of Roosevelt regiment, 17, 19–20; on shooting saboteurs, 47; on Wilson's negotiations with the Germans, 313, 319

Harding, William, 100

Hardwick, Thomas W.: backing Roosevelt division, 17; loss in Georgia 1918 primary, 345; opposition to conscription, 14, 16; opposition to 1918 Sedition Act, 73; proposal of draftee bonus, 29

Harmsworth, Alfred. See Northcliffe, Lord

Harper, Samuel, 174

Harris, Ernst L., 199

Harries, Meirion, and Susie Harries, 133, 428–29n.25

Harris, William J., 345

Harrison, Pat, 345, 364

Hart, Albert Bushnell, 81, 82–83, 374

Harvey, George, 21, 49, 96, 258. See also *North American Review*; *War Weekly* of the *North American Review*

Harvey's Weekly, 362

Hastings, William H., 28

Hays, Will, 346, 351

Haywood, William ("Big Bill"), 131, 132, 134–35

Hearst, William Randolph: appraisal of, 114; backers of, 108, 113; background of, 6; general wartime views of, 110–11; on Japan and Russia, 188; opposition to retaining Wilhelm as kaiser, 315; raising of funds for destroyed French cities, 112; for recognizing Bolshevik

Hearst, William Randolph (*cont.*)
regime, 164; scheme for peace,
215; toasting Wilson, 113. *See
also* Brisbane, Arthur;
Deutsches Journal; Hale,
William Bayard; *New York
American*; *San Francisco
Examiner*
Hearst press: adoption of Irish
cause, 108; attack on Lloyd
George Trades Union Con-
gress speech, 237; backing
William Boyce Thompson,
162; backing Wilson's 1917
annual message, 228; blasting
by Theodore Roosevelt, 69, 90;
on Brest-Litovsk, 165–66; endorsement of Benedict XV
peace bid, 218, 221; general
condemnations of, 82, 111–12;
on George Chamberlain's
army reforms, 269; on Lloyd
George speech (June 1917),
210; and 1917 New York
mayoralty election, 125; on
1918 congressional election,
351, 354; praising War Department, 271; pro-Bolshevik, 164,
176; and Root, 46; seeking
conference of belligerents (July
1917), 215; war prognosis (July
1917), 205; and Wilson, 66
Heckscher, August, 401n.73
Heflin, Tom, 12, 16, 98–99, 349
Helm, Harvey, 14
Herron, George D., 250, 251
Hertling, Georg von: attack on
Wilson (July 11, 1918), 254;
becoming German chancellor,
206; condemnation of Lloyd
George's Trades Union Congress speech, 236; freshly
stating war aims (Feb. 25,
1918), 248–49; House on war
aims of, 246; replaced by
Maximilian of Baden, 310;
response to Wilson's Fourteen
Points speech (Jan. 24, 1918),
245; Wilson on war aims of,
247
Hibben, John Grier, 83
Hickey, Donald R., 103
Hill, David Jayne, 83
Hillquit, Morris: counsel for Max
Eastman, 78; drafting of
Socialist Party St. Louis
platform (Apr. 1917), 118;
endorsement of Lloyd
George's Trades Union Congress speech, 237; favoring
Bolshevik regime, 128, 171;
loss in congressional race of
1918, 353; and People's
Council of America, 139, 143;
remaining in Socialist Party,
120; running for mayor of
New York (1917), 124–27;
seeking to attend Stockholm
conference, 122; supported by
Viereck, 106; Walling on, 120
Hindenburg, Paul von: and armistice, 310, 311, 324, 326;
drafting of comprehensive war
aims (spring 1917), 214
Hindenburg Line, 14, 295, 301
Hintze, Paul von, 310
Hirano Maru (Japanese ship), 314
Hitchcock, Gilbert: on aircraft
flaws, 275; attack on U.S.
mobilization system, 269, 271;
background of, 269; praising
Lodge address (Sept. 23, 1918),

307; recognition of contribution, 278; on Wilson negotiation with Germany, 319, 323, 325

Holtzendorff, Henning von, 33–34

Hooker, Elon, 83

Hoover, Herbert, 187, 191, 352

Hornaday, William T., 84

House, Edward Mandell: on aiding Bolsheviks, 162, 166; on aiding Russian provisional government, 155, 219–20; on armistice, 363; attack by Penrose, 268; background of, 330–31; backing of Hearst plan to restore French cities, 112; on Burleson, 67, 70; comments on Wilson leadership style, 370; discovery of British war aims (Nov. 1917), 223; discussion of war aims with Balfour (Apr. 1917), 207–8; establishment of the Inquiry, 232–33; evaluation of, 3, 371–72; favoring Hoover mission to Russia, 191; on Fourteen Points speech and aftermath (Jan. 8, 1918), 234, 235, 237, 246, 247; on French survival, 32–33; on Garfield's fuel policies, 266; House-Grey memorandum (1916), 330, 371; on initial Allied needs, 9; on Italy, 203–4, 331; on Japanese presence in Siberia, 187, 194; on Lodge speech (Aug. 23, 1918), 308; and Ludendorff offensive, 285, 291; mission to Paris (Oct. 1918), 328–35, 338–40, 438n.33; on naval race with Britain, 44; on 1917 New York mayoralty race, 126;

offering plan for a league of nations, 309; opposition to amalgamation, 263; opposition to prosecuting Industrial Workers of the World, 134; opposition to repressing Socialists, 124; on Pershing, 289; on Pershing's unconditional surrender demand, 336, 337; on responding to Benedict XV, 219–20, 221; on Russian recovery, 219; on Sisson documents, 173; suggestion of Hughes for aircraft inquiry, 276; wanting Baker replaced by Lane, 267; on Wilson call for Democratic Congress (Oct. 1918), 350; on Wilson negotiations with Central Powers, 306, 313; on Wilson's Flag Day speech (June 14, 1917), 213; on Wilson's negotiations with the Germans, 324; on Wilson's speech (Feb. 11, 1918), 248

House of Representatives, U.S.: Conscription Act (1917), 10–17, 22; Espionage Act (1917), 65–66; Garfield fuel order (1918), 266; investigation of Heflin accusations, 99; investigation of National Security League, 348; Ireland petition (1917), 108; Military Affairs Committee, 275; 1918 congressional election, 353; Overman Act (1918), 273; revised Conscription Act (1918), 294; Sedition Act (1918), 72, 74; Trading with the Enemy Act (1917), 70

Houston, David, 322, 363
Howard, Roy W., 361
Howe, Frederick C., 75
Huber, F. A., 116
Huddleston, George, 15, 345
Hughes, Charles Evans: backing
    Mitchel for New York mayor
    (1917), 124; investigation of
    aircraft industry, 276, 372;
    joining League for National
    Unity, 348; as possible
    president, 376
Hull, William Isaac, 140
Hungary, 212; separation from
    Austria, 320, 321. *See also*
    Austro-Hungarian Empire
Hunter, Robert, 120
Hurd, Richard M., 97, 101
Hurley, Edward N., 43, 113
Husting, Paul O., 342
Huysman, Camille, 122
Hylan, John Francis, 125–27

indemnities. *See* reparations
Industrial Workers of the World
    (IWW): activities of, 130–31;
    and Algie Simons, 120; at-
    tacked by American Protective
    League, 26, 88; background of,
    131; drafting of Registration
    Day activities, 27; persecutions
    of, 131–35, 373–74; and Sedi-
    tion Act (1918), 71–72; and
    Wilson, 375
influenza epidemic: and German
    army and civilians, 299, 305,
    314; and Great Britain, 362;
    and U.S. army and civilians,
    89, 181, 183, 299
Ingram, Alton Earl, 152
Inquiry, the, 232–35, 239

Insull, Samuel, 85
International Harvester, 149, 170
International Socialist Review,
    120
invasion scenarios, 12, 13–14, 104,
    204
Inviting War to America (Benson),
    119
Iraq. *See* Mesopotamia
Ireland, 109, 224, 308, 362
Irish Americans, 108-9, 356. See
    also *Gaelic American*
Irish World, 109
Ironside, William E., 184
Isaacs, Rufus Daniel. *See* Reading
    Lord
Ishii, Kukujiro, 194–95. *See also*
    Lansing and Ishii agreement
Issues and Events: attacks on Lloyd
    George's Trades Union Con-
    gress speech, 237; attacks on
    Roosevelt, 91; background of,
    6, 105; on censorship, 70; on
    Wilson reply to Benedict XV,
    222; on Wilson speech (Feb.
    11, 1918), 248
Istanbul. *See* Constantinople
Italy, and territorial claims: Bene-
    dict XV and, 218; Burian on,
    255; Cecil on, 208; Charles I
    on, 250; coal shortages, 34;
    Cobb-Lippmann memo-
    randum on, 333; and Congress
    of Oppressed Austrian
    Peoples, 252–53; Czernin on,
    246; Hertling on, 245; Hillquit
    on, 237; House on, 223, 331;
    Lansing on, 244; Lloyd George
    on, 235; Lodge on, 307; Roo-
    sevelt on, 224; Wilson on, 240,
    244. *See also* London, Treaty

of (1915); Trentino; Trieste; *and individual leaders*; *military campaigns*

Izvestiia, 159, 163–64, 244

Jacobi, Abraham, 105
James, Edwin, 290
James, Ollie, 57, 269
Jameson, J. Franklin, 174
Japan: domination of China's Peking government, 186; goals on Asian continent, 186; House seeking British naval alliance against, 331; Lansing's concern over, 180; penetration of Manchuria, 185; presence of, opposed in Siberia, 187–88, 191, 193; Siberia activity, 189, 194, 197, 200; sympathy towards, 188–89, 190, 193; Trotsky's concern over, 167–68; William Mason on imperialistic aims, 243; Wilson's concern over, 166, 187, 193, 194,198–99, 411n.45, 414n.68. *See also* Ishii, Kukujro; Lansing and Ishii agreement
Jeffersonian, The, 68, 345
Jehovah's Witnesses, 87–88
Jellicoe, John, 34, 36, 38
Jensen, Joan M., 89
Jewish League of American Patriots, 46
Joffre, Joseph, 23, 24, 206, 280
Johnson, Hiram: on censorship, 13, 64; on Fourteen Points, 248; George Creel on, 49; and Raymond Robins, 170; on Sedition Act, 72–73, 74; on slacker raids, 89
Johnson, Hugh, 25, 362–63

Johnson, Royal C., 12
Jones, Andrieus, 89
Jones, Rufus, 75
Jones, Wesley, 13
Jordan, David Starr, 75, 106, 140
Joy, Henry B., 83
Judson, William V., 149, 155, 157
Jugoslavs. *See* Yugoslavs
Jusserand, Jules, 17, 200
Justice Department: Bureau of Investigation (BOI), 85; and Creel Committee, 53; indictment of Jeremiah O'Leary, 109; and Industrial Workers of the World, 134; and 1917 espionage bill, 64, 67, 75; total number of prosecutions, 79; turf war with Treasury Department, 85. *See also* Gregory, Thomas
Jutland, Battle of (1916), 36, 310

Kahn, Julius, 11, 13, 17, 47, 351
Kahn, Otto, 105
Kalamatiano, Xenophon, 172
Kaledin, Aleksey Maksimovich, 161
Kallen, Horace, 116
Kalmykov, Ivan, 197
Kansas City Star, 90, 92
Kato, Kanji, 197
Kazin, Michael, 98, 143, 357
Keegan, John, 31–32
Kellogg, Frank B., 12
Kennan, George F.: on Czech Legion, 196, 411n.45; on Hoover appointment to Russia, 181; on North Sea involvement, 181, 184–85, 410n.25; on Raymond Robins, 157; on Root mission, 403n.17;

Kennan, George F. (*cont.*)
on Siberian venture, 414n.68;
on Sisson documents, 174–75;
on support of Russian coun-
terrevolutionaries, 161; on
Trotsky bid to Robins, 406n.62
Kennedy, David M.: on Congress
and free press, 66; on Ford
senatorial candidacy, 343; on
Pershing, 431n.18; on Roosevelt division, 24; on vigilante
organizations, 86, 89–90; on
Wilson call for Democratic
Congress, 440; on Wilson's
role in Wisconsin congressional race, 342
Kent, William, 84, 138
Kenyon, William S., 48, 96
Kerensky, Alexander: lack of U.S.
support, 373; minister of
justice, 147; minister of war,
154; overthrown, 159; prime
minister, 155, 158
Kiel, 1918 mutiny, 327
King, William H.: and aircraft
scandal, 276; attack on Industrial Workers of the World,
133; favoring Siberian intervention, 190; and National
German-American Alliance,
105; opposition to July 1917
Reichstag resolution, 215;
peace conditions of, 218;
sponsor of Trading with the
Enemy Act, 69; on Wilson's
negotiating with the Germans,
325
Kirby, William F., 15, 270, 313
Kirchway, Freda, 121
Kitchin, Claude: attack on Creel,
59; chair of House Ways and
Means Committee, 351; and
1918 congressional election,
344; opposition to conscription, 11; and "soak and the
rich" policies, 356; and Wil-
son's negotiations with the
Germans, 364
Knight, Austin, 193, 411n.45
Knights of Columbus, 46
Knock, Thomas C.: on civil liber-
ties, 401n.73; on House
October 1918 negotiations
in Paris, 438n.33; on 1918
congressional election, 356,
440n.33; on Wilson's league,
241
Knox, Alfred, 194
Knox, Philander, 275, 316
Kola, myth of military supplies,
180, 184
Kolchak, Aleksandr, 19
Kopelin, Louis, 121, 127, 228. See
also *Appeal to Reason; New
Appeal*
Kornilov, Lavr, 157
Kotlas, 182
Kreisler, Fritz, 102
Kriemhilde Stellung, 296, 301
Kuhn, Joseph E., 377n.3
Kuhn, Loeb banking firm, 82

Labor War Board, 372
La Follette, Robert Marion: attack
on Fourteen Points, 242; attack
on Lloyd George's Trades
Union Congress speech, 237;
backed by Viereck, 106; background of, 114; controversy
over Sept. 20, 1917, speech, 84,
114–16, 376; opposition to
conscription, 13–14; pessi-

mistic war outlook, 231; and special 1918 Wisconsin senatorial election, 342; support of bonus for draftees, 29; on war against Austria, 227; and Wilson's Armistice Day speech, 364

La Guardia, Fiorello, 9, 353

Lamar, William H., 67, 77–78, 140

Lammasch, Heinrich, 250

Landis, Kenesaw Mountain, 129, 135

Lane, Franklin Knight: accusation of leaking cabinet discussions, 371; on aircraft production, 274; fear of German invasion of Canada, 204; foreseeing of long war, 231; House's choice for war secretary, 267; on 1918 congressional election, 350, 355; praise of Czech Legion, 198; seeing conflict as holy war, 52

Lansdowne, Lord, 224–25, 228, 248, 376

Lansing, Robert: appraisal of, 372; and autumn 1918 negotiations with Germany, 322, 325, 359; on Benedict XV peace plea, 220; and Creel Committee, 50; on false November 7 armistice, 360; fear of Bolshevik movement, 162, 164, 172, 232, 313; fear of victorious Germany, 204; on Fourteen Points, 244; on Hapsburg Empire, 225–26, 253; opposition to publishing Sisson documents, 173; opposition to Stockholm conference, 122; opposition to U.S. aiding Bolsheviks, 169;

and Raymond Robins, 170, 176; and Root mission, 149, 150, 151–52; and Russia's provisional government, 151; seeking banning of German press, 64; seeking to aid General Kaledin, 161; and Siberian intervention, 192, 193, 199–200, 201; on Sixtus letter, 251; welcoming Russia's March revolution, 148; and White Sea intervention, 179–80, 183, 184; and William Boyce Thompson, 162

Lansing and Ishii agreement, 196, 372

Larson, Cedric, 61

Lasch, Christopher: on Root mission, 403n.17; on Siberian venture, 412n.56, 414n.68; on Sisson documents, 175

Latvia, 172

Law, Bonar, 224

Lawrence, David, 49, 315

League for National Unity (LNU), 348–49

league of nations, as general concept: and Czernin, 246; and Hertling, 245, 248; and Lloyd George, 236; and 1917 Reichstag resolution, 214; and Payer, 306; Sonnino opposition to, 334; and Stockholm conference (1917), 123; and Theodore Roosevelt, 316–17

League of Nations, and Wilson: Cobb–Lippmann memorandum on, 333; early vision of, 241, 309–10; evaluation of stance, 368; and "five points" speech (Sept. 27, 1918), 309;

League of Nations (*cont.*)
Fourteen Points speech and, 241, 245; House critique of, 306, 311; message to Russian provisional government (spring 1917), 211; and Mt. Vernon (July 4,1918) speech, 253; and 1918 congressional elections, 357; president's general thoughts upon, 309; role in House's Oct. 1918 negotiations in Paris, 335, 339; war message (Apr. 2, 1917), 210

League to Enforce Peace, 309, 317, 368

Lebanon, 208

Lee, Algernon, 122

Leinster (ship), 314

Leiter, Joseph, 21

Lejeune, John R., 290, 303, 373

Lenin, V. I.: backing Brest-Litovsk Treaty, 168; contact with Robins, 162–63, 170, 414n.68; endorsement of peace program by Hillquit, 128; endorsement of peace program by Viereck, 106; and Fourteen Points, 163, 244; leading November revolution, 159; peace program of, 159, 241–42; presentation of rival to Wilsonian peace terms, 2, 229, 373; release from prison, 158; seeing Russia still under siege, 169; writing for Hearst, 164. *See also* Sisson, Edgar: and forged documents

Lenroot, Irvine L., 12, 342

Letts, 333

Lever, Asbury, 12

Lever Act, 273

Levin, N. Gordon, 414n.68

Lewis, J. Hamilton: attack on Hertling speech, 249; backing Benedict XV peace bid, 218; on civil liberties, 47; claiming Wilson as nonpartisan, 346; endorsement of Wilson's Fourteen Point speech, 242; seeking war against Austria, Bulgaria, and Turkey, 228; on Siberia intervention, 190; support of Reichstag 1917 resolution, 215

Lewis, Merton E., 112

Liberator, 79

Liberty aircraft engine, 275, 276

Liberty Loans: and German Americans, 104, 106; and Hearst, 100; and Hillquit, 125, 126; and Nonpartisan League, 136; successful campaign, 3

Liggett, Hunter: Armistice Day attack of, 362; on Metz drive, 295; and Meuse–Argonne campaign, 298, 301; on Sedan drive, 304; tactics of, 373

Lincoln, W. Bruce, 182, 197, 406n.62

Lindbergh, Charles A., Sr., 138

Link, Arthur S.: on Fourteen Points, 422n.38; on House October 1918 negotiations in Paris, 340; on implications of German collapse, 361; on Siberian venture, 414n.68; on Wilson address (Apr. 6, 1918) ("force to the utmost"), 252; on Wilson and civil liberties, 375, 401n.73; on Wilson and secret treaties, 208; on Wilson reply to Benedict XV, 221; on Wilson's Fourteen Points

address, 241; on Wilson's plea
for Democratic Congress,
440n.33
Linthicum, John L., 378n.16
Lippmann, Walter: on Colonel
House, 330; and the Inquiry,
233, 234; on New York 1917
mayoralty election, 126;
opposition to government
censorship, 70, 124; seeking
government publicity bureau,
49. *See also* Cobb–Lippmann
memorandum
Literary Digest: deploring Bolshevik rule, 160, 165, 171, 172;
nature of, 5; on newspapers on
conscription, 10; on newspapers on German note (Oct.
12, 1918), 315; on newspapers
on retaining Hohenzollerns,
325; on Siberia intervention,
190; warning of German sabotage, 98; on Wilson reply to
Benedict XV, 221
Lithuania, 214, 224, 308, 310, 333
Little, Frank, 133
Livermore, Seward W.: on Congress and Baker, 267; on New
York 1917 mayoralty race, 127;
on 1918 Congressional election, 356, 357; on Vardaman,
345; on Wilson's censorship, 66
Lloyd George, David: acceptance
of Wilson's promise of support
(March 1918), 283–84; advocating for Balkan strategy, 267;
anger over Wilson's aide-
mémoire, 194; and Benedict
XV peace plan, 218; disappointment with U.S. military
performance during Allied of-

fensive, 301; doubtful of U.S.
fighting performance, 9; fear of
Ludendorff offensive, 283;
head of munitions effort,
257–68; on July 1917 Reichstag
resolution, 214, 215; on Lansdowne letter, 224; meeting
with William Boyce
Thompson, 162; negotiations
with House (Oct. 1918), 331,
334, 335, 338, 339; noting
European exhaustion, 205;
on Pershing's independent
demands, 336; presentation
of peace conditions (June 29,
1917), 209–10; presentation
of plan to divide German,
Ottoman territory to House,
223; seeking more U.S. forces,
289; setting down German
surrender terms (Oct. 7, 1918),
311; stressing need for amalgamation during Ludendorff
offensive, 286, 287, 288; Trades
Union Congress address (Jan.
5, 1918), 235–37, 238, 242,
331–32; and Wilson's armistice
conditions, 312, 315, 322, 324;
on Wilson's "four principles"
speech (July 4, 1918), 254; on
Wilson's Fourteen Points
address, 248
Lochner, Louis, 140, 143, 144
Lockhart, H. Bruce, 155, 157
Lodge, Henry Cabot: address
(Aug. 23, 1918) articulating
peace agenda, 307–8, 376; on
aircraft shortage, 275, 276;
attack on book *Two Thousand
Questions*, 60; on Bisbee labor
deportations, 133; on Bulgaria,

Lodge, Henry Cabot (*cont.*) 227; on censorship, 64; and congressional election of 1918, 350, 351, 352, 352; on conscription legislation, 17; on Czech Legion, 198; defense of Daniels, 40–41; defense of Roosevelt on defense matters, 92; evaluation of, 376; favoring banning books from army camps, 75; on German American press, 100; on league of nations, 317; mocked by Creel, 48; opposition to 1918 Sedition Act, 79; prediction of difficult war, 32; and Roosevelt regiment, 19–20; stressing need to investigate unpreparedness, 268; on Wilson's Fourteen Points speech (Jan. 8, 1918), 242; on Wilson's negotiations with Germans, 311, 313, 316, 318, 319, 323, 325

London, Jack, 119–20

London, Meyer: attack on National Security League, 348; background of, 128; backing Wilson's reply to Benedict XV, 222; on Bolshevik regime, 166; loss of congressional seat (1918), 353; opposition to censorship, 64, 68, 70, 74; opposition to conscription, 14; opposition to war against Austria, 227; praise of Wilson's Fourteen Points address, 243; seeking conference to discuss peace terms, 216; on Wilson's negotiations with the Germans, 306. *See also* Socialist Party

London, Treaty of, with Italy (1915), 207–8, 223, 240, 242, 333

Longworth, Nicholas, 258

Lost Battalion, 297

Lowden, Frank, 103, 141–42

Lowell, A. Lawrence, 112

Lowry, Bullitt, 338

Ludendorff, Erich: and armistice, 310, 311, 320, 324, 326; blaming retreat on influenza, 299; defeated at Amiens (Aug. 8, 1918), 294; fear of American army, 279–80; predicts Allied breakthrough (Oct. 1), 301; seeking diplomatic action (June 1917), 305; stressing need for quick blow, 283; and submarine warfare, 34, 41

Ludendorff offensives: fifth offensive (Friedensturm) (July 14–19), 292; first offensive (Michael) (Mar. 21–Apr. 5, 1917), 282–85; fourth offensive (Gneisenau) (June 9–13), 291–92; German strength at start, 364; second offensive (Georgette) Apr. 9–29, 285–86; third offensive (Blücher) (May 27–June 6), 289–91

Luebke, Frederick C., 103–4

Lundeen, Ernest, 28, 138, 227

Lusitania, 60, 96, 102; and La Follette, 114–15, 116

Luxembourg, 214, 360

Lvov, George E., 147, 153, 155

Lydecker, Charles E., 83

MacArthur, Douglas, 295, 302, 304

MacDonald, Ramsay, 214

Macgowen, Kenneth, 114

MacMillan, Margaret, 249, 337–38
Madden, Martin B., 58, 268
Maddox, Robert, 412n.56, 414n.68
Magnes, Judah, 139, 141, 143
Magyars. *See* Hungary
Mahan, Alfred Thayer, 34
Maisal, Robert, 55
Malone, Dudley Field, 79
Mamatey, Victor, 240, 246
Manchester Guardian, publication
    of secret treaties, 159
Manchuria, 185–86, 197
Manders, Mary Sue, 431n.18
Mann, James, 11, 21, 347
March, Peyton: appointment as
    chief of staff, 272, 372; on
    conscription law, 24–25;
    opposition to north Russia
    intervention, 179, 180; and
    Pershing, 282, 336; and Siberia
    intervention, 192, 193; and
    Wilson's negotiations with
    the Germans, 322
Markham, Edwin, 107
Marne: first battle (1914), 24;
    second battle (1917), 292
Marquis, Don, 81
Marshall, George C., 295, 296
Marshall, Thomas A., 132, 342
Martin, Thomas S., 259
Masaryk, Thomas, 218, 321,
    414n.68
Mason, William E.: on Alsace-
    Lorraine, 242; backing
    Roosevelt regiment, 20; on
    conscription, 28, 98; on
    People's Council convention,
    141; on U.S. military effi-
    ciency, 269
Masses, 76–78
Masters, Edgar Lee, 107

Maurer, James, 84, 139
Maurice, Frederick, 297
Maxim, Hudson, 84
Maximilian ("Max") of Baden,
    310–11, 315, 320, 326, 359
Mayo, Henry T., 37
McAdoo, William Gibbs: accom-
    plishments of, 2; administra-
    tion of railroads, 265; attack on
    Roosevelt, 92; doubts sending
    troops to Europe, 9; fear of
    British navalism, 43–44; fear of
    national bankruptcy, 322; loans
    to the Allies, 2, 33, 229; oppo-
    sition to American Protection
    League, 85–86, 87; praised by
    Hearst, 113; seeing pacifist
    speeches as treasonous, 46;
    suggestion of Root for Russian
    mission, 149
McArthur, Clifton, 12
McClellan, George B., 75
McClure, S. S., 51, 243
McCooey, John H., 126
McCormick, Cyrus H., 149
McCormick, Medill, 265
McCormick, Vance, 349
McCoy, Frank, 20
McCumber, Porter: on Creel Com-
    mittee, 59; favoring Fourteen
    Points, 317; opposition to
    armistice, 311–12; prediction
    of long war, 231; on Reichstag
    resolution, 215; on Wilson's
    Armistice Day speech, 364
McElroy, Robert, 82, 83, 96
McFadden, David, 406n.62,
    411n.45
McGuire, James G., 75
McKellar, Kenneth, 11, 72
McKeown, Thomas, 12

McLemore, Jeff, 344, 348

Menken, Solomon Stanwood, 82, 83

Merriam, Charles E., 51

Mesopotamia: Cobb–Lippmann memorandum on, 333; Hearst press on, 221; the Inquiry on, 240; Lloyd George on, 209, 236, 335; *New Republic* on, 210; and Sykes-Picot treaty, 208

Metropolitan, 90

Metropolitan Opera House, on German music, 102

Metz, U.S. military objective, 261, 295, 301, 311, 372–73

Meuse–Argonne campaign, 294, 295, 296–304, 365

Mezes, Sidney, 232–33, 234

Michaelis, Georg, 206, 214, 215, 217, 222

Miles, Basil, 173

Miller, Clarence B., 72, 227, 265

Miller, David Hunter, 233, 234, 309

Miller, John, 13

Miller, Kelly, 75

Millett, Allan, 261

Milner, Alfred, 163, 286, 309, 334

Milwaukee Leader, 70, 71, 117, 120, 342

Milyukov, Paul, 147, 148, 153

Mitchell, John Purroy, 10, 111, 124, 126–27

Mitchell, William ("Billy") L., 274, 294

Mittleuropa (Neumann), 212; concept of, 234

Mock, James Robert, 61

Monroe, Harriet, 107

Montenegro, 235, 240, 246, 311

Montfaucon Hill, 296

Moran, Thomas, 54

More Excellent Way, A (Jones), 75

Morgan, J. P. & Company, 33; attack on, 28, 344, 345. *See also* Davison, Henry P.; Stettinius, Edward, Sr.

Morgenthau, Henry, 124, 349

Morin, John, 15

Morris, Edmund, 25

Morris, Roland S., 199

Mosier, John, 429n.34, 431n.18

Mott, John R., 149, 152

Mott, T. Bentley, 149

Muck, Karl, 102

Mugridge, Ian, 114

Murmansk: background of, 177; Bolshevik control of, 178, 182; Bolsheviks reenter, 184; *Olympia* sent to, 180; Peyton March on, 179; and Trotsky, 168, 169; Wilson on use of U.S. forces, 192; Wilson reluctant to intervene, 180

Myers, Henry, 12, 133, 364

Nash, George H., 352

Nation: on Armistice, 364; background of, 5; backing Wilson's Fourteen Points address, 243; censoring of journal, 76, 374; on German music, 101; on Industrial Workers of the World, 132; on La Follette, 116; on Lloyd George's Trades Union Congress speech, 236–37; on Ludendorff offensive, 284; on 1918 congressional election, 346, 351, 354; opposition to Ford Senate candidacy, 343; opposition to Hearst, 111; opposition to Sedition Act, 75; opposition to Siberian intervention, 191, 196,

198; opposition to Wilson's Mount Vernon address (July 4, 1918), 254; on Reichstag 1917 resolution, 215; on Sisson documents, 174; on Theodore Roosevelt, 91; on Wilson's note (Oct. 23, 1918), 325; on Wilson's speech (Sept. 27, 1918), 309. See also Strunsky, Simeon; Villard, Oswald Garrison
National Association for the Advancement of Colored People (NACCP), 46, 119
National Association of Manufacturers, 349
National Chamber of Commerce, 204
National City Bank, 170
National Civic Federation, 162
National Civil Liberties Bureau, 70, 74–75
National German-American Alliance, 104–5
National Guard, 8, 10
National Labor Publicity Organization, 55
National Party, 121
National Security League (NSL): background and activity of, 82–83, 374; backing conscription, 10; denouncement of La Follette, 115; on German American press, 100; opposition from Creel, 84; repressing dissent, 61, 94; role in 1918 congressional elections, 347–48; sponsoring Chamberlain, 268; and Wilson administration, 375. See also Van Tyne, Claude

Navy, U.S.: Atlantic Fleet, 37; and convoys, 38–39, 42, 57, 370; early condition of, 34–35; General Board of, 35, 44; initial strategy of, 35–36; and mines, 35, 42–43; Naval War College, 36; Navy Department, 88; role in Atlantic campaign, 42–43. See also Daniels, Josephus; Roosevelt, Franklin Delano; and individual admirals
Navy League, 83
Nearing, Scott, 143, 144, 164, 243, 353
Nebeker, Frank K., 134
Nelson, James Carlson, 182
Nelson, Knute, 29, 65, 100, 273
Neu, Charles S.: on House October 1918 negotiations in Paris, 330, 340; on Siberian expedition, 413; on Wilson's 1918 leverage with Allies, 325; on Wilson's note (Oct. 23, 1918), 435
Neumann, Friedrich, 212
New, Harry S., 275, 316
New Appeal, 127, 166. See also Kopelin, Louis
Newberry, Truman, 343–44
New Republic: on Armistice, 364; background of, 5; backing Brest-Litovsk treaty, 165; backing Wilson's address (Feb. 11, 1918), 248; on Benedict XV peace bid, 219; on Bolshevik regime, 167, 171; on censorship, 68, 70, 75, 76, 78; on Chamberlain's war council proposal, 269; on Lloyd George's speech (June 29,

New Republic (cont.)
1917), 210; on Lodge's speech (Aug. 23, 1918), 308; on Ludendorff 1918 offensive, 284; on 1917 New York mayoralty race, 127; on 1918 congressional elections, 347, 351, 354, 356; opposition to Siberian venture, 191, 196, 198; opposition to Wilson's Flag Day address, 213; on partisanship of Wilson appointments, 346–47; on peace terms, 114; on rationale for German behavior, 216; on Rose Pastor Stokes sentence, 129; on Russian military effort, 155; on Stockholm conference, 123; on Wilson's negotiations with the Germans, 318, 325; on Wilson's 1917 annual message, 217. *See also* Croly, Herbert; Lippmann, Walter

New York American: attack on Britain, 111; attack on Theodore Roosevelt, 91; backing Wilson's note (Oct. 14, 1918), 319; backing Wilson's note (Oct. 23, 1918), 325; burnt copies, 112; circulation of, 110; defense of Creel, 58; endorsement of Bolsheviks, 164, 171; endorsement of Wilson, 113; favoring Roosevelt battalion, 20; favoring Stockholm Conference, 123; opposition to espionage bill, 66; opposition to Lodge's speech (Aug. 23, 1918), 308; prediction of future war, 110; on Socialist Party, 68, 127. *See also* Hale, William

Bayard; Hearst, William Randolph; Hearst press

New York Call, 49, 70, 74, 107, 117

New Yorker Staats-Zeitung, 90, 104. *See also* Ridder, Bernard

New York Evening Post, 69, 159, 162, 174, 208. *See also* Bohn, Frank; Strunsky, Simeon; Villard, Oswald Garrison

New York Times: and aircraft production, 275; on Bisbee deportations, 132; condemnation of sinking of *Hirano Maru*, 314; desire to have Creel fired, 58; endorsement of Austria's bid for peace (Sept. 1918), 306; endorsement of Lodge's peace terms (Aug. 23, 1918), 308; endorsement of Wilson's call for Democratic Congress, 351; favoring Japanese troops in Siberia, 188; favoring war against Austria, 226; fear of German subversion, 97, 103; on 1917 New York mayoralty race, 125, 126, 127; opposition to Benedict XV peace bid, 218; opposition to negotiated peace, 311; opposition to People's Council of America, 140; opposition to publication of secret treaties, 159–60; opposition to Roosevelt regiment, 21; praising Kerensky, 156; on results of 1918 congressional race, 355; on War Department competence, 270. *See also* James, Edwin

New York Tribune: backing Sisson documents, 174; on conscription debate, 10; on October

1918 negotiations with Germans, 315; opposition to Brisbane, 114; opposition to Hearst press, 111; on phony armistice, 361; praise for Wilson's Flag Day address, 213; praise for Wilson's Fourteen Points address, 243; praise for Wilson's reply to Benedict XV, 221; on press censorship, 64–65. *See also* Broun, Haywood; Simonds, Frank

New York *World*: advocating for free press, 76; on Bolshevik revolution, 160, 165; opposition to Garfield's fuel order, 266; opposition to German peace bid (Oct. 6, 1918), 311; opposition to Roosevelt regiment, 21; opposition to slacker raids, 89; opposition to unconditional surrender, 325–26; opposition to Vardaman purge, 348; praise for Wilson's Four Points speech (Feb. 11, 1918), 248; praise for Wilson's note (Oct. 14, 1918), 319; praise for Wilson's response to Benedict XV peace bid, 221; on Reichstag 1917 resolution, 215; seeking "sane censorship," 65. *See also* Cobb, Frank

Nicholas II (tsar of Russia), 147

Nivelle, Robert, 31, 203

Nock, Albert Jay, 49

Nonpartisan Leader, 136, 137

Nonpartisan League, 106, 114, 135–39, 353

Norris, George, 29, 69

North, Frank Mason, 349

North American Review: background of, 5; foreseeing exhaustion of belligerents, 32; on German language, 101; on Ludendorff offensive, 231; opposition to Reichstag resolution, 215; opposition to Roosevelt regiment, 21; praise for Siberian intervention, 196; on secret treaties, 248; seeking draconian peace, 325. *See also* Harvey, George; *War Weekly* of the *North American Review*

Northcliffe, Lord, 33, 224–25, 231, 309

Norton, Patrick, 99

Notestein, Wallace, 53–54

Nuorteva, Santeri, 174

O'Brian, John Lord, 74

O'Connell, William H., 112

O'Hare, Kate Richards, 124, 130

Ohlinger, Gustavus, 105

O'Leary, Jeremiah, 99

Olds, Frank, 99

Olympia (ship), 180

Omsk, anti-Bolshevik regime, 189, 199

open covenants, 136, 238, 245, 246

Open Door policy, 414n.68. *See also* Lansing and Ishii agreement

Orlando, Vittorio, 289, 311

Orth, Charles D., 348

Ossendowsky, Anton Martynovich, 173

Ottoman Empire: and Benedict XV, 220; capitulation, 327; congressional debate on, 227; disintegration of, 206, 301, 310;

Ottoman Empire (*cont.*)
Hertling on, 245; House and
Balfour on (Apr. 1917), 207;
House on, 220; Lloyd George
on, 209, 223, 235–36; Roosevelt on, 224, 226, 316; Sykes–
Picot agreement and, 208;
Wilson on, 223, 225, 240, 245,
251. *See also* Sykes–Picot
agreement
Our Benevolent Feudalism
(Ghent), 120
Outlook: attack on Benedict XV
peace note, 219; background
of, 5, 47; for curbing civil liberties, 47; defense of Sisson
documents, 174; denounce-
ment of La Follette 1917
peace terms resolution, 114;
denouncement of Lord Lansdowne, 225; endorsement of
Lodge's speech (Aug. 23,
1918), 308; endorsement of
Wilson's address (July 4,
1918), 253; endorsement of
Wilson's Fourteen Points
address, 243; favoring censorship, 65; favoring Japanese
Siberia intervention, 188;
favoring war against Austria,
226; fear of Ludendorff offensive, 284; on German com-
posers, 101; on Ireland's
self-rule, 109; on mobilization
crisis, 269–70; Post Office
action against, 75–76; on
Russian wartime defeats, 155;
on Wilson's negotiations with
the Germans, 314. *See also*
Abbott, Lyman; Hagedorn,
Hermann

Overman, Lee, 65, 72, 273, 275
Overman Act, 273, 278
Owen, Robert L., 162

Pacelli, Eugenio, 217
Page, Walter Hines: endorsement
of Wilson's reply to Benedict
XV, 221; evaluation of, 371;
fear of Europe-wide famine,
32; fear of German domination
of eastern Europe, 205; on
futility of war, 205; opposition
to negotiation, 247; seeing
Britain in peril, 33, 37
Painlevé, Paul, 205
Palestine: Cobb–Lippmann memo-
randum on, 333; and Constan-
tinople Agreements, 207;
Hearst chain on, 221; House
and Balfour (Apr. 1917) on,
207; the Inquiry on, 240;
Lloyd George on, 209, 223,
236, 335; Lodge on, 307;
Roosevelt on, 308
Palmer, A. Mitchell, 88
Palmer, Frederick, 260, 288, 298
Pan-Germany, concept of, 212–13
Papen, Franz von, 112
Parker, Alton B., 124
Parker, Frank, 304
Paris, economic pact (1916), 209
Pasha, Paul Bolo, 112
Pašić, Nikola, 218
Passchendaele, 31, 203, 236
Patton, George S., 291, 294
Payer, Frederick von, 306, 326
Pennsylvania Federation of Labor,
170
People's Council of America for
Democracy and Peace (PCA),
55, 139–44, 373, 374

People's Counselor, 142

Penrose, Boies: attack on Daniels, 40; backing Will Hays, 346; and Creel Committee, 57, 59; finding mobilization incompetent, 268; praise of Armistice Day speech, 364

Perkins, Dexter, 54

Perry, Ralph Barton, 47, 81

Pershing, John Joseph: Allied leaders critical of progress made by, 301–3; appointment as commander of American Expeditionary Force, 260; appointment of self as commander of Group of American Armies, 301; arrival in France, 260–62; background of, 8, 103, 259–60; and Belleau Wood, 429n.34; blaming War Department, 299; on Cantigny battle, 288; creation of Second Army, 301; debate over retention as commander, 289; defense of tactics, 299; denial of atrocity stories, 96; endorsement of Archangel intervention, 179; endorsement of Siberia intervention, 190; evaluation of, 4, 300, 364, 431n.18; finding French favoring Wilson's Fourteen Points speech, 245; finding U.S. troops badly equipped, 277; on France's condition, 33, 205; and heated debates over amalgamation, 263, 280–82, 284–85, 287, 288, 332; historians critical of tactics, 300, 431n.18; on maintaining Russian front, 157–58; and Meuse–Argonne campaign, 296, 297, 299, 300, 301–2; opposition of drive to Metz, 261, 295, 372–73; ordering Armistice Day attack, 362; request for massive American aid (June 2, 1918), 289; responsibility for supply incompetence, 277; and Roosevelt division, 20–21, 23; seeing U.S. Army as indispensable to victory, 291; seeking drive to Sedan, 303–4; seeking unconditional surrender, 335–37; setting armistice terms, 323; and St. Mihiel, 294, 296

Pétain, Henri Philippe: assuming command, 31; on Ludendorff offensive, 283; and Pershing armistice terms, 335; request for American forces, 261, 280, 288; seeking amalgamation of American troops, 281; setting armistice terms, 323

Peterson, H. C., 26, 74, 135

Petrograd Formula, 148

Phelan, James D., 108

Phelps-Dodge corporation, 132

Philipp, Emanuel, 141, 342

Phillimore, Sir Walter, 309

Pichon, Stephen, 245

Picot, François Georges. *See* Sykes–Picot agreement

Pierce, Palmer E., 259

Pinchot, Amos, 49, 68, 76, 77

Pittman, Key, 116, 313

Plunkett, Sir Horace, 330–31

Poetry Society of America, 407

Pogue, Forrest C., 428n.25

Poincaré, Raymond, 250, 263

Poindexter, Miles: attack on *American Weekly*, 107; attack on Industrial Workers of the World, 133; on Borglum firing, 275; endorsement of slacker raids, 89; favoring Sedition Act, 72; on intervention in Siberia, 188–89, 190; and Wilson's negotiating with the Germans, 312, 316, 319, 322–23, 325

Poland: Benedict XV on, 217, 220; Cecil on, 209; Cobb–Lippmann memorandum on, 333; and Congress of Oppressed Austrian Peoples, 252–53; Czernin on, 246; Hertling on, 245; Hindenburg on, 214; House on, 207, 331; Lansing on, 244; Lloyd George on, 209, 235; Lodge on, 307; Max of Baden on, 310; Payer on, 306; Roosevelt on, 223–24; self-government of, 321; Wilson on, 240–41, 244, 247

Polar Bear Expedition, 183

Polk, Frank L., 173, 187, 194, 195

Pomerene, Atlee, 319

Poole, DeWitt Clinton, 161, 172, 173, 190

Poole, Ernest, 120

Poole, F. C.: commanding British forces in Murmansk, 178, 179; commanding U.S. troops, 182–84; landing of troops in Archangel, 181; overthrow of Archangel regime, 183

Pope, George, 349

Post Office Department, 75, 106, 374. *See also* Burleson, Albert Sidney; Lamar, William H.

Pou, Edward William, 10–11, 59, 248

Poverty (Hunter), 120

Prager, Robert Paul, 102–3

Pravda, 159, 164, 169

pre-armistice agreement, 339

press opinion, American: apathy towards 1918 Sedition Act, 75; backing conscription of Irishmen, 109; backing Wilson's Apr. 6, 1918 ("force to the utmost") speech, 252; backing Wilson's July 4, 1918, speech, 254; backing Wilson's Sept. 17, 1918, speech, 309; celebrating battle of Cantigney, 288; celebrating battle of Seicheprey, 286; division over Wilson's first note to Germany (Oct. 8, 1918), 313–14; enthusiasm over Wilson address (Feb. 11, 1918), 248; favoring war message (Apr. 6, 1917), 210; favoring Wilson's December 1917 annual message, 228; favoring Wilson's Flag Day address (June 14, 1917), 211; and generally backing Sisson papers, 174; hostile to German note (Oct. 12, 1918), 315; hostile to Germany note (Oct. 20, 1918), 323; hostile to Prince Max note (Oct. 6, 1918), 311; ignoring attack on Herbert Bigelow, 142; lineup on conscription, 10, 26; opposition to Benedict XV peace appeal, 218; opposition to People's Council of America, 143; opposition to Reichstag resolution (July

1917), 214; split over Japan's role in Siberia, 188–89; turning negative regarding Bolshevik revolution, 165; welcoming American Siberian intervention, 196; on Wilson's second note to Germany (Oct. 14, 1918), 319; on Wilson's third note to Germany (Oct. 23, 1918), 325. See also *Current Opinion*; *Literary Digest*; *and individual journals*

Prison Memoirs of an Anarchist (Berkman), 75

progressive movement, 51, 61, 373

Providence Journal, 99

public opinion, American: backing Wilson's reply to Benedict XV's peace appeal, 221; favoring Fourteen Points address (Jan. 8, 1918), 114, 243–44; favoring Lloyd George's Trades Union Congress speech, 236–37; favoring March 1917 Russian revolution, 148; favoring Wilson's "peace without victory" speech (Jan. 22, 1917), 144; favoring Wilson's War Message (Apr. 6, 1917), 144; on Garfield fuel measure, 266; initial national war apathy, 48; on Newton Baker, 267. See also *Current Opinion*; *Literary Digest*; press opinion, American

Quin, Percy E., 22, 74, 227

Radosh, Ronald, 56, 123

Raemacher, Louis, 110

Rainey, James, 431n.18

Rathenau, Walter, 39–40

Rathom, John Revelstoke, 99

Reading, Lord, 180, 283. See also Baker–Reading agreement

Red Cross, 193. See also American Red Cross Commission to Russia

Redfield, William C., 114

Reed, James: attack on Creel Committee reference book, 60; Creel attack on, 59; defense of administration mobilization efforts, 269; favoring enlistee bonus, 29; favoring Roosevelt regiment, 17; opposition to conscription, 16; opposition to Sedition Act, 73; pro-Hearst, 113; on Wilson's negotiations with Germany, 312, 318, 319

Reed, John, 68, 77, 78

Reichstag resolution (July 19, 1917): Allied and American reaction, 214, 376; endorsement by Viereck, 106; text, 214

Reinsch, Paul, 190

Renner, Karl, 321

reparations: Ashurst favoring, 218; contained within Oct. 1918 final Allied armistice terms, 359, 360; House negotiations, 338, 339, 340, 438n.33; Lloyd George favoring, 235, 335; McCumber resolution demanding, 312; offered by Max of Baden, 310; opposition from Benedict XV, 216–17; opposition from Hearst, 215; opposition from Lansdowne, 224; opposition from Lenin, 159;

reparations (*cont.*)
opposition from Nonpartisan League, 136; opposition from People's Council 139; Roosevelt favoring, 224

Rhineland: and armistice terms, 360, 362; French demand for, 335, 337, 338; House acceptance of French demands regarding, 335, 438n.33; major Allied goal, 262; Pershing's conditions regarding, 336; united Allied demand regarding (Oct. 1918), 311; Wilson's skepticism concerning, 336, 338

Rhodes, Cecil, 105, 106

Ribot, Alexandre, 205, 211

Richard, Carl J.: on Siberia "mission creep," 414n.68; on Wilson and Bolshevism, 201; on Wilson and Japan, 411n.45; on Wilson and war prisoners in Siberia, 412n.56

Rickenbacker, Eddie, 93

Ridder, Bernard, 104, 222. See also *New Yorker Staats-Zeitung*

Riggs, E. Francis, 166

Robertson, William, 262, 281

Robins, Raymond: background of, 157; contacts with Lenin and Trotsky, 162–63, 167–68, 175, 201, 414n.68; evaluation of diplomacy, 175, 406n.62; jurisdiction problems within Russia, 158; seeking aid for Bolshevik Russia, 169–70; and Sisson documents, 173

Robinson, James Harvey, 68

Robinson, Joseph, 116

Rochester, Edward S., 56

Rocky Mountain News, Creel's writings in, 58

Rogers, Henry, 77

Roosevelt, Edith, 92

Roosevelt, Eleanor, 40

Roosevelt, Franklin Delano, 32, 34, 35, 40

Roosevelt, Kermit, 91

Roosevelt, Quentin, 92–93, 316

Roosevelt, Theodore: and American Defense Society, 83, 84; on Arizona labor unrest, 132; attack on Fourteen Points, 316, 351; background of, 90; contribution to Vigilantes, 82; and domestic reform, 93; endorsement of Wilson's 1917 annual message, 228; evaluation of, 93–94, 375, 376; favoring Siberia intervention, 190; favoring unconditional surrender, 324–25, 349; general views on dissent, 90–94, 401n.73; on German Americans, 69, 90, 91, 92, 107; giving global world vision (Oct. 1917), 223–24, 254; hatred of Wilson, 90–91, 149; health of, 92; and Hearst, 69, 91, 111, 112; on Henry Cabot Lodge speech (Aug. 23, 1918), 308; illness of, 271; on Irish self-government, 108; on Jews and Bolshevik revolution, 165; on a league of nations, 316–17; on military inadequacies, 263–64, 267, 270–71; and National Security League, 82; and New York mayoralty race, 124, 126, 127; and 1918 congressional election, 351–52,

354; opposition to censorship, 69, 73; opposition to Henry Ford senatorial candidacy, 343; opposition to La Follette, 115; opposition to Lansdowne letter, 225; opposition to Non-partisan League, 137; opposition to Wilson's October 22, 1918, note to Germany, 313; and *Outlook*, 5; presentation of peace proposals, 308; and proposed division, 17–24; on submarine warfare, 40; travels to Washington to promote war cabinet, 270; welcoming Russian provisional government, 154; on Wilson's Fourteen Points speech, 243

Root, Elihu: approval of Wilson's War Message, 45; fear of German victory, 204; and National Security League, 82, 83, 347–48, 374; praise for Kerensky, 154, 156; role in 1918 congressional election, 346, 347–48; on Roosevelt division, 18; on "treason," 46

Root mission to Russia, 77, 149–52, 372, 373, 403n.17

Rudin, Harry R., 362, 435n.69

Ruggles, James A., 166, 168

Rumania: Allied leaders seek contact with, 163; and Benedict XV, 220; Cobb–Lippmann memorandum on, 333; and Congress of the Oppressed Austrian Peoples, 252–53; German preliminary peace with, 251; House and Balfour (Apr. 1917) on, 207; House on, 331; Lloyd George on, 235; Lodge on, 307; Payer on, 306; united Allied demand regarding (Oct. 1918), 311; Wilson on, 212, 240. *See also* Bucharest, Treaty of

Russell, Charles Edward: on Benedict XV peace bid, 219; on Creel Committee, 51; opposition to Hillquit in 1917 New York mayoralty race, 126; opposition to La Follette, 115; prowar Socialist, 119; serving on Root commission, 149, 150, 151, 152; and Social Democratic League, 121; writing for *Masses*, 76

Russia, and March 1917 revolution, 147–48; American reactions to provisional government, 154–56; Brusilov offensive, 154–55; first coalition of Prince Lvov (May 16–July 16, 1917), 153–55; Kornilov rebellion, 157–58; Lansing on, 148, 155–56; and Petrograd Formula, 148; railroad system of, 152–53, 170; second coalition of Kerensky (May 16–Oct. 8, 1917), 155–58; third coalition of Kerensky (Oct. 8–Nov. 7, 1917), 158–60; Wilson on, 148, 154. *See also* American Red Cross Commission to Russia; Root mission to Russia

Russia, and November 1917 Bolshevik revolution, 159; Allied leaders on, 163; Czernin on, 246; Hearst on, 164; Hertling on, 245; Lansing on, 162, 164, 172, 232, 313; making preliminary armistice with

Russia (*cont.*)
Germany, 162; military defeats of, 169; negative reactions to, 160, 171; Payer on, 306; positive reactions to, 160, 171; September 1918 government of Admiral Kolchak, 199; signing of supplementary treaty to Brest-Litovsk (Aug. 1917), 181; signing of Treaty of Brest-Litovsk, 164, 168, 251; U.S. diplomatic corps on, 161, 169, 171–72; Wilson on, 160–61, 163–64, 166–67, 171, 172, 223, 233, 239. *See also* Archangel; Graves, William S.; Murmansk; Robins, Raymond; Sisson: and forged documents; Vladivostok; *and individual leaders*
Russia, and publication of secret treaties, 148, 154, 159–60, 208
Rutherford, Joseph F., 87–88
Ryan, John D., 275, 276
Rye, Tom C., 345
Ryerson, Donald, 51

Sabine, George H., 51
Salzman, Neil V., 406n.62
San Francisco Examiner, 110
Sarrail, Maurice, 377n.3
Saturday Evening Post, 246
Saulsbury, Willard, 364
Sayre, John Nevin, 67
Schaffer, Ronald, 401n.73
Scheideman, Philip, 361
Scherer, James A. B., 113
Schiff, Jacob, 82, 105
Schild, George, 403n.17
Schrader, Frederick Franklin, 75, 105
Schwabe, Klaus, 252, 361, 435n.69

Scott, Hugh L., 9, 149, 150, 151, 257
Seabury, Samuel, 124
Second International, 106, 121, 213. *See also* Stockholm conference
secret treaties, 235, 239, 247, 248. *See also* Constantinople Agreements; London, Treaty of, with Italy (1915); Sykes–Picot agreement
Sedan, military goal of, 294, 296, 301, 303–4, 359, 360
Sedition Act (1918): censorship involved in, 74–75; compared to 1917 Espionage Act, 71; debate on, 3, 71–74; and Debs, 130; enactment of, 74, 374; scholars on, 401n.73
Seicheprey, engagement at, 286
self-determination of nations: Beck on, 244; Hertling on, 248; Lansing on, 244; Lenin on, 158; Lloyd George on, 236; and Wilson, 247, 249
Semenov, Grigori, 188, 197
Senate, U.S.: Committee on Foreign Relations, 341, 350; Conscription Act (1917), 11–17, 21–22; debate over war aims and German surrender, 311–13, 316–17, 322–23, 325; Espionage Act (1917), 64–66; and Garfield fuel order, 266; and La Follette, 115–16; and National German-American Alliance, 105; 1918 congressional election, 116, 353; Overman Act (1918), 273; revised conscription act (1918), 294; Sedition Act (1918), 72–74; Trading with the Enemy Act (1917), 69–70

Senate, U.S., Committee on Military Affairs: on conscription, 11; investigation of air force, 275; investigation of mobilization, 265–66, 267–68, 270; potential leadership, 351

Serbia: Allied demands regarding (Oct. 1918), 311; and Benedict XV, 220; Charles I on, 250; Cobb–Lippmann memorandum on, 333; House and Balfour (Apr. 1917) on, 207; House on, 331; Lloyd George on, 235; Lodge on, 307; opposition by Fred Britten, 242; Wilson on, 240. *See also* Pašić, Nikola

Services of Supply, 272

Seymour, Charles, 438n.33

Sharp, William G., 245

Shaw, Albert, 60

Shaw, Anna Howard, 51

Shaw, George Bernard, 107

Sheppard, Morris, 116, 319

Sherman, Lawrence: attack on Industrial Workers of the World, 133; attack on Wilson, 273; deploring Prager lynching, 103; favoring Japanese troops in Russia, 190; opposition to conscription, 15; opposition to Creel, 58; opposition to recognizing Bolshevik Russia, 267; opposition to Sedition Act, 73; presentation of peace agenda, 216

Sherman, Stuart P., 52–53, 91

Sherwood, Isaac, 14

Shields, John K., 218, 345

Shipping Board, U.S., 43, 265, 271

Shotwell, James T., 232, 233

Shouse, Jowett, 15

Siberia. *See* Czech Legion; Trans-Siberian Railway; Vladivostok

Sigel, Franz, 105

Simmons, Fernifold, 313, 319

Simonds, Frank, 32, 99

Simons, Algie: former radical, 120; opposition to Hillquit, 126; opposition to Socialist party, 119, 120; serving on Creel Committee, 51; and Social Democratic League, 56, 121

Sims, William Sowden, 36–37, 41, 42

Sinclair, Upton, 51, 76, 78, 119–20, 121

Singer corporation, 170

Sinn Fein, 109

Sisson, Edgar: and forged documents, 56, 173–75, 176, 373; sent to Russia, 152, 158; serving on Creel Committee, 56

Sisson, Thomas, 15

Sharpe, Henry G., 265

Sixtus (prince of Bourbon-Parma), 250

slacker raids, 88–89, 375

Slayden, James L., 14, 249, 344, 345–46

Sloan, John, 76

Slovaks. *See* Czechoslovak National Council; Czechs

Smith, Al, 253, 353

Smith, Hoke, 64

Smith, J. Allen, 58

Smith, John M. C., 13, 15

Smith, John Walter, 164

Smith, William Alden, 218, 343

Smoot, Reed, 89, 242, 346, 350, 375

Smuts, Jan Christian, 205, 235, 248, 289

Smythe, Donald: on amalgamation, 282; on Cantigny battle, 428n.25; on Newton Baker, 258; Pershing criticized by, 281, 431n.18; on Roosevelt regiment, 23; on St. Mihiel battle, 295

Snell, John, 217

Social Democratic League (SDL), 55–56, 120–21

Socialist Party (U.S.): condition of, 117–18, 374; election of 1918, 353; endorsed by Viereck, 106; endorsement of Bolshevik regime, 129; fighting conscription, 123; and 1917 elections, 127; peace program of, 128; repression of, 128–30; St. Louis platform (1917), 118–19, 129; in Wisconsin, 342. *See also individual leaders*; *journals*

Soissons, engagements at, 288, 293

Solf, Wilhelm, 314–16, 321–22, 323–24, 326

Sonnino, Georgio Sidney, 218, 309, 334

South Manchurian Railroad, 186

Spargo, John: and National Party, 121; opposition to censorship, 71; opposition to People's Council of America, 140; opposition to Socialist St. Louis platform, 119, 120; serving on Creel Committee, 51; and Social Democratic League, 120–21

Spring Rice, Cecil Arthur, 17, 44

Squier, George O., 275, 276

Stagg, Amos Alonzo, 112

State Department, 50, 88, 170, 190, 195–96. *See also* Bullitt, William C.; Lansing, Robert

Stead's Review, 60

Steffens, Lincoln, 48, 132

Sterrett (ship), 314

Stettinius, Edward, Sr., 271

Stevens, John F., 153, 185

Stevenson, David, 229, 418n.57

Stewart, George, 182

Stimson, Henry L., 20, 372

St. Mihiel, Battle of, 294–96

Stockholm conference (1917), 108, 121–23, 229

Stokes, James Graham Phelps, 119, 120–21, 129

Stokes, Rose Pastor, 129, 374

Stokowski, Leopold, 102

Stone, Melville, 290

Stone, William J.: attack on Theodore Roosevelt, 21, 73, 92; backing censorship, 65; backing William Boyce Thompson, 162; denial of Wilson's partisan, 346; favoring war against Austria, 226

Stowell, Ellery C., 140

Strakhovsky, Leonid I., 156, 403n.17

Straus, Oscar, 125

Striner, Richard: on amalgamation, 282; on Attorney General Gregory, 75; on Roosevelt regiment, 23–24; on Wilson and civil liberties, 401n.73; on Wilson's peace agenda, 255, 422n.38

Strunsky, Simeon, 123, 219

submarines: Germany's use of, 33–34, 36, 40; operation of, 38

Suchan coal fields, 20

Sullivan, Mark, 49, 81, 322, 324, 361
Summerall, Charles P., 303, 304, 361
Summers, Maddin, 159, 161, 170
Sunday, Billy, 20, 46, 96–97
Sun Yat-sen, 186
Supreme War Council: creation of, 204; and declaration of war against Austria, 226; definition of nature of armistice, 314, 338, 371; House appointed to, 329; recommendation for northern Russian intervention, 178–79; recommendation for Siberian intervention, 186–87, 191–92; seeking amalgamation, 284, 287, 288; undercutting of Wilson's Fourteen Points address, 246–47. *See also* Bliss, Tasker; Foch, Ferdinand; Haig, Douglas; Pershing, John Joseph; Pétain, Henri Philippe
Swanson, Claude, 364
Sykes–Picot agreement (1916), 208, 240, 333
Syria: and Constantinople Agreements, 207; Hearst chain on, 221; the Inquiry on, 240; Lloyd George on, 236, 335; and Sykes–Picot agreement, 208; Theodore Roosevelt on, 224

Taft, William Howard: and Admiral Sims, 36; backing Lloyd George's Trades Union Congress speech, 236; denouncement of Bolshevik regime, 160, 165; denouncement of La Follette, 115; endorsement of northern Russia intervention, 190; endorsement of Sisson documents, 174; fear concerning Ludendorff offensive, 284; on Fourteen Points, 316; head of Labor War Board, 372; on Irish self-rule, 108; negative charisma of, 376; and New York 1917 mayoralty race, 124; and 1918 congressional race, 346, 349, 351, 354, 355; noting popular apathy, 48; opposition to Chamberlain war council proposal, 270; opposition to Hertling speech (Feb. 25, 1918), 249; opposition to Lansdowne letter, 225; opposition to Roosevelt regiment, 21; opposition to Sedition Act, 73; on Wilson's negotiations with the Germans, 319, 324. *See also* League to Enforce Peace
Tammany Hall, 125, 127
Tarbell, Ida, 51, 81
Tarkington, Booth, 51, 81
Tarnowski, Adam, 225–26
Taylor, Hannis, 28
Tereshchenko, Mikhail I., 153–54
Thomas, Charles S., 318, 323
Thomas, Norman, 67
Thomas, Robert Y., Jr., 16, 313
Thompson, C. S., 84
Thompson, William ("Big Bill") Hale, 141, 142, 363
Thompson, William Boyce, 156–57, 158, 162
Thronveit, Trygve, 249, 401n.73, 440n.33
Tiagra, U.S. forces attacked at, 183
Tillman, Benjamin, 97
Tooze, Adam, 201
Townley, Arthur C., 135, 136, 137, 138, 139

Trading with the Enemy Act (1917), 69–70, 100, 374
Trani, Eugene P., 168, 403n.17, 410n.25, 414n.68
Trans-Siberian Railway: and American forces, 182, 199, 200; and Chinese Eastern Railroad, 153; and Czech Legion, 178, 190, 192; and Japan, 194; scope and condition of, 153; and Trotsky, 168
Trask, David F.: on amalgamation, 282; defense of House October 1918 negotiations, 438n.33; on league of nations, 368; on Pershing, 431; on Wilson's naval policy, 40; on Wilson's note (Oct. 23, 1918), 435n.69
Treasury Department, 85. See also McAdoo, William Gibbs
Trentino, 208, 255, 311, 333
Trieste, 207, 255, 307, 333
Trotsky, Leon: becoming commissar for foreign affairs, 158; challenge to Wilson, 229; claim of "finance capital" causing U.S. to enter war, 160; freed from prison, 158; and Murmansk intervention, 169, 178, 180; and Raymond Robins, 162–63, 167–68, 201, 406n.62, 414n.68; seeking Allied aid, 169
Tumulty, Joseph: backing Hylan in 1917 New York mayoralty race, 126; congratulations to Brisbane, 113; finding Roosevelt and Lodge partisan in 1898, 351–52; offer of commission in Roosevelt regiment, 20; opposition to Debs trial, 134; opposition to Henry Ford senatorial candidacy, 343

Turkey. See Ottoman Empire
Turner, Frederick Jackson, 54
Tuscan (ship), 42
Two Thousand Questions and Answers about the War, 60
Tyrol, 208, 240

U-151, 42
Ufa, Russian Provisional government, 199
Ukraine, 168, 169, 287, 306
United Confederate Veterans, 26
United Irish-American Societies of New York, 108
United Press, 360
Unterberger, Betty Miller: on Czech Legion, 189–90, 191; on decision to invade Siberia, 411n.45, 414n.68; on war declaration against Austria, 226, 227–28
Untermeyer, Louis, 76
Untermeyer, Samuel, 46

Vail, Theodore N., 348
Van Dyke, Henry, 96, 125–26
Van Tyne, Claude, 60, 114
Vanderbilt, Cornelius, III, 82, 374
Vanderveer, George F., 134
Vandiver, Frank, 261, 429n.34
Vardaman, James K.: backing La Follette, 116; favoring bonus for draftees, 29; favoring Roosevelt regiment, 17; fear of Blacks in army, 16; loss in 1918 primary, 345–46; opposition to censorship, 70, 73
Vare, William S., 21
Vaughn, Stephen L., 50, 52–53, 60–61
Vaux, engagement at, 290–91
Veblen, Thorstein, 134

Victor Emmanuel II (king of Italy), 56

Viereck, George Sylvester: attacked by Roosevelt, 90; defense of German territorial ambitions, 213; establishment of Agricultural and Industrial Labor Relief Bureau, 106–7; favoring papal peace bid, 219; on Fourteen Points, 244; general views of, 106–8; harassment of, 107–8; publication of *Viereck's: The American Weekly*, 6; on Russian defeat, 166; on Wilson's Russian overture, 167. See also *American Weekly*

Viereck's: The American Weekly. See *American Weekly*

Vigilantes (organization), 81–82, 84

Villa, Pancho, 21, 259

Villard, Oswald Garrison: defense of Victor Berger, 124; on 1918 congressional election, 357; protest of censorship, 68; publication of *Nation*, 5, 76; on quick war mobilization, 271; on Trading with the Enemy Act, 70. See also *Nation*; *New York Evening Post*

Vimy Ridge, Battle of (1917), 31

Vinson, Carl, 345

Viviani, René. See Balfour–Viviani mission

Vladivostok: Allies' seizure of Vladivostok, 190; background of, 185; and Czech Legion, 189–90; debate over intervention, 186–87, 190–92; evaluation of U.S. policy, 200–202, 373; General Graves's contingent sent to, 195–200; and Japan, 185–86, 187–89, 194–95,

199; and Trotsky and, 168; Wilson on intervention, 180, 192–94, 198–99, 369

Volodga, U.S. military goal, 182

Vrooman, Carl S., 138

Wadsworth, James, 271

Wald, Lillian, 47, 48, 140, 215

Walker, S. J., 103

Walling, William English: attack on Hillquit, 126; on Creel Committee, 51; on East St. Louis riots, 97; noting Bolshevik appeal, 231–32; opposition to Socialist Party war stance, 119, 120; on Stockholm conference, 123

Walsh, David I., 353

Walsh, Joseph, 57

Walsh, Thomas, 72, 16

Walworth, Arthur, 411n.45

War College, U.S. Army, 9–10, 18, 259, 300

War Cyclopedia, 53

War Department: assumption of intelligence work, 88; condemnation of, by Roosevelt, 264; draft preparation, 25; overall evaluation, 372; perception as inefficient by Pershing, 281; praise from Hearst, 271; prewar mobilization plan, 9; reorganization by Baker, 258; seeking wide presidential authority, 272. See also Baker, Newton Diehl; General Staff, U.S. Army; March, Peyton

War Industries Board, 138, 258, 271–72

War Weekly of the *North American Review*: attack on Creel and Creel Committee, 57, 59;

War Weekly of the *North American Review* (*cont.*)
backing Peyton March, 272; on Brest-Litovsk treaty, 165; on censorship, 76; condemnation of Henry Ford 1918 senatorial candidacy, 343; denouncement of Hertling terms, 249; efforts to censor, 76, 374; favoring intervention in Russia, 188, 190; on Irish conscription, 109; nature of, 5, 57, 362; on 1918 congressional election, 347, 351, 354; opposition to Chamberlains's war cabinet, 270; opposition to Henry Ford senatorial candidacy, 343; opposition to lynch law, 103; praise for Czech Legion, 196; praise for Wilson on Russia, 164, 167; praise for Wilson's Fourteen Points speech, 243; praise for Wilson's Mount Vernon address (July 4, 1918), 254; praise for Wilson speech (Sept. 27, 1918), 309; publication of atrocity story, 96; on Rose Pastor Stokes, 129; support for Overman Act, 273; on Vardaman, 346; on war cabinet proposal, 270; on Wilson's "force to the utmost" speech (Apr. 6, 1918), 252
Warburg, Paul M., 104
Warren, Charles W., 64, 372
Warren, Francis, 259
Warth, Robert D., 123
Washburn, Stanley, 149–50
Watson, James E., 58, 59, 72
Watson, Tom, 68, 69, 345

Wawro, Geoffrey: on Belleau Wood, 429n.34; on Cantigny, 428n.25; on Hunter Liggett, 301; on Pershing, 431n.18; on St. Mihiel, 295
Webb, Edwin, 65, 71
Weeks, John, 164, 265, 271, 353
Weinstein, James, 127
Weintraub, Stanley, 362
Wertz, Edwin S., 130
Westenhaver, David, 130
Westinghouse Air Break Company, 170
What Germany Can Do for Ireland (McGuire), 75
Wheeler, Henry, 132
Where Do You Stand? (Hagedorn), 104
White, John Albert, 411n.45, 412n.56, 414n.68
White, William Allen, 81
Why Is Your Country at War and What Happens to You After the War, and Related Subjects (Lindbergh), 138
Why War? (Howe), 75
Wilbur, Ray Lyman, 140
Wilhelm II (kaiser of Germany): abdication, 361; backing Hindenburg's wide-ranging war aims, 214; on Benedict XV's peace bid, 217; exaggeration of power, 326; fear of overthrow of regime, 320; on German submarine warfare, 36, 41; hostility towards, 46, 54, 113, 312, 325; seeing need to end war, 294, 310; Wilson on his retaining office, 322
Williams, John Sharp: on censorship, 47; defense of conscrip-

tion, 13; defense of Wilson's
mobilization system, 269; on
negotiating with Germany,
218, 318–19; opposition to
bonus for draftees, 29; opposition to La Follette, 116; opposition to Lenroot, 342
Williams, T. Harry, 431n.18
Williams, William Appleman,
414n.68
Wilson, Edith, 350
Wilson, Henry (British army), 319,
324
Wilson, Henry B. (U.S. Navy), 37,
360
Wilson, William B., 132, 134
Wilson, Woodrow: address for Red
Cross building dedication,
210–11; address to Atlantic
Fleet (Aug. 11, 1917), 39, 216;
on Admiral Sims decoration,
36; advocating for Irish self-
government, 108; on aiding
Poles, Cossacks, 161; and aircraft scandals, 274–77; on
amalgamation, 262–63, 283,
285, 369; on American Defense
Society, 84; American Federation of Labor address (Nov.
12, 1917), 142, 160, 223; on
American Protective League,
86, 89; Annual Message (Dec.
4, 1917), 71, 160–62, 225–28,
264, 374–75; "Appeal to the
American People" (Apr. 15,
1917), 210–11; Armistice Day
address to Congress, 363–64;
and army scandals, 265, 266,
268, 272–73, 278; backing
Czech independence, 253,
320–21; on Balfour–Viviani

mission, 206; Baltimore ("force
to the utmost") speech (Apr. 6,
1918), 251–52; on ban of
Masses, 79; on ban of *Nation*,
78; on ban of *Outlook*, 76; and
battleship construction, 40, 44;
and Bisbee deportations, 132,
375; call for Democratic Congress, 349–53, 355, 370,
440n.33; call for unity, 45; on
Charles's secret letter to Poincaré, 251; and Cobb interview
(Mar. 19, 1917), 144; condemning lynching dissenters,
103; condemning Soviet "barbarism" (Sept. 1918), 172; and
conscription, 9–10, 17, 18–19,
24, 29; creation of Creel Committee, 49–50; decision to intervene in Siberia, 192–94, 195,
197, 198–99; defense of Creel
personally, 59; denial of partisanship (May 27, 1918),
341–42; early ambivalence
towards Bolshevik Russia, 160;
encouraging messages to provisional government (Aug. 14,
1917), 156; encouraging messages to provisional government (May 26, 1917), 154;
endorsement of Ford candidacy, 343–44; endorsement of
Sisson documents, 173; evaluation of, 2, 367–76; evaluation
of Fourteen Points speech,
246–47, 368, 422n.38; evaluation of House mission, 340,
435n.69; evaluation of negotiations, 327, 369, 435n.69;
evaluation of Russian policy,
175–76, 184–85, 200–202,

Wilson, Woodrow (*cont.*)
410n.25, 411n.45, 412n.56,
414n.68; extension of credit to
Russian provisional government, 148–49; fear of Bolshevism, 313; feud with Roosevelt,
90–91, 92; final negotiations
with the Germans, 312–14,
317–20, 323–26, 369, 371; Flag
Day address (June 6, 1917), 3,
98, 212–13, 374; Four Points
speech (Feb. 11, 1918), 247–50,
368; Fourteen Points speech
(Jan. 8, 1918), 144, 163–64,
233, 237–46; Fourth Liberty
Loan speech (Sept. 27, 1918),
308–9; general evaluation of
civil liberties record, 144–45,
374–75, 401n.73; on German
Americans, 101; on Hearst
press, 113; and House October
1918 negotiations in Paris, 329,
334–35, 336, 338, 339–40;
ignoring William Boyce
Thompson, 162; imposing of
restrictions on German aliens,
99; and Inquiry, 234; institution of convoys, 58; intervention in Wisconsin primary,
342–43; for "just" commercial
claims of Russia, Austria, and
Germany, 233; meeting with
Root commission, 151, 152;
message to All-Russia Congress of Soviets (Mar. 11,
1918), 166–67; Mount Vernon
(five principles) speech (July 4,
1918), 171, 253–55, 315, 369;
nationalizing railroads, 265;
New York Red Cross speech
(May 18, 1918), 171, 252; and
1917 New York mayoralty
race, 126; and 1918 election
results, 355–57; and Non-
partisan League, 138–39; and
northern Russia, 180–81, 184;
opposition to Allied war aims,
212, 223; opposition to La Follette, 115; opposition to repression, 48; "Peace without
victory" speech (Jan. 27, 1917),
106, 144, 209, 241; on People's
Council of America, 141, 142;
and Pershing, 260, 282, 289,
336–37; pondering Siberian
involvement, 187, 188, 191; on
press censorship, 65, 66, 68–69,
70–71; on protests against
draft, 27, 28; on Raymond
Robins, 170; recognition of
Czechoslovak independence,
320; Registration Day remarks
(June 5, 1917), 26; on Reichstag 1917 resolution, 216;
rejecting Austrian peace bid
(Sept. 16, 1918), 306; reply to
Benedict XV (Aug. 27, 1917),
200–223, 229, 418n.57; and
secret treaties, 208, 238; and
Sedition Act (1918), 74; seeing
U.S. as "Associated Power,"
209; signing of Espionage Act
(1917), 66; signing of Trading
with the Enemy Act, 70; and
Southern primaries, 344–46;
speech to League to Enforce
Peace (May 27, 1916), 241;
support for jailing Rose Pastor
Stokes, 129; on Warburg resignation, 104; War Message
(April 2, 1917), 3, 10, 98, 114,
144, 148, 209, 210

Wilson and the Issues (Creel), 49
Wise, James W., 14, 16
Wise, Stephen, 125, 143
Wiseman, William, 370
Woman's Peace Party, 140, 243.
    See also Addams, Jane
Wood, L. Hollingsworth, 384n.9
Wood, Leonard: on air warfare,
    274; attacked by Baker, 270;
    evaluation of, 375; and Roo-
    sevelt division, 20; suggested
    for Russian campaign, 190;
    visiting European front, 263
Woodward, David: on amalgam-
    ation, 282; on Army Reorgani-
    zation Bill (1916), 271; on
    Belleau Wood, 429n.34; on
    Brest-Litovsk, 165; on British
    and French weaknesses, 331;
    on effort to reach Sedan, 304;
    on Lloyd George's Trades
    Union Congress speech, 236;
    on Ludendorff tactics, 287;
    on Pershing, 260, 277, 337,
    431n.18; on prewar army, 8;
    on Roosevelt division, 24;
    on Seicheprey engagement,

286; on Wilson's war guilt
    stance, 212
Works, John, 141
World Student Christian
    Federation, 149
World Tomorrow, 67

York, Alvin, 297–98
Young, Art, 76, 77
Young, Lafayette, 97
Young Men's Christian Association
    (YMCA), 149, 193
Young People's Socialist League,
    129, 193
Yuan Shih-k'ai, 186
Yugoslavs: and Congress of Op-
    pressed Austrian Peoples, 252;
    Lansing on, 244, 253; Lodge,
    307; Roosevelt on, 224; Wilson
    on, 320–21. *See also* Monte-
    negro; Serbia

Zimmermann, Arthur, 36
Zinoviev, Gregory, 167
Zionism, 223, 308, 333. *See also*
    Palestine

Justus D. Doenecke

is professor emeritus of history at New College of Florida. He is the author of numerous books including *Storm on the Horizon: The Challenge to American Intervention, 1939–1941*, winner of the Herbert Hoover Book Award, and *Nothing Less than War: A New History of America's Entry into World War I*.